THE SCHOOL IN THE UNITED STATES

THE SCHOOL IN THE UNITED STATES

A Documentary History

James W. Fraser

Northeastern University
Boston, MA

Boston Burr Ridge, IL Dubuque, IA Madison, WI
New York San Francisco St. Louis
Bangkok Bogotá Caracas Lisbon London Madrid Mexico City
Milan New Delhi Seoul Singapore Sydney Taipei Toronto

McGraw-Hill Higher Education

A Division of The **McGraw·Hill** *Companies*

THE SCHOOL IN THE UNITED STATES: A DOCUMENTARY HISTORY

Published by McGraw-Hill, an imprint of The McGraw-Hill Companies, Inc., 1221 Avenue of the Americas, New York, NY 10020. Copyright © 2001 by The McGraw-Hill Companies, Inc. All rights reserved. No part of this publication may be reproduced or distributed in any form or by any means, or stored in a database or retrieval system, without the prior written consent of The McGraw-Hill Companies, Inc., including, but not limited to, in any network or other electronic storage or transmission, or broadcast for distance learning.

Some ancillaries, including electronic and print components, may not be available to customers outside the United States.

This book is printed on acid-free paper.

1 2 3 4 5 6 7 8 9 0 DOC/DOC 0 9 8 7 6 5 4 3 2 1 0

ISBN 0–07–232448–1

Vice president and editor-in-chief: *Thalia Dorwick*
Editorial director: *Jane E. Vaicunas*
Sponsoring editor: *Beth Kaufman*
Developmental editor: *Cara Harvey*
Marketing manager: *Daniel M. Loch*
Project manager: *Christine Walker*
Production supervisor: *Sandy Ludovissy*
Coordinator of freelance design: *Michelle D. Whitaker*
Freelance cover designer: *Kristyn A. Kalnes*
Cover images: *©Corbis*
Photo research coordinator: *John C. Leland*
Supplement coordinator: *Sandra M. Schnee*
Compositor: *Black Dot Group*
Typeface: *10/12 Times Roman*
Printer: *R. R. Donnelley & Sons Company/Crawfordsville, IN*

The credits section for this book begins on page 357 and is considered an extension of the copyright page.

Library of Congress Cataloging-in-Publication Data

Fraser, James W., 1944–
    The school in the United States : a documentary history / James W. Fraser. — 1st ed.
        p.   cm.
    Includes bibliographical references and index.
    ISBN 0–07–232448–1
    1. Education—United States—History. 2. Schools—United States—History. I. Title.

    LA205 .F68   2001
    370'.973—dc21   00–032895
                                                                                       CIP

www.mhhe.com

*To My Colleagues in the School of
Education at Northeastern University
Students * Faculty * Staff*

CONTENTS

CHAPTER 8   SCHOOLS IN THE COLD WAR ERA, 1950-1970   222

CHAPTER 9   CIVIL RIGHTS, INTEGRATION, AND SCHOOL REFORM,
           1954-1980   255

CHAPTER 10   RIGHTS AND OPPORTUNITIES IN AMERICAN
            EDUCATION, 1965-1980   293

CHAPTER 11   REFORM EFFORTS OF THE 1980s AND 1990s   319

ABOUT THE AUTHOR

James W. Fraser is Professor of History and Education and Dean of the School of Education at Northeastern University, Boston, Massachusetts. Prior to his appointment as Dean of the new School of Education, Fraser was the Director of the Center for Innovation in Urban Education at Northeastern from 1993–1999. Fraser also regularly teaches a graduate seminar at Northeastern in the History of American Education.

Before coming to Northeastern University, Fraser was Professor of Education and Dean of the Division of Educational Studies and Public Policy at Lesley College, Cambridge, Massachusetts. In 1987–88, he served as Special Assistant to the Massachusetts Chancellor of Higher Education and was responsible for the report of the Joint Task Force on Teacher Preparation. This report resulted in a complete restructuring of the teacher education programs in Massachusetts. Professor Fraser's previous teaching career includes positions at the University of Massachusetts at Boston, Boston University, and Public School 76 in Manhattan, where he taught fourth grade.

Professor Fraser holds a Ph.D. degree from Columbia University (1975) and an M.Div. from Union Theological Seminary, New York (1970). He is an ordained minister in the United Church of Christ and pastor of Grace Church in East Boston.

Fraser has published numerous books and articles in the history of education and related educational policy issues. His most recent publications include *Between Church and State: Religion and Public Education in a Multicultural America* (New York: St. Martin's Press, 1999); *Reading, Writing, and Justice: School Reform as If Democracy Matters* (Albany, N.Y.: State University of New York Press, 1997); *Mentoring the Mentor: A Critical Dialogue with Paulo Freire,* coedited with Paulo Freire, Donaldo Macedo, Tanya McKinnon, and William T. Stokes (New York: Peter Lang, 1997); and *Freedom's Plow: Teaching in the Multicultural Classroom*, coedited with Theresa Perry (New York: Routledge, 1993). He is also editor of the series, "Transforming Teaching" published by Routledge, New York.

ABOUT THE COVER

The three cover photographs provide symbols of some of the major themes of The School in the United States. Schools in the United States have never been static institutions but rather ever evolving in their roles and their constituencies. The first photograph is from a school run by the Freedmen's Bureau for newly freed African American students—see Chapter Five—in Beaufort, South Carolina. This picture was taken in the 1860's, during, or very soon after, the Civil War. The second picture was taken of a group of young people at the Kingsboro Federal Housing Project in Brooklyn, New York in the 1940s. Chapter Six and Eight discuss many of the issues that these young people would have faced in their own schooling. Finally, the back cover photograph could have been taken at almost any time, but in fact is of two girls arriving at the Dewitt S. Morgan School (School 86) in Indianapolis, Indiana in 1990. The classroom these girls entered is discussed in Chapters Ten and Eleven.

PREFACE

While I have taught about the history of education in the United States in one context or another for more than twenty years, I have long been frustrated with my inability to find just the right textbook for the course. Many wonderful books have been published in the field of the history of education. Careful studies of some of the major events and major figures, critical reviews of the changing role of the school, and thoughtful new inquiries into the place of the school in different communities are all available. In the last few years, several excellent textbooks have also appeared. This is a much richer field than it was when I began teaching in the 1970s. But still the book I have sought has not been available. I wanted something that engaged students more directly in learning, a volume that included many primary documents—first-person accounts or other reports and narratives published in the appropriate era so that students could make their own evaluations and engage directly with some of the major debates. I also wanted something that provided an overview of the range of issues from the time of the first European encounter to the present—a skeleton that students and instructor could use together to place different case studies in a larger historical context. And I wanted something that provided students with a basic framework for reviewing other works. I suspected I was not alone in wanting this sort of collection of materials. Too often, an instructor in history of education courses is reduced to the standard procedure of using secondary sources and supplementing them with photocopies, library research assignments, and far too much time wasted chasing documents instead of studying them. Like many others who teach the history of education, I want students to read documents as diverse as Jefferson's "Bill for the More General Diffusion of Knowledge," W. E. B. DuBois's critique of manual education in *The Souls of Black Folk,* one of the works of John Dewey, and *A Nation at Risk,* the 1983 document produced by the Reagan administration's Department of Education. These documents, and others like them, are regular staples in good history courses, but they are not available in one place. Finally, I have decided to create my own text. I tried it first with my own students and now offer it here.

→ APPROACH

Historians of education, like most historians, have been a contentious lot for decades. In the early and middle years of the twentieth century, the history of education became an important element in teacher preparation. Educators designed textbooks and courses to inspire future teachers to take their place in the continuing growth and success of the American school as an agency of increasing democratization. Beginning in the 1960s, historians began to challenge that view. Lawrence Cremin and Bernard Bailyn, for example, argued that the history of education should be taught as history, not as inspirational literature for novice teachers. Later in the same decade, a generation of historians, led by Michael Katz, also began to question whether the growth of schooling was as benign as earlier generations had argued. More and more historians came to the conclusion that the history of American schooling had often been one of new forms of oppression that imposed the values and expectations of a dominant class on other classes, races, and cultures. As the civil rights agenda began to make itself felt among academic disciplines, attention to the specific educational experiences of African Americans, Hispanic Americans, Asian Americans, and, of course, women came to the fore. The ironic fact that the vast majority of teachers had been women for the past hundred and fifty years—while the historians, philosophers, and administrators had been overwhelmingly male—was not lost on historians such as Nancy Hoffman, whose *Woman's True Profession* began a movement that focused on the voices of teachers rather than on the "experts" who wrote about teaching. Not surprisingly, the conservative trends of the 1980s also affected the academic debates, as other historians, such as Diane Ravitch, began to challenge the language of critique. And at century's end, still other historians, such as David Tyock and Lonny Cuban, began to look again more closely at the specific institution that has carried so much of the nation's educational responsibility—the public school—and ask whether we have understood nearly as well as we might what actually went on in the schools over time, how major reform movements were incorporated or ignored, and how teaching and learning took place in the daily lives of real students and teachers. It has been an exciting, if sometimes stressful, field.

A basic questions remains: How does all of this relate to the needs of future teachers or education historians? Neither group will benefit by a return to the inspirational history of the 1950s. But future teachers quickly lose interest in the debates among historians, while historians can quickly adopt a prematurely narrow view that limits their ability to see the big picture. A documentary history, such as this, is designed to provide lively reading and class discussions by considering the actual words of teachers and other school leaders. It represents an approach to teaching history that is generally more interesting to nonhistorians and more provocative to historians.

This volume will explore the major debates of each era through a review of selected documents of the time, both famous ones and less known selections. Through the consideration of a number of topics that have emerged over the last almost four hundred years of schooling in the United States, the book will attempt to support students as they confront many of the philosophical issues that they will face as teachers. Schools have changed drastically over the last four centuries, and the social role that they have played in the lives of citizens has evolved in every decade. It is important for future teachers and for historians of education to remember that different institutional structures have existed at different points in the history of schooling in the United States; this means that different structures can also exist in the future. The current bureaucratic and hierarchical models of schooling are not the only options.

This is not a history of slow progression towards the great institution of the modern school. Inspirational history for teachers went out of vogue some time ago. Unfortunately, it has too often been replaced by a virtual historical amnesia that allows today's professionals to know very little, if anything, of the emergence of contemporary models of schooling. *The School in the United States* is meant to be both an informative and a hopeful book. If schools have evolved and changed in decades past, they can evolve and change in the future; and teachers, allied with students, parents, and others, can make schools change for the better. But in order to be effective agents of change, to work well in the institutions as they exist today, teachers need to understand the roots of the current reality . . . they need to be well-informed about the history of the American school. It is to that end that this volume is dedicated.

✢ AUDIENCE

My goal in this volume is to provide students—future teachers, emerging historians, and those interested in learning more about the history of education for professional or academic reasons, or simply out of their own curiosity—a way to immerse themselves in some of the major debates that have consumed teachers, students, administrators, and philosophers over the centuries. It has been my experience engaging oneself deeply anddirectly in these very real debates makes history come alive far more than does simply reading *about* the issues and debates. It is one thing for a student to read about Horace Mann's role from the perspective of an historian who is an admirer or a critic of Mann. It is quite different for that student to read Mann's own words and then the words of some of his sharpest contemporary critics, such as the Massachusetts Democrats who advocated abolishing his position. The latter approach leads students to a much deeper engagement with the issues and certainly sparks more lively class sessions in my seminars. Students read one way if they are preparing for class discussions and examinations; they read far more thoughtfully if they are preparing for a class debate in which they will defend or attack the author's position. I prefer the kind of energy that emerges from the latter type of class activity.

I imagine this volume used in several different ways:

- As a primary text for a history of education course, providing a supporting framework for various monographs and student-initiated research projects.
- As a documentary supplement to one of the excellent textbooks that have recently appeared in the field, such as Joel Spring's *The American School, 1642–1996* or Wayne Urban and Jennings Wagoner's *American Education: A History.*
- As a tool for structuring a class around some of the major debates in American education, debates that might be reenacted in the class. Students would need to prepare for these debates first by reading the documents and then by researching further on the issues—whether they are issues of the early nineteenth century or the late twentieth.

The School in the United States: A Documentary History is designed as a textbook for history of education courses, whether these courses are offered through Education Departments and other teacher education programs or through History Departments. While courses of this sort cover much of the same material, those in Education Departments—whether they are called History of Education, Foundations of Education, or Introduction to Education—often have more of a professional focus, while courses in History Departments treat education as one of many topics appropriate for historical inquiry. This volume is specifically designed for use in both kinds of courses. The book is structured so that it can stand alone as a core text or be used in connection with other materials. Supplemented with additional materials, it can serve both undergraduate and graduate students quite well. While teachers of undergraduate courses often like a text—which *The School in the United States* can be—instructors in graduate courses often prefer a combination of monographs and primary documents. In the latter case, the documents are made available through *The School in the United States.* The purpose of this book is to help students of American history, and especially prospective teachers, gain a feel for the historical, philosophical, and cultural roots of public schooling as it is experienced by teachers, students, parents, and others in the community today. Too often, the history of education is framed only in terms of contemporary debates. We should always study history in order to enlighten current debates, but history is also a matter of understanding the past on its own terms, with as much accuracy as possible.

✦ Using A Documentary History in the College Classroom

The School in the United States assumes the possibility of many different approaches to teaching the history of American education. This volume provides a chronological overview of schooling in the United States from the early 1600s to the beginning of the twenty-first century; in this sense, it can be the text which carries the course. It can also serve as a companion to a more traditional textbook. Most importantly, by providing a collection of primary documents in one easily accessible place, it allows students to review the debates, which can become the focus of the course. An instructor can supplement this volume with the secondary sources that seem appropriate, with a textbook (more likely in lower-division undergraduate courses) or with a series of other books and articles (probably the norm for advanced courses, especially graduate seminars). In all cases, the documents that speak for themselves in this text can be adapted to the needs of quite different groups of students.

The collection of materials provides examples of the kinds of primary documents that I believe are essential to an understanding of the history of the school as it has emerged in the United States over the past four centuries. I have had the good fortune to try these materials out with willing students and supportive colleagues at Northeastern University, particularly in my graduate seminar in the History of Education in the United States. The text seems to have worked for these students, and I hope it will do the same for a wider audience of future teachers and historians.

This book is not designed as a teacher-proof curriculum for history of education courses. Because it relies heavily on primary documents, it is designed to provide a basis for engaged classroom debates and discussions. It is left to the teacher to arrange those debates and to explore, through supplemental materials, the rich arguments that historians have mounted concerning issues in the history of American education. This text is designed to allow students in a history of education course, or others interested in these topics, to be historians themselves. It is up to the instructor to encourage rich and thoughtful interpretation and analysis. *The Instructor's Guide* that is available along with this volume is designed to facilitate a lively interaction in a variety of different classroom settings. It includes several sample syllabi for classes that might use this book in different ways. It also provides questions for classroom discussion and examples of the kinds of classroom debates that a teacher can facilitate by using documents that represent different perspectives on a single issue.

✦ WHY THESE DOCUMENTS?

Schools and debates about schooling have created a vast literature in the United States over the past four hundred years. Any effort to develop a documentary history of any reasonable length will inevitably disappoint some. As the editor, I could happily have produced a book of double this length and still not included everything I wanted. Students, however, would properly rebel at both the price and the volume of reading.

In this book, I have used five primary criteria in selecting documents:

- There are some authors and documents that no reasonable history of education could exclude. These include such voices as those of Thomas Jefferson, Horace Mann, W. E. B. DuBois, Margaret Haley, and John Dewey. I have attempted to provide representative samples that are both illustrative and engaging.
- The voices of teachers must be heard throughout the book. Whether the voice is Mary Augusta Roper's from the 1850s, Cora Bigelow's from the early twentieth century, or Herb Kohl's in a more recent reflection on his first year in the classroom, teacher voices are an essential part of this history. From the thousands available, I have tried to pick samples that give a flavor of each time and a sense of the promise and problems of the profession.
- Textbooks have been a major part of the school experience for generations of students. From the colonial *New England Primer* to the *McGuffey's Readers* to the more modern Scott, Foresman readers, samples of the stories through which students learned to read are important.
- The history of education is also a history of national debates about schooling. Presidential speeches—from Jefferson to Johnson—Congressional actions, and Supreme Court decisions have shaped the world in which teachers teach and philosophers ponder.
- Finally, I have tried to include documents that shed light on unique moments in the history of schooling. The Virginia Council in London's 1636 "Instructions to the Governor of Virginia," sheds light on the education of the young, both European and Native American; other documents bring to life the battle over desegregation in the Boston Public Schools in the 1840s and 1850s, the experiences of an early twentieth-century immigrant girl like Mary Antin, or the New York City School Department's efforts to accommodate Puerto Rican immigrants in the 1950s. These readings are important if one is to understand schools and the impact of schooling on a wide range of the nation's citizens.

As each section of the book and each major document opens, I have offered a brief introduction. My primary goal is to let the documents speak for themselves. At the same time, I think this is best facilitated when students understand the historical context in which the document was written, who wrote it, and why. My introductions are designed to spark interest and understanding, not to substitute for further reading among the range of available histories of education.

The greatest success for any such collection is its capacity to provoke student curiosity about the context in which these documents were written and their desire to study more primary sources. In order to stimulate that curiosity, I have included a bibliography that suggests further readings on each of the topics introduced in this volume. The bibliography should be of use to students as they develop research papers on specific sections of this book. It also provides background information to help students understand the documents offered here. And, most importantly, it provides a jumping-off place for those who get hooked on the study of the history of American education, so that they can continue their research in many different directions.

�🠒 ACKNOWLEDGMENTS

I owe a special debt to my students and colleagues over the years at Northeastern University, and before that, at Lesley College, Wheelock College, The University of Massachusetts at Boston, Boston University, and Wellesley College. I have been privileged to work with many wonderful people who have allowed me to test and build my own approach to the history of American education. To all of those who assumed the roles of Horace Mann, Bishop Hughes, and many others in class debates, my thanks. My fellow historians, beginning with my mentor, Lawrence A. Cremin, have shaped my thinking about every one of these documents. Their wisdom is reflected throughout this book; the errors are my own.

In planning this book, I have also benefited from the enthusiasm and support of my editors at McGraw-Hill, Beth Kaufman and Cara Harvey. Without them, this manuscript might have stayed on the shelf for a very long time. Gina Serotti, a history student and a future teacher at Northeastern University, provided invaluable research assistance. I am also deeply grateful to the historians and archivists who made it possible to locate some of these documents. My former department chair, William Fowler, now the President of the Massachusetts Historical Society, along with the Society's superb reference librarian, Nicholas Graham, made my work much easier. My former colleague, David Ment, Librarian at Teachers College, Columbia University was also most helpful. Jennifer Dawson and Jacqueline Ramos did an extraordinary amount of typing in a very short time.

Those who reviewed this manuscript, Malcolm B. Campbell, Bowling Green State University; John Georgeoff, Purdue University; Frank Guldbrandsen, University of Minnesota; B. Edward McClellan; Edna Mitchell, Mills College; Colleen A. Moore, Central Michigan University; Norman Rose, Sonoma State University, shaped it in ways that I hope they will recognize.

Finally, of course, my family, and especially my wife Katherine, provided essential patience and support.

I hope that this volume is as useful to other instructors and students as it has been to me and mine. Most of all, I hope it will allow a new generation of teachers and scholars to understand the history of schooling in the United States in greater depth, and thus to be able to make their own contributions to a system of schooling in the twenty-first century that is more democratic and more effective for all of the nation's students.

Jim Fraser
Northeastern University, Boston, Massachusetts

CHAPTER ONE

THE SCHOOL IN COLONIAL AMERICA, 1620-1770

Introduction

Schools existed in the North American colonies that would eventually become the United States almost from the beginning of European settlement. English settlers created schools, which would become a dominant institution in the United States of the nineteenth and twentieth centuries, as part of their effort to build a little England in their new home. But in order to understand the schools of colonial America, it is important to understand how they differed from, as well as how they were similar to, modern schools. First, schools were a relatively small part of English education. Family, church, community, and apprenticeship all ranked far above formal schooling as means to gain a good and useful education. In addition, schools were introduced into the lands which would become the United States at a unique historic moment—a time when three cultures were meeting in ways unimaginable to the English people who had designed the institution.

In colonial America, these three cultures were meeting—and clashing—in new and powerful ways. All cultures educate—all cultures find ways to induct the young into society—but they do so in many different ways. The Native Americans who initially welcomed but quickly came to oppose the new immigrants had their own long-established pattern of informal apprenticeship, followed by dramatic testing rituals and

1

rites of passage at adolescence. African Americans, who were brought into the colonies within a decade of the first white settlement, brought traditions similar to those of the Native Americans, making structured rituals of education and testing part of their community norms. The Europeans had yet another set of community rituals—from baptism and confirmation to apprenticeship—and they also had the institution of the school.

However, the three cultures did not meet as equals. The Europeans had gunpowder, and they meant to control the political and cultural destinies not only of their own descendants, but of the Native Americans they met and the African Americans whom they brought to these shores in chains. These realities are essential for understanding colonial education and the inheritance it passed on to later generations. The United States was a multicultural society long before it was a nation, and its different cultures had radically different educational traditions and patterns. But multiculturalism does not necessarily mean equality. Within the diverse cultures in colonial society, one culture had the power to impose its institutions on the others.

In most of North America, this meant that English institutions would dominate. The educational pattern that had emerged in England in the sixteenth and seventeenth centuries involved a mix of institutions that included:

- *The family,* which had basic responsibility for the instruction of all youth in the household in both literacy and basic work-related skills (which meant farm life for the vast majority).
- *The church,* which preached and catechized the whole congregation, as well as special gatherings of youth, so that they would understand the true faith. (While the English went through a series of Civil Wars to decide what was the true faith—Roman Catholic or one of several versions of Protestantism— very few doubted that the true faith, as they defined it, should be taught to all citizens through an established state church.)
- *The whole community,* which shared basic values and expectations of youth, punished deviance, and organized apprenticeship patterns.
- And finally, *the school,* which served as an adjunct to the more important institutions, providing some skills in literacy and mathematical skills and preparing selected (male) leaders for college.

Most of the North American colonies were founded with this model more or less intact.

One of the earliest issues the English faced had to do with the education of the new peoples they were encountering. The Virginia Company, based in London, instructed their Governor to ensure that the Indians were inducted into Christianity and English culture whether they wanted to be or not. It was not the last time schooling would be imposed by those in power on others who did not want it. Later documents indicate the same approach to Indian education continued years later. The colonial era also saw great debates about the appropriate education of African-American slaves. Initially, some European settlers feared that literacy, and especially conversion to Christianity, might make the slaves eligible for freedom. In time, however, the governing authorities decided differently. Slaves could be educated, and they could convert to Christianity and join the European churches, but they would remain slaves. In the colonial era, this legislation unleashed a significant effort to educate the slaves in the rudiments of Christianity and a somewhat less enthusiastic, but still real, effort to encourage literacy among the slaves. Only much later, as literate slaves rebelled in the nineteenth century, did the southern states outlaw literacy among their slaves.

Slave owners were also not the only ones frightened by literacy. Virginia Governor Berkeley's oft-quoted statement reflected the thinking of many: "I thank God, *there are no free schools* nor *printing,* and I hope we shall not have these [for a] hundred years; for *learning* has brought disobedience, and heresy, and sects into the world, and *printing* has divulged them, and libels against the best government. God keep us from both!" It would be well after the American Civil War before the racial and class divisions of the South began to lose their power over those who advocated schooling for all. And only after the civil rights movement of the twentieth century did the face of southern education really change.

Puritan New England had a stronger commitment to schooling. The Puritans saw education as one essential element in the larger structure of the society's educational configuration. In Boston, which was founded in 1630, family, church, and of course the community, were there from the beginning, but schools were added within five years. In April 1635, Boston Latin School was created by public vote. As was recorded, "At a general meeting upon public notice agreed that our brother Philemon Pormort shall be intreated to become schoolmaster for the teaching and nurturing of children with us." Pormort apparently agreed, although within a few years he was in trouble with the authorities for supporting the "heretic" Anne Hutcheson and was forced into exile in New Hampshire. His successor, Daniel Maude, continued the school in his own home until 1645, when the first schoolhouse for the Latin School was built.

Just as the first schools were opening, legislators were creating laws to ensure their availability—at least to the English. For example:

- In 1642, the first education-related legislation passed the Massachusetts legislature. It required that the head of every household teach every child in that household—male and female, biological children, apprentices, or servants—"to read and understand the principles of religion and the capital laws of the country."
- In 1647, more detailed legislation also required the creation of schools. "It being one chief project of that old deluder Satan," began one of the most famous pieces of education-related legislation ever written, "to keep men from the knowledge of the Scriptures . . . It is therefore ordered, that every township in this jurisdiction, after the Lord hath increased them to the number of fifty householders, shall then forthwith appoint one within their town to teach all such children as shall resort to him to write and read, whose wages shall be paid either by the parents or masters of such children, or by those inhabitants in general. . . . And it is further ordered, that where any town shall increase to the number of 100 families or householders, they shall set up a grammar school, the master thereof being able to instruct youth so far as they may be fitted for the university."

It is important to note what these laws did not require as well as what they did. Neither law required children to attend school; instead, parents needed to ensure that their children would learn, and the community had to ensure that schools were available. Thus, schools did not have to be the vehicle of learning—and for many they weren't, especially for many girls, but also for some boys.

Benjamin Franklin's *Autobiography* provides an excellent description of how colonial schooling actually worked for European Americans. Franklin was born in Boston in 1714. About a decade later, his formal schooling began after he had already learned to read and write at home:

> I was put to the grammar school [Boston Latin School] at eight years of age, my father intending to devote me as the tithe of his sons to the service of the church. My early readiness in learning to read . . . and the opinion of all his friends that I should certainly make a good scholar, encouraged him in this purpose of his. . . . I continued, however, at the grammar school rather less than a year. . . . my father, burdened with a numerous family, was unable without inconvenience to support the expense of a college education, considering, moreover, as he said to one of his friends in my presence, the little encouragement that line of life afforded for those educated for it. [Franklin and his father agreed that preaching would not be a very rewarding line of life for Franklin.] He gave up his first intentions, took me from the grammar school, and sent me to a school for writing and arithmetic . . .

The Grammar school was useful if Franklin was preparing for ministry (and therefore college), but once Franklin switched goals, there was no further value in that school, so he dropped out and went to a "school for writing and arithmetic." Although one could view such a move as downward mobility, the arithmetic included bookkeeping and business skills, combined with further work in English rather than Latin. In other words, the whole system focused not so much on ordered progression through a hierarchy, but rather on providing useful skills. This was exactly what Franklin needed.

✦Virginia Council [London], Instructions to Sir Thomas Gates, Knight, Governor of Virginia, 1636

The London-based Virginia Council gave clear instructions to one of their early governors, Sir Thomas Gates, regarding his responsibility to educate the native peoples in the ways of English Christianity. Their instructions revealed overt hostility to the religions, cultures, and educational systems of the original inhabitants of the New World; their orders also demonstrated their conviction that Christianity and English civilization both offered important opportunities to native children.

You shall, with all propenseness and diligence, endeavor the conversion of the natives to the knowledge and worship of the true God and their Redeemer, Christ Jesus, as the most pious and noble end of this plantation, which the better to effect you must procure from them some convenient number of their children to be brought up in your language and manners. And if you find it convenient, we think it reasonable you first remove . . . them from their . . . priests by a surprise of them all and detain them prisoners, for they are so wrapped up in the fog and misery of their iniquity, and so terrified with their continual tyranny, chained under with the bond of Death unto the Devil, that while [the priests] live among them to poison and infect . . . their minds, you shall never make any great progress into this glorious work, nor have any civil peace or concur with them. And in case of necessity or conveniency, we pronounce it not cruelty nor breach of charity to deal more sharply with them and to proceed even to dash with these murderers of souls and sacrificers of gods' images to the devil . . . .

→VIRGINIA STATUTES ON THE EDUCATION OF INDIAN CHILDREN HELD HOSTAGE, FROM THE VIRGINIA STATUTES AT LARGE, 1656

Twenty years after the London-based Council sent its instructions, the Virginia legislature began to outline its own plan for the education of Indian children held hostage among them. The purpose it outlined for their schooling influenced the purpose of schooling for many in future generations. The legislature specified that it was the responsibility of those in charge of these youth to "do their best to bring them up in Christianity, civility, and the knowledge of necessary trades." Although the specific focus on Christianity faded during the twentieth century, the emphasis on American civilization and on useful work has changed surprisingly little.

If the Indians shall bring in any children as gauges of their good and quiet intentions to us and amity with us, then the parents of such children shall choose the persons to whom the care of such children shall be entrusted; and the country by us their representatives do engage that we will not use them as slaves, but do their best to bring them up in Christianity, civility, and the knowledge of necessary trades. And on the report of the commissioners of each respective county that those under whose tuition they are do really intend the bettering of the children in these particulars, then a salary shall be allowed to such men as shall deserve and require it.

→SOUTH CAROLINA STATUTE ON CONVERSION OF SLAVES TO CHRISTIANITY, DIGEST OF THE PUBLIC STATUTE LAW OF SOUTH CAROLINA, 1711

State legislatures and other governing authorities stepped in to resolve the controversy over the education of slaves in religion and literacy. Slave owners were worried about losing their "property rights" if slaves took on more of the attributes of free citizens. This legislation from South Carolina is but one example of similar laws passed throughout the nation. Masters were free to educate their slaves, secure in the knowledge that they would still be slaves no matter what level of education or piety they achieved.

Since charity and the Christian religion which we profess obliges us to wish well to the souls of all men, and that religion may not be made a pretence to alter any man's property and right, and that no persons may neglect to baptize their Negroes or slaves, or suffer them to be baptized for fear that thereby they should be manumitted and set free: Be it therefore enacted, that it shall be, and is hereby declared, lawful for any Negroe or Indian slave, or any other slave or slaves whatsoever, to receive and profess the Christian faith, and be thereunto baptized. But that notwithstanding such slave or slaves shall receive and profess the Christian religion, and be baptized, he or they shall not thereby be manumitted or set free, or his or their owner, master, or mistress lose his or their civil right, property, and authority over such slave or slaves, but that the slave or slaves, with respect to his or their servitude, shall remain and continue in the same state and condition that he or they was in before the making of this act.

↱A Missionary Report from Mr. Taylor to the Society in North Carolina on the Baptism of Slaves, April 23, 1719

Clearly the acts of a colonial legislature did not satisfy everyone, as this letter from a missionary to the religious society that supported his work indicates. In Anglican North Carolina, Taylor was attempting to inculcate the slaves of one plantation in English Christianity by having them memorize selections from the Episcopal Book of Common Prayer. The plantation owner, however, feared that his slaves would be freed unless the British Parliament enacted a law preventing it.

In this year I caused a pretty many of the children to learn our catechism, and catechized them in public. In this year I baptized one adult white young woman and thirty white children, and one adult Negro young woman, and one mustee [a person of European and Indian ancestry] young woman and three mustee young children, in all thirty-six. I hope I took a method with the Negro young man, and with the mustee young woman whom I baptized which will please the Society, which was this. I made them get our Church Catechism perfectly without book, and then I took some pains with them to make them understand it, and especially the baptismal covenant, and to persuade them, faithfully and constantly to perform the great things they were to promise at their baptism and ever after to perform to God. And then I caused them to say the catechism one Lord's Day, and the other Lord's Day before a large congregation without book, which they did both distinctly, and so perfectly that all that heard them admired their saying it so well. And with great satisfaction to myself I baptized these two persons . . .

I had for some time great hopes of being the minister that should convert and baptize the rest of Esquire Duckenfield's slaves, which I was very desirous and ambitious to be, and I would have begrudged no pains but would, most freely and with the greatest pleasure, have done all I could to promote and accomplish this so great, and so good work. And in order thereunto, I was preparing four more of them for baptism, and had taught one of those four [his] catechism very perfectly and the other three a good part of it, and now as I was about this good work, the enemies to the conversion and baptism of slaves industriously and very busily buzzed into the peoples' ears that all slaves that were baptized were to be set free. And this silly bugbear so greatly scared Esquire Duckenfield that he told me plainly I should baptize no more of his slaves till the Society had got a law made in England that no baptized slave should be set free because he is baptized, and sen[t] it here. And many more are of the same mind, and so this good work was knocked in the head, which is a great trouble to me because so many slaves are so very desirous to become Christians without any expectation of being set free when they are baptized. I fear this good work will not be revived and prosper here till such a law is enacted by the Parliament of Great Britain and this people are acquainted with it, for I perceive nothing else will satisfy them.

✦Virginia's Cure, or An Advisive Narrative Concerning Virginia, London, 1662

As the next two documents show, caste, class, and race were not the only determinants in limiting the spread of schooling in the southern colonies. Because the territory was settled in plantations and farms scattered over large areas, formal schooling was logistically difficult. And the hierarchical attitudes of many, like Governor Berkeley, made schools an object of distrust. These two statements from Virginia show why an advocate for education like Thomas Jefferson would face an uphill battle in advocating for schools throughout the Commonwealth even a century later.

Their almost general want of schools for the education of their children is another consequence of their scattered planting, of most sad consideration, most of all bewailed of parents there; and therefore the arguments drawn from thence most likely to prevail with them cheerfully to embrace the remedy. This want of schools, as it renders a very numerous generation of Christians' children born in Virginia (who naturally are of beautiful and comely persons and generally of more ingenious spirits than these in England) unserviceable for any great employments either in Church or State; so likewise it obstructs the hopefullest way they have for the conversion of the heathen, which is, by winning the heathen . . . to bring in their children to be taught and instructed in our schools together with the children of the Christians.

I shall humbly . . . endeavor to contribute towards the compassing this remedy by propounding:

1. That your Lordship would be pleased to acquaint the King with the necessity of promoting the building [of] towns in each county of Virginia, upon the consideration of the forementioned sad consequences of their present manner of living there.

2. That your Lordship . . . be pleased to move the pitiful and charitable heart of His Gracious Majesty (considering the poverty and needs of Virginia) for a collection to be made in all the churches of his three kingdoms . . . for the promoting a work of so great charity to the souls of many thousands of his loyal subjects, their children, and the generations after them, and of numberless poor heathen; and that the ministers of each congregation be enjoined with more than ordinary care and pains to stir up the people to a free and liberal contribution towards it . . . .

✦Sir William Berkeley, Governor of Virginia, response to "Enquiries to the Governor of Virginia," from the Lords' Commissioners of Foreign Plantations, 1671

What course is taken about instructing the people within your government in the christian religion; and what provision is there made for the paying of your ministry?

Answer: The same course that is taken in England out of towns; every man according to his ability instructing his children. We have forty-eight parishes, and our ministers are well paid, and by my consent should be better *if they would pray oftener and preach less.* But of all other commodities, so of this, *the worst are sent us,* and we had few that we could boast of, since the persecution in *Cromwell's* tyranny drove divers worthy men hither. But, I thank God, *there are no free schools* nor *printing,* and I hope we shall not have these hundred years; for *learning* has brought disobedience, and heresy, and sects into the world, and *printing* has divulged them, and libels against the best government. God keep us from both!

✦MASSACHUSETTS' OLD DELUDER SATAN LAW, 1647

Comparing this Massachusetts legislation of 1647 with contemporary educational laws, one might become wistful for the rhetoric of the past. In fact, however, the legislature was simply placing their commitment to education in the context of the state-approved Puritan faith. If the Puritan version of Protestant Christianity, which demanded that each believer read and study the Bible on their own, were to prevail, then literacy was absolutely essential. In 1642, they passed their first significant school law, requiring that every head of household ensure the literacy of all children resident in that home. Now, five years later, they added to the package by requiring that every town offer a school as one means of supporting the householders in their quest to educate children. It is important to note, however, that the responsibility for literacy continued to rest on the family. The school was an adjunct, an option that might or might not be selected as the vehicle for accomplishing state-mandated skills.

It being one chief project of that old deluder Satan to keep men from the knowledge of the Scriptures, as in former times by keeping them in an unknown tongue, so in these latter times by persuading from the use of tongues, that so at least the true sense and meaning of the original might be clouded by false glosses of saint-seeming deceivers, that learning may not be buried in the grave of our fathers in the church and commonwealth, the Lord assisting our endeavors:

It is therefore ordered, that every township in this jurisdiction, after the Lord hath increased them to the number of fifty householders, shall then forthwith appoint one within their town to teach all such children as shall resort to him to write and read, whose wages shall be paid either by the parents or masters of such children, or by the inhabitants in general by way of supply, as the major part of those that order the prudentials of the town shall appoint. Provided, those that send their children be not oppressed by paying much more than they can have them taught for in other towns. And it is further ordered, that where any town shall increase to the number of 100 families or householders, they shall set up a grammar school, the master thereof being able to instruct youth so far as they may be fitted for the university. Provided, that if any town neglect the performance hereof above one year, that every such town shall pay five pounds to the next school till they shall perform this order.

✦BENJAMIN FRANKLIN, AUTOBIOGRAPHY 1714-1718

Benjamin Franklin wrote his famous Autobiography *in four stages in his middle and late years. It was not fully published until 1868. The portion cited here involves events that took place in 1714–1718. His report of his own childhood and education remains a classic description of the experience of many a white youth within the schools of the colonial era. Boston Latin School proudly claims Franklin as a graduate while, in fact, he dropped out after only a few months. But no one, least of all Franklin, thought that his departure was a problem. He moved on first to another school to learn the specific skills in bookkeeping that it offered him and then to an apprenticeship that prepared him for his first occupation as a printer. At the same time, his voracious reading and keen observation of those around him prepared him intellectually for his role as one of the prime shapers of the new American nation.*

My elder brothers were all put apprentices to different trades. I was put to the grammar school at eight years of age, my father intending to devote me as the tithe of his sons to the service of the church. My early readiness in learning to read (which must have been very early, as I do not remember when I could not read) and the opinion of all his friends that I should certainly make a good scholar, encouraged him in this purpose of his. My uncle Benjamin, too, approved of it and proposed to give me all his shorthand volumes of sermons to set up with, if I would learn his shorthand. I continued, how–ever, at the grammar school rather less than a year, though in that time I had risen gradually from the middle of the class of that year to be at the head of the same class, and was removed into the next class, whence I was to be placed in the third at the end of the year. But my father, burdened with a numerous family, was unable without inconvenience to support the expense of a college education, considering, moreover, as he said to one of his friends in my presence, the little encouragement that line of life afforded to those educated for it. He gave up his first intentions, took me from the grammar school, and sent me to a school for writing and arithmetic kept by a then famous man, Mr. Geo. Brownell. He was a skillful master, and successful in his profession, employing the mildest and most encouraging methods. Under him I learned to write a good hand pretty soon, but I failed in the arithmetic and made no progress in it. At ten years old, I was taken home to help my father in his business, which was that of a tallow chandler and soap boiler—a business he was not bred to but had assumed on his arrival in New England, because he found his dyeing trade, being in little request, would not maintain his family. Accordingly, I was employed in cutting wick for the candles, filling the molds for cast candles, attending the shop, going of errands, etc. . . .

I continued thus employed in my father's business for two years, that is, till I was twelve years old; and my brother John, who was bred to that business, having left my father, married and set up for himself at Rhode Island, there was every appearance that I was destined to supply his place and be tallow chandler. But my dislike to the trade continuing, my father had apprehensions that if he did not put me to one more agreeable, I should break loose and go to sea, as my brother Josiah had done, to his great vexation. In consequence he sometimes took me to walk with him and see join-ers, bricklayers, turners, braziers, etc., at their work, that he might observe my inclina-tion and endeavor to fix it on some trade that would keep me on land. It has ever since been a pleasure to me to see good workmen handle their tools; and it has been useful to me to have learned so much by it as able to do little jobs myself in my house, when a workman could not readily be got, and to construct little machines for my experiments when the intention of making these was warm in my mind. My father determined at last for the cutler's trade, and placed me for some days on trial with Samuel, son of my uncle Benjamin, who was bred to that trade in London and had just established himself in Boston. But the sum he exacted as a fee for my apprenticeship displeased my father, and I was taken home again.

From my infancy I was passionately fond of reading, and all the little money that came into my hands was laid out in the purchasing of books. I was very fond of voy-ages. My first acquisition was Bunyan's works in separate little volumes. I afterwards sold them to enable me to buy R. Burton's historical collections; they were small chap-men's books and cheap, forty or fifty in all. My father's little library consisted chiefly of books in polemic divinity, most of which I read. I have since often regretted that at a time when I had such a thirst for knowledge, more proper books had not fallen in my way, since it was now resolved I should not be bred to divinity. There was among them Plutarch's *Lives,* in which I read abundantly, and I still think that time spent to great advantage. There was also a book of Defoe's called an *Essay on Projects* and another of Dr. Mather's called *Essays to do Good,* which perhaps gave me a turn of thinking that had an influence on some of the principal future events of my life.

This bookish inclination at length determined my father to make me a printer, though he had already one son (James) of that profession. In 1717 my brother, James, returned from England with a press and letters to set up his business in Boston. I liked it much better than that of my father, but still had a hankering for the sea. To prevent the apprehended effect of such an inclination, my father was impatient to have me bound to my brother. I stood out some time, but at last was persuaded and signed the indenture, when I was yet but twelve years old.

✦THE NEW ENGLAND PRIMER, 1768

The New England Primer *was the premiere textbook for basic literacy in colonial New England. Children learned the alphabet and their catechism through it at the same time. Moving from "In Adam's Fall We Sinned all," through "Zaccheus he Did Climb the Tree, Our Lord to see," children were inducted into a holistic worldview. The primer continued in use for some time after the Revolution, although references to the English King were removed. One could date the beginnings of American civil religion with the replacement of an earlier Calvinist "Whales in the Sea God's Voice obey," with "Washington brave his country did save."*

The New England Primer. Boston: Printed and Sold By John Perkins, 1768. MHS Neg.#1313, #1314, #1315, #1316, #1319, and #1490. Reprinted courtesy of the Massachusetts Historical Society.

THE
New-England
PRIMER
Improved.

For the more eafy attaining the
true reading of Englifh.

To which is added,

The Affembly of Divines, and Mr. COTTON's *Catechifm.*

BOSTON: Printed for, and
Sold by JOHN PERKINS, in
Union Street.   1 7 6 8.

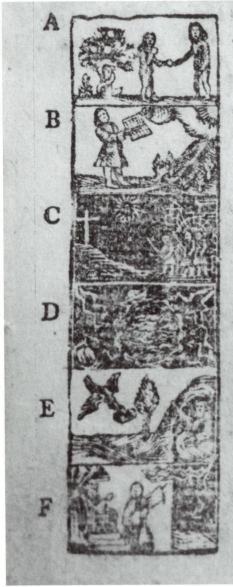

A In ADAM's Fall,
   We sinned all.

B Heaven to find,
   The BIBLE Mind.

C CHRIST crucify'd,
   For Sinners dy'd.

D The Deluge drown'd
   The Earth around.

E ELIJAH hid,
   By Ravens fed.

F The Judgment made
   Felix afraid.

G — As runs the Glafs,
Our Life doth pafs.

H — My Book and Heart
Muft never part.

I — Job feels the Rod,
Yet bleffes GOD.

K — Proud Korah's Troops
Was fwallow'd up.

L — Lot fled to Zoar,
Saw fiery Shower
On Sodom pour.

M — Mofes was he
Who Ifrael's Hoft
Led thro' the Sea.

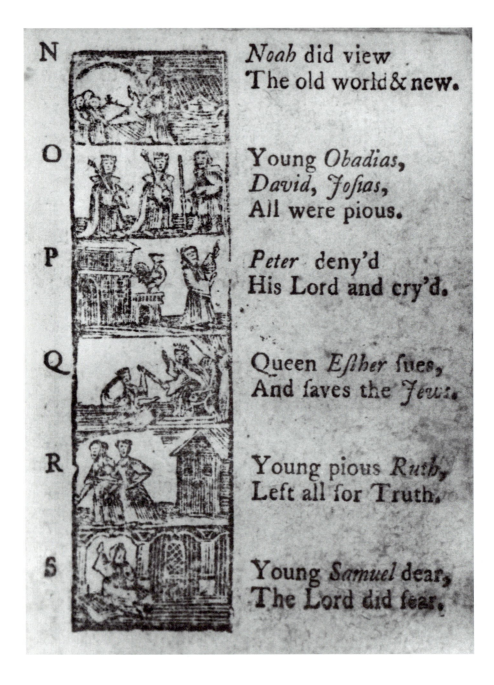

N — *Noah* did view
The old world & new.

O — Young *Obadias*,
David, Josias,
All were pious.

P — *Peter* deny'd
His Lord and cry'd.

Q — Queen *Esther* sues,
And saves the *Jews.*

R — Young pious *Ruth,*
Left all for Truth.

S — Young *Samuel* dear,
The Lord did fear.

T Young *Timothy*
Learnt Sin to fly.

U *Vashti* for Pride,
Was set aside.

W Whales in the Sea,
GOD's Voice obey.

X *Xerxes* did die,
And so must I.

Y While Youth do chear
Death may be near.

Z *Zaccheus* he
Did climb the Tree,
Our Lord to see.

WHO was the first Man ?————Adam.
Who was the first Woman ?   Eve.
Who was the first Murderer ?   Cain.
Who was the first Martyr ?   Abel.
Who was the first Translated ?   Enoch.
Who was the oldest Man ?   Methuselah.
Who built the Ark ?   Noah.
Who was the Patientest Man ?   Job.
Who was the meekest Man ?   Moses.
Who led Israel into Canaan ?   Joshua.
Who was the strongest Man ?   Samson.
Who kill'd Goliah ?   David.
Who was the wisest Man ?   Solomon.
Who was in the Whale's Belly ?   Jonah
Who saves lost men ?   Jesus Christ.
Who is Jesus Christ ?   the Son of God.
Who was the Mother of Christ ?   Mary.
Who betray'd his Master ?   Judas.
Who deny'd his Master ?   Peter.
Who was the first Christian Martyr ? Stephen.
Who was chief Apostle of the Gentiles ? Paul.

The Infant's Grace before and after Meat.

Bless me, O Lord, and let my food strengthen
me to serve thee, for Jesu Christ sake. Amen.
I Desire to thank God who gives me food
to eat every Day of my Life.   Amen.

CHAPTER TWO

THE AMERICAN REVOLUTION AND SCHOOLS FOR THE NEW REPUBLIC, 1770-1820

Introduction

The colonial pattern of schooling was imported from England, as were most colonial institutions. After the American Revolution, citizens of the new nation needed to decide what to keep and what to discard from their English inheritance. Clearly, they intended to keep schools, but they also intended to change them. The *New England Primer's* editorial change, from "Whales in the Sea, God's Voice obey," to "Washington brave his country did save," was symbolic of the changes to come as a new generation sought to create a uniquely American form of education for the young citizens of the new republic.

Thomas Jefferson is certainly the best remembered of the leaders of the revolutionary generation who addressed issues of schooling. The Virginia legislature rejected his proposed "Bill for the More General Diffusion of Knowledge" in 1779. However, that document and his subsequent, "Notes on the State of Virginia," written while he was representing American interests in Paris in 1783, represent perhaps the best (and certainly the best known) statement of the demands a democratic revolution places on schooling. When Jefferson argued that the best safeguard against tyranny is "to illuminate, as far as practicable, the minds of the people at large," he articulated the American faith in education as clearly as would ever be done. Of course, students of history recognize the irony that Jefferson's definition of "the people at large" was fairly limited. Jefferson seldom included women in his definition of citizens, and his own role as a slaveholder dramatically undermined all of his democratic rhetoric, including his call for universal schooling. A further irony exists: Although Jefferson was a prime voice for the development of schools for all citizens in Virginia and throughout the new nation, his home state did not adopt any of his recommendations until long after his death. Indeed, only at the hands of its first post-Civil War government, with the voices of newly freed slaves included in the debate, did Virginia adopt Jefferson's earlier proposals. For all of his failings, however, Jefferson outlined a democratic political vision and system of education in his writings that later generations would embrace far more fervently than the author ever dreamed possible.

Less remembered than Jefferson, but probably more effective in the educational politics of their generation, were two other philosophers of education, Benjamin Rush and Noah Webster. Rush, though he disagreed with much of Jefferson's politics, shared in Jefferson's opinion that a new form of education was needed in the new nation. In a series of lectures that were later published, including "Thoughts Upon the Mode of Education in a Republic" in 1786 and "Thoughts Upon Female Education" in 1787, Rush outlined his version of republican virtues and education, including a specific, if somewhat limited, vision of the educational needs of female citizens.

Noah Webster, best remembered for his dictionary, probably did more to shape the education of the revolutionary era than any of his contemporaries. In his 1790 "On the Education of Youth in America," Webster outlined his goals. In his dictionary, he put these goals into practice, creating a new American form of the language, consciously different from the English of the mother country.

While Jefferson, Rush, Webster, and others wrote about the kind of education the new nation needed, the new political structures began to actually create educational institutions. Each of the newly freed thirteen colonies wrote a new constitution. Many of these earliest constitutions deemed a system of free public schooling essential to democracy. In Massachusetts, for example, John Adams, later to be the second president of the United States, was called on to draft a new constitution in 1780. Adams included in his draft a state mandate for the development of a school system and other means of encouraging a literate citizenry. Adams framed his rationale for schooling in somewhat arcane language, but his basic ideas would be adopted by each succeeding generation of leaders who wanted to expand the role of schooling in the American republic:

> Wisdom, and knowledge, as well as virtue, diffused generally among the body of the people, being necessary for the preservation of their rights and liberties; and as these depend on spreading the opportunities and advantages of education in the various parts of the country, and among the different orders of the people . . . [schools should be established] to countenance and inculcate the principles of humanity and general benevolence, public and private charity, industry and frugality, honesty and punctuality in their dealings; sincerity, good-humour, and all social affections, and generous sentiments among the people.

Thus as the new state governments took shape, the school was emerging with a new role: It should not only support literacy, but encourage a quasi-religious morality among citizens.

The federal government also took an early lead in educational issues. While schooling was left to the states, the national government did have a role in maintaining an educated populace. Even before the Constitution was adopted, while still under the Articles of Confederation in 1787, Congress adopted the Northwest Ordinance, setting up a government for the new territories of the northwest (the present states of Michigan, Wisconsin, Ohio, Indiana, and Illinois). The ordinance included its famous edict that "Religion, Morality and knowledge being necessary to good government and the happiness of mankind, Schools and the means of education shall forever be encouraged." This link between good government, schools, and morality would continue for a long time to come.

Congress and the presidents, from Washington on, also had to address the education of the Indian populations, with whom they were developing a series of treaties. Throughout the nation's history, the government's attitude towards Native Americans has been ambivalent, but the Civilization Fund Act of 1819 represents one of the earliest efforts to force Indians into the American system of society and government and the use of schools to accomplish the task. Almost without exception, at least until the era of the New Deal in the 1930s, federal policy assumed that schooling for Indians meant schooling that separated them from their cultures—and usually their lands—by making them adopt the culture and ethics of European Americans. Respect for cultural diversity was not on the horizon.

Of course, the issues were more complex than these brief documents indicate. Jefferson understood all too well that women, Native Americans, and African Americans were excluded from the Republic his schools were designed to serve. Who would be included—in the schools and in definitions of democracy—would be debated for the next two hundred years of American history. Attending to the real diversity of the nation's citizens and to the institutionalization of the revolutionary era's dreams for schools would be left to later generations. In the field of schooling, the founders' primary contribution was a vision of what they thought schooling should be. Deciding who would be included in this vision, and making it come alive, was left to future generations. It is in the next era—the time of the Common School Movement, between 1820 and 1860—that the issues raised during the revolutionary era first received significant attention, even as schools were becoming a universal part of American society.

✢Thomas Jefferson, A Bill for the More General Diffusion of Knowledge, 1779

In 1779, in the midst of the American Revolution, a young Thomas Jefferson proposed three interconnected bills to the Virginia legislature: one to make the College of William and Mary more democratic, one proposing a public library system, and the third to create a statewide school system for his newly independent home state. None of the bills passed. Indeed, none of the southern states had a meaningful system of public education in place until after the Civil War. But in his "Bill for the More General Diffusion of Knowledge," Jefferson outlined in very clear terms the rationale for a system he believed was appropriate for educating the youth of a new democracy.

Whereas it appeareth that however certain forms of government are better calculated than others to protect individuals in the free exercise of their natural rights, and are at the same time themselves better guarded against degeneracy, yet experience hath shewn, that even under the best forms, those entrusted with power have, in time, and by slow operations, perverted it into tyranny; and it is believed that the most effectual means of preventing this would be, to illuminate, as far as practicable, the minds of the people at large, and more especially to give them knowledge of those facts, which history exhibiteth, that, possessed thereby of the experience of other ages and countries, they may be enabled to know ambition under all its shapes, and prompt to exert their natural powers to defeat its purposes; And whereas it is generally true that people will be happiest whose laws are best, and are best administered, and that laws will be wisely formed, and honestly administered, in proportion as those who form and administer them are wise and honest; whence it becomes expedient for promoting the publick happiness that those persons, whom nature hath endowed with genius and virtue, should be rendered by liberal education worthy to receive, and able to guard the sacred deposit of the rights and liberties of their fellow citizens, and that they should be called to that charge without regard to wealth, birth, or other accidental condition or circumstance; but the indigence of the greater number disabling them from so educating, at their own expence, those of their children whom nature hath fitly formed and disposed to become useful instruments for the public, it is better that such should be sought for and educated at the common expence of all, than that the happiness of all should be confided to the weak or wicked:

Be it therefore enacted by the General Assembly, that in every county within this commonwealth, there shall be chosen annually, by the electors qualified to vote for Delegates, three of the most honest and able men of their county, to be called the Aldermen of the county; and that the election of the said Aldermen shall be held at the same time and place, before the same persons, and notified and conducted in the same manner as by law is directed for the annual election of Delegates for the county.

The person before whom such election is holden shall certify to the court of the said county the names of the Aldermen chosen, in order that the same may be entered of record, and shall give notice of their election to the said Aldermen within a fortnight after such election.

The said Aldermen on the first Monday in October, if it be fair, and if not, then on the next fair day, excluding Sunday, shall meet at the court-house of their county, and proceed to divide their said county into hundreds, bounding the same by water courses, mountains, or limits, to be run and marked, if they think necessary, by the county surveyor, and at the county expence, regulating the size of the said hundreds, according to the best of their discretion, so as that they may contain a convenient number of children to make up a school, and be of such convenient size that all the children within each hundred may daily attend the school to be established therein, distinguishing each hundred by a particular name; which division, with the names of the several hundreds, shall be returned to the court of the county and be entered of record, and shall remain unaltered until the increase or decrease of inhabitants shall render an alteration necessary, in the opinion of any succeeding Aldermen, and also in the opinion of the court of the county.

The electors aforesaid residing within every hundred shall meet on the third Monday in October after the first election of Aldermen, at such place, within their hundred, as the said Aldermen shall direct, notice thereof being previously given to them by such person residing within the hundred as the said Aldermen shall require who is hereby enjoined to obey such requisition, on pain of being punished by amercement and imprisonment. The electors being so assembled shall choose the most convenient place within their hundred for building a school-house. If two or more places, having a greater number of votes than any others, shall yet be equal between themselves, the Aldermen, or such of them as are not of the same hundred, on information thereof, shall decide between them. The said Aldermen shall forthwith proceed to have a school-house built at the said place, and shall see that the same be kept in repair, and, when necessary, that it be rebuilt; but whenever they shall think necessary that it be rebuilt, they shall give notice as before directed, to the electors of the hundred to meet at the said school-house, on such day as they shall appoint, to determine by vote, in the manner before directed, whether it shall be rebuilt at the same, or what other place in the hundred.

At every of these schools shall be taught reading, writing, and common arithmetick, and the books which shall be used therein for instructing the children to read shall be such as will at the same time make them acquainted with Graecian, Roman, English, and American history. At these schools all the free children, male and female, resident within the respective hundred, shall be intitled to receive tuition gratis, for the term of three years, and as much longer, at their private expence, as their parents, guardians, or friends shall think proper.

Over every ten of these schools (or such other number nearest thereto, as the number of hundreds in the county will admit, without fractional divisions) an overseer shall be appointed annually by the Aldermen at their first meeting, eminent for his learning, integrity, and fidelity to the commonwealth, whose business and duty it shall be, from time to time, to appoint a teacher to each school, who shall give assurance of fidelity to the commonwealth, and to remove him as he shall see cause; to visit every school once in every half year at the least; to examine the schollars; see that any general plan of reading and instruction recommended by the visiters of William and Mary College shall be observed; and to superintend the conduct of the teacher in every thing relative to his school.

Every teacher shall receive a salary of _____ by the year, which, with the expences of building and repairing the school-houses, shall be provided in such manner as other county expences are by law directed to be provided and shall also have his diet, lodging, and washing found him, to be levied in like manner, save only that such levy shall be on the inhabitants of each hundred for the board of their own teacher only.

And in order that grammar schools may be rendered convenient to the youth in every part of the commonwealth, Be it farther enacted, that on the first Monday in November, after the first appointment of overseers for the hundred schools, if fair, and if not, then on the next fair day, excluding Sunday, after the hour of one in the afternoon, the said overseers appointed for the schools in the counties of Princess Ann, Norfolk, Nansemond and Isle-of-Wight, shall meet at Nansemond court-house; those for the counties of Southampton, Sussex, Surry, and Prince George, shall meet at Sussex court-house; those for the counties of Brunswick, Mecklenburg, and Lunenburg, shall meet at Lunenburg court-house; those for the counties of Dinwiddie, Amelia, and Chesterfield, shall meet at Chesterfield court-house; those for the counties of Powhatan, Cumberland, Goochland, Henrico, and Hanover, shall meet at Henrico court-house; those for the counties of Prince Edward, Charlotte, and Halifax, shall meet at Charlotte court-house; those for the counties of Henry, Pittsylvania, and Bedford, shall meet at Pittsylvania court-house; those for the counties of Buckingham, Amherst, Albermarle, and Fluvanna, shall meet at Albermarle court-house; those for the counties of Botetourt, Rockbridge, Montgomery, Washington, and Kentucky, shall meet at Botetourt court-house; those for the counties of Augusta, Rockingham, and Greenbrier, shall meet at Augusta court-house; those for the counties of Accomack and Northampton, shall meet at Accomack court-house; those for the counties of Elizabeth City, Warwick, York, Gloucester, James City, Charles City, and New-Kent, shall meet at James City court-house; those for the counties of Middlesex, Essex, King and Queen, King William and Caroline, shall meet at King and Queen court-house; those for the counties of Lancaster, Northumberland, Richmond, and Westmoreland, shall meet at Richmond court-house; those for the counties of King George, Stafford, Spotsylvania, Prince William, and Fairfax, shall meet at Spotsylvania court-house; those for the counties of Loudoun and Fauquier, shall meet at Loudoun court-house; those for the counties of Culpeper, Orange, and Louisa, shall meet at Orange court-house; those for the counties of Shenandoah and Frederick, shall meet at Frederick court-house; those for the counties of Hampshire and Berkeley, shall meet at Berkeley court-house; and those for the counties of Yohogania, Monongalia, and Ohio, shall meet at Monongalia court-house; and shall fix on such place in some one of the counties in their district as shall be most proper for situating a grammar school-house; endeavouring that the situation be as central as may be to the inhabitants of the said counties, that it be furnished with good water, convenient to plentiful supplies of provision and fuel, and more than all things that it be healthy. And if a majority of the overseers present should not concur in their choice of any one place proposed, the method of determining shall be as follows: If two places only were proposed, and the votes be divided, they shall decide between them by fair and equal lot; if more than two places were proposed, the question shall be put on those two which on the first division had the greater number of votes; or if no two places had a greater number of votes than the others, as where the votes shall have been equal between one or both of them and some other or others, then it shall be decided by fair and equal lot (unless it can be agreed by a majority of votes) which of the places having equal numbers shall be thrown out of the competition, so that the question shall be put on the remaining two, and if on this ultimate question the votes shall be equally divided, it shall then be decided finally by lot.

The said overseers having determined the place at which the grammar school for their district shall be built, shall forthwith (unless they can otherwise agree with the proprietors of the circumjacent lands as to location and price) make application to the clerk of the county in which the said house is to be situated, who shall thereupon issue a writ, in the nature of a writ of ad quod damnum, directed to the sheriff of the said county commanding him to summon and impanel twelve fit persons to meet at the place, so destined for the grammar school house, on a certain day, to be named in the said writ, not less than five, nor more than ten, days from the date thereof; and also to give notice of the same to the proprietors and tenants of the lands to be viewed, if they be to be found within the county, and if not then to their agents therein if any they have. Which freeholders shall be charged by the said sheriff impartially, and to the best of their skill and judgment to view the lands round about the said place, and to locate and circumscribe, by certain metes and bounds, one hundred acres thereof, having regard therein principally to the benefit and convenience of the said school, but respecting in some measure also the convenience of the said proprietors, and to value and appraise the same in so many several and distinct parcels as shall be owned or held by several and distinct owners or tenants, and according to their respective interest and estates therein. And after such location and appraisement so made, the said sheriff shall forthwith return the same under the hands and seals of the said jurors, together with the writ, to the clerk's office of the said county and the right and property of the said proprietors and tenants in the said lands so circumscribed shall be immediately divested and be transferred to the commonwealth for the use of the said grammar school, in full and absolute dominion, any want of consent or disability to consent in the said owners or tenants notwithstanding. But it shall not be lawful for the said overseers so to situate the said grammar school-house, nor to the said jurors so to locate the said lands, as to include the mansion-house of the proprietor of the lands, nor the offices, curtilage, or garden, thereunto immediately belonging.

The said overseers shall forthwith proceed to have a house of brick or stone, for the said grammar school, with necessary offices, built on the said lands, which grammar school-house shall contain a room for the school, a hall to dine in, four rooms for a master and usher, and ten or twelve lodging rooms for the scholars.

To each of the said grammar schools shall be allowed out of the public treasury, the sum of   pounds, out of which shall be paid by the Treasurer, on warrant from the Auditors, to the proprietors or tenants of the lands located, the value of their several interest as fixed by the jury, and the balance thereof shall be delivered to the said overseers to defray the expence of the said buildings.

In these grammar schools shall be taught the Latin and Greek languages, English grammar, geography, and the higher part of numerical arithmetick, to wit, vulgar and decimal fractions, and the extraction of the square and cube roots.

A visitor from each county constituting the district shall be appointed, by the overseers, for the county, in the month of October annually, either from their own body or from their county at large, which visitors or the greater part of them, meeting together at the said grammar school on the first Monday in November, if fair, and if not, then on the next fair day, excluding Sunday, shall have power to choose their own Rector, who shall call and preside at future meetings, to employ from time to time a master, and if necessary, an usher, for the said school, to remove them at their will, and to settle the price of tuition to be paid by the scholars. They shall also visit the school twice in every year at the least, either together or separately at their discretion, examine the scholars, and see that any general plan of instruction recommended by the visitors of William and Mary College shall be observed. The said masters and ushers, before they enter on the execution of their office, shall give assurance of fidelity to the commonwealth.

A steward shall be employed, and removed at will by the master, on such wages as the visitors shall direct; which steward shall see to the procuring [of] provisions, fuel, servants for cooking, waiting, house cleaning, washing, mending, and gardening on the most reasonable terms; the expence of which, together with the steward's wages, shall be divided equally among all the scholars boarding either on the public or private expence. And the part of those who are on private expence, and also the price of their tuitions due to the master or usher, shall be paid quarterly by the respective scholars, their parents, or guardians, and shall be recoverable, if withheld, together with costs, on motion in any Court of Record, ten days notice thereof being previously given to the party, and a jury impannelled to try the issue joined, or enquire of the damages. The said steward shall also, under the direction of the visiters, see that the houses be kept in repair, and necessary enclosures be made and repaired, the accounts for which, shall, from time to time, be submitted to the Auditors, and on their warrant paid by the Treasurer.

Every overseer of the hundred schools shall, in the month of September annually, after the most diligent and impartial examination and enquiry, appoint from among the boys who shall have been two years at the least at some one of the schools under his superintendance, and whose parents are too poor to give them farther education, some one of the best and most promising genius and disposition, to proceed to the grammar school of his district; which appointment shall be made in the court-house of the county, on the court day for that month if fair, and if not, then on the next fair day, excluding Sunday, in the presence of the Aldermen, or two of them at the least, assembled on the bench for that purpose, the said overseer being previously sworn by them to make such appointment, without favor or affection, according to the best of his skill and judgment, and being interrogated by the said Aldermen, either on their own motion, or on suggestions from the parents, guardians, friends, or teachers of the children, competitors for such appointment; which teachers shall attend for the information of the Aldermen. On which interregatories the said Aldermen, if they be not satisfied with the appointment proposed, shall have right to negative it; whereupon the said visiter may proceed to make a new appointment, and the said Aldermen again to interrogate and negative, and so toties quoties until an appointment be approved.

Every boy so appointed shall be authorised to proceed to the grammar school of his district, there to be educated and boarded during such time as is hereafter limited; and his quota of the expences of the house together with a compensation to the master or usher for his tuition, at the rate of twenty dollars by the year, shall be paid by the Treasurer quarterly on warrant from the Auditors.

A visitation shall be held, for the purpose of probation annually at the said grammar school on the last Monday in September, if fair, and if not, then on the next fair day, excluding Sunday, at which one third of the boys sent thither by appointment of the said overseers, and who shall have been there one year only, shall be discontinued as public foundationers, being those who, on the most diligent examination and enquiry, shall be thought to be of the least promising genius and disposition; and of those who shall have been there two years, all shall be discontinued, save one only the best in genius and disposition, who shall be at liberty to continue there four years longer on the public foundation, and shall thence forward be deemed a senior.

The visiters for the districts which, or any part of which, be southward and westward of James river, as known by that name, or by the names of Fluvanna and Jackson's river, in every other year, to wit, at the probation meetings held in the years, distinguished in the Christian computation by odd numbers, and the visiters for all the other districts at their said meetings to be held in those years, distinguished by even numbers, after dilligent examination and enquiry as before directed, shall chuse one among the said seniors, of the best learning and most hopeful genius and disposition, who shall be authorised by them to proceed to William and Mary College, there to be educated, boarded, and clothed, three years; the expence of which annually shall be paid by the Treasurer on warrant from the Auditors.

✢THOMAS JEFFERSON, NOTES ON THE STATE OF VIRGINIA, 1783

Four years after the failure of his proposal for a general system of schooling, Jefferson wrote from Paris, where he was then serving as American ambassador, about the conditions of his home state and especially his continuing commitment to a system of public education. In these notes, Jefferson explains the reasoning behind his detailed plans for a school system.

Many of the laws which were in force during the monarchy being relative merely to that form of government, or inculcating principles inconsistent with republicanism, the first assembly which met after the establishment of the commonwealth, appointed a committee to revise the whole code, to reduce it into proper form and volume, and report it to the assembly. This work has been executed by three gentlemen, and reported; but probably will not be taken up till a restoration of peace shall leave to the legislature leisure to go through such a work. . . .

Another object of the revisal is, to diffuse knowledge more generally through the mass of the people. This bill proposes to lay off every county into small districts of five or six miles square, called hundreds, and in each of them to establish a school for teaching reading, writing, and arithmetic. The tutor to be supported by the hundred, and every person in it entitled to send their children three years gratis, and as much longer as they please, paying for it. These schools to be under a visitor who is annually to chuse the boy of best genius in the school, of those whose parents are too poor to give them further education, and to send him forward to one of the grammar schools, of which twenty are proposed to be erected in different parts of the country, for teaching Greek, Latin, geography, and the higher branches of numerical arithmetic. Of the boys thus sent in any one year, trial is to be made at the grammar schools one or two years, and the best genius of the whole selected, and continued six years, and the residue dismissed. By this means twenty of the best geniuses will be raked from the rubbish annually, and be instructed, at the public expence, so far as the grammar schools go. At the end of six years instruction, one half are to be discontinued (from among whom the grammar schools will probably be supplied with future masters); and the other half, who are to be chosen for the superiority of their parts and disposition, are to be sent and continued three years in the study of such sciences as they shall chuse, at William and Mary college, the plan of which is proposed to be enlarged, as will be hereafter explained, and extended to all the useful sciences. The ultimate result of the whole scheme of education would be the teaching all the children of the State reading, writing, and common arithmetic; turning out ten annually, of superior genius, well taught in Greek, Latin, geography, and the higher branches of arithmetic; turning out ten others annually, of still superior parts, who, to those branches of learning, shall have added such of the sciences as their genius shall have led them to; the furnishing to the wealthier part of the people convenient schools at which their children may be educated at their own expence.

The general objects of this law are to provide an education adapted to the years, to the capacity and the condition of every one, and directed to their freedom and happiness. Specific details were not proper for the law. These must be the business of the visitors entrusted with its execution. The first stage of this education being the schools of the hundreds, wherein the great mass of the people will receive their instruction, the principle foundations of future order will be laid here. Instead, therefore, of putting the Bible and Testament into the hands of the children at an age when their judgments are not sufficiently matured for religious inquiries, their memories may here be stored with most useful facts from Grecian, Roman, European, and American history. The first elements of morality too may be instilled into their minds; such as; when further developed as their judgments advance in strength, may teach them how to work out their greatest happiness, by shewing them that it does not depend on the condition of life in which chance has placed them, but is always the result of a good conscience, good health, occupation, and freedom in all just pursuits.

Those whom either the wealth of their parents or the adoption of the state shall destine to higher degrees of learning, will go on to the grammar schools, which constitute the next stage, there to be instructed in the languages. The learning [of] Greek and Latin, I am told, is going into disuse in Europe. I know not what their manners and occupations may call for: but it would be very ill-judged in us to follow their example in this instance. There is a certain period of life, say from eight to fifteen or sixteen years of age, when the mind like the body is not yet firm enough for laborious and close operations. If applied to such, it falls an early victim to premature exertion; exhibiting, indeed, at first, in these young and tender subjects, the flattering appearance of their being men while they are yet children, but ending in reducing them to be children when they should be men. The memory is then most susceptible and tenacious of impressions; and the learning of languages being chiefly a work of memory, it seems precisely fitted to the powers of this period, which is long enough too for acquiring the most useful languages, ancient and modern. I do not pretend that language is science. It is only an instrument for the attainment of science. But that time is not lost which is employed in providing tools for future operation: more especially as in this case the books put into the hands of the youth for this purpose may be such as will at the same time impress their minds with useful facts and good principles. If this period be suffered to pass in idleness, the mind becomes lethargic and impotent, as would the body it inhabits if unexercised during the same time. The sympathy between body and mind during their rise, progress, and decline, is too strict and obvious to endanger our being misled while we reason from the one to the other. As soon as they are of sufficient age, it is supposed they will be sent on from the grammar schools to the university, which constitutes our third and last stage, there to study those sciences which may be adapted to their views. By that part of our plan which prescribes the selection of the youths of genius from among the classes of the poor, we hope to avail the state of those talents which nature has sown as liberally among the poor as the rich, but which perish without use, if not sought for and cultivated. But of all the views of this law none is more important, none more legitimate, than that of rendering the people the safe, as they are ultimate, guardians of their own liberty. For this purpose the reading in the first stage, where they will receive their whole education, is proposed, as has been said, to be chiefly historical. History, by apprising them of the past, will enable them to judge of the future; it will avail them of the experience of other times and other nations; it will qualify them as judges of the actions and designs of men; it will enable them to know ambition under every disguise it may assume; and knowing it, to defeat its views. In every government on earth is some trace of human weakness, some germ of corruption and degeneracy, which cunning will discover, and wickedness insensibly open, cultivate, and improve. Every government degenerates when trusted to the rulers of the people alone. The people themselves therefore are its only safe depositories. And to render even them safe, their minds must be improved to a certain degree. This indeed is not all that is necessary, though it be essentially necessary. An amendment of our constitution must here come in aid of the public education. The influence over government must be shared among all the people. If every individual which composes their mass participates of the ultimate authority, the government will be safe; because the corrupting the whole mass will exceed any private resources of wealth; and public ones cannot be provided but by levies on the people. In this case every man would have to pay his own price. The government of Great Britain has been corrupted, because but one man in ten has a right to vote for members of parliament. The sellers of the government, therefore, get nine-tenths of their price clear. It has been thought that corruption is restrained by confining the right of suffrage to a few of the wealthier of the people: but it would be more effectually restrained by an extension of that right to such numbers as would bid defiance to the means of corruption.

✦BENJAMIN RUSH, THOUGHTS UPON THE MODE OF EDUCATION PROPER IN A REPUBLIC, 1786

Benjamin Rush, although not remembered in the same league as Jefferson or Adams or even dictionary writer Noah Webster, was known during the revolutionary era as one of Pennsylvania's greatest citizens. A doctor and a professor of chemistry, he was also a political leader who signed the Declaration of Independence. He wrote about education as one who saw himself as a leader in the business of nation building. His "Plan for the Establishment of Public Schools and the Diffusion of Knowledge in Pennsylvania" was based on the still novel assumption that it was a proper use of tax money to support schools. Like Jefferson, Rush believed that "A free government can only exist in an equal diffusion of literature. Without learning, men become savages or barbarians, and where learning is confined to a few people, we always find monarchy, aristocracy, and slavery." To replace these evils with democracy, Rush proposed a tax-supported system of public education for Pennsylvania that would include the state university at Philadelphia and four colleges spread around the state, that would prepare citizens for the university; an academy in each county that would offer the scholarly languages needed for the colleges; and a free school in each township that would offer mathematics, as well as reading and writing in English and German. While outlining the kind of system he thought his home state needed, Rush also provided an extended essay covering his thoughts on the unique kind of education appropriate for the new republic. While his recommendations are similar to Jeffersons, in some ways, they are directly contradictory in others especially regarding the teaching of religion.

The business of education has acquired a new complexion by the independence of our country. The form of government we have assumed has created a new class of duties to every American. It becomes us, therefore, to examine our former habits upon this subject, and in laying the foundations for nurseries of wise and good men, to adapt our modes of teaching to the peculiar form of our government.

The first remark that I shall make upon this subject is that an education in our own is to be preferred to an education in a foreign country. The principle of patriotism stands in need of the reinforcement of *prejudice,* and it is well known that our strongest prejudices in favor of our country are formed in the first one and twenty years of our lives. The policy of the Lacedamonians is well worthy of our imitation. When Antipater demanded fifty of their children as hostages for the fulfillment of a distant engagement, those wise republicans refused to comply with his demand but readily offered him double the number of their adult citizens, whose habits and prejudices could not be shaken by residing in a foreign country. Passing by, in this place, the advantages to the community from the early attachment of youth to the laws and constitution of their country, I shall only remark that young men who have trodden the paths of science together, or have joined in the same sports, whether of swimming, skating, fishing, or hunting, generally feel, through life, such ties to each other as add greatly to the obligations of mutual benevolence.

I conceive the education of our youth in this country to be peculiarly necessary in Pennsylvania while our citizens are composed of the natives of so many different kingdoms in Europe. Our schools of learning, by producing one general and uniform system of education, will render the mass of the people more homogeneous and thereby fit them more easily for uniform and peaceable government.

I proceed, in the next place, to inquire what mode of education we shall adopt so as to secure to the state all the advantages that are to be derived from the proper instruction of youths; and here I beg leave to remark that the only foundation for a useful education in a republic is to be laid in Religion. Without this, there can be no virtue, and without virtue there can be no liberty, and liberty is the object and life of all republican governments.

Such is my veneration for every religion that reveals the attributes of the Deity, or a future state of rewards and punishments, that I had rather see the opinions of Confucius or Mohammed inculcated upon our youth than see them grow up wholly devoid of a system of religious principles. But the religion I mean to recommend in this place is the religion of Jesus Christ.

It is foreign to my purpose to hint at the arguments which establish the truth of the Christian revelation. My only business is to declare that all its doctrines and precepts are calculated to promote the happiness of society and the safety and well-being of civil government. A Christian cannot fail of being a republican. The history of the creation of man and of the relation of our species to each other by birth, which is recorded in the Old Testament, is the best refutation that can be given to the divine right of kings and the strongest argument that can be used in favor of the original and natural equality of all mankind. A Christian, I say again, cannot fail of being a republican, for every precept of the Gospel inculcates those degrees of humility, self-denial, and brotherly kindness which are directly opposed to the pride of monarchy and the pageantry of a court. A Christian cannot fail of being useful to the republic, for his religion teacheth him that no man "liveth to himself." And lastly, a Christian cannot fail of being wholly inoffensive, for his religion teacheth him in all things to do to others what he would wish, in like circumstances, they should do to him.

I am aware that I dissent from one of those paradoxical opinions with which modern times abound: that it is improper to fill the minds of youth with religious prejudices of any kind and that they should be left to choose their own principles after they have arrived at an age in which they are capable of judging for themselves. Could we preserve the mind in childhood and youth a perfect blank, this plan of education would have more to recommend it, but this we know to be impossible. The human mind runs as naturally into principles as it does after facts. It submits with difficulty to those restraints or partial discoveries which are imposed upon it in the infancy of reason. Hence the impatience of children to be informed upon all subjects that relate to the invisible world. But I beg leave to ask, Why should we pursue a different plan of education with respect to religion from that which we pursue in teaching the arts and sciences? Do we leave our youth to acquire systems of geography, philosophy, or politics till they have arrived at an age in which they are capable of judging for themselves? We do not. I claim no more, then, for religion than for the other sciences, and I add further that if our youth are disposed after they are of age to think for themselves, a knowledge of *one* system will be the best means of conducting them in a free inquiry into other systems of religion, just as an acquaintance with one system of philosophy is the best introduction to the study of all the other systems in the world.

I must beg leave upon this subject to go one step further. In order more effectually to secure to our youth the advantages of a religious education, it is necessary to impose upon them the doctrines and discipline of a particular church. Man is naturally an ungovernable animal, and observations on particular societies and countries will teach us that when we add the restraints of ecclesiastical to those of domestic and civil government, we produce in him the highest degrees of order and virtue. That fashionable liberality which refuses to associate with any one sect of Christians is seldom useful to itself or to society and may fitly be compared to the unprofitable bravery of a soldier who wastes his valor in solitary enterprises without the aid or effect of military associations. Far be it from me to recommend the doctrines or modes of worship of any one denomination of Christians. I only recommend to the persons entrusted with the education of youth to inculcate upon them a strict conformity to that mode of worship which is most agreeable to their consciences or the inclinations of their parents.

Under this head, I must be excused in not agreeing with those modern writers who have opposed the use of the Bible as a schoolbook. The only objection I know to it is its division into chapters and verses and its improper punctuation which render it a more difficult book to read *well* than many others, but these defects may easily be corrected, and the disadvantages of making children early and intimately acquainted with the means of acquiring happiness both here and hereafter. How great is the difference between making young people acquainted with the interesting and entertaining truths contained in the Bible, and the fables of Moore and Croxall, or the doubtful histories of antiquity! I maintain that there is no book of its size in the whole world that contains half so much useful knowledge for the government of states or the direction of the affairs of individuals as the Bible. To object to the practice of having it read in schools because it tends to destroy our veneration for it is an argument that applies with equal force against the frequency of public worship and all other religious exercises.

The first impressions upon the mind are the most durable. They survive the wreck of the memory and exist in old age after the ideas acquired in middle life have been obliterated. Of how much consequence, then, must it be to the human mind in the evening of life to be able to recall those ideas which are most essential to its happiness, and these are to be found chiefly in the Bible. The great delight which old people take in reading the Bible, I am persuaded, is derived chiefly from its histories and precepts being *associated* with the events of childhood and youth, the recollection of which forms a material part of their pleasures.

I do not mean to exclude books of history, poetry, or even fables from our schools. They may and should be read frequently by our young people, but if the Bible is made to give way to them altogether, I foresee that it will be read in a short time only in churches and in a few years will probably be found only in the offices of magistrates and in courts of justice.

Next to the duty which young men owe to their Creator, I wish to see a SUPREME REGARD TO THEIR COUNTRY inculcated upon them. When the Duke of Sully became prime minister to Henry the IVth of France, the first thing he did, he tells us, "was to subdue and forget his own heart." The same duty is incumbent upon every citizen of a republic. Our country includes family, friends, and property, and should be preferred to them all. Let our pupil be taught that he does not belong to himself, but that he is public property. Let him be taught to love his family, but let him be taught at the same time that he must forsake and even forget them when the welfare of his country requires it.

He must watch for the state as if its liberties depended upon his vigilance alone, but he must do this in such a manner as not to defraud his creditors or neglect his family. He must love private life, but he must decline no station, however public or responsible it may be, when called to it by the suffrages of his fellow citizens. He must love popularity, but he must despise it when set in competition with the dictates of his judgment or the real interest of his country. He must love character and have a due sense of injustices, but he must be taught to appeal only to the laws of the state, to defend the one and punish the other. He must love family honor, but he must be taught that neither the rank nor antiquity of his ancestors can command respect without personal merit. He must avoid neutrality in all questions that divide the state, but he must shun the rage and acrimony of party spirit. He must be taught to love his fellow creatures in every part of the world, but he must cherish with a more intense and peculiar affection the citizens of Pennsylvania and of the United States.

I do not wish to see our youth educated with a single prejudice against any nation or country, but we impose a task upon human nature repugnant alike to reason, revelation, and the ordinary dimensions of the human heart when we require him to embrace with equal affection the whole family of mankind. He must be taught to amass wealth, but it must be only to increase his power of contributing to the wants and demands of the state. He must be indulged occasionally in amusements, but he must be taught that study and business should be his principal pursuits in life. Above all, he must love life and endeavor to acquire as many of its conveniences as possible by industry and economy, but he must be taught that this life "is not his own" when the safety of his country requires it. These are practicable lessons, and the history of the commonwealths of Greece and Rome show that human nature, without the aids of Christianity, has attained these degrees of perfection.

While we inculcate these republican duties upon our pupil, we must not neglect at the same time to inspire him with republican principles. He must be taught that there can be no durable liberty but in a republic and that government, like all other sciences, is of a progressive nature. The chains which have bound the science in Europe are happily unloosed in America. *Here* it is open to investigation and improvement. While philosophy has protected us by its discoveries from a thousand natural evils, government has unhappily followed with an unequal pace. It would be to dishonor human genius only to name the many defects which still exist in the best systems of legislation. We daily see matter of a perishable nature rendered durable by certain chemical operations. In like manner, I conceive that it is possible to analyze and combine power in such a manner as not only to increase the happiness but to promote the duration of republican forms of government far beyond the terms limited for them by history or the common opinions of mankind.

To assist in rendering religious, moral, and political instruction more effectual upon the minds of our youth, it will be necessary to subject their bodies to physical discipline. To obviate the inconveniences of their studious and sedentary mode of life, they should live upon a temperate diet, consisting chiefly of broths, milk, and vegetables. The black broth of Sparta and the barley broth of Scotland have been alike celebrated for their beneficial effects upon the minds of young people. They should avoid tasting spirituous liquors. They should also be accustomed occasionally to work with their hands in the intervals of study and the busy seasons of the year in the country. Moderate sleep, silence, occasional solitude, and cleanliness should be inculcated upon them, and the utmost advantage should be taken of a proper direction of those great principles in human conduct—sensibility, habit, imitation, and association.

The influence [of] these physical causes will be powerful upon the intellects as well as upon the principles and morals of young people.

To those who have studied human nature, it will not appear paradoxical to recommend in this essay a particular attention to vocal music. Its mechanical effects in civilizing the mind and thereby preparing it for the influence of religion and government have been so often felt and recorded that it will be unnecessary to mention facts in favor of its usefulness in order to excite a proper attention to it.

In the education of youth, let the authority of our masters be as *absolute* as possible. The government of schools, like the government of private families, should be *arbitrary*, that it may not be *severe*. By this mode of education, we prepare our youth for the subordination of laws and thereby qualify them for becoming good citizens of the republic. I am satisfied that the most useful citizens have been formed from those youth who have never known or felt their own wills till they were one and twenty years of age, and I have often thought that society owes a great deal of its order and happiness to the deficiencies of parental government being supplied by those habits of obedience and subordination which are contracted at schools.

I cannot help bearing a testimony, in this place, against the custom which prevails in some parts of America (but which is daily falling into disuse in Europe) of crowding boys together under one roof for the purpose of education. The practice is the gloomy remains of monkish ignorance and is as unfavorable to the improvements of the mind in useful learning as monasteries are to the spirit of religion. I grant this mode of secluding boys from the intercourse of private families has a tendency to make them scholars, but our business is to make them men, citizens, and Christians. The vices of young people are generally learned from each other. The vices of adults seldom infect them. By separating them from each other, therefore, in their hours of relaxation from study, we secure their morals from a principal source of corruption, while we improve their manners by subjecting them to those restraints which the difference of age and sex naturally produce in private families. . . .

The *present time* is peculiarly favorable to the establishment of these benevolent and necessary institutions in Pennsylvania. The minds of our people have not as yet lost the yielding texture they acquired by the heat of the late Revolution. They will *now* receive more readily than five or even three years hence new impressions and habits of all kinds. The spirit of liberty *now* pervades every part of the state.

➔BENJAMIN RUSH, THOUGHTS UPON FEMALE EDUCATION, 1787

In addition to his general thoughts on the education needed for a newly democratic nation, Benjamin Rush had quite specific designs for the education he thought women needed. This essay, which was originally a speech to the Board of Visitors of the young Ladies' Academy at Pennsylvania given July, 1787, outlines what was at the time a very liberal approach to the education of women in the new nation. As in his earlier essay, so here Rush's desire to create a distinctly American and democratic form of education is clear in this essay as is his hope that democratic women will have a level of independence far greater than their predecessors.

Gentlemen,

I have yielded with diffidence to the solicitations of the Principal of the Academy, in undertaking to express my regard for the prosperity of this seminary of learning by submitting to your candor a few thoughts upon female education.

The first remark that I shall make upon this subject is that female education should be accommodated to the state of society, manners, and government of the country in which it is conducted.

This remark leads me at once to add that the education of young ladies in this country should be conducted upon principles very different from what it is in Great Britain and in some respects different from what it was when we were a part of a monarchical empire.

There are several circumstances in the situation, employments, and duties of women in America which require a peculiar mode of education.

I.   The early marriages of our women, by contracting the time allowed for education, renders it necessary to contract its plan and to confine it chiefly to the more useful branches of literature.

II. The state of property in America renders it necessary for the greatest part of our citizens to employ themselves in different occupations for the advancement of their fortunes. This cannot be done without the assistance of the female members of the community. They must be the stewards and guardians of their husbands' property. That education, therefore, will be most proper for our women which teaches them to discharge the duties of those offices with the most success and reputation.

III. From the numerous avocations to which a professional life exposes gentlemen in America from their families, a principal share of the instruction of children naturally devolves upon the women. It becomes us therefore to prepare them, by a suitable education, for the discharge of this most important duty of mothers.

IV. The equal share that every citizen has in the liberty and the possible share he may have in the government of our country make it necessary that our ladies should be qualified to a certain degree, by a peculiar and suitable education, to concur in instructing their sons in the principles of liberty and government.

V.   In Great Britain the business of servants is a regular occupation, but in America this humble station is the usual retreat of unexpected indigence; hence the servants in this country possess less knowledge and subordination than are required from them; and hence our ladies are obliged to attend more to the private affairs of their families than ladies generally do of the same rank in Great Britain. "They are good servants," said an American lady of distinguished merit in a letter to a favorite daughter, "who will do well with good looking after." This circumstance should have great influence upon the nature and extent of female education in America.

The branches of literature most essential for a young lady in this country appear to be:

I.   A knowledge of the English language. She should not only read but speak and spell correctly. And to enable her to do this, she should be taught the English grammar and be frequently examined in applying its rules in common conversation.

II.   Pleasure and interest conspire to make the writing of a fair and legible hand a necessary branch of female education. For this purpose she should be taught not only to shape every letter properly but to pay the strictest regard to points and capitals . . . .

III. Some knowledge of figures and bookkeeping is absolutely necessary to qualify a young lady for the duties which await her in this country. There are certain occupations in which she may assist her husband with this knowledge, and should she survive him and agreeably to the custom of our country be the executrix of his will, she cannot fail of deriving immense advantages from it.

IV.   An acquaintance with geography and some instruction in chronology will enable a young lady to read history, biography, and travels, with advantage, and thereby qualify her not only for a general intercourse with the world but to be an agreeable companion for a sensible man. To these branches of knowledge may be added, in some instances, a general acquaintance with the first principles of astronomy and natural philosophy, particularly with such parts of them as are calculated to prevent superstition, by explaining the causes or obviating the effects of natural evil.

V.   Vocal music should never be neglected in the education of a young lady in this country. Besides preparing her to join in that part of public worship which consists in psalmody, it will enable her to soothe the cares of domestic life. The distress and vexation of a husband, the noise of a nursery, and even the sorrows that will sometimes intrude into her own bosom may all be relieved by a song, where sound and sentiment unite to act upon the mind. . . .

VI.   Dancing is by no means an improper branch of education for an American lady. It promotes health and renders the figure and motions of the body easy and agreeable. I anticipate the time when the resources of conversation shall be so far multiplied that the amusement of dancing shall be wholly confined to children. But in our present state of society and knowledge, I conceive it to be an agreeable substitute for the ignoble pleasures of drinking and gaming in our assemblies of grown people.

VII. The attention of our young ladies should be directed as soon as they are prepared for it to the reading of history, travels, poetry, and moral essays. These studies are accommodated, in a peculiar manner, to the present state of society in America, and when a relish is excited for them in early life, they subdue that passion for reading novels which so generally prevails among the fair sex. I cannot dismiss this species of writing and reading without observing that the subjects of novels are by no means accommodated to our present manners. They hold up *life,* it is true, but it is not yet *life* in America. Our passions have not as yet "overstepped the modesty of nature," nor are they "torn to tatters," to use the expressions of the poet, by extravagant love, jealousy, ambition, or revenge. . . .

VIII. It will be necessary to connect all these branches of education with regular instruction in the Christian religion. For this purpose the principles of the different sects of Christians should be taught and explained, and our pupils should early be furnished with some of the most simple arguments in favor of the truth of Christianity. A portion of the Bible (of late improperly banished from our schools) should be read by them every day and such questions should be asked, after reading it, as are calculated to imprint upon their minds the interesting stories contained in it.

Rousseau has asserted that the great secret of education consists in "wasting the time of children profitably." There is some truth in this observation. I believe that we often impair their health and weaken their capacities by imposing studies upon them which are not proportioned to their years. But this objection does not apply to religious instruction. There are certain simple propositions in the Christian religion that are suited in a peculiar manner to the infant state of reason and moral sensibility. A clergyman of long experience in the instruction of youth informed me that he always found children acquired religious knowledge more easily than knowledge upon other subjects, and that young girls acquired this kind of knowledge more readily than boys. The female breast is the natural soil of Christianity, and while our women are taught to believe its doctrines and obey its precepts, the wit of Voltaire and the style of Bolingbroke will never be able to destroy its influence upon our citizens.

IX. If the measures that have been recommended for inspiring our pupils with a sense of religious and moral obligation be adopted, the government of them will be easy and agreeable. I shall only remark under this head that *strictness* of discipline will always render *severity* unnecessary and that there will be the most instruction in that school where there is the most order.

I have said nothing in favor of instrumental music as a branch of female education because I conceive it is by no means accommodated to the present state of society and manners in America. The price of musical instruments and the extravagant fees demanded by the teachers of instrumental music form but a small part of my objections to it. . . .

I cannot dismiss the subject of female education without remarking that the city of Philadelphia first saw a number of gentlemen associated for the purpose of directing the education of young ladies. By means of this plan the power of teachers is regulated and restrained and the objects of education are extended. By the separation of the sexes in the unformed state of their manners, female delicacy is cherished and preserved. Here the young ladies may enjoy all the literary advantages of a boarding school and at the same time live under the protection of their parents. Here emulation may be excited without jealousy, ambition without envy, and competition without strife.

The attempt to establish this new mode of education for young ladies was an experiment and the success of it hath answered our expectations. Too much praise cannot be given to our principal and his assistants, for the abilities and fidelity with which they have carried the plan into execution. The proficiency which the young ladies have discovered in reading, writing, spelling, arithmetic, grammar, geography, music, and their different catechisms since the last examination is a less equivocal mark of the merits of our teachers than anything I am able to express in their favor.

But the reputation of the academy must be suspended till the public are convinced by the future conduct and character of our pupils of the advantages of the institution. To you, therefore, YOUNG LADIES, an important problem is committed for solution; and that is, whether our present plan of education be a wise one and whether it be calcu-lated to prepare you for the duties of social and domestic life. I know that the elevation of the female mind, by means of moral, physical, and religious truth, is considered by some men as unfriendly to the domestic character of a woman. But this is the prejudice of little minds and springs from the same spirit which opposes the general diffusion of knowledge among the citizens of our republics. If men believe that ignorance is favorable to the government of the female sex, they are certainly deceived, for a weak and ignorant woman will always be governed with the greatest difficulty.

I have sometimes been led to ascribe the invention of ridiculous and expensive fashions in female dress entirely to the gentlemen in order to divert the ladies from improving their minds and thereby to secure a more arbitrary and unlimited authority over them. It will be in your power, LADIES, to correct the mistakes and practice of our sex upon these subjects by demonstrating that the female temper can only be governed by reason and that the cultivation of reason in women is alike friendly to the order of nature and to private as well as public happiness.

↠Noah Webster, On the Education of Youth in America, Boston, 1790

While his name continues to find fame through the omnipresent Webster's Dictionary, Noah Webster himself has been virtually forgotten. He was, in fact, the single most influential person in the early development of a uniquely American version of the English language. His dictionary as well as his Speller, Grammar, and Reader were designed to clearly differentiate a democratic American English from the more flowery language of monarchical England. The fact that to this day people in the United States use a simpler form of spelling—"honor" rather than "honour," for example—is due to Webster's work. In addition to his schoolbooks, Webster was one of the most prolific authors of the revolutionary generation on the question of the appropriate kind of education for the youth of the new nation. While he and Rush differed in substantial and interesting ways, the differences were minor compared to their common emphasis on the need for a new educational system in the United States.

Education is a subject which has been exhausted by the ablest writers, both among the ancients and moderns. I am not vain enough to suppose I can suggest any new ideas upon so trite a theme as education in general; but perhaps the manner of conducting the youth in America may be capable of some improvement. Our constitutions of civil government are not yet firmly established; our national character is not yet formed; and it is an object of vast magnitude that systems of education should be adopted and pursued which may not only diffuse a knowledge of the sciences but may implant in the minds of the American youth the principles of virtue and of liberty and inspire them with just and liberal ideas of government and with an inviolable attachment to their own country. It now becomes every American to examine the modes of education in Europe, to see how far they are applicable in this country and whether it is not possible to make some valuable alterations, adapted to our local and political circumstances. Let us examine the subject in two views. First, as it respects arts and sciences. Secondly, as it is connected with morals and government. In each of these articles let us see what errors may be found and what improvements suggested in our present practice.

The first error that I would mention is a too general attention to the dead languages, with a neglect of our own.

This practice proceeds probably from the common use of the Greek and Roman tongues before the English was brought to perfection. There was a long period of time when these languages were almost the only repositories of science in Europe. Men who had a taste for learning were under a necessity of recurring to the sources, the Greek and Roman authors. These will ever be held in the highest estimation both for style and sentiment, but the most valuable of them have English translations, which, if they do not contain all the elegance, communicate all the ideas of the originals. The English language, perhaps, at this moment, is the repository of as much learning as one half the languages of Europe. In copiousness it exceeds all modern tongues, and though inferior to the Greek and French in softness and harmony, yet it exceeds the French in variety; it almost equals the Greek and Roman in energy and falls very little short of any language in the regularity of its construction.

In deliberating upon any plan of instruction, we should be attentive to its future influence and probable advantages. What advantage does a merchant, a mechanic, a farmer, derive from an acquaintance with the Greek and Roman tongues? It is true, the etymology of words cannot be well understood without a knowledge of the original languages of which ours is composed. But a very accurate knowledge of the meaning of words and of the true construction of sentences may be obtained by the help of dictionaries and good English writers, and this is all that is necessary in the common occupations of life. But suppose there is some advantage to be derived from an acquaintance with the dead languages, will this compensate for the loss of five or perhaps seven years of valuable time? Life is short, and every hour should be employed to good purposes. If there are no studies of more consequence to boys than those of Latin and Greek, let these languages employ their time, for idleness is the bane of youth. But when we have an elegant and copious language of our own, with innumerable writers upon ethics, geography, history, commerce, and government—subjects immediately interesting to every man—how can a parent be justified in keeping his son several years over rules of syntax, which he forgets when he shuts his book, or which, if remembered, can be of little or no use in any branch of business? This absurdity is the subject of common complaint; men see and feel the impropriety of the usual practice, and yet no arguments that have hitherto been used have been sufficient to change the system or to place an English school on a footing with a Latin one in point of reputation.

It is not my wish to discountenance totally the study of the dead languages. On the other hand, I should urge a more close attention to them among young men who are designed for the learned professions. The poets, the orators, the philosophers, the historians of Greece and Rome furnish the most excellent models of style and the richest treasures of science. The slight attention given to a few of these authors in our usual course of education is rather calculated to make pedants than scholars, and the time employed in gaining superficial knowledge is really wasted.

> A little learning is a dangerous thing,
> Drink deep, or taste not the Pierian spring.

But my meaning is that the dead languages are not necessary for men of business, merchants, mechanics, planters, etc., nor of utility sufficient to indemnify them for the expense of time and money which is requisite to acquire a tolerable acquaintance with the Greek and Roman authors. Merchants often have occasion for a knowledge of some foreign living language as the French, the Italian, the Spanish, or the German, but men whose business is wholly domestic have little or no use for any language but their own, much less for languages known only in books. . . .

If language is to be taught mechanically or by rote, it is a matter of little consequence whether the rules are in English, Latin, or Greek, but if children are to acquire
ideas, it is certainly easier to obtain them in a language which they understand than in
a foreign tongue. The distinctions between the principal parts of speech are founded in
nature and are within the capacity of a school boy. These distinctions should be
explained in English, and when well understood will facilitate the acquisition of other
languages. Without some preparation of this kind, boys will often find a foreign language extremely difficult and sometimes be discouraged. We often see young persons
of both sexes puzzling their heads with French when they can hardly write two sentences of good English. They plod on for some months with much fatigue, little
improvement, and less pleasure, and then relinquish the attempt.

The principles of any science afford pleasure to the student who comprehends
them. In order to render the study of language agreeable, the distinctions between words
should be illustrated by the differences in visible objects. Examples should be presented to the senses, which are the inlets of all our knowledge. That *nouns are the
names of things and that adjectives express their qualities* are abstract definitions which
a boy may repeat five years without comprehending the meaning. But that *table* is the
name of an article and *hard* or *square* is its property is a distinction obvious to the senses and consequently within a child's capacity.

There is one general practice in schools which I censure with diffidence, not
because I doubt the propriety of the censure, but because it is opposed to deep-rooted
prejudices: this practice is the use of the Bible as a schoolbook. There are two reasons
why this practice has so generally prevailed: the first is that families in the country are
not generally supplied with any other book; the second, an opinion that the reading of
the scriptures will impress upon the minds of youth the important truths of religion and
morality. The first may be easily removed, and the purpose of the last is counteracted
by the practice itself.

If people design the doctrines of the Bible as a system of religion, ought they to
appropriate the book to purposes foreign to this design? Will not a familiarity, contracted by a careless, disrespectful reading of the sacred volume, weaken the influence
of its precepts upon the heart?

Let us attend to the effect of familiarity in other things.

The rigid Puritans who first settled the New England states often chose their bury-
ing ground in the center of their settlements. Convenience might have been a motive for
the choice, but it is probable that a stronger reason was the influence which they supposed the frequent burials and constant sight of the tombs would have upon the lives of
men. The choice, however, for the latter purpose was extremely injudicious, for it may
be laid down as a general rule that those who live in a constant view of death will
become hardened to its terrors.

No person has less sensibility than the surgeon who has been accustomed to the
amputation of limbs. No person thinks less of death than the soldier who has frequently walked over the carcasses of his slain comrades or the sexton who lives among
the tombs.

Objects that affect the mind strongly, whether the sensations they excite are
painful or pleasurable, always lose their effect by a frequent repetition of their impressions. Those parts of the scripture, therefore, which are calculated to strike terror to the
mind lose their influence by being too frequently brought into view. The same objection will not apply to the history and morality of the Bible, select passages of which

may be read in schools to great advantage. In some countries, the common people are not permitted to read the Bible at all. In ours, it is as common as a newspaper and in schools is read with nearly the same degree of respect. Both these practices appear to be extremes. My wish is not to see the Bible excluded from schools, but to see it is used as a system of religion and morality.

These remarks suggest another error which is often committed in our inferior schools: I mean that of putting boys into difficult sciences while they are too young to exercise their reason upon abstract subjects. For example, boys are often put to the study of mathematics at the age of eight or ten years and before they can either read or write. In order to show the impropriety of such a practice, it is necessary to repeat what was just now observed, that our senses are the avenues of knowledge. This fact proves that the most natural course of education is that which employs, first the senses or powers of the body or those faculties of the mind which first acquire strength, and then proceeds to those studies which depend on the power of comparing and combining ideas. The art of writing is mechanical and imitative; this may therefore employ boys as soon as their fingers have strength sufficient to command a pen. A knowledge of letters requires the exercise of a mental power, memory, but this is coeval almost with the first operations of the human mind, and with respect to objects of sense, is almost perfect even in childhood. Children may therefore be taught reading as soon as their organs of speech have acquired strength sufficient to articulate the sounds of words.

But those sciences a knowledge of which is acquired principally by the reasoning faculties should be postponed to a more advanced period of life. In the course of an English education, mathematics should be perhaps the last study of youth in schools. Years of valuable time are sometimes thrown away in a fruitless application to sciences, the principles of which are above the comprehension of the students.

There is no particular age at which every boy is qualified to enter upon mathematics to advantage. The proper time can be best determined by the instructors, who are acquainted with the different capacities of their pupils.

Another error which is frequent in America is that a master undertakes to teach many different branches in the same school. In new settlements, where people are poor and live in scattered situations, the practice is often unavoidable, but in populous towns it must be considered as a defective plan of education. For suppose the teacher to be equally master of all the branches which he attempts to teach, which seldom happens, yet his attention must be distracted with a multiplicity of objects and consequently painful to himself and not useful to the pupils. Add to this the continual interruptions which the students of one branch suffer from those of another, which must retard the progress of the whole school. It is a much more eligible plan to appropriate an apartment to each branch of education, with a teacher who makes that branch his sole employment. The principal academies in Europe and America are on this plan, which both reason and experience prove to be the most useful. . . .

But the principal defect in our plan of education in America is the want of good teachers in the academies and common schools. By good teachers I mean men of unblemished reputation and possessed of abilities competent to their stations. That a man should be master of what he undertakes to teach is a point that will not be disputed, and yet it is certain that abilities are often dispensed with, either through inattention or fear of expense.

To those who employ ignorant men to instruct their children, permit me to suggest one important idea: that it is better for youth to have *no* education than to have a bad one, for it is more difficult to eradicate habits than to impress new ideas. The tender shrub is easily bent to any figure, but the tree which has acquired its full growth resists all impressions.

Yet abilities are not the sole requisites. The instructors of youth ought, of all men, to be the most prudent, accomplished, agreeable, and respectable. What avail a man's parts, if, while he is the "wisest and brightest," he is the "meanest of man-kind?" The pernicious effects of bad example on the *minds* of youth will probably be acknowledged, but with a view to *improvement* it is indispensably necessary that the teachers should possess good breeding and agreeable manners. In order to give full effect to instructions, it is requisite that they should proceed from a man who is loved and respected. But a low-bred clown or morose tyrant can command neither love nor respect, and that pupil who has no motive for application to books but the fear of a rod will not make a scholar.

The rod is often necessary in school, especially after the children have been accustomed to disobedience and a licentious behavior at home. All government originates in families, and if neglected there, it will hardly exist in society, but the want of it must be supplied by the rod in school, the penal laws of the state, and the terrors of divine wrath from the pulpit. The government both of families and schools should be absolute. There should in families be no appeal from one parent to another, with the prospect of pardon for offenses. The one should always vindicate, at least apparently, the conduct of the other. In schools the matter should be absolute in command, for it is utterly impossible for any man to support order and discipline among children who are indulged with an appeal to their parents. A proper subordination in families would generally supersede the necessity of severity in schools, and a strict discipline in both is the best foundation of good order in political society.

From a strange inversion of the order of nature, the cause of which it is not necessary to unfold, the most important business in civil society is in many parts of America committed to the most worthless characters. The education of youth, an employment of more consequence than making laws and preaching the gospel, because it lays the foundation on which both law and gospel rest for success, this education is sunk to a level with the most menial services. In most instances we find the higher seminaries of learning entrusted to men of good characters and possessed of the moral virtues of social affections. But many of our inferior schools, which, so far as the heart is concerned, are as important as colleges, are kept by men of no breeding, and many of them, by men infamous for the most detestable vices. Will this be denied? Will it be denied that before the war it was a frequent practice for gentlemen to purchase convicts who had been transported for their crimes and employ them as private tutors in their families?

Gracious Heavens! Must the wretches who have forfeited their lives and been pronounced unworthy to be inhabitants of a *foreign* country be entrusted with the education, the morals, the character of *American* youth?

The only practicable method to reform mankind is to begin with children, to banish, if possible, from their company every low-bred, drunken, immoral character. Virtue and vice will not grow together in a great degree, but they will grow where they are planted, and when one has taken root, it is not easily supplanted by the other. The great art of correcting mankind, therefore, consists in prepossessing the mind with good principles.

For this reason society requires that the education of youth should be watched with the most scrupulous attention. Education, in a great measure, forms the moral characters of men, and morals are the basis of government. Education should therefore be the first care of a legislature, not merely the institution of schools but the furnishing of them with the best men for teachers. A good system of education should be the first article in the code of political regulations, for it is much easier to introduce and establish an effectual system for preserving morals than to correct by penal statutes the ill effects of a bad system. I am so fully persuaded of this that I shall almost adore that great man who shall change our practice and opinions and make it respectable for the first and best men to superintend the education of youth.

Another defect in our schools, which, since the Revolution, is become inexcusable, is the want of proper books. The collections which are now used consist of essays that respect foreign and ancient nations. The minds of youth are perpetually led to the history of Greece and Rome or to Great Britain; boys are constantly repeating the declamations of Demosthenes and Cicero or debates upon some political question in the British Parliament. These are excellent specimens of good sense, polished style, and perfect oratory, but they are not interesting to children. They cannot be very useful, except to young gentlemen who want them as models of reasoning and eloquence in the pulpit or at the bar.

But every child in America should be acquainted with his own country. He should read books that furnish him with ideas that will be useful to him in life and practice. As soon as he opens his lips, he should rehearse the history of his own country; he should lisp the praise of liberty and of those illustrious heroes and statesmen who have wrought a revolution in her favor.

A selection of essays respecting the settlement and geography of America, the history of the late Revolution and of the most remarkable characters and events that distinguished it, and a compendium of the principles of the federal and provincial governments should be the principal schoolbook in the United States. These are interesting objects to every man; they call home the minds of youth and fix them upon the interests of their own country, and they assist in forming attachments to it, as well as in enlarging the understanding. . . .

In several states, we find laws passed establishing provision for colleges and academies where people of property may educate their sons, but no provision is made for instructing the poorer rank of people even in reading and writing. Yet in these same states, every citizen who is worth a few shillings annually is entitled to vote for legislators. This appears to me a most glaring solecism in government. The constitutions are *republican* and the laws of education are *monarchical*. The *former* extend civil rights to every honest, industrious man, the *latter* deprive a large proportion of the citizens of a most valuable privilege.

In our American republics, where government is in the hands of the people, knowledge should be universally diffused by means of public schools. Of such consequence is it to society that the people who make laws should be well informed that I conceive no legislature can be justified in neglecting proper establishments for this purpose.

When I speak of a diffusion of knowledge, I do not mean merely a knowledge of spelling books and the New Testament. An acquaintance with ethics and with the general principles of law, commerce, money, and government is necessary for the yeomanry of a republican state. This acquaintance they might obtain by means of books calculated for schools and read by the children during the winter months and by the circulation of public papers.

"In Rome it was the common exercise of boys at school to learn the laws of the twelve tables by heart, as they did their poets and classic authors." What an excellent practice this in a free government!

It is said, indeed by many, that our common people are already too well informed. Strange paradox! The truth is, they have too much knowledge and spirit to resign their share in government and are not sufficiently informed to govern themselves in all cases of difficulty.

There are some acts of the American legislatures which astonish men of information, and blunders in legislation are frequently ascribed to bad intentions. But if we examine the men who compose these legislatures, we shall find that wrong measures generally proceed from ignorance either in the men themselves or in their constituents. They often mistake their own interest, because they do not foresee the remote consequences of a measure.

It may be true that all men cannot be legislators, but the more generally knowledge is diffused among the substantial yeomanry, the more perfect will be the laws of a republican state.

Every small district should be furnished with a school, at least four months in a year, when boys are not otherwise employed. This school should be kept by the most reputable and well informed man in the district. Here children should be taught the usual branches of learning, submission to superiors and to laws, the moral or social duties, the history and transactions of their own country, the principles of liberty and government. Here the rough manners of the wilderness should be softened and the principles of virtue and good behavior inculcated. The *virtues* of men are of more consequence to society than their *abilities,* and for this reason the *heart* should be cultivated with more assiduity than the *head.*

Such a general system of education is neither impracticable nor difficult, and excepting the formation of a federal government that shall be efficient and permanent, it demands the first attention of American patriots. Until such a system shall be adopted and pursued, until the statesman and divine shall unite their efforts in *forming* the human mind, rather than in lopping its excrescences after it has been neglected, until legislators discover that the only way to make good citizens and subjects is to nourish them from infancy, and until parents shall be convinced that the *worst* of men are not the proper teachers to make the *best,* mankind cannot know to what a degree of perfection society and government may be carried. America affords the fairest opportunities for making the experiment and opens the most encouraging prospect of success.

In a system of education that should embrace every part of the community, the female sex claim no inconsiderable share of our attention.

The women in America (to their honor it is mentioned) are not generally above the care of educating their own children. Their own education should therefore enable them to implant in the tender mind such sentiments of virtue, propriety, and dignity as are suited to the freedom of our governments. Children should be treated as children, but as children that are in a future time to be men and women. By treating them as if they were always to remain children, we very often see their childishness adhere to them, even in middle life. The silly Language called *baby talk,* in which most persons are initiated in infancy, often breaks out in discourse at the age of forty and makes a man appear very ridiculous. In the same manner, vulgar, obscene, and illiberal ideas imbibed in a nursery or a kitchen often give a tincture to the conduct through life. In order to prevent every evil bias, the ladies, whose province it is to direct the inclinations of children on their first appearance and to choose their nurses, should be possessed, not only of amiable manners, but of just sentiments and enlarged understandings.

But the influence of women in forming the dispositions of youth is not the sole reason why their education should be particularly guarded; their influence in controlling the manners of a nation is another powerful reason. Women, once abandoned, may be instrumental in corrupting society, but such is the delicacy of the sex and such the restraints which custom imposes upon them that they are generally the last to be corrupted. There are innumerable instances of men who have been restrained from a vicious life and even of very abandoned men who have been reclaimed by their attachment to ladies of virtue. A fondness for the company and conversation of ladies of character may be considered as a young man's best security against the attractives of a dissipated life. A man who is attached to good company seldom frequents that which *is bad*. For this reason, society requires that females should be well educated and extend their influence as far as possible over the other sex.

But a distinction is to be made between a *good* education and a *showy* one, for an education, merely superficial, is a proof of corruption of taste and has a mischievous influence on manners. The education of females, like that of males, should be adapted to the principles of the government and correspond with the stage of society. Education in Paris differs from that in Petersburg, and the education of females in London or Paris should not be a model for the Americans to copy.

In all nations, a good education is that which renders the ladies correct in their manners, respectable in their families, and agreeable in society. That education is always *wrong* which raises a woman above the duties of her station.

In America, female education should have for its object what is *useful*. Young ladies should be taught to speak and write their own language with purity and elegance, an article in which they are often deficient. The French language is not necessary for ladies. In some cases it is convenient, but, in general, it may be considered as an article of luxury. As an accomplishment, it may be studied by those whose attention is not employed about more important concerns.

Some knowledge of arithmetic is necessary for every lady. Geography should never be neglected. *Belles-lettres* learning seems to correspond with the dispositions of most females. A taste for poetry and fine writing should be cultivated, for we expect the most delicate sentiments from the pens of that sex which is possessed of the finest feelings.

A course of reading can hardly be prescribed for all ladies. But it should be remarked that this sex cannot be too well acquainted with the writers upon human life and manners. The *Spectator* should fill the first place in every lady's library. Other volumes of periodical papers, though inferior to the *Spectator,* should be read, and some of the best histories.

With respect to novels, so much admired by the young and so generally condemned by the old, what shall I say? Perhaps it may be said with truth that some of them are useful, many of them pernicious, and most of them trifling. A hundred volumes of modern novels may be read without acquiring a new idea. Some of them contain entertaining stories, and where the descriptions are drawn from nature and from characters and events in themselves innocent, the perusal of them may be harmless.

Were novels written with a view to exhibit only one side of human nature, to paint the social virtues, the world would condemn them as defective, but I should think them more perfect. Young people, especially females, should not see the vicious part of mankind. At best, novels may be considered as the toys of youth, the rattle boxes of sixteen. The mechanic gets his pence for his toys, and the novel writer, for his books, and it would be happy for society if the latter were in all cases as innocent playthings as the former.

In the large towns in America, music, drawing, and dancing constitute a part of female education. They, however, hold a subordinate rank, for my fair friends will pardon me when I declare that no man ever marries a woman for her performance on a harpsichord or her figure in a minuet. However ambitious a woman may be to command admiration *abroad,* her real merit is known only at *home.* Admiration is useless when it is not supported by domestic worth. But real honor and permanent esteem are always secured by those who preside over their own families with dignity.

Before I quiet this subject, I beg leave to make some remarks on a practice which appears to be attended with important consequences; I mean that of sending boys to Europe for an education or sending to Europe for teachers. This was right before the Revolution, at least so far as national attachments were concerned, but the propriety of it ceased with our political relation to Great Britain.

In the first place, our honor as an independent nation is concerned in the establishment of literacy institutions adequate to all our own purposes, without sending our youth abroad or depending on other nations for books and instructors. It is very little to the reputation of America to have it said abroad that after the heroic achievements of the late war these independent people are obliged to send to Europe for men and books to teach their children A B C.

But in another point of view, a foreign education is directly opposite to our political interest and ought to be discountenanced, if not prohibited.

Every person of common observation will grant that most men prefer the manners and the government of that country where they are educated. Let ten American youths be sent, each to a different European kingdom, and live there from the age of twelve to twenty, and each will give the preference to the country where he has resided.

The period from twelve to twenty is the most important in life. The impressions made before that period are commonly effaced; those that are made during that period *always* remain for many years and *generally* through life.

Nine-nine persons of a hundred who pass that period in England or France will prefer the people, their manners, their laws, and their government to those of their native country. Such attachments are injurious, both to the happiness of the men and to the political interest of their own country. As to private happiness, it is universally known how much pain a man suffers by a change of habits in living. The customs of Europe are and ought to be different from ours, but when a man has been bred in one country, his attachments to its manners make them, in a great measure, necessary to his happiness. On changing his residence, he must therefore break his former habits, which is always a painful sacrifice; or the discordance between the manners of his own country and his must give him incessant uneasiness; or he must introduce into a circle of his friends the manners in which he was educated. These consequences may follow, and the last, which is inevitable, is a pubic injury. The refinement of manners in every country should keep pace exactly with the increase of its wealth, and perhaps the greatest evil America now feels is in improvement of taste and manners which its wealth cannot support.

A foreign education is the very source of this evil; it gives young gentlemen of fortune a relish for manners and amusements which are not suited to this country, which, however, when introduced by this class of people will always become fashionable.

But a corruption of manners is not the sole objection to a foreign education; an attachment to a *foreign* government, or rather a want of attachment to our *own,* is the natural effect of a residence abroad during the period of youth. It is recorded of one of the Greek cities that in a treaty with their conquerors it was required that they should give a certain number of *male children* as hostages for the fulfillment of their engagements. The Greeks absolutely refused, on the principle that these children would imbibe the ideas and embrace the manners of foreigners or lose their love for their own country, but they offered the same number of *old* men without hesitation. This anecdote is full of good sense. A man should always form his habits and attachments in the country where he is to reside for life. When these habits are formed, young men may travel without danger of losing their patriotism. A boy who lives in England from twelve to twenty will be an *Englishman* in his manners and his feelings, but let him remain at home till he is twenty and form his attachments, he may be several years abroad and still be an *American.* There may be exceptions to this observation, but living examples may be mentioned to prove the truth of the general principle here advanced respecting the influence of habit.

It may be said that foreign universities furnish much better opportunities of improvements in the sciences that the American. This may be true and yet will not justify the practice of sending young lads from their own country. There are some branches of science which may be studied to much greater advantage in Europe than in America, particularly chemistry. When these are to be acquired, young gentlemen ought to spare no pains to attend the best professors. It may, therefore, be useful, in some cases, for students to cross the Atlantic to *complete* a course of studies, but it is not necessary for them to go early in life nor to continue a long time. Such instances need not be frequent even now, and the necessity for them will diminish in proportion to the future advancement of literature in America.

It is, however, much questioned whether in the ordinary course of study a young man can enjoy greater advantages in Europe than in America. Experience inclines me to raise a doubt whether the danger to which a youth must be exposed among the sons of dissipation abroad will not turn the scale in favor of our American colleges. Certain it is that four fifths of the great literary characters in America never crossed the Atlantic.

But if our universities and schools are not so good as the English or Scotch, it is the business of our rules to improve them, not to endow them merely; for endowments alone will never make a flourishing seminary; but to furnish them with professors of the first abilities and the most assiduous application and with a complete apparatus for establishing theories by experiments. Nature has been profuse to the Americans, in genius and in the advantages of climate and soil. If this country, therefore, should long be indebted to Europe for opportunities of acquiring any branch of science in perfection, it must be by means of a criminal neglect of its inhabitants.

The difference in the nature of the American and European governments is another objection to a foreign education. Men form modes of reasoning or habits of thinking on political subjects in the country where they are bred; these modes of reasoning may be founded on fact in all countries, but the same principles will not apply in all governments because of the infinite variety of national opinions and habits. Before a man can be a good legislator, he must be intimately acquainted with the temper of the people to be governed. No man can be thus acquainted with the people without residing among them and mingling with all companies. For want of this acquaintance, a Turgot and a Price may reason most absurdly upon the constitutions of the American states;

and when any person has been long accustomed to believe in the propriety or impropriety of certain maxims or regulations of government, it is very difficult to change his opinions or to persuade him to adapt his reasoning to new and different circumstances.

One half the European Protestants will now contend that the Roman Catholic religion is subversive of civil government. Tradition, books, education have concurred to fix this belief in their minds, and they will not resign their opinions, even in America, where some of the highest civil offices are in the hands of Roman Catholics.

It is therefore of infinite importance that those who direct the councils of a nation should be educated in that nation. Not that they should restrict their personal acquaintance to their own country, but their first ideas, attachments, and habits should be acquired in the country which they are to govern and defend. When a knowledge of their own country is obtained and an attachment to its laws and interest deeply fixed in their hearts, then young gentlemen may travel with infinite advantage and perfect safety. I wish not therefore to discourage traveling, but, if possible, to render it more useful to individuals and to the community. My meaning is that *men* should travel and not *boys*.

It is time for the Americans to change their usual route and travel through a country which they never think of or think beneath their notice: I mean the United States.

While these states were a part of the British Empire, our interest, our feelings, were those of Englishmen; our dependence led us to respect and imitate their manners and to look up to them for our opinions. We little thought of any national interest in America, and while our commerce and governments were in the hands of our parent country and we had no common interest, we little thought of improving our acquaintance with each other or of removing prejudices and reconciling the discordant feelings of the inhabitants of different provinces. But independence and union render it necessary that the citizens of different states should know each others' characters and circumstances, that all jealousies should be removed, that mutual respect and confidence should succeed and a harmony of views and interest be cultivated by a friendly intercourse.

A tour through the United States ought now to be considered as a necessary part of a liberal education. Instead of sending young gentlemen to Europe to view curiosities and learn vices and follies, let them spend twelve or eighteen months in examining the local situation of the different states—the rivers, the soil, the population, the improvements and commercial advantages of the whole—with an attention to the spirit and manners of the inhabitants, their laws, local customs, and institutions. Such a tour should at least precede a tour to Europe, for nothing can be more ridiculous than a man traveling in a foreign country for information when he can give no account of his own. When, therefore, young gentlemen have finished an academic education, let them travel through America. Travel through America and afterwards to Europe if their time and fortunes will permit. But if they cannot make a tour through both, that in America is certainly to be preferred, for the people of America, with all their information, are yet extremely ignorant of the geography, policy, and manners of their neighboring states. Except a few gentlemen whose public employments in the army and in Congress have extended their knowledge of America, the people in this country, even of the higher classes, have not so correct information respecting the United States as they have respecting England or France. Such ignorance is not only disgraceful but is materially prejudicial to our political friendship and federal operations.

Americans, unshackle your minds and act like independent beings. You have been children long enough, subject to the control and subservient to the interest of a haughty parent. You have now an interest of your own to augment and defend: you have an empire to raise and support by your exertions and a national character to establish and extend by your wisdom and virtues. To effect these great objects, it is necessary to frame a liberal plan of policy and build it on a broad system of education. Before this system can be formed and embraced, the Americas must *believe* and *act* from the belief that it is dishonorable to waste life in mimicking the follies of other nations and basking in the sunshine of foreign glory.

✦United States Congress, Northwest Ordinance, July 13, 1787

Few sentences of legislation have been cited as often as the one from the Northwest Ordinance that stated, "Religion, morality, and knowledge being necessary to good government and the happiness of mankind, schools and the means of education shall forever be encouraged." While most of the 1787 legislation dealt with setting up the five new states that would eventually be admitted as Ohio, Indiana, Illinois, Michigan, and Wisconsin, the one sentence constituted the new national government's first commitment to support schools. There is certainly a Jeffersonian ring to the plea that education is important for securing "religion, morality, knowledge . . . and good government." And the authorities in the new territories did take the admonishment seriously; public support for schools became part of the new constitution in all five states.

It is hereby ordained and declared, by the authority aforesaid, That the following articles shall be considered as articles of compact between the original States, and the people and States in the said territory, and forever remain unaltered, unless by common consent, to wit: . . .

Religion, morality, and knowledge being necessary to good government and the happiness of mankind, schools and the means of education shall forever be encouraged. The utmost good faith shall always be observed towards the Indians; their lands and property shall never be taken from them without their consent; and in their property, rights, and liberty, they never shall be invaded or disturbed, unless in just and lawful wars authorized by Congress; but laws founded in justice and humanity shall from time to time be made, for preventing wrongs being done to them, and for preserving peace and friendship with them.

✦United States Congress, Civilization Fund Act, March 3, 1819

From its earliest years, the United States government struggled with the issue of how best to relate to the Indians. Early administrations viewed the various tribes as separate nations with whom the United States could wage war or conclude peace treaties. All too many—inside and outside of the government—preferred war and the taking of Indian lands. At the same time, others argued that the best course was to "civilize" the Indians, inducting them slowly into citizenship. While European missionaries had gone to the Indians from the earliest settlements in the sixteenth century, missionary efforts expanded in the national period. In 1810, some of the largest Protestant denominations expanded their Indian missions with government support. The Civilization Fund of 1819 formalized government support, allowing direct payments to "capable persons of good moral character," (that is, Protestant missionaries) who sought to bring European culture and religion to the various tribes.

An Act making provision for the civilization of the Indian tribes adjoining the frontier settlements:

Be it enacted by the Senate and House of Representatives of the United States of America, in Congress assembled, That for the purpose of providing against the further decline and final extinction of the Indian tribes, adjoining the frontier settlements of the United States, and for introducing among them the habits and arts of civilization, the President of the United States shall be, and he is hereby authorized, in every case where he shall judge improvement in the habits and condition of such Indians practicable, and that the means of instruction can be introduced with their own consent, to employ capable persons of good moral character, to instruct them in the mode of agriculture suited to their situation; and for teaching their children in reading, writing, and arithmetic, and performing such other duties as may be enjoined, according to such instructions and rules as the President may give and prescribe for the regulation of their conduct, in the discharge of their duties.

And be it further enacted, That the annual sum of ten thousand dollars be, and the same is hereby appropriated, for the purpose of carrying into effect the provisions of this act; and an account of the expenditure of the money, and proceedings in execution of the foregoing provisions, shall be laid annually before Congress.

Approved, March 3, 1819.

CHAPTER 3

THE COMMON SCHOOL
MOVEMENT, 1820-1860

Introduction

The pattern of public schooling we know today—tax-supported, free, and essentially compulsory—emerged in the United States during the four decades prior to the Civil War. As we have seen already, schools existed from the early 1600s in the colonies that would become the United States. But the role schools played changed significantly after the American Revolution. While the colonial school had been an adjunct to family, church, and community—offering on an elective basis those skills not learned at home, at church, or through apprenticeship—schools became the central institution of education during the early nineteenth century. And while Jefferson, Rush, and Webster argued in favor of schooling, it was the leaders of a succeeding generation—the school reformers of the 1820s–1850s—who actually implemented their ideas.

Horace Mann, who served as the first Secretary of the Massachusetts State Board of Education from 1837 to 1848, was perhaps the most articulate and certainly the most often-heard voice in the common school movement. Mann never tired of reminding audiences of the importance of the common school enterprise. As he wrote in his last (1848) Annual Report to the Board, "Without undervaluing any other human agency, it may be safely affirmed that the Common School, improved and energized, as it can easily be, may become the most effective and benignant of all the forces of civilization." Clearly, Mann's goals were not modest. But he had two basic reasons for placing so much faith in the schools. First, schools were becoming universal. The words "common school" meant common to all. In an era of increasing diversity, when no one religion could claim such loyalty, the church could no longer serve as a unifying force. But the school, reaching all citizens, could replace the church as the carrier of culture and creator of national unity. Secondly, the school reached citizens when they were young, when they could be molded into good Americans—at least, as Mann and his fellow school reformers defined the term. Adults would not be as easy to influence.

While Mann's was the most prominent voice in the common school movement, similar reformers, including Henry Barnard in Connecticut and Calvin Stowe and Samuel Lewis in Ohio, could be found in virtually every state of the Northeast and the Midwest (then simply called the West). All of the leaders who were involved in the creation of the Common Schools had a sense that they were participants in a heroic movement and treated each other in this way.

As the next section will show, the South did not follow the same course until after the Civil War. But by the 1850s, in spite of opposition, state-supported and more-or-less compulsory public schools were available in virtually all of the North and West of the then United States.

Two important anchors stabilized and strengthened the common school movement. One was an assumption, articulated by Mann in his Twelfth Report, that a generic Protestantism would serve the needs of the nation well. As historian Timothy L. Smith has written of the "common faith," which lay behind the emergence of the common school, "By the middle of the nineteenth century, leading citizens assumed that Americanism and Protestantism were synonyms and that education and Protestantism were allies." This was not the assumption of the more secular revolutionary generation, but with the major religious revivals of the early nineteenth century, and the significant growth of Catholic immigration, the nation's older leaders shifted their views towards a "vision of the future [which] was not the heavenly city of the eighteenth-century enlightenment but the New Jerusalem of the Christian millennium" (Timothy L. Smith, "Protestant Schooling and American Nationality, 1800–1850," *Journal of American History*).

The second equally important anchor of the common school movement was the replacement of the traditional male schoolmaster with the much lower-paid female schoolteacher. No one was more effective than Catharine Beecher in convincing school reformers that the key to their whole enterprise was the preparation and hiring of low-cost female teachers. Beecher was anxious to create a niche outside the home for single women like herself and was willing to accept second-class citizenship as the means to an education and professional career for women. Beecher was careful to include a moral dimension to her argument: she was among the advocates of the idea that women were more suited to teaching the young than men. As she said, "What is the most important and peculiar duty of the female sex? It is the physical, intellectual, and moral education of children. It is the care of the health, and the formation of the character, of the future citizen of this great nation." Her 1835 *Essay on the Education of Female Teachers* (New York: Van Nostrand & Dwight, 1835), which is included here, is one of many such talks she gave in a lifetime devoted to transforming the teaching profession from an overwhelmingly male to an overwhelmingly female profession.

Of course, not everyone was as enthusiastic in support of common schools as Mann, Beecher, and their allies. Historian Michael Katz has documented a series of failed school tax proposals that working-class voters rejected because they believed that the schools would primarily serve middle- and upper-class students, while the tax burden would fall on all citizens. [See Katz's *The Irony of Early School Reform:*

Educational Innovation in Mid-Nineteenth Century Massachusetts (1968) and *Class, Bureaucracy, and Schools* (1971) for more details.] Many well-off voters also saw no reason why they should pay taxes to support the education of other people's children, especially because they were quite prepared to use their own funds to pay for the education of their own children. Yet others feared the increased power of the state as it came to control more and more spheres of public life and public consciousness. (See, for example, Maxine Greene, *The Public School and the Private Vision.*)

Opposition to the common school movement took many forms. In 1840, the Massachusetts legislature, over Mann's vigorous objections, voted to abolish the State Board of Education and the office of Secretary, that Mann held. The vote was eventually overturned, and Mann held office for another eight years. But the reasons for the legislature's actions, reported in the selections from the *Common School Journal* included in this chapter, cast an illuminating light on the political battles surrounding education reform in the 1840s. Mann's opponents were not antieducation, but they were democratic localists who objected to what they saw as a state takeover of a local matter. Voices clamoring for community control of education have emerged in every era since Mann's time. They have supported different causes and expressed different concerns, but the question of who should hold the authority and responsibility for the education and enculturation of the youth is as unresolved an issue today as it was in Mann's time.

One group more than any other had cause to worry about the common school movement—and worry they did. While Timothy Smith broke new ground as a historian in making his statement about the links between Americanism, Protestantism, and education, a number of Catholic leaders were making the same argument by the 1840s. New York City's Catholic bishop at that time, John Hughes, took the lead in opposing the schools of the Public School Society, which, he rightly saw, were not nonsectarian but merely pan-Protestant. For him, the requirement that Catholic students attend such schools was a direct attack on his faith and on the religious freedom on which the nation prided itself. So he said:

> Should the professors of some weak or unpopular religion be oppressed today, the
> experiment may be repeated tomorrow on some other. Every successful attempt in that
> way will embolden the spirit of encroachment and diminish the power of resistance;
> and, in such an event, the monopolizers of education, after having discharged the
> office of public tutor, may find it convenient to assume that of public preacher.

Clearly Hughes and his allies meant to stop the movement towards a common Protestant culture and a common Protestant faith. They understood, far better than Mann or others, that in many ways the common school of the 1840s and 1850s was actually a state-supported Protestant parochial school. They certainly meant to have none of it. The "Petition of the Catholics of New York for a Portion of the Common School Fund," a petition signed by a number of Catholic laymen and included in this chapter, represents Hughes's arguments at their clearest.

It was, in fact, a fear of Catholicism—and especially rising Catholic immigration— which provided much of the fuel for the common school movement. In Boston, for example, the changes had been quite dramatic. In 1830, Boston was—as it had been in 1730—a city whose citizens were of predominantly English origin and Protestant faith. The highest number of immigrants in any one year—from all parts of the globe—was, up to that year, 4,000. By 1849, however, 29,000 immigrants a year were coming from

Ireland alone. And by 1860, the majority of Boston's citizens were Irish-Catholic. It was an extraordinary transformation. Driven by the potato famine, which gave many Irish-Catholics a choice between immigration and death, the immigration moved large numbers of desperately poor Catholics into one of the world's most Protestant and English-oriented cities.

The English-origin civic leaders did not intend to easily surrender their economic and cultural control. While violent clashes arose between poor and working-class Protestants and Catholics, such as the riots that led to the burning of the Ursuline Convent in Charlestown in 1834, Boston's elite had a different response. After all, Catholic immigrants could provide low-cost workers who could fuel an economic upsurge for the region. The challenge was to "Americanize" them, which meant "Protestantizing" them to the greatest degree possible. In 1845, the city's Mayor, Josiah Quincy, provided his version of the solution: "All children must be taught to respect and revere law and order . . . " [the School Committee must] "save society not with the cannon and the rifle but with the spelling book, grammar, and the Bible."

Horace Mann's work cannot be understood apart from this charged social and cultural situation. Mann was a school reformer, and he was also part of a national drive to define the nature of America's culture. The common school would replace the church as the carrier of the culture. It would not reflect any one Protestant sect, but the very definition Mann gave to nonsectarianism: "Reading the Bible without note or comment," was a deeply Protestant approach to the scriptures.

In the context of this same struggle, compulsory school laws also suddenly emerged. The schools of the colonial era and the early Republic were totally voluntary. Now, if a common culture was to be built, the common people had to be required to attend. For many Catholics, the issue was instead how to find a way to stay out. The result was a powerful alternative system of education—the Catholic parochial school system. But it is only possible to understand the Catholic system in the context of the very Protestant flavor of the public schools.

The debates about schooling between 1820 and 1860 among the nation's cultural elite focused almost exclusively on schooling whites. It was not surprising the South was left out of the movement, for the issue of slavery divided the South's population far too deeply for them to participate in anything that focused on commonality. But racism was not confined to the South. In the North, African Americans were free, but they were still restricted in terms of attending school. While Mann himself was an abolitionist, one can search in vain for material on the education of his state's African-American population within his education reports.

But not everyone was willing to ignore the issue. In the South, state legislatures reacted with increased fear toward African-American literacy after a number of slave uprisings, led by literate blacks, had taken place. At the same time, free blacks and their white allies ensured that illiteracy was not as prevalent among African Americans as the legislatures wished.

In the North, the issue of African-American education also received significant attention, in spite of the silence of the common school's most vocal leaders. In Boston, an independent African-American school was founded soon after the turn of the century. By 1821, a subcommittee of the Boston School Committee was charged with looking after the "African School." And in 1834, the School Committee built the Abiel Smith School, with four teachers and 300 students, operating as a segregated school on Beacon Hill.

A later generation of African Americans and white abolitionist allies began a campaign for integration in the 1840s. Led by William C. Nell (an African American) and William Lloyd Garrison (a European-American abolitionist), this coalition petitioned the School Committee to end segregation in 1840, 1844, 1845, 1846, and 1849. In 1849, they took the issue to court in the *Roberts* case, which is included in the readings. The plaintiffs lost this case; on April 8, 1850, Massachusetts Chief Justice Lemuel Shaw ruled that "separate but equal" facilities were legally acceptable. Decades later, Judge Shaw's decision was cited by the U.S. Supreme Court in *Plessy v. Ferguson,* the 1896 decision allowing segregation throughout the nation. This ruling was finally overturned in *Brown v. Board of Education* in 1954. However, in the nineteenth century, the issue did not end in the courts but in the legislature. In April 1855, the Massachusetts public schools were legally integrated. The Smith School was closed and the Boston Public Schools fully integrated—at least for the time being. This chapter closes with the 1846 Petition to the School Committee for Integrated Schools, the School Committee's rejection of the petition, materials from the *Roberts* case before the Massachusetts Supreme Judicial Court, and finally the legislature's 1855 action abolishing racial segregation in the public schools of the Commonwealth. It is important to realize how long the struggle for true educational equality has been going on.

✦ HORACE MANN, TENTH AND TWELFTH ANNUAL REPORTS TO THE MASSACHUSETTS BOARD OF EDUCATION, 1846 AND 1848

Horace Mann's twelve annual reports, written between 1837 and 1848, were his most powerful and effective tool in building support for his notion of the kind of school the new nation needed. Many of the reports had a specific theme, but each pushed the need for the public to support a common school education if democracy was to thrive. Mann elaborated this theme in detail in his Tenth Report in 1846. As the short selection from that report, included here, demonstrates, Mann firmly believed in transfer of private resources to the public good through taxation when necessary for a cause such as public education. This twelfth—and last—report, also included here, was Mann's opportunity to sum up. He had already resigned his position to take the congressional seat to which he had been elected. In this report, he affirmed the importance of the schools while stressing their fundamentally religious character. What looked like state-sponsored Protestantism to others was, to Mann, simply the affirmation of universal religious and ethical values.

Tenth Annual Report (1846)

I believe in the existence of a great, immutable principle of natural law, or natural ethics,—a principle antecedent to all human institutions and incapable of being abrogated by any ordinances of man,—a principle of divine origin, clearly legible in the ways of Providence as those ways are manifested in the order of nature and in the history of the race,—which proves the *absolute right* of every human being that comes into the world to an education; and which, of course, proves the correlative duty of every government to see that the means of that education are provided for all.

In regard to the application of this principle of natural law,—that is, in regard to the extent of the education to be provided for all, at the public expense,—some differences of opinion may fairly exist, under different political organizations; but under a republican government, it seems clear that the minimum of this education can never be less than such as is sufficient to qualify each citizen for the civil and social duties he will be called to discharge;—such an education as teaches the individual the great laws of bodily health; as qualified for the fulfillment of parental duties; as is indispensable for the civil functions of a witness or a juror; as is necessary for the voter in municipal affairs; and finally, for the faithful and conscientious discharge of all those duties which devolve upon the inheritor of a portion of the sovereignty of this great republic.

The will of God, as conspicuously manifested in the order of nature, and in the relations which he has established among men, places the *right* of every child that is born into the world to such a degree of education as will enable him and, as far as possible, will predispose him, to perform all domestic, social, civil and moral duties, upon the same clear ground of natural law and equity, as it places a child's *right,* upon his first coming into the world to distend his lungs with a portion of the common air, or to open his eyes to the common light or to receive that shelter, protection and nourishment which are necessary to the continuance of his bodily existence. And so far is it from being wrong or a hardship, to demand of the possessors of property their respective shares for the prosecution of this divinely-ordained work, that they themselves are guilty of the most far-reaching injustice, who seek to resist or to evade the contribution. The complainers are the wrong-doers. The cry, "Stop thief," comes from the thief himself.

To any one who looks beyond the mere surface of things, it is obvious, that the primary and natural elements or ingredients of all property consist in the riches of the soil, in the treasures of the sea, in the light and warmth of the sun, in the fertilizing clouds and streams and dews, in the winds, and in the chemical and vegetative agencies of nature. In the majority of cases, all that we call property, all that makes up the valuation or inventory of a nation's capital, was prepared at the creation, and was laid up of old in the capacious store-house of nature. For every unit that a man earns by his own toil or skill, he receives hundreds and thousands, without cost and without recompense, from the All-bountiful Giver. . . .

These few references show how vast a proportion of all the wealth which men presumptuously call their own, because they claim to have earned it, is poured into their lap, unasked and unthanked for, by the Being, so infinitely gracious in his physical, as well as in his moral bestowments.

But for whose subsistence and benefit, were these exhaustless treasuries of wealth created? Surely not for any one man, nor for any one generation; but for the subsistence and benefit of the whole race, from the beginning to the end of time. . . .

The three following propositions, then, describe the broad and ever-during foundation on which the Common School system of Massachusetts reposes:

> The successive generations of men, taken collectively, constitute one great Commonwealth.

> The property of this Commonwealth is pledged for the education of all its youth, up to such a point as will save them from poverty and vice, and prepare them for the adequate performance of their social and civil duties.

The successive holders of this property are trustees, bound to the faithful execution of their trust, by the most sacred obligations; because embezzlement and pillage from children and descendants are as criminal as the same offences when perpetrated against contemporaries.

Twelfth Annual Report (1848)

Without undervaluing any other human agency, it may be safely affirmed that the Common School, improved and energized, as it can easily be, may become the most effective and benignant of all the forces of civilization. Two reasons sustain this position. In the first place, there is a universality in its operation, which can be affirmed of no other institution whatever. If administered in the spirit of justice and conciliation, all the rising generation may be brought within the circle of its reformatory and elevating influences. And, in the second place, the materials upon which it operates are so pliant and ductile as to be susceptible of assuming a greater variety of forms than any other earthly work of the Creator. The inflexibility and ruggedness of the oak, when compared with the lithe sapling or the tender germ, are but feeble emblems to typify the docility of childhood, when contrasted with the obduracy and intractableness of man. It is these inherent advantages of the Common School, which, in our own State, have produced results so striking, from a system so imperfect, and an administration so feeble. In teaching the blind, and the deaf and dumb, in kindling the latent spark of intelligence that lurks in an idiot's mind, and in the more holy work of reforming abandoned and outcast children, education has proved what it can do, by glorious experiments. These wonders, it has done in its infancy, and with the lights of a limited experience; but, when its faculties shall be fully developed, when it shall be trained to wield its mighty energies for the protection of society against the giant vices which now invade and torment it;—against intemperance, avarice, war, slavery, bigotry, the woes of want and the wickedness of waste, then, there will not be a height to which these enemies of the race can escape, which it will not scale, nor a Titan among them all, whom it will not slay.

I proceed, then, in endeavoring to show how the true business of the schoolroom connects itself, and becomes identical, with the great interests of society. The former is the infant, immature state of those interests; the latter, their developed, adult state. As "the child is father to the man," so may the training of the schoolroom expand into the institutions and fortunes of the State.

Moral Education

Moral Education is a primal necessity of social existence. The unrestrained passions of men are not only homicidal, but suicidal; and a community without a conscience would soon extinguish itself. Even with a natural conscience, how often has Evil triumphed over Good! From the beginning of time, Wrong has followed Right, as the shadow the substance. As the relations of men became more complex, and the business of the world more extended, new opportunities and new temptations for wrong-doing have been created. With the endearing relations of parent and child, came also the possibility of infanticide and parricide; and the first domestic altar that brothers ever reared was stained with fratricidal blood. Following close upon the obligations to truth, came falsehood and perjury, and closer still upon the duty of obedience to the Divine law, came disobedience. With the existence of private relations between men, came fraud; and with the existence of public relations between nations, came aggression, war, and slavery. And so, just in proportion as the relations of life became more numerous, and the interests of society more various and manifold, the range of possible and of actual offenses has been continually enlarging. As for every new substance there may be a new shadow, so for every new law there may be a new transgression. No form of the precious metals has ever been used which dishonest men have not counterfeited; and no kind of artificial currency has ever been legalized which rogues have not forged. The government sees the evils that come from the use of intoxicating drinks, and prohibits their sale; but unprincipled men pander to depraved appetites, and gather a harvest of dishonest profits. Instead of licensing lotteries, and deriving a revenue from the sale of tickets, the State forbids the mischievous traffic; but while law-abiding men disdain to practice an illicit trade, knavish brokers, by means of the prohibition itself, secure a monopoly of the sales, and pocket the infamous gain. The government imposes duties on imported goods; smugglers evade the law, and bring goods into the country clandestinely, or perjurers swear to false invoices, and escape the payment of duty, and thus secure to themselves the double advantage of increased sales, and enhanced profits upon what is sold. Science prepares a new medicine to heal or alleviate the diseases of men; crime adulterates it, or prepares, as substitute, some cheap poison that resembles it, and can be sold instead of it. A benefactor of the race discovers an agent which has the marvelous power to suspend consciousness, and take away the susceptibility of pain; villain uses it to rob men or pollute women. Houses are built. The incendiary burns them that he may purloin the smallest portion of their goods. The press is invented to spread intelligence; but libellers use it to give wings to slander. And, so, throughout all the infinitely complex and ramified relations of society, wherever there is a right there may be a wrong; and wherever a law is made to repress the wrong, it may be evaded by artifice or overborne by violence. In fine, all means and laws designed to repress injustice and crime, give occasion to new injustice and crime. For every lock that is made, a false key is made to pick it; and for every Paradise that is created, there is a Satan who would scale its walls. . . .

Against these social vices, in all ages of the world, the admonitions of good men have been directed. The moralist has exposed their deformity in his didactic page; the satirist has chastised them in his pungent verse; the dramatist has held them up to ridicule on the mimic stage; and, to some extent, the Christian minister has exhibited their gross repugnancy to the character of a disciple of Jesus. Still they continue to exist; and,—to say nothing of heathen nations—the moral condition of all Christendom is, in this respect, like the physical condition of one of the nations that compose it;—that extraordinary people, I mean, whose dwellings, whose flocks, whose agriculture, whose merchandise, and who, themselves, are below the level of the ocean; and against them, at all times, this ocean rages, and lifts itself up; and whenever or wherever it can find a breach, or make one, it rushes in, and overwhelms men and their possessions in one common inundation. Even so, like a weltering flood, do immoralities and crimes break over all moral barriers, destroying and profaning the securities and the sanctities of life. Now, how best shall this deluge be repelled? What mighty power, or combination of powers, can prevent its inrushing, or narrow the sweep of its ravages?

The race has existed long enough to try many experiments for the solution of this greatest problem ever submitted to its hands; and the race has experimented, without stint of time or circumscription of space, to mar or modify legitimate results. Mankind have tried despotisms, monarchies, and republican forms of government. They have tried the extremes of anarchy and of autocracy. They have tried Draconian codes of law; and, for the lightest offences, have extinguished the life of the offender. They have established theological standards, claiming for them the sanction of Divine authority, and the attributes of a perfect and infallible law; and then they have imprisoned, burnt, massacred, not individuals only, but whole communities at a time, for not bowing down to idols which ecclesiastical authority had set up. These and other great systems of measure have been adopted as barriers against error and guilt; they have been extended over empires, prolonged through centuries, and administered with terrible energy; and yet the great ocean of vice and crime overleaps every embankment, pours down upon our heads, saps the foundations under our feet, and sweeps away the securities of social order, of property, liberty, and life.

At length, these experiments have been so numerous, and all of them have terminated so disastrously, that a body of men has risen up, in later items, powerful in influence, and not inconsiderable in numbers, who, if I may use a mercantile phrase, would abandon the world as a total loss;—who mock at the idea of its having a benevolent or even an intelligent Author or Governor; and who, therefore, would give over the race to the dominion of chance, or to that of their own licentious passions, whose rule would be more fatal than chance.

But to all doubters, disbelievers, or despairers in human progress, it may still be said, there is one experiment which has never yet been tried. It is an experiment which, even before its inception, offers the highest authority for its ultimate success. Its formula is intelligible to all; and it is as legible as though written in starry letters on an azure sky. It is expressed in these few and simple words:—*"Train up a child in the way he should go, and when he is old he will not depart from it."* This declaration is positive. If the conditions are complied with, it makes no provision for a failure. Though pertaining to morals, yet, if the terms of the direction are observed, there is no more reason to doubt the result, than there would be in an optical or a chemical experiment.

But this experiment has never yet been tried. Education has never yet been brought to bear with one hundredth part of its potential force, upon the natures of children, and, through them, upon the character of men, and of the race. In all the attempts to reform mankind which have hitherto been made, whether by changing the frame of government, by aggravating of softening the severity of the penal code, or by substituting a government-created, for a God-created, religion;—in all these attempts, the infantile and youthful mind, its amenability to influences, and the enduring and self-operating character of the influences it receives, have been almost wholly unrecognized. Here, then, is a new agency, whose powers are but just beginning to be understood, and whose mighty energies, hitherto, have been but feebly invoked; and yet, from our experience, limited and imperfect as it is, we do know that, far beyond any other earthly instrumentality, it is comprehensive and decisive. . . .

Religious Education

On this subject, I propose to speak with freedom and plainness, and more at length than I should feel required to do, but for the peculiar circumstances in which I have been placed. It is a matter of notoriety, that the views of the Board of Education—and my own, perhaps still more than those of the Board—on the subject of religious instruction in our Public Schools, have been subjected to animadversion. Grave charges have been made against us, that our purpose was to exclude religion; and to exclude that, too, which is the common exponent of religion—the Bible—from the Common Schools of the State; or, at least, to derogate from its authority, and destroy its influence in them. Whatever prevalence a suspicion of the truth of these imputations may have heretofore had, I have reason to believe that further inquiry and examination have done much to disabuse the too credulous recipients of so groundless a charge. Still, amongst a people so commendably sensitive on the subject of religion, as are the people of Massachusetts, any suspicion of irreligious tendencies, will greatly prejudice any cause, and, so far as any cause may otherwise have the power of doing good, will greatly impair that power.

It is known, too, that our noble system of Free Schools for the whole people, is strenuously opposed;—by a few persons in our own State, and by no inconsiderable numbers in some of the other states of this Union;—and that a rival system of "Parochial" or "Sectarian Schools," is now urged upon the public by a numerous, a powerful, and a well-organized body of men. It has pleased the advocates of this rival system, in various public addresses, in reports, and through periodicals devoted to their cause, to denounce our system as irreligious and anti-Christian. They do not trouble themselves to describe what our system is, but adopt a more summary way to forestall public opinion against it, by using general epithets of reproach, and signals of alarm.

In this age of the world, it seems to me that no student of history, or observer of mankind, can be hostile to the precepts and the doctrines of the Christian religion, or opposed to any institutions which expound and exemplify them; and no man who thinks, as I cannot but think, respecting the enduring elements of character, whether public or private, can be willing to have his name mentioned while he is living, or remembered when he is dead, as opposed to religious instruction, and Bible instruction for the young. In making this final Report, therefore, I desire to vindicate my conduct from the charges that have been made against it; and, so far as the Board has been implicated in these charges, to leave my testimony on record for their exculpation. Indeed, on this point, the Board and myself must be justified or condemned together; for I do not believe they would have enabled me, by their annual reelections, to carry forward any plan for excluding either the Bible or religious instruction from the schools; and had the Board required me to execute such a purpose, I certainly should have given them the earliest opportunity to appoint my successor. I desire, also, to vindicate the system with which I have been so long and so intimately connected, not only from the aspersion, but from the suspicion, of being an irreligious, or anti-Christian, or an un-Christian system. I know, full well, that it is unlike the systems which prevail in Great Britain, and in many of the continental nations of Europe, where the Established Church controls the education of the young, in order to keep itself established. But this is presumptive evidence in its favor, rather than against it.

All the schemes ever devised by governments, to secure the prevalence and permanence of religion among the people, however variant in form they may have been, are substantially resolvable into two systems. One of these systems holds the regulation and control of the religious belief of the people to be one of the functions of government, like the command of the army or the navy, or the establishment of courts, or the collection of revenues. According to the other system, religious belief is a matter of individual and parental concern; and, while the government furnishes all practicable facilities for the independent formation of that belief, it exercises no authority to prescribe, or coercion to enforce it. The former is the system, which, with very few exceptions, has prevailed throughout Christendom, for fifteen hundred years. Our own government is the almost solitary example among the nations of the earth, where freedom of opinion, and the inviolability of conscience, have been even theoretically recognized by the law. . . .

The very terms, *Public School,* and *Common School,* bear upon their face, that they are schools which the children of the entire community may attend. Every man, not on the pauper list, is taxed for their support. But he is not taxed to support them as special religious institutions; if he were, it would satisfy, at once, the largest definition of a Religious Establishment. But he is taxed to support them, as a *preventive* means against dishonesty, against fraud, and against violence; on the same principle that he is taxed to support criminal courts as a *punitive* means against the same offenses. He is taxed to support schools, on the same principle that he is taxed to support paupers; because a child without education is poorer and more wretched than a man without bread. He is taxed to support schools, on the same principle that he would be taxed to defend the nation against foreign invasion, or against rapine committed by a foreign foe; because the general prevalence of ignorance, superstition, and vice, will breed Goth and Vandal at home, more fatal to the public well-being, than any Goth or Vandal from abroad. And, finally, he is taxed to support schools, because they are the most effective means of developing and training those powers and faculties in a child, by which, when he becomes a man, he may understand what his highest interests and his highest duties are; and may be, in fact, and not in name only, a free agent. The elements of a political education are not bestowed upon any school child, for the purpose of making him vote with this or that political party, when he becomes of age; but for the purpose of enabling him to choose for himself, with which party he will vote. So the religious education which a child receives at school, is not imparted to him for the purpose of making him join this or that denomination, when he arrives at years of discretion, but for the purpose of enabling him to judge for himself, according to the dictates of his own reason and conscience, what his religious obligations are, and whither they lead. But if a man is taxed to support a school, where religious doctrines are inculcated which he believes to be false, and which he believes that God condemns; then he is excluded from the school by the Divine law, at the same time that he is compelled to support it by the human law. This is a double wrong. It is politically wrong, because, if such a man educates his children at all, he must educate them elsewhere, and thus pay two taxes, while some of his neighbors pay less than their due proportion of one; and it is religiously wrong, because he is constrained, by human power, to promote what he believes the Divine Power forbids. The principle involved in such a course is pregnant with all tyrannical consequences. It is broad enough to sustain any claim of ecclesiastical domination, ever made in the darkest ages of the world. Every religious persecution, since the time of Constantine, may find its warrant in it, and can be legitimately defended upon it. If a man's estate may be taken from him to pay for teaching a creed which he believes to be false, his children can be taken from him to be taught the same creed; and he, too, may be punished to any extent, for not voluntarily surrendering both his estate and his offspring. If his children can be compulsorily taken and taught to believe a creed which the parent disbelieves, then the parent can be compulsorily taken and made to subscribe to the same creed. And, in regard to the extent of the penalties which may be invoked to compel conformity, there is no stopping-place between taking a penny and inflicting perdition. It is only necessary to call a man's reason and conscience and religious faith, by the name of recusancy, or contumacy, or heresy, and so to inscribe them on the statute book; and then the nonconformist or dissenter may be subdued by steel, or cord, or fire; by anathema and excommunication in this life, and the terrors of endless perdition in the next. Surely, that system cannot be an irreligious, an anti-Christian, or an un-Christian one, whose first and cardinal principle it is, to recognize and protect the highest and dearest of all human interests and of all human rights. . . .

It is still easier to prove that the Massachusetts school system is not anti-Christian nor un-Christian. The Bible is the acknowledged expositor of Christianity. In strictness, Christianity has no other authoritative expounder. This Bible is in our Common Schools, by common consent. Twelve years ago, it was not in all the schools. Contrary to the genius of our government, if not contrary to the express letter of the law, it had been used for sectarian purposes,—to prove one sect to be right, and others to be wrong. Hence, it had been excluded from the schools of some towns, by an express vote. But since the law and the reasons on which it is founded, have been more fully explained and better understood; and since sectarian instruction has, to a great extent, ceased to be given, the Bible has been restored. I am not aware of the existence of a single town in the State, in whose schools it is not now introduced, either by a direct vote of the school committee, or by such general desire and acquiescence, as supersede the necessity of a vote. In all my intercourse, for twelve years, whether personal or by letter, with all the school officers in the State, and with tens of thousands of individuals in it, I have never heard an objection made to the use of the Bible in school, except in one or two instances; and, in those cases, the objection was put upon the ground, that daily familiarity with the book, in school, would tend to impair a reverence for it.

If the Bible, then, is the exponent of Christianity; if the Bible contains the communications, precepts, and doctrines, which make up the religious system, called and known as Christianity; if the Bible makes known those truths, which, according to the faith of Christians, are able to make men wise unto salvation; and if this Bible is in the schools, how can it be said that Christianity is excluded from the schools; or how can it be said that the school system, which adopts and uses the Bible, is an anti-Christian, or an un-Christian system? It that which is the acknowledged exponent and basis of Christianity is in the schools, by what tergiversation in language, or paralogism in logic, can Christianity be said to be shut out from the schools? If the Old Testament were in the schools, could a Jew complain, that Judaism was excluded from them? If the Koran were read regularly and reverently in the schools, could a Mahomedan say that Mahomedanism was excluded? Or, if the Mormon Bible were in the schools, could it be said that Mormonism was excluded from them?

Is it not, indeed, too plain, to require the formality of a syllogism, that if any man's creed is to be found in the Bible, and the Bible is in the schools, then that man's creed is in the schools? This seems even plainer than the proposition, that two and two make four; that is, we can conceive of a creature so low down in the scale of intelligence, that he could not see what sum would be produced by adding two and two together, who still could not fail to see, that, if a certain system, called Christianity, were contained in, and inseparable from, a certain book called the Bible, then wherever the Bible might go, there the system of Christianity must be. . . .

And further; our law explicitly and solemnly enjoins it upon all teachers, without any exception, "to exert their best endeavors, to impress on the minds of children and youth committed to their care and instruction, the principles of piety, justice, and a sacred regard to truth, love to their country, humanity and universal benevolence, sobriety, industry, and frugality, chastity, moderation, and temperance, and those other virtues which are the ornament of human society, and the basis upon which a republican constitution is founded." Are not these virtues and graces part and parcel of Christianity? In other words, can there be Christianity without them? While these virtues and these duties towards God and man, are inculcated in our schools, any one who says that the schools are anti-Christian or un-Christian, expressly affirms that his own system of Christianity does not embrace any one of this radiant catalogue; that it rejects them all; that it embraces their opposites! . . .

This topic invites far more extended exposition; but this must suffice. In bidding an official Farewell to a system, with which I have been so long connected, to which I have devoted my means, my strength, my health, twelve years of time, and, doubtless, twice that number of years from what might otherwise have been my term of life, I have felt bound to submit these brief views in its defense. In justice to my own name and memory; in justice to the Board of which I was originally a member, and from which I have always sought counsel and guidance; and in justice to thousands of the most wise, upright, and religious-minded men in Massachusetts, who have been my fellow-laborers in advancing the great cause of Popular Education, under the auspices of this system, I have felt bound to vindicate it from the aspersions cast upon it, and to show its consonance with the eternal principles of equity and justice. I have felt bound to show, that, so far from its being an irreligious, an anti-Christian, or an un-Christian system, it is a system which recognizes religious obligations in their fullest extent; that it is a system which invokes a religious spirit, and can never be fitly administered without such a spirit; that it inculcates the great commands, upon which hang all the law and the prophets; that it welcomes the Bible, and therefore welcomes all the doctrines which the Bible really contains, and that it listens to these doctrines so reverently, that, for the time being, it will not suffer any rash mortal to thrust in his interpolations of their meaning, or overlay, the text with any of the "many inventions" which the heart of man has sought out. It is a system, however, which leaves open all other means of instruction,—the pulpits, the Sunday schools, the Bible classes, the catechisms, of all denominations,—to be employed according to the preferences of individual parents. It is a system which restrains itself from teaching, that what it does teach is all that needs to be taught, or that should be taught; but leaves this to be decided by each man for himself, according to the light of his reason and conscience; and on his responsibility to that Great Being, who, in holding him to an account for the things done in the body, will hold him to the strictest account for the manner in which he has "trained up" his children.

Such, then, in a religious point of view, is the Massachusetts system of Common Schools. Reverently, it recognizes and affirms the sovereign rights of the Creator; sedulously and sacredly it guards the religious rights of the creature; while it seeks to remove all hindrances, and to supply all furtherances to a filial and paternal communion between man and his Maker. In a social and political sense, it is a *Free* school system. It knows no distinction of rich and poor, of bond and free, or between those who, in the imperfect light of this world, are seeking, through different avenues, to reach the gate of heaven. Without money and without price, it throws open its doors, and spreads the table of its bounty, for all the children of the State. Like the sun, it shines, not only upon the good; and, like the rain, its blessings descend, not only upon the just, but upon the unjust, that their injustice may depart from them, and be known no more.

→ CATHARINE E. BEECHER, AN ESSAY ON THE EDUCATION OF FEMALE TEACHERS FOR THE UNITED STATES, 1835

Catharine Beecher was a tireless advocate for expanding women's opportunities by educating them and allowing them to be teachers. Along with her allies, Beecher succeeded in changing the teaching profession from being overwhelmingly male to overwhelmingly female. Future chapters tell the stories of women who went west to teach in the new settlements and later south to teach the newly freed slaves. Prior to Beecher's generation, most women simply would not have worked outside the home. Beecher convinced women, their families, and local and state governments that women's maternal natures and their willingness to work at lower salaries made them ideal candidates for this fast-growing profession. At the same time, she argued forcefully for women's education, made all the more necessary by their new role.

Another object to be aimed at in regard to female education is, to introduce into schools such a course of intellectual and moral discipline, and such attention to mental and personal habits, as shall have a decided influence in fitting a woman for her peculiar duty. What is the most important and peculiar duties of the female sex? It is the physical, intellectual, and moral education of children. It is the care of the health, and the formation of the character, of the future citizen of this great nation.

Woman, whatever are her relations in life, is necessarily the guardian of the nursery, the companion of childhood, and the constant model of imitation. It is her hand that first stamps impressions on the immortal spirit, that must remain forever. And what demands such discretion, such energy, such patience, such tenderness, love, and wisdom, such perspicacity to discern, such versatility to modify, such efficiency to execute, such firmness to persevere, as the government and education of all the various characters and tempers that meet in the nursery and school-room? Woman also is the presiding genius who must regulate all those thousand minutiae of domestic business, that demand habits of industry, order, neatness, punctuality, and constant care. And it is for such varied duties that woman is to be trained. For this her warm sympathies, her lively imagination, her ready invention, her quick perceptions, all need to be cherished and improved; while at the same time those more foreign habits, of patient attention, calm judgment, steady efficiency, and habitual self-control, must be induced and sustained.

Is a weak, undisciplined, unregulated mind fitted to encounter the responsibility, weariness, and watching of the nursery; to bear the incessant care and perplexity of governing young children; to accommodate with kindness and patience to the peculiarities and frailties of a husband; to control the indolence, waywardness, and neglect of servants; and to regulate all the variety of domestic cares? The superficial accomplishments of former periods were of little avail to fit a woman for such arduous duties; and for this reason it is, that as society has advanced in all other improvements, the course of female education has been gradually changing, and some portion of that mental discipline, once exclusively reserved for the other sex, is beginning to exert its invigorating influence upon the female character. At the same time the taste of the age is altered; and, instead of the fainting, weeping, vapid, pretty play-thing, once the model of female loveliness, those qualities of the head and heart that best qualify a woman for her duties, are demanded and admired.

None will deny the importance of having females properly fitted for their peculiar duties; and yet few are aware how much influence a teacher may exert in accomplishing this object. School is generally considered as a place where children are sent, not to form their habits, opinions, and character, but simply to learn from books. And yet, whatever may be the opinion of teachers and parents, children do, to a very great extent, form their character under influences bearing upon them at school. They are proverbially creatures of imitation, and accessible to powerful influences. Six hours every day are spent with teachers, whom they usually love and respect, and whose sentiments and opinions, in one way or another, they constantly discover. They are at the same time associated with companions of all varieties of temper, character, and habit. Is it possible that this can exist without involving constant and powerful influences, either good or bad? The simple fact that a teacher succeeds in making a child habitually accurate and thorough in all the lessons of school, may induce mental habits that will have a controlling influence through life. If the government of schools be so administered as to induce habits of cheerful and implicit obedience, if punctuality, neatness, and order in all school employment's are preserved for a course of years, it must have some influence in forming useful habits. On the contrary, if a child is tolerated in disobedience and neglect, if school duties are performed in a careless, irregular, and deficient manner, pernicious habits may be formed that will operate disastrously through life. It is true that mismanagement and indulgence at home may counteract all the good influences of school; and the faithful discharge of parental duty may counteract, to some extent, the bad influences of school: but this does not lessen the force of these considerations. . . .

Thus, in those parts of our country which have been most moral and intelligent, the education of the lower classes is deteriorating, as it respects moral and religious restraints, while the statistics of education, coming from other parts of the nation, are most appalling. We find that in one of our smallest middle states, thirty thousand adults and children are entirely without education and without schools. In one of the largest middle states, four hundred thousand adults and children are thus destitute. In one of the best educated western states, one third of the children are without schools; while it appears, that, in the whole nation, there are a million and half of children and, nearly as many adults, in the same deplorable ignorance, and without any means of instruction. At the same time, thousands and thousands of degraded foreigners, and their ignorant families, are pouring into this nation at every avenue. All these ignorant native and foreign adults are now voters, and have a share in the government of the nation. All these million children, in a very a few years, will take the same stand; while other millions, as ignorant and destitute, are hastening in their rear. What is the end of these things to be? How long will it take, at this rate, for the majority of votes, and of the physical force of the nation, to be in the hands of ignorance and vice? That terrific crisis is now before us; and a few years will witness its consummation, unless such energetic and persevering efforts are made as time never saw.

Here, we have no despotic monarch to endow seminaries for teachers, and every child in the nation to school for seven successive years, to place a Bible in every school, and enforce a system of moral and religious instruction. It is the people who must voluntarily do it, or it will remain undone. Public sentiment must be aroused to a sense of danger; the wealthy and intelligent must pour out their treasures to endow seminaries for teachers; moral and religious education, and the best methods of governing and regulating the human mind, must become a science; those who have had most experience, and are best qualified in this department, must be called upon to contribute their experience and combined efforts, to qualify others for these duties; men of talent and piety must enter this as the noblest and most important missionary field; females who have time and talents, must be called to aid in the effort; seminaries for teachers, with their model schools, must be established in every state; agents must be employed to arouse and enlighten the people; and when the people are sufficiently awake to the subject, legislative and national aid must be sought.

The object aimed at is one immense and difficult enough to demand the highest exercise of every energy, and every mode of influence. If Prussia, with her dense population, finds one teacher for every ten children needful, the sparseness of population in our wide territories surely demands an equal supply. At this rate, *ninety thousand* teachers are this moment wanted to supply the destitute; and to these must be added every year *twelve thousand,* simply to meet the increase of population. But if we allow thirty pupils as the average number for every teacher, then we need *thirty thousand* teachers for present wants, and an annual addition of *four thousand* for increase of population. And yet, what has been done—what is now doing—to meet this enormous demand? While Prussia, for years, has been pouring out her well-educated teachers from her forty-five seminaries, at the rate of one for every ten pupils; while France is organizing her Normal schools in all her departments for the education of her teachers; what is done in America, wealthy, intelligent, and free America, whose very existence is depending on the virtuous education of her children? In New England, we hear of one solitary institution for the preparation of teachers; and, in New York, eight are just starting into being; and this is all! Now, at this moment, we need at least thirty thousand teachers, and four thousand every year in addition, just to supply the increase of youthful population. And we must educate the nation, or be dashed in pieces, amid all the terrors of the wild fanaticism, infidel recklessness, and political strife, of an ungoverned, ignorant, and unprincipled populace. What patriot, what philanthropist, what Christian, does not see that all that is sacred and dear in home, and country, and liberty, and religion, call upon him to waken every energy, and put forth every effort?

Does the heart fail, and the courage sink, at the magnitude of the work, and the apparent destitution of means? We have the means—we have the power. There is wealth enough, and benevolence enough, and self-denying laborers enough. Nothing is wanting but a knowledge of our danger, our duty, and our means, and a willing mind in exerting our energies. Our difficulties and danger have been briefly noticed. It is the object of this essay to point out one important measure in the system of means that must be employed.

When we consider the claims of the learned professions, the excitement and profits of commerce, manufactures, agriculture, and the arts; when we consider the aversion of most men to the sedentary, confining, and toilsome duties of teaching and governing young children; when we consider the scanty pittance that is allowed to the majority of teachers; and that few men will enter a business that will not support a family, when there are multitudes of other employments that will afford competence, and lead to wealth; it is chimerical to hope that the supply of such immense deficiencies in our national education is to come chiefly from that sex. It is woman, fitted by disposition, and habits, and circumstances, for such duties, who, to a very wide extent, must aid in educating the childhood and youth of this nation; and therefore it is, that females must be trained and educated for this employment. And, most happily, it is true, that the education necessary to fit a woman to be a teacher, is exactly the one that best fits her for that domestic relation she is primarily designed to fill.

But how is this vast undertaking to be accomplished? How can such a multitude of female teachers as are needed, be secured and fitted for such duties? The following will show how it can be done, if those most interested and obligated shall only will to have it done.

Men of patriotism and benevolence can commence by endowing two or three seminaries for female teachers in the most important stations in the nation, while to each of these seminaries shall be attached a model school, supported by the children of the place where it is located. In these seminaries can be collected those who have the highest estimate of the value of moral and religious influence, and the most talents and experience for both intellectual and moral education.

When these teachers shall have succeeded in training classes of teachers on the best system their united wisdom can devise, there will be instructors prepared for other seminaries for teachers, to be organized and conducted on the same plan; and thus a regular and systematic course of education can be disseminated through the nation.

Meantime, proper efforts being made by means of the press, the pulpit, and influential men employed as agents for this object, the interest of the whole nation can be aroused, and every benevolent and every pious female in the nation, who has the time and qualifications necessary, can be enlisted to consecrate at least a certain number of years to this object. There is not a village in this nation that cannot furnish its one, two, three, and in some cases ten or even twenty, laborers for this field.

And, as a system of right moral and religious education gains its appropriate influence, as women are more and more educated to understand and value the importance of their influence in society, and their peculiar duties, more young females will pursue their education with expectation that, unless paramount private duties forbid, they are to employ their time and talents in the duties of a teacher, until they assume the responsibilities of domestic life. Females will cease to feel that they are educated just to enjoy themselves in future life, and realize the obligations imposed by Heaven to live to do good. And when, females are educated as they ought to be, every woman at the close of her school education, will be well-qualified to act as a teacher.

The establishment of institutions for the education of female teachers, would also most successfully remedy all the difficulties in regard to female education which have been exhibited. When female teachers are well-trained for their profession, a great portion of the higher female schools will be entrusted to their care, and they will be prepared to co-operate in propagating a uniform and thorough system of female education, both intellectual and moral. When such teachers are scattered through the land, they will aid in enlightening the public mind in regard to permanently endowed institutions for females. By this means, also, essential aid will be rendered in advancing improvements in regard to physical education, in introducing useful exercise, in promoting a national taste for music, and in various other modern improvements.

Add to these views the fact, that there is now a great amount of female benevolence and activity unemployed for want of suitable opportunities. The writer of this article has had painful occasion to realize this. Having for years been in a situation which secured an extensive acquaintance in all parts of the country, and having been regarded as a source of information by many who were anxious to obtain teachers, and also by females who were desirous to secure either the education or the situation of a teacher, it has been heart-sickening to witness the intense interest that exists in all parts of the nation to obtain good teachers, and at the same time to know the earnest longing of many energetic and benevolent females to secure such situations as were offered, and yet to feel utterly unable to lend any aid to either.

The want of health to undertake such a correspondence and to assume such responsibilities as were demanded, together with the pressure of other obligations, made it an imperious duty to turn a deaf ear to all such applications. But it is believed that, during the last two years, the writer could have supplied more than a hundred towns and villages of the west with teachers, who would have been comfortably, and in many cases most liberally, supported, had the teachers been on the ground and at command. At the same time, extensive acquaintance, correspondence, and traveling, have led to the conviction that there are hundreds of benevolent and self-denying females, who are actually pining for something more worthy of their interest and efforts than they can now find in their limited spheres.

Many such are to be found in the higher circles. In more cases than one, confidential communications have been received, stating that the writer was in the possession of leisure, and property, and education, and yet without any thing to do that equaled her desires or abilities; expressing her interest in the cause of education, her desire to become a teacher, and the unwillingness of friends to promote her wishes, on the ground that they were wild and impracticable. To this were added entreaties for advice and assistance, if such wishes and plans were not deemed visionary and unreasonable.

In other classes of society, the increase of manufactures has removed so much domestic employment from female hands among the common yeomanry of the country, that multitudes of females in this class most joyfully would embrace the employment of teachers, could any method be devised for preparing and locating them. Few know or realize the amount of Christian benevolence which is slumbering in female bosoms, which could be most delightfully and beneficially employed to elevate and save our country. A great proportion of this is to be found among those who have not the means of securing an education; and many who could discharge the humbler duties of instruction, have no means of obtaining proper locations.

We need institutions endowed at public expense, and so constituted, that, while those who are able shall pay the full value of their privileges, those who have not the ability shall be furnished gratuitously with what they cannot purchase; while all who receive these advantages shall consider themselves pledged to devote themselves to the cause of education, and also to refund their expenses, whenever future earnings, or a change in their situation, will enable them to do it. And if men of wealth will furnish the means, if they will collect the talent and experience that are ready to engage in the enterprise, they will soon find multitudes of laborers hastening to the field. As things now are, few females of discretion and good sense would attempt, unaided, what their friends, and most of the community, would deem the Quixotic enterprise of preparing themselves to be teachers, and then set out to seek a situation in the destitute portions of our country. But let benevolent men unite in endowing institutions for those who are unprepared, and secure some organization of suitable persons, whose business it shall be to provide places for those who are prepared; let statistics of the wants of the country be sent abroad, and the cry go forth "Whom shall we send, and who will go for us?" and from amid the green hills and white villages of New England, hundreds of voices would respond, "Here am I, send me," while kindred voices, through the whole length of the land, would echo the reply.

In behalf of such, then, it is, that the writer would address this intelligent and patriotic assembly, and through them the benevolent and philanthropic of the nation: Give us the opportunity of aiding to preserve the interest and institutions of our country. Send us to the thousands of destitute children whom we should rejoice to train up in virtue, and prepare for Heaven. We relinquish the pursuit of wealth, the paths of public honor, and the strife for patronage and power; give us the humble, sacred, delightful pleasures of benevolence. While, on earth, we seek not the plaudits of fame, and wear no fabrics of splendor and renown; while, like the little insects that build beneath the waters, we toil unnoticed and unknown, give us the pleasing consciousness that we are silently raising monuments of beauty and glory, that shall stand in the light of Heaven through everlasting years.

✦ THE COMMON SCHOOL JOURNAL, DEBATE OVER PLAN TO ABOLISH THE BOARD OF EDUCATION, 1840

Not everyone supported Horace Mann in his crusade to organize common schools. Some argued schools were a private family matter. Mann's strongest opponents in Massachusetts did support publicly financed and controlled schools, but they wanted the individual cities and towns of the Commonwealth to maintain local control. They distrusted Mann's advocacy for a state Board of Education, even if its authority was severely limited, and they predicted, correctly, that once a board was in place, its authority would only grow. The debate came to a head in 1840 when, during Mann's third year in office, the state legislature came very close to abolishing the state board and Mann's office as its secretary. The debate, reproduced here from Mann's Common School Journal, *is enlightening regarding the continuing battle over local versus state and federal control of education.*

We have been requested, by many of our subscribers and correspondents, to give some account, in the pages of this Journal, of the abortive attempt, made last winter, in the House of Representatives, to abolish the Board of Education and to break up the Normal Schools.—Ed.

House of Representatives, March 7th, 1840
The Committee on Education having been directed, by an order of the House of the third instant, to consider the expediency of abolishing the Board of Education and the Normal Schools, and to report by bill or otherwise, have attended that duty, and respectfully submit the following

Report

In entering upon the duties intrusted to them, your Committee were fully aware of the difficulties with which it is encompassed. Their inquiry extends to the principles, operation, and probable effects of an institution, organized by a former Legislature, to promote the great interest of Common Schools. A period of nearly three years has elapsed, since the act of the Legislature which established the Board of Education; two successive legislatures have acquiesced in its existence, and the three annual reports of the Board and their Secretary have borne strong testimony to its beneficial influence. Under these circumstances, for your Committee to give an opposite testimony might seem to savor of temerity, not to say, of presumption. But our Committee in the faithful performance of their duty, do not shrink from encountering this charge; they cannot allow themselves to be deterred from expressing the deliberate conclusions of their judgment, by the fear of this or any other imputation. Their apprehensions spring from a different source. An attempt may be made to identify the interest of Common Schools with the existence of the Board of Education; and any objections to that Board may, perhaps, be regarded by some, as a covert assault upon our long-established system of public instruction. But, since our system of public schools did not owe its origin to the Board of Education, but was in existence for two centuries before that Board was established, a proposal to dispense with its further services cannot be reasonably considered as indicating any feelings of hostility or of indifference towards our system of Common Schools. It is, indeed, the attachment of your Committee to that system, which has induced them to investigate, with care and attention the tendencies of the Board of Education. And, it is the conclusion to which they have arrived, that the operations of that Board are incompatible with those principles upon which our Common Schools have been founded and maintained, that leads them to make this Report.

The first question to be considered is, what is the power of the Board of Education? Upon this point, very great difference of opinion appear to prevail. By the terms of the Act, the Board seems to have only a power of recommending, but it is the opinion of many, that this power of recommendation, exercised by such a Board, must of necessity be soon converted into a power of regulation; and even if it were not, the vantage ground which such a board occupies, must obviously give it, for all practical purposes, an equivalent power. One manifest means by which this power of recommending measures may become, and, in several instances, has already become, equivalent to a power of regulation, is to be found in the circumstance, that the Legislature will naturally lend a ready ear to the suggestions of the Board, and will be apt, without much examination, to clothe with a legal sanction such rules and regulations, as the Board may recommend. It would thus appear, that the Board has a tendency, and a strong tendency, to engross to itself the entire regulation of our Common Schools, and practically to convert the Legislature into a mere instrument for carrying its plans into execution. If, however, this result should be disclaimed, and the Legislature is left as independent as before, and with the same feeling of responsibility for all enactments on the subject of schools, the Board seems to be useless; for the Legislature will not lack suggestions from a variety of other quarters, equally well-adapted to furnish them. If then the Board has any actual power, it is a dangerous power, trenching directly upon the rights and duties of the Legislature; if it has no power, why continue its existence, at annual expense to the Commonwealth?

As a mere organ for the collection and diffusion of information on the subject of education, the Board seems to your Committee to be, in several respects, very much inferior to those voluntary associations of teachers, which preceded the existence of the Board, and which, perhaps, suggested the idea of it. In these voluntary associations a vast number of persons are interested; a spirit of emulation exists; and each member is anxious to distinguish himself by his contributions to the common cause. Indeed, the Board of Education has found itself obliged to have recourse to these very associations, as a principal means for carrying out its plans. But it is obvious to your Committee, that conventions of teachers called by authority, and subjected to a foreign control, will not feel themselves free to act; they will not feel a due responsibility, and will not share the zeal and emulation to be expected in associations purely voluntary. As your Committee have already stated, these associations of teachers were in existence before the Board was established; and from the best information your Committee have been able to obtain, instead of increasing, they have, in some places, declined in interest and utility, since they were taken under the patronage of the Board.

Considering the degree of interest which pervades this community, on the subject of education, and the large number of intelligent persons whose lives are devoted to that profession, your Committee do not apprehend that any discoveries, which may be made in the art or science of teaching, will remain undisseminated, through want of zeal to spread information, or of disposition to acquire it. Your Committee can well imagine that in a different state of society, such as is to be found in the newly-settled States, where Common Schools are a novelty, and teachers are generally ill-qualified for their office, some artificial means, such as a Board of Education, might be useful, in stimulating a spirit of inquiry and in disseminating knowledge. But, among us, with so many accomplished teachers, a public Board, established for the benefit of the profession of teaching, seems as little needed as a public Board for the benefit of divinity, medicine, or the law. Undoubtedly, in all these professions, great improvements might be made; but it is better to leave them to private industry and free competition, than for the Legislature to put them under the superintendence of an official Board.

The true way to judge of the practical operations of the Board of Education is not merely to consult the statutes by which the Board is established, but also to examine its own reports. They will furnish an unquestionable means of discovering what are the objects, which the Board actually proposes for itself. A very cursory examination of these documents will suffice to show, that, so far from continuing our system of public instruction, upon the plan upon which it was founded, and according to which it has been so long and so successfully carried on, the aim of the Board appears to be, to remodel it altogether after the example of the French and Prussian systems.

These systems have a central Board, which supplies the ignorance and incapacity of the administrators of local affairs, and which models the schools of France and Prussia all upon one plan, as uniform and exact as the discipline of an army. On the other hand, our system of public instruction has proceeded upon the idea, that the local administrators of affairs, that is to say, the school committees of the several towns and districts, are qualified to superintend the schools, and might best be trusted with that superintendence. This different method of operating is not confined to public schools, but extends to every other department of life. In France or Prussia, the smallest bridge cannot be built, or any village road repaired, until a central Board has been consulted, a plan, which, in its practical operations, and notwithstanding the science of the central Board, and the skill of the engineers whom it has at command, is found not at all comparable with our system of local authority.

De Tocqueville, whose work upon America has been so much admired, dwells at great length and with great emphasis, upon the advantages which New England derives from its excellent system of local authority; while he points out the want of local public spirit in the countries of Europe, and the deficiency of interest in local affairs, as the greatest obstacle in the way of public improvements. This system of local authority is as beneficial to the schools, as to any thing else. It interests a vast number of people in their welfare, whose zeal and activity, if they find themselves likely to be overshadowed by the controlling power of a central Board, will be apt to grow faint. Improvements, which a teacher or school committee have themselves hit upon, will be likely to be pushed with much more spirit, than those which are suggested, or, as it were, commanded, by a foreign and distant power.

After all that has been said about the French and Prussian systems, they appear to your Committee to be much more admirable, as a means of political influence, and of strengthening the hands of the government, than as a mere means for the diffusion of knowledge. For the latter purpose, the system of public Common Schools, under the control of persons most interested in their flourishing condition, who pay taxes to support them, appears to your Committee much superior. The establishment of the Board of Education seems to be the commencement of a system of centralization and of monopoly of power in a few hands, contrary, in every respect, to the true spirit of our democratical institutions; and which, unless speedily checked, may lead to unlooked for and dangerous results.

As to the practical operation of this centralizing system, your Committee would observe, that some of the rules and regulation already devised by the Board of Education, and doubtless considered by it as of very useful tendency, have proved, when carried into execution in the schools, very embarrassing, and have engrossed much of the time and attention of the teachers, which might better have been bestowed upon the instruction of their pupils, than in making out minute and complicated registers of statistics. The Board passes new regulations respecting the returns to be made out by the school committees, and sends forth its blanks; the school committees are abruptly notified of them, without being informed of the reasons upon which they are founded. The rules and regulations become so numerous and complicated, as to be difficult of apprehension, as well as of execution. Indeed, a periodical commentary seems necessary, from the Secretary of the Board, in order to enable school committees to discharge their duties. Your committee are strongly of opinion, that nothing but a prevailing impression, well- or ill-founded, that a compliance with the rules and regulations of the Board is necessary to secure to towns their annual share of the school fund, has enabled those rules and regulations to be at all regarded. The multiplicity and complexity of laws, with respect to any subject, are matter of just complaint; and is especially the case with respect to Common Schools, the teachers of which have a great variety of arduous duties, which must, of necessity, be performed, and which ought not to be aggravated by any requirements, not essential to the welfare of the schools. A central Board, the members of which are not practical teachers, will be easily led to imagine, that minute statistical facts and other like information, may be obtained at much less expense of valuable time, than is actually needed for procuring them.

Your Committee have already stated, that the French and Prussian system of public schools appears to have been devised, more for the purpose of modifying the sentiments and opinions of the rising generation, according to a certain government standard, than as a mere means of diffusing elementary knowledge. Undoubtedly, Common Schools may be used as a potent means of engrafting in to the minds of children, political, religious and moral opinions; but, in a country like this where such diversity of sentiments exists, especially upon theological subjects and where morality is considered a part of religion, and is, to some extent, modified by sectarian views, the difficulty and danger of attempting to introduce these subjects into our school, according to one fixed and settled plan, to be devised by a central Board, must be obvious. The right to mould the political, moral, and religious, opinions of his children, is a right exclusively and jealously reserved by our laws to every parent; and for the government to attempt directly or indirectly, as to these matters, to stand in the parent's place, is an undertaking of very questionable policy. Such an attempt cannot fail to excite a feeling of jealousy, with respect to our public schools, the results of which could not but be disastrous.

A prominent measure, already brought forward by the Board of Education, as a mean of moulding the sentiments of the rising generation, is the project of furnishing under the sanction of the Board, a school library for each district in the Commonwealth. It is professed, indeed, that the matter selected for this library will be free both from sectarian, and political objections. Unquestionably, the Board will endeavor to render it so. Since, however, religion and politics, in this free country, are so intimately connected with every other subject, the accomplishment of that object is utterly impossible nor would it be desirable, if possible. That must, indeed, be an uninteresting course of reading, which would leave untouched either of these subjects; and he must be a heartless writer, who can treat religious or political subjects, without affording any indication of his political or religious opinions. Books, which confine themselves to the mere statement of undisputed propositions, whether in politics, religion, or morals, must be meager, indeed; nor is it possible to abstract, from treatises on these subjects, all that would give offence, without abstracting, at the same time, the whole substance of the matter. Mere abstract propositions are of very little interest: it is their practical application to particular cases, in which all readers, and especially young readers, are principally interested. It is not sufficient, and it ought not to be, that a book contains nothing which we believe to be false. If it omits to state what we believe to be true, if it founds itself upon vague generalities which will equally serve the purpose of all reasoners, alike; this very omission to state what we believe to be the truth becomes, in our eyes, a fault of the most serious character. A book, upon politics, morals, or religion, containing no party or sectarian views, will be apt to contain no distinct views of any kind and will be likely to leave the mind in a state of doubt and skepticism, much more to be deplored than any party or sectarian bias.

If a taste for reading exists in our Common Schools, considering the cheapness and multiplicity of books, and the vast number of pen devoted to the supply of intellectual wants, it cannot be doubted that, according to the ordinary rules of demand and supply, books adapted for the purpose of a school library will be furnished, as fast as they are needed; and out of the books, thus produced, every school committee would be at liberty to make a selection, adapted to the wants and wishes of their district. The question whether the public money should be appropriated, to aid the school districts in providing themselves with books, is a question as to which your Committee do not feel themselves called upon to express any opinion. That question, however, is very different from the question whether the Commonwealth shall aid, by an appropriation of the public money, and by lending its countenance and patronage, to give an artificial circulation to a particular set of books. Your Committee have no doubts as to the inexpediency of such a proceeding.

Another project, imitated from France and Prussia, and set on foot under the superintendence of the Board of Education, is the establishment of Normal Schools. Your Committee approach this subject with some delicacy, inasmuch as one half the expense of the two Normal schools already established has been sustained by private munificence. If, however, no benefit, in proportion to the money spent, is derived from these schools, it is our duty, as legislators, in justice not only to the Commonwealth but to the private donor, to discontinue the project. Comparing the two Normal Schools already established with the academies and high school of the Commonwealth, they do not appear to your Committee to present any peculiar or distinguishing advantages.

Academies and high schools cost the Commonwealth nothing; and they are fully adequate, in the opinion of your Committee, to furnish a component supply of teachers. In years past, they have not only supplied our own schools with competent teachers, but have annually furnished hundreds to the West and the South. There is a high degree of competition existing between these academies, which is the best guaranty for excellence. It is insisted by the Board, however, that the art of teaching is a peculiar art, which is particularly and exclusively taught at Normal Schools; but it appears to your Committee, that every person, who has himself undergone a process of instruction, must acquire, by that very process, the art of instructing others. This certainly will be the case with every person of intelligence; if intelligence be wanting, no system of instruction can supply its place. An intelligent mechanic, who has learned his trade, is competent, by that very fact, to instruct others in it; and needs no Normal School to teach him the art of teaching his apprentices.

Considering that our district schools are kept, on an average for only three or four months in the year, it is obviously impossible, and perhaps it is not desirable, that the business of keeping these schools should become a distinct and separate profession, which the establishment of Normal Schools seems to anticipate.

Even if these schools did furnish any peculiar and distinguishing advantages, we have no adequate security that the teacher, thus taught at the public expense, will remain in the Commonwealth; and it seems hardly just that Massachusetts, in the present state of her finances, should be called upon to educate, at her own cost, teachers for the rest of the Union.

If it be true, that the teachers of any of our district schools are insufficiently qualified for the task, the difficulty originates, as it appears to your Committee, not in any deficiency of the means of obtaining ample qualifications, but in insufficiency of compensation. Those districts, which are inclined to pay competent wages, can at all times be supplied with competent teachers and the want of means or inclination to pay an adequate salary, is not a want which Normal Schools have any tendency to supply.

From the number of scholars who have hitherto attended the Normal Schools, established by the Board of Education, it does not appear that any want of such institutions is seriously felt. The number of pupils falls far short of the average number in our academies and high schools.

It may be suggested, that to abolish these Normal Schools, when they have been in operation for so short a time, is not to give the experiment a fair trial. But the objections of your Committee, as will appear from the considerations above submitted, are of a general and fundamental nature; and they do not consider it advisable to persevere in an experiment, of the inutility of which they are perfectly satisfied. In fact, these schools do not appear to your Committee to have any stronger claims on the public

treasury, for an appropriation of two thousand dollars a year, than many of our academies and high schools.

Should the Normal Schools be discontinued by the Legislature, it is but just and
reasonable, in the opinion of your Committee, that the sums, advanced by the individual who has generously contributed to the support of those schools, should be refunded;
which might be done, by an appropriation of probably five or six hundred dollars, in
addition to the money not yet expended, in the hands of the treasurer of the fund.

The Secretary of the Board of Education stated, in his argument before your
Committee on the subject of Normal Schools that engagements with the teachers of
those schools and other parties interested, had been entered into for a term of three
years; and he argued, that it would be improper for the Legislature to disturb these contracts. With respect to these contracts, your Committee are decidedly of the opinion,
that they ought never to have been made, except with express understanding of a lia-
bility to be rescinded or modified, at the pleasure of the Legislature. If, however, they
have been otherwise made, and if any individuals shall appear to have any reasonable
claim to be remunerated for any disappointment, occasioned by discontinuing the
schools, the Legislature have the power to make such remuneration; and your
Committee believe, that the sooner such a settlement is made, the better, inasmuch as
an increase in the number of the schools as contemplated by the Board, would increase
the difficulty and cost of such a settlement.

In conclusion, the idea of the State controlling Education whether by establishing
a central Board, by allowing that Board to sanction a particular Library, or by organizing Normal Schools, seems to your Committee a great departure from the uniform spirit
of our institutions, a dangerous precedent, and an interference with a matter more properly belonging to those hands, to which our ancestors wisely intrusted it. It is greatly to
be feared, that any attempt, to form all our schools and all our teachers upon one model,
would destroy all competition, all emulation, and even the spirit of improvement itself.
When a large number of teachers and school committees are all aiming at improvement,
as is doubtless the case, to a great extent, in this Commonwealth, improvements seem
much more likely to be found out and carried into practice, than when the chief right of
experimenting is vested in a central Board.

With these views, your Committee have come to the conclusion, that the interest
of our Common Schools would rest upon a safer and more solid foundation, if the
Board of Education and the Normal Schools were abolished. Your Committee would
therefore recommend the passage of the following bill.

For the Committee,

Allen W. Dodge

An Act to Abolish the Board of Education

*Be it enacted by the Senate and House of Representatives in General Court assembled,
and by the authority of the same, as follows:*

Sec. 1. The Board of Education and the office of Secretary to the Board of Education
are hereby abolished; and the act passed April 20, 1837, entitled 'An Act
Relating to Common Schools,' is hereby repealed.

Sec. 2. The act passed March 31, 1838, entitled 'An Act to Defray the Expenses of
the Board of Education,' and also the act passed April 21, 1838, entitled 'An

Act to Prescribe the Duties and Fix the Compensation of the Secretary of the Board of Education,' are hereby repealed.

Sec. 3. So much of the First section of the act passed April 13, 1838, entitled 'An Act concerning Schools' that requires that copies of the annual reports, made by school committees to the towns, shall be sent to the Secretary of the Commonwealth, and also the fifth, sixth, and seventh, sections of the said act, are hereby repealed.

Sec. 4. The resolves passed April 19, 1838, entitled Resolves Relative to Qualifying Teachers for Common Schools, and the act passed March 26, 1839, entitled An Act to incorporate the Trustees of the Plymouth County Normal School, are hereby repealed.

Sec. 5. So much of the third section of the act passed March 18, 1839, entitled 'An Act concerning Schools,' as authorizes the Board of Education to prescribe the time when the school committees of the several towns shall make their annual returns to the Secretary of the Commonwealth, is hereby repealed, and said returns shall be made on or before the fifteenth day of November annually.

Sec. 6. So much money as shall remain in the hands of the treasurer of the Normal School fund, after defraying the expenses that may be incurred up to the close of the current terms of the said schools, respectively, shall be paid over to the honorable Edmund Dwight; and for so much additional money as may be necessary to make up the sum heretofore contributed by the said Dwight to the said fund, His Excellency the Governor is hereby authorized to draw his warrant in favor of the said Dwight, to be paid out of any moneys in the treasury of the Commonwealth, not otherwise appropriated.

Remarks of Mr. A. W. Dodge of Hamilton, in the House of Representatives, March 18th, 1840, on the Bill for abolishing the Board of Education and the Normal Schools:

Mr. Dodge, of Hamilton, said that, in opposing the Board of Education, he need not be supposed to be opposing the *cause* of Education. With the same end, gentlemen might differ about the means. The power of this Board appeared harmless; but, from its unrestrained nature, it was, in fact, dangerous.

He said, that he did not believe in the statement of the Board, that the system of the Common Schools was in a sinking and rotten condition. Did not gentlemen think that children were now better educated in the Common Schools, than when they themselves were boys?

He thought it idle, to suppose that the Commonwealth, by accepting the donation for the support of Normal Schools, had tied its hands in such a manner, that it could not rescind the bargain. He should refer to the Normal Schools themselves, at another stage of the debate.

He alluded to the Abstract of the School Returns, which had been said to be evidence of the desire of the towns to support the Board. The Secretary was directed to make extracts from the reports of school committees. He could of course extract such portions as advocated the institution and existence of the Board, and reject portions of an opposite bearing: and these extracts were offered to the Legislature as the "unbiased testimony" of the Commonwealth.

Mr. D. proceeded to argue from the system of *registers* in schools which was introduced by the Board; and exhibited a blank form, as at first used. This was too large and inconvenient. The Board had since altered it to be smaller and more convenient; but the *power* to require a still more cumbrous and useless one still remains.

The Board of Education have made an agreement with a publishing house in this city, for the publication of a 'School Library.' School Libraries were very good and useful institutions, and he wished there were more of them; but what authority did the Board find in the statute for giving their sanction to these books? There was none. To be sure, the Board say that they do not require, but only *recommend,* the adoption of these books; but it may be easily seen what a powerful and injurious effect a recommendation even from such a source might have.

Mr. D. made a calculation of the amount which might, on an average, be used for the purpose of supplying libraries, and inquired, whether it were wise that this thirty thousand dollars, which might be used for the necessary purpose of employing teachers, should be exhausted on the merely collateral benefit of supplying books.

From these and other details, said Mr. D., I am induced to say that the Board of Education, by what it has done and what it is preparing to do, has transcended its powers, and is entering upon the greatest innovation upon the Common-School privileges. The Board, he thought, were attempting entirely to remodel the school system, and draw it into a similarity to the French and Prussian systems. Were gentlemen prepared for this?

The powers of the Board looked harmless; the Board appeared to doubt, occasionally, whether or no, it had this or that power. But it might gradually induce the Legislature to grant it one right after another, until its influence would be entirely absolute. He compared the organization of the Board to widely-extended police in an absolute government; where the magistrates in the small districts being numerous, so that the office being effective, the officers might be insignificant, and the registration and returns being all made to one office, the centralization is complete.

Some gentlemen had said that we had better not now stop this experiment; he (Mr. D.) thought it better to stop it now, than after, by a longer continuance, it had become more thoroughly interwoven with, and injurious to, the school system of Massachusetts.

✣ PETITION OF THE CATHOLICS OF NEW YORK FOR A PORTION OF THE COMMON SCHOOL FUND: TO THE HONORABLE BOARD OF ALDERMEN OF THE CITY OF NEW YORK, 1840

The petition included here is a clear example of the views of one group of citizens who disagreed sharply with school reformers like Horace Mann. From the earliest days of the republic to the present, some have argued, as did Mann, that public funds and public control of schools should always be aligned. Others have argued that groups who held different views on essential matters of faith and culture should have the freedom to take their share of the public funds and educate children according to the dictates of their own consciences. One of the clearest examples of this conflict was in the great "school wars" in New York City in the 1840s. While the Public School Society wanted to consolidate its control over all of the schools, Roman Catholics, led by Bishop John Hughes, argued that such consolidation threatened their basic freedom to educate their children in an atmosphere sympathetic to the Catholic faith. The debate about the appropriate use of public funds for different kinds of schools remains unresolved in the twenty-first century, but the New York crisis of 1840 provides one of its most dramatic moments. The petition from a number of Roman Catholic lay leaders gives eloquent testimony to their reasons for their perspective.

The Petition of the Catholics of New York, Respectfully represents:

That your Petitioners yield to no class in their performance of, and disposition to perform all the duties of citizens. They bear, and are willing to bear, their portion of every common burden; and feel themselves entitled to a participation in every common benefit.

This participation, they regret to say, has been denied them for years back, in reference to Common School Education in the city of New York, except on conditions with which their conscience, and, as they believe their duty to God, did not, and do not leave them at liberty to comply.

The rights of conscience, in this country, are held by the constitution and universal consent to be sacred and inviolate. No stronger evidence of this need adduced than the fact, that one class of citizens are exempted from the duty or obligation of defending their country against an invading foe, out of delicacy and deference to the rights of conscience which forbids them to take up arms for any purpose.

Your Petitioners only claim the benefit of this principle in regard to the public education of their children. They regard the public education which the State has provided as a common benefit, in which they are most desirous and feel that they are entitled to participate; and therefore they pray your Honorable Body that they may be permitted to do so, without violating their conscience.

But your Petitioners do not ask that this prayer be granted without assigning their reasons for preferring it.

In ordinary cases men are not required to assign the motives of conscientious scruples in matters of this kind. But your petitioners are aware that a large, wealthy, and concentrated influence is directed against their claim by the Corporation called the Public School Society. And that this influence, acting on a public opinion already but too much predisposed to judge unfavorably of the claims of your petitioners, requires to be met by facts which justify them in thus appealing to your Honorable Body, and which may at the same time, convey a more correct impression to the public mind. Your petitioners adopt this course the more willingly, because the justice and impartiality which distinguish the decisions of public men, in this country, inspire them with the confidence that your Honorable Body will maintain, in their regard, the principle of the rights of conscience, if it can be done without violating the rights of others, and on no other condition is the claim solicited.

It is not deemed necessary to trouble your Honorable Body with a detail of the circumstances by which the monopoly of the public education of children in the city of New York, and of the funds provided for that purpose at the expense of the State, have passed into the hands of a private corporation, styled in its Act of Charter, "The Public School Society of the City of New York." It is composed of men of different sects or denominations. But that denomination, Friends, which is believed to have the controlling influence, both by its numbers and otherwise, holds as a peculiar sectarian principle that any formal or official teaching of religion is, at best, unprofitable. And your petitioners have discovered that such of their children as have attended the public schools, are generally, and at an early age, imbued with the same principle that they become untractable, disobedient, and even contemptuous towards their parents unwilling to learn anything of religion as if they had become illuminated, and could receive all the knowledge of religion necessary for them by instinct or inspiration. Your petitioners do not pretend to assign the cause of this change in their children, they only attest the fact, as resulting from their attendance at the public schools of the Public School Society.

This Society, however, is composed of gentlemen of various sects, including even one or two Catholics. But they profess to exclude all sectarianism, from their schools. If they do not exclude sectarianism, they are avowedly no more entitled to the school funds than your petitioners or any other denomination of professing Christians. If they do, as they profess, exclude sectarianism, then your petitioners contend that they exclude Christianity and leave to the advantage of infidelity the tendencies which are given to the minds of youth by the influence of this feature and pretension of their system.

If they could accomplish what they profess, other denominations would join your petitioners in remonstrating against their schools. But they do not accomplish it. Your petitioners will show your Honorable Body that they do admit what Catholics call sectarianism, (although others may call it only religion) in a great variety of ways.

In their 22d report, as far back as the year 1827, they tell us, page 14, that they *"are aware of the importance of early RELIGIOUS INSTRUCTION,"* and that none but what is *"exclusively general and scriptural in its character should be introduced into the schools under their charge."* Here, then, is their own testimony that they did introduce and authorize "religious instruction" in their schools. And that they solved, with the utmost composure, the difficult question on which the sects disagree, by determining *what kind* of *"religious instruction"* is *"exclusively general and scriptural in its character."* Neither could they impart this "early religious instruction" themselves. They must have left it to their teachers and these, armed with official influence, could impress those "early religious instructions" on the susceptible minds of the children, with the authority of dictators.

The Public School Society in their report for the year 1832, page 10, describe the effect of these "early religious instruction," without, perhaps, intending to do so; but yet precisely as your petitioners have witnessed it, in such of their children as attended those schools. *"The age at which children are usually sent to school affords a much better opportunity to mold their minds to peculiar and exclusive forms of faith than any subsequent period of life."* In page 11, of the same report, they protest against the injustice of supporting "religion in any shape" by public money; as if the early religious instruction which they had themselves authorized in their schools five years before, was not "religion in some shape," and was not supported by public taxation. They tell us again in more guarded language, "The Trustees are deeply impressed with the importance of imbuing the youthful mind with religious impressions, and they have endeavored to attain this object, as far as the nature of the institution will admit." Report of 1837.

In their Annual Report they tell us, that "They would not be understood as regarding religious impressions in early youth as unimportant; on the contrary, they desire to do all which may with propriety be done, to give a right direction to the minds of the children intrusted to their care. Their schools are uniformly opened with reading of the Scriptures, and the class-books are such as recognize and enforce the great and generally acknowledged principles of Christianity." Page 7.

In their 34th Annual Report, for the year 1839, they pay a high compliment to a deceased teacher for "the moral and religious influence exerted by her over the three hundred girls daily attending her school," and tell us that "it could not but have had a lasting effect on many of their susceptible minds." Page 7. And yet in all these "early religious instruction, religious impressions, and religious influence," essentially anti-Catholic, your petitioners are to see nothing sectarian; but if in giving the education which the State requires, they were to bring the same influences to bear on the "susceptible minds" of their own children, in favor, and not against, their own religion, then this society contends that it would be sectarian!

Your petitioners regret that there is no means of ascertaining to what extent the teachers in the schools of this Society carried out the views of their principles on the importance of conveying "early religious instructions" to the "susceptible minds" of their children. But they believe it is in their power to prove, that in some instances, the Scriptures have been explained, as well as read to the pupils.

Even the reading of the Scriptures in those schools your petitioners cannot regard otherwise than as sectarian; because Protestants would certainly consider as such the introduction of the Catholic Scriptures, which are different from theirs, and the Catholics have the same ground of objection when the Protestant version is made use of.

Your petitioners have to state further, as grounds of their conscientious objections to those schools, that many of the selections in their elementary reading lessons contain matter prejudicial to the Catholic name and character. The term *Popery* is repeatedly found in them. This term is known and employed as one of insult and contempt towards the Catholic religion, and it passes into the minds of children with the feeling of which it is the outward expression. Both the historical and religious portions of the reading lessons are selected from Protestant writers, whose prejudices against the Catholic religion render them unworthy of confidence in the mind of your petitioners, at least so far as their own children are concerned.

The Public School Society have heretofore denied that their books contained anything reasonably objectionable to Catholics. Proofs of the contrary could be multiplied, but it is unnecessary, as they have recently retracted their denial, and discovered, after fifteen years' enjoyment of their monopoly, that their books do contain objectionable passages. But they allege that they have proffered repeatedly to make such corrections as the Catholic Clergy might require. Your petitioners conceive that such a proposal could not be carried into effect by the Public School Society without giving just ground for exception to other denominations. Neither can they see with what consistency that Society can insist, as it has done, on the perpetuation of its monopoly, when the Trustees thus avow their incompetency to present unexceptionable books, without the aid of the Catholic, or any other Clergy. They allege, indeed, that with the best intentions they have been unable to ascertain the passages which might be offensive to Catholics. With their intentions, your petitioners cannot enter into any question. Nevertheless, they submit to your Honorable Body, that Society is eminently incompetent to the superintendent of public education, if they could not see that the following passage was unfit for the public schools, and especially unfit to be placed in the hands of Catholic children.

They will quote the passage as one instance, taken from Putnam's Sequel, page 266:

> Huss, John, a zealous reformer from Popery, who lived in Bohemia, towards the close
> of the fourteenth, and beginning of the fifteenth centuries. He was bold and

persevering; but at length, trusting himself to the deceitful Catholics he was by them brought to trial, condemned as a heretic, and burnt at the stake.

The Public School Society may be excused for not knowing the historical inaccuracies of this passage; but surely assistance of the Catholic Clergy could not have been necessary to an understanding of the word "deceitful," as applied to all who profess the religion of your petitioners.

For these reasons, and others of the same kind, your petitioners cannot, in conscience, and consistently with their sense of duty to God, and to their offspring, intrust the Public School Society with the office of giving "a right direction to the minds of their children." And yet this Society claims that office, and claims for the discharge of it the Common School Funds, to which your petitioners, in common with other citizens, are contributors. In so far as they are contributors, they are not only deprived of any benefit in return, but their money is employed to the damage and detriment of their religion, in the minds of their own children, and of the rising generation of the community at large. The contest is between the *guarantied* rights, civil and religious, of the citizen of the one hand, and the pretensions of the Public School Society on the other; and whilst it has been silently going on for years, your petitioners would call the attention of your Honorable Body to its consequences on that class for whom the benefits of public education are most essential—the children of the poor.

This class (your petitioners speak only so far as relates to their own denomination), after a brief experience of the schools of the Public School Society, naturally and deservedly withdrew all confidence from it. Hence the establishment by your petitioners of schools for the education of the poor. The expense necessary for this, was a second taxation, required not by the laws of the land, but by the no less imperious demands of their conscience.

They were reduced to the alternative of seeing their children growing up in entire ignorance, or else taxing themselves anew for private schools, whilst the funds provided for education, and contributed in part by themselves, were given over to the Public School Society, and by them employed as has been stated above.

Now your petitioners respectfully submit, that without this confidence, no body of men can discharge the duties of education as intended by the State, and required by the people. The Public School Society are and have been at all times, conscious that they had not the confidence of the poor. In their twenty-eighth report, they appeal to the ladies of New York to create or procure it, by "the persuasive eloquence of female kindness;" page 5. And from this they pass, on the next page to the more efficient eloquence of coercion under penalties and privations to be visited on all persons, "whether emigrants or otherwise," who being in the circumstances of poverty referred to, should not send their children to some "public or other daily school." In their twenty-seventh report, pages 15 and 16, they plead for the doctrine, and recommend it to public favor by the circumstance that it will affect but "few natives." But why should it be necessary at all, if they possessed that confidence of the poor, without which they need never hope to succeed? So well are they convinced of this, that no longer ago than last year, they gave up all hope of inspiring it, and loudly called for coercion by *"the strong arm of the civil power"* to supply its deficiency. Your petitioners will close this part of their statement with the expression of their surprise and regret that gentlemen who are themselves indebted much to the respect which properly cherished for the rights of conscience, should be so unmindful of the same rights in the case of your petitioners. Many of them are by religious principle so pacific that they would not take up arms in the defense of the liberties of their country, though she should call them to her aid; and yet, they do not hesitate to invoke the "strong arm of the civil power" for the purpose of abridging the private liberties of their fellow-citizens, who may feel equally conscientious.

Your petitioners have to deplore, as a consequence of this state of things, the ignorance and vice to which hundreds, nay thousands of their children are exposed. They have to regret, also that the education which they can provide, under the disadvantages to which they have been subjected, is not as efficient as it should be. But should your Honorable Body be pleased to designate their schools as entitled to receive a just proportion of the public funds which belong to your petitioner in common with other citizens, their school could be improved for those who attend, others now growing up in ignorance could be received, and the ends of the Legislature could be accomplished—a result which is manifestly hopeless under the present system.

Your petitioners will now invite the attention of your Honorable Body to the objection and misrepresentations that have been urged by the Public School Society to granting the claim of your petitioners. It is urged by them that it would be appropriating money raised by general taxation to the support of the Catholic religion. Your petitioners join issue with them and declare unhesitatingly, that if this objection can be established the claim shall be forthwith abandoned. It is objected that though we are taxed as citizens, we apply for the benefits of education as "Catholics." Your petitioners, to remove this difficulty, beg to be considered in their application in the identical capacity in which they are taxed—viz. as citizens of the commonwealth. It has been contended by the Public School Society that the law disqualifies schools which admit any profession of religion, from receiving any encouragement's from the School Fund. Your petitioners have two solutions for this pretended difficulty. 1. Your petitioners are unable to discover any such disqualification in the law, which merely delegates to your Honorable Body the authority and discretion of determining what schools or societies shall be entitled to its bounty. 2. Your petitioners are willing to fulfill the conditions of the law so far as religious teaching is proscribed during school hours. In fine your petitioners, to remove all objections, are willing that the material organization of their schools, and the disbursement of the funds allowed for them, shall be conducted, and made, by persons unconnected with the religion of your petitioners, even the Public School Society, if it should please your Honorable Body to appoint them for that purpose. The public may then be assured that the money will not be applied to the support of the Catholic religion.

It is deemed necessary by your petitioners to save the Public School Society the necessity of future misconception, thus to state the things which are not petitioned for. The members of that Society, who have shown themselves so impressed with the importance of conveying their *notions* of "early religious instruction" to the "susceptible minds" of Catholic children, can have no objection that the parents of the children, and teachers in whom the parents have confidence, should do the same, provided no law is violated thereby, and no disposition evinced to bring the children of other denominations within its influence.

Your petitioners, therefore, pray that your Honorable Body will be pleased to designate, as among the schools entitled to participate in the Common School Fund, upon complying with the requirements of the law, and the ordinances of the corporation of the city or for such other relief as to your Honorable Body shall seem meet,

St. Patrick's School, St. Peter's School, St. Mary's School, St. Joseph's School, St. James School, St. Nicholas School, Transfiguration Church School, and St. John's School.

And your petitioners further request, in the event of your Honorable Body's determining to hear your petitioners on the subject of their petition, that such time may be appointed as may be most agreeable to your Honorable Body and that a full session of your Honorable Board be convened for that purpose.

And your petitioners, &c.

Thomas O'Connor, Chairman
Gregory Dillon, Andrew Carrigan, Peter Duffy, Vice chairmen
B. O'Conner, James Kelly, J. M'Louglin, Secretaries
Of a general meeting of the Catholics of the City of New York, convened in the
    school-room of St. James Church, Sept. 21, 1840

✦ The Desegregation of the Boston Public Schools, 1846-1855

Given Boston's turbulent experience with school integration in the 1970s, few realize that the legal desegregation of the Boston Public Schools took place more than a century earlier, in 1855. The various documents included here—the 1846 petition by the African-American community for desegregated schools, the School Committee's response, the records of the 1849 Sarah C. Roberts v. The City of Boston court case, and finally the legislature's act ending segregation in 1855—together tell of an early and important effort by the African-American community to control its own fate.

Report to the Primary School Committee on the Petition of Sundry Colored Persons for the Abolition of the Schools for Colored Children (Boston, June 15, 1846)

To the Primary School Committee of the City of Boston:
The undersigned colored citizens of Boston, parents and guardians of children now attending the exclusive Primary Schools for children in this City, respectfully represent;—that the establishment of exclusive schools for our children is a great injury to us, and deprives us of those equal privileges and advantages in the public school to which we are entitled as citizens. These separate schools cost more and do less for the children than other schools, since all experience teaches that where a small and despised class are shut out from the common benefit of any public institutions of learning and confined to separate schools, few or none interest themselves about the school—neglect ensues, abuses creep in, the standard of scholarship degenerates, and the teachers and the scholars are soon considered, and of course, become, an inferior class.

But to say nothing of any other reasons for this change, it is sufficient to say that the establishment of separate schools for our children is believed to be unlawful, and it is felt to be if not in intention, in fact, insulting. If, as seems to be admitted, you are violating our rights, we simply ask you to cease doing so.

We therefore earnestly request that such exclusive schools be abolished, and that our children be allowed to attend the Primary Schools established in the respective Districts in which we live.

[Signed]

George Putnam
And Eighty-five Others

Report of the Primary School Committee in Response to the Petition

This report was adopted by the Committee by a vote of 59 to 16. A dissenting minority report, advocating integrated schools, was also presented.

What we claim is, That, under the law giving to the School Committee "the general charge and superintendence of all the public schools," and the power to "determine the number and qualifications of the scholars to be admitted into the school," the Committee have the right to distribute, assign, and classify, all children, belonging to the schools in the City according to their best judgment:

In applying these principles to the case of colored children, we maintain,

1. That their peculiar physical, mental, and moral structure, requires an educational treatment, different, in some respects, from that of white children. Teachers of schools in which they are intermingled, remark, that, in those parts of study and instruction in which progress depends on memory, or on the imitative faculties, chiefly, the colored children will often keep pace with the white children, but, when progress comes to depend chiefly on the faculties of invention, comparison, and reasoning, they quickly fall behind.
2. That the number of colored children, in Boston, is so great, that they can be advantageously placed in separate schools, where all needful stimulus, arising from numbers and competition, may be felt, without their being degraded or discouraged.
3. That they live so compactly, that in very few (if in any) cases, is it at all inconvenient to attend the special Schools provided for them.
4. That the facts, connected with the origin and history of these Schools, show, that, with out them, the colored people would have remained ignorant and degraded, and very few would have been found in the Schools.
5. That if these special Schools were now abolished, the number of colored children in the Public Schools would be greatly diminished, while serious injury would also be done to the other Schools, and no benefit would result.
6. That the majority of the colored, and most of the white people, prefer the present system.

As, then, there is no statute, nor decision of the civil Courts, against classifying children in schools according to a distinction in races, color, or mental and physical peculiarities, the Committee believe that we have the right to classify on these principles; nor do they believe, that, by so doing, we defeat the intent, or violate the spirit, of the law, the Constitution, or the invaluable common-school system established by our fathers; nor in any way infringe the rights of the colored child, or degrade the colored people. These Schools were established for their special benefit: for the same reason we would have them vigorously sustained. No man, colored or white, who understands their real value to the colored people, would seek their destruction.

Sarah C. Roberts v. *The City of Boston,* 5 **Mass. Reports (1849)**

(The facts of the case:)

The plaintiff is a colored child, of five years of age, a resident of Boston, and living with her father, since the month of March, 1847, in Andover street, in the sixth primary school district. In the month of April, 1847, she being of suitable age and qualifications (unless her color was a disqualification) applied to a member of the district primary school committee, having under his charge the primary school nearest to her place of residence, for a ticket of admission to that school, the number of scholars therein warranting her admission, and no special provision having been made for her, unless the establishment of the two schools for colored children exclusively is to be considered.

The member of the school committee, to whom the plaintiff applied, refused her application, on the ground of her being a colored person, and of the special provision made as aforesaid. The plaintiff thereupon applied to the primary school committee of the district, for admission to one of their schools, and was in like manner refused admission, on the ground of her color and the provision aforesaid. She thereupon petitioned the general primary school committee, for leave to enter one of the schools nearest her residence. That committee referred the subject to the committee of the district, with full powers, and the committee of the district thereupon again refused the plaintiff's application, on the sole ground of color and the special provision aforesaid, and the plaintiff has not since attended any school in Boston. Afterwards, on the 15th of February, 1848, the plaintiff went into the primary school nearest her residence, but without any ticket of admission or other leave granted, and was on that day ejected from the school by the teacher.

The school established in Belknap Street (a school for Negro children) is twenty-one hundred feet distant from the residence of the plaintiff, measuring through the streets, and in passing from the plaintiff's residence to the Belknap Street school, the direct route passes the ends of two streets in which there are five primary schools . . . . The distance from the plaintiff's residence to the nearest primary school is nine hundred feet. The plaintiff might have attended the school in Belknap Street, at any time, and her father was informed, but he refused to have her attend there.

Argument of Charles Sumner, Esq. Against the Constitutionality of Separate Colored Schools in the Case of *Sarah C. Roberts* vs. *The City of Boston* (1849)

I.   I begin with the principle, that, according to the spirit of American institutions, and especially of the Constitution of Massachusetts, *all men, with out distinction of color or race, are equal before the law.*

I might, perhaps, leave this proposition without one word of comment. The equality of men will not be directly denied on this occasion, and yet it has been so often assailed of late, that I trust I shall not seem to occupy your time superfluously in endeavoring to show what is understood by this term, when used in laws, or constitutions, or other political instruments.

The equality which was declared by our fathers in 1776, and which was made the fundamental law of Massachusetts in 1780, *was equality before the law.* Its object was to efface all political or civil distinctions, and to abolish all institutions founded upon birth. "All men are created equal," says the Declaration of Independence. "All men are *born* free and equal," says the Massachusetts Bill of Rights. These are not vain words. Within the sphere of their influence no person can be *created,* no person can be *born,* with civil or political privileges, not enjoyed equally by all his fellow-citizens, nor can any institution be established recognizing any distinctions of birth. This is the Great Charter of every person who draws his vital breath upon this soil, whatever may be his condition, and whoever may be his parents. He may be poor, weak, humble, black— he may be of Caucasian, of Jewish, of Indian, or of Ethiopian race—he may be of French, of German, of English, of Irish extraction—but before the Constitution of Massachusetts, all these distinctions disappear. He is not poor, or weak or humble, or black—nor Caucasian, nor Jewish, nor Indian, nor Ethiopian—nor French, nor German, nor English, nor Irish; he is a MAN,—the equal of all his fellowmen. He is one of the children of the State, which, like an impartial parent, regards all its offspring with an equal care. To some it may justly allot higher duties, according to their higher capacities, but it welcomes all to its equal, hospitable board. The State, imitating the divine justice, is no respecter of persons.

II.   I now pass to the second stage of this argument, and ask attention to this proposition. The legislature of Massachusetts, in entire harmony with the Constitution, has made no discrimination of color or race, in the establishment of Public Schools.

If such discrimination were made by the laws, they would be unconstitutional and void. But the legislature of Massachusetts has been too just and generous, too mindful of the Bill of Rights, to establish any such privilege of *birth.* The language of the statutes is general, and applies equally to all children, of whatever color or race.

The provisions of the law regulating this subject are entitled, *Of the Public Schools* (Revised Statutes, chap. 23). It is to these that we must look in order to ascertain what constitutes a Public School. None can be legally such which are not established in conformity with the law. They may, in point of fact, be more or less public: yet, if they do not come within the terms of the law, they do not form a part of the beautiful system of our public schools—they are not public schools.

I conclude . . . that there is but one kind of public school established by the laws of Massachusetts. This is the general Public School, free to all the inhabitants. There is nothing in these laws establishing any exclusive or separate school for any particular class, whether rich or poor, whether Catholic or Protestant, whether white or black. In the eye of the law there is but *one class,* in which all interests, opinions, conditions and colors commingle in harmony—excluding none, comprehending all.

III. The Courts of Massachusetts have never recognized any discrimination, founded on color or race, in the administration of the Public Schools, but have recognized the equal rights of all the inhabitants.

There are a few decisions only of our Court bearing on this subject, but they all breathe one spirit. The sentiment of equality animates them. In the case of *Commonwealth* vs. *Davis,* 6 Mass R. 146, while declaring the equal rights of all the inhabitants both in the grammar and district schools, the Court said: "The schools required by the statute are to be maintained for the benefit of the whole town, *as it is the wise policy of the law to give all the inhabitants equal privileges for the education of their children in the public schools.* Nor is it in the power of the majority to deprive the minority of this *privilege* . . . Every inhabitant of the town has a right to participate in the benefits of both descriptions of schools, and it is not competent for a town to establish a grammar school for the benefit of one part of the town to the exclusion of the other, although the money raised for the support of schools may be in other respects fairly apportioned."

IV.   The exclusion of colored children from the Public Schools, open to white children, is a source of practical inconvenience to them and their parents, to which white persons are not exposed, and is, therefore, a violation of Equality. The black and the white are not equal before the law.

It appears from the statement of facts, that among the rules of the Primary School Committee, is one to this effect: *"Scholars to go to the school nearest their residence.* Applicants for admission to our schools (with the exception and provision referred to in the preceding rule) are especially entitled to to enter the schools nearest to their places of residence." The exception here is "of those for whom special provision has been made" in separate schools; that is, colored children.

I may go, however, beyond the facts of this case, and show that the inconvenience arising from the exclusion of colored children, is of such a character as seriously to affect the comfort and condition of the African race in Boston. The two primary schools open to these children are in Belknap Street and in Sun Court. I need not add that the whole city is dotted with schools open to white children. The colored parents, anxious that their children should have the benefit of education, are compelled to live in the neighborhood of the schools, to gather about them, as in the East people come from a distance to rest near a fountain or a well. They have not, practically, the same liberty of choosing their homes, which belongs to the white man. Inclination, or business, or economy, may call them to another part of the city; but they are restrained on account of their children. There is no such restraint upon the white man, for he knows that wherever in the city inclination, or business, or economy, may call him, he will find a school open to his children near his door. Surely this is not equality before the law.

Or if a colored person, yielding to the necessities of his position, removes to a distant part of the city, his children may be compelled, at an inconvenience which will not be called trivial, to walk a long distance in order to enjoy the advantages of the school. In our severe winters, this cannot be disregarded by children so tender in years as those of the primary schools. There is a respectable colored person, I am told, who became some time since a resident at East Boston, separated by the water from the main land. There are, of course, proper public schools at East Boston, but none that were then open to colored children. This person, therefore, was obliged to send his children, three in number, daily, across the ferry to the distant African school. The tolls for these children amounted to a sum which formed a severe tax upon a poor man.

V.   The separation of children in the Public Schools of Boston, on account of color or race, is in the nature of Caste, and is a violation of Equality.

The facts in this case show expressly that the child was excluded from the school nearest to her dwelling, the number in the school at the time warranting her admission, "on the sole ground of color." The first Majority Report presented to the School Committee, to which reference is made in the statement of facts, gives, with more fullness, the grounds of this discrimination, saying, "It is one of races, not of color, merely. The distinction is one which the Almighty has seen fit to establish, and it is founded deep in the physical, mental, and moral natures of the two races. No legislation, no social customs, can efface this distinction."

Words more apt than these to describe the heathenish relation of Caste, could not be chosen.

It will be vain to say that this distinction, though seeming to be founded on color, is in reality founded on natural and physical peculiarities, which are independent of color. These peculiarities, whatever they may be, are peculiarities of race, and any discrimination on account of them constitutes the relation of Caste. Disguise it as you will, it is this hateful institution. But the words Caste and Equality are contradictory. They mutually exclude each other. Where Caste is, there cannot be Equality, Where Equality is, there cannot be Caste.

It is unquestionably true that there is a distinction between the Ethiopian and Caucasian race. Each has received from the hand of God certain characteristics of color and form. The two may not readily intermingle, although we are told by Homer that Jupiter

>—did not disdain to grace
>The feast of Ethiopia's blameless race.

One may be uninteresting or offensive to the other, precisely as different individuals of the same race and color may be uninteresting or offensive to each other. *But this distinction can furnish no ground for any discrimination before the law.*

We abjure nobility of all kinds; but here is a nobility of the skin. We abjure all hereditary distinctions; but here is an hereditary distinction, founded not on the merit of the ancestor, but on his color. We abjure all privileges derived from birth; but here is a privilege which depends solely on the accident, whether an ancestor is black or white. We abjure all inequality before the law; but here is an inequality which touches not an individual, but a race. We revolt at the relation of caste; but here is a case which is established under a Constitution, declaring that all men are born equal.

Condemning caste and inequality before the law, let us now consider more particularly the powers of the Schools Committee. Here it will be necessary to enter into some details.

VI. The Committee of Boston, charged with the superintendence of the Public Schools, have no *power* under the Constitution and laws of Massachusetts, to make any discrimination on account of color or race, among children in the Public Schools.

It has been already seen that this power is inconsistent with the Constitution and laws of Massachusetts, and with all adjudications of the Supreme Court. The stream cannot rise higher than the fountain-head, and if there be nothing in these elevated sources, from which this power can draw its sanction, it must be considered nullity.

But it is said that the Committee, in thus classifying the children, have not violated any principle of Equality, inasmuch as they have provided a school with competent instructors for the colored children, where they have equal advantages of instruction with those enjoyed by the white children. It is said that excluding the colored children from the Public Schools open to white children, they furnish them an equivalent.

In point of fact, it is not an equivalent. We have already seen that it is the occasion of inconveniences to the colored children and their parents, to which they would not be exposed, if they had access to the nearest public schools, besides inflicting upon them the stigma of Caste. Still further, and this consideration cannot be neglected, the matters taught in the two schools may be precisely the same; but a school, exclusively devoted to one class, must differ essentially, in its spirit and character, from that public school known to the law, where all classes meet together in equality. It is a mockery to call it an equivalent.

But there is yet another answer. Admitting that it is an equivalent, still the colored children cannot be compelled to take it. Their rights are Equality before the law; nor can they be called upon to renounce one jot of this. They have an equal right with white children to the general public schools. A separate school, thought well-endowed, would not secure to them that precise Equality, which they would enjoy in the general public schools. The Jews in Rome are confined to a particular district, called the Ghetto. In Frankfort they are condemned to a separate quarter, known as the Jewish quarter. It is possible that the accommodations allotted to them are as good as they would be able to occupy, if left free to choose throughout Rome and Frankfort; but this compulsory segregation from the mass of citizens is of itself an *inequality* which we condemn with our whole souls. It is a vestige of ancient intolerance directed against a despised people. It is of the same character with the separate schools in Boston.

Who can say, that this does not injure the blacks? Theirs, in its best estate, is an unhappy lot. Shut out by a still lingering prejudice from many social advantages, a despised class, they feel this proscription from the Public Schools as a peculiar brand. Beyond this, it deprives them of those healthful animating influences which would come from a participation in the studies of their white brethren. It adds to their discouragements. It widens their separation from the rest of the community, and postpones that great day of reconciliation which is sure to come.

The whole system of public schools suffers also. It is a narrow perception of their high aim which teaches that they are merely to furnish to all the scholars an equal amount in knowledge, and that, therefore, provided all be taught, it is of little consequence where, and in what company it be done. The law contemplates not only that they all shall be taught *all together.* They are not only to receive equal quantities of knowledge, but all are to receive it in the same way. All are to approach together the same common fountain; nor can there be any exclusive source for any individual or any class. The school is the little world in which the child is trained for the larger world of life. It must, therefore, cherish and develop the virtues and the sympathies which are employed in the larger world. And since, according to our institutions, all classes meet without distinction of color, in the performance of civil duties, so should they all meet without distinction of color, in the school, beginning there those relations of equality which our Constitution and laws promise to all.

As the State receives strength from the unity and solidarity of its citizens, without distinction of class, so the school receives new strength from the unity and solidarity of all classes beneath its roof. In this way the poor, the humble, and the neglected, share not only the companionship of their presence, in drawing towards the school a more watchful superintendence. A degraded or neglected class, if left to themselves, will become more degraded or neglected. To him that hath shall be given; and the world, true to these words, turns from the poor and outcast to the rich and fortunate. It is the aim of our system of Public Schools, by the blending of all classes, to draw upon the whole school the attention which is too apt to be given only to the favored few, and thus secure to the poor their portion of the fruitful sunshine. But the colored children, placed apart by themselves, are deprived of this blessing.

Nothing is more clear than that the welfare of classes, as well as of individuals, is promoted by mutual acquaintance. The French and English, for a long time regarded as natural enemies, have at last, from a more intimate communion, found themselves to be natural friends. Prejudice is the child of ignorance. It is sure to prevail where people do not know each other. Society and intercourse are means established by Providence for human improvement. They remove antipathies, promote mutual adaptation and conciliation, and establish relations of reciprocal regard. Who so sets up barriers to these, thwarts the way of Providence, crosses the tendencies of human nature, and directly interferes with the laws of God.

Sarah C. Roberts v. *City of Boston*, Decision of the Supreme Judicial Court

The great principle, advanced by the learned and eloquent advocate of the plaintiff, is, that, by the constitution and laws of Massachusetts, all persons without distinction of age or sex, birth or color, origin or condition, are equal before the law. This, as a broad general principle, such as ought to appear in a declaration of rights, is perfectly sound; it is not only expressed in terms, but pervades and animates the whole spirit of our constitution of free government. But, when this great principle comes to be applied to the actual and various conditions of persons in society, it will not warrant the assertion, that men and women are legally clothed with the same civil and political powers, and that children and adults are legally to have the same functions and be subject to the same treatment; but only that the right, of all, as they are settled and regulated by law, are equally entitled to the paternal consideration and protection of the law, for their maintenance and security. What those rights are, to which individuals, in the infinite variety of circumstances by which they are surrounded in society, are entitled, must depend on laws adapted to their respective relations and conditions.

Conceding, therefore, in the fullest manner, that colored persons, the descendants of Africans, are entitled by law, in this commonwealth, to equal rights, constitutional and political, civil and social, the question then arises, whether the regulation in question, which provides separate schools for colored children, is a violation of any of these rights.

Legal rights must, after all, depend upon the provisions of law; certainly all those rights of individuals which can be asserted and maintained in any judicial, tribunal. The proper providence of a declaration of rights and constitution of government, after directing its form, regulating its organization and the distribution of its powers, is to declare great principles and fundamental truths, to influence and direct the judgment and conscience of legislators in making laws, rather than to limit and control them, by directing what precise laws they shall make. The provision, that it shall be the duty of legislatures and magistrates to cherish the interests of literature and the sciences, espe-cially the university at Cambridge, public schools, and grammar schools, in the towns, is precisely of this character. Had the legislature failed to comply with this injunction, and neglected to provide public schools in the towns, or should they so far fail in their duty as to repeal all laws on the subject, and leave all education to depend on private means, strong and explicit as the direction of the constitution is, it would afford no rem-edy or redress to the thousands of the rising generation, who now depend on these schools to afford them a most valuable education, and an introduction to useful life.

In the absence of special legislation on this subject, the law has vested the power in the committee to regulate the system of distribution and classification; and when this power is reasonably exercised, without being abused or perverted by colorable pre-tenses, the decision of the committee must be deemed conclusive. The committee, apparently upon great deliberation, have come to the conclusion, that the good of both classes of schools will be best promoted, by maintaining the separate primary schools for colored and for white children, and we can perceive no ground to doubt, that this is the honest result of their experience and judgment.

It is urged, that this maintenance of separate schools tends to deepen and perpet-uate the odious distinction of caste, founded in a deep-rooted prejudice in public opin-ion. This prejudice, if it exists, is not created by law, and probably cannot be changed by law. Whether this distinction and prejudice, existing in the opinion and feelings of the community, would not be as effectually fostered by compelling colored and white children to associate together in the same schools, may well be doubted; at all events, it is a fair and proper question for the committee to consider and decide upon, having in view the best interests of both classes of children placed under their superintendence, and we cannot say, that their decision upon it is not founded on just grounds of reason and experience, and in the results of a discriminating and honest judgment.

The increased distance, to which the plaintiff was obliged to go to school from her father's house, is not such, in our opinion, as to render the regulation in question unreasonable, still less illegal.

"An Act in Amendment of 'An Act Concerning Public School . . . ,' " Chapter 256, Massachusetts Acts and Resolves, 1854–1855 (Boston, 1855)

[While the Massachusetts Supreme Court ruling in the Roberts case allowed segrega-tion to continue, the Massachusetts legislature ended the practice with the brief 1855 law that follows.

In determining the qualifications of scholars to be admitted into any public school or any district school in this Commonwealth, no distinction shall be made on account of the race, color, or religious opinions of the applicant or scholar.

Any child who, on account of his race, color, or religious opinions, shall be excluded from any public or district school in this Commonwealth, for admission to which he may be otherwise qualified, shall recover damages therefore in an action of tort, to be brought in the name of said child by his guardian or next friend, in any court of competent jurisdiction to try the same, against the city or town by which such school is supported.

CHAPTER 4

SCHOOLING MOVES WEST, 1835-1860

Introduction

During the early decades of the nineteenth century, European Americans rapidly settled the lands west of the Alleghenies, forming the new states of Ohio, Indiana, Illinois, Michigan and Wisconsin. The center of gravity for the United Sates was shifting west. And with the North and South growing further apart in their irreconcilable differences over slavery, the West was seen as the hope of the future. But who would control the culture of the West? Not only was there competition between the cultures of the North and South, but new European immigrants were moving directly to the West. As German and Irish Catholics moved into the new areas, members of the nation's older Protestant elite worried about the character of the region and, therefore, of the nation. What better institution to "rescue" the West than the public school as envisioned by Horace Mann and his many eastern allies? If the New England model of schooling could be established in what was to be the Midwest, then perhaps New England culture—and cultural dominance—could also be established. Thus, by the 1830s, a major effort emerged to shape the culture of the West, with the public school at the center of the action.

In 1835, Lyman Beecher, one of the nation's best known preachers, who had recently moved from Boston to Cincinnati, published *A Plea for the West*. Asking for Eastern funds to support institutions in the West, he wrote:

> The thing required for the civil and religious prosperity of the West, is universal education, and moral culture, by institutions commensurate to that result—the all-pervading influences of schools, and colleges, and seminaries, and pastors, and churches. When the West is well-supplied in this respect, though there may be great relative defects, there will be, as we believe, the stamina and vitality of a perpetual civil and religious prosperity.

Eastern funds and eastern recruits were essential. But, as Beecher insisted, schooling was the key to the civil and religious prosperity of the region.

Beecher and his allies, including his daughter Catharine Beecher and his son-in-law Calvin Stowe, were part of the nucleus of people who started public schools in Ohio. Other teams of ministers and educators helped found public schools in the other states of the Midwest. Even more than on the East Coast, schooling took off in the Midwest. The school was the ideal institution to help shape the culture of the new region.

By the late 1840s, midwestern schools were well-established, but they still lacked teachers. As a result, one of the nation's first major internal missionary campaigns was developed. The Board of National Popular Education, founded by Catharine Beecher, and other groups sponsored by various religious and charitable organizations, began raising funds and recruiting young women to go west as school teachers. As an earlier version of the Teacher Corps, the Board of National Popular Education offered young women adventure in a new place, a sense of purpose and meaningful effort, and a fresh start in life. Many responded. The official publications of the Board reported the successes of the adventure. Some of the teachers' private correspondence reported the hardships more vividly. Both are included in this chapter.

While midwestern schools initially relied on eastern funds and eastern teachers, it was for midwestern schools themselves that the most successful textbook ever known in the United States was published. A small Cincinnati publishing house offered William Holmes McGuffey $1,000 for a primer, a speller, and four readers. The first readers were published in 1836; McGuffey received his $1,000, and the publisher became a millionaire. Between 1836 and 1920, over 122,000,000 copies of the readers were sold. *McGuffey's Reader* reflected American white middle-class Protestant morality as it existed circa 1836, but later editions also became one of the major shapers of American morality in the decades ahead. As generations of school children learned to read from these stories, they also learned what it meant to be an American and a participant in a larger society that had clear expectations of its citizens.

Reading most of the material published in the Midwest before the Civil War, one would conclude that only Europeans and their descendants lived there. That was far from the truth. All of the states of the upper Midwest were free states, and numbers of free Blacks lived there, often in less-than-easy circumstances. And while most of the previous Indian residents had died or been moved farther west, there continued to be Indian communities and conflicts in the region. Subsequent chapters include most of the material on Indian and African-American educational experiences, but this chapter closes with one Indian's speech emphatically rejecting European culture, religion, and schooling. Nevertheless, by the time of the Civil War, no part of the country had such a clearly established and organized system of public schools, so much popular support for the institution, or such widespread participation.

✦ Selections from McGuffey's Sixth Eclectic Reader, 1836 (with many subsequent editions)

For generations of Americans, especially young people living in the Midwest and West between the late 1830s and the early 1900s, McGuffey's Readers *was the basic textbook for all schooling. In his forward to a republication of the readers, historian Henry Steele Commager noted that "part of the greatness of the* McGuffey Readers *was that they were there at the right time—they were there to be read by millions of children from all parts of the country . . .". Just as the schools were growing, a textbook came along that fit the morality and the patriotism of the institution and the times. The examples that follow are typical of* McGuffey: *Patrick Henry's speech advocating the cause of the American revolution before the Virginia Legislature, and the indomitable Lyman Beecher's sermon calling on the nation's increasingly diverse peoples to view the Puritan founders of Massachusetts as their true forebearers. While later editions of the readers became less overtly religious, the patriotic themes, the celebration of the virtues of European Protestant ethics, and the focus on male leadership continued throughout. The readings that follow are from the 1879 edition.*

Speech Before the Virginia Convention

Patrick Henry, 1736–1799, was born in Hanover County, Virginia. He received instruction in Latin and mathematics from his father, but seemed to develop a greater fondness for hunting, fishing, and playing the fiddle than for study. Twice he was set up in business, and twice failed before he was twenty-four. He was then admitted to the bar after six weeks of study of the law. He got no business at first in his profession, but lived with his father-in-law. His wonderful powers of oratory first showed themselves in a celebrated case which he argued in Hanover Court-house, his own father being the presiding magistrate. He began very awkwardly, but soon rose to a surprising height of eloquence, won his case against great odds, and was carried off in triumph by the delighted spectators. His fame was now established; business flowed in, and he was soon elected to the Virginia Legislature, where, in 1765, he made his famous speech on his resolutions against the Stamp Act, of which the following selection is a portion. He was a delegate to the Congress of 1774, and during the Revolution he was, for several years, Governor of Virginia. In 1788, he earnestly opposed the adoption of the Federal Constitution. When he died, he left a large family and an ample fortune. In person, Mr. Henry was tall and rather awkward, with a face stern and grave. When he spoke on great occasions, his awkwardness forsook him, his face lighted up, and his eyes flashed with a wonderful fire. In his life, he was good-humored, honest, and temperate. His patriotism was of the noblest type; and few men in those stormy times did better service for their country than he.

> It is natural for man to indulge in the illusions of hope. We are apt to shut our eyes against a painful truth, and listen to the song of that siren till she transforms us into beasts. Is this the part of wise men, engaged in a great and arduous struggle for liberty? Are we disposed to be of the number of those, who, having eyes, see not, and having ears, hear not the things which so nearly concern their temporal salvation? For my part, whatever anguish of spirit it may cost, I am willing to know the whole truth; to know the worst, and to provide for it.
>
>   I have but one lamp by which my feet are guided; and that is the lamp of experience. I know of no way of judging the future but by the past; and, judging by the past, I wish to know what there has been in the conduct of the British ministry for the last ten years to justify those hopes with which gentlemen have been pleased to solace themselves and the house? Is it that insidious smile with which our petition has been lately received? Trust it not: it will prove a snare to your feet. Suffer not yourselves to be betrayed with a kiss. Ask yourselves, how this gracious reception of our petition comports with those warlike preparations which cover our waters and darken our land. Are fleets and armies necessary to a work of love and reconciliation? Have we shown ourselves so unwilling to be reconciled that force must be called in

to win back our love? Let us not deceive ourselves. These are the implements of war and subjugation,—the last arguments to which kings resort.

I ask, gentlemen, what means this martial array, if its purpose be not to force us into submission? Can gentlemen assign any other possible motive for it? Has Great Britain any enemy in this quarter of the world, to call for all this accumulation of navies and armies? No, she has none. They are meant for us: they can be meant for no other. They are sent over to bind and rivet upon us those chains which the British ministry have been so long forging. And what have we to oppose to them? Shall we try argument? We have been trying that for the last ten years. Have we any thing new to offer upon the subject? Nothing. We have held the subject up in every light in which it was capable; but it has been all in vain. Shall we resort to entreaty and humble supplication? What terms shall we find which have not been already exhausted? Let us not, I beseech you, deceive ourselves longer. We have done everything that could be done, to avert the storm which is now coming on. We have petitioned; we have remonstrated; we have supplicated; we have prostrated ourselves at the foot of the throne, and implored its interposition to arrest the tyrannical hands of the ministry and parliament. Our petitions have been slighted; our remonstrances have produced additional violence and insult; our supplications disregarded; and we have been spurned with contempt from the foot of the throne.

In vain, after these things, may we indulge the fond hope of peace and reconciliation. There is no longer any room for hope. If we wish to be free; if we mean to preserve inviolate those inestimable privileges for which we have been so long contending; if we mean not basely to abandon the noble struggle in which we have been so long engaged, and which we have pledged ourselves never to abandon until the glorious object of our contest shall be obtained—we must fight! I repeat it, we must fight! An appeal to arms and the God of Hosts, is all that is left us.

They tell us that we are weak; unable to cope with so formidable an adversary. But when shall we be stronger? Will it be the next week, or the next year? Will it be when we are totally disarmed, and when a British guard shall be stationed in every house? Shall we gather strength by irresolution and inaction? Shall we acquire the means of effectual resistance by lying supinely on our backs, and hugging the delusive phantom of hope, until our enemies shall have bound us hand and foot? We are not weak, if we make a proper use of those means which the God of nature hath placed in our power.

Three millions of people, armed in the holy cause of liberty, and in such a country as that which we possess, are invincible by any force which our enemy can send against us. Besides, we shall not fight our battles alone. There is a just God who presides over the destinies of nations; and who will raise up friends to fight our battles for us. The battle is not to the strong alone; it is to the vigilant, the active, the brave. Besides, we have no election. If we were base enough to desire it, it is now too late to retire from the contest. There is no retreat but in submission and slavery! Our chains are forged. Their clanking may be heard on the plains of Boston! The war is inevitable; and, let it come! I repeat, let it come!

It is vain to extenuate the matter. Gentlemen may cry peace, peace; but there is no peace. The war is actually begun. The next gale that sweeps from the north, will bring to our ears the clash of resounding arms! Our brethren are already in the field! Why stand we here idle? What is it that gentlemen wish? What would they have? Is life so dear, or peace so sweet, as to be purchased at the price of chains and slavery? Forbid it, Almighty God! I know not what course others may take; but as for me, give me liberty or give me death.

The Memory of Our Fathers

Lyman Beecher, 1775–1863, a famous Congregational minister of New England, was born in New Haven, graduated from Yale College in 1797, and studied theology with Dr. Timothy Dwight. His first settlement was at East Hampton, L.I. at a salary of three hundred dollars a year. He was pastor of the church in Litchfield, C.T. from 1810 till 1826, when he removed to Boston, and took charge of the Hanover Street Church. In the religious controversies of the time, Dr. Beecher was one of the most prominent characters. From 1832 to 1842, he was President of Lane Theological Seminary, in the suburbs of Cincinnati. He then returned to Boston, where he spent most of the closing years of his long and active life. His death occurred in Brooklyn, N.Y. As a theologian, preacher, and advocate of education, temperance, and missions, Dr. Beecher occupied a very prominent place for nearly half a century. He left a large family of sons and two daughters, who are well known as among the most eminent preachers and authors in America.

> We are called upon to cherish with high veneration and grateful recollections, the memory of our fathers. Both the ties of nature and the dictates of policy demand this. And surely no nation had ever less occasion to be ashamed of its ancestry, or more occasion for gratulation in that respect; for while most nations trace their origin to barbarians, the foundations of our nation were laid by civilized men, by Christians. Many of them were men of distinguished families, of powerful talents, of great learning and of pre-eminent wisdom, of decision of character, and of most inflexible integrity. And yet not unfrequently they have been treated as if they had no virtues; while their sins and follies have been sedulously immortalized in satirical anecdote.
>
> The influence of such treatment of our fathers is too manifest. It creates and lets loose upon their institutions, the vandal spirit of innovation and overthrow; for after the memory of our fathers shall have been rendered contemptible, who will appreciate and sustain their institutions? "The memory of our fathers" should be the watchword of liberty throughout the land; for, imperfect as they were, the world before had not seen their like, nor will it so, we fear, behold their like again. Such models of moral excellence, such apostles of civil and religious liberty, such shades of the illustrious dead looking down upon their descendants with approbation or reproof, according as they follow or depart from the good way, constitute a censorship inferior only to the eye of God; and to ridicule them is national suicide.
>
> The doctrines of our fathers have been represented as gloomy, superstitious, severe, irrational, and of a licentious tendency. But when other systems shall have produced a piety as devoted, a morality as pure, a patriotism as disinterested, and a state of society as happy, as have prevailed where their doctrines have been most prevalent, it may be in season to seek an answer to this objection.
>
> The persecutions instituted by our fathers have been the occasion of ceaseless obloquy upon their fair fame. And truly, it was a fault of no ordinary magnitude, that sometimes they did persecute. But let him whose ancestors were not ten times more guilty, cast the first stone, and the ashes of our fathers will no more be disturbed. Theirs was the fault of the age, and it will be easy to show that no class of men had, at that time, approximated so nearly to just apprehensions of religious liberty; and that it is to them that the world is now indebted for the more just and definite views which now prevail.
>
> The superstition and bigotry of our fathers are themes on which some of their descendants, themselves far enough from superstition, if not from bigotry, have

delighted to dwell. But when we look abroad, and behold the condition of the world, compared with the condition of New England, we may justly exclaim, "Would to God that the ancestors of all the nations had been not only almost, but altogether such bigots as our fathers were."

✦ CALVIN E. STOWE, REPORT ON ELEMENTARY PUBLIC INSTRUCTION IN EUROPE, 1837

While Calvin Stowe never held public office—he was a professor of New Testament at Lane Theological Seminary in Cincinnati—he did have an influence in Ohio not unlike that of Horace Mann in Massachusetts. A tireless advocate for an expanded public school system in his adopted state, he also wanted a school that inculcated the young with his version of morality and knowledge. A year before Horace Mann made his trip to view the schools of Prussia, Calvin Stowe made a trip there. His subsequent report to the Ohio legislature is part report and part advocacy for his own model for Ohio. As Stowe selectively described what he saw in Europe, he made it very clear what he believed legislatures should create in the United States.

Internal Arrangements of the Prussian Schools

I will now ask your attention to a few facts respecting the internal management of the schools in Prussia and some other parts of Germany, which were impressed on my mind by a personal inspection of those establishments.

One of the circumstances that interested me most was the excellent order and rigid economy with which all the Prussian institutions are conducted. Particularly in large boarding schools, where hundreds, and sometimes thousands of youths are collected together, the benefits of the system are strikingly manifest. Every boy is taught to wait upon himself—to keep his person, clothing, furniture, and books, in perfect order and neatness; and no extravagance in dress, and no waste of fuel or food, or property of any kind is permitted. Each student has his own single bed, which is generally a light mattrass, laid upon a frame of slender bars of iron, because such bedsteads are not likely to be infested by insects, and each one makes his own bed and keeps it in order. In the house, there is a place for every thing and every thing must be in its place. In one closet are the shoe brushes and blacking, in another the lamps and oil, in another the fuel. At the doors are good mats and scrapers, and every thing of the kind necessary for neatness and comfort, and every student is taught, as carefully as he is taught any other lesson, to make a proper use of all these articles at the right time, and then to leave them in good order at their proper places. Every instance of neglect is sure to receive its appropriate reprimand, and if necessary, severe punishment. I know nothing that can benefit us more than the introduction of such oft-repeated lessons on carefulness and frugality into all our educational establishments; for the contrary habits of carelessness and wastefulness, notwithstanding all the advantages which we enjoy, have already done us immense mischief. Very many of our families waste and throw away nearly as much as they use; and one third of the expenses of housekeeping might be saved by system and frugality. It is true, we have such an abundance of every thing that this enormous waste is not so sensibly always to be so with us. The productions of our country for some years past have by no means kept pace with the increase of consumption, and many an American family during the last season has felt a hard pressure, where they never expected to feel one.

Especially should this be made a branch of female education, and studied faithfully and perseveringly by all who are to be wives and mothers, and have the care of families.

The universal success also and very beneficial results, with which the arts of drawing and designing, vocal and instrumental music, moral instruction and the Bible, have been introduced into schools, was another fact peculiarly interesting to me. I asked all the teachers with whom I conversed, whether they did not sometimes find children who were actually incapable of learning to draw and to sing. I have had but one reply, and that was, that they found the same diversity of natural talent in regard to these as in regard to reading, writing, and the other branches of education; but they had never seen a child who was capable of learning to read and write, who could not be taught to sing well and draw neatly, and that too without taking any time which would at all interfere with, indeed which would not actually promote his progress in other studies. In regard to the necessity of moral instruction and the beneficial influence of the Bible in schools, the testimony was no less explicit and uniform. I inquired of all classes of teachers, and men of every grade of religious faith, instructors in common schools, high schools, and schools of art, of professors in colleges, universities, and professional seminaries, in cities in the country, in places where there was a uniformity and in places where was a diversity of creeds, of believers and unbelievers, of rationalists and enthusiasts, of Catholics and Protestants; and I never found but one reply, and that was, that to leave the moral faculty uninstructed was to leave the most important part of the human mind undeveloped, and to strip education of almost every thing that can make it valuable; and that the Bible, independently of the interest attending it, as containing the most ancient and influential writings ever recorded by human hands, and comprising the religious system of almost the whole of the civilized world, is in itself the best book that can be put into the hands of children to interest, to exercise, and to unfold their intellectual and moral powers. Every teacher whom I consulted, repelled with indignation the idea that moral instruction is not proper for schools; and spurned with contempt the allegation, that the Bible cannot be introduced into common schools without encouraging a sectarian bias in the matter of teaching; an indignation and contempt which I believe will be fully participated in by every high-minded teacher in christendom.

A few instances, to illustrate the above-mentioned general statements, I here subjoin—Early in September I visited the Orphan House at Halle, an institution founded by the benevolence of Franke, about the year 1700, and which has been an object of special favor with the present king of Prussia. It now contains two thousand seven hundred to three thousand boys, most of them orphans sustained by charity. After examining its extensive grounds, its commodious and neat buildings, its large book store, its noble printing establishment, for printing the Bible in the Oriental and modern languages, its large apothecary's shop, for the dispensation of medicine to the poor, and the exquisitely beautiful statue of its founder, erected by Frederic William III; I was invited by Drs. Guerike and Netto to go into the dinning hall and see the boys partake of their supper. The hall is a very long and narrow room, and furnished the whole length of each side with short tables like the mess tables on board a man of war, each table accommodating about twelve boys. The tables were without cloths, but very clean, and were provided with little pewter basins of warm soup, and just as many pieces of dark and coarse, but very wholesome, bread, as there were to be boys at the table. When the bell rang, the boys entered in a very quiet and orderly manner, each with a little pewter spoon in his hand. When they had arranged themselves at table, at a signal from the teacher one of the boys ascended a pulpit near the center of the hall, and in the most appropriate manner supplicated the blessing of God upon their frugal repast. The boys then each took his bit of bread in one hand, and with his spoon in the other, made a very quiet and healthful meal. They then united in singing two or three verses of a hymn, and retired in the same quiet and orderly manner in which they had entered. It being warm weather, they were dressed in jackets and trousers of clean, coarse brown linen; and a more cheerful, healthy, intelligent set of youthful faces and glistening eyes I never saw before; and notwithstanding the gravity with which they partook of their supper and left the hall, when fairly in the yard, there was such a pattering of little feet, such a chattering of German, and such skipping and playing, as satisfied me that none of their boyish spirits had been broken by the discipline of the school.

At Weisenfels, near Lutzen where the great battle was fought in the Thirty Years' War, there is a collection of various schools, under the superintendent of Dr. Harnisch, in what was formerly a large convent. Among the rest there is one of those institutions peculiar to Prussia, in which the children of very destitute families are taken and educated at the public expense, to become teachers in poor villages where they can never expect to receive a large compensation; institutions of a class which we do not *need here,* because no villages in this country *need* be poor. Of course, though they have all the advantages of scientific advancement enjoyed in the most favored schools, frugality and self-denial form an important part of their education. Dr. Harnisch invited me to this part of the establishment to see these boys dine. When I came to the room, they were sitting at their writing tables, engaged in their studies as usual. At the ringing of the bell they arose. Some of the boys left the room, and the others removed the papers and books from the tables, and laid them away in their places. Some of the boys who had gone out, then re-entered with clean, coarse tablecloths in their hands, which they spread over their writing tables. These were followed by others with loaves of brown bread, and plates provided with cold meat and sausages, neatly cut in slices, and jars of water, which they arranged on the table. Of these materials, after a short religious service, they made a cheerful and hearty meal; then arose, cleared away their tables, swept their room, and after a suitable season of recreation, resumed their studies. They are taught to take care of themselves, independent of any help, and their only luxuries are the fruits and plants which they cultivate with their own hands, and which grow abundantly in the gardens of the institution . . . .

Character of the System

The striking features of this system, even in the hasty and imperfect sketch which my limits allow me to give, are obvious even to superficial observation. No one can fail to observe its great completeness, both as to the number and kind of subjects embraced in it, and as to its adaptedness to develop every power of every kind, and give it a useful direction. What topic in all that is necessary for a sound business education is here omitted? I can think of nothing, unless it be one or two of the modern languages, and these are introduced whenever it is necessary, as has already been seen in the study sheet of Dr. Diesterweg's seminary, inserted on a preceding page of this report. I have not taken the course as precisely as it exists in any one school, but have combined from an investigation of many institutions, the features which I supposed would most fairly represent the whole system. In the Rhinish provinces of Prussia, in a considerable part of Bavaria, Baden, and Wirtemberg, French is taught as well as German; in the schools of Prussian Poland, German and Polish are taught; and even English, in the Russian schools of Cronstadt and Archangel, where so many English and American merchants resort for the purposes of trade. Two languages can be taught in a school quite as easily as one, provided the teacher be perfectly familiar, as any one may see by visiting Mr. Solomon's school in Cincinnati, where all the instruction is given both in German and English.

What faculty of mind is there that is not developed in the scheme of instruction sketched above? I know of none. The perceptive and reflective faculties, the memory and the judgment, the imagination and the taste, the moral and religious faculty, and even the various kinds of physical and manual dexterity, all have opportunity for development and exercise. Indeed, I think the system in its great outlines, as nearly complete as human ingenuity and skill can make it; though undoubtedly some of its arrangements and details admit of improvement; and some changes will of course be necessary in adapting it to the circumstances of different countries.

The entirely practical character of the system is obvious throughout. It views every subject on the practical side, and in reference to its adaptedness to use. The dry technical abstract parts of science are not those first presented; but the system proceeds, in the only way which nature ever pointed out, from practice to theory, from parts to demonstrations. It has often been a complaint in respect to some systems of education, that the more a man studied, the less he knew of the actual business of life. Such a complaint cannot be made in reference to this system, for being intended to educate for the actual business of life, this object is never for a moment lost sight of.

Another striking feature of the system is its moral and religious character. Its morality is pure and elevated, its religion entirely removed from its narrowness of sectarian bigotry. What parent is there, loving his children and wishing to have them respected and happy, who would not desire that they should be educated under such a kind of moral and religious influence as has been described? Whether a believer in revelation or not, does he not know that without sound morals there can be no happiness, and that there is no morality like the morality of the New Testament? Does he not know that without religion, the human heart can never be at rest, and that there is no religion like the religion of the Bible? Every well-informed man knows, that, as a general fact, it is impossible to impress the obligations of morality with any efficiency on the heart of a child, or even on that of an adult, without an appeal to some mode which is sustained by the authority of God; and for what code will it be possible to claim this authority if not for the code of the Bible?

But perhaps some will be ready to say, the scheme is indeed an excellent one, provided only it were practicable; but the idea of introducing so extensive and complete a course of study into our common schools is entirely visionary and can never be realized. I answer, that it is not theory which I have been exhibiting, but a matter of fact, a copy of actual practice. The above system is no visionary scheme emanating from the closet of a recluse, but a sketch of the course of instruction now actually pursued by thousands of schoolmasters in the best district schools that have ever been organized. It can be done, for it has been done, it is now done, and it ought to be done. If it can be done in Europe, I believe it can be done in the United States: If it can be done in Prussia, I know it can be done in Ohio. The people have but to say the word and provide the means, and the thing is accomplished; for the word of the people here is even more powerful than the word of the King there; and the means of the people here are altogether more abundant for such an object than the means of the sovereign there. Shall this object, then, so desirable in itself, so entirely practicable, so easily within our reach, fail of accomplishment? For the honor and welfare of our State, for the safety of our whole nation, I trust it will not fail; but that we shall soon witness in this commonwealth the introduction of a system of common school instruction, fully adequate to all the wants of our population.

✦ BOARD OF NATIONAL POPULAR EDUCATION, CORRESPONDENCE, 1849-1850

While eastern missionaries and their allies were succeeding in establishing schools and systems of schooling in the Midwest, their very success led to a desperate shortage of teachers. Turning back to the East Coast was the obvious step. Eastern teachers were not only literate, they shared the values of the midwestern school leaders in terms of both literacy and piety. A number of organizations began sending teachers west, the largest founded by Catharine Beecher and led by William Slade, former Governor of Vermont. Obvious as the move seems, it was a radical departure from previous sex-role stereotypes for a religious society to recruit young single women and send them hundreds of miles from home to begin their work as teachers. This nineteenth-century Teacher Corps was the forerunner of similar efforts after the Civil War to send missionaries to the South to teach newly freed slaves. In both cases, young women were offered adventure as well as a sense of purpose for their lives. Beginning with its second Annual Report, the Board also included extracts from letters of teachers. While these letters were carefully selected to portray the work in its most positive and romantic light—they were part of a continuing recruitment and fundraising campaign—they also give one a glimpse of the morality, dedication, and sense of adventure among these teachers. The letters also leave litle doubt that it was a Protestant public school system that the National Board meant to establish.

St. Paul, Minnesota
Aug. 8, 1849
A new school house is about being prepared, so that Miss B. and myself will be kept from idleness. In performing my duty as a teacher and a Christian I have been supported far better than I had dared to hope—so true is it that God never forsakes his children. For encouragement to continue my labors, I have but to look at what this town was two years ago, and what it is at present. I rejoice that I have been thrown here at so early a period in the history of this Territory, and trust that, as one of the many now weaving the future web of society, my thread may be ever redolent with Christian love, and my

efforts ever on the side of Christian Education. This is truly, an important field, and when the germ now budding shall have reached maturity, mighty will be the results. I believe Minnesota is yet to be a leader in the cause of Religion and Education.

Oct. 31. [1849]

My labors have been abundantly blessed during the past season. Not only the day school but the Sabbath school has doubled in interest. I have in my mind an idea of starting a "Youth's Total Abstinence Society," which I think would operate well. This is a young community, and it is impossible to tell what may be the result even of a day.

The Governor told me that we should be supplied with a room and furniture to make a school comfortable. Besides improvement in educational matters, there is a decided advancement in the cause of religion, and morality. Laws have been passed for the suppression of gambling and drinking. . . . The different towns are filling up somewhat slowly, but the probability is, that, next spring, the emigration will be greater than ever.

This is a great country to make one grow. All the faculties are brought into action. I feel as if it was one of heaven's best blessings, that I was sent here, where there can be no shirking of labor—no release from responsibility, and no lack of room to work in. May God bless you and the cause in which you labor, and grant you full faith in the promise, that "in due season you shall reap if you faint not."

From another Teacher in Minnesota
Nov. 12, 1849

I find no difficulty in managing the most turbulent spirits. But were there no Bible to teach me the secret of success in this department of my labors, I should be like the mariner without a compass. As it is, I am often allowed to look at the effect of the great principles of *right* and *wrong,* upon minds unused to the sweet, the subduing power of the gospel. Through the influence of the precept, "Be ye kind one to another, tender hearted, forgiving one another, even as God for Christ's sake hath forgiven you," the habits of some of my scholars are so far changed, that instead of raising the clenched fist at every little affront, they refer all their childish feuds to me. The satisfaction which they manifest with my decisions, is a rich reward for all my exertions and privations. I conduct my Sabbath school with so little parade that I presume the Priest does not know of its existence. I infer from this, from the circumstance that the Catholic children attend regularly. My prospects for continued and increasing usefulness are flattering. I am happy—very happy.

From a Teacher in Southern Indiana
Nov. 12, 1849

I very soon learned after coming here, that much prejudice existed against eastern teachers, and many unkind remarks were made; but, this feeling is fast passing away. Indeed, some of the very individuals have since apologized to me, and now treat me with much respect, while those who have children, have wished to send to my school, and are now waiting with much impatience for admission . . . All who are able, join with me each morning in reading from the Bible. These are seasons of deep interest—and the effect on the school is most salutary. Indeed I could not commence the duties of the day without it, with any hope that I should get through successfully. I often talk with them about the lesson, endeavoring to impress on their minds the necessity of having a new heart—of loving the Savior, and in general am listened to with much apparent interest. . . . My pupils are constant in their attendance, and have an increasing interest in their studies. The community generally have a very high opinion of the teachers sent out by the Board, and the confidence in them, as far as I have had an opportunity to judge, is increasing. I am content and happy. I do not regret that I left home, although I often *feel* that I am *not at home.* Society is divided, which is to be expected, where it is composed of so many different elements. There are Swiss, French, Irish, and Dutch. I love the work; and if I can be useful shall continue to be happy. I feel grateful for the favors received at Hartford. My stay there was of much benefit—the preparatory course aiding me essentially in my work as a teacher.

✦ Mary Augusta Roper, Letters from Mill Point, Michigan, 1852-1854

The purposes for which the Board of National Popular Education selected a certain kind of letter for publication are reflected in other unpublished letters contained in the Board's files. Polly Welts Kaufman's Women Teachers on the Frontier *traces the lives of these women primarily through their correspondence. Kaufman's careful study gives the reader a sense of the adventure offered to a generation of women who escaped the social restrictions of their home towns, as well as their sense of dedication to the welfare of others. At the same time, the difficulty and the loneliness of the enterprise is clear. Moving far away from family and friends, without easy communications, living in a strange place, and dealing with illness made the experience precarious for many. Mary Augusta Roper of Templeton, Massachusetts was sent by the National Board to Mill Point, Michigan in the 1850s. Her letters to the women in Hartford, Connecticut who selected and trained the teachers, written between 1852 and 1854, illustrate the challenges many of these teachers faced.*

Mill Point, Ottawa County, Michigan
October 18 '52
Committee for Selecting Teachers, Hartford, C.T.

Ladies,

Since leaving Hartford last May, I have been actively engaged in the school of this place, which has been quite large, averaging 40 scholars. No time has been left unoccupied, to be filled up with unavailing regrets, that home and friends are so far away, and I had been unconscious that time had flown so rapidly until the arrival of Miss Bell at Grand Haven reminded me that another class had been collected and scattered over the broad west, and I had not written one word to you.

　　Lest the circumstances in which I have been placed excuse the delay, I have waited on one account to see the end of a difference of parties which would not be

---

Kaufman, Polly Welts. *Women Teachers on the Frontier.* New Haven: Yale University Press, 1984. Reprinted by permission of Yale University Press.

decided until the annual school meeting, which took place a few days since, but for you to understand the position in which I have been placed I must describe the place and people.

Mill Point is a village separated from Grand Haven entirely by water, containing about 400 inhabitants. A collection of foreigners mostly, who are employed in the steam mills which give the place its name. There are only four families in the place of intelligence. A few other families possess influence but are bad men. A few men in the place wished for a teacher from Governor Slade's class to supply the place of Miss E. Chandler (a lady sent out several years ago and who had taught in this place a year) who was going to leave on account of her health wishing a smaller school. The other party said "they had had a pious teacher long enough" and wished for a Universalist in principle. Mr. Smith was appointed school Director, and he, with the advice of two other of the officers, applied for a teacher, and I was sent here. At the same time a lady destitute of religious principle was hired to teach the children of the dissatisfied ones. No effort was left untried to injure my school. I fortunately succeeded in gaining the affection and confidence of my scholars, so that all avenues to that were closed up.

Completely foiled in their attempts to break up the school in this, they resorted to another expedient which has alike failed. They cautiously circulated suspicions of my good character, and growing bold, finally asserted with barefaced boldness the most indecent stories. At first no attention was paid to it by my friends, but they finally met the Authors of the slander, and before they left them, received the acknowledgement that a miserable fellow—a personal enemy of Mr. Smith, made such by Mr. S. on one occasion reproving him for profanity, had been induced to commence the slander, to gratify his hatred of Mr. Smith. It caused a great excitement at the time, but did not interrupt my school, although I suffered severely at the time.

At the last school meeting a great effort was made to take from Mr. Smith the office of Director, had it been accomplished, I should not have continued the school, but the cause of right and virtue triumphed, they failed to elect an officer consequently, my employers are still at the head of affairs. They assure me of their unbounded confidence and respect and will not hear on any account of my leaving unless it is so unpleasant that I should *greatly* prefer a location elsewhere. I am firmly attached to my scholars, and I think I can say that they are to me. Attempts have been made repeatedly upon members of my school, to induce them to find fault with school, and leave it for the other, but never have they in but one instance succeeded, and that was the case of two Dutch [German] boys of passionate tempers, who combined in their character the worst traits I ever met in children, their absence was an advantage rather than a loss to the school.

I open my school with prayer and I never have seen any disposition to levity during devotions. We have a large Sabbath School, with only three teachers, we have hitherto felt the want of books, but a large library is on its way hither from my native place, a donation from the church of which I am a member.

We have had no regular preaching but are now making an effort to raise money for the support of a minister, and I think shall succeed. The same opposition has been made to that movement as to all others of such a nature, but it has succeeded beyond our expectations. I think that eventually the cause of religion will triumph but there is a great amount of irreligion, skepticism if not infidelity now.

Miss Bell arrived safely and has commenced her school under favorable circumstances, but she has to fill the place of one of the most successful teachers the state affords, viz. Miss Mary White, her scholars were singularly attached to her, always speaking of her with all the tenderness of a mother.

Mill Point and Grand Haven are favored with the most beautiful natural scenery, the views from Lake Michigan's shores are very fine, sand hills of the purest white sand lying as steep as it is possible for sand to lie and in some instances covered with wild roses to the water's edge. Our sunsets on the Lake are magnificent in the extreme, and now in midsummer when the forests are robed in their varied hues the effect is fine.

Lake Michigan announces the approach of winter by his deep, wild roar and it is a beautiful scene to see his snow-crested breakers, dashing in fury and dying upon the shores.

I have heard from no member of the class of last spring, a wide correspondence of my own has prevented my writing to them and I have received no letters.

I shall ever retain the most grateful recollections of the kindness experienced at Hartford. I have found the facts learned by visiting schools there most important, enabling me to have a standard of school discipline in my own mind which if never reached, is a constant incentive to active exertion.

With an humble wish that your society may receive Heaven's blessing I will close.

Respectfully yours,

Mary Augusta Roper

Mill Point, Ottawa County, Michigan
June 10, 1853

Miss Swift,
Dear Madam,

I received your kind letter of December, last, but words cannot express the support and consolation it afforded me in those hours of trial, and I now find myself surrounded by circumstances calling once more for your advice.

You expressed a wish that I might continue my school here for two years. I have found it impossible to do so. As the first year was drawing to a close, the time for which I was engaged at first because Mr. Smith was Director only for that time, the opposition had been so violent to every measure he had taken, he decided to make no farther effort to hire a Teacher. This is founded, as I think I have written you before, on his decided opposition to the almost frightful immorality existing here.

My school before its close had become reduced in number to less than one half its first size, still numbering the scholars of the most intelligent unprejudiced portion of the people, even those who joined in railing Mr. Smith would send their oldest daughters to me, and the smaller ones away. And as far as I know all the fault that has been found with me has been "that my scholars loved me" too much.

An old Irish woman whose dirty little ones cried to come back says, "Oh! She's no Teacher, she don't *lick* them at all, she ought'er at 'em with the broomstick."

Perhaps it may be well to give a short account of my manner of conducting the school. I never used the rod unless when a scholar refused to obey me and I believe I can recall but three instances of the kind. A record was kept of the Attendance, Deportment, and Recitations of each scholar, the last numbering three grades Perfect, Good, & Bad lessons so that each Scholar & Parent, if they chose, knew the true standing of all. The highest number received the prize.

At the close of the last term, I received a present of $30 from the people, and the satisfaction expressed by all whose opinion I valued. Mrs. Smith assured me she had never sent the children to a Teacher where she had been so gratified with their improvement.

I did not write you directly because I knew it would be your wish for me to engage again and I had received repeated intimation that I could engage in the Union School at Grand Rapids from my kind friends Dr. Shepard's family of that place whose elegant home has been my own from the first. Several circumstances have prevented. The Principal has been succeeded by a gentleman from the east, bringing two assistants with him so that all Vacancies are filled, and at the close of the last term I felt completely worn out in mind and body and knew that I must have rest. The ague has taken away my strength so entirely that my friends tell me that it would not be possible for me to teach as the least fatigue brings it on. Under these circumstances it is my earnest wish to return home and regain my health and spirits in the peaceful quiet of home, its shade. But I await your advice.

I know my experience the past year has in a measure disheartened me but I feel that through its heavy trials an all-sustaining arm has held me up. A victim of misrepresentation from the first and the basest calumny, it created a sensitiveness about entering society I never felt before, and I have remained with those few who knew me aright and scarcely know any others. I have tried indeed to live near to God and have ever realized the promise "ye shall not seek me in vain."

Miss Bell I do not meet often but always hear that she is happy. I saw Miss Chandler before she returned East, she said she had always regretted advising Mr. Smith to send for another Teacher, but she had no idea of the opposition she would meet with.

I thank little Helen for her affectionate remembrance, and wish to be remembered to her. I cannot close without an apology for my letter, it has been written while a chill has been on me.

Respectfully yours,

Mary A. Roper

If it is convenient I would like to receive an answer soon.

Templeton, [Mass.] July 22, 1854

Miss N. Swift,

Just one year has passed away since my arrival in my mountain home and I once more address you asking a word of advice in regard to my future.

You will remember, perhaps, some of the circumstances of my return from Mill Point, my location in the spring of 1852. I shall never forget the depression of spirit I was suffering when I penned that last letter to you asking if it was not best for me to return—nor the salutary lesson of that year's experience in which I learned that a life of nineteen years in New England had not fitted me for a position in which the "Wisdom of a serpent and the harmlessness of a dove" were certainly needed.

But my health is now reestablished and my desire to be active somewhere brings home the question, where I can best labor? In the stillness [and] the quiet of my home I have reviewed that eventful year—brought home its trials, its stern teachings, to my soul and strove to learn their source—their aim. With an humbled heart I have seen my shortcomings—been comforted with the pure motives with which I labored and realized with heartfelt joy the fullness of the promise "My grace is sufficient to thee." In view of it I can feel to shrink from no mental or physical suffering where Christ, duty, point the way in my future and if my trials are peculiar to a location or be the result of evil in my heart, may He but give me grace to endure them until their end is accomplished.

When the Circular for August appeared, I decided to ask your advice in regard to my return to the West considering the state of my health while there and all the circumstances. I have a friend in Petersburg O[hi]o—A teacher in the Collegiate Female Seminary of that place who will gladly find me a position in that place or state if I choose.

If it is convenient I should like an answer soon. My humble attainments you know—They are advanced only by *experience* and by an attention to instrumental music for a few months.

Respectfully yours,

Mary Augusta Roper
Love to Helen.

✦ THE SPEECH OF RED JACKET, THE SENECA CHIEF, TO A MISSIONARY, CIRCA 1830

The missionary preachers and schoolteachers who moved into the new European-American settlements west of the Alleghenies during the first half of the nineteenth century focused their energies almost exclusively on the development of white settlements. While of mixed opinions on slavery, the majority were probably moderate abolitionists; not concerned enough about slavery to do much about it, but also not much interested in introducing the institution into the new territories of the West. As the midwestern states were admitted to the union, they were admitted as free states. While the Great Plains wars with the Indian tribes lay ahead, most of the Native Americans had already died from disease or war or retreated west of the Mississippi by the time the settlers arrived. The focus, then, was simply on white settlement and the establishment of European notions of civilization. There were exceptions, however—for example, among members of the Iroquois tribes that remained in upstate New York. In these cases, the settlers sought to convert the Indians to their religion and their notions of culture and schooling. As would happen throughout the nation's development, not all indigenous peoples were as eager to accept western notions of education as the missionaries hoped. New York's Governor DeWitt Clinton developed a great respect for the Seneca leader, Red Jacket, who responded verbally to the missionaries with as clear a rejection of their teachings as any that has been recorded.

Friend and Brother, it was the will of the Great Spirit that we should meet together this day. He orders all things, and he has given us a fine day for our council. He has taken his garment from before the sun, and caused it to shine with brightness on us. Our eyes are opened, that we see clearly: our ears are unstopped, that we have been able to hear distinctly the words that you have spoken; for all these favors we thank the Great Spirit, and him only.

Brother, this council fire was kindled by you; it was at your request that we came together at this time; we have listened with attention to what you have said; you requested us to speak our minds freely; this gives us great joy, for we now consider that we stand upright before you, and can speak what we think; all have heard your voice, and all speak to you as one man; our minds are agreed.

Brother, you say you want an answer to your talk before you leave this place. It is right you should have one, as you are a great distance from home, and we do not wish to detain you; but we will first look back a little and tell you what our fathers have told us, and what we have heard from the white people.

Brother, listen to what we say. There was a time when our forefathers owned this great land. Their seats extended from the rising to the setting sun. The Great Spirit had made it for the use of the Indians. He had created the buffalo, the deer, and other animals for food. He had made the bear and the beaver, and their skins served us for clothing. He had scattered them over the country, and taught us how to take them. He had caused the earth to produce corn for bread, all this he had done for his red children, because he loved them. If we had any disputes about hunting grounds, they were generally settled without the shedding of much blood; but an evil day came upon us; your forefathers crossed the great waters, and landed on this island. Their numbers were small; they found tribes, and not enemies; they told us they had fled from their own country for fear of wicked men, and come here to enjoy their religions. They asked for a small seat; we took pity on them, granted their request, and they sat down among us; we gave them corn and meat; they gave us poison in return.

The white people had now found our country, tidings were carried back, and more came among us, yet we did not fear them, we took them to be friends; they called us brothers; we believed them, and gave them a larger seat. At length their numbers had greatly increased; they wanted more land; they wanted our country. Our eyes were opened, and our minds became uneasy. Wars took place; Indians were hired to fight against Indians; and many of our people were destroyed. They also brought strong liquors among us; it was strong and powerful, and has slain thousands.

Brother, our seats were once large, and yours were very small; you have now become a great people, and we have scarcely a place left to spread our blankets; you have got our country, but are not satisfied; you want to force your religion upon us.

Brother, continue to listen. You say that you are sent to instruct us how to worship the *Great Spirit* agreeable to his mind, and if we do not take hold of the religion you white people teach, we shall be unhappy hereafter; you say that you are right, and we are lost; how do we know this to be true? We understand that your religion is written in a book; if it was intended for us as well as you, why has not the Great Spirit given it to us, and not only to us, but why did he not give to our forefathers the knowledge of that book, with the means of understanding it rightly? We only know what you tell us about it; how shall we know when to believe, being so often deceived by the white people?

Brother, you say there is but one way to worship and serve the Great Spirit; if there is but one religion, why do you white people differ so much about it? Why not all agree, as you can all read the book?

Brother, we do not understand these things; we are told that your religion was given to your forefathers, and has been handed down from father to son. We also have a religion which was given to our forefathers, and has been handed down to us, their children. We worship that way. *It teaches us to be thankful for all the favors we receive; to love each other, and to be united; we never quarrel about religion.*

Brother, the Great Spirit has made us all; but he has made a great difference between his white and red children; he has given us a different complexion, and different customs; to you he has given the arts; to these he has not opened our eyes; we know these things to be true. Since he has made so great a difference between us in other things, why may we not conclude that he has given us a different religion according to our understanding; the Great Spirit does right; he knows what is best for his children; we are satisfied.

Brother, we do not wish to destroy your religion, or take it from you; we only want to enjoy our own.

Brother, you say, that you have not come to get our land or our money, but to enlighten our minds. I will now tell you that I have been at your meetings, and saw you collecting money from the meeting. I cannot tell what this money was intended for, but suppose it was for your minister, and if we should conform to your way of thinking, perhaps you may want some from us.

Brother, we are told that you have been preaching to white people in this place; these people are our neighbors, we are acquainted with them; we will wait a little while and see what effect your preaching has upon them.

[The same document also reports a statement by Red Jacket on another occasion in which he alluded to the crucifixion of Christ]

Brother, if your white men murdered the son of the Great Spirit, we Indians had nothing to do with it, and it is none of our affair. If he had come among us we would not have killed him; we would have treated him well, you must make amends for that crime yourselves.

CHAPTER 5

SLAVERY, RECONSTRUCTION, AND THE SCHOOLS OF THE SOUTH, 1820-1903

Introduction

In 1935, W. E. B. DuBois wrote in *Black Reconstruction in America* that, "Public education for all at public expense was, in the South, a Negro idea" (pp. 168–69). He was several decades ahead of most other historians in correctly interpreting the history of school development in the states of the former Confederacy. Only recently have historians come to realize the depth and significance of the role Reconstruction played in the expansion of public schools in the South. And while historians did tell of the experiences of northern philanthropists and northern missionary teachers in working with newly freed slaves during and after the Civil War, few noted the essential role the recently freed African Americans themselves played in seeking literacy and in building a system of public schooling.

Northern missionaries who went south during and after the Civil War were greatly surprised to find that, in spite of southern laws and all of the efforts to stamp out literacy among slaves, there were many literate slaves. While they constituted a small minority of the total ex-slave population, these individuals had learned to read and write in spite of great danger during their years of slavery. Frederick Douglass was hardly a typical slave. He had gained his freedom before the war and was among the great abolitionist and national leaders of the Civil War generation. Nevertheless, his autobiographical account of how he learned to read and write—in spite of severely repressive measures designed to keep him illiterate—exemplifies the experience of many others.

James D. Anderson's *The Education of Blacks in the South, 1860–1935* (Chapel Hill: The University of North Carolina Press, 1988) provides a very important historical corrective to much of the history written prior to the 1980s. Anderson describes the educational scene at slavery's end:

> Blacks emerged from slavery with a strong belief in the desirability of learning to read and write. This belief was expressed in the pride with which they talked of other ex-slaves who learned to read or write in slavery and in the esteem in which they held literate blacks. It was expressed in the intensity and the frequency of their anger at slavery for keeping them illiterate. "There is one sin that slavery committed against me," professed one ex-slave, "which I will never forgive. It robbed me of my education." The former slaves' fundamental belief in the value of literate culture was expressed most clearly in their efforts to secure schooling for themselves and their children. Virtually every account by historians or contemporary observers stresses the ex-slaves' demand for universal schooling. In 1879, Harriet Beecher Stowe said of the freedmen's campaign for education: "They rushed not to the grog-shop but to the schoolroom—they cried for the spelling-book as bread, and pleaded for teachers as a necessity of life." Journalist Charles Nordhoff reported that New Orleans's ex-slaves were "almost universally . . . anxious to send their children to school." Booker T. Washington, a part of this movement himself, described most vividly his people's struggle for education: "Few people who were not right in the midst of the scenes can form any exact idea of the intense desire which the people of my race showed for education. It was a whole race trying to go to school. Few were too young, and none too old, to make the attempt to learn." When supervising the first contrabands at Fortress Monroe in 1861, Edward L. Pierce "observed among them a widespread desire to learn to read."

The power of this commitment to literacy comes through in the documents that remain. In particular, the New England Freedmen's Aid Society records shift in tone from offering help to passive blacks to respecting and cooperating with newly freed slaves.

It is important to read first-person accounts of what happened in the South in the immediate aftermath of the Civil War. The records of the New England Freedmen's Aid Society, now available at the Massachusetts Historical Society, provide one such window into the important educational effort that swept the South during the 1860s and 1870s. A somewhat different, and very powerful first-person account of what it was like to teach former slaves in the South is contained in the journal of Charlotte Forten. Forten was among the first northern teachers to go south. She volunteered early in the Civil War to teach some of the first slaves to be freed by the Union Army. Her perspective—which comes through very clearly in her diary—is also different because she herself was an African American, a free black who had taught school in Massachusetts prior to the war.

Reconstruction, and the literacy campaigns that went with it, came to an abrupt halt in 1876 with the withdrawal of Union troops and the return of white segregationist governments across the South. Many northern allies turned to other matters after 1876, leaving southern blacks at the mercy of the reconstituted segregationist governments. While the public schools founded under Reconstruction did continue, they survived only as ill-funded, segregated institutions until the middle of the twentieth century, if not later.

Under the difficult circumstances of post-1876 South, Booker T. Washington emerged as a leading voice in the African-American community. Washington urged other blacks to at least partially accommodate the white power structure to gain a degree of freedom and autonomy for black institutions, especially his own institute at Tuskegee, Alabama. Washington was by far the most widely recognized African-American voice in the United States during the late nineteenth century. He was able to channel northern philanthropy into southern schools as long as the schools stayed focused on practical matters. He—and his supporters—viewed his industrial education as a first step in the long, slow process of increasing the educational opportunities available to southern blacks.

Some of Washington's African-American contemporaries challenged his ideas, believing he was too much an accommodationist and a gradualist. But by far his strongest challenge came from W. E. B. DuBois, destined to be one of the greatest of African-American leaders of the first half of the twentieth century. DuBois had no patience with Washington's industrial education. For him, the key was to develop an intellectual elite, a "talented tenth" who could receive the best of what a classical education could offer, who could be philosophical and moral leaders in the campaign for freedom. Examples from the Washington-DuBois debates are reproduced here in some detail. It is essential to understand these educational struggles within the African-American community and also read them as illustrative of all debates about the meaning and purpose of education for any people.

✦ FREDERICK DOUGLASS, THE NARRATIVE OF THE LIFE OF FREDERICK DOUGLASS: AN AMERICAN SLAVE, 1845

The Narrative of the Life of Frederick Douglass: An American Slave *was published in 1845. It immediately brought national fame to Douglass, and it also provided an intimate portrait of what slavery was really like. Douglass was born as a slave about 1817 on the eastern shore of Maryland. He escaped in 1838 and moved to New Bedford, Massachusetts. After the publication of his autobiography, he became a leader, along with William Lloyd Garrison, in the Massachusetts Anti-Slavery Society, a confidant— and sometimes opponent—of both John Brown and Abraham Lincoln, and probably the most respected leader of the African-American community in the years immediately after the Civil War. Douglass's great accomplishments came later in life. In the account that follows, he was a young slave, desperate—like many others—to gain the window of freedom that literacy would open on a larger world.*

Very soon after I went to live with Mr. And Mrs. Auld, she very kindly commenced to teach me the A, B, C. After I had learned this, she assisted me in learning to spell words of three or four letters. Just at this point of my progress, Mr. Auld found out what was going on, and at once forbade Mrs. Auld to instruct me further, telling her, among other things, that it was unlawful, as well as unsafe, to teach a slave to read. To use his own words, further, he said, "If you give a nigger an inch, he will take an ell. A nigger should know nothing but to obey his master—to do as he is told to do. Learning would *spoil* the best nigger in the world. Now," said he, "if you teach that nigger (speaking of myself) how to read, there would be no keeping him. It would forever unfit him to be a slave. He would at once become unmanageable, and of no value to his master. As to himself, it could do him no good, but a great deal of harm. It would make him discontented and unhappy." These words sank deep into my heart, stirred up sentiments within that lay slumbering, and called into existence an entirely new train of thought. It was a new and special revelation, explaining dark and mysterious things, with which my youthful understanding had struggled, but struggled in vain. I now understood what had been to me a most perplexing difficulty—to wit, the white man's power to enslave the black man. It was a grand achievement, and I prized it highly. From that moment, I understood the pathway from slavery to freedom. It was just what I wanted, and I got it at a time when I the least expected it. Whilst I was saddened by the thought of losing the aid of my kind mistress, I was gladdened by the invaluable instruction which, by the merest accident, I had gained from my master. Though conscious of the difficulty of learning without a teacher, I set out with high hope, and a fixed purpose, at whatever cost of trouble, to learn how to read. The very decided manner with which he spoke, and strove to impress his wife with the evil consequences of giving me instruction, served to convince me that he was deeply sensible of the truths he was uttering. It gave me the best assurance that I might rely with the utmost confidence on the results which, he said, would flow from teaching me to read. What he most dreaded, that I most desired. What he most loved, that I most hated. That which to him was a great evil, to be carefully shunned, was to me a great good, to be diligently sought; and the argument which he so warmly urged, against my learning to read, only served to inspire me with a desire and determination to learn. In learning to read, I owe almost as much to the bitter opposition of my master, as to the kindly aid of my mistress. I acknowledge the benefit of both. . . .

I lived in Master Hugh's family about seven years. During this time, I succeeded in learning to read and write. In accomplishing this, I was compelled to resort to various stratagems. I had no regular teacher. My mistress, who had kindly commenced to instruct me, had, in compliance with the advice and direction of her husband, not only ceased to instruct, but had set her face against my being instructed by any one else. It is due, however, to my mistress to say of her, that she did not adopt this course of treatment immediately. She at first lacked the depravity indispensable to shutting me up in mental darkness. It was at least necessary for her to have some training in the exercise of irresponsible power, to make her equal to the task of treating me as though I were a brute.

My mistress was, as I have said, a kind and tender-hearted woman; and in the simplicity of her soul she commenced, when I first went to live with her, to treat me as she supposed one human being ought to treat another. In entering upon the duties of a slaveholder, she did not seem to perceive that I sustained to her the relation of a mere chattel, and that for her to treat me as a human being was not only wrong, but dangerously so. Slavery proved as injurious to her as it did to me. When I went there, she was a pious, warm, and tender-hearted woman. There was no sorrow or suffering for which she had not a tear. She had bread for the hungry, clothes for the naked, and comfort for every mourner that came within her reach. Slavery soon proved its ability to divest her of these heavenly qualities. Under its influence, the tender heart became stone, and the lamb-like disposition gave way to one of tiger-like fierceness. The first step in her downward course was in her ceasing to instruct me. She now commenced to practice her husband's precepts. She finally became even more violent in her opposition than her husband himself. She was not satisfied with simply doing as well as he had commanded; she seemed anxious to do better. Nothing seemed to make her more angry than to see me with a newspaper. She seemed to think that here lay the danger. I have had her rush at me with a face made all up of fury, and snatch from me a newspaper, in a manner that fully revealed her apprehension. She was an apt woman; and a little experience soon demonstrated, to her satisfaction, that education and slavery were incompatible with each other.

From this time I was most narrowly watched. If I was in a separate room any considerable length of time, I was sure to be suspected of having a book, and was at once called to give an account of myself. All this, however, was too late. The first step had been taken. Mistress, in teaching me the alphabet, had given me the *inch,* and no precaution could prevent me from taking the *ell.*

The plan which I adopted, and the one by which I was most successful, was that of making friends of all the little white boys whom I met in the street. As many of these as I could, I converted into teachers. With their kindly aid, obtained at different times and in different places, I finally succeeded in learning to read. When I was sent of errands, I always took my book with me, and by going one part of my errand quickly, I found time to get a lesson before my return. I used also to carry bread with me, enough of which was always in the house, and to which I was always welcome; for I was much better off in this regard than many of the poor white children in our neighborhood. This bread I used to bestow upon the hungry little urchins, who, in return, would give me that more valuable bread of knowledge. I am strongly tempted to give the names of two or three of those little boys, as a testimonial of the gratitude and affection I bear them; but prudence forbids;—not that it would injure me, but it might embarrass them; for it is almost an unpardonable offence to teach slaves to read in this Christian country. It is enough to say of the dear little fellows, that they lived on Philpot Street, very near Durgin and Bailey's shipyard. I used to talk this matter of slavery over with them. I would sometimes say to them, I wished I could be as free as they would be when they got to be men. "You will be free as soon as you are twenty-one, *but I am a slave for life!* Have not I as good a right to be free as you have?" These words used to trouble them; they would express for me the liveliest sympathy, and console me with the hope that something would occur by which I might be free.

I was now about twelve years old, and the thought of being *a slave for life* began to bear heavily upon my heart. Just about this time, I got hold of a book entitled, *The Columbian Orator.* Every opportunity I got, I used to read this book. Among much other interesting matter, I found in it a dialogue between a master and his slave. The slave was represented as having run away from his master three times. The dialogue represented the conversation which took place between them, when the slave was retaken the third time. In this dialogue, the whole argument in behalf of slavery was brought forward by the master, all of which was disposed of by the slave. The slave was made to say some very smart as well as impressive things in his reply to his master— things which had the desired though unexpected effect; for the conversation resulted in the voluntary emancipation of the slave on the part of the master.

In the same book, I met with one of Sheridan's mighty speeches on and in behalf of Catholic emancipation. These were choice documents to me. I read them over and over again with unabated interest. They gave tongue to interesting thoughts of my own soul, which had frequently flashed through my mind, and died away for want of utterance. The moral which I gained from the dialogue was the power of truth over the conscience of even a slaveholder. What I got from Sheridan was a bold denunciation of slavery, and a powerful vindication of human rights. The reading of these documents enabled me to utter my thoughts, and to meet the arguments brought forward to sustain slavery; but while they relieved me of one difficulty, they brought on another even more painful than the one of which I was relieved. The more I read, the more I was led to abhor and detest my enslavers. I could regard them in no other light than a band of successful robbers, who had left their homes, and gone to Africa, and stolen us from our homes, and in a strange land reduced us to slavery. I loathed them as being the meanest as well as the most wicked of men. As I read and contemplated the subject, behold! That very discontentment which Master Hugh had predicted would follow my learning to read had already come, to torment and sting my soul to unutterable anguish. As I writhed under it, I would at times feel that learning to read had been a curse rather than a blessing. It had given me a view of my wretched condition, without the remedy. It opened my eyes to the horrible pit, but to no ladder upon which to get out. In moments of agony, I envied my fellow-slaves for their stupidity. I have often wished myself a beast. I preferred the condition of the meanest reptile to my own. Any thing, no matter what, to get rid of thinking! It was this everlasting thinking of my condition that tormented me. There was no getting rid of it. It was pressed upon me by every object within sight or hearing, animate or inanimate. The silver trump of freedom had roused my soul to eternal wakefulness. Freedom now appeared, to disappear no more forever. It was heard in every sound, and seen in every thing. It was ever present to torment me with a sense of my wretched condition. I saw nothing without seeing it, I heard nothing without hearing it, and felt nothing without feeling it. It looked from every star, it smiled in every calm, breathed in every wind, and moved in every storm.

I often found myself regretting my own existence, and wishing myself dead; and but for the hope of being free, I have no doubt but that I should have killed myself, or done something for which I should have been killed. While in this state of mind, I was eager to hear any one speak of slavery. I was a ready listener. Every little while, I could hear something about the abolitionists. It was some time before I found what the word meant. It was always used in such connections as to make it an interesting word to me. If a slave ran away and succeeded in getting clear, or if a slave killed his master, set fire to a barn, or did any thing very wrong in the mind of a slaveholder, it was spoken of as the fruit of *abolition.* Hearing the word in this connection very often, I set about learning what it meant. The dictionary afforded me little or no help. I found it was "the act of abolishing;" but then I did not know what was to be abolished. Here I was perplexed. I did not dare to ask any one about its meaning, for I was satisfied that it was something they wanted me to know very little about. After a patient waiting, I got one of our city papers, containing an account of the number of petitions from the north, praying for the abolition of slavery in the District of Columbia, and of the slave trade between the States. From this time I understood the words *abolition* and *abolitionist,* and always drew near when that word was spoken, expecting to hear something of importance to myself and fellow-slaves. The light broke in upon me by degrees. I went one day down on the wharf of Mr. Waters; and seeing two Irishmen unloading a scow of stone, I went, unasked, and helped them. When he had finished, one of them came to me and asked me if I were a slave. I told him I was. He asked, "Are ye a slave for life?" I told him that I was. The good Irishman seemed to be deeply affected by the statement. He said to the other that it was a pity so fine a little fellow as myself should be a slave for life. He said it was a shame to hold me. They both advised me to run away to the north; that I should find friends there, and that I should be free. I pretended not to be interested in what they said, and treated them as if I did not understand them; for I feared they might be treacherous. White men have been known to encourage slaves to escape, and then, to get the reward, catch them and return them to their masters. I was afraid that these seemingly good men might use me so; but I nevertheless remembered their advice, and from that time I resolved to run away. I looked forward to a time at which it would be safe for me to escape. I was too young to think of doing so immediately; besides, I wished to learn how to write, as I might have occasion to write my own pass. I consoled myself with the hope that I should one day find a good chance. Meanwhile, I would learn to write.

The idea as to how I might learn to write was suggested to me by being in Durgin and Bailey's ship-yard, and frequently seeing the ship carpenters, after hewing, and getting a piece of timber ready for use, write on the timber the name of that part of the ship for which it was intended. When a piece of timber was intended for the larboard side, it would be marked thus—"L." When a piece was for the starboard side, it would be marked thus—"S." A piece for the larboard side forward, would be marked thus— "L.F." When a piece was for starboard side forward, it would be marked thus—"S.F." For larboard aft, it would be marked thus—"L.A." For starboard aft, it would be marked thus—"S.A." I soon learned the names of these letters, and for what they were intended when placed upon a piece of timber in the shipyard. I immediately commenced copying them, and in a short time was able to make the four letters named. After that, when I met with any boy who I knew could write, I would tell him I could write as well as he. The next word would be, "I don't believe you. Let me see you try it." I would then make the letters which I had been so fortunate as to learn, and ask him to beat that. In this way I got a good many lessons in writing, which it is quite possible I should never have gotten in any other way. During this time, my copy-book was the board fence, brick wall, and pavement; my pen and ink was a lump of chalk. With these, I learned mainly how to write. I then commenced and continued copying the Italics in Webster's Spelling Book, until I could make them all without looking on the book. By this time, my little Master Thomas had gone to school, and learned how to write, and had written over a number of copy-books. These had been brought home, and shown to some of our near neighbors, and then laid aside. My mistress used to go to class meeting at the Wilk Street meeting-house every Monday afternoon, and leave me to take care of the house. When left thus, I used to spend the time in writing in the spaces left in Master Thomas's copy-book, copying what he had written. I continued to do this until I could write a hand very similar to that of Master Thomas. Thus, after a long, tedious effort for years, I finally succeeded in learning how to write.

✦ THE NEW ENGLAND FREEDMEN'S AID SOCIETY—OFFICIAL RECORDS, 1862-1872

Boston was the center of northern abolitionist activity in the decades leading up to the Civil War. It is not surprising, then, that the city's leaders responded quickly to the federal government's call to help educate of the newly freed slaves. (In the early years of the war, the army called the freed slaves "contrabands" because they were still viewed

Minutes. February 1, 1862, February 7, 1862, and September 10, 1862. Volume of Minutes, 1862-74. Ms. N-10 New England Freedmen's Society Records. Reprinted courtesy of the Massachusetts Historical Society.

Annual Meeting. 1872. Volume of Minutes, 1862-74. Ms. N-10 New England Freedmen's Aid Society Records. Reprinted courtesy of the Massachusetts Historical Society.

as property forfeited by the rebelling southerners.) It is most interesting, in these three brief excerpts from the records of the New England Freedmen's Aid Society, to see the evolving view of the African-American communities of the South. In the organizational meetings of the society in 1862, the newly freed are viewed as "unfortunate human beings," passive and helpless. By 1867, experience in the South had taught the societies that schooling could—and should—be a cooperative effort between northern philanthropic efforts and southern African-American communities. And by the 1870s, the focus was in turning the schools over to the local communities and focusing instead on teacher education. This represents a dramatic change in the views of at least one small group of northern whites. Of course, all of this occurred before the Union army withdrew from the southern states and returned power to southern white leaders in the later 1870s. Nevertheless, the three readings that follow support James Anderson's conclusion: Whites went south initially thinking they would have to do everything for the former slaves, only to discover that they were welcome only if they respected ex-slaves enough to engage in cooperative efforts with them.

February 1, 1862

The undersigned were appointed a committee to bring to your notice a letter recently received in this city from E. S. Pierce, Esq., Agent of the U. S. Government for the "Contrabands," at Port Royal. In that letter, the writer urges the importance of immediately sending out teachers for the 8,000 unfortunate human beings now within the lines of our army in South Carolina.

February 7, 1862

I. The object of the Educational Commission shall be the industrial, social, intellectual, moral, and religious improvement of persons released from slavery in the course of the War for the Union. . . .

II. The educational commission shall employ as its laborers, persons of undoubted loyalty to the Federal Government, who shall not permit their work to interfere with the proper discipline and regulating of the camps; and it will expect and gratefully welcome any facilities which the Government may be pleased to grant, such as passes for teachers, and supplies, and rations, and due protection for said teachers while engaged in their work.

New York City, Sept. 10, 1867

I.   *Resolved,* That the best interests of the freed people require the permanent establishment of free schools in the South: that, as in the Northern free-school system, the people should cooperate in their support; and, therefore, that no new schools should be established, except where co-operation can be secured.

II. *Resolved,* That our teachers and agents in the South should organize the people into associations to raise means to aid in the establishment and support of their schools.

III. *Resolved,* That, in the opinion of this meeting, all books should be sold at a price to be fixed by the Teachers' Committee; and that none should be given away except by special permission of the Committee. . . .

Lyman Abbot, General Secretary

1872

The annual meeting of the N. E. Freedmen's Aid Society was held yesterday afternoon, in the Freeman Place Chapel, the vice-president, Mr. William Lloyd Garrison in the chair. . . . From this report, it appeared that the number of teachers at the South had been greatly reduced, the attention being turned especially to the normal schools. These are under the most experienced teachers and their good results are already apparent, the graduates being the best teachers which can be procured for their peculiar work. In Maryland two teachers are retained, the expense being chiefly borne by the citizens of Baltimore. More than two hundred scholars are now in the school. A letter was read from one of the teachers giving an encouraging report of progress. The work in Richmond has ceased on account of the action of the local authorities in receiving colored pupils into their schools. In Virginia, there are two schools with five teachers and two hundred and thirty-seven scholars. In North Carolina there is one school kept by two teachers and educating seventy-seven scholars. In South Carolina, there are five schools, twenty-one teachers, and six hundred and sixty-five pupils. In Georgia, eleven schools, thirty-three teachers and twelve hundred scholars.

→ THE NEW ENGLAND FREEDMEN'S AID SOCIETY— CORRESPONDENCE, 1865-1874

While the official records provide a glimpse into the thinking of the northern social leaders who supported the society, the society's correspondence with the teachers who went south provides a better look at the reality of daily life in the schools. As with the National Board in the 1850s, so in the 1860s and 1870s, young people from across the north—mostly women, but also some men—responded to the call to go south to aid in the instruction of the newly freed citizens. The letters that follow give a sense of what life was like, revealing not only the official records and reports of the Society, but also the more personal concerns and stories of the teachers.

Winchester
Mar 14, 1865

Yours of the 9th is at hand. I hope those two good teachers from Boston will be sent out so as to be here the 1st of April. The school numbered ninety-one at present. Perhaps Miss Moore will leave in a day or two, but a short vacation will be no injury. Don't fail to send a supply of books. Many of them can purchase their books, if they can find them to purchase. There seems to be but one thing to render the success of the enterprise uncertain, viz: "the occupation of the town by our troops." From present appearances, I think there is little doubt that the town will be held. I will meet the teachers at the depot . . . four miles from this place at anytime, if I can be notified.

N. E. Brackett

N.E. Brackett. Letters to Edward D. Cheney, March 14, 1865 and September 29, 1869. Ms. N-10 New England Freedmen's Aid Society Records. Reprinted courtesy of the Massachusetts Historical Society.

N.E. Brackett. Letter to Caroline Alfred, January 8, 1874. Ms. N-10 New England Freedmen's Aid Society Records. Reprinted courtesy of the Massachusetts Historical Society.

Boston
Sept 29, 1869

Mr. Jillson,
Dear Sir,

We have had the pleasure of a visit from our friend, Mr. Tomlinson, and have arranged with him in regard to our work in South Carolina. We hope to keep up as many schools in the state as last year and shall employ the native teachers as far as possible. In order to do so, we must have the co-operation of the colored people themselves and Mr. Tomlinson agrees with us that they should pay one half of the teachers' salaries whenever they are able.

But we see no prospect of our being able to do anything in South Carolina beyond this year, except in keeping up the Shaw School at Charlestown. It seems to us that the time has already come when the people can and ought to support and manage the schools themselves and the legislating of last year shows a disposition to do so, although the desired result was not obtained.

We give you this timely notice that in your plans for the promotion of public education you may know on what help from us you can rely. We shall be very glad to give you any aid in our power and hope that this year's work will show a great progress in the schools.

Will you be kind enough to give us any information you think would be interesting to us in regard to your plans for the schools in South Carolina?

Yours very respectfully,

Edward D. Cheney

Columbus, Ga
January 8th, 1874

My Dear Mr. Cheney:

Enclosed please find Report from Dec. which I should have forwarded earlier, but during Christmas vacation both Marian Lucy and myself were on the sick list and I did not find the time to settle accounts.

Our school seems quite prosperous, though not quite as large as usual at this time of year, owing no doubt to the harsh times which press very heavily on this people . . .

We have rather more pupils, who come from the country, and who walk long distances, and a smaller number who board in the city, than we have had for the last three years, and this is quite conclusive evidence of poverty. During Aunt Lucy's illness she was visited by pupils of whom, I dare say, you have heard, and in the course of conversation one day she spoke of the gratitude which to him the colored people had always evinced, and also of their forgiving spirit instancing one case which it seems to me is worth preserving. A certain Rev. Mr. DeLawson, an Episcopal minister, was noted under the old regime for his cruel treatment of his slaves. I fancy he did not amount to much as a preacher, for he raised then—as now—vegetables for market and sent "Hannah" to town with them every morning. The stripping and whipping of Hannah were inevitable if she failed to sell the entire contents of her wagon. But Hannah was a favorite and she was thus spared the beating by the kindness of some of his patrons and they gave her small pieces of money for herself so that she had gotten together about $60.00 in small pieces of silver which she gave to the Rev. to keep for her. When "the freedom" came Hannah wanted to go by herself and meekly asked the preacher for his six penses, but he, evidently intending to do his small part toward the fulfillment of the Scripture "from him that hath not, shall be taken away even that which he hath," utterly refused to give her a cent.

She had no clothes, but she went away and now in her old age has managed to make a comfortable home for herself. The old mistress had been even harder with Hannah than the master (an almost universal experience) but last summer "old missus" was very sick with a lingering fever and with no one to do for her.

Hannah left her comfortable home, tended to her day and night, killed her own chickens to make broth for her, and took the entire care of her for two months without any prospect of wages. Could either you or I have done as much?

The old preacher brings vegetables to market himself now, but it seems to me his strawberries are always sour.

We are all "tolerably" well now. We have had a most delightful winter, though it was very cold at Christmas

The children were quite disappointed at not having a Christmas tree and so was I, but I mean to get up an entertainment for them some time next month.

Did you receive a box of _____ some week or two since? They will, I am sure, prove very beautiful creatures if they live.

You spoke of a Library to be added to this one. Are you intending to send the books this year?

Mr. Harris is expecting to come to Columbus this month and then most likely there will be a change of one Trustee.

With love to the cousins, I am cordially yours

Caroline Alfred

✦ CHARLOTTE FORTEN, THE JOURNAL OF CHARLOTTE FORTEN, 1862

European-Americans were the only ones to go south to teach the newly freed slaves. The Moorland-Spingarn Research Center at Howard University has made available The Journal of Charlotte Forten, *a free African American who also joined the movement of northern women to the schools of the South. Forten was born as a free black in Philadelphia in 1837. She later moved to Salem, Massachusetts, where she taught in the Epes Grammar School in the late 1850s. As the readings below indicate, with the coming of the war, she was anxious to go south to teach in the schools of the recently freed slaves. One of the earliest experiments of the federal government in opening schools for the ex-slaves was in Port Royal, South Carolina, where the military had taken over control of the coastal islands as part of the effort to blockade southern ports. The portions*

Stevenson, Brenda, ed. *The Journals of Charlotte Forten Grimke.* New York: Oxford University Press, 1988. Reprinted by permission of the Moorland-Spingarn Research Center, Howard University.

of the journal that follow cover the weeks after her initial decision, her travels south, and her initial impressions of the schools. The danger she describes was not exaggerated. She was literally teaching on the edge of the battle line during the early stages of the Civil War. In such a context the mix of her commitment to the cause of abolition, her descriptions of teaching, and her wonderful notes about flowers, climate and daily life are all the more intriguing.

Wednesday, September 3 [1862]. Have been anxious and disappointed at not hearing from Dr. P[eck]. But a letter from Mrs. J. to-day tells me that she has seen him, and that he is very sanguine about my going. Dr. [Seth] R.[ogers] and others to whom he spoke about it, wish it. The Com.[mission] meets to-day, and then he will write immediately and let me know the final decision. Last week I heard from home that there was no doubt of my being able to go from the Phil[adelphia] Com[mittee]. Mr. [J. Miller] McK.[im] had spoken to them about it. So if I cannot go from Boston I am sure of going from P.[hiladelphia] but w'ld rather go under Boston auspices. Since I have been here have read *Cecil Breems.* I liked it better than I feared, but not nearly so well as *John Brent.* Still it interested me much. It has the heroic element and much *real* tragedy in it. A picture of Winthrop that I saw at the W.[hittier]'s interested me much. Beautiful, with all a woman's gentleness, and a woman's and man's high heroism and grandeur of soul, and a poet's dreamy grace besides.

    Monday, September 8. No further news from B.[oston]. I am determined to go to-morrow and see for my-self what the trouble is. Have paid a last visit to the W.[ater] C.[ure]. Am so grieved that I shall not see Dr. [Seth] R.[ogers]. He has gone to N.[ahant]. S.[allie] walked here to see me. We sat on the doorstep in the lovely moonlight, and talked for hours. We talked of self-sacrifice. What a girl S.[allie] is! Full of originality and genius—strange and wayward to the last degree. What will become of her? What will her life be? I ask myself often. She interests me deeply.

    Wednesday, October 21. To-day rec'd a note from Mr. McK.[im] asking me if I c'ld possibly be ready to sail for Port Royal, perhaps tomorrow. I was astonished, stupefied, and, at first thought it impossible, but on seeing Mr. McK.[im] I found there was a excellent opportunity for me to go. An old Quaker gentleman is going there to keep store, accompanied by his daughter, and he is willing to take charge of me. It will probably be the only opportunity that I shall have of going this winter, so at any cost I *will* go. And so now to work. In greatest haste.

    Met John P.[ierce] on the cars. He was very kind.

    At Sea. October 27, Monday. Let me see. Where am I? What do I want to write? I am in a state of utter bewilderment. It was on Wed. I rec'd the note. On Thursday I said "good bye" to the friends that are so dear, and the city that is so hateful, and went to N.Y. Spent the night with Mrs. [Peter] W.[illiams]. The next morn did not hurry myself, having heard that the Steamer "United States" w'ld not sail till twelve. Mrs. W.[illiams] and I went to "Lovejoy's" to meet the Hunns' and found there a card from Mr. H.[unn] bidding me hasten to the steamer, as it was advertised to sail at nine. It was then between ten and eleven. After hurrying down and wearying ourselves, found when I got on board that it was not to sail till twelve. But I did not go ashore again. It was too bad, for I had not time to get several things that I wanted much, among them *Les Miserables,* which my dear brother H.[enry] had kindly given me the money for. He had not had time to get it in Phila[delphia].

Enjoyed the sail down the harbor perfectly. The shipping is a noble sight. Had no symptoms of sea-sickness until eve. when being seated at the table inexpressibly singular sensation caused me to make a hasty retreat to the aft-deck, where by keeping perfectly still sitting on a coil of ropes spent a very comfortable eve. and had a pleasant conversation with one of the passengers. Did not get out of sight of land until after dark, I regretted that.

Early this morn. Mr. [John] H.[unn] came to our door to tell us that we were in sight of the blockading fleet in Charlestown harbor. Of course, we sprang to the window eagerly; and saw the masts of the ships looking like a grove of trees in the distance. We were not near enough to see the city. It was hard to realize that we were even so near the barbarous place.

Later. We are again in sight of land. Have passed Edisto and several other islands, and can now see Hilton Head. Shall reach it about one. 'Tis nearly eleven now. The S.[outh] C.[arolina] shore is flat and low—a long line of trees. It does not look very inviting. We are told that oranges will be ripe when we get to Beaufort, and that in every way this is just the loveliest season to be there, which is very encouraging.

We approach Hilton Head. Our ship has been boarded by Health Officer and Provost Marshal. We shall soon reach the landing. All is hurry and confusion on board. I must lay thee aside, friend journal, and use my eyes for seeing all there is to be seen. When we reach our place of destination I will give to thee, oh faithful friend, the result of my observations. So *au revoir.*

Tuesday night. 'T'was a strange sight as our boat approached the landing at Hilton Head. On the wharf was a motley assemblage—soldiers, officers, and "contrabands" of every hue and size. They were mostly black, however, and certainly the most dismal specimens I ever saw. H.[ilton] H.[ead] looks like a very desolate place; just a long, low sandy point running out into the sea with no visible dwellings upon it but the soldiers' white-roofed tents.

Thence, after an hour's delay, during which we signed a paper, which was virtually taking the oath of allegiance, we left the "United States," most rocking of rockety propellers—and took a steamboat for Beaufort. On board the boat was General [Rufus] Saxton, to whom we were introduced. I like his face exceedingly. And his manners were very courteous and affable. He looks like a thoroughly *good* man.—From H.[ilton] H.[ead] to B.[eaufort] the same low line of sandy shore bordered by trees; almost the only object of interest to me were the remains of an old Huguenot Fort, built many, many years ago.

Arrived at B.[eaufort]; we found that we had yet not reached our home. Went to Mr. [Mansfield] French's, and saw there Reuben T.[omlinson], whom I was very glad to meet, and Mrs. [Francis] Gage, who seemed to be in rather a dismal state of mind. B.[eaufort] looks like a pleasant place. The houses are large and quite handsome, built in the usual Southern style with verandahs around them, and beautiful trees. One magnolia tree in Mr. F[rench's] yard is splendid—quite as large as some of our large shade trees, and with the most beautiful foliage, a dark, rich, glossy green.

Went into the Commissary's Office to wait for the boat which was to take us to St. Helena's Island which is about six miles from B.[eaufort]. 'Tis here that Miss [Laura] Towne has her school, in which I am to teach, and that Mr. Hunn will have his store. While waiting in the office we saw several military gentleman [sic], *not* very creditable specimens, I sh'ld say. The little Commissary himself, Capt. T., is a perfect little popinjay, and he and a Colonel somebody who didn't look any too sensible, talked in a very smart manner, evidently for our especial benefit. The word *nigger* was plentifully used, whereupon I set them down at once as *not* gentleman [sic]. Then they talked a great deal about rebel attacks and yellow fever, and other alarming things, with significant nods and looks at each other. We saw through them at once, and were not at all alarmed by any of their representations. But if they are a fair example of army officers, I sh'ld pray to see as little of them as possible.

To my great joy I found that we were able to be rowed by a crew of negro boatmen. Young Mr. F.[rench]—whom I like—accompanied us, while Mr. H.[unn] went with a flat to get our baggage. The row was delightful. It was just at sunset—a grand Southern sunset; and the gorgeous clouds of crimson and gold were reflected in the waters below, which were smooth and calm as a mirror. Then, as we glided along, the rich sonorous tones of the boatmen broke upon the evening stillness. Their singing impressed me much. It was so sweet and strange and solemn. "Roll, Jordan, Roll" was grand, and another

> Jesus make de blind to see
> Jesus make de deaf to hear
> Jesus make de cripple walk
> Walk in, dear Jesus,

And the refrain,

> No man can hender me.

It was very, very impressive. I want to hear these men sing [John Greenleaf] Whittier's "Song of the Negro Boatmen." I am going to see if it can't be brought about in some way.

It was nearly dark when we reached St. Helena's, where we found Miss T.[owne]'s carriage awaiting us, and then we three and our driver, had a long drive along the lonely roads in the dark night. How easy it sh'ld have been for a band of guerillas— had any chanced that way—to seize and hang us. But we found nothing of the kind. We were in a jubilant state of mind and sang "John Brown" with a will as we drove through the pines and palmettos. Arrived at the Superintendent's house[;] we were kindly greeted by him and the ladies and shown into a lofty *ceilinged* parlor where a cheerful wood fire glowed in the grate, and we soon began to feel quite at home in the very heart of Rebeldom; only that I do not at all realize yet that we are in S.[outh] C.[arolina]. It is all a strange wild dream, from which I am constantly expecting to awake. But I can write no more now. I am tired, and still feel the motion of the ship in my poor head. Good night, dear A!

Wednesday, October 29. A lovely day, but rather cool, I sh'ld think, for the "sunny South." The ship still reals [sic] in my head, and everything is most unreal, yet I went to drive . . . We drove to Oaklands, our future home. It is very pleasantly situated, but the house is in rather a dilapidated condition, as are most of the houses here, and the yard and garden have a neglected look, when it is cleaned up, and the house made habitable; I think it will be quite a pleasant place. There are some lovely roses growing there and quantities of ivy creeping along the ground, even under the house, in wild luxuriance—the negroes on the place are very kind and polite. I think I shall get on amicably with them.

After walking about and talking with them, and plucking some roses and ivy to send home, we left Oaklands and drove to the school. It is kept by Miss [Ellen] Murray and Miss Towne in the little Baptist Church, which is beautifully situated in a grove of live oaks. Never saw anything more beautiful than these trees. It is strange that we do not hear of them at the North. They are the first objects that attract one's attention here. They are large, noble trees with small, glossy green leaves. Their beauty consists in the long bearded moss with which every branch is heavily draped. This moss is singularly beautiful, and gives a solemn, almost funeral, aspect to the trees.

We went into the school, and heard the children read and spell. The teachers tell us that they have made great improvement in a very short time, and I noticed with pleasure how bright, how eager to learn many of them seem. The singing delighted me most. They sang beautifully in their rich, sweet, clear tones, and with that peculiar swaying motion which I had noticed before in the older people, and which seems to make their singing all the more effective. Besides several other tunes they sang "Marching Along" with much spirit, and then one of their own hymns, "Down in the Lonesome Valley," which is sweetly solemn and most beautiful. Dear children! Born in slavery, but free at last? May God preserve you all the blessings of freedom, and may you be in every possible way fitted to enjoy them. My heart goes out to you. I shall be glad to do all that I can to help you.

As we drove homeward I noticed that the trees are just beginning to turn; some beautiful scarlet berries were growing along the roadside, and everywhere the beautiful live oak with its moss drapery. The palmettos disappoint me much. Most of them have a very jagged appearance, and are yet stiff and ungraceful. The country is very level— as flat as that in eastern Penn[sylvania]. There are plenty of woods, but I think they have not the grandeur of our Northern woods. The cotton fields disappoint me too. They have a very straggling look, and the pods are small, not at all the great snowballs that I had imagined. Altogether the country w'ld be rather desolate looking were it not for my beautiful and evergreen oaks.

Friday, October 31. Miss T[owne] went to B.[eaufort] to-day, and I taught for her. I enjoyed it much. The children are well-behaved and eager to learn. It will be a happiness to teach here. I like Miss [Ellen] Murray so much. She is of English parentage, born in the Provinces. She is one of the most whole-souled, warm-hearted women I ever met. I felt drawn to her from the first (before I knew she was English) and of course I like her none the less for that. Miss Towne also is a delightful person. "A Charming lady" Gen. Saxton calls her, and my heart echoes the words. She is housekeeper, physician, everything, here. The most indispensable person on the place, and the people are devoted to her. And indeed she is quite a remarkable young lady. She is one of the earliest comers, and has done much good in teaching and superintending the negroes. She is quite young; not more than twenty-two or three, I sh'ld think, and is superintendent of two plantations. I like her energy and decision of character. Her appearance, too, is very interesting. Mr. [Richard] S. [oule], the superintendent, is a very kind, agreeable person. I like him.

Wednesday, November 5. Had my first regular teaching experience, and to you and you only friend beloved, will acknowledge that it was *not* a very pleasant one. Part of my scholars are very tiny—babies, I call them—and it is hard to keep them quiet and interested while I am hearing the larger ones. They are too young even for the alphabet, it seems to me. I think I must write home and ask somebody to send me picture-books and toys to amuse them with. I fancied Miss T.[owne] looked annoyed when, at one time, the little ones were usually restless. Perhaps it was only my fancy. Dear Miss M.[urray] was kind and considerate as usual. She is very lovable. Well, I *must* not be discouraged. Perhaps things will go on better to-morrow. I am sure I enjoyed the walk to school. Through those lovely woods, just brightening to scarlet now. Met the ladies about halfway, and they gave me a drive to the church. . . .

Monday, November 10. We taught—or rather, commenced teaching—the children "John Brown," which they entered into eagerly. I felt the full to the significance of *that* song being sung here in S.[outh] C.[arolina] by little negro children, by those whom he—the glorious old man—died to save. Miss [Laura] T.[owne] told them about him. A poor mulatto man is in one of our people's houses, a man from the North, who assisted Mr. [Samuel D.] Phillips (a nephew of Wendell P.[hillips]) when he was here, in teaching school; he seems to be quite an intelligent man. He is suffering from fever. I shall be glad to take as good care of him as I can. It is so sad to be ill, helpless, and poor, and so far away from home. This eve, though, I felt wretchedly, had a long exercise in irregular French verbs. The work of reviewing did me good. Forgot bodily ills—even so great an ill as a bad cold in the head for a while.

Thursday, November 13. Was there ever a lovelier road than that through part of my way to school lies? . . . Talked to the children a little while to-day about the noble Toussaint. They listened very attentively. It is well that they sh'ld know what one of their own color c'ld do for his race. I long to inspire them with courage and ambition (of a noble sort), and high purposes. It is noticeable how very few mulattoes there are here. Indeed in our school, with one or two exceptions, the children are all black. A little mulatto child strayed into the school house yesterday—a pretty little thing with large beautiful black eyes and lovely long lashes. But so dirty! I longed to seize and thoroughly cleanse her. The mother is a good-looking woman, but quite black. "Thereby," I doubt not, "hangs a tale." This eve. Harry, one of the men on the place, came in for a lesson. He is most eager to learn, and is really a scholar to be proud of. He learns rapidly. I gave him his first lesson in writing to-night, and his progress was wonderful. He held his pen almost perfectly right the first time. He will very soon learn to write, I think. I must inquire who w'ld like to take lessons at night. Whenever I am well enough it will be a real pleasure to teach them. . . .

Monday, November 17. Had a dreadfully wearying day in school, of which the less said the better. Afterward drove the ladies to "The Corner," a collection of negro houses, whither Miss T.[owne] went on a doctoring expedition. The people there are very pleasant. Saw a little baby, just borne today—and another—old Venus' great grandchild for whom I made the little pink frock. These people are very grateful. The least kindness that you do them they insist on repaying in some way. We have had a quantity of eggs and potatoes brought us despite our remonstrances. Today one of the women gave me some Tanias. Tania is a queer-looking root. After it is boiled it looks a little like potato, but is much larger. I don't like the taste.

Thursday, November 27. Thanksgiving Day. This, according to Gen. [Rufus] Saxton's noble Proclamation, was observed as a day of "Thanksgiving and praise." It has been a lovely day—cool, delicious air, golden, gladdening sunlight, deep blue light, with soft white clouds floating over it. . . . This morning a large number—Superintendents, teachers, and freed people, assembled in the little Baptist church. It was a sight that I shall not soon forget—that crowd of eager, happy black faces from which the shadow of slavery had forever passed. "Forever free!" "Forever free!" Those magical words were all the time singing themselves in my soul, and never before have I felt so truly grateful to God.

✦ Booker T. Washington, The Future of the American Negro, 1899

Other documents by Washington were more famous, but none stated his view on the proper education of southern African Americans than his book, The Future of the American Negro, *published in 1899. In this selection, Washington makes his argument that education for basic economic development (industrial education) must precede education for "high culture."*

In order that the reader may understand me and why I lay so much stress upon the importance of pushing the doctrine of industrial education for the Negro, it is necessary, first of all, to review the condition of affairs at the present time in the Southern States. For years I have had something of an opportunity to study the Negro at first-hand; and I feel that I know him pretty well—him and his needs, his failures and his successes, his desires and the likelihood of their fulfillment. I have studied him and his relations with his white neighbors, and striven to find how these relations may be made more conducive to the general peace and welfare both of the South and of the country at large.

In the Southern part of the United States there are twenty-two millions of people who are bound to the fifty millions of the North by ties which neither can tear asunder if they would. The most intelligent in a New York community has his intelligence darkened by the ignorance of a fellow-citizen in the Mississippi bottoms. The most wealthy in New York City would be more wealthy but for the poverty of a fellow-being in the Carolina rice swamps. The most moral and religious men in Massachusetts have their religion and morality modified by the degradation of the man in the South whose religion is a mere matter of form or of emotionalism. The vote of the man in Maine that is cast for the highest and purest form of government is largely neutralized by the vote of the man in Louisiana whose ballot is stolen or cast in ignorance. Therefore, when the South is ignorant, the North is ignorant; when the South is poor, the North is poor; when the South commits crime, the nation commits crime. For the citizens of the North there is no escape; they must help raise the character of the civilization in the South, or theirs will be lowered. No member of the white race in any part of the country can harm the weakest or meanest member of the black race without the proudest and bluest blood of the nation being degraded.

It seems to me that there never was a time in the history of the country when those interested in education should the more earnestly consider to what extent the mere acquiring of the ability to read and write, the mere acquisition of a knowledge of literature and science, makes men producers, lovers of labor, independent, honest, unselfish, and, above all, good. Call education by what name you please, if it fails to bring about these results among the masses, it falls short of the highest end. The science, the art, the literature, that fails to reach down and bring the humblest up to the enjoyment of the fullest blessings of our government is weak, no matter how costly the buildings or apparatus used or how modern the methods of instruction employed. The study of arithmetic that does not result in making men conscientious in receiving and counting the ballots of their fellow-men is faulty. The study of art that does not result in making the strong less willing to oppress the weak means little. How I wish that from the most cultured and highly endowed university in the great North to the humblest log cabin school-house in Alabama, we could burn, as it were, into the hearts and heads of all that usefulness, that service to our brother, is the supreme end of education. Putting the thought more directly as it applies to conditions in the South, can you make the intelligence of the North affect the South in the same ratio that the ignorance of the South affects the North? Let us take a not improbable case: A great national case is to be decided, one that involves peace or war, the honor or dishonor of our nation—yea, the very existence of the government. The North and West are divided. There are five million votes to be cast in the South; and, of this number, one-half are ignorant. Not only are one-half the voters ignorant; but, because of the ignorant votes they cast, corruption and dishonesty in a dozen forms have crept into the exercise of the political franchise to such an extent that the conscience of the intelligent class is seared in its attempts to defeat the will of the ignorant voters. Here, then, you have on the one hand an ignorant vote, on the other an intelligent vote minus a conscience. The time may not be far off when to this kind of jury we shall have to look for the votes which shall decide in a large measure the density of our democratic institutions.

When a great national calamity stares us in the face, we are too much given to depending on a short "campaign of education" to do on the hustlings what should have been accomplished in the school.

With this idea in view, let us examine with more care the condition of civilization in the South and the work to be done there before all classes will be fit for the high duties of citizenship. In reference to the Negro race, I am confronted with some embarrassment at the outset, because of the various and conflicting opinions as to what is to be its final place in our economic and political life.

Within the last thirty years—and, I might add, within the last three months—it has been proven by eminent authority that the Negro is increasing in numbers so fast that it is only a question of a few years before he will far outnumber the white race in the South, and it has also been proven that the Negro is fast dying out, and it is only a question of a few years before he will have completely disappeared. It has also been proven that education helps the Negro and that education hurts him, that he is fast leaving the South and taking up residence in the North and West, and that his tendency is to drift toward the lowlands of the Mississippi bottoms. It has been proven that education unfits the Negro for work and that education makes him more valuable as a laborer, that he is our greatest criminal and that he is our most law-abiding citizen. In the midst of these conflicting opinions, it is hard to hit upon the truth.

But, also, in the midst of this confusion, there are a few things of which I am certain—things which furnish a basis for thought and action. I know that whether the Negroes are increasing or decreasing, whether they are growing better or worse, whether they are valuable or valueless, that a few years ago some fourteen of them were brought into this country, and that now those fourteen are nearly ten millions. I know that, whether in slavery or freedom, they have always been loyal to the Stars and Stripes, that no school-house has been opened for them that has not been filled, that the 2,000,000 ballots that they have the right to cast are as potent for weal or woe as an equal number cast by the wisest and most influential men in America. I know that wherever Negro life touches the life of the nation it helps or it hinders, that wherever the life of the white race touches the black it makes it stronger or weaker. Further, I know that almost every other race that has tried to look the white man in the face has disappeared. I know, despite all the conflicting opinions, and with a full knowledge of all the Negroes' weaknesses, that only a few centuries ago they went into slavery in this country pagans, that they came out Christians; they went into slavery as so much property, they came out American citizens; they went into slavery without a language, they came out speaking the proud Anglo-Saxon tongue; they went into slavery with the chains clanking about their wrists, they came out with the American ballot in their hands.

I submit it to the candid and sober judgment of all men, if a race that is capable of such a test, such a transformation, is not worth saving and making a part, in reality as well as in name, of our democratic government. That the Negro may be fitted for the fullest enjoyment of the privileges and responsibilities of our citizenship, it is important that the nation be honest and candid with him, whether honesty and candor for the time being pleases or displeases him. It is with an ignorant race as it is with a child: it craves at first the superficial, the ornamental signs of progress rather than the reality. The ignorant race is tempted to jump, at one bound, to the position that it has required years of hard struggle for others to reach.

It seems to me that, as a general thing, the temptation in the past in educational and missionary work has been to do for the new people that which was done a thousand years ago, or that which is being done for a people a thousand miles away, without making a careful study of the needs and conditions of the people whom it is designed to help. The temptation is to run all people through a certain educational mould, regardless of the condition of the subject or the end to be accomplished. This has been the case too often in the South in the past, I am sure. Men have tried to use, with these simple people just freed from slavery and with no past, no inherited traditions of learning, the same methods of education which they have used in New England, with all its inherited traditions and desires. The Negro is behind the white man because he has not had the same chance, and not from any inherent difference in his nature and desires. What the race accomplishes in these first fifty years of freedom will at the end of these years, in a large measure, constitute its past. It is, indeed, a responsibility that rests upon this nation—the foundation laying for a people of its past, present, and future at one and the same time.

One of the weakest points in connection with the present development of the race is that so many get the idea that the mere filling of the head with a knowledge of mathematics, the sciences, and literature, means success in life. Let it be understood, in every corner of the South, among the Negro youth at least, that knowledge will benefit little except as it is harnessed, except as its power is pointed in a direction that will bear upon the present needs and conditions of the race. There is in the heads of the Negro youth of the South enough general and floating knowledge of chemistry, of botany, of zoology, of geology, of mechanics, of electricity, of mathematics, to reconstruct and develop a large part of the agricultural, mechanical, and domestic life of the race. But how much of it is brought to a focus along lines of practical work? In cities of the South like Atlanta, how many colored mechanical engineers are there? Or how many machinists? How many civil engineers? How many architects? How many house decorators? In the whole State of Georgia, where 80 percent of the colored people depend upon agriculture, how many men are there who are well-grounded in the principles and practices of scientific farming? Or dairy work? Or fruit culture? Or floriculture?

For example, not very long ago I had a conversation with a young colored man who is a graduate of one of the prominent universities of this country. The father of this man is comparatively ignorant, but by hard work and the exercise of common sense, he has become the owner of two thousand acres of land. He owns more than a score of horses, cows, and mules and swine in large numbers, and is considered a prosperous farmer. In college, the son of this farmer has studied chemistry, botany, zoology, surveying, and political economy. In my conversation I asked this young man how many acres his father cultivated in cotton and how many in corn? With a far-off gaze up into the heavens he answered he did not know. When I asked him the classification of the soils on his father's farm, he did not know. He did not know how many horses or cows his father owned nor of what breeds they were, and seemed surprised that he should be asked such questions. It never seemed to have entered his mind that on his father's farm was the place to make his chemistry, his mathematics, and his literature penetrate and reflect itself in every acre of land, every bushel of corn, every cow, and every pig.

Let me give other examples of this mistaken sort of education. When a mere boy, I saw a young colored man, who had spent several years in school, sitting in a common cabin in the South, studying a French grammar. I noted the poverty, the untidiness, the want of system and thrift, that existed about the cabin, notwithstanding his knowledge of French and other academic studies.

Again, not long ago I saw a colored minister preparing his Sunday sermon just as the New England minister prepares his sermon. But this colored minister was in a broken-down, leaky, rented log cabin, with weeds in the yard, surrounded by evidences of poverty, filth, and want of thrift. This minister had spent some time in school studying theology. How much better it would have been to have had this minister taught the dignity of labor, taught the theoretical and practical farming in connection with his theology, so that he could have added to his meager salary, and set an example for his people in the matter of living in a decent house, and having a knowledge of correct farming! In a word, this minister should have been taught that his condition, and that of his people, was not that of a New England community; and he should have been trained as to meet the actual needs and conditions of the colored people in this community, so that a foundation might be laid that would, in the future, make a community like New England communities.

Since the Civil War, no one object has been more misunderstood than that of the object and value of industrial education for the Negro. To begin with, it must be borne in mind that the condition that existed in the South immediately after the war, and that now exists, is a peculiar one, without a parallel in history. This being true, it seems to me that the wise and honest thing to do is to make a study of the actual condition and environment of the Negro, and do that which is best for him, regardless of whether the same thing has been done for another race in exactly the same way. There are those among the white race and those among the black race who assert, with a good deal of earnestness, that there is no difference between the white man and the black man in this country. This sounds very pleasant and tickles the fancy; but, when the test of hard, cold logic is applied to it, it must be acknowledged that there is a difference—not an inherent one, not a racial one, but a difference growing out of unequal opportunities in the past.

If I may be permitted to criticize the educational work that has been done in the South, I would say that the weak point has been in the failure to recognize this difference.

Negro education, immediately after the war in most cases, was begun too nearly at the point where New England education had ended. Let me illustrate. One of the saddest sights I ever saw was the placing of a three-hundred-dollar rosewood piano in a country school in the South that was located in the midst of the "Black Belt." Am I arguing against the teaching of instrumental music to the Negroes in that community? Not at all; only I should have deferred those music lessons about twenty-five years. There are numbers of such pianos in thousands of New England homes. But behind the piano in the New England home there are one hundred years of toil, sacrifice, and economy; there is the small manufacturing industry, started several years ago by hand power, now grown into a great business; there is ownership in land, a comfortable home, free from debt, and a bank account. In this "Black Belt" community where this piano went, four-fifths of the people owned no land, many lived in rented one-room cabins, many were in debt for food supplies, many mortgaged their crops for the food on which to live, and not one had a bank account. In this case, how much wiser it would have been to have taught the girls in this community sewing, intelligent and economical cooking, house-keeping, something of dairying and horticulture? The boys should have been taught something of farming in connection with their common-school education, instead of awakening in them a desire for a musical instrument which resulted in their parents going into debt for a third-rate piano or organ before a home was purchased. Industrial lessons would have awakened, in this community, a desire for homes, and would have given the people the ability to free themselves from industrial slavery to the extent that most of them would have soon purchased homes. After the home and the necessaries of life were supplied could come the piano. One piano lesson in a home of one's own is worth twenty in a rented log cabin.

All that I have just written, and the various examples illustrating it, show the present helpless condition of my people in the South—how fearfully they lack the primary training for good living and good citizenship, how much they stand in the need of a solid foundation on which to build their future success. I believe, as I have many times said in various addresses in the North and in the South, that the main reason for the existence of this curious state of affairs is the lack of practical training in the ways of life.

There is, too, a great lack of money with which to carry on the educational work in the South. I was in a country in a Southern State not long ago where there are some thirty thousand colored people and about seven thousand whites. In this country, not a single public school for Negroes had been open that year longer than three months, not a single colored teacher had been paid more than $15 per month for his teaching. Not one of these schools was taught in a building that was worthy of the name of school-house. In this country, the State or public authorities do not own a single dollar's worth of school property—not a school-house, a blackboard, or a piece of crayon. Each colored child had spent on him that year for his education about fifty cents, while each child in New York or Massachusetts had had spent on him that year for education not far from $20. And yet each citizen of this country is expected to share the burdens and privileges of our democratic form of government just as intelligently and conscientiously as the citizens of New York or Boston. A vote in this country means as much to the nation as a vote in the city of Boston. Crime in this country is as truly an arrow aimed at the heart of the government as a crime committed in the streets of Boston.

A single school-house built this year in a town near Boston to shelter about three hundred pupils cost more for building alone than is spent yearly for the education, including buildings, apparatus, teachers, for the whole colored school population of Alabama. The Commissioner of Education for the State of Georgia not long ago reported to the State legislature that in that State there were two hundred thousand children that had entered no school the year past and one hundred thousand more who were at school but a few days, making practically three hundred thousand children between six and eighteen years of age that are growing up in ignorance in one Southern State alone. The same report stated that outside of the cities and towns, while the average number of school-houses in a country was sixty, all of these sixty school-houses were worth in lump less than $2,000, and the report further added that many of the school-houses in Georgia were not fit for horse stables. I am glad to say, however, that vast improvement over this condition is being made in Georgia under the inspired leadership of State Commissioner Glenn, and in Alabama under the no less zealous leadership of Commissioner Abercrombie.

These illustrations, so far as they concern the Gulf States, are not exceptional cases; nor are they overdrawn.

Until there is industrial independence, it is hardly possible to have good living and a pure ballot in the country districts. In these States, it is safe to say that not more than one black man in twenty owns the land he cultivates. Where so large a proportion of a people are dependent, live in other people's houses, eat other people's food, and wear clothes they have not paid for, it is pretty hard to expect them to live fairly and vote honestly.

I have thus far referred mainly to the Negro race. But there is another side. The longer I live and the more I study the question, the more I am convinced that it is not so much a problem as to what the white man will do with the Negro as what the Negro will do with the white man and his civilization. In considering this side of the subject, I thank God that I have grown to the point where I can sympathize with a white man as much as I can sympathize with a black man. I have grown to the point where I can sympathize with a Southern white man as much as I can sympathize with a Northern white man.

As bearing upon the future of our civilization, I ask of the North what of their white brethren in the South—those who have suffered and are still suffering the consequences of American slavery, for which both North and South were responsible? Those of the great and prosperous North still owe to their less fortunate brethren of the Caucasian race in the South, not less than to themselves, a serious and uncompleted duty. What was the task the North asked the South to perform? Returning to their destitute homes after years of war to face blasted hopes, devastation, a shattered industrial system, they asked them to add to their own burdens that of preparing in education, politics, and economics, in a few short years, for citizenship, four millions of former slaves. That the South, staggering under the burden, made blunders, and that in a measure there has been disappointment, no one need be surprised. The educators, the statesmen, the philanthropists, have imperfectly comprehended their duty toward the millions of poor whites in the South who were buffeted for two hundred years between slavery and freedom, between civilization and degradation, who were disregarded by both master and slave. It needs no prophet to tell the character of our future civilization when the poor white boy in the country districts of the South receive one dollar's worth of education and the boy of the same class in the North twenty dollars' worth, when one never enters a reading-room or library and the other has reading-rooms and libraries in every ward and town, when one hears lectures and sermons once in two months and the other can hear a lecture or a sermon every day in the year.

The time has come, it seems to me, when in this matter we should rise above party or race or sectionalism into the region of duty of man to man, of citizen to citizen, of Christian to Christian; and if the Negro, who has been oppressed and denied his rights in a Christian land, can help the whites of the North and South to rise, can be the inspiration of their rising, into this atmosphere of generous Christian brotherhood and self-forgetfulness, he will see in it a recompense for all that he has suffered in the past.

✦ W. E. B. DuBois, The Souls of Black Folk, 1903

*At the end of the nineteenth century, Booker T. Washington had become the acknowl-
edged voice of the African-American community in the South and generally in the
nation. He had found a respectful audience in both white and black communities in a
way no other African American had since the end of Reconstruction a quarter-century
earlier. However, with the new century, a young Harvard graduate rose to challenge
Washington. Believing that Washington's vision was too narrow and ultimately sold the
African-American community short, DuBois argued, first in* The Souls of Black Folk
*and then in a long line of subsequent publications, that the African-American commu-
nity needed a larger vision and a wider dream if liberation was to be found. The previous reading from Washington, combined with the two selections from* The Souls of
Black Folk *that follow, clearly frame the DuBois-Washington debate.*

Of Mr. Booker T. Washington and Others

Easily the most striking thing in the history of the American Negro since 1876 is the
ascendancy of Mr. Booker T. Washington. It began at the time when war memories and
ideals were rapidly passing; a day of astonishing commercial development was dawn-
ing; a sense of doubt and hesitation overtook the freedmen's sons—then it was that his
leading began. Mr. Washington came, with a single definite programme, at the psychological moment when the nation was a little ashamed of having bestowed so much sentiment on Negroes, and was concentrating its energies on Dollars. His programme of
industrial education, conciliation of the South, and submission and silence as to civil
and political rights, was not wholly original; the Free Negroes from 1830 up to war-
time had striven to build industrial schools, and the American Missionary Association
had from the first taught various trades; and Price and others had sought a way of honorable alliance with the best of Southerners. But Mr. Washington first indissolubly
linked these things; he put enthusiasm, unlimited energy, and perfect faith into this programme, and changed it from a by-path into a veritable Way of Life. And the tale of the
methods by which he did this is a fascinating study of human life.

It startled the nation to hear a Negro advocating such a programme after many
decades of bitter complaint; it startled and won the applause of the South, it interested
and won the admiration of the North; and after a confused murmur of protest, it
silenced, if it did not convert, the Negroes themselves.

To gain the sympathy and cooperation of the various elements comprising the
white South was Mr. Washington's first task; and this, at the time Tuskegee was
founded, seemed, for a black man, well-nigh impossible. And yet ten years later it was
done in the word spoken at Atlanta: "In all things purely social we can be as separate
as the five fingers, and yet one as the hand in all things essential to mutual progress."
This "Atlanta Compromise" is by all odds the most notable thing in Mr. Washington's
career. The South interpreted it in different ways: the radicals received it as a complete
surrender of the demand for civil and political equality; the conservatives, as a generously conceived working basis for mutual understanding. So both approved it, and today its author is certainly the most distinguished Southerner since Jefferson Davis, and
the one with the largest personal following.

Next to this achievement comes Mr. Washington's work in gaining place and consideration in the North. Others less shrewd and tactful had formerly essayed to sit on these two stools and had fallen between them; but as Mr. Washington knew the heart of the South from birth and training, so by singular insight he intuitively grasped the spirit of the age which was dominating the North. And so thoroughly did he learn the speech and thought of triumphant commercialism, and the ideals of material prosperity, that the picture of a lone black boy poring over a French grammar amid the weeds and dirt of a neglected home soon seemed to him the acme of absurdities. One wonders what Socrates and St. Francis of Assisi would say to this.

And yet this very singleness of vision and thorough oneness with his age is a mark of the successful man. It is as though Nature must needs make men narrow in order to give them force. So Mr. Washington's cult order has gained unquestioning followers, his work has wonderfully prospered, his friends are legion, and his enemies are confounded. To-day he stands as the one recognized spokesman of his ten million fellows, and one of the most notable figures in a nation of seventy millions. One hesitates, therefore, to criticize a life which, beginning with so little, has done so much. And yet the time is come when one may speak in all sincerity and utter courtesy of the mistakes and shortcomings of Mr. Washington's career, as well as of his triumphs, without being thought captious or envious, and without forgetting that it is easier to do ill than well in the world.

The criticism that has hitherto met Mr. Washington has not always been of this broad character. In the South especially, has he had to walk warily to avoid the harshest judgements—and naturally so, for he is dealing with the one subject of deepest sensitiveness to that section. Twice—once when at the Chicago celebration of the Spanish-American War he alluded to the color-prejudice that is "eating away the vitals of the South," and once [when] he dined with President Roosevelt—has the resulting Southern criticism been violent enough to threaten seriously his popularity. In the North the feeling has several times forced itself into words, that Mr. Washington's counsels of submission overlooked certain elements of true manhood, and that his educational programme was unnecessarily narrow. Usually, however, such criticism has not found open expression, although too, the spiritual sons of the Abolitionists have not been prepared to acknowledge that the schools founded before Tuskegee, by men of broad ideals and self-sacrificing spirit, were wholly failures or worthy of ridicule. While, then, criticism has not failed to follow Mr. Washington, yet the prevailing public opinion of the land has been but too willing to deliver the solution of a wearisome problem into his own hands, and say, "If that is all you and your race ask, take it."

Among his own people, however, Mr. Washington has encountered the strongest and most lasting opposition, amounting at times to bitterness, and even to-day continuing strong and insistent even though largely silenced in outward expression by the public opinion of the nation. Some of this opposition is, of course, mere envy; the disappointment of displaced demagogues and the spite of narrow minds. But aside from this, there is among educated and thoughtful colored men in all parts of the land a feeling of deep regret, sorrow, and apprehension at the wide currency and ascendancy which some of Mr. Washington's theories have gained. These same men admire his sincerity of purpose, and are willing to forgive much to honest endeavor, which is doing something worth the doing. They cooperate with Mr. Washington as far as they conscientiously can; and, indeed, it is no ordinary tribute to this man's tact and power that, steering as he must between so many diverse interests and opinions, he so largely retains the respect of all.

But the hushing of the criticism of honest opponents is a dangerous thing. It leads some of the best of the critics to unfortunate silence and paralysis of effort, and others to burst into speech so passionately and intemperately as to lose listeners. Honest and earnest criticism from those whose interests are most nearly touched—criticism of writers by readers, or government by those governed, or leaders by those led—this is the soul of democracy and the safeguard of modern society. If the best of the American Negroes receive by outer pressure a leader whom they had not recognized before, manifestly there is here a certain palpable gain. Yet there is also irreparable loss—a loss of that peculiarly valuable education which a group receives when by search and criticism it finds and commissions its own leaders. The way in which this is done is at once the most elementary and the nicest problem of social growth. History is but the record of such group-leadership; and yet how infinitely changeful is its type and character! And of all types and kinds, what can be more instructive than the leadership of a group within a group?—that curious double movement where real progress may be negative and actual advance be relative retrogression. All this is the social student's inspiration and despair.

Now in the past the American Negro has had instructive experience in the choosing of group leaders, founding thus a peculiar dynasty which in the light of present conditions is worthwhile studying. When sticks and stones and beasts form the sole environment of a people, their attitude is largely one of determined opposition to and conquest of natural forces. But when to earth and brute is added an environment of men and ideas, then the attitude of the imprisoned group may take three main forms—a feeling of revolt and revenge; an attempt to adjust all thought and action to the will of the greater group; or, finally, a determined effort at self-realization and self-development despite environing opinion. The influence of all these attitudes at various times can be traced in the history of the American Negro, and in the evolution of his successive leaders.

Before 1750, while the fire of African freedom still burned in the veins of the slaves, there was in all leadership or attempted leadership but the one motive of revolt and revenge—typified in the terrible Maroons, the Danish blacks, and Cato of Stono, and veiling all the Americas in fear of insurrection. The liberalizing tendencies of the later half of the eighteenth century brought, along with kindlier relations between black and white, thoughts of ultimate adjustment and assimilation. Such aspiration was especially voiced in the earnest songs of Phyllis, in the martyrdom of Attucks, the fighting of Salem and Poor, the intellectual accomplishments of Banneker and Derham, and the political demands of the Cuffes.

Stern financial and social stress after the war cooled much of the previous humanitarian ardor. The disappointment and impatience of the Negroes at the persistence of slavery and serfdom voiced itself in two movements. The slaves in the South, aroused undoubtedly by vague rumors of the Haytian revolt, made three fierce attempts at insurrection—in 1800 under Gabriel in Virginia, in 1822 under Vesey in Carolina, and in 1831 again in Virginia under the terrible Nat Turner. In the Free states, on the other hand, a new and curious attempt at self-development was made. In Philadelphia and New York, color-prescriptions led to a withdrawal of Negro communicants from white churches and the formation of a peculiar socio-religious institution among the Negroes known as the African Church—an organization still living and controlling in its various branches over a million of men.

Walker's wild appeal against the trend of the times showed how the world was changing after the coming of the cotton-gin. By 1830, slavery seemed hopelessly fastened on the South, and the slaves thoroughly cowed into submission. The free Negroes of the

North, inspired by the mulatto immigrants from the West Indies, began to change the basis of their demands; they recognized the slavery of slaves, but insisted that they themselves were freemen, and sought assimilation and amalgamation with the nation on the same terms with other men. Thus, Forten and Purvis of Philadelphia, Shad of Wilmington, DuBois of New Haven, Barbadoes of Boston, and others, strove singly and together as men, they said, not as slaves; as "people of color," not as "Negroes." The trend of the times, however, refused them recognition save in individual and exceptional cases, considered them as one with all despised blacks, and they soon found themselves striving to keep even the rights they formerly had of voting and working and moving as freemen. Schemes of migration and colonization arose among them; but these they refused to entertain, and they eventually turned to the Abolition movement as a final refuge.

Here, led by Remond Nell, Wells-Brown, and Douglass, a new period of self-assertion and self-development dawned. To be sure, ultimate freedom and assimilation was the ideal before the leaders, but the assertion of the manhood rights of the Negro by himself was the main reliance, and John Brown's raid was the extreme of its logic. After the war and emancipation, the great form of Fredrick Douglass, the greatest of American Negro leaders, still led the host. Self-assertion, especially in political lines, was the main programme, and behind Douglass came Elliot, Bruce, and Langston, and the Reconstruction politicians, and less conspicuous but of greater social significance, Alexander Crummell and Bishop Daniel Payne.

Then came the Revolution of 1876, the suppression of the Negro votes, the changing and shifting of ideals, and the seeking of new lights in the great night. Douglass, in his old age, still bravely stood for the ideals of his early manhood—ultimate assimilation *through* self-assertion, and on no other terms. For a time Price arose as a new leader, destined, it seemed, not to give up, but to re-state the old ideals in a form less repugnant to the white South. But he passed away in his prime. Then came the new leader. Nearly all the former ones had become leaders by the silent suffrage of their fellows, had sought to lead their own people alone, and were usually, save Douglass, little known outside their race. But Booker T. Washington arose as essentially the leader not of one race but of two—a compromiser between the South, the North, and the Negro. Naturally the Negroes resented, at first bitterly, signs of compromise which surrendered their civil and political rights, even though this was to be exchanged for larger chances of economic development. The rich and dominating North, however, was not only weary of the race problem, but was investing largely in Southern enterprises, and welcomed any method of peaceful cooperation. Thus, by national opinion, the Negroes began to recognize Mr. Washington's leadership; and the voice of criticism was hushed.

Mr. Washington represents in Negro thought the old attitude of adjustment and submission; but adjustment at such a peculiar time as to make his programme unique. This is an age of unusual economic development, and Mr. Washington's programme naturally takes an economic cast, becoming a gospel of Work and Money to such an extent as apparently almost completely to overshadow the higher aims of life. Moreover, this is an age when the more advanced races are coming closer in contact with the less developed races, and the race-feeling is therefore intensified; and Mr. Washington's programme practically accepts the alleged inferiority of the Negro races. Again, in our own land, the reaction from the sentiment of war time has given impetus to race-prejudice against Negros, and Mr. Washington withdraws many of the high demands of Negros as men and American citizens. In other periods of intensified prejudice all the Negro's tendency to self-assertion has been called forth; at this period a policy of submission is advocated. In the history of nearly all other races and peoples, the doctrine preached at such crises has been that manly self-respect is worth more than lands and houses, and that a people who voluntarily surrender such respect, or cease striving for it, are not worth civilizing.

In answer to this, it has been claimed that the Negro can survive only through submission. Mr. Washington distinctly asks that black people give up, at least for the present, three things—

First, political power,
Second, insistence on civil rights,
Third, higher education of Negro youth—

and concentrate all their energies on industrial education, the accumulation of wealth, and the conciliation of the South. This policy has been courageously and insistently advocated for over fifteen years, and has been triumphant for perhaps ten years. As a result of this tender of the palm-branch, what has been the return? In these years there have occurred:

1. The disfranchisement of the Negro.
2. The legal creation of a distinct status of civil inferiority for the Negro.
3. The steady withdrawal of aid from institutions for the higher training of the Negro.

These movements are not, to be sure, direct results of Mr. Washington's teachings; but his propaganda has, without a shadow of a doubt, helped their speedier accomplishment. The question then comes: Is it possible, and probable, that nine millions of men can make effective progress in economic lines if they are deprived of political rights, made a servile caste, and allowed only the most meagre chance for developing their exceptional men? If history and reason give any distinct answer to these questions, it is an emphatic *No*. And Mr. Washington thus faces the triple paradox of his career:

1. He is striving nobly to make Negro artisans business men and property-owners; but it is utterly impossible, under modern competitive methods, for workingmen and property-owners to defend their rights and exist without the right of suffrage.
2. He insists on thrift and self-respect, but at the same time counsels a silent submission to civic inferiority such as is bound to sap the manhood of any race in the long run.
3. He advocates common-school and industrial training, and depreciates institutions of higher learning; but neither the Negro common-schools, nor Tuskegee itself, could remain open a day were it not for teachers trained in Negro colleges, or trained by their graduates.

This triple paradox in Mr. Washington's position is the object of criticism by two classes of colored Americans. One class is spiritually descended from Toissant [Toussaint] the Savior, through Gabriel, Vesey, and Turner, and they represent the attitude of revolt and revenge; they hate the white South blindly and distrust the white race generally, and so far as they agree on definite action, think that the Negro's only hope lies in emigration beyond the borders of the United States. And yet, by the irony of fate, nothing has more effectually made this programme seem hopeless than the recent course of the United States toward weaker and darker peoples in the West Indies, Hawaii, and the Philippines—for where in the world may we go and be safe from lying and brute force?

The other class of Negroes who cannot agree with Mr. Washington has hitherto said little aloud. They deprecate the sight of scattered counsels, of internal disagreement; and especially they dislike making their just criticism of a useful and earnest man an excuse for a general discharge of venom from small-minded opponents. Nevertheless, the questions involved are so fundamental and serious that it is difficult to see how men like the Grimkes, Kelly Miller, J. W. E. Bowen, and other representatives of this group, can much longer be silent. Such men feel in conscience bound to ask of this nation three things:

1. The right to vote.
2. Civic equality.
3. The education of youth according to ability.

They acknowledge Mr. Washington's invaluable service in counseling patience and courtesy in such demands; they do not ask that ignorant black men vote when ignorant whites are debarred, or that any reasonable restriction in the suffrage should not be applied; they know that the low social level of the mass of the race is responsible for much discrimination against it, but they also know, and the nation knows, that relentless color-prejudice is more often a cause than a result of the Negro's degradation; they seek the abatement of this relic of barbarism, and not its systematic encouragement and pampering by all agencies of social power from Associated Press to the Church of Christ. They advocate, with Mr. Washington, a broad system of Negro common schools supplemented by thorough industrial training; but they are not supprised that a man of Mr. Washington's insight cannot see, that no such educational system ever has rested or can rest on any other basis than that of the well-equipped college and university, and they insist that there is a demand for a few such institutions throughout the South to train the best of the Negro youth as teachers, professional men, and leaders.

This group of men honor Mr. Washington for his attitude of conciliation toward the white South; they accept the "Atlanta Compromise" in its broadest interpretation; they recognize, with him, many signs of promise, many men of high purpose and fair judgement, in this section; they know that no easy task has been laid upon a region already tottering under heavy burdens. But, nevertheless, they insist that the way to truth and right lies in straightforward honesty, not indiscriminate flattery; in praising those of the South who do well and criticizing uncompromisingly those who do ill; in taking advantage of the opportunities at hand and urging their fellows to do the same, but at the same time in remembering that only a firm adherence to their higher ideals and aspirations will ever keep those ideals within the realm of possibility. They do not expect that the free right to vote, to enjoy civic rights, and to be educated, will come in a moment; they do not expect to see the bias and prejudices of years disappear at the blast of a trumpet; but they are absolutely certain that the way for a people to gain their reasonable rights is not by voluntarily throwing them away and insisting that they do not want them; that the way for a people to gain respect is not by continually belittling and ridiculing themselves; that, on the contrary, Negroes must insist continually, in season, and out of season that color discrimination is barbarism, and that black boys need education as well as white boys.

In failing thus to state plainly and unequivocally the legitimate demands of their people, even at the cost of opposing an honored leader, the thinking classes of American Negroes would shirk a heavy responsibility—a responsibility to themselves, a responsibility to the struggling masses, a responsibility to the darker races of men whose future depends so largely on this American experiment, but especially a responsibility to this nation—this common Fatherland. It is wrong to encourage a man or a people in evil-doing; it is wrong to aid and abet a national crime simply because it is unpopular not to do so. The growing spirit of kindliness and reconciliation between the North and South after the frightful difference of a generation ago ought to be a source of deep congratulation to all, and especially to those whose mistreatment caused the war; but if that reconciliation is to be marked by the industrial slavery and civic death of those same black men, with permanent legislation into a position of inferiority, then those black men, if they are really men, are called upon by every consideration of patriotism and loyalty to oppose such a course by all civilized methods, even though such opposition involves disagreement with Mr. Booker T. Washington. We have no right to sit silently by while the inevitable seeds are sown for a harvest of disaster to our children, black and white.

First, it is the duty of black men to judge the South discriminatingly. The present generation of Southerners are not responsible for the past, and they should not be blindly hated or blamed for it. Furthermore, to no class is the indiscriminate endorsement of the recent course of the South toward Negroes more nauseating than to the best thought of the South. The South is not "solid"; it is a land in the ferment of social change, wherein forces of all kinds are fighting for supremacy; and to praise the ill the South is to-day perpetrating is just as wrong as to condemn the good. Discriminating and broad-minded criticism is what the South needs—needs it for the sake of her own white sons and daughters, and for the insurance of robust, healthy mental and moral development. To-day even the attitude of the Southern whites toward the blacks is not, as so many assume, in all cases the same; the ignorant Southerner hates the Negro, the workingmen fear his competition, the money-makers wish to use him as a laborer, some of the educated see a menace in his upward development, while others—usually the sons of the masters—wish to help him to rise. National opinion has enabled this last class to maintain the Negro common schools, and to protect the Negro partially in property, life, and limb. Through the pressure of the money-makers, the Negro is in danger of being reduced to semi-slavery, especially in the country districts; the workingmen, and those of the educated who fear the Negro, have united to disenfranchise him, and some have urged his deportation; while the passions of the ignorant are easily aroused to lynch and abuse any black man. To praise this intricate whirl of thought and prejudice is nonsense; to inveigh indiscriminately against "the South" is unjust; but to use the same breath in praising Governor Aycock, exposing Senator Morgan, arguing with Mr. Thomas Nelson Page, and denouncing Senator Ben Tillman, is not only sane, but the imperative duty of thinking black men.

It would be unjust to Mr. Washington not to acknowledge that in several instances he has opposed movements in the South which were unjust to the Negro; he sent memorials to the Louisiana and Alabama constitutional conventions, he has spoken against lynching, and in other ways has openly or silently set his influence against sinister schemes and unfortunate happenings. Notwithstanding this, it is equally true to assert that on the whole the distinct impression left by Mr. Washington's propaganda is, first, that the South is justified in its present attitude toward the Negro because of the Negro's degradation; secondly, that the prime cause of the Negro's failure to rise more quickly is his wrong education in the past; and thirdly, that his future rise depends primarily on his own efforts. Each of these propositions is a dangerous half-truth. The supplementary truths must never be lost sight of; first, slavery and race-prejudice are potent if not sufficient causes of the Negro's position; second, industrial and common-school training were necessarily slow in planting because they had to await the black teachers trained by higher institutions—it being extremely doubtful if any essentially different development was possible, and certainly a Tuskegee was unthinkable before 1880; and, third, while it is a great truth to say that the Negro must strive and strive mightily to help himself, it is equally true that unless his striving be not simply seconded, but rather aroused and encouraged, by the initiative of the richer and wiser environing group, he cannot hope for great success.

In his failure to realize and impress this last point, Mr. Washington is especially to be criticized. His doctrine has tended to make the whites, North and South, shift the burden of the Negro problem to the Negro's shoulders and stand aside as critical and rather pessimistic spectators; when in fact the burden belongs to the nation, and the hands of none of us are clean if we bend not our energies to righting these great wrongs.

The South ought to be led, by candid and honest criticism, to assert her better self and do her full duty to the race she has cruelly wronged and is still wronging. The North—her co-partner in guilt—cannot salve her conscience by plastering it with gold. We cannot settle this problem by diplomacy and suaveness, by "policy" alone. If worse come to worst, can the moral fibre of this country survive the slow throttling and murder of nine millions of men?

The black men of America have a duty to perform, a duty stern and delicate—a forward movement to oppose a part of the work of their greatest leader. So far as Mr. Washington preaches Thrift, Patience, and Industrial Training for the masses, we must hold up his hands and strive with him, rejoicing in his honors and glorying in the strength of this Joshua called of God and of man to lead the headless host. But so far as Mr. Washington apologizes for injustice, North or South, does not rightly value the privilege and duty of voting, belittles the emasculating effects of caste distinctions, and opposes the higher training and ambition of our brighter minds—so far as he, the South, or the Nation, does this—we must unceasingly and firmly oppose them. By every civilized and peaceful method we must strive for the rights which the world accords to men, clinging unwaveringly to those great words which the sons of the Fathers would fain to forget: "We hold these truths to be self-evident: That all men are created equal; that they are endowed by their Creator with certain unalienable rights; that among these are life, liberty, and the pursuit of happiness."

Of the Training of Black Men

In rough approximation we may point out four varying decades of work in Southern education since the Civil War. From the close of the war until 1876, was the period of uncertain groping and temporary relief. There were army schools, mission schools, and schools of the Freedman's Bureau in chaotic disarrangement seeking system and cooperation. Then followed ten years of constructive definite effort toward the building of complete school systems in the South. Normal schools and colleges were founded for the freedom, and teachers trained there to man the public schools. There was the inevitable tendency of war to underestimate the prejudices of the master and ignorance of the slave, and all seemed clear sailing out of the wreckage of the storm. Meantime, starting in this decade, yet especially developing from 1885 to 1895, began the industrial revolution of the South. The land saw glimpses of a new destiny and the stirring of new ideals. The educational system, striving to complete itself, saw new obstacles and a field of work ever broader and deeper. The Negro colleges, hurriedly founded, were inadequately equipped, illogically distributed, and of varying efficiency and grade; the normal and high schools were doing little more than common-school work, and the common schools were training but a third of the children who ought to be in them, and training these too often poorly. At the same time, the white South, by reason of its sudden conversion from the slavery ideal, by so much the more became set and strengthened in its racial prejudice, and crystallized it into harsh law and harsher custom; while the marvelous pushing forward of the poor white daily threatened to take even bread and butter from the mouths of the heavily handicapped sons of the freedmen. In the midst, then, of the larger problem of Negro education sprang up the more practical question of work, the inevitable economic quandary that faces a people in the transition from slavery to freedom, and especially those who make that change amid hate and prejudice, lawlessness and ruthless competition.

The industrial school springing to notice in this decade, but coming to full recognition in the decade beginning with 1895, was the proffered answer to this combined educational and economic crisis, and an answer of singular wisdom and timeliness. From the very first in nearly all the schools some attention had been given in training in handiwork, but now was this training first raised to a dignity that brought it in direct touch with the South's magnificent industrial development, and given an emphasis which reminded black folk that before the Temple of Knowledge swing the Gates of Toil.

Yet, after all, they are but gates, and when turning our eyes from the temporary and the contingent in the Negro problem to the broader question of the permanent uplifting and civilization of the black men in America, we have a right to inquire, as this enthusiasm for material advancement mounts to its height, if after all the industrial school is the final and sufficient answer in the training of the Negro race; and to ask gently, but in all sincerity, the ever-recurring query of the ages, Is not life more than meat, and the body more than raiment? And men ask this to-day all the more eagerly because of sinister signs in recent educational movements. The tendency is here, born of slavery and quickened to renewed life by the crazy imperialism of the day, to regard human beings as among the material resources of a land to be trained with an eye single to future dividends. Race-prejudices, which keep brown and black men in their "places," we are coming to regard as useful allies with such a theory, no mater how much they may dull the ambition and sicken the hearts of struggling human beings. And above all, we daily hear that an education that encourages aspiration, that sets the loftiest ideals and seeks as an end culture and character rather than bread-winning, is the privilege of white men and the danger and delusion of black.

Especially has criticism been directed against the former educational efforts to aid the Negro. In the four periods I have mentioned, we find first, boundless, planless enthusiasm and sacrifice; then the preparation of teachers for a vast public-school system; then the launching and expansion of that school system amid increasing difficulties; and finally the training of workmen for the new and growing industries. This development has been sharply ridiculed as a logical anomaly and flat reversal of nature. Soothly we have been told that first industrial and manual training should have taught the Negro to work, then simple schools should have taught him to read and write, and finally, after years, high and normal schools could have completed the system, as intelligence and wealth demanded.

That a system logically so complete was historically impossible, it needs but a little thought to prove. Progress in human affairs is more often a pull than a push, a surging forward of the exceptional man, and the lifting of his duller brethren slowly and painfully to his vantage-ground. Thus it was no accident that gave birth to universities centuries before the common schools, that made fair Harvard the first flower of our wilderness. So in the South: the mass of the freedmen at the end of the war lacked the intelligence so necessary to modern workingmen. They must first have the common school to teach them to read, write, and cipher; and they must have higher schools to teach teachers for the common schools. The white teachers who flocked South went to establish such a common-school system. Few held the idea of founding colleges; most of them at first would have laughed at the idea. But they faced, as all men since them have faced, that central paradox of the South—the social separation of the races. At that time it was the sudden volcanic rupture of nearly all relations between black and white, in work and government and family life. Since then, a new adjustment of relations in economic and political affairs has grown up—an adjustment subtle and difficult to grasp, yet singularly ingenious, which leaves still that frightful chasm at the color-line across which men pass at their peril. Thus, then and now, there stand in the South two separate worlds; and separate not simply in the higher realms of social intercourse, but also in church and school, on railway and street-car, in hotels and theatres, in streets and city sections, in books and newspapers, in asylums and jails, in hospitals and graveyards. There is still enough of contact for large economic and group cooperation, but the separation is so thorough and deep that it absolutely precludes for the present between the races anything like that sympathetic and effective group-training and leadership of the one by the other, such as the American Negro and all backward peoples must have for effectual progress.

This the missionaries of '68 soon saw; and if effective industrial and trade schools were impracticable before the establishment of a common-school system, just as certainly no adequate common schools could be founded until there were teachers to teach them. Southern whites would not teach them; Northern whites in sufficient numbers could not be had. If the Negro was to learn, he must teach himself, and the most effective help that could be given him was the establishment of schools to train Negro teachers. This conclusion was slowly but surely reached by every student of the situation until simultaneously, in widely separated regions, without consultation or systematic plan, there arose a series of institutions designed to furnish teachers for the untaught. Above the sneers of critics at the obvious defects of this procedure must ever stand its one crushing rejoinder: in a single generation, they put thirty thousand black teachers in the South; they wiped out the illiteracy of the majority of the black people of the land, and they made Tuskegee possible.

Such higher training-schools tended naturally to deepen broader development: at first, they were common and grammar schools, then some became high schools. And finally, by 1900, some thirty-four had one year or more of studies of college grade. This development was reached with different degrees of speed in different institutions: Hampton is still a high school, while Fisk University started her college in 1871, and Spelman Seminary about 1896. In all cases the aim was identical—to maintain the standards of the lower training by giving teachers and leaders the best practicable training; and above all, to furnish the black world with adequate standards of human culture and lofty ideals of life. It was not enough that the teachers of teachers should be trained in technical normal methods; they must also, so far as possible, be broadminded, cultured men and women, to scatter civilization among a people whose ignorance was not simply of letters, but of life itself.

It can thus be seen that the work of education in the South began with higher institutions of training, which threw off as their foliage common schools, and later industrial schools, and at the same time strove to shoot their roots ever deeper toward college and university training. That this was an inevitable and necessary development, sooner or later, goes without saying; but there has been, and still is, a question in many minds if the natural growth was not forced, and if the higher training was not either overdone or done with cheap and unsound methods. Among white Southerners, this feeling is widespread and positive. A prominent Southern journal voiced this in a recent editorial.

"The experiment that has been made to give the colored students classical training has not been satisfactory. Even though many were able to pursue the course, most of them did so in a parrot-like way, learning what was taught, but not seeming to appropriate the truth and import of their instruction, and graduating without sensible aim or valuable occupation for their future. The whole scheme has proved a waste of time, efforts, and the money of the state."

While most fair-minded men would recognize this as extreme and overdrawn, still without doubt many are asking, Are there a sufficient number of Negroes ready for college training to warrant the undertaking? Are not too many students prematurely forced into this work? Does it not have the effect of dissatisfying the young Negro with his environment? And do these graduates succeed in real life? Such natural questions cannot be evaded, nor on the other hand must a Nation naturally skeptical as to Negro ability assume an unfavorable answer without careful inquiry and patient openness to conviction. We must not forget that most Americans answer all queries regarding the Negro *a priori,* and that the least that human courtesy can do is to listen to evidence.

The advocates of the higher education of the Negro would be the last to deny the incompleteness and glaring defects of the present system: too many institutions have attempted to do college work, the work in some cases has not been thoroughly done, and quantity rather than quality has sometimes been sought. But all this can be said of higher education throughout the land; it is the almost inevitable incident of educational growth, and leaves the deeper question of the legitimate demand for the higher training of Negroes untouched. And this latter question can be settled in but one way—by a first-hand study of the facts. If we leave out of view all institutions which have not actually graduated students from a course higher than that of a New England high school, even though they be called colleges; if then we take the thirty-four remaining institutions, we may clear up many misapprehensions by asking searchingly, What kind of institutions are they? what do they teach? and what sort of men do they graduate?

And first we may say that this type of college, including Atlanta, Fisk, and Howard, Wilberforce and Claflin, Shaw, and the rest, is peculiar, almost unique. Through the shining trees that whisper before me as I write, I catch glimpses of a boulder of New England granite, covering a grave, which graduates of Atlanta University have placed there—

> Grateful memory of their former teacher and friend and of the unselfish life he lived, and the novel work he wrought; that they, their children, and their children's children might be blessed.

CHAPTER 6

GROWTH AND DIVERSITY IN SCHOOLS AND STUDENTS, 1880-1960

❖ Introduction

❖ Third Plenary Council of Baltimore, 1884

❖ Mary Antin, *The Promised Land*, 1912

❖ Lewis Meriam, *The Problem of Indian Administration*, 1928

❖ The Asian Experience in California, 1919-1920

❖ Beatrice Griffith, *American Me,* 1948

❖ Teaching Children of Puerto Rican Background in the New York City Schools, 1954

Introduction

Students in the United States have always been a diverse lot. How the schools have handled this diversity has changed dramatically over the years, however. Before the nation was founded, the thirteen colonies all had immigrants from many different European countries mingling with Africans and their descendents, both slave and free, as well as with Indians who predated both on these shores. Spanish-speaking residents of Puerto Rico and much of the American southwest did not immigrate to the United States, they simply happened to be in lands conquered by the growing nation. Asian immigrants began coming to the United States in the middle of the nineteenth century. All of these groups had to engage with schools in one way or another.

Schools as they existed in the United States were imported from Europe and especially England. They were often alien places to many from other countries and cultures. The result, far too often, has been a definition of schooling as an institution for the dominant classes. At times others were excluded from schools. At times they were welcomed, but only on the dominant culture's terms. At yet other times, they were segregated in separate schools. Including and respecting a diverse population within schools remains a major issue in schooling at the beginning of the twenty-first century.

While the last chapter focused on the African-American experience, this chapter looks at the ways in which schools related to a wide range of other groups—nineteenth-century Roman Catholics, turn-of-the-century Jewish immigrants from eastern Europe, Asian immigrants on the West Coast, Mexican-Americans in California, and Puerto Rican migrants to the New York City Public Schools in the 1950s. The individual documents are illustrative; no one should assume that all Catholics followed the directives of their bishops to attend parochial schools; and certainly not all Jewish immigrants had as positive an experience with American schools as Mary Antin. Taken as a whole, however, the readings give a flavor of the responses of people from different cultures to U.S. schools.

By the time the Third Plenary Council of the nation's Roman Catholic bishops met in Baltimore in 1884, the Catholic leadership had given up on any meaningful chance to gain public support for their separate schools. For all the energy put into the campaign by New York's Bishop John Hughes and others, Catholics remained a minority in the nation, and the majority was not about to lend financial support to their schools. The bishops decided that the alternative was to withdraw from the public schools and develop an alternative school system that reflected Catholic faith and values. While the resulting Roman Catholic parochial school system became the most popular alternative to the public school ever seen in the United States, the decision to create an alternative system, despite financial difficulty, was certainly of interest to other groups.

Mary Antin's experience in fully embracing the public schools represents the opposite end of the spectrum. For Antin, as for many immigrants, the public schools represented a wonderful opportunity not only to enter the American nation but to become an American. Her autobiography, *The Promised Land*, has been critiqued for casting a romantic haze around the immigrant experience. Nevertheless, it remains a powerful first-person account. And hundreds of thousands of other young people who flocked to these shores between 1880 and 1920 shared her enthusiasm for the schools of Boston and other locales.

The Native American experience with education has always been unique. More than any other group, Native Americans were truly a conquered people who had no say in their decision to become part of the United States. The U.S. government developed a wide range of programs to acculturate Indians to European-American ways. At their worst, these programs were designed to "kill the Indian but save the human." Other educators and missionaries were more respectful of Indian culture. But few Europeans were successful in developing a respectful engagement with Indians. By the 1920s, the failure of U.S. educational practices in regard to Native Americans was becoming clearer and clearer. As a result, the U.S. Department of the Interior commissioned a survey, subsequently known as the Meriam report for its author, Lewis Meriam, which offered a devastating critique of previous efforts at Indian education. It took an additional three decades before some of the issues raised in the Meriam report were truly addressed, but the report did represent a turning point toward developing an education that was more respectful and less imperialistic. In addition, the report offers the twenty-first century student a good picture of the nature of Indian education as it existed in the late nineteenth and early twentieth centuries.

The Latino experience with schooling has long been problematic. In the middle of the nineteenth century, the United States conquered northern Mexico, adding the states of California, Arizona, New Mexico, and Texas to the union. Many Mexican citizens suddenly became American citizens, but the change in political citizenship did not change their cultural or linguistic traditions. Schools often treated these new citizens as distinctly second-class citizens. The passing of a century did not fully ameliorate these issues. The reports describing the difficulties of Mexican-American students in the Los Angeles public schools from the 1940s provide a picture of what school life was like for many children on the West Coast. In the 1950s, large numbers of Puerto Rican citizens began immigrating to New York City. The circular issued by the New York Board of Education offers a glimpse at how they were welcomed into the city's schools.

No one set of documents can cover all the groups of people who have interacted with American schools, nor the many different perspectives of individuals within each group. Nevertheless, the documents in this chapter should give the reader some sense of the incredibly diverse experiences of many children over many years in public schools in the United States.

THIRD PLENARY COUNCIL OF BALTIMORE, 1884

The first Roman Catholic bishop in the United States was appointed shortly after the Revolution. Bishop John Carroll was based in Baltimore, and he and a small number of priests ministered to a small Catholic population clustered in the middle colonies. By 1850, Catholicism had become the nation's largest single denomination, with parishes, priests, and bishops spread throughout the land. During the middle of the century, the bishops held three national meetings, or ecumenical councils, in Baltimore to develop a detailed understanding of what it meant to be an American Catholic. Each of these meetings addressed the issue of the proper education for a Catholic school child. At the third and final meeting, the bishops issued a decree that was quite unmistakable in its direction. In spite of the difficulties and financial constraints, the bishops insisted "that near every church a parish school, where one does not yet exist, is to be built and maintained in perpetuum . . ." and "that all Catholic parents should be bound to send their children to the parish school . . ." The direction was set, and the Catholic parochial school system was fully launched.

One of our first cares has been to provide for the more perfect education of aspirations to the holy Priesthood. It has always been the Church's endeavor that her clergy should be eminent in learning. For she always considered that nothing less than this is required by their sacred office of guarding and dispensing Divine truth. "The lips of the priest shall keep knowledge," says the Most High, "and the people shall seek the law at his mouth" (Malachy 2:7). This is true in all times; for no advance in secular knowledge, no diffusion of popular education, can do away with the office of the teaching ministry, which Our Lord has declared shall last forever. In every age it is and shall be the duty of God's priests to proclaim the salutary truths which our Heavenly Father has given to each generation in the way that will move their minds and hearts to embrace and love them; to defend them, when necessary, against every attack of error. From this it is obvious that the priest should have a wide acquaintance with every department of learning that has bearing on religious truth. Hence, in our age, when so many misleading theories are put forth on every side, when every department of natural truth and fact is actively explored for objections against revealed religion, it is evident how extensive and thorough should be the knowledge of the minister of the Divine Word, that he may be able to show forth worthily the beauty, the superiority, the necessity of the Christian religion, and to prove that there is nothing in all that God has made to contradict anything that God has taught.

Hence, the priest who has the noble ambition of attaining to the high level of his holy office, he may well consider himself a student all his life; and of the leisure hours which he can find amid the duties of his ministry, he will have very few that he can spare for miscellaneous reading, and none at all to waste. And hence, too, the evident duty devolving on us, to see that the course of education in our ecclesiastical colleges and seminaries be as perfect as it can be made.

Scarcely, if at all, secondary to the Church's desire for the education of the clergy, is her solicitude for the education of the laity. It is not for themselves, but for the people, that the Church wishes her clergy to be learned, as it is not for themselves only, but for the people that they are priests. Popular education has always been a chief object of the Church's care; in fact, it is not too much to say that the history of civilization and education is the history of the Church's work. In the rude ages, when semibarbarous chieftains boasted of their illiteracy, she succeeded in diffusing that love of learning which covered Europe with schools and universities; and thus, from the barbarous tribes of the early middle ages, she built up the civilized nations of modern times. Even subsequent to the religious dissensions of the sixteenth century, whatever progress has been made in education is mainly due to the impetus which she had previously given. In our own country, notwithstanding the many difficulties attendant on first beginnings and unexampled growth, we already find her schools, academics, and colleges everywhere, built and sustained by voluntary contributions, even at the cost of great sacrifices, and comparing favorably with the best educational institutions in the land.

These facts abundantly attest the Church's desire for popular instruction. The beauty of truth, the refining and elevating influences of knowledge, are meant for all, and she wishes them to be brought within the reach of all. Knowledge enlarges our capacity for self-improvement and for promoting the welfare of our fellow men; and in so noble a work the Church wishes every hand to be busy. Knowledge, too, is the best weapon against pernicious errors. It is only "a little learning" that is "a dangerous thing." In days like ours, when error is so pretentious and aggressive, every one needs to be as completely armed as possible with sound knowledge, not only the clergy, but the people also that they may be able to withstand the noxious influences of popularized irreligion.

In the great coming combat between truth and error, between Faith and Agnosticism, an important part of the fray must be borne by the laity, and woe to them if they are not well-prepared. And if, in the olden days of vassalage and serfdom, the Church honored every individual, no matter how humble his position, and labored to give him the enlightenment that would qualify him for future responsibilities, much more now, in the era of popular rights and liberties, when every individual is an active and influential factor in the body politic, does she desire that all should be fitted by suitable training for an intelligent and conscientious discharge of the important duties that will devolve upon them.

Few, if any, will deny that a sound civilization must depend upon sound popular education. But education, in order to be sound and to produce beneficial results, must develop what is best in man, and make him not only clever but good. A one-sided education will develop a one-sided life; and such a life will surely topple over, and so will every social system that is built up of such lives. True civilization requires that not only the physical and intellectual, but also the moral and religious, well-being of the people should be promoted, and at least with equal care. Take away religion from a people, and morality would soon follow; morality gone, even their physical condition will ere long degenerate into corruption which breeds decrepitude, while their intellectual attainments would only serve as a light to guide them to deeper depths of vice and ruin. This has been so often demonstrated in the history of the past, and is, in fact so self-evident, that one is amazed to find any difference of opinion about it. A civilization without religion, would be a civilization of "the struggle for existence, and the survival of the fittest," in which cunning and strength would become the substitutes for principle, virtue, conscience and duty. As a matter of fact, there never has been a civilization worthy of the name without religion; and from the facts of history the laws of human nature can easily be inferred.

Hence, education, in order to foster civilization, must foster religion. Now the three great educational agencies are the home, the Church, and the school. These mould men and shape society. Therefore, each of them, to do its part well, must foster religion. But many, unfortunately, while avowing that religion should be the light and the atmosphere of the home and of the Church, are content to see it excluded from the school, and even advocate as the best school system [that] which necessarily excludes religion.

Few surely will deny that childhood and youth are the periods of life when the character ought especially to be subjected to religious influences. Nor can we ignore the palpable fact that the school is an important factor in the forming of childhood and youth, so important that its influence often outweighs that of home and Church. It cannot, therefore, be desirable or advantageous that religion should be excluded from the school. On the contrary, it ought there to be one of the chief agencies for molding the young life to all that is true and virtuous, and holy. To shut religion out of the school, and keep it for home and the Church, is logically, to train up a generation that will consider religion good for home and the Church, but not for the practical business of real life. But a more false and pernicious notion could not be imagined. Religion, in order to elevate a people, should inspire their whole life and rule their relations with one another. A life is not dwarfed, but ennobled by being lived in the presence of God.

Therefore the school, which principally gives the knowledge fitting for practical life, ought to be preeminently under the holy influence of religion. From the shelter of home and school, the youth must soon go out into the busy way of trade or traffic or professional practice. In all these, the principles of religion should animate and direct him. But he cannot expect to learn these principles in the workshop or the office or the counting room. Therefore, let him be well and thoroughly imbued with them by the joint influences of home and school, before he is launched out on the dangerous sea of life.

All denominations of Christians are now awaking to this great truth, which the Catholic Church has never ceased to maintain. Reason and experience are forcing them to recognize that the only practical way to secure a Christian people, is to give the youth a Christian education. The avowed enemies of Christianity in some European countries are banishing religion from the schools, in order gradually to eliminate it from among the people. In this they are logical, and we may well profit by the lesson. Hence the cry for Christian education is going up from all religious bodies throughout the land. And this is no narrowness and "sectarianism" on their part; it is an honest and logical endeavor to preserve Christian truth and morality among the people by fostering religion in the young. Nor is it any antagonism to the State; on the contrary, it is an honest endeavor to give to the State better citizens, by making them better Christians. The friends of Christian education do not condemn the State for not imparting religious instruction in the public schools as they are now organized; because they well know it does not lie within the province of the State to teach religion. They simply follow their conscience by sending their children to denominational schools, where religion can have its rightful place and influence.

Two objects therefore, dear brethren, we have in view, to multiply our schools, and to perfect them. We must multiply them, till every Catholic child in the land shall have within its reach the means of education. There is still much to do ere this be attained. There are still thousands of Catholic children in the United States deprived of the benefit of a Catholic school. Pastors and parents should not rest till this defect be remedied. No parish is complete till it has schools adequate to the need of its children, and the pastor and people of such a parish should feel that they have not accomplished their entire duty until the want is supplied.

But then, we must also perfect our schools. We repudiate the idea that the Catholic school need be in any respect inferior to any other school whatsoever. And if hitherto, in some places, our people have acted on the principle that it is better to have an imperfect Catholic school than to have none, let them now push their praiseworthy ambition still further, and not relax their efforts till their schools be elevated to the highest educational excellence. And we implore parents not to hasten to take their children from school, but to give them all the time and all the advantages that they have the capacity to profit by, so that, in after life, their children may "rise up and call them blessed."

We need hardly remind you, beloved brethren, that while home life would not, as a rule, be sufficient to supply the absence of good or counteract the evil of dangerous influences in the school, it is equally true, that all that the Christian school could accomplish would be inadequate without the cooperation of the Christian home. Christian schools sow the seed, but Christian homes must first prepare the soil, and afterwards foster the seed and bring it to maturity.

Decrees of the Council—Title IV

After full consideration of these matters, we conclude and decree:

1. That near every church a parish school, where one does not yet exist, is to be built and maintained *in perpetuum* within two years of the promulgation of this council, unless the bishop should decide that because of serious difficulties a delay may be granted.
2. That all Catholic parents should be bound to send their children to the parish school, unless it is evident that a sufficient training in religion is given either in their own homes, or in other Catholic schools; or when because of sufficient reason, approved by the bishop, with all due precautions and safeguards, it is licit to send them to other schools. What constitutes a Catholic school is left to the decision of the bishop.

✦ MARY ANTIN, THE PROMISED LAND, 1912

The years between 1880 and 1920 saw a massive immigration from southern and eastern Europe to the United States. The populations in the schools—and the sheer number of children attending school, especially in the cities of the Northeast and Midwest— were radically different after the arrival of these immigrants. While Mary Antin provides a romantic version of the immigrant experience in The Promised Land *(Boston: Houghton Mifflin, 1912), her story of her own encounter with the public schools as a young Russian girl freshly arrived in Boston gives us one view of the turn-of-the-century educational experience.*

The apex of my civic pride and personal contentment was reached on the bright September morning when I entered the public school. That day I must always remember, even if I live to be so old that I cannot tell my name. To most people, their first day at school is a memorable occasion. In my case, the importance of the day was a hundred times magnified, on account of the years I had waited, the road I had come, and the conscious ambitions I had entertained.

I am wearily aware that I am speaking in extreme figures, in superlatives. I wish I knew some other way to render the mental life of the immigrant child of reasoning age. I may have been ever so much an exception in acuteness of observation, powers of comparison, and abnormal self-consciousness; none the less were my thoughts and conduct typical of the attitude of the intelligent immigrant child toward American institutions. And what the child thinks and feels is a reflection of the hopes, desires, and purposes of the parents who brought him overseas, no matter how precocious and independent the child may be. Your immigrant inspectors will tell you what poverty the foreigner bring in his baggage, what want in his pockets. Let the overgrown boy of twelve, reverently drawing his letters in the baby class, testify to the noble dreams and high ideal that may be hidden beneath the greasy caftan of the immigrant. Speaking for the Jews, at least, I know I am safe in inviting such an investigation.

Who were my companions on my first day of school? Whose hand was in mine, as I stood, overcome with awe, by the teacher's desk, and whispered my name as my father prompted? Was it Frieda's steady, capable hand? Was it her loyal heart that throbbed, beat for beat with mine, as it had done through all our childish adventures? Frieda's heart did throb that day, but not with my emotions. My heart pulsed with joy and pride and ambition; in her heart, longing fought with abnegation. For I was led to the schoolroom, with its sunshine and its singing and the teacher's cheery smile; while she was led to the workshop, with its foul air, care-lined faces, and the foreman's stern command. Our going to school was the fulfillment of our father's best promises to us, and Frieda's share in it was to fashion and fit the calico frocks in which the baby sister and I made our first appearance in a public schoolroom.

I remember to this day the gray pattern of calico, so affectionately did I regard it hung upon the wall—my consecration robe awaiting the beatific day. And Frieda, I am sure, remembers it, too, so longingly did she regard it as the crisp, starchy breadths of it slid between her fingers. But whatever were her longings, she said nothing of them; she bent over the sewing—machine humming an Old-World melody. In every straight, smooth seam, perhaps, she tucked away some lingering impulse of childhood; but she matched the scrolls and flowers with the utmost care. If a sudden shock of rebellion made her straighten up for an instant, the next instant she was bending to adjust a ruffle to the best advantage. And when the momentous day arrived, and the little sister and I stood up to be arrayed it was Frieda herself who patted and smoothed my stiff new calico, who made me turn round and round, to see that I was perfect; who stooped to pull out a basting-thread. If there was anything in her heart besides sisterly pride and love and good-will, as we parted that morning, it was a sense of loss and a woman's acquiescence to her fate; for we had been close friends, and now our ways would lie apart. Longing she felt, but no envy. She did not grudge me what she was denied. Until that morning we had been children together, but now, at the fiat of her destiny, she became a woman, with all a woman's cares; whilst I, so little younger than she, was bidden to dance at the May festival of untroubled childhood.

I wish, for my comfort, that I could say I had some notion of the difference of our lots, some sense of the injustice to her, of the indulgence to me. I wish I could even say that I gave serious thought to the matter. There had always been a distinction between us rather out of proportion to the difference in our years. Her good health and domestic instincts had made it natural for her to become my mother's right hand, in the years preceding the emigration, when there were no more servants or dependents. Then there was the family tradition that Mary was the quicker, the brighter of the two, and that hers could be no common lot. Frieda was relied upon for help, and her sister for glory. And when I failed as a milliner's apprentice, while Frieda made excellent progress at the dressmaker's, our fates, indeed, were sealed. It was understood, even before we reached Boston, that she would go to work and I to school. In view of the family prejudices, it was the inevitable course. No injustice was intended. My father sent us hand in hand to school, before he had ever thought of America. If, in America, he had been able to support his family unaided, it would have been the culmination of his best hopes to see all his children at school, with equal advantages at home. But when he had done his best, and was still unable to provide even bread and shelter for us all, he was compelled to make us children self-supporting as fast as it was practicable. There was no choosing possible; Frieda was the oldest, the strongest, the best prepared, and the only one who was of legal age to be put to work.

My father has nothing to answer for. He divided the world between his children in accordance with the laws of the country and the compulsion of his circumstances. I have no need of defending him. It is myself that I would like to defend, and I cannot. I remember that I accepted the arrangements made for my sister and me without much reflection, and everything that was planned for my advantage I took as a matter of course. I was no heartless monster, but a decidedly self-centered child. If my sister had seemed unhappy, it would have troubled me; but I am ashamed to recall that I did not consider how little it was that contented her. I was so preoccupied with my own happiness that I did not half perceive the splendid devotion of her attitude towards me, the sweetness of her joy in my good luck. She not only stood by approvingly when I was helped to everything; she cheerfully waited on me herself. And I took everything from her hand as if it were my due.

The two of us stood a moment in the doorway of the tenement house on Arlington Street, that wonderful September morning when I first went to school. It was I that ran away, on winged feet of joy and expectation; it was she whose feet were bound in the treadmill of daily toil. And I was so blind that I did not see the glory lay on her, and not on me.

Father himself conducted us to school. He would not have delegated that mission to the President of the United States. He had awaited the day with impatience equal to mine, and the visions he saw as he hurried us over the sun-flecked pavements transcended all my dreams. Almost his first act on landing on American soil, three years before, had been his application for naturalization. He had taken the remaining steps in the process with eager promptness, and at the earliest moment allowed by the law, he became a citizen of the United States. It is true that he left home in search of bread for his hungry family, but he went blessing the necessity that drove him to America. The boasted freedom of the New World meant to him far more than the right to reside, travel, and work wherever he pleased; it meant the freedom to speak his thoughts, to throw off the shackles of superstition, to test his own fate, unhindered by political or religious tyranny. He was only a young man when he landed—thirty-two; and most of his life had been held in leading-strings. He was hungry for his untasted manhood.

Three years passed in sordid struggle and disappointment. He was not prepared to make a living even in America, where the day laborer eats wheat instead of rye. Apparently the American flag could not protect him against the pursuing Nemesis of his limitations; he must expiate the sins of his fathers who slept across the seas. He had been endowed at birth with a poor constitution, a nervous, restless temperament, and an abundance of hindering prejudices. In his boyhood, his body was starved, that his mind might be stuffed with useless learning. In his youth, this dearly gotten learning was sold, and the price was the bread and salt which he had not been trained to earn for himself. Under the wedding canopy, he was bound for life to a girl whose features were still strange to him; and he was bidden to multiply himself, that sacred learning might be perpetuated in his sons, to the glory of the God of his fathers. All this while he had been led about as a creature without a will, a chattel, an instrument. In his maturity, he awoke, and found himself poor in health, poor in purse, poor in useful knowledge, and hampered on all sides. At the first nod of opportunity he broke away from his prison, and strove to atone for his wasted youth by a life of useful labor; while at the same time he sought to lighten the gloom of his narrow scholarship by freely partaking of modern ideas. But his utmost endeavor still left him far from his goal. In business, nothing prospered with him. Some fault of hand or mind or temperament led him to failure where other men found success. Wherever the blame for his disabilities be placed, he reaped their bitter fruit. "Give me bread!" he cried in America. "What will you do to earn it?" the challenge came back. And he found that he was master of no art, of no trade; because he had only the most antiquated methods of communicating it.

So in his primary quest he had failed. There was left him the compensation of intellectual freedom. That he sought to realize in every possible way. He had very little opportunity to prosecute his education, which in truth, had never been begun. His struggle for a bare living left him no time to take advantage of the public evening school; but he lost nothing of what was to be learned through reading, through attendance at public meetings, through exercising the rights of citizenship. Even here he was hindered by a natural inability to acquire the English language. In time, indeed, he learned to read, to follow a conversation or lecture; but he never learned to write correctly, and his pronunciation remains extremely foreign to this day.

If education, culture, the higher life were shining things to be worshipped from afar, he still had a means left whereby he could draw one step nearer to them. He could send his children to school, to learn all those things that he knew by fame to be desirable. The common school, at least, perhaps high school; for one or two, perhaps even college! His children should be students, should fill his house with books and intellectual company; and thus he would walk by proxy in the Elysian Fields of liberal learning. As for the children themselves, he knew no surer way of their advancement and happiness.

So it was with a heart full of longing and hope that my father led us to school on that first day. He took long strides in his eagerness, the rest of us running and hopping to keep up.

At last the four of us stood around the teacher's desk; and my father, in his impossible English, gave us over in her charge, with some broken word of his hopes for us that his swelling heart could no longer contain. I venture to say that Miss Nixon was struck by something uncommon in the group we made, something outside of Semitic features and the abashed manner of the alien. My little sister was as pretty as a doll, with her clear pink-and-white face, short golden curls, and eyes like blue violets when you caught them looking up. My brother might have been a girl, too, with his cherubic contours of face, rich red color, glossy black hair, and fine eyebrows. Whatever secret fears were in his heart, remembering his former teachers, who had taught with the rod, he stood up straight and uncringing before the American teacher, his cap respectfully doffed. Next to him stood a starved-looking girl with eyes ready to pop out, and short dark curls that would not have made much of a wig for a Jewish bride.

All three children carried themselves rather better than the common run of "green" pupils that were brought to Miss Nixon. But the figure that challenged attention to the group was the tall, straight father, with his earnest face and fine forehead, nervous hands eloquent in gesture, and a voice full of feeling. This foreigner, who brought his children to school as if it were an act of consecration, who regarded the teacher of the primer class with reverence, who spoke of visions, like a man inspired, in a common schoolroom, was not like other aliens, who brought their children in dull obedience to the law; was not like the native fathers, who brought their unmanageable boys, glad to be relieved of their care. I think Miss Nixon guessed what my father's best English could not convey. I think she divined that by the simple act of delivering our school certificates to her he took possession of America.

Initiation

It is not worthwhile to refer to voluminous school statistics to see just how many "green" pupils entered school last September, not knowing the days of the week in English, who next February will be declaiming patriotic verses in honor of George Washington and Abraham Lincoln, with a foreign accent, indeed, but with plenty of enthusiasm. It is enough to know that this hundred-fold miracle is common to the schools in every part of the United States where immigrants are received. And if I was one of Chelsea's hundred in 1894, it was only to be expected, since I was one of the older of the "green" children, and had had a start in my irregular schooling in Russia, and was carried along by a tremendous desire to learn, and had my family to cheer me on.

I was not a bit too large for my little chair and desk in the baby class, but my mind, of course, was too mature by six or seven years for the work. So as soon as I could understand what the teacher said in class, I was advanced to the second grade. This was within a week after Miss Nixon took me in hand. But I do not mean to give my dear teacher all the credit for my rapid progress, nor even half the credit. I shall divide it with her on behalf of my race and family. I was Jew enough to have an aptitude for language in general, and to bend my mind earnestly to the task; I was Antin enough to read each lesson with my heart, which gave me an inkling of what was coming next, and so carried me along by leaps and bounds. As for the teacher, she could best explain what theory she followed in teaching us foreigners to read. I can only describe the method, which was so simple that I wish holiness could be taught in the same way.

There were about half a dozen of us beginners in English, in age from six to fifteen. Miss Nixon made a special class of us, and aided us so skillfully and earnestly in our endeavors to "see-a-cat," and "hear-a-dog-bark," and "look-at-the-hen," that we turned over page after page of ravishing history, eager to find out how the common world looked, smelled, and tasted in the strange speech. The teacher knew just when to let us help each other out with a word in our own tongue—it happened that we were all Jews—and so, working all together, we actually covered more ground in a lesson than the native classes, composed entirely of little tots.

But we stuck—stuck fast—at the definite article; and sometimes the lesson resolved itself into a species of lingual gymnastics, in which we all looked as if we meant to bite our tongues off. Miss Nixon was pretty, and she must have looked well with her white teeth showing in the act; but at the time I was too solemnly occupied to admire her looks. I did take great pleasure in her smile of approval, whenever I pronounced well; and her patience and perseverance in struggling with us over that thick little word are becoming to her even now, after fifteen years. It is not her fault if any of us to-day give a buzzing sound to the dreadful English *th*.

I shall never have a better opportunity to make public declaration of my love for the English language. I am glad that American history runs, chapter for chapter, the way it does; for thus America came to be the country I love so dearly. I am glad, most of all, that Americans began by being Englishmen, for thus did I come to inherit this beautiful language in which I think. It seems to me that in any other language happiness is not so sweet, logic is not so clear. I am not sure that I could believe in my neighbors as I do if I thought about them in un-English words. I could almost say that my conviction of immortality is bound up with the English of its promise. And as I am attached to my prejudices, I must love the English language!

Whenever the teachers did anything special to help me over my private difficulties, my gratitude went out to them, silently. It meant so much to me that they halted the lesson to give me a lift, that I needs must love them for it. Dear Miss Carrol of the second grade, would be amazed to hear what small things I remember, all because I was so impressed at the time with her readiness and sweetness in taking notice of my difficulties.

Says Miss Carrol, looking straight at me:

"If Johnnie has three marbles, and Charlie has twice as many, how many marbles has Charlie?"

I raise my hand for permission to speak.

"Teacher, I don't know vhat is tvice?"

Teacher beckons me to her, and whispers to me the meaning of the strange word, and I am able to write the sum correctly. It's all in the day's work with her; with me, it is a special act of kindness and efficiency.

She whom I found in the next grade became so dear a friend that I can hardly name her with the rest, though I mention none of them lightly. Her approval was always dear to me, first because she was "Teacher," and afterwards, as long as she lived, because she was my Miss Dillingham. Great was my grief, therefore, when, shortly after my admission to her class, I incurred discipline, the first, and next to the last, time in my school career.

The class was repeating in chorus the Lord's Prayer, heads bowed on desks. I was doing my best to keep up by the sound; my mind could not go beyond the word "hallowed," for which I had not found the meaning. In the middle of this prayer, a Jewish boy across the aisle trod on my foot to get my attention. "You must not say that," he admonished in a solemn whisper; "It's Christian." I whispered back that it wasn't, and went on to the "Amen." I did not know but what he was right, but the name of Christ was not in the prayer, and I was bound to do everything that the class did. If I had any Jewish scruples, they were lagging away behind my interest in school affairs. How American this was: two pupils side by side in the schoolroom, each holding to his own opinion, but both submitting to the common law; for the boy at least bowed his head as the teacher ordered.

But all Miss Dillingham knew of it was that two of her pupils whispered during morning prayer, and she must discipline them. So I was degraded from the honor row to the lowest row, and it was many a day before I forgave that young missionary; it was not enough for my vengeance that he suffered punishment with me. Teacher, of course, heard us both defend ourselves, but there was a time and a place for religious arguments, and she meant to help us remember that point.

I remember to this day what a struggle we had over the word "water," Miss Dillingham and I. It seemed as if I could not give the sound of *w:* I said "vater" every time. Patiently my teacher worked with me, inventing mouth exercises for me, to get my stubborn lips to produce that *w;* and when at last I could say "village" and "water" in rapid alteration, without misplacing the two initials, that memorable word was sweet on my lips. For we had conquered, and Teacher was pleased.

Getting a language in this way, word by word, has a charm that may be set against the disadvantages. It is like gathering a posy blossom by blossom. Bring the bouquet into your chamber, and these nasturtiums stand for the whole flaming carnival of them tumbling over the fence out there; these yellow pansies recall the velvet crescent of color glowing under the bay window; this spray of honeysuckle smells like the wind-tossed masses of it on the porch, ripe and bee-laden; the whole garden in a glass tumbler. So it was with one who gathers words, loving them. Particular words remain associated with important occasions in the learner's mind. I could thus write a history of my English vocabulary that should be at the same time an account of my comings and goings, my mistakes and my triumphs, during the years of my initiation.

If I was eager and diligent, my teachers did not sleep. As fast as my knowledge of English allowed, they advanced me from grade to grade, without reference to the usual schedule of promotions. My father was right, when he often said, in discussing my prospects, that ability would be promptly recognized in the public schools. Rapid as was my progress, on account of the advantages with which I started, some of the other "green" pupils were not far behind me; within a grade or two, by the end of the year. My brother, whose childhood had been one hideous nightmare, what with the stupid *rebbe* [rabbi], the cruel whip, and the general repression of life in the pale, surprised my father by the progress he made under intelligent, sympathetic guidance. Indeed, he soon had a reputation in the school that the American boys envied; and all through the school course he more than held his own with pupils his own age. So much for the right and wrong way of doing things.

There is a record of my early progress in English much better than my recollections, however accurate and definite these may be. I have several reasons for introducing it here. First, it shows what the Russian Jew can do with an adopted language; next, it proves that vigilance of our public school teachers of which I spoke; and last, I am proud of it! That is an unnecessary confession, but I could not be satisfied to insert it into the record here, with my vanity unavowed.

This is a document, copied from an educational journal, a tattered copy of which lies in my lap as I write—treasured for fifteen years, you see, by my vanity.

Editor, Primary Education:

This is the uncorrected paper of a Russian child twelve years old, who studied English only four months. She had never, until September, been to school even in her own country and has learned English spoken *only* at school. I shall be glad if the paper of my pupil and the above explanation may appear in your paper.

M.S. Dillingham
Chelsea, Mass.

Snow

Snow is frozen moisture which comes from the clouds. Now the snow is coming down in feather-flakes, which makes nice snow-balls. But there is still one kind of snow more. This kind of snow is called snow-crystals, for it comes down in little curly balls. These snow-crystals aren't quite as good for snow-balls as the feather-flakes, for they (the snow-crystals) are dry: so they can't keep together as feather-flakes do.

The snow is dear to some children for they like sleighing.

As I said at the top—the snow comes from the clouds.

Now the trees are bare, and no flowers are to see in the fields and gardens (we all know why), and the whole world seems like asleep without the happy bird songs which left us till spring. But the snow which drove away all these pretty and happy things, try, (as I think) not to make us at all unhappy; they covered up the branches of the trees, the fields, the gardens and houses, and the whole world looks like dressed in a beautiful white—instead of green—dress, with the sky looking down on it with a pale face.

And so the people can find some joy in it, too, without the happy summer.

Mary Antin

And now that it stands there, with *her* name over it, I am ashamed of my flippant talk about vanity. More to me than all the praise I could hope to win by the conquest of fifty languages is the association of this dear friend with my earliest efforts at writing; and it pleases me to remember that to her I owe my very first appearance in print. Vanity is the least part of it, when I remember how she called me to her desk, one day after school was out, and showed me my composition—my own words, that I had written out of my own head—printed out, clear black and white, with my name at the end! Nothing so wonderful had ever happened to me before. My whole consciousness was suddenly transformed. I suppose that was the moment when I became a writer. I always loved to write—I wrote letters whenever I had an excuse—yet it never occurred to me to sit down and write my thoughts for no person in particular, merely to put the word on paper. But now, as I read my own words, in a delicious confusion, the idea was born. I stared at my name: *Mary Antin.* Was that really I? The printed characters composing it seemed strange to me all of a sudden. If that was my name, and those were the words out of my own head, what relation did it all have to *me,* who was alone there with Miss Dillingham, and the printed page between us? Why, it meant that I could write again, and see my writing printed for people to read! I could write many, many, many things: I could write a book! The idea was so huge, so bewildering, that my mind scarcely could accommodate it.

I do not know what my teacher said to me; probably very little. It was her way to say only a little, and look at me, and trust me to understand. Once she had occasion to lecture me about living a shut-up life; she wanted me to go outdoors. I had been repeatedly scolded and reproved on that score by other people, but I had only laughed, saying that I was too happy to change my ways. But when Miss Dillingham spoke to me, I saw that it was a serious matter; and yet she only said a few words, and looked at me with that smile of hers that was only half a smile, and the rest a meaning. Another time she had a great question to ask me, touching my life to the quick. She merely put her question, and was silent; but I knew what answer she expected, and not being able to give it then, I went away sad and reproved. Years later I had my triumphant answer, but she was no longer there to receive it; and so her eyes look at me, from the picture on the mantel there, with a reproach I no longer merit.

I ought to go back and strike out all that talk about vanity. What reason have I to be vain, when I reflect how at every step I was petted, nursed, and encouraged? I did not even discover my own talent. It was discovered first by my father in Russia, and next by my friend in America. What did I ever do but write when they told me to write? I suppose my grandfather, who drove a spavined horse through the lonely country lanes, sat in the shade of crisp-leaved oaks to refresh himself with a bit of black bread; and an acorn falling beside him, in the immense stillness, shook his head with the echo, and left him wondering. I suppose my father stole away from the synagogue one long festival day, and stretched himself out in the sun-warmed grass, and lost himself in dreams that made the world of men unreal when he returned to them. And so what is there left for me to do, who do not have to drive a horse nor interpret ancient lore, but put my grandfather's question into words and set to music my father's dream? The tongue am I of those who lived before me, as those that are to come will be the voice of my unspoken thoughts. And so who shall be applauded if the song be sweet, if the prophecy be true?

I never heard of any one who was so watched and coaxed, so passed along from hand to helping hand, as was I. I always had friends. They sprang up everywhere, as if they stood waiting for me to come. Here was my teacher, the moment she saw that I could give a good paraphrase of her talk on "Snow," bent on finding out what more I could do. One day she asked me if I had ever written poetry. I had not, but I went home and tried. I believe it was more snow, and I know it was wretched. I wish I could produce a copy of that early effusion; it would prove that my judgement is not severe. Wretched it was—worse, a great deal, than reams of poetry that is written by children about whom there is no fuss made. But Miss Dillingham was not discouraged. She saw that I had no idea of metre, so she proceeded to teach me. We repeated miles of poetry together, smooth lines that sang themselves, mostly out of Longfellow. Then I would go home and write—oh, about the snow in our back yard!—but when Miss Dillingham came to read my verses, they limped and they lagged and they dragged, and there was no tune that would fit them.

At last came the moment of illumination: I saw where my trouble lay. I had supposed that my lines matched when they had an equal number of syllables, taking no account of accent. Now I knew better; now I could write poetry! The everlasting snow melted at last, and the mud puddles dried in the spring sun, and the grass on the common was green, and I still wrote poetry! Again I wish I had some example of my springtime rhapsodies, the veriest rubbish of the sort that ever a child perpetrated. Lizzie McDee, who had red hair and freckles, and a Sunday-school manner on weekdays, and was below me in the class, did a great deal better. We used to compare verses; and while I do not remember that I ever had the grace to own that she was the better poet, I do know that I secretly wondered why the teachers did not invite her to stay after school and study poetry, while they took so much pains with me. But so it was always with me: somebody did something for me all the time.

→ LEWIS MERIAM, THE PROBLEM OF INDIAN ADMINISTRATION, 1928

Throughout the seventeenth, eighteenth, and nineteenth centuries, educators and mis-sionaries had sought to bring European-style schooling to the Indians. Beginning in 1875, many within the federal government advocated a shift in policy, removing Indians from their familiar surroundings to boarding schools far removed from tribe, family, and friends so that the process of acculturating them into a European-American lifestyle and learning system would be more effective. In 1928, after a half-century of boarding schools and three centuries of other forms of schooling, Lewis Meriam was asked by the U.S. Department of the Interior to examine the education of Indians, and especially the role of the federal government in that effort. His report is devastating, but also very informative. The "Meriam Report," as it came to be known, represented a turning point of sorts and the beginning of a slow reorganization of federal priorities in Indian education.

The work of the government directed toward the education and advancement of the Indian himself, as distinguished from the control and conservation of his property, is largely ineffective. The chief explanation of the deficiency in this work lies in the fact that the government has not appropriated enough funds to permit the Indian Service to employ an adequate personnel properly qualified for the task before it.

Absence of Well-Considered, Broad Education Program

The outstanding evidence of the lack of an adequate, well-trained personnel is the absence of any well-considered, broad educational program for the Service as a whole. Here the word *education* is used in its widest sense and includes not only school train-ing of adults to aid them in adjusting themselves to the dominant social and economic life which confronts them, but it also embraces education in economic production and in living standards necessary for the maintenance of health and decency.

Formal Education of Indian Children

For several years, the general policy of the Indian Service has been directed away from the boarding school for Indian children and toward the public schools and Indian day schools. More Indian children are now in public schools maintained by the state or local governments than in special Indian schools maintained by the nation. It is, however, still the fact that the boarding school, either reservation or nonreservation, is the dom-inant characteristic of the school system maintained by the national government for its Indian wards.

The survey staff finds itself obliged to say frankly and unequivocally that the pro-visions for the care of the Indian children in boarding schools are grossly inadequate.

The outstanding deficiency is in the diet furnished the Indian children, many of whom are below normal health. The diet is deficient in quantity, quality, and variety. The effort has been made to feed the children on a per capita of eleven cents a day, plus what can be produced on the school farm, including the dairy. At a few, very few, schools, the farm and the dairy are sufficiently productive to be a highly important fac-tor in raising the standard of the diet, but even at the best schools these sources do not fully meet the requirements for the health and development of the children. At the worst schools, the situation is serious in the extreme. The major diseases of the Indians are tuberculosis and trachoma. Tuberculosis unquestionably can be best combated by a preventive, curative diet and proper living conditions, and a considerable amount of evidence suggests that the same may prove true of trachoma. The great protective foods are milk and fruit and vegetables, particularly fresh green vegetables. The diet of the Indian children in boarding schools is generally notably lacking in these preventive foods. Although the Indian Service has established a quart of milk a day per pupil as the standard, it has been able to achieve this standard in very few schools. At the special school for children suffering from trachoma, now in question at Fort Defiance, Arizona, milk is not part of the normal diet. The little produced is mainly consumed in the hospital, where children acutely ill are sent. It may be seriously questioned whether the Indian Service could do very much better than it does without more adequate appropriations.

Next to dietary deficiencies comes overcrowding in dormitories. The boarding schools are crowded materially beyond their capacities. A device frequently resorted to in an effort to increase dormitory capacity without great expense is the addition of large sleeping porches. They are in themselves reasonably satisfactory, but they shut off light and air from the inside rooms, which are still filled with beds beyond their capacity. The toilet facilities have in many cases not been increased proportionately to the increase in pupils, and they are fairly frequently not properly maintained or conveniently located. The supply of soap and towels has been inadequate.

The medical service rendered the boarding school children is not up to a reasonable standard. Physical examinations are often superficial and enough provision is not made for the correction of remediable defects.

The boarding schools are frankly supported in part by the labor of the students. Those above the fourth grade ordinarily work for half a day and go to school for half a day. A distinction in theory is drawn between industrial work undertaken primarily for the education of the child and production work done primarily for the support of the institution. However, teachers of industrial work undertaken ostensibly for education say that much of it is, as a matter of fact, production work for the maintenance of the school. The question may very properly be raised as to whether much of the work of Indian children in boarding schools would not be prohibited in many states by the child labor laws, notably the work in the machine laundries. At several schools, the laundry equipment is antiquated and not properly safe-guarded. To operate on a half-work, half-study plan makes the day very long, and the child has almost no free time and little opportunity for recreation. Not enough consideration has been given the question of whether the health of the Indian children warrants the nation in supporting the Indian boarding schools in part through the labor of these children.

The medical attention given Indian children in the day schools maintained by the government is also below a reasonable standard.

In securing teachers for the government schools, and in recruiting other employees for the boarding schools, the Indian service is handicapped by low salaries and must accordingly adopt low standards for entrance. Although some of the nonreservation schools purport to be high schools, the qualifications of their teaching force do not entitle them to free and unrestricted recognition as accredited high schools. At best, they have been able to secure limited recognition from local universities. The teaching, taken as a whole, is not up to the standards set by reasonably progressive white communities.

Some years ago, in an effort to raise standards, the Indian Service adopted a uniform curriculum for all Indian schools. Modern experience has demonstrated that the effective device for raising standards is not curriculum control, but the establishment of high minimum qualifications for the teaching staff. The uniform curriculum works badly because it does not permit of relating teaching to the needs of the particular Indian children being taught. It requires the same work for Indian children who are the first generation to attend school and who do not speak English as it does for those who are of the third generation of school children, who have long been in contact with the whites, and speak English in the home.

The discipline in the boarding schools is restrictive rather than developmental. Routine institutionalism is almost the invariable characteristic of the Indian boarding school.

Although the problem of the returned Indian student has been much discussed, and it is recognized that in many instances the child returns to his home poorly adjusted to conditions that confront him, the Indian Service has lacked the funds to attempt to aid the children when they leave school either to find employment away from the reservation or to return to their homes and work out their salvation there. Having done almost no work of this kind, it has not subjected its schools to the test of having to show how far they have actually fitted the Indian children for life. Such a test would undoubtedly have resulted in a radical revision of the industrial training offered in the schools. Several of the industries taught may be called vanishing trades, and others are taught in such a way that the Indian students cannot apply what they have learned in their own homes, and they are not far enough advanced to follow their trades in a white community in competition with white workers without a period of apprenticeship. No adequate arrangements have been made to secure for them the opportunity of apprenticeship.

School System

The first and foremost need in Indian education is a change in point of view. Whatever may have been the official governmental attitude, education for the Indian in the past has proceeded largely on the theory that it is necessary to remove the Indian child as far as possible from his home environment; whereas the modern point of view in education and social work lays stress on upbringing in the natural setting of home and family life. The Indian educational enterprise is peculiarly in need of the kind of approach that recognizes this principle; that is less concerned with a conventional school system and more with the understanding of human beings.

The methods must be adopted to individual abilities, interests, and needs. Indian tribes and individual Indians within the tribes vary so greatly that a standard content and method of education, no matter how carefully they might be prepared, would be worse than futile.

Routinization must be eliminated. The whole machinery of routinized boarding school and agency life works against that development of initiative and independence which should be the chief concern of Indian education in and out of school. The routinization characteristic of the boarding schools, with everything scheduled, no time left to be used at the child's own initiative, every moment determined by a signal or an order, leads just the other way.

For the effort to bring Indian children schools up to standard by prescribing from Washington a uniform course of study for all Indian schools and by sending out from

Washington uniform examination questions must be substituted the only method of fixing standards that has been found effective in other school systems, namely, that of establishing reasonably high minimum standards for entrance into positions in the Indian school system. Only thus can the Service get first-class teachers and supervisors who are competent to adapt the educational system to the needs of the pupils they are to teach, with due consideration of the economic and social conditions of the Indians in their jurisdiction and of the nature and abilities of the individual child.

The curriculum must not be uniform and standardized. The text books must not be prescribed. The teacher must be free to gather material from the life of the Indians about her, so that the little children may proceed from the known to the unknown and not be plunged at once into a world where all is unknown and unfamiliar. The little desert Indian in an early grade who is required to read in English from a standard school teacher about the ship that sails the sea has no mental background to understand what it is all about and the task of the teacher is rendered almost impossible. The material, particularly the early material, must come from local Indian life, or at least be within the scope of the child's experience.

To get teachers and school supervisors who are competent to fit the school to the needs of the children, the Indian Service must raise its entrance requirements and increase its salary scale . . . The Indian schools, as a matter of fact, require better teachers than do the city school systems for white children. The teacher in the Indian schools has the harder task and cannot secure so much assistance from supervisory officers.

The objection to the heavy assignments of purely productive labor must not be construed as a recommendation against industrial education. On the contrary, it is specifically recommended that the industrial education be materially improved. The industrial teachers must be free to plan the industrial teaching from the educational standpoint, largely unhampered by the demands for production to support the schools or the Service. The work must be an educational enterprise, not a production enterprise. The persons selected for industrial teachers must be chosen because of their capacity to teach and not because of their capacity to do the work themselves with the aid of the pupils as helpers. The industries taught must be selected not because they supply the needs of the institution, but because they train the pupil for work which he may get at home on the reservation or in some white community to which there is some possibility of his going.

The industrial training must be subjected to the tests of practical use. The Indian Service must attempt to place the Indians who leave the school and help them to become established in productive enterprise either on the reservation or in white communities. It must be prepared to enter into cooperative arrangements with employers so that boys and girls shall have opportunity to gain experience in commercial employment while still having some official connection with the school. In this way, the school can place its emphasis on helping the pupil acquire the necessary fundamental skills and then getting him a job which there is a local demand. The schools cannot train for all occupations, but they can aid the boy or girl in acquiring those types of skills that are common to many occupations. The Service should make a survey of the economic opportunities for its pupils and plan its industrial training to meet these ends.

In the discussion of health, it has been recommended that the over-crowding of boarding schools be corrected through the maximum possible elimination of young children from these schools. From the educational standpoint, the young child does not belong in a boarding school. For normal, healthy development, he needs his family, and his family needs him. Young children, at least up to the sixth grade, should normally be provided for either in Indian Service day schools or in public schools. Not until they have reached adolescence and finished the local schools should they normally be sent to a boarding school.

Because of the nature of the Indian country, the boarding school will for many years to come be essential to provide secondary education of a type adapted to the needs of Indian youth. It can stress provision for their special needs in a way that the typical high school designed for white children already adjusted to the prevailing economic and social system could not do. It must emphasize training in health, in family, and in community life, in productive efficiency, and in the management and use of property and income to a degree probably unnecessary in general public schools.

Although the boarding school must be distinctive in the emphasis on the special needs of the Indians, it should not be so distinctive that it will not dovetail into the general educational system of the country. The promising Indian boy or girl who has attended an Indian boarding school and who desires to go on with his education should not encounter any educational barrier because of the limitations of the Indian boarding schools. The faculties and their courses of study should be such that they can meet the standards set for accredited high schools. It may prove necessary for the Indian youth who wishes to go on to higher institutions to spend a little longer time in the boarding school than he would have spent in an accredited high school, but the way should exist and should be plainly marked.

The Indian Service should encourage promising Indian youths to continue their education beyond the boarding schools and to fit themselves for professional, scientific, and technical callings. Not only should the educational facilities of the boarding schools provide definitely for fitting them for college entrance, but the Service should aid them in meeting the costs.

The present policy of placing Indian children in public schools near their homes instead of in boarding schools or even in Indian Service day schools is, on the whole, to be commended. It is a movement in the direction of the normal transition, it results, as a rule, in good race contacts, and the Indians like it. The fact must be recognized, however, that often Indian children and Indian families need more service than is ordinarily rendered by public schools, as has been elaborated in the discussion of boarding schools. The Indian Service must, therefore, supplement the public school work by giving special attention to health, industrial, and social training, and the relationship between home and school. The transition must not be pushed too fast. The public schools must be really ready to receive the Indians, and for some years the government must exercise some supervision to see that the Indian children are really getting the advantage offered by the public school system. The policy of having a federal employee perform the duties of attendance officer is sound, but more emphasis should be placed on work with families in this connection, in an effort not so much to force attendance as to remove the causes of nonattendance.

The Indian day schools should be increased in number and improved in quality and should carry children at least through the sixth grade. The Hopi day schools are perhaps the most encouraging feature of the Indian school system. More can perhaps be done in providing transportation to day schools. Where Indians come in to camp near the day schools, special activities should be undertaken for them. In general, the day schools should be made community centers for reaching adult Indians in the vicinity as well as children, and they should be tied into the whole program adopted for the jurisdiction.

✦ THE ASIAN EXPERIENCE IN CALIFORNIA, 1919-1920

The state of California has long been the main point of entry for Asians coming to the United States, and for most of its first century as a state it offered a fairly inhospitable welcome. Efforts at Chinese exclusion date from the middle of the nineteenth century. As the material included in this 1919 report issued by the state of California indicates, by the beginning of the twentieth century, efforts were also underway to limit Japanese immigration. The report, titled California and the Oriental: Japanese, Chinese, and Hindus *is interesting for the three perspectives offered. The opening letter from the Governor of California to the Secretary of State clearly rejects Japanese immigration. The study conducted under the Governor's auspices is critical, but less hostile. And finally, attached to the study is a petition from the Japanese Association to President Woodrow Wilson, asserting their right to be full citizens in the state and students in the schools of California. The contrasting perspectives could not be starker.*

Sacramento, June 19, 1920

State of California, Governor's Office
Hon. Bainbridge Colby
Secretary of State, Washington, D.C.

Sir:

I have the honor to transmit herewith the official report prepared and filed with me by the State Board of Control of California on the subject of Oriental immigration, population, and land ownership.

The subject is one of such transcendent importance to the people of California, and is so potential with future difficulties between the United States of America and the Oriental countries, that I deem it my duty in forwarding the report to outline in brief the history of the development of the Japanese problem in California, together with the legislation already enacted and that now pending. In doing so I trust I may be able clearly to lay before you the necessity of action by our Federal Government in the attainment of a permanent solution of this matter.

While the report deals with the problem as an entire Asiatic one, the present acute situation is occasioned specifically by the increase in population and land ownership of the Japanese. Forty years ago the California race problem was essentially a Chinese problem. At that time our Japanese population was negligible. The Chinese immigrants, however, were arriving in such numbers that the people of the entire Pacific slope became alarmed at a threatened inundation of our white civilization by this Oriental influx.

Popular feeling developed to such a pitch that many unfortunate incidents occurred of grave wrong done to individual Chinese as the result of mob and other illegal violence. Our country became awakened at the growing danger, and Congress passed the Chinese Exclusion Act, providing for the exclusion of all Chinese laborers and the registration of all Chinese at the time lawfully within the country. The statute was sufficiently comprehensive effectively to exclude further Chinese immigration and to make difficult, if not impossible, the evasion of the spirit of the act. As a result of this enactment, there has been a substantial reduction in the Chinese population of California.

Let me repeat that in submitting this report and transmitting this letter with its recommendations, the people of California only desire to retain the commonwealth of California for its own people; they recognize the impossibility of that peace-producing assimilability which comes only when races are so closely akin that intermarriage within a generation or two obliterates original lines. The thought of such a relationship is impossible to the people of California, just as the thought of intermarriage of whites and blacks would be impossible to the minds of the leaders of both races in the southern states; just as the intermarriage of any immigrant African would not be considered by the people of the Eastern States.

California is making this appeal primarily, of course, for herself, but in doing so she feels that the problem is hers solely because of her geographical position on the Pacific slope. She stands as one of the gateways for Oriental immigration to this country. Her people are the first affected, and unless the race ideals and standards are preserved here at the national gateway, the conditions that will follow must soon affect the rest of the continent.

I trust that I have clearly presented the California point of view, and that in any correspondence or negotiations with Japan which may ensue as the result of the accompanying report, or any action which the people of the State of California may take thereon, you will understand that it is based entirely on the principle of race self-preservation and the ethnological impossibility of successfully assimilating this constantly increasing flow of Oriental blood.

I have the honor to remain,

Yours very respectfully,
Wm. D. Stephens

Governor of California

Schools

Orientals attend the American public schools. In fact, until 1921, in some of the districts, the Japanese constituted the major part of the attendance, whites and Japanese attending the same schools together. The legislature of 1921, however, provided for separate schools for orientals as follows: "The governing body of the school district shall have power . . . to establish separate schools for Indian children and for children of Chinese, Japanese, or Mongolian parentage. When such separate schools are established, Indian children or children of Chinese, Japanese, or Mongolian parentage must not be admitted into any other school."

Japanese Language Schools

The Japanese, besides attending the American public schools, thereby acquiring the English language and a knowledge of American customs, in many districts, also attend private Japanese schools conducted in the Japanese language in which are taught the language, laws, customs, history, and religion of Japan. How many there are at present of these Japanese language schools was not ascertained definitely. In a report submitted October 17, 1921, to the Superintendent of Public Instruction by the secretary of the Japanese Association of America, there was listed forty "Japanese Language Institutes" in northern and central California and fourteen in southern California. However, in a memorial address, prepared by the Japanese Association of America (in California), to the President of the United States, on the occasion of his visit to California in 1919, the Japanese Association stated that there were in California seventy-five such Japanese language schools, which they designate as "supplementary" schools.

While the Japanese schools are said by the Japanese to be primarily for the study of the Japanese language, and not intended to perpetuate the traditions and moral concepts of Japan, nevertheless, when an attempt was made in the Territorial Legislature of Hawaii to require teachers in these Japanese language schools to qualify for a certificate to teach, by passing an examination in the English language, American history, and American civics, the measure introduced in the legislature for this purpose was strongly opposed by Japanese educators and editors on the ground that it would force Japanese schools in that territory to close. This opposition defeated the bill. . . .

On June 3, 1921, Governor William D. Stephens signed Assembly Bill Number 836, which added section one thousand five hundred thirty-four to the Political Code. This section, based on the Hawaiian law for the regulation of foreign language schools, provides that:

1. No person shall conduct or teach in a private school, conducted in the language of a foreign nation, without first obtaining a permit to do so from the superintendent of public instruction.
2. Each applicant shall be examined as to his knowledge of American history and institutions and his ability to read, write and speak the English language. The latter provision, however, is to be liberally construed up to the first of July, 1923.
3. Before issuing a permit, the superintendent of public instruction shall require the applicant to file an affidavit pledging himself to abide by the requirements of the law, the regulations of the superintendent of public instruction, and to so direct the minds of the pupils as will tend to make them good and loyal American citizens.
4. No such private school shall be conducted in the morning before school hours, during the hours the public schools are in session, nor for a longer period each day than one hour, nor more than six hours per week, nor more than thirty-eight weeks per year. Pupils over the age of seventeen, who are not required to attend the public schools, are exempt from these provisions.
5. The superintendent of public instruction shall have full supervision of courses of study and the textbooks used.
6. Each school shall be open to the inspection of the superintendent of public instruction, who shall have power to revoke the permit granted and discontinue the school if it has not complied with the law.
7. Failure to comply with the law shall be a misdemeanor punishable by a fine of not less than twenty-five dollars, which fine shall be paid into the unapportioned school fund of the county in which the school is located.
8. The superintendent of public instruction shall be empowered to appoint city and county superintendents of schools to act as deputies without pay to investigate such schools.
9. Applicants are required to pay a fee of two dollars.

In conformity with this law, which became effective July 30, 1921, applications from two hundred eighteen Japanese, seventy-seven Chinese, one Korean, three Americans, and two Germans had been received up to October 22, 1921.

Examinations have been held at Sacramento, Stockton, San Francisco, and Los Angeles. Each applicant was permitted to answer in English or his native language. While many of the applicants have shown an excellent understanding of the subject matter, the greater number have most definitely exposed the result of being crammed for the examinations. Although the standard set was that of an eighth grade pupil, many were unable to pass satisfactory examinations.

Japanese Home Influence Nullifies American School Teachings

It seems apparent that the teachings of the American public schools do not offset the Japanese home influence, for, after years of residence in California, the Japanese still continue to congregate in racial groups, speak the Japanese language among themselves, and adhere to the customs of the mother country. There is little evidence of their assimilation. Dr. Sidney L. Gulick, author of numerous books and articles on the Japanese question, lecturer in the Imperial University of Japan, and who is by no means unfriendly to the Japanese, has expressed this very aptly in his book, *The American-Japanese Problem,* in which, addressing himself to the subject as it relates to the teaching of Japanese children in the schools of Hawaii, he writes as follows:

> It is not to be assumed that the education they (Japanese children) receive in the public schools, which they leave at fourteen or fifteen years of age, is adequate to prepare them for citizenship during the six or seven years after they get out from under the influence of their American teachers. Most of the boys will be isolated from English-speaking Americans; they will be associated chiefly with men of their own race, imbibing, therefore, the Oriental ideas as they approach manhood. The mere fact, accordingly, of American birth, public school education, and the requisite age should not be regarded as adequate qualification for the suffrage; for it is to be remembered that during the entire period of schooling, not only have they been in Oriental homes, but the Japanese at heart have been diligently drilled in Japanese schools by Japanese teachers, many of whom have little acquaintance and no sympathy with American institutions or a Christian civilization.
>
> If, as Asiatics, they maintain their traditional conceptions of God, nature, and men, of male and female, of husband and wife, of parent and child, of ruler and ruled, of the state and the individual, the permanent maintenance in Hawaii of American democracy, American homes, and American liberty is impossible.

Concerning the Japanese language schools in California, the Japanese Association of America, in the memorial to the President, above-mentioned, has the following to say:

> Aside from the schools for instructing Japanese in English there are seventy-five so-called 'supplementary' schools for teaching children the Japanese language. These are attended by the Japanese pupils after the public schools close for the day. These are primarily for the study of the Japanese language and are not intended to perpetuate the traditions and moral concepts of Japan. Of course, these are criticised by hostile Americans. But says Professor Millis, "They are supplementary schools, and at the worst, there is much less in them to be adversely criticised than in the

parochial schools attended by so many children of the South and European immigrants. No real problem is yet evident connected with Japanese children on American soil."

A Response

Memorial Presented to the President While at San Francisco on September 18, 1919 from The Japanese Association of America, No. 444 Bush Street, San Francisco, California

Honorable Woodrow Wilson
President of the United States of America,
San Francisco, California

Mr. President: The Japanese Association of America, on behalf of resident Japanese in the State of California, extends greetings to you and begs to add its voice of welcome to that of the great state which you now honor by your presence. It sincerely hopes that the noble task in which you are now engaged may be fully realized, and that world peace and happiness may be the ultimate rewards of the labors for humanity to which your great efforts are devoted.

The Japanese people of this state, trusting implicitly in the lofty spirit of justice and fair dealing which have characterized your every public act and expression, take advantage of your presence in California to lay before you a few facts and figures bearing upon their relations to the community in which they reside, and they venture to ask for them your respectful and disinterested consideration.

The cry against our people may be historically traced as far back as 1887, when there were no more than 400 Japanese in the entire state. The so-called Japanese question did not, however, assume an acute character until 1906, when the school question arose. Unfortunately that question was settled by the politicians and not determined upon its true merits. At any rate, ever since that date, the Japanese "question" has become an issue of a most complicated nature—political, economic, racial, diplomatic—always resulting in the suffering of the Japanese residents. A few of the more familiar cases might be mentioned. The "Gentlemen's Agreement," under the workings of which America prohibits Japanese immigration, has been so strictly administered by the Japanese government that there has been no immigration from Japan. The alien land law of this state, enacted in 1913, prohibits Japanese ownership of land and limits the terms of lease to three years.

This limitation strikes at the very foundations of farming so far as the Japanese are concerned, and the limitation is substantially interfering with all Japanese agricultural enterprises. Not satisfied with these annoying measures, innumerable anti-Japanese bills were introduced at the last session of the State Legislature. One of those proposed to deprive the Japanese of the right to lease land while another proposed to segregate Japanese children in the public schools.

These facts, not to mention others, have tended to strain the historic friendly relations between the United States and Japan. We regret the situation. However, the Japanese residents, on the whole, have so far entertained the faith that the American Government would eventually protect them and render them justice and peace. A great deal of anxiety has, in the meantime, been experienced by them. This is but natural, and this unrest has been reflected across the ocean. Some of us who feel that we are better acquainted with the situation, have taken the position that our best course must come from education and we have been doing our utmost in what we characterize as an "Americanization campaign." We point out to our fellow-countrymen the better elements in American civilization, urging them to strive for their own improvement and better fit themselves for American life, hoping thereby to be relieved of the anxiety created and reinforced by the constant agitation against them. Our Americanization campaign will prove fruitless unless backed by true sympathy on the part of Americans. We regret to say that even to these efforts on our part there has been given but little response or sympathy.

May we not then appeal to you, Mr. President, and ask your powerful aid in so adjusting our condition on this coast that we may engage in legitimate pursuits and live in peace?

A brief statement may here be made concerning the anti-Japanese agitation in California. Before taking up the alleged reasons upon which the agitation is based, we may be allowed to quote one of the best general statements on the subject, which was prepared by Professor P.J. Treat of Stanford University, an acknowledged authority on Oriental history. He says:

"It was in 1905 that the first suspicion of friction appeared. And in the next nine years a series of incidents occasioned some ill feeling, but it must be remembered that the friction was always between popular groups; the official relations were always cordial.

The occasions for controversy were found in both the United States and in the far East. In the United States it arose from the agitation for the exclusion of the Japanese immigrants. This movement began in California about 1905. It had a small basis in fact, for there were relatively few Japanese in this country, but if their number continued to increase as rapidly as it had since 1900, a real social and economic problem would be soon presented. Instead of meeting this problem through diplomatic channels, the agitators, remembering the Chinese exclusion movement of an earlier generation, commenced direct action. This took the form of the so-called 'schoolboy incident' in San Francisco. Using the excuse that school facilities were lacking after the great fire in 1906, the school board ordered all Oriental students to attend a designated school. The Japanese, recognizing the motive which prompted this action, justly resented it. And it was the more ungracious because at the time of the earthquake and fire the Japanese Red Cross had contributed to the relief of San Francisco more money than all other foreign countries combined. They had eagerly seized this opportunity of showing their appreciation of all that the United States had done for Japan in the past. The action of a local school board soon became a national and an international question. With the legal aspects we are not concerned here. The matter was settled, between the federal government and San Francisco, by a compromise. The Japanese students were admitted to all the schools as of old, and President Roosevelt promised to take up the question of immigration with Japan.

When the matter was presented in proper form, the Japanese at once met our requests. Practically all thoughtful Japanese realized the dangers involved in a mass immigration of people from a land with low standards of living to one where they were high. The understanding took the form of the "Gentlemen's Agreement," under which Japan promised not to give passports to laborers desiring to emigrate to the United States, and our Government, in turn, agreed not to subject the Japanese to the humiliation of an exclusion act. Since this agreement went into effect in 1907, it has met every need. No one has found ground for questioning the scrupulous good faith of the Japanese foreign office in the issue of passports. In fact, the admission of Japanese under the passport system has worked out with fewer abuses than the admission of Chinese under the exclusion laws which we administer ourselves.

Unfortunately, this good understanding did not quiet the agitation on the Pacific Coast. In the California Legislature in 1909, 1911, and 1913, a number of measures were proposed which would have caused discrimination against the Japanese residents of the state. These were reported to the Japanese press, and even though not passed, they kept alive the resentment. Japanese who accepted our views regarding immigration did not hesitate to assert that such Japanese as were admitted to our country should enjoy rights and privileges equal to those of any alien. A crisis was reached when, in 1913, a bill was proposed at Sacramento which would deny to Japanese the right to acquire land or to lease it for more than three years. The purpose of this bill was to prevent the accumulation of agricultural land by the industrious and thrifty Japanese farmers. But the danger was largely imaginary because, due to the "Gentlemen's Agreement," very few Japanese could enter the country, and in 1913, less than 13,000 acres were actually owned by them. In spite of the efforts of the national administration, the bill was passed in a modified form, which made it apply only to aliens ineligible for citizenship. This class included, specifically, the Chinese, and, by interpretation, all aliens who were not "free white persons" or persons of African nativity or descent.". . .

Finally we beg to state a few facts concerning the more important of our positive efforts to uplift the Japanese residents. These may be classified under four headings: An organized movement for Americanization, the protection of Japanese immigrants, religious work, and schools for immigrants and their children.

The origin of our more or less organized movement for Americanization can be traced back to 1900. We first directed our effort to what we called social education and economic development. We tried to impart to our fellow countrymen elementary facts of American civilization so that they could better fit themselves for American life. We tried to teach them that assimilation was the first step for their success. Then we tried to convince them that by contributing to the national interests of America they could attain their own economic development.

In 1918, when the American government laid down the general plan of the "Americanization campaign," we made it the foundation of our work. In fact, we joined the movement. The Japanese associations of San Francisco, Los Angeles, Portland, and Seattle assumed the responsibility of directing the campaign in the coast states, Nevada, Utah, and Colorado.

The San Francisco Association employs a man educated in America to canvass the northern half of the state. His function was to organize, in conjunction with the local associations, work for the campaign. Meetings were held at which men and women familiar with America addressed the Japanese. These addresses are for the purpose of acquainting the local Japanese with America. The topics discussed are such as American history, spirit, politics, economics, industry, religion, education, society, customs and manners, hygiene, care of children, cooking, housekeeping, etc. Besides lectures, pamphlets on these subjects have been prepared, and these are freely distributed. We have asked the Japanese schools, churches, Y.M.C.A., Y.W.C.A. clubs and other associations, newspapers and magazines to help us in our campaign, and they are enthusiastically responding. The Japanese Agricultural Association is also doing most effective work. We are also making a special effort to facilitate learning of the English language. We are helping to organize classes for women and children newly arrived and securing proper teachers for them. We are also helping them to select textbooks so that they can learn the language, and, at the same time, become familiar with America. Such is the nature and scope of our Americanization campaign.

To protect new arrivals, mostly women and children, we are cooperating with every institution connected with immigration at the time of their arrival, and after their landing in America. We distribute at ports of departure pamphlets on what they should know on the voyage and in America. We send one of our secretaries to the immigration station every time a ship arrives to facilitate the needs of newcomers. We do what we can for the unfortunate immigrants, acting as go-between [for] such and the Federal Bureau of Immigration. We make special efforts to protect wives whose husbands, for various reasons, fail to meet them at the station. We do our best to see that Japanese immigrants are accorded proper treatment from immigration officials. Our relations with these officials have been very cordial, and we are grateful.

The earlier Japanese immigrants were mostly students, and for many years students formed the bulk of Japanese immigrants. They began to come to America about forty years ago. The Christian missionaries saw a chance to do proselyting work among the young Japanese. First they taught them English and helped them to secure jobs. As the number of Japanese increased, missions were established. These conducted religious meetings, and schools and provided rooming facilities. The various denominations together now maintain fifty-nine missions in America and Canada. These are doubtless helping the Japanese in many ways. But Professor Millis says: "These missions are for Japanese alone, and a recognition of a difference between them and other races [is] a condition which lessens their value as an assimilative force." This inductment is, we are inclined to think, worthy of serious consideration by all who are interested in religious instruction as well as in the real Christianization of the Japanese. A stigma is attached to "mission" Christianity in the mind of many Japanese Christians, and they prefer to attend American churches, and they do. The mission work, if properly instituted, will no doubt have a far-reaching influence in Americanizing Japanese immigrants.

Aside from the schools for instructing Japanese in English, there are seventy-five so-called "supplementary" schools for teaching children the Japanese language. These are attended by the Japanese pupils after the public schools close for the day. They are primarily for the study of the Japanese language and are not intended to perpetuate the traditions and moral concepts of Japan. Of course, these are criticized by hostile Americans. But says Professor Millis, "They are supplementary schools, and at the worst, there is much less in them to be adversely criticized than in the parochial schools attended by many children of the South and European immigrants. No real problem is yet evident connected with Japanese children on American soil." These are some of the more obvious facts concerning the status of Japanese residents in California.

In conclusion, Mr. President, the undersigned, in their unofficial capacity as representatives of their countrymen, have thought this a fitting opportunity for directing your attention to the status of our people on this coast. We approach you in no spirit of complaint. If we have grievances, we recognize that such grievances are inseparable from the conditions which now exist and that they must be borne with patience. It is our firm belief, however, that fuller knowledge and better understanding on the part of the

American people of our aims and aspirations as residents of the great State of California will tend to disabuse some prejudices and make our condition happier. We would convince the people of California that our presence and our activities are not a menace to the commonwealth, but that its dearest interests are our own. We are happy to be able to count with confidence upon your love of justice and we ask your powerful help in so shaping public thought and opinion that every obstacle to harmony may be removed. It is the earnest desire of the Japanese people in this state to dwell in peace and good will with their American neighbors, and they desire to so direct their energies that the best interests of the state and communities in which they live may be subserved.

If it is our good fortune to impress you with the sincerity of these, our purpose and aims, we shall feel that your visit to the West has been most fortunate and we shall remain gratified and grateful.

We have the honor to remain, Sir,

Most respectfully yours,

The Japanese Association of America

✦ BEATRICE GRIFFITH, AMERICAN ME, 1948

At the conclusion of World War II, *Beatrice Griffith set out to capture the experience of a range of young Californians in coming to terms with the culture of their rapidly growing state. She interviewed young people, studied their schools, and reported the results in* American Me *in 1948. Her report on the experience of Mexican-Americans in the Los Angeles area is filled with warmth, humor, and powerful judgments about the workings of racism in the United States just as the World War was ending and the Cold War with the Soviet Union beginning. She began this report with an extended oral history, offering an extended autobiographical statement by one of her interviewees. This is followed by Griffith's own analysis of the state of Mexican-American schooling in the places she studied.*

One-World Kids

That afternoon we went drunk to school. I was feeling fine. Feeling fine cause I was just sixteen, had a dime, and gave a penny to the Salvation Army. I hadn't felt so fine for a long time, not since I thought one day at junior high I would be somebody. So I gave myself with respect and dressed like a Square at school, and gave everybody good manners. But nobody would believe that I wanted to make something of myself, and they only laughed. And that light-skinned cholo teacher who talked real dainty Spanish, she gave me the reputation of a gangster in that school. She used to ask me, "Wild woman, what alley did you come from?" But when she saw me dressed like a Square and giving myself with respect, she couldn't believe it and laughed, too. So it was no go. But I sure felt good for a while.

Well, this noon we both walked past the vocational school where the schools send their bad kids. Singing all the way, Jitterbug and me. Only we couldn't walk very good. The girls yelled at us from behind the board fence, so we started back. When we got to the school door I threw my cigarette away and walked down the hall real fine. But one thing we forgot, we forgot to stop singing. So the principal came out and Jitterbug ran into one of the classrooms and sat down at a desk. But me—I walked straight into her office, I'm that dumb, and started talking. I told that principal I was going to be somebody big, real famous. But she wouldn't listen. She was only crying and calling me honey and asking me, "How could you do this to me, honey? You were my sweetheart girl, look at the appreciation you gave me."

But one thing she didn't know, it wasn't to her, it was to me and my mother I was doing it, being drunk.

I saw Jitterbug coming from the room across the hall, and the teacher talking rough to her, pushing her along the hall, telling her, "We don't allow drunkards in this school." She yelled loud enough for another school to hear. Jitterbug never drank before today, and now already they think she is a Lost Weekend. So I tried to stop talking, cause I remembered how fakey they are at this school. You give them the trust and then they don't keep the truth, so everything is dirty.

The principal was telling me that I was a dear sweet girl, and all that jive. And next door Jitterbug was crying, asking them for the favor not to tell her mother. Jitterbug never asked any favors of anybody, only one. Just to play "Beat Bad Boogie" and "Ave Maria" when she died. That's all. But those teachers would promise not to tell her mother, and then would do her dirty and tell everything to the cops and her mother sure.

The principal was talking a lot of talk. "You aren't happy are you, honey? Why do you smoke marijuana, honey? Tell me where you got the whiskey, honey."

So I told her the truth that a drunk man bought it for us, but she believed it for a lie. Then she looked at me with those missionary eyes and gave me that long-distance embarrassment, and promised her word not to tell my mother.

That day after school, while we was waiting for the old streetcar to take us home (all but Jitterbug, and the cops from Juvenile took her home), we tried to buy some ice-cream cones at the drug store. But sometimes they wouldn't sell you any. Today was one of those days. We all crowded in there. I wanted to get some aspirin and went back in the store. When I heard them calling the girls, "You dirty Pachucas, get out of this store," I came up front.

"I bought some aspirin, mister. How about a glass of water?" I asked him.

But he yelled at me, "There's a gas station across the street, if you want water. We don't want you Pachucas here. Now, get out."

So I told him, "Maldita sea tu madre, and your grandmother, and your great-grandmother's mother's mother, and all their cows and goats. You don't stop to know if we are Pachucas or not, just because we dress this way."

The girls were sore. Everybody was mad, waiting outside that drugstore. Largo wrote her name real big on the Coca-Cola sign by the brick wall. "Remember, Cuata, when they used to make you scrub all the names off the basement walls at school just cause Negra put them there and they thought it was you?"

"Sure, man, just cause I was dark they thought those names were mine. Some were, but not all. I worked a lot for that chick cause my skin is dark—but then it took my mother a lot of months to get it just that color I guess."

I was getting tired of hanging around and waiting for that streetcar, and none of the guys showed up yet.

Mostly when the girls wait for the streetcar they talk about that school and the teachers. All the troubles come out on that corner cause we have to wait sometimes a long time. If the conductor sees a big bunch of us he won't stop, so we hang around.

Fushia was sore cause she got expelled from school today. "Just cause there was a big commotion when Yoyo and Chonto drove by the school, they thought it was me. Always those teachers give the blame someplace else. How come they aren't ever fair? They sit me in a room with a pencil and tell me, 'Now honey, write down on that paper why you're bad.' So when I drew a picture of Joan Crawford with a big overlip, old lady Wiggins got real real mad. Then they gave me a summons, nice and polite from the office. 'Well dearie, that's the last. We've tried our best with you. We're simply fed up. We just can't go on. We can no longer help you,' and all that jive, she told me. But it was dirty not to hear my story."

Some of the guys drove by then, and there was a lot of commotion. Simon, Wapa, and Gege all got in the car and drove away downtown. Lola scratched her name on a brick that didn't have none. "Sure those teachers should know how to help girls with their problems, not shut them out because they're hard. Remember Miss Stevanson and those teachers at Lockwood, that other special school? They'd give you chances and chances. That's why we went in there real rugged and came out all squarey, with no overlip, no short skirts, or pompadours or zombie shoes. They didn't try to control our clothes, and no teacher's-pet stuff."

Caldonia lit a cigarette and sat down on the curb. "And they didn't yell at you. They were honest and equal. It's not the strictness that counts. I've sat in a lot of principals' offices for hours, with them trying to get me to take down my pompadour. But strictness and nothing else doesn't get control. Some teachers can keep you after school for hours, but couldn't make me mind ever." She passed me a cigarette then, cause another streetcar had just banged on up the street without stopping.

"Heck yes, if they expect a courteous answer they should set the example for someone to follow, and not yell at you like you are deaf. Remember that old teacher in junior high who used to yell at us, 'you stupid B27's, she'd yell. 'You blockheads.' But that day she called my mother a Mexican dumbbell was too bad for her. She was so surprised when I slapped her she just stared pop-eyed, while I walked down the stairs to the principal's office. That began all my trouble."

Changa bought some gum across at the grocery store and passed it around. "Sure, I remember her. Deeply in my heart, to the last inch of my heart, to the deepest part of my heart, I shall always remember that s.o.b. How could I forget her?"

"Yeah, and Miss Stevanson never threw it to you that you were a Mexican, and would explain all the big long words, cause she came out strong for work. Remember, Changa, it took me two weeks to learn to say 'vulgar profanity'? But if you tried hard she didn't fail you. She was with respect and was fair, and those beautiful hair and eyes! Things would be different here if she was our teacher. She'd have control."

Huera let out a yell at the streetcar that almost stopped, then it banged the bell and went on. "Cholo cabron, why doesn't he stop? I gotta get home."

I told the girls to pipe down, cause that old store guy would call the police if he heard so much noise, but it was no use. Everybody was talking at once.

"Why, even if Stevanson wasn't for Roosevelt, she never let a Gabacho girl say something bad about him. I bet if Roosevelt was alive this school would be different. Remember the CCC's he gave us and all those things? And remember when Roosevelt talked on the radio? Man, it was real keen—made you all warm inside, like Lena Horne singing. Let's put his name here by ours, real big!" Cuata and Vicki started in making a big Roosevelt name on the Coca-Cola sign, standing high on the wall. We watched to see if the drugstore boss came out.

"Sure the school would be different. Cause Roosevelt knew our language even if he didn't speak Spanish, cause he knew the language the poor people talk. He knew the languages of all the people who don't speak American, and the poor people who speak American but not with rich money. We could write him and tell him about what we want in this school, and he'd do something, I bet," I told him, "cause my aunt wrote him when her house was going to be sold, and it wasn't."

"Yeah, but it's different now. With Roosevelt alive you felt safe, like inside the house when it's raining outside. Or you've just had a long drag of tea and everything is comfortable and smooth. Cause he would protect you, there was nothing to fear like being hungry. He knew about being hungry, I guess, cause he gave us NYA and hospitals and WPA and lots of other things people need when they haven't money and can't speak." Beaver picked up a piece of dirt and threw it smack in the face of the cute little blonde chick in that Coca-Cola sign. "Make that name Roosevelt bigger—so everybody can see it."

I remember what my mother said, "The only thing Roosevelt did to hurt his people was to die. If Americans could give their lives to save him, you'd have to stand in line." But I think my mother isn't so sad that my brother is dead in Germany now, cause Roosevelt is with him and all the dead soldiers and sailors. She says she felt more comfortable, and I guess she does.

Just then a bunch of high-school chicks came by and gave us those looks of theirs. They're so stuck up they probably say they're Spanish and not Mexican. But we did them nothing, not since that day they called us dirty Pachucas and we beat them up.

I sat down on the fireplug. "Come on. Let's write a letter to Roosevelt like if he were still alive, and tell him what we want for a school."

I began to write.

Dear President Roosevelt,

The next time one of those dames asks what will make our school better, we're going to tell them what we're telling you. But you'll probably get this letter before they ask us. So here goes!

We want to know out of that school the things you are supposed to know in life. How to fill out papers for work. How to put money in the bank. To know about the world we're living in. Not to know nothing about nothing. To know about the stars and moon, about shorthand and penmanship and power machines, so we can sew for our kids when we have them. And how to give them understanding.

We want lots of clubs for all of us, not only honor clubs where you have wings like angels. To know what we're reading about, how to talk with people when they say, 'Did you see this and that about Europe and Russia?' And how to say back, 'Oh yes. I know. And did you know this and that, about some current events?' And if we could have one period to study health about ourselves, how our organs are made, and what to do if we get sick, that would be good.

And we would like, President Roosevelt, a course in beauty—combing hair, how to fix your make-up, what style and all that. Not this professional grooming course they give us, that means cutting paper dolls out of newspapers.

In grammar school we studied about things that were so fine, all about life in other countries, like you knew about. You know, all that one-world business. We live in one world too—the Mexican world. But we want to go places and do things everywhere. To get out of these little grapes-of-wrath houses we live in.

But mostly, President Roosevelt, we want to know about the living of life real real good.

Your friends,

The One-World Kids

The Schools [Griffith's sociological analysis]

It is in the schools that children of Mexican ancestry learn of America: American life, American history, her great men, her cities, and government. Here they make their dreams—and often lose them. The school records of these youngsters are affected by the same factors that influence any other underprivileged children—poverty, bad housing, undernourishment, and ill health. Added to these are the bilingualism and segregation which make even worse the hard lot of underprivileged childhood.

To children required to live in segregated areas, the insecurity and sense of inferiority that comes early in childhood is intensified by school segregation. Throughout the Southwest, many Mexican-American children see the big school bus going through the streets of their town picking up the "Americans," one by one, to take them blocks away to the big school, with its auditorium, cafeteria, and play equipment. The "Mexican" youngsters often walk down the long road to the small school where "specially trained" teachers teach them about that almost unknown world that is America.

The segregated "Mexican schools" usually lack the play facilities, cafeteria, and auditorium of the big school, and there are also differences in teaching personnel. "It is not uncommon for the teachers to be sent to the "Mexican" school as a matter of administrative discipline. Again, they may be transferred to the school because of difficulty with children and parents. One administrator described such a situation accurately when he said, "There isn't a teacher in *that* school who could be kept in the Anglo school. The parents wouldn't stand for it. Mexicans don't care."

The two most common excuses justifying segregation of Mexican-American children are: "They don't speak good English," and "They're dirty." The truth is that where Mexican parents are given a chance, their youngsters come to school as clean, and sometimes cleaner than, the other children. Their clothes may be poorer, but parental pride keeps the blackened washtubs boiling in the backyard. As for not speaking good English— they speak good or bad English according to the opportunity given them to hear it.

Stereotyped thinking of prejudiced teachers often results in false generalizations about Spanish-speaking children. One school reported "severe problems" regarding the cleanliness, tardiness, and truancy among the Mexican-Americans who comprised 2 percent of the school's population. After some investigation it was found that "only three Mexican-American families were dirty. The rate of uncleanliness was actually greater among the Anglo-American families in the school. The same conclusion had to be drawn in terms of tardiness and truancy."

Another frequent complaint is: "They are so clannish . . . Mexican children always hang around together—they don't mix." The facts are that Mexican-American youngsters, particularly the younger ones, mix as well as any group if given encouragement. They are, however, sensitive and proud, and if they are made to feel a group apart, it is natural for them to cling together rather than push themselves where they are not welcome.

The pattern of segregation is occasionally lost to the casual observer. Teachers may say, "Why, we don't have segregation here—you see the children together there in the yard." Actually, after recess, the Mexican-American children may attend separate classes in the basement, or other rooms set aside for them, with "special teachers." Then, too, the children may attend classes together, yet graduate on different nights, as happened in one school in Los Angeles County.

It should not be inferred that most California schools are segregated, for such is not the case. The percentage throughout other Southwest states is considerably higher as a rule. Increasingly the schools in California are yielding to community pressure and abandoning the segregated school systems. Saticoy schools in Ventura County, El Monte, Chino, and all districts in Riverside County are among the schools that are no longer segregated. In several instances, the fair-minded and democratic school principals have led the fight to abandon segregation.

In 1945, parents of over five thousand Mexican-American children in Santa Ana, California, hired David Marcus, Los Angeles attorney, and proceeded to sue the Orange County Board of Education in an attempt to secure unsegregated schools for their sons and daughters. On March 22, 1946, Judge Paul J. McCormack handed down a permanent injunction against further segregation. He found such a policy "arbitrary and discriminatory and in violation of their constitutional rights and illegal and void." When the Orange County Board of Education appealed the case to the Ninth Circuit Court of Appeals in San Francisco, Justices Stevens and Denman handed down two court opinions which were scathing denunciations of this Board of Education. They then directed the Los Angeles Federal Grand Jury to review the facts for the purpose of returning an indictment against the Board.

One of the most damaging results of segregating Mexican-American children is that their bilingual handicap is intensified. They speak Spanish in the home and with their playmates, and when they do not play with Anglo-American children at school, they grow up thinking in Spanish, and acting with "Mexican" reactions to American situations. Contrary to the opinion of some teachers and parents, the Spanish-speaking child does *not* learn English more quickly in a school where there are only Mexican-American children. The English vocabulary with which a great many Spanish-speaking children enter school is negligible. It is safe to say that at the end of the first school year the vocabulary of these children consists of those words that the teacher has stressed, and those heard most often among their "American" playmates. The importance of unsegregated kindergartens for equipping the little Mexican-American youngsters with a minimum English vocabulary with which to enter school cannot be minimized.

The fallacy of the belief that segregated schools teach English better than unsegregated is well-demonstrated by the noticeable accent with which English is spoken by thousands of children who were born and raised in America, but educated in "Mexican" schools.

Another stereotyped belief held by some teachers is the conviction that Mexican-American children are inferior mentally. One elementary school teacher who attended a teachers' summer workshop in Los Angeles on "the Education of Mexican and Spanish-Speaking Pupils," showed how deeply ingrown this belief can be: "I've had a very entertaining experience but as far as I am concerned, they are still dirty, stupid, and dumb."

Too often a teachers' interest in her pupils is determined by the intelligence quotients registered in the class. Where this is so, the bilingual child starts out with a definite handicap, which is seldom eliminated in later school years.

Let's take an example, a Spanish-speaking child from a poor home and large family. Juanito's father and mother are immigrants from Mexico who speak little English. They are migratory workers in the seasonal crops, and return to the city when the harvesting season is over. Juanito works with them. During his nine years of living, he has missed a couple of months or more of schooling each year since he enrolled in the first grade. He is undernourished, nervous, and restless. He understands little of the English spoken around him when he enters school. He hears only Spanish in his crowded home and from the loud radio constantly playing Mexican songs. His father, tired and weary from his long work, may drink little or much to ease his own frustrations—to quench the thirst of the hot Mexican food.

Juanito comes to school, washed up or not, after a breakfast of beans and flour tortillas. When he is given his Binet test, there is a confusion in his mind as to what the words mean, what the teacher means, what the whole business means. He may "get through," but he may also have such an emotional or lingual block that he fails to get an I.Q. above 70. Does this mean that Juanito is innately a dull child? Can his teacher honestly say his "inborn capacity has been adequately measured?"

These youngsters, confronted with intelligence tests in schools, are under a real disadvantage. George I. Sanchez, professor of Latin-American Education at the University of Texas, says that, "There are no adequate group tests that do justice to the Mexican-American child." Nevertheless, the Mexican-American child is constantly being compared with his "American" classmates by most of his teachers, and usually to his detriment. Too many teachers fail to realize that "there is no Nordic corner on brains." They disregard the personal, social, and cultural differences of their pupils. They forget that Binet himself warned that the tests could be safely used only if the various individuals have the same or approximately the same environmental opportunities.

The fact of the matter is, these children follow the same biological curve as any other group. Doctor Elizabeth Woods, psychologist for the Los Angeles City Schools, says, "Some are super, some slow, but in general their average is like that of any other children."

H. A. Overstreet puts it another way. "Tests of intelligence are as often as not tests of what communities do to the minds of their people. We know that I.Q.s can be improved by better surroundings. A generally low test score, therefore, in any part of the country and among large numbers of its inhabitants, may merely reveal that in that region society is an enemy of its people."

Probably the most important factor of all, however, in the school life of the Spanish-speaking child is the attitude of the teachers. One school administrator said, "If I find a teacher who can reach a Spanish-speaking child, I find that she influences that child's whole life very often. If she gets into his being and the child takes her understanding into his own complex little life, the influence is incalculable later on . . ." It takes most of these children about ten minutes in a class to determine a teacher's attitude. From then on, the behavior pattern is predetermined for many.

Unfortunately, however, the sympathetic and understanding teacher is not the usual one by any means. Besides these there are the teachers who are sentimental and those who are indifferent and prejudiced—and the latter group predominates.

In speaking of the sentimental attitude, Dr. Ethel P. Andrus, nationally known educator, said, "Some teachers wrap the Mexican child up in a Zarape. He's delightful, cute, picturesque, and dramatic—but that is not making him an American. He is a person apart. If America is to survive, these children must be part of us . . . *not apart from us.* The Zarape attitude is the sentimental approach that some of the best teachers are guilty of practicing."

It is the sentimental teachers who place an emphasis on handicrafts in place of academic work, saying, "You can't force these children into the Anglo-Saxon mold or pattern of schooling. They are different—they are elemental in their conception of

things. They have different temperaments. The best program for them is one of intensive handicrafts in informal classrooms."

Such attitudes, and the common belief that they are good only in art, are mali-
cious. Inasmuch as the Mexican-American children are not expected to measure up
with other children academically, the teachers need not bother. Just praise them in the
lower grades, celebrate Cinco de Mayo, brush them up in the jarabe tapatio . . . make
pets out of the cutest ones . . . and pass them on to the next grade. "We just let them
slide through if they don't measure up." In the higher grade levels, they are advised
to take woodwork, machine and print shop, gardening, art, sewing, or cosmetology
. . . "That's the best thing for them. Why give them big ideas—they're a simple
people."

They're not so simple. Children are shrewd, and Mexican-American youngsters
are particularly sensitive. The sentimentalists don't fool all of the children they teach,
as the remark of one junior high girl shows. "You know, that teacher used to hate me
until I played 'Dream of Love' and 'Bésame Mucho' on the piano. 'Oh, I didn't know
you played such beautiful music,' she said . . . and a lot of stuff like that. She gave me
the soft line . . . 'You Mexican girls are so artistic,' she'd say, just so I'd play more. But
I knew she hated me, so I wouldn't wear that old Mexican costume and dance for her."

It is questionable whether sentimental principals and teachers basically like
these children. Their sentimentality is a cover-up, a conscience soother, a failure to
admit the equality of the Mexican group. "If America is to be strong, they must be a
part of us," accepting the responsibilities of citizenship as do any other Americans.
Furthermore, the sentimental teacher does not Americanize the children . . . she
Mexicanizes them.

This is not intended as a criticism of those comparatively few teachers who show
respect for these children as Americans by wanting to strengthen their pride in the Old
Country's culture. That, too, is needed. It is good if directed properly, if the teacher
keeps in mind the fact that the Mexican-Americans are, after all, Americans, and it is
our culture they will live by, be judged by; it is our way of life they know so little about,
and are so eager to learn.

The most common attitude is that of indifference. The principal of a school in San
Fernando Valley, which has a large Mexican population, voiced the indifferent attitude
neatly enough when she said, "If you teach them attitudes and responses and how to be
good citizens, how to wash and iron and scrub and bake, that's all you need to do. Why
teach them to read and write and spell? Why worry about it . . . they'll only pick beets
anyway."

This attitude usually accompanies the happy belief that "they don't want to be any
better. No matter what you teach them, they'll only marry, have lots of kids, and let the
dishes stay dirty as they do now."

Instead of accepting these children as a challenge to their initiative, such teachers
usually request to be placed in other schools where they do not have to observe "those
dirty and stupid Mexican kids." If placement in other schools out of the Mexican neighborhoods were always effected, and these teachers replaced by sympathetic ones, it
would be a beneficial arrangement all the way around. Unfortunately this is not always
possible, and so some just sweat it out, with the children bearing the brunt of prejudice.

Others of the indifferent group prefer to stay in the "Mexican schools" because
less is demanded of them as teachers and community leaders. They can slide along from

year to year, half doing a vital job, complaining about their hard lot to everyone who will listen.

Against the many examples of indifference and prejudice, ignorance and sentimentality, the sincere work of capable, patient, and sincere teachers and principals stands out bright as sunlight. It is from their successful classes that Mexican-American children carry away the kind of dreams of achievement and plans that go to make America a great nation.

The hope and encouragement such teachers give are the best insurance agents against the Mexican-American child leaving school for factory and field work, even when economic pressures are great. One successful principal was told, "You seem to get a better class of Mexican pupils in your school than we do. They look so much more intelligent and brighter than ours." She replied, "Well, we insist that they be intelligent . . . We demand that they make the effort to come up to a standard . . . so we get work that is a standard."

Sometimes the teachers succeed just because of the high standards they demand of the children. Or they may get results if, combined with high expectations, they have a close relationship with the children and their Mexican parents. In schools where a real effort is made to minimize the wide cultural gulf, discipline is not the problem it is in other areas where poverty, racial antagonisms, and lack of home supervision foster rebellious and resentful youngsters.

An example of "accepting each child as he is" is shown in the attitude of one elementary teacher toward pupils who slept in their clothes. "There are too many kids sleeping together in small overcrowded homes, sleeping both ways with five in a bed. I figure my job is to teach them and not to smell them. Children can't sleep cold, that's all."

There is one school located in the heart of a congested Mexican-Negro district where the relationship between the teachers and parents is exceptionally good. In the Americanization classes and parties, the teachers and mothers share the benefits of "intercultural relations" on a practical basis by exchanging cooking recipes and folk dances. The PTA attendance is large (contrary to the usual Mexican PTA attendance), and the health education and immunization programs are successful.

✦ Teaching Children of Puerto Rican Background in the New York City Schools, 1954

While the schools of Los Angeles were struggling to come to terms with the educational needs of the children of its longest-term residents—the citizens of its Mexican-American community—the New York City Public Schools were experiencing a new wave of immigrants. New York had long been the entry point for European immigrants, and the city's schools often served as the first point of contact with the new culture. The schools had helped assimilate generations of Irish, Italian, Russian, and many other European immigrant children. After World War II, Puerto Ricans also began moving to New York in large numbers. The public school administration responded with a major effort known as "The Puerto Rican Study," a multipronged effort conducted in the early 1950s to review the curriculum and the means of instruction so as to engage these new students. The study, and the 1954 brochure for teachers, "Teaching Children of Puerto Rican Background," part of which is included here, provide an interesting glimpse of the attitudes of the school administrators. At one moment wise and respectful, in the next filled with low expectations, the study reflects all of the ambiguity with which generations of newcomers have, in fact, been greeted.

There are in the New York City Schools today a large number of children of Puerto Rican background. Many of them have difficulties communicating in English. They come from a background different from that of our continental American way of living and learning. They present a situation similar, in some respects, to that of previous waves of newcomers to our city. The adjustment of the New York City schools to these latest arrivals again offers our staff a challenging opportunity.

These Spanish-speaking children have become a part of the student body of New York City. They are being helped to take their places and participate effectively in our city life, each child to the full extent of his individual potentialities. They are learning English as a second language and are adjusting to our ways of living on the continent and in the City of New York in particular. . . .

Local schools and the districts have been studying for some time the problem of organizing classes for children of Puerto Rican background. Many clues to effective plans of organization have been investigated. The superiority of any one plan has not been established, however. Practices that are successful in one situation do not always seem to meet the needs of other situations. *Pending further study, therefore, the following pages are offered as descriptions of practices found successful in many instances, and not as prescriptions to be followed by all schools.* They describe procedures used in the reception of pupils, in the organization of classes, in the assignment of pupils to both orientation and regular classes, and in providing for adequate guidance until proper adjustment has been made. In the main these suggestions are tentative, based on practices which thus far have seemed successful.

Reception of New Arrivals

A. *Advance Preparation.* Schools situated in areas where large numbers of Puerto Rican families live have found it helpful to prepare all directions and routine notices in Spanish and to post them along with the English signs in corridors and rooms where they will be most useful. Reading the instructions in their own language enables parents to help in the routines to be followed.

   It is good practice also to have prepared in advance a welcome booklet in Spanish, which is distributed during registration. Information given should answer questions about the school and its educational goals and practices. The welcome booklet can be a constant source of reference for the parents during the time the student remains in the school.

B. *During Registration.* Since many of the newcomers from Puerto Rico arrive at the school with little ability to make themselves understood, the assistance of a Spanish-speaking person, familiar with Puerto Rican backgrounds, is invaluable during registration. Ideally, this person is a member of the supervisory or teaching staff; however, parent or student translators can receive the newcomer with a friendly greeting in Spanish and thus do much to establish the initial rapport. Some elementary schools arrange to have bilingual parents on duty at regular times during the week; other schools on various levels make use of the older students organized as a bilingual group within the service squad or the General Organization.

In addition to greeting the children and parents upon their arrival, the bilingual group assists the schools in the following ways:

1. to convey to the newcomers that certain documents, such as birth certificate, previous school record, and evidence of vaccination are expected.
2. to answer questions that arise after parents and pupils have had an opportunity to read the welcome booklets distributed by the school.
3. to assure parents of the schools' readiness to cooperate in all matters involving the well-being of their children.
4. to explain to parents the value of Parents' Associations and urge participation in such organizations.
5. to give information about the club and extracurricular programs of secondary schools.
6. to answer questions (if any) about special orientation classes.
7. to reassure students that someone who speaks their language will be available to help translate for them.
8. to inform parents of requirements of school attendance, and of notification to the school when the family moves. . . .

Assignment to Regular Classes

Assignment to Regular Classes After the Orientation Period. Experience has shown that many children will be able to profit from the work in the regular class after approximately six months. Children above the age of nine who have had no previous school experience may need a longer time in the orientation class. The administrator is guided by the following considerations in making the reassignment to a regular class.

A. *Teacher Judgment.* This should include results of observation of the pupil in all aspects of school living. His readiness to take his place in a regular class with students of his own age group should be a deciding factor. With a very young child, this might mean ability to express himself orally and to understand spoken English and ability to adjust to class routine. With an older child, this might mean ability to use reading as a tool for further learning and ability to participate in committee work.

B. *Judgment of Other School Personnel.* Anyone who comes in contact with the pupil—the principal, special teachers assigned to the program, the guidance counselor, other members of the teaching staff—may be asked to evaluate the readiness of the pupil to be transferred to a regular class. Simple forms have been worked out for this purpose by various schools.

C. *More formal evaluative procedures.* The results of all examinations the teacher has given to ascertain degree of mastery of subject matter should be taken into account. These tests may have been simple questions and answers, dictation of previously prepared material, the reading of an experience chart, or the answers to questions based on a reading selection. The ability of the child to communicate orally should be the fundamental consideration. Formal standardized tests in English or Spanish have not proved useful thus far. . . .

Curriculum and Procedures

The schools are adapting their curriculum and teaching procedures in various ways to meet the special needs of the Puerto Rican child. The immediate concern is the orientation of the pupils to the school, the home, and community environment. A few of the major responsibilities of the school in which there are Puerto Rican children are:

1. To plan for those experiences in social and community living which will lead to effective participation in our everyday New York City life.
2. To encourage the use of the English language for the communication of needs, wants, ideas, and desires.
3. To guide physical, intellectual, emotional, and social growth toward satisfactory personal and social adjustment.
4. To inculcate ideals of responsibility leading to active and effective citizenship.

To achieve these ideals, the school must stress:

a. Oral and written communication in English
b. Everyday living in a big city
c. Citizenship and our American heritage
d. Health and nutrition
e. Personal and community hygiene
f. Safety
g. Guidance—personal, educational, and vocational

This manual is a guide, especially for teachers who have had only limited experience in teaching children whose native language is not English. It will be helpful to them and to more experienced teachers in selecting and organizing units, in varying procedures, and in obtaining and using materials. Since it is undesirable to follow a predetermined program, and since the variables in each school and in each group make it impossible to do so, teachers will adapt the suggestions and procedures given here. After teachers have had some experience, they will select and develop units with their own groups, based on the experiences and needs of the individuals concerned.

A curriculum devised for the education of Puerto Rican children should:

1. *Allow for flexibility.*
   Everyday experiences and needs as they arise should form the basis for units of learning. The needs will vary from one school age to another.
2. *Make use of the background experiences of the child.*
   His life in Puerto Rico, his trip to the United States, his previous educational training, and his ability to use Spanish should be the starting point for new learnings.
3. *Provide for direct experiences.*
   Tours of the school and trips in the community as well as activities in the classroom are important for language readiness.
4. *Plan for different levels of language ability.*
   Even where attempts are made to group children homogeneously, it is usually necessary to provide experiences and activities on different levels. For example, there may be in the same class children who read Spanish well, and those who

have difficulty in reading Spanish; those with some knowledge of English and those with little previous contact with English; those who learn rapidly and those who learn slowly.

5. *Use varied approaches to obtain the desired objectives.*
   In addition to providing for direct experiences, wide use should be made of media such as selected audio-visual aids.

6. *Stress language growth in all activities.*
   All play and work experiences should be made to yield new vocabulary, idioms, and sentence patterns and encourage spontaneous conversation.

7. *Make provision for repetition of newly acquired vocabulary, idioms, and sentence patterns in a variety of situations.*
   New learnings should be reinforced by practice in activities involving all curriculum areas.

8. *Emphasize growth in oral expression.*
   Speaking and aural comprehension are of primary importance. Reading and writing may be deferred for pupils unable to communicate orally. With older pupils, reading and writing are sometimes used to reinforce the learning of language patterns.

9. *Be paced to meet the individual needs of each child.*
   A feeling of security and progress stemming from mastery of each step must accompany all learning.

10. *Provide for full participation of the pupils in all school-wide activities where language competency is not of paramount importance.*
    Opportunities for immediate active participation in health education and shop programs, assemblies, activities of the students' General Organization, service squads, and monitorial service should be given.

11. *Take cognizance of the cultural and linguistic contributions that the Puerto Rican children can make.*
    Emotional needs such as the desire for status, belonging, and achievement may be satisfied by having pupils serve as interpreters or student helpers. They may also explain the Puerto Rican background to the class or school. . . .

Developing Communication Skills

For most of our Puerto Rican children, the school has a major responsibility to develop the essential communication skills in oral and written English. The program for the teaching of English as a second language may consist of many facets. Some of these are: building a rich background of experience, teaching language patterns through a planned sequence, using Spanish to develop comprehension, and others. Some schools may emphasize one of these, while another school may reject it almost completely. Moreover, combinations of various elements of the program may vary from school to school. No clear experimental evidence of the most effective type of program is available as yet. The procedures described below are therefore to be considered *tentative* and *suggestive*.

In general, communication skills are built around meaningful concepts gained through a rich background of experience. Thus, the school and the teacher can promote growth in language competence by providing an environment so rich that children want to inquire and talk about it. In this way, the children are given direct contact with the materials on which the new language is based. For children who speak little or no English, comprehension may be developed through such media as pictures, objects, models, dramatization, and pantomime. Much practice is needed to fix associations with the new words and sentence patterns developed through the use of the materials.

The materials should be attractively arranged so as to invite initiative and stimulate conversation. The classroom environment should be such as to encourage children to use the English language. . . .

The teacher should not:

1. Speak loudly or at an exaggerated rate (either too quickly or too slowly). The children should become accustomed to a normal tone, and a normal rate in which the small words take their proper unstressed place, as, for example, "the book on the desk" is not to be said, "thee book on thee desk."
2. Speak in isolated words.
3. Imitate the sounds and intonation of the child.
4. Adapt her speech pattern to that of the child. Expressions such as, "You go library," should not be reinforced by being repeated by the teacher.
5. Underestimate the ability of the pupil to utter a complete sentence with proper prompting by her.
6. Become discouraged because constant repetition is necessary.
7. Assume that there is an automatic transfer of learning from a sound in one word to the same sound in a new word. By giving some time to the sounds mentioned in this report, and by pointing out that the same sound occurs in other words, phrases, and sentences, transfer of learning may be expected.
8. Expect mastery of contractions, such as, "won't," "can't," "don't," "couldn't," "wouldn't," etc., to come easily without special training.
9. Confuse the children by requiring the use of several sentence patterns at one time.
10. Forget her own experience in learning a second language, perhaps in high school or college; and that learning *her* first language actually covered a period of several years.

CHAPTER 7

THE PROGRESSIVE ERA, 1890-1950

Introduction

Perhaps no reform movement in American education lasted so long or had so much influence as progressive education. Often associated with the work of John Dewey, progressive education dominated the educational landscape for a decade before the twentieth century began and for much of the first half of the century. Well into the 1950s, education-related debates often focused on the virtues and vices of progressive education.

Progressive education had as many definitions as it had proponents—or, later, critics. Lawrence A. Cremin's, *The Transformation of the School: Progressivism in American Education, 1876–1957* (New York: Alfred A. Knopf, 1961) has long been viewed as the definitive history of progressive education. For Cremin, progressive education could not be understood apart from the larger progressive movement which swept the country in the early twentieth century, electing first Teddy Roosevelt and later Woodrow Wilson as progressive presidents. For Cremin, the key to understanding the movement was clear. "The word *progressive* provides the clue to what it really was: the educational phase of American Progressivism writ large. In effect, progressive education began as progressivism in education: a many-sided effort to use the schools to improve the lives of individuals." (p. viii.)

In my own examination of progressivism, I have come to the surprising (to me, at least) conclusion that progressive education actually meant so many things; that it was an educational reform effort with so many facets—that it is a virtually meaningless term. Like the words *school reform* at the twentieth century's end, *progressive education* came to be a catch phrase for whatever any particular speaker thought should be done in education for the first several decades of the century. Only by clustering progressives into subgroups can we make any sense of the era. I propose at least four separate strands of school reform, all of which called themselves "progressive." They are:

- administrative progressives, who sought consolidated management
- militant teachers, who sought a greater role for themselves
- child-centered curriculum reformers
- advocates of testing and measurement

Selected readings from advocates of each of these strands are included in this chapter.

One can imagine the debates that must have taken place between administrative progressives like James Jackson Storrow, and his counterparts across the country, and the teacher leaders in their cities. Both called themselves progressives. But the administrative leaders believed that progressivism meant centralized authority in a board of "the brightest and best" citizens working closely with a professional administrator. The fact that the "brightest and best" were usually from old-line English stock, and those they viewed as their corrupt opponents were more often Irish-Catholics or representatives of other immigrant groups was, to the administrative progressives, incidental. Militant teachers viewed the same boards and their hand-picked professional superintendents as distant spectators who did not understand the realities that teachers faced. For the teachers, the key was to shift power *away* from centralized bureaucracies into the hands of individual teachers. In addition to the ethnic issues that divided these two groups, the vast majority of the board members and superintendents were male, and most of the teachers were female. This created gender differences of great significance.

The curriculum reformers tended to be closer to the teachers than to the administrative progressives. However, for them the child—and not the teacher or the administration—was the central focus of school reform. The advocates of a child-centered curriculum believed passionately that traditional schools were boring and that only by eliciting the full and active participation of every child in the learning process would real education take place. They opposed regimentation in every form and advocated the creation of a small-scale democracy in every classroom to promote active learning and help develop future adults who would be active participants in a larger democratic society.

Finally, the educational testing advocates saw themselves as scientists who were above the squabbles of the other groups. For them, the key to successful education was the scientific measurement of the innate ability each child possessed. Once that was measured—through the Stanford-Binet or other intelligence tests—the school curriculum could be shaped to support that child. The notion that education might change children or society was foreign to the test advocates.

As the Great Depression of the 1930s replaced the prosperity of the teens and twenties, those who believed that progressive education meant using the school to build a larger progressive society became more and more militant. George Counts became quite critical of other progressives who focused only on the individual child when it was all of society that needed to change. He and John Dewey called on teachers to be leaders in building the new society and replacing the corrupt and defeated capitalism of early twentieth-century America. To lump all of these extraordinarily diverse actors under a single banner of progressivism is to misunderstand both their similarities and their differences. But to fail to attend to the lasting impact all of these groups had is equally to miss some of the most interesting developments in the history of American education.

✦ JAMES JACKSON STORROW, SON OF NEW ENGLAND, 1932

Every major city in the United States had groups of business leaders who advocated school reform in the early years of the twentieth century. These administrative progressives took over local school boards and hired a new breed of educational leader, the professionally trained school superintendent, to be the chief executive officer of each school system. Administrative progressives believed schools could benefit from a dose of business sense. The premiere leader of the administrative progressive movement in Boston was James Jackson Storrow. An investment banker and urban reformer, Storrow designed major changes in Boston's city plan, ran for mayor in a heated campaign in 1909, and later took the lead in uniting a number of smaller automobile companies into General Motors. Along the way, he also was involved in a significant effort to improve the Boston Public Schools. He describes this effort in his family-authorized biography, Son of New England: James Jackson Storrow, 1864–1926, *written soon after Storrow's death by Henry Greenleaf Pearson, a portion of which appears here. The story begins with Storrow's election to Boston's highly politicized twenty-four member School Committee in 1901. As reported, Storrow—like his fellow administrative progressives in other cities—quickly moved to reduce the committee to a five-member group of elite citizens who would then turn management over to a carefully chosen professional administrator.*

At the beginning of his term [in 1901], Storrow, who was not in the habit of letting grass grow under his feet, expected to make himself speedily familiar with the character and the working of this branch of the city government of which he was to be a part; but it proved a very difficult thing to do. Indeed, so clumsy and antiquated was the organization of the School Committee, and so much was it affected by the political atmosphere of the municipal administration, with its undercover methods, that even at the end of his three-year term he felt that he had learned little and, except for one innovation of his own, had accomplished even less. What the experience taught him, however, was really more important than what he expected to learn, for he became convinced that it was not possible to achieve anything constructive so long as the Committee continued to be constituted as it was.

Storrow's first term of service may be summarized in his own account of the conditions which he found existing in the School Committee. To preface it with the stage-setting: The furniture and its arrangement in the School Committee room of the building on Mason Street were expressive of the character of the body. The plan was that of a legislative chamber: a desk on a high platform for the presiding officer; facing him, a semicircle of twenty-three desks for the members of the Committee. The secretary had a table in front of the rostrum; at the rear was a space reserved for the public and the reporters. Procedure always conformed exactly to that of a legislative body: Nothing was ever said in a conversational tone; every word was spoken as part of a speech.

As the multitudinous details of the School Committee's business could not possibly be attended to in full session, small committees were needed, and enough of them to provide at least one chairmanship for each of the twenty-four members. As Storrow describes the working of the system:

> Each subcommittee is forever creating upon its own motion, business for itself. It is always hacking at or placing patches upon our school system. The other members of the board have no notice of its sessions; they do not know what scheme the chairman

may be hatching; and when it is hatched out, it needs only two of his fellow members to put it through. Even the superintendent, the actual executive head of the school system, and who ought to be held directly responsible for the efficiency of the schools, is for the most part not consulted. In fact, if the superintendent were obliged to be present at these continual meetings of these subcommittees, besides the meetings of the full Board, he would have a sorry time of it. For one thing, it would be a physical impossibility . . .

The workings of these subcommittees are entirely autocratic, and on the star chamber plan. But it is here the business of the School Board is carried on; here the plans are matured; here the appointments of teachers are passed or held up; here the new textbooks are settled upon and the school supplies bought, the janitors appointed and the budget for the year laid out.

The new member of the School Board, besides finding out that the most far-reaching innovation to the school system can thus be originated and matured by three members of the Board sitting privately in one of these small subcommittee rooms, also soon discovers that the business of the whole School Board is so conducted at its fortnightly meetings that almost any plan can be rushed through before the average member has a chance to pass an intelligent judgment upon it. There are often one hundred matters voted upon at one session of the Board. A large part of the business never gets there; what little does, if it does not pass through the avalanche of votes taken at every meeting, is only discussed in formal speeches, which are intended to attract attention rather than enlighten, and be sensational enough to secure a headline in the next morning's paper rather than change the conviction of fellow members.

From Storrow's account, it is easy to see that many members of the Committee were concerned chiefly in representing the local constituency which had elected them, in getting jobs for teachers and janitors in the schools of their districts, and in obtaining whatever else was desirable and profitable for Charlestown, South Boston, or Dorchester, as the case may be. Since the "master" of each school was beholden to the district committee for his appointment, it was with his members that he was wont to consult, rather than with the superintendent. As has been said, however, the number of members approving this system was in 1902 smaller than ever before, and among the representatives of the Public School Association were such highly regarded citizens as Grafton D. Cushing and Robert Treat Paine, Jr.; also George O. A. Ernst, who was just entering on his labors on behalf of the Boston Schools; George E. Brock and Thomas J. Kenny, who later became members of the reorganized School Committee; and Randal G. Morris. . . .

Meanwhile, as has been stated, Storrow found himself impotent in any other direction; then, in the second year of his term, the majority maintained by Public School Association representatives was reduced, and in the third year, the group formed a helpless minority. Several incidents, more or less scandalous, showed the deterioration of the Committee, and its low estate became a matter of general comment.

Once Storrow was convinced that the reform of the School Committee as an organization was essential and that no one else was likely to make any move, he decided to undertake it himself. As his term of service drew to a close in 1904, he did not stand for reelection, but instead made plans for an appeal to the Legislature. In order to find out what was the best type of school board, he applied to professor Paul Hanus of the Division of Education at Harvard ("I have a wild Utopian idea of possibly trying to remodel the School Committee," he wrote), and thus obtained the assistance of Henry W. Holmes, now Dean of the Graduate School of Education, who made a careful study of the different methods of school administration in American cities and gave Storrow a report with recommendations, of which the essential point was a School Committee of five, its members appointed by the mayor. Indeed, this provision constituted practically alone the bill which Storrow finally decided to lay before the Legislature:

> We spent six months in drawing up a bill of a new school organization [he wrote afterwards], with many modern improvements, such as a longer term for the superintendent, etc., etc., but before we went up to the Legislature we pitched out all the modern improvements and came down to the transferring of the authority of the old Board to the new, feeling that if we got the new men on the new Board we would get any reasonable request granted by the Legislature, and in fact this was just what happened.

Next, he handled the campaign as he had handled that for the Charles River Basin. He formed no committee or association; he took all the responsibility, supplied the driving energy, and employed helpers to obtain signatures to his petition, to attend to publicity, and otherwise to get support for his project. At the hearing on his bill before the Committee on Cities he had important assistance from two ex-mayors of Boston—Josiah Quincy and Nathan Mathews—but the chief speaker was himself. Asked afterwards by someone who would emulate him to describe "his method of insuring favorable action by the Legislature," he replied simply, "I should be very glad indeed to tell you how you could accomplish what you desire, but I must confess that I do not know of any method of insuring favorable action by the Legislature upon such a proposition—or upon any other. The only method I know of is to expend all the energy and good sense one possesses in presenting the merits of one's case to the committee having it under consideration and to the members of the Legislature. They must be induced to take an interest in the matter, and convinced that the change is one the public interest requires."

Though, as was to be expected, Storrow's measure was opposed by the beneficiaries of the old system, their opposition proved so extravagant that it carried little weight with the Legislature. The objection of the Public School Association and of an organization known as the Independent Women Voters that appointment of five members of the Committee by the mayor would deprive women of their only opportunity to exercise the suffrage had more weight; their suggestion that the Committee be chosen by ballot was accepted by Storrow. With this change, the measure became law.

"Presenting the merits of one's case" to the voters of Boston in a municipal campaign was, however, a vastly different matter from talking informingly and persuasively to legislators individually and in groups; it was an undertaking with the methods of which Storrow was entirely unfamiliar and for which he was in many ways unsuited. Furthermore, as it happened, the elements of the campaign this year were so strangely mixed as to baffle even the seasoned politicians. At the outset, the Democratic control had been snatched from "smiling Jim Donovan," the city boss, by John F. Fitzgerald, "the young Napoleon of the North End." Besides these two factions in the party camp, there was a third, led by a woman, which, resenting the demolition of the old School Committee, went into action with a blind rage of vindictiveness. On the other side, the reformers were by no means in agreement as to methods, and Storrow, a newcomer, was felt by the seasoned campaigners of the P.S.A. to be imperiling its success by his independent acts. Some of his ideas he put into effect with a rapidity that astonished and alarmed them; but when they reasoned with him they were equally astonished at the way in which he listened to their argument and with no pride of opinion abandoned his own project.

After a good deal of negotiating, which on the Democratic side finally brought out the police, the School Committee slates were made up: one was as bad as possible; the other, composed of men of high character (G. E. Brock, D. A. Ellis, T. J. Kenny, W. S. Kenney, J. J. Storrow) was expected to appeal to all voters who wished to take the school system out of politics, and in that department of the city government, at least, to establish and maintain high standards of administration. Thanks to the endorsements that these five men received both from the two political parties and from the nonpartisan associations, thanks to vigorous campaigning in which the reform elements at last came together, thanks finally to the scandals in which some of their opponents were involved and which at this time became a matter of general knowledge, public opinion was roused to the point of voting to clean house. In fact, although on election day, the first Monday in December, Fitzgerald, the Democratic candidate for mayor, was successful, the greater triumph went to the Public School Association, which elected its entire ticket.

When this new Committee met on January 1, 1906, and as its first act elected Storrow chairman, it faced a strange situation. Only ten days before, the Superintendent of Schools had died suddenly, his death having been brought on, as most people believed, by a vituperative attack made on him at one of the last sessions of the old Committee by its most discredited member. The new Board therefore had as a pressing duty the selection of his successor. The most promising man for the position, Stratton D. Brooks, for some years past one of the assistant superintendents, or supervisors, as they were called, had just been elected Superintendent of Schools of Cleveland, and had gone thither to take up his new duties. Before his departure, however, Storrow had talked with him and obtained from him a comprehensive plan for reorganizing the school system. After the Committee had ransacked the nation, they returned to Brooks and persuaded the City of Cleveland to release him. Before the first of March, Storrow had taken the program of reform from its pigeonhole and given it to Brooks to put into execution.

In the hands of the new Board and its Superintendent lay the fate of 99,000 pupils and 3,300 employees, and the disposition of funds amounting annually to $3,673,800.

From the beginning, the new School Committee was agreed that it could not possibly perform its work unless it limited itself to functions proper to a body of final authority. Accordingly, it lodged executive duties in the Superintendent, under whom were six Assistant Superintendents, a business agent, and a schoolhouse custodian. In the course of his reorganizing and reforming, Brooks had many a sharp contest, with much clamor from the public, especially on behalf of recalcitrant teachers. The old order was not of a kind to melt under the genial influence of a warm sun. Blows had to be given and received, and Brooks was every inch a fighter. When protests against his masterful ways poured in on the School Committee, they were listened to respectfully, but they did not impair its support of its executive officer. When a man received responsibility with which Storrow was connected he knew what he could count on. . . .

To give a picture of Storrow's School Committee at work: The five men usually assembled on Mondays at half-past four, in the large room formerly consecrated to oratory. ("When I found how the new School Committee was made up," one of the Assistant Superintendents told an appreciative audience, "and saw that there was not an orator among them, I said, 'Thank God, the schools are safe.'") At this session, they held hearings for any citizen or group who had complaints or proposals to make. Some of the questions that Storrow put to these visitors, like his investigation of the fire drill, were not calculated to make them "quite so proud of themselves as they had been;" other questions were asked on purpose to see whether they would stand to their guns. Disconcerted, perhaps, at first, the visitor realized before he left the room that he had been paid the compliment of a genuine interview with a man, not in the least antagonistic, who wanted "real results." These hearings were followed by discussion amongst the members of the Committee, in which the measures to be voted on at the formal session in the evening were put into final shape. While they talked, the menu of the Adams House was passed about and each man gave his order for dinner. During dinner the talk continued, and presently it was time for the stated meeting.

At this session, the public was admitted, though usually, in the absence of speechmaking, it preferred not to come, and the audience consisted of two or three reporters. Motions were passed with a mere formality of discussion—all moot points had been settled beforehand—and at the end of half or three-quarters of an hour, the meeting adjourned. Then began the real business of the evening. In the Superintendent's office, with coats off, in relaxed positions, the atmosphere growing thicker and thicker from cigar smoke, these five men ran the gamut of Brooks's problems with him. The conversation was discursive—the school system, it seemed, opened the door to every subject known to the mind of man; it was not gay, not intense; but always it was absorbingly human. And it was as human beings that they dealt with what was before them. Storrow here was not the businessman absenting himself hurriedly from the world of high finance to perform a hard duty. He was merely a citizen—a sample citizen—threshing out with his municipal neighbors matters of common interest, coming to the work with zest and receiving from it refreshment. Like the talk of a group of familiars at a country store, their session was long, leisurely, and late, and it was frequently well after midnight when they broke up and went home to their waiting wives.

✦ Margaret Haley, Why Teachers Should Organize, 1904

When Margaret Haley spoke to the National Education Association in 1904 on the need for teachers to organize, she was already the best-known teacher advocate in the United States. Founder and leader of the Chicago Teachers Federation, Haley was a powerful and effective voice for the rights of teachers. In 1904, the NEA was dominated by the male elite of education. To this less-than-friendly audience, Haley asserted that teachers needed:

- *Increased salaries*
- *Job security and pensions*
- *An end to overwork in overcrowded schoolrooms*
- *Recognition of teachers as educators instead of "factoryized education"*

For Haley and her counterparts, change had to come quickly, so that teachers could be professionals who felt proud of themselves and of their service to the nation's children. An organized body of teachers—a union—Haley believed, was the key to change.

The responsibility for changing existing conditions so as to make it possible for the public schools to do its work rests with the people, the whole people. Any attempt on the part of the public to evade or shift this responsibility must result in weakening the public sense of civic responsibility and the capacity for civic duty, besides further isolating the public school from the people, to the detriment of both.

The sense of responsibility for the duties of citizenship in a democracy is necessarily weak in a people so lately freed from monarchical rule as are the American people, and who still retain in their educational, economic, and political systems so much of their monarchical inheritance, with growing tendencies for retaining and developing the essential weaknesses of that inheritance instead of overcoming them. . . .

Practical experience in meeting the responsibilities of citizenship directly, not in evading or shifting them, is the prime need of the American people. However clever or cleverly disguised the schemes for relieving the public of these responsibilities by vicarious performance of them, or however appropriate those schemes in a monarchy, they have no place in a government of the people, by the people, for the people, and such schemes must result in defeating their object; for to the extent that they obtain, they destroy in a people the capacity for self-government.

If the American people cannot be made to realize and meet their responsibility to the public school, no self-appointed custodians of the public intelligence and conscience can do it for them. Horace Mann, speaking of the dependence of the prosperity of the schools on the public intelligence, said:

> The people will sustain no better schools and have no better education than they
> personally see the need of; and therefore the people are to be informed and elevated
> as a preliminary step toward elevating the schools.

Sometimes, in our impatience at the slowness with which the public moves in these matters, we are tempted to disregard this wise counsel.

The methods as well as the objects of teachers' organizations must be in harmony with the fundamental object of the public school in a democracy, to preserve and develop the democratic ideal. It is not enough that this ideal be realized in the administration of the schools, and the methods of teaching; in all its relations to the public, the public school must conform to this ideal.

Nowhere in the United States today does the public school, as a branch of the public service, receive from the public either the moral or financial support needed to enable it properly to perform its important function in the social organism. The conditions which are militating most strongly against efficient teaching, and which existing organizations of the kind under discussion here are directing their energies toward changing, briefly stated, are the following:

1. Greatly increased cost of living, together with constant demands for higher standards of scholarship and professional attainments and culture, to be met with practically stationary and wholly inadequate teachers' salaries.
2. Insecurity of tenure of office and lack of provision for old age.
3. Overwork in overcrowded schoolrooms, exhausting both in mind and body.
4. And, lastly, lack of recognition of the teacher as an educator in the school system, due to the increased tendency toward "factoryizing education," making the teacher an automaton, a mere factory hand, whose duty it is to carry out mechanically and unquestioningly the ideas and orders of those clothed with the authority of position, and who may or may not know the needs of the children or how to minister to them.

The individuality of the teacher and her power of initiative are thus destroyed, and the result is courses of study, regulations and equipment which the teachers have had no voice in selecting, which often have no relation to the children's needs, and which prove a hindrance instead of a help in teaching.

Dr. John Dewey, of the University of Chicago, in the *Elementary School Teacher* for December 1903, says:

As to the teacher: If there is a single public-school system in the United States where there is official and constitutional provision made for the submitting questions of methods of discipline and teaching, and the questions of the curriculum, text-books, etc., to the discussion of those actually engaged in the work of teaching, that fact has escaped my notice. Indeed, the opposite situation is so common that it seems, as a rule, to be absolutely taken for granted as the normal and final condition of affairs. The number of persons to whom any other course has occurred as desirable, or even possible—to say nothing of necessary—is apparently very limited. But until the public-school system is organized in such a way that every teacher has some regular and representative way in which he or she can register judgment upon matters of educational importance, with the assurance that this judgment will somehow affect the school system, the assertion that the present system is not, from the internal standpoint, democratic seems to be justified. Either we come here upon some fixed and inherent limitation of the democratic principle, or else we find in this fact an obvious discrepancy between the conduct of the school and the conduct of social life—a discrepancy so great as to demand immediate and persistent effort at reform.

A few days ago, Professor George F. James, dean of pedagogy of the State University of Minnesota, said to an audience of St. Paul teachers:

One hundred thousand teachers will this year quit an occupation which does not yield them a living wage. Scores and hundreds of schools are this day closed in the most prosperous sections of this country because the bare pittance offered will not attract teachers of any kind.

Professor James further maintained that schoolteachers are not only underpaid, but that they are paid much less proportionately than they received eight years ago.

It is necessary that the public understand the effect which teaching under these conditions is having upon the education of the children.

A word, before closing, on the relations of the public school teachers and the public schools to the labor unions. As the professional organization furnishes the motive and ideal which shall determine the character and methods of the organized effort of teachers to secure better conditions for teaching, so is it the province of the educational agencies in a democracy to furnish the motive and ideal which shall determine the character and methods of the organization of its members for self-protection.

There is no possible conflict between the good of society and the good of its members, of which the industrial workers are the vast majority. The organization of these workers for the mutual aid has shortened the hours of labor, raised and equalized the wages of men and women, and taken the children from the factories and workshops. These humanitarian achievements of the labor unions—and many others which space forbids enumerating—in raising the standard of living of the poorest and weakest members of society, are a service to society which for its own welfare it must recognize. More than this, by intelligent comprehension of the limitations of the labor unions and the causes of these limitations, by just, judicious, and helpful criticism and cooperation, society must aid them to feel the inspiration of higher ideals, and to find the better means to realize these ideals.

If there is one institution on which the responsibility to perform this service rests most heavily, it is the public school. If there is one body of public servants of whom the public has a right to expect the mental and moral equipment to face the labor question, and other issues vitally affecting the welfare of society and urgently pressing for a rational and scientific solution, it is the public school teachers, whose special contribution to society is their own power to think, the moral courage to follow their convictions, and the training of citizens to think and to express thought in free and intelligent action.

The narrow conception of education which makes the mechanics of reading, and arithmetic, and other subjects, the end and aim of schools, instead of a means to an end—which mistakes the accidental and incidental for the essential—produces the unthinking, mechanical mind in a teacher and pupil, and prevents the public schools as an institution, and the public school teachers as a body, from becoming conscious of their relation to society and its problems, and from meeting their responsibilities. On the other hand, that teaching which is most scientific and rational gives the highest degree of power to think and to select the most intelligent means of expressing thought in every field of activity. The ideals and methods of the labor unions are in a measure a test of the efficiency of the schools and other educational agencies.

How shall the public school and the industrial workers, in their struggle to secure the rights of humanity through a more just and equitable distribution of the products of their labor, meet their mutual responsibility to each other and to society?

Whether the work of coordinating these two great educational agencies, manual and mental labor, with each other and with the social organism, shall be accomplished through the affiliation of the organizations of brain and manual workers is a mere matter of detail and method to be decided by the exigencies in each case. The essential thing is that the public school teachers recognize the fact that their struggle to maintain the efficiency of the schools through better conditions for themselves is a part of the same great struggle which the manual workers—often misunderstood and unaided— have been making for humanity through their efforts to secure living conditions for themselves and their children; and that lack of the unfavorable conditions of both is a common cause.

Two ideals are struggling for supremacy in American life today: one, the industrial ideal, dominating through the supremacy of commercialism, which subordinates the worker to the products and the machine; the other, the ideal of democracy, the ideal of the educators, which places humanity above all machines, and demands that all activity shall be the expression of life. If this ideal of the educators cannot be carried over into the industrial field, then the ideal of industrialism will be carried over into the school. Those two ideals can no more continue to exist in American life than our nation could have continued half-slave and half-free. If the school cannot bring joy to the work of the world, the joy must go out of its own life, and work in the school, as in the factory, will become drudgery.

Viewed in this light, the duty and responsibility of the educators in the solution of the industrial question is one which must thrill and fascinate while it awes, for the very depth of the significance of life is shut up in this question. But the first requisite is to put aside all prejudice, all preconceived notions, all misinformation and half-information, and to take to this question what the educators have long recognized must be taken to scientific investigation in other fields. There may have been justification for failure to do this in the past, but we cannot face the responsibility of continued failure and maintain our title as thinkers and educators. When men organize and go out to kill, they go surrounded by pomp, display, and pageantry, under the inspiration of music and with the admiration of the throng. Not so the army of industrial toilers who have been fighting humanity's battles, unhonored and unsung.

It will be well indeed if the teachers have the courage of their convictions and face all that the labor unions have faced with the same courage and perseverance.

Today, teachers of America, we stand at the parting of the ways: Democracy is not on trial, but America is.

✦ ELLA FLAGG YOUNG, ISOLATION IN THE SCHOOL, 1901

While Margaret Haley of Chicago was the nation's best known organizer of militant teachers into the first fledgling teacher unions, her close ally, Ella Flagg Young, was the most significant theoretical voice in the teacher's movement of the progressive era. A colleague of John Dewey at the University of Chicago and later the Superintendent of the Chicago Public Schools, Young provided a powerful voice for the belief that a democratic society required a democratic system of education—one in which the teacher was a respected citizen and not a passive cog in a machine run from above, especially one run by "administrative progressives" like Storrow and his counterparts in cities across the country. The selections from Young's Isolation in the School *(Chicago: The University of Chicago Press, 1901) that appear here give some flavor of Young's philosophy, which animated teacher organizations across the nation.*

Two objections will be urged against the implication that all should be active, not only in realizing, but in setting, the aim of the school. (1) The school cannot have so many different aims as there are teachers connected with it. If active participation in originating and cooperating means diversity, then this objection is well-grounded. (2) Teachers are satisfied with the present method. The relations are pleasant in the system. No one feels downtrodden. Consideration must be shown; teachers are too busy to have the duty of assisting in planning the course of study added to their labors. Anyway, they have no ideals to set up. . . .

The greatest question before civilized nations today is whether the law of the mental life-process shall be recognized in education as original in all minds, or as peculiar to certain types only. Or, to put it in another way, shall the mental powers of the few be exercised according to law, and those of the many be isolated from that which evolves power—the initiative in action—or shall all be active as organic parts of the thinking world? Rude self-assertion and hopeless self-renunciation are the attendants upon an abnormal mental restraint, as disease and weakness are the attendants upon physical inaction. As a high degree of energy and reasonable powers of endurance are the result of a regimen in accord with the law underlying the life-process of the physical organism, so a well-poised self-assertion and a judicious self-renunciation are the results of an activity in harmony with the law underlying the mental life-process. . . .

Following close upon this question of activity in the mental life as presented by modern theory is that pertaining to the function of the school in this government. In its general aim, the function of the private and the public school is the same, but because the latter is directly dependent upon the state for its life, it has been subjected to a closer scrutiny both as to methods and results. Critics of democracy and critics of the public schools unite in making essentially the same criticism on our form of government and on our schools, though they express themselves differently. The first, the critics of democracy, say that its tendency is to breed many commonplace, average men upon whom the responsibilities of the state will fall, instead of a few great men who might easily assume the duties of statesmanship. Critics of the public school say that it is dominated by the theory of uniformity, and they ask why teachers who help make the school a mere mill, grinding uniform grists, are retained. The obverse of this is found among the teachers. An energetic and thoughtful part of the corps is strenuously decrying that form of systematism of the schools which tends to make automatons of the teachers. This opposition began before criticism of the method of the schools was well-defined in the minds of those on the outside. Here we have a curious condition of affairs. The objects of the critics and the teachers seem widely different. The first aim, to purge the schools of the present type of teacher; the second aim, to displace the mechanical action of the school. Investigation will show their ultimate aims to be identical. With truth, the schools are frequently pointed out as the greatest unifying agent extant in this land, whose people represent all European peoples, and yet who have a common faith in the integral principles of the constitution of its national and state organizations.

How varied are the races that have come from Europe! Though of the Aryan stock, the branches have each their marked peculiarities. Not alone the differences in the Celtic, the Romanic, the Germanic, the Slavonic, and the Graeco-Italian blend, but the differences growing out of the social customs of the many nations into which long ago the races had divided have been brought into the public school to be minimized, obliterated, harmonized in the process of unification. A survey of the past two hundred years shows the children of the poor and the rich, of the English-speaking and the non-English-speaking races, of the various religious faiths, all meeting on a common ground and with a common interest—the mastery of the printed page. As the young have striven side by side in the common school, they have learned, not from the printed page, but through experience, that the soul is not classified according to its worldly possessions, the particular language spoken in the home, or the faith in which it is reared. Differences in race customs might have been so intensified by the segregation of immigrants of different nationalities that open hostility would have been the prevailing attitude of different settlements toward each other. So potent has been the public school in creating a sentiment favorable to oneness, to Americanism, that sectional antagonism based on racial characteristics maintained in their original forms is unknown. In childhood, millions of America's citizens have learned something of the fundamentals in the unity of the human race. The comradeship in experience developed by the democratic spirit pervading the methods in instruction and discipline, is a more positive factor in the sympathetic appreciation existing between members of different religious and social organizations than the association in private or denominational schools can ever be.

It is the free public school that has made the child of foreign parentage strive to take on the habits of dress, speech, and thought that would identify him with the people whose ancestors were merged into this social and political society at an earlier date than were his. . . .

The school cannot take up the question of the development of training for citizenship in a democracy while the teachers are still segregated in two classes, as are the citizens in an aristocracy.

No more un-American or dangerous solution of the difficulties involved in maintaining a high degree of efficiency in the teaching corps of a large school system can be attempted than that which is effected by what is termed "close supervision." Frequent visitations to the schools in the district, or ward, bring the minutiae of each schoolroom into the foreground, and develop a feeling of responsibility for matters of petty detail which are of a purely personal nature; and hence it follows that a ranking officer may be so near to the daily work as to have an exaggerated, or mistaken, conception of the obligations of a superintendent in determining the method in regard to even the nonessentials in the conduct of the school. In a short time the teachers must cease to occupy the position of initiators in the individual work of instruction and discipline, and must fall into a class of assistants, whose duty consists in carrying out instructions of a higher class which originates method for all. The reaction from close supervision with one set of dominant ideas to close supervision with another set has been the basis of procedure in every large system, with little recognition of the fundamental difficulty in the theory. In colleges and universities, the benumbing theory of close supervision of the members of the faculties is unknown; and yet it is generally held as an inspiring, natural one for elementary schools. There must come a recognition of the law of life in those schools. The rights and obligations that inhere in members in different parts of the system must be subjected to careful analysis, and then the teaching corps must be unfettered in its activity in striving to realize those things which will evolve themselves in a free play of thought in the individual and the community.

To secure this freedom of thought, there must be, within the various parts of the school, organizations for the consideration of questions of legislation. Such organizations have been effected in some universities and in a few schools systems, but in the latter, they lack some essential features for securing freedom of thought; and yet they are deemed satisfactory; so little does the teaching corps know about origination of thought on questions concerning education. Without doubt, councils for discussion and recommendation may be organized, and seem to have an eminently successful life, and yet come far short of their potentialities. The voice of authority of position not only must not dominate, but must not be heard in the councils. There should be organized, throughout every system, school councils whose membership in the aggregate should include every teacher and principal. The membership of each school council should be small enough to make the discussions deliberative, not sensational. The necessity for such an organization that shall insure a free play of thought and its expression, rather than courage in opposing and declaiming, because restive under restraint, cannot be made too emphatic. There should be a central council composed of delegates from the other councils. The representation in the central council should not be determined by ranking positions in the schools. It is fair to assume that the delegates would be selected with care. After recommendations have been made to the superintendent, and he, with the assistant or district superintendents and the supervisors of special studies, has discussed them, if there are any points of difference in judgment, the district superintendents should meet the first councils and present the objections. The attendance of members of the supervising force upon the meetings for the reconsideration of questions would clarify the thought of all, provided there was no suspicion of an effort to have the objections sustained because of the official position of the objectors.

If the result of the second discussion shows the original recommendation by the council again sustained, and the superintendent, upon receipt of the report, believes the majority of teachers and principals mistaken, there should be no further effort made to secure the adoption of his views by vote of the councils. *He should act in accordance with his own judgment, and be held responsible for the outcome.* No one would receive the decision of the superintendent as something strange, unknown, to be incorporated in the work. The deliberations would have familiarized all with the essentials involved, and those sharp breaks in theory and practice which have been made in the past would no longer be possible. Education would be a continuous process, based on theory; not mere experimentation, based on personal preferences. . . .

In America today, more than leeway in individual opinion is needed; more than the recognition of the individual and his development. From the entrance upon the first year in the kindergarten till the close of the student life, if the school functions as an intrinsic part of this democracy, the child, the youth, and the teacher will each be an organic factor in an organization where rights and duties will be inseparable; where the free movement of thought will develop great personalities.

✦ GRACE C. STRACHAN, EQUAL PAY FOR EQUAL WORK, 1910

While Margaret Haley and the Chicago teachers focused on a wide range of issues affecting teachers, Grace Strachan and the other leaders of New York City's Interborough Association of Women Teachers had a single focus: the unequal salaries paid to women teachers. One of the clearest symbols of the unequal status of women in the teaching profession was the fact that not only did they regularly occupy the lower rungs of the profession—they were the classroom teachers, while men were the super-intendents—but that even at the level of classroom teacher, most cities and towns had two different salary scales, one for women and one for men. From early in the nine-teenth century onward, women had been recruited to the teaching profession because they were seen as more maternal than men, but also because school boards could hire them more cheaply. During the progressive era, the second part of the argument no longer held water—at least for the women involved. Although it took some time, the campaign for equal pay was generally successful, and one of the legacies of the pro-gressive era was a gradual end to the two-level pay scale. Still, schools tended to pro-mote men to the higher-paying ranks much faster than women for many years to come.

Salary—A periodical allowance made as compensation to a person for his official or professional services or for his regular work.—*Funk and Wagnalls.*

Notice the words, *a person.* Here is no differentiation between male persons and female persons.

Yet the City of New York pays a "male" person for certain "professional services" $900, while paying a "female" person only $600 for the same "professional services." Stranger still, it pays for certain experience for a "male" person $105, while paying a "female" person only $40 for the identical experience. These are but samples of the "glaring inequalities" in the teachers' salary schedules.

Why is the male in the teaching profession differentiated from the male in every other calling, when his salary is concerned?

Why does the city differentiate the woman it hires to teach its children from the woman it hires to take stenographic notes, use a typewriter, follow up truants, inspect a tenement, or issue a license?

Why are not the appointees from the eligible lists established by the Department of Education, entitled to the same privileges and rights as appointees from the Civil Service lists from other City and State Departments?

Some ask, "Shall the single woman, in teaching, be given the married woman's wage?" I do not know what they mean, I say, "Why not the single woman in teaching just as much as the single woman in washing, in farming, in dressmaking, in nursing, in telephoning?"

Again, some ask, is there such a thing as "equal work" by two people?

Technically, no. No two people do exactly the same work in the same way. This is true of all professional and official work. Compare Mayor Gaynor's work with Mayor McClellan's. Will anyone say their work as mayor is "Equal Work"? And yet the pay is the same. Do all policemen do "Equal Work"? Yet they receive equal pay. So with firemen, school physicians, tenement house inspectors. The taxpayers, no doubt, believe that, judged by his work, Mayor Gaynor is worth a far higher salary than many of his predecessors. But a great corporation like the City of New York cannot attempt to pay each of its employees according to the work of that particular street cleaner or fireman or stenographer, and so must be content with classifying its positions, and fixing a salary for each. So should it do for its teachers. That is all we ask.

The Family-to-Support Argument:

It is rather a sad commentary on our profession that its men members are the only men who object to women members of the same profession getting the same pay for the same work. Who ever heard of a man lawyer fighting a woman lawyer in this way? A man doctor arguing that another doctor should give her services for less pay simply because she happened to be a woman? And leaving the professions, what attitude do we find the men who form our "Labor Unions" taking on this question? They form a solid phalanx on the side of "Equal Pay." The most powerful of all unions in many respects—"Big Six"—has a by-law making it a misdemeanor to pay a woman less than a man working the same form. All Labor Unions fight "two prices on a job."

Is it not sad to see men, American men, shoving aside, trampling down, and snatching the life preservers from their sisters? I say life preservers seriously and mean it literally. For to the woman obliged to support herself, is not her wage-earning ability truly a life preserver? How can any man expect one whom she is legally privileged to assist, take from a woman any part of the wages she has earned and remain worthy even in his own eyes? The excuses he makes to himself and to hers in the attempt to justify his act, tends to belittle him more and more.

And yet some men whose blood sisters have by teaching provided the money to enable them, their brothers, to become teachers, oppose those very sisters in their efforts to obtain "Equal Pay for Equal Work." Can one ask for stronger proof of the insidious danger to our manhood which lurks in the unjust standards of salary for services rendered? The true man, the good man, ought to put the woman who earns a respectable living on a pedestal, as a beacon of encouragement to other women to show them one who wanted clothes to wear, and food to eat and a place to live, and who obtained them by honorable labor.

I am firmly convicted that while teaching is a natural vocation for most women, it is rarely the true vocation of a man. And that those who enter the vocation without the love for it which overshadows even the pocket returns, invariably deteriorate. Their lives are spent largely among those whom they consider their subordinates—in a position or in a salary, if not in intellect—the children and the woman teachers. They grow to have an inordinate opinion of themselves. No matter how ridiculous or absurd or unfair may be the attitudes they take and the things they say, there is no one to say,

"Nonsense!" as would one of his peers in the outer world. The novelist Davis Graham Phillips, in the following description of one of his characters, expresses my opinion better than I can myself: "Peter was not to blame for his weaknesses. He has not had the chance to become otherwise. He had been deprived of that hand-to-hand strife which alone makes a man strong. Usually, however, the dangerous truth as to his weaknesses was well-hidden by the fictitious seeming of strength which obstinacy, selfishness, and adulation of a swarm of sycophants and dependents combine to give a man of means and position." Recently, in one of our schools, a male assistant to the principal resigned. The vacancy thus caused was filled by a woman. This woman is doing the same work as the man did, but with greater satisfaction to the principal. *But* she is being paid $800 a year less than the man was.

In another school I know, there was a woman assistant to principal. As a grade teacher she had married and resigned, expecting—as most girls do when they marry— that she wouldn't have to work outside the home any more. But her husband became a victim of tuberculosis, and they went to Colorado in search of health for him. Time passed, their funds were exhausted, the invalid was unable to work, and so they came back, and the wife—after certifying, as by our by-laws require, that her husband was unable to support her and had been so for two years—was reappointed. Later she secured promotion to assistant to principal. During the day she labored in a large, progressive school, composed almost wholly of children born in Russia, or of Russian parentage. At night she taught a class of foreign men. Now, although she actually had a family to support, she was receiving $800 a year less than a man in her position would receive. A married man? Oh, no, not necessary. He might be a millionaire bachelor, or the pet of a wealthy wife—it is only necessary for him to be a "male" assistant to principal. Possibly on account of her family responsibilities, probably because she was ambitious, she strove for a principalship. During the school year, she traveled to Columbia University and took postgraduate courses after school and on Saturdays; during the summer, when she should have been resting, she was studying with Professor This and Professor That. Last September she took the examination for a principal's license: in October, she died—typhoid, the doctors said. The husband she had cheerfully and lovingly supported for years survived her but a few weeks.

Why have I dwelt on this? To show the absurdity of the "family wage" argument of the male teacher . . . . Under a system of equal pay, where services should be paid for irrespective of sex, some men to-day remain single because of relative economic independence, which they desire to maintain. These men are, however, relatively few. Women are as instinctive and as normal as men are, and independence, which they feared to lose, would prevent very few from marrying when they should make marriages which were attractive to them. Independence of women would improve marriage, since fewer women would marry because of necessity. By the same means, divorce would be decreased, and human happiness would have a boom.

Our Association early in 1908 gathered some statistics. They showed 377 women—11 of them married and 6 widows—supporting 707 others besides themselves. These teachers are all women, but the people depending wholly upon them or partly upon them are their mothers or their fathers or both or a brother or a sister or a niece or a nephew. These are actual figures collated from written answers to our questionnaire. You see, then, that here is an average of two people for every woman to support besides herself. Now, what salary is offered to these young women of twenty-one years of age, after they have spent all these years in preparing for the position of teacher? What salary is she being paid by the City of New York, the greatest city in the world, with the greatest public school system in the world? $11.53 a week. A woman in charge of one of the stations in the city gets more than that. Does the latter have to spend as much money on clothes? No. She can wear the same clothes from one end of the year to the other, if she wants to, and then not be criticized. But I know when I go into a classroom, among the things that I notice is the teacher's dress—whether it is neat, whether it is appropriate. She must be a model for her class. Besides, the teacher must live in a respectable neighborhood and make a good appearance at home and abroad, and she must continue her studies in order to give satisfactory service.

✦ CORA BIGELOW, WORLD DEMOCRACY AND SCHOOL DEMOCRACY, 1918

Cora Bigelow was the leader of the elementary school teachers' organization in Boston; a group she was able to turn briefly into one of the first teacher unions in the nation in 1919. She wrote the following article for their monthly Boston Teachers News Letter *in December, 1918, a month after World War I ended. Bigelow's brief piece reflects the views of at least one group of classroom teachers who embraced the progressive vision of a reformed school as part of a larger reformed society, with teachers leading the effort. Although Bigelow has kind words for school administrators, she—and many others like her across the country—clearly stood in opposition to the administrative progressives and their efforts to centralize authority in a professional elite. For Bigelow, progressive education meant teacher power: adequate compensation for teachers and a central role in the development of the school's curriculum and goals.*

World democracy and school democracy should go hand in hand. The world has reached a crisis where national autocracy must disappear. Business and commercial autocracy also must go. Autocracy, wherever it occurs in school affairs, must follow the trend of the times and give place to democracy.

Democracy has developed rapidly in the professional life of American schools, to the great advantage of the schools. It is not unusual for school superintendents and other professional officials to seek conferences regularly with teachers in the endeavor to work out school problems. There is no loss of dignity on the part of these higher officials and not the faintest assumption of arrogance on the part of teachers who meet in such conferences. It is but the earnest, natural, and democratic "getting together" of those mutually interested in the progress of education.

So long as the conferences deal solely with academic subjects, they are looked upon favorably by school committees in general, who themselves represent the financial end of school planning. But the moment conferences take up the subject of school business, however closely connected with school efficiency, they are called mercenary and self-seeking and are at once in great disfavor, if not in disgrace. School teaching is the one occupation where reasonable regard for one's own financial welfare is seemingly not a virtue.

Many school committees appear to expect professional progress to go on in the mind and soul of the teachers without equal regard for their bodily welfare. Professional heights, though fully recognized by the professional school officials, do not enable the teachers to meet their financial requirements of the times. Is it mercenary and selfish for teachers to show an interest in being able to meet their just debts?

School committees and teachers alike represent the average intelligence of the community, the former are temporarily representing the public, while the latter are permanently employed by the public. Any teacher who resigns may be elected to the school committee and fill the office admirably, but not one in many of the members of school committees (who has not previously been a teacher) can become an acceptable teacher. This being true, why are school committees in our cities and towns apparently fearful of advising with teachers in school planning?

The world has reached a time when there must be true cooperation in every walk of life, not operating from one party and cooperating from the other. Cooperation is mutual effort of equal earnestness. American teachers are ready to fulfill their part of the contract, and will accept at once any disposition on the part of school authorities to consummate such a mutual effort.

The professional officials connected with most American schools long since successfully adopted the democratic plan of mutual effort to develop the schools. There will never be peace and contentment in school systems until school committees become as democratic as the professional school officials, until school autocracy is exchanged for school democracy, and until school committees apply the deep, broad democratic principles to their temporary power, which are not being worked on in the great world issues, as the good which can come out of the present world war against autocracy.

The teachers are ready and the professional school officials have already become democratic. When will the other factor in American school affairs join hands with these two in honest endeavor to put the American schools on the broad basis of American democracy?

Then, and not until then, will the present cause of discord diminish. Democracy stands for mutual benefits derived from earnest mutual effort, regularly sustained.

❖ JOHN DEWEY, THE SCHOOL AND SOCIETY, 1899

The curriculum reformers—the advocates of the child-centered school—regarded the work of John Dewey as their theoretical base. The range of reformers, some predating Dewey and others building consciously on his work, included some of the best known names in progressive education—Francis W. Parker, Randolph S. Bourne, Carleton Washburne, Agnes DeLima, and William H. Kilpatrick. These child-centered advocates developed their own progressive schools or their own differing brands of the child-centered curriculum. Still, to gain a sense of the flavor of the movement, it is best to start with Dewey's own work, such as the selection included here from The School and Society. *Dewey was often called "the father of progressive education" by both friends and detractors of the movement. He saw himself as primarily a philosopher. During his long life from 1859 to 1952, he started the Laboratory School at the University of Chicago in 1896, testing many of the progressive theories, and wrote a steady stream of commentaries on education, culminating in* Democracy and Education *in 1916.*

We are apt to look at the school from an individualistic standpoint, as something between teacher and pupil, or between teacher and parent. That which interests us most is naturally the progress made by the individual child of our acquaintance, his normal physical development, his advance in ability to read, write, and figure, his growth in the knowledge of geography and history, improvement in manners, habits of promptness, order, and industry—it is from such standards as these that we judge the work of the school. And rightly so. Yet the range of the outlook needs to be enlarged. What the best and wisest parent wants for his own child, that must the community want for all of its children. Any other ideal for our schools is narrow and unlovely; acted upon, it destroys our democracy. All that society has accomplished for itself is put, through the agency of the school, at the disposal of its future members. All its better thoughts of itself it hopes to realize through the new possibilities thus opened to its future self. Here individualism and socialism are at one. Only by being true to the full growth of all the individuals who make it up, can society by any chance be true to itself. And in the self-direction thus given, nothing counts as much as the school, for, as Horace Mann said, "Where anything is growing, one former is worth a thousand reformers."

Whenever we have in mind the discussion of a new movement in education, it is especially necessary to take the broader, or social, view. Otherwise, changes in the school institution and tradition will be looked at as the arbitrary inventions of particular teachers, at the worst transitory fads, and at the best merely improvements in certain details—and this is the plane upon which it is too customary to consider school changes. It is as rational to conceive of the locomotive or the telegraph as personal devices. The modification going on in the method and curriculum of education is as much a product of the changed social situation, and as much an effort to meet the needs of the new society that is forming, as are changes in modes of industry and commerce.

It is to this, then, that I especially ask your attention: the effort to conceive what roughly may be termed the "New Education" in the light of larger changes in society. Can we connect this "New Education" with the general march of events? If we can, it will lose its isolated character; it will cease to be an affair which proceeds only from the over-ingenious minds of pedagogues dealing with particular pupils. It will appear as part and parcel of the whole social evolution, and, in its more general features at least, as inevitable. Let us then ask after the main aspects of the social movement; and afterward turn to the school to find what witness it gives of effort to put itself in line. And since it is quite impossible to cover the whole ground, I shall for the most part confine myself in this chapter to one typical thing in the modern school movement—that which passes under the name of manual training—hoping, if the relation of that to changed social conditions appears, we shall be ready to concede the point as well regarding other educational innovations.

I make no apology for not dwelling at length upon the social changes in question. Those I shall mention are writ so large that he who runs may read. The change that comes first to mind, the one that overshadows and even controls all others, is the industrial one—the application of science resulting in the great inventions that have utilized the forces of nature on a vast and inexpensive scale. The growth of a worldwide market as the object of production, of vast manufacturing centers to supply this market, of cheap and rapid means of communication and distribution between all its parts. Even as to its feebler beginnings, this change is not much more than a century old; in many of its most important aspects, it falls within the short span of those now living. One can hardly believe there has been a revolution in all history so rapid, so extensive, so complete. Through it the face of the earth is made over, even as to its physical forms; political boundaries are wiped out and moved about, as if they were indeed only lines on a paper map; population is hurriedly gathered into cities from the ends of the earth; habits of living are altered with startling abruptness and thoroughness; the search for the truths of nature is infinitely stimulated and facilitated, and their application to life made not only practicable, but commercially necessary. Even our moral and religious ideas and interests, the most conservative because the deepest-lying things in our nature, are profoundly affected. That this revolution should not affect education in some other than a formal and superficial fashion is inconceivable.

Back of the factory system lies the household and neighborhood system. Those of us who are here today need go back only one, two, or at most three generations, to find a time when the household was practically the center in which were carried on, or about which were clustered, all the typical forms of industrial occupation. The clothing worn for the most part made in the house; the members of the household were usually familiar also with the shearing of the sheep, the carding and spinning of the wool, and the plying of the loom. Instead of pressing a button and flooding the house with electric light, the whole process of getting illumination was followed in its toilsome length from the killing of the animal and the trying of fat to the making of wicks and dipping of candles. The supply of flour, of lumber, of foods, of building materials, of household furniture, even of metal ware, of nails, hinges, hammers, etc., was produced in the immediate neighborhood, in shops which were constantly open to inspection and often centers of neighborhood congregation. The entire industrial process stood revealed, from the production on the farm of the raw materials till the finished article was actually put to use. Not only this, but practically every member of the household had his own share in the work. The children, as they gained in strength and capacity, were gradually initiated into the mysteries of the several processes. It was a matter of immediate and personal concern, even to the point of actual participation.

We cannot overlook the factors of discipline and of character-building involved in this kind of life: training in habits of order and of industry, and in the idea of responsibility, of obligation to do something, to produce something, in the world. There was always something which really needed to be done, and a real necessity that each member of the household should do his own part faithfully and in cooperation with others. Personalities which became effective in action were bred and tested in the medium of action. Again, we cannot overlook the importance for educational purposes of the close and intimate acquaintance got with nature at first hand, with real things and materials, with the actual processes of their manipulation, and the knowledge of their social necessities and uses. In all this there was continual training of observation, of ingenuity, constructive imagination, of logical thought, and of the sense of reality acquired through first-hand contact with actualities. The educative forces of the domestic spinning and weaving, of the sawmill, the gristmill, the cooper shop, and the blacksmith forge, were continuously operative.

No number of object-lessons, got up as object-lessons for the sake of giving information, can afford even the shadow of a substitute for acquaintance with the plants and animals of the farm and garden acquired through actual living among them and caring for them. No training of sense-organs in school, introduced for the sake of training, can begin to compete with the alertness and fullness of sense-life that comes through daily intimacy and interest in familiar occupations. Verbal memory can be trained in committing tasks, a certain discipline of the reasoning powers can be acquired through lessons in science and mathematics; but, after all, this is somewhat remote and shadowy compared with the training of attention and of judgment that is acquired in having to do things with a real motive behind and a real outcome ahead. At present, concentration of industry and division of labor have practically eliminated household and neighborhood occupations—at least for educational purposes. But it is useless to bemoan the departure of the good old days of children's modesty, reverence, and implicit obedience, if we expect merely by bemoaning and by exhortation to bring them back. It is radical conditions which have changed, and only an equally radical change in education suffices. We must recognize our compensations—the increase in toleration, in breadth of social judgment, the larger acquaintance with human nature, the sharpened alertness in reading signs of character and interpreting social situations, greater accuracy of adaptation to differing personalities, contact with greater commercial activities. These considerations mean so much to the city-bred child of today. Yet there is a real problem: how shall we retain these advantages, and yet introduce into the school something representing the other side of life—occupations which exact personal responsibilities and which train the child in relation to the physical realities of life?

When we turn to the school, we find that one of the most striking tendencies at present is toward the introduction of so-called manual training, shopwork, and the household arts—sewing and cooking.

This has not been done "on purpose," with a full consciousness that the school must now supply that factor of training formerly taken care of in the home, but rather by instinct, by experimenting and finding that such work takes a vital hold of pupils and gives them something which was not to be got in any other way. Consciousness of its real import is still so weak that the work is often done in a half-hearted, confused, and unrelated way. The reasons assigned to justify it are painfully inadequate or sometimes even positively wrong.

If we were to cross-examine even those who are most favorably disposed to the introduction of this work into our school system, we should, I imagine, generally find the main reasons to be that such work engages the full spontaneous interest and attention of the children. It keeps them alert and active, instead of passive and receptive; it makes them more useful, more capable, and hence more inclined to be helpful at home; it prepares them to some extent for the practical duties of later life—the girls to be more efficient house managers, if not actually cooks and seamstresses; the boys (were our educational system only adequately rounded out into trade schools) for their future vocations. I do not underestimate the worth of these reasons. Of those indicated by the changed attitude of the children, I shall indeed have something to say in the next chapter, when speaking directly of the relationship of the school to the child. But this point of view is, upon the whole, unnecessarily narrow. We must conceive of work in wood and metal, of weaving, sewing, and cooking, as methods of living and learning, not as distinct studies.

We must conceive of them in their social significance, as types of the processes by which society keeps itself going, as agencies for bringing home to the child some of the primal necessities of community life, and as ways in which these needs have been met by the growing insight and ingenuity of man; in short, as instrumentalities through which the school itself shall be made a genuine form of active community life, instead of a place set apart in which to learn lessons.

A society is a number of people held together because they are working along common lines, in a common spirit, and with reference to common aims. The common needs and aims demand a growing interchange of thought and growing unity of sympathetic feeling. The radical reason that the present school cannot organize itself as a natural social unit is because just this element of common and productive activity is absent. Upon the playground, in game and sport, social organization takes place spontaneously and inevitably. There is something to do, some activity to be carried on, requiring natural divisions of labor, selection of leaders and followers, mutual cooperation and emulation. In the schoolroom, the motive and the cement of social organization are alike wanting. Upon the ethical side, the tragic weakness of the present school is that it endeavors to prepare future members of the social order in a medium in which the conditions of the social spirit are eminently wanting.

The difference that appears when occupations are made the articulating centers of school life is not easy to describe in words; it is a difference in motive, of spirit and atmosphere. As one enters a busy kitchen in which a group of children are actively engaged in the preparation of food, the psychological difference, the change from more or less passive and inert recipiency and restraint to one of buoyant, outgoing energy, is so obvious as fairly to strike one in the face. Indeed, to those whose image of the school is rigidly set, the change is sure to give a shock. But the change in the social attitude is equally marked. The mere absorbing of facts and truths is so exclusively individual an affair that it tends very naturally to pass into selfishness. There is no obvious social motive for the acquirement of mere learning, there is no clear social gain in success thereat. Indeed, almost the only measure for success is a competitive one, in the bad sense of that term—a comparison of results in the recitation or in the examination to see which child has succeeded in getting ahead of others in storing up, in accumulating, the maximum of information. So thoroughly is this the prevailing atmosphere that for one child to help another in his task has become a school crime. Where the school work consists in simply learning lessons, mutual assistance, instead of being the most natural form of cooperation and association, becomes a clandestine effort to relieve one's neighbor of his proper duties. Where active work is going on, all this is changed. Helping others, instead of being a form of charity which impoverishes the recipient, is simply an aid in setting free the powers and furthering the impulse of the one helped. A spirit of free communication, of interchange of ideas, suggestions, results, both successes and failures of previous experiences, become the dominating note of the recitation. So far as emulation enters in, it is in the comparison of individuals, not with regard to the quantity of information personally absorbed, but with reference to the quality of work done—the genuine community standard of value. In an informal but all the more pervasive way, the school life organizes itself on a social basis.

Within this organization is found the principle of school discipline or order. Of course, order is simply a thing which is relative to an end. If you have the end in view of forty or fifty children learning certain set lessons, to be recited to a teacher, your discipline must be devoted to securing that result. But if the end in view is the development of a spirit of social cooperation and community life, discipline must grow out of and be relative to such an aim. There is little of one sort of order where things are in process of construction; there is a certain disorder in any busy workshop; there is not silence; persons are not engaged in maintaining certain fixed physical postures; their arms are not folded; they are not holding their books thus and so. They are doing a variety of things, and there is the confusion, the bustle, that results from activity. But out of the occupation, out of doing things that are to produce results, and out of doing these in a social and cooperative way, there is born a discipline of its own kind and type. Our whole conception of school discipline changes when we get this point of view. In critical moments, we all realize that the only discipline that stands by us, the only training that becomes intuition, is that got through life itself. That we learn from experience, and from books or the sayings of others *only* as they are related to experience, and not mere phrases. But the school has been so set apart, so isolated from the ordinary conditions and motives of life, that the place where children are sent for discipline is the one place in the world where it is most difficult to get experience—the mother of all discipline worth the name. It is only when a narrow and fixed image of traditional school discipline dominates that one is in any danger of overlooking that deeper and infinitely wider discipline that comes from having a part to do in constructive work, in contributing to a result which, social in spirit, is nonetheless obvious and tangible in form—and hence in a form with reference to which responsibility may be exacted and accurate judgment passed.

The great thing to keep in mind, then, regarding the introduction into the school of various forms of active occupation, is that through them the entire spirit of the school is renewed. It has a chance to affiliate itself with life, to become the child's habitat, where he learns through directed living, instead of being only a place to learn lessons having an abstract and remote reference to some possible living to be done in the future. It gets a chance to be a miniature community, an embryonic society. This is the fundamental fact, and from this arise continuous and orderly streams of instruction. Under the industrial regime described, the child, after all, shared in the work, not for the sake of the sharing, but for the sake of the product. The educational results secured were real, yet incidental and dependent. But in the school, the typical occupations followed are freed from all economic stress. The aim is not the economic value of the products, but the development of social power and insight. It is this liberation from narrow utilities, this openness to the possibilities of the human spirit, that makes these practical activities in the school allies of art and centers of science and history.

The unity of all the sciences is found in geography. The significance of geography is that it presents the earth as the enduring home of the occupations of man. The world without its relationship to human activity is less than a world. Human industry and achievement, apart from their roots in the earth, are not even a sentiment, hardly a name. The earth is the final source of all man's food. It is his continual shelter and protection, the raw material of all his activities, and the home to whose humanizing and idealizing all his achievement returns. It is the great field, the great mine, the great source of the energies of heat, light, and electricity; the great scene of ocean, stream, mountain, and plain, of which all our agriculture and mining and lumbering, all our manufacturing and distributing agencies, are but the partial elements and factors. It is through occupations determined by this environment that mankind has made its historical and political progress. It is through these occupations that the intellectual and emotional interpretation of nature has been developed. It is through what we do in and with the world that we read its meaning and measure its value.

In educational terms, this means that these occupations in the school shall not be mere practical devices or modes of routine employment, the gaining of better technical skill as cooks, seamstresses, or carpenters, but active centers of scientific insight into natural materials and processes, points of departure whence children shall be led out into a realization of the historic development of man. The actual significance of this can be told better through one illustration taken from actual schoolwork than by general discourse.

There is nothing which strikes more oddly upon the average intelligent visitor than to see boys as well as girls of ten, twelve, and thirteen years of age engaged in sewing and weaving. If we look at this from the standpoint of preparation of the boys for sewing on buttons and making patches, we get a narrow and utilitarian conception— a basis that hardly justifies giving prominence to this sort of work in the school. But if we look at it from another side, we find that this work gives the point of departure from which the child can trace and follow the progress of mankind in history, getting an insight also into the materials used and the mechanical principles involved. In connection with these occupations, the historic development of man is recapitulated. For example, the children are first given the raw material—the flax, the cotton plant, the wool as it comes from the back of the sheep (if we could take them to the place where the sheep are sheared, so much the better). Then a study is made of these materials from the standpoint of their adaptation to the uses to which they may be put. For instance, a comparison of the cotton fiber with wool fiber is made. I did not know, until the children told me, that the reason for the late development of the cotton industry as compared with the woolen is that the cotton fiber is so very difficult to free by hand from the seeds. The children in one group worked thirty minutes freeing cotton fibers from the boll and seeds, and succeeded in getting out less than one ounce. They could easily believe that one person could gin only one pound a day by hand, and could understand why their ancestors wore woolen instead of cotton clothing. Among other things discovered as affecting their relative utilities was the shortness of the cotton fiber as compared with that of wool, the former averaging, say, one-third of an inch in length, while the latter run to three inches in length; also that the fibers of cotton are smooth and do not cling together, while the wool has a certain roughness which makes the fibers stick, thus assisting the spinning. The children worked this out for themselves with the actual material, aided by questions and suggestions from the teacher.

They then followed the processes necessary for working the fibers up into cloth. They reinvented the first frame for carding the wool—a couple of boards with sharp pins in them for scratching it out. They redevised the simplest process for spinning the wool—a pierced stone or some other weight through which the wool is passed, and which as it is twirled draws out the fiber; next the top, which was spun on the floor, while the children kept the wool in their hands until it was gradually drawn out and wound upon it. Then the children are introduced to the invention next in historic order, working it out experimentally, thus seeing its necessity, and tracing its effects, not only upon that particular industry, but upon modes of social life—in this way passing in review the entire process up to the present complete loom, and all that goes with the application of science in the use of our present available powers. I need not speak of the science involved in this—the study of the fibers, of geographical features, the conditions under which raw materials are grown, the great centers of manufacture and distribution, the physics involved in the machinery of production; nor, again, of the historical side—the influence which these inventions have had upon humanity. You can concentrate the history of all mankind into the evolution of the flax, cotton, and wool fibers into clothing. I do not mean that this is the only, or the best, center. But it is true that certain very real and important avenues to the consideration of the history of the race are thus opened—that the mind is introduced to much more fundamental and controlling influences than appear in the political and chronological records that usually pass for history.

Now, what is true of this one instance of fibers used in fabrics (and, of course, I have only spoken of one or two elementary phases of that) is true in its measure of every material used in every occupation, and of the processes employed. The occupation supplies the child with a genuine motive; it gives him experience at first hand; it brings him into contact with realities. It does all this, but in addition it is liberalized throughout by translation into its historic and social values and scientific equivalencies. With the growth of the child's mind in power and knowledge it ceases to be a pleasant occupation merely and becomes more and more a medium, an instrument, an organ of understanding—and is thereby transformed.

This, in turn, has its bearing upon the teaching of science. Under present conditions, all activity, to be successful, has to be directed somewhere and somehow by the scientific expert—it is a case of applied science. This connection should determine its place in education. It is not only that the occupations, the so-called manual or industrial work in the school, give the opportunity for the introduction of science which illuminates them, which makes them material, freighted with meaning, instead of being mere devices of hand and eye; but that the scientific insight thus gained becomes an indispensable instrument of free and active participation in modern social life. Plato somewhere speaks of the slave as one who in his actions does not express his own ideas, but those of some other man. It is our social problem now, even more urgent than in the time of Plato, that method, purpose, understanding, shall exist in the consciousness of the one who does the work, that his activity shall have meaning to himself.

When occupations in the school are conceived in this broad and generous way, I can only stand lost in wonder at the objections so often heard, that such occupations are out of place in the school because they are materialistic, utilitarian, or even menial in their tendency. It sometimes seems to me that those who make these objections must live in quite another world. The world in which most of us live is a world in which everyone has a calling and occupation, something to do. Some are managers and others are subordinates. But the great thing for one as for the other is that each shall have had the education which enables him to see within his daily work all there is in it of large and human significance. How many of the employed are today mere appendages to the machines which they operate! This may be due in part to the machine itself, or the régime which lays so much stress upon the products of the machine; but it is certainly due in large part to the fact that the worker has had no opportunity to develop his imagination and his sympathetic insight as to the social and scientific values found in his work. At present, the impulses which lie at the basis of the industrial system are either practically neglected or positively distorted during the school period. Until the instincts of construction and production are systematically laid hold of in the years of childhood and youth, until they are trained in social directions, enriched by historical interpretation, controlled and illuminated by scientific methods, we certainly are in no position even to locate the source of our economic evils, much less to deal with them effectively.

If we go back a few centuries, we find a practical monopoly of learning. The term *possession* of learning is, indeed, a happy one. Learning was a class matter. This was a necessary result of social conditions. There were not in existence any means by which the multitude could possibly have access to intellectual resources. These were stored up and hidden away in manuscripts. Of these there were at best only a few, and it required long and toilsome preparation to be able to do anything with them. A high-priesthood of learning, which guarded the treasury of truth and which doled it out to the masses under severe restrictions, was the inevitable expression of these conditions. But, as a direct result of the industrial revolution of which we have been speaking, this has been changed. Printing was invented; it was made commercial. Books, magazines, papers were multiplied and cheapened. As a result of the locomotive and telegraph, frequent, rapid, and cheap intercommunication by mail and electricity was called into being. Travel has been rendered easy; freedom of movement, with its accompanying exchange of ideas, indefinitely facilitated. The result has been an intellectual revolution. Learning has been put into circulation. While there still is, and probably always will be, a particular class having the special business of inquiry in hand, a distinctively learned class is henceforth out of the question. It is an anachronism. Knowledge is no longer an immobile solid; it has been liquefied. It is actively moving in all the currents of society itself.

It is easy to see that this revolution, as regards the materials of knowledge, carries with it a marked change in the attitude of the individual. Stimuli of an intellectual sort pour in upon us in all kinds of ways. The merely intellectual life, the life of scholarship and learning, thus gets a very altered value. Academic and scholastic, instead of being titles of honor, are becoming terms of reproach.

But all this means a necessary change in the attitude of the school, one of which we are as yet far from realizing the full force. Our school methods, and to a very considerable extent our curriculum, are inherited from the period when learning and command of certain symbols, affording as they did the only access to learning, were all-important. The ideals of this period are still largely in control, even where the outward methods and studies have been changed. We sometimes hear the introduction of manual training, art, and science into the elementary, and even the secondary, schools deprecated on the ground that they tend toward the production of specialists—that they detract from our present scheme of generous, liberal culture. The point of this objection would be ludicrous if it were not often so effective as to make it tragic. It is our present education which is highly specialized, one-sided, and narrow. It is an education dominated almost entirely by the mediaeval conception of learning. It is something which appeals for the most part simply to the intellectual aspect of our natures, our desire to learn, to accumulate information, and to get control of the symbols of learning; not to our impulses and tendencies to make, to do, to create, to produce, whether in the form of utility or of art. The very fact that manual training, art, and science are objected to as technical, as tending toward mere specialism, is of itself as good testimony as could be offered to the specialized aim which controls current education. Unless education had been virtually identified with the exclusively intellectual pursuits, with learning as such, all these materials and methods would be welcome, would be greeted with the utmost hospitality.

While training for the profession of learning is regarded as the type of culture, or a liberal education, the training of a mechanic, a musician, a lawyer, a doctor, a farmer, a merchant, or a railroad manager is regarded as purely technical and professional. The result is that which we see about us everywhere—the division into "cultured" people and "workers," the separation of theory and practice. Hardly 1 percent of the entire school population ever attains to what we call higher education; only 5 percent to the grade of our high school; while much more than half leave on or before the completion of the fifth year of the elementary grade. The simple facts of the case are that in the great majority of human beings, the distinctively intellectual interest is not dominant. They have the so-called practical impulse and disposition. In many of those in whom by nature intellectual interest is strong, social conditions prevent its adequate realization. Consequently, by far the larger number of pupils leave school as soon as they have acquired the rudiments of learning, as soon as they have enough of the symbols of reading, writing, and calculating to be of practical use to them in getting a living. While our educational leaders are talking of culture, the development of personality, etc., as the end and aim of education, the great majority of those who pass under the tuition of the school regard it only as a narrowly practical tool with which to get bread and butter enough to eke out a restricted life. If we were to conceive our educational end and aim in a less exclusive way, if we were to introduce into educational processes the activities which appeal to those whose dominant interest is to do and to make, we should find the hold of the school upon its members to be more vital, more prolonged, containing more of culture.

But why should I make this labored presentation? The obvious fact is that our social life has undergone a thorough and radical change. If our education is to have any meaning for life, it must pass through an equally complete transformation. This transformation is not something to appear suddenly, to be executed in a day by conscious purpose. It is already in progress. Those modifications of our school system which often appear (even to those most actively concerned with them, to say nothing of their spectators) to be mere changes of detail, mere improvement within the school mechanism, are in reality signs and evidences of evolution. The introduction of active occupations, of nature-study, of elementary science, of art, of history; the relegation of the merely symbolic and formal to a secondary position; the change in the moral school atmosphere, in the relation of pupils and teachers—of discipline; the introduction of more active, expressive, and self-directing factors—all these are not mere accidents, they are necessities of the larger social evolution. It remains but to organize all these factors, to appreciate them in the fullness of meaning, and to put the ideas and ideals involved into complete, uncompromising possession of our school system. To do this means to make each one of our schools an embryonic community life, active with types of occupations that reflect the life of the larger society and are permeated throughout with the spirit of art, history, and science. When the school introduces and trains each child of society into membership within such a little community, saturating him with the spirit of service, and providing him with the instruments of effective self-direction, we shall have the deepest and best guaranty of a larger society which is worthy, lovely, and harmonious.

⇸ LEWIS M. TERMAN, NATIONAL INTELLIGENCE TESTS, 1919

If there is any part of the progressive heritage that continues to impact contemporary students, it is the belief, strongly held by one faction of progressive educators, that educational testing is the key to understanding students and improving their education. Edward L. Thorndike voiced his confidence in educational measurement when he wrote in 1918 that, "Whatever exists at all exists in some amount. To know it thoroughly involves knowing its quality as well as its quantity." From this confidence in scientific measurement came the IQ test, the SAT, and all the rest of the range of educational testing that has impacted the lives of virtually every American student for the last century. The voice most consistently calling for testing was Lewis M. Terman, a long-time member of the faculty at Stanford University, member of the Commission that developed tests for the U. S. Army during World War I, and popularizer of the Stanford-Binet intelligence tests. In this selection, from his 1919 book, The Intelligence of School Children, *he wrote of his faith in a plea to schoolteachers to adopt his perspective.*

The Binet tests, a method of assaying intelligence. In order to find out how much gold is contained in a given vein of quartz, it is not necessary to uncover all the ore and extract and weigh every particle of the precious metal. It is sufficient merely to ascertain by borings the linear extent of the lode and to take a small amount of the ore to the laboratory of an assayer, who will make a test and render a verdict of so many ounces of gold per ton of ore.

A half-century ago, Francis Galton predicted that it would sometime be possible to obtain a general knowledge of the intellectual capacities of a man by sinking shafts, as it were, at a few critical points. Already Galton's dream is in process of realization, for in the last decade, mental testing has become one of the most fruitful branches of psychological science. The credit for pointing the way belongs largely to the French psychologist, Alfred Binet, who, after more than fifteen years of patient research, gave to the world in 1908 the system of mental tests now known as the Binet-Simon Intelligence Scale. In various revised forms, the method has come into general use in public schools, institutions for defectives, prisons, reform schools, and juvenile courts in the United States and in Europe. Our debt to Binet is very great, for he succeeded in bringing psychology down from the clouds and making it useful to men.

The Binet scale is made up of an extended series of tests in the nature of problems, success in which demands the exercise of the intellectual processes. As left by Binet, the scale consisted of fifty-four tests, ranging in difficulty from tests which are passed by the average child of three years, to tests which are difficult enough for the average adult. The Standard Revision has increased the number of tests to ninety and has extended the scale far enough to measure the intelligence of superior adults.

The ninety tests in the revised scale constitute an extremely variegated series. This is necessary, since their purpose is to measure the subject's *general intelligence*, not his special ability in a particular line. They include tests of memory, language comprehension, size of vocabulary, orientation in time and space, eye-hand coordinations, knowledge about familiar things, judgment, ability to find likenesses and differences between common objects, arithmetical reasoning, resourcefulness and ingenuity in difficult practical situations, ability to detect absurdities, apperception, the speed and richness of association of ideas, the power to combine the dissected parts of a form board or a group of ideas into a unitary whole, the capacity to generalize from particulars, the ability to deduce a rule from connected facts, etc. Thus the tests give a kind of composite picture of the subject's general mental ability, and since standards of comparison have been established for each of the individual tests by trying it out on hundreds of unselected normal children of all ages, it is possible to express the total result of an examination in terms of "mental age" norms.

Why a mental test is significant. Are we justified in attributing real diagnostic significance to the little intellectual "stunts" called for by an intelligence scale? Some of these may even appear trivial. What does it signify, for example, whether a given ten-year-old subject names forty words or a hundred words in three minutes? Whether he puts together the parts of a form board in thirty seconds or in two minutes? Whether he defines thirty words or sixty words of a hundred-word list? Whether his definitions of words are stated in terms of "use" or in terms "superior to use"? Whether a series of five digits or only a series of three digits can be repeated backwards after a single auditory presentation? Whether there are three, two, one, or no successes in the attempt to draw a diamond-shaped figure from copy?

The secret lies in the standardization of the tests upon normal children of different ages. Without such a standardization, the tests would mean nothing. Standardization is coming to play the same role in psychology that it has long played in the various branches of applied science. The architect or bridge engineer plans his structure with constant reference to foot-pounds of strain which various materials will withstand. The physician analyzes a drop of blood and, by comparison of corpuscle count and haemoglobin with the norms for health and disease, is able to render an important diagnosis. The psychologist working with mental tests may be compared with the palaeontologist who finds in a gravel bed of some prehistoric age a skull cap, a fragment of a jaw, and a broken humerus. Although the layman might not even recognize the human origin of such remnants, the palaeontologist is able to tell us that the bones are those of a middle-aged male, that the species to which he belonged had not yet learned to stand erect, that he probably did not know the use of fire (worn teeth indicate that he subsisted on uncooked foods), that his intelligence was inferior (cranial contents only two thirds that of modern man), and that he had probably evolved but limited power of speech (diminutive points of attachment for the speech muscles). A little technical acquaintance with the standards of shape, size, and structure of human bones has transformed the meaningless fragments into a "missing link"—*Homo neanderthalensis*.

Perhaps no two things could be more alike to casual inspection than the balls of two thumbs; yet one who has been taught to read fingerprints can ordinarily find from forty to seventy separate and individually sufficient points of identification. Just as many a man has been hanged on the evidence of his fingerprints, so many an individual might safely be committed to an institution for the feebleminded on the evidence of ten or a dozen intelligence tests which have been standardized according to age norms.

The meaning of mental age. Both the individual tests of the Binet scale and the scale as a whole have been standardized on the basis of age norms. The tests themselves are located in age groups in such a way as to bring it about that the *average* child of eight years will earn by the scale a "mental age" of eight years, the *average* twelve-year-old a "mental age" of twelve years, etc. Such an arrangement was arrived at empirically by trying out a series of tests upon hundreds of normal children of different ages. The Stanford Revision, for example, was based on tests of 1,700 children and 400 adults.

To illustrate the use of the scale, let us suppose we are testing a child of eight years. If our subject passes successfully as far as the average child of eight years, we say that his mental age is eight years, or in this case, normal. If he goes as far as the average ten-year-old, we say that he has a mental age of ten years. If he earns no more credit than the average six-year-old, his mental age is six years. Binet merely took a standard of comparison which everyone uses (namely, the standard of age) and made it definite by finding out what intellectual performances representative children of different ages are capable of.

It is necessary that the reader should at the outset arrive at a correct understanding of what the term *mental age* is and is not intended to signify. Two misconceptions are to be avoided:

1. That each "mental age" is a separate and qualitatively distinct level of mental attainment, contrasting markedly with both the mental age which precedes it and that which follows it. Such a use of the term is not in harmony with the facts. Mental development is consecutive and gradual. There is probably no mental power, capacity, or function which has a Minerva birth. The "faculty" in question develops first in rudimentary form, then grows gradually stronger and more definite until, by imperceptible stages, it reaches a state of maturity.

2.   Another misunderstanding comes from the assumption that those who use the term believe a given mental age is a stage of development which all normal individuals pass through at the corresponding actual age. Such a belief would imply that the age of ten years, for example, all children who do not belong to some special type (defective, genius, etc.) should be found at the ten-year mental age, eight-year children at the eight-year mental age, etc. It is one of the main purposes of this book to show how widely children of a given age differ in mental age, and how greatly children of adjacent ages overlap each other in mental age.

The real meaning of the term is perfectly straightforward and unambiguous. By a given mental age, we mean *that degree of general mental ability which is possessed by the average child of corresponding chronological age.*

Mental age a basis for school grading. The significance of mental age for the teacher lies in the fact that it can be used as a basis for grading the pupils so as to secure class groups of homogeneous ability. As will be shown in succeeding chapters, the pupils of given grades, or even the pupils of one grade in a single classroom, are far from equal in general intelligence or in ability to master the school work. Generally speaking, not far from a fourth of the pupils in any given grade have a mental level too low to make satisfactory work in that grade possible, while another fourth have reached a mental level which would enable them to succeed in a higher grade.

The intelligent quotient. The mental age merely indicates the level of development which a child has reached at a given time. Considered apart from chronological age it does not tell us whether a child is bright, dull, or average. Of three children all testing at the mental age of eight years, one might very well be exceptionally superior, one average, and one feebleminded. Such would be the case if their chronological ages were six, eight, and twelve years. In addition to an index of absolute mental level, we need an index of relative brightness. Such is the intelligence quotient (IQ), which is the ratio of mental age to chronological age. The six-year-old of eight-year mental age has an IQ of 8/6 or 133; the twelve-year-old with a mental age of eight years, an IQ of 8/12, or 67. In computing the IQ of an adult subject, years of chronological age in excess of sixteen are disregarded, as the development of native intelligence seems practically to cease not far from this age.

An idea of how greatly school children differ in brightness is shown by the analysis of the IQs of one-thousand representative children in which it was found that:

The lowest 1% go to 70 or below, the highest 1% reach 130 or above
The lowest 2% go to 73 or below, the highest 2% reach 128 or above
The lowest 3% go to 76 or below, the highest 3% reach 125 or above
The lowest 5% go to 78 or below, the highest 5% reach 122 or above
The lowest 10% go to 85 or below, the highest 10% reach 116 or above
The lowest 15% go to 88 or below, the highest 15% reach 113 or above
The lowest 20% go to 91 or below, the highest 20% reach 110 or above
The lowest 25% go to 92 or below, the highest 25% reach 108 or above
The lowest 33% go to 95 or below, the highest 33% reach 106 or above

The intelligent quotient a basis for prediction. Just as mental age indicates the school grade in which a child normally belongs at a given time, so the IQ is the basis for prediction in regard to the child's later mental development. The possibility of such prediction comes from the fact that the IQ has been found in the large majority of cases to remain fairly constant, at least for the ages between three or four and fourteen or fifteen. For illustration, we will take the case of a four-year-old child who is found to have a mental age of five years, and whose IQ is therefore 125. The probability is that child will continue to have a mental age not far from 25 percent above his chronological age, with consequences which may be expressed as follows:

Chronological Age	Probable Mental Age	Probable School Ability
4 years	5 years	Upper kindergarten
6 years	7 ½ years	Second school grade
8 years	10 years	High fourth grade
10 years	12 ½ years	Low seventh grade
12 years	15 years	First year high school

It would, of course, be absurd to expect the IQ to maintain itself at an absolutely constant figure. Fluctuations occur for at least three reasons: (1) There may be in exceptional cases a certain amount of irregularity in the actual rate of mental development. (2) The results of a test may be influenced to some extent by the conditions under which it is given, the state of the child's health, his attitude toward the test, fatigue, and other temporary or accidental factors. Retests after a brief interval indicate that errors from this source are ordinarily not large. (3) There is inevitably a certain amount of error in every IQ rating, due to imperfections in the scale used. If the scale has been so standardized that it yields mental ages which are too low, the IQ found will be too low; if the scale errs in the direction of being too generous, the resulting IQ will be too high. A scale may err in one direction at one level and in the opposite direction at another level. It was the most serious fault of the original Binet scale that in the lower range of tests it yielded mental ages which were too high, and in the upper range mental ages which were too low. The effect of such errors is greatly to exaggerate the amount of fluctuation to which mental growth is subject. It was the main purpose of the Standard Revision to reduce these constant errors. Chapter XI shows in detail the degree of constancy which may be expressed for the IQ when the Standard Revision is used. While the law of constancy is subject to minor revisions, few things are more certain than the essential untruth of the widespread belief that mental development knows no regularity, and that the dullard of to-day becomes the genius of tomorrow. The fact is that, apart from minor fluctuations due to temporary factors, and apart from occasional instances of arrest or deterioration due to acquired nervous disease, the feebleminded remain feeble-minded, the dull remain dull, the average remain average, and the superior remain superior. There is nothing in one's equipment, with the exception of character, which rivals the IQ in importance.

Effects of environment on the IQ. The question is always raised whether, in estimating a child's intelligence on the basis of the IQ it is not necessary to make allowance for the influence of social environment. For example, it is often argued that the child cannot know his age if he has never heard it, cannot read and report the memory passages if he has never attended school, cannot count from 20 to 1 if he has never been taught to count from 1 to 20, cannot name the days of the week or the months of the year unless he has heard others name them, and that therefore the IQ can have little significance except possibly as an index of the subject's social and educational environment.

It is, of course, true that an individual who for his entire life had been entirely deprived of human environment (assuming such a thing to be possible) could not pass a satisfactory Binet test, however normal his original endowment may have been. To use an extreme illustration, a child of ten years who had been reared in a cage, whose wants had been supplied while he was asleep, or by means of ingenious mechanical contrivances, who had never seen a human being, could hardly be expected to make a brilliant showing in defining words in the vocabulary test, detecting absurdities, repeating sentences, reading the Binet passage, answering comprehension questions, or naming sixty words. We may go further and assume that such a subject would be as little successful with the three-year as with the ten-year test.

Needless to say, the Binet scale was not intended for subjects of the type we have just described. Its use in a given case takes for granted that the ordinary and all but inevitable social contacts have been made, that the subject is not deaf or blind, and that he has had reasonable opportunity to learn the language in which the tests are given. Children who have attended school for any considerable time meet all of these requirements, whatever the social status of the home.

As a matter of fact, limited acquaintance with the language employed in the examination does not put the subject at great disadvantage in many of the tests. In some it does, and in testing subjects who are under this handicap the vocabulary test and a few others may very well be omitted. Following are two illustrations which show that the validity of the scale does not hinge entirely upon the subject's knowledge of English:

1.   Kohs tested a Belgian refugee child of nine years who had been in America but two years. Although this child's acquaintance with the English language was very limited, the IQ earned on the Stanford-Binet scale was 99. The child was also doing schoolwork of average quality in the fourth grade.
2.   Dickson tested a Japanese boy, aged five years, two months, who had never attended school and who had had little opportunity to learn English; yet this boy earned a mental age of seven years and an IQ of 133.

That lack of schooling does not prevent a subject from earning an average or superior score in the test is shown by the cases of S. S. and Gypsy Mary.

S. S. was tested at the age of seven years. He had never been to school, and although his home advantages were excellent, he had had no formal instruction and had never learned to read. The parents believed, perhaps rightly, that the important needs of childhood, apart from simple moral instruction, are food, fresh air, and freedom to play. Nevertheless, S. earned a mental age of ten years, eight months, and an IQ of 153.

In 1916, a gypsy girl of sixteen years was given the Stanford Binet test in a clinic in Oakland, California. This girl had been stolen by the gypsies when she was about four years old, had lived with them continuously until a few days before the test was made, and had never attended a school. The IQ found was approximately 100.

It is not denied that the cultural status of the home (even apart from heredity) may affect the result of the test to some extent, although the influence has never been accurately determined. If it were considerable, we should find a marked rise of IQ in the case of children who had been removed from an inferior to a satisfactory home environment. Our data on this point are not extensive, but of a dozen or more children of this kind whom we have retested, not one showed improvement. Two such children, Walter and Frank, have been under observation for several years. Until the ages of five and seven years they lived in an exceptionally poor home. The mother was dull, the father illiterate and a drunkard. Both of the parents died within a year, and the boys were adopted by a woman of decidedly more than average ability who treated them as her own sons. At the time of adoption, one tested at 73, the other at 82. Four years later, the IQ's were 70 and 77. It is a general rule that children of borderline intelligence improve little if at all in IQ as they get older, notwithstanding their increased school experience and the extra attention they receive in special classes.

That the environment of the home affects the result of the test but little is further shown by the fact that occasionally in a very inferior home, all of the children except one test low, as would be expected, while that one tests exceptionally high. In one such family (Portuguese) there are three children who test between 76 and 88, while a brother of these tests at 130. The latter is making a very superior record in high school, which he entered at the age of thirteen years. The others have not been able to complete the eighth grade. All have had the same home environment and the same educational opportunities.

Scales for group testing. To test each year the intelligence of all the children by the Binet method would involve a larger task than the school is likely to undertake. There is accordingly a wide field for tests which can be applied to an entire group, or class, at once. The various scales have been devised for this purpose. The group scales are given as written tests and can be applied to an entire class of fifty or more pupils in about an hour. To score the records requires about ten minutes for each pupil, or a total of about five or six hours for a class of average size. This can be done evenings or at odd times. Most group scales have the advantage of requiring little special psychological training either for giving the tests or scoring them. An unfortunate limitation of such scales is that they are not satisfactory in the lower grades, where the need for testing is greatest. As measures of intelligence they are probably somewhat less accurate than scales for individual testing, but their obvious advantages make them deserving of wide use with pupils of the upper grades and high school.

However, no group scale will ever do away with the necessity of individual testing. Rather it makes the need for individual testing more obvious. All the pupils in the fourth grade and beyond should be given a test by the group method every year, and those whose scores are either very high or very low in the group examination should be given a Binet test. As will be shown later, it is highly desirable that every pupil be given a mental test within the first half-year of his school life.

✧ George Counts, Dare the School Build a New Social Order? 1932

One of the most powerful voices of dissent in the 1930s emerged from the heart of progressive education itself. In the midst of the Great Depression, George S. Counts found himself increasingly frustrated with the fact that the child-centered wing of progressivism was drowning out all of the rest. "Like a baby shaking a rattle, we seem to be utterly content with action, provided it is sufficiently vigorous and noisy," he said. "The weakness of Progressive Education thus lies in the fact that it has elaborated no theory of social welfare, unless it be that of anarchy or extreme individualism." In a series of speeches to teacher union gatherings, Counts electrified his audience with his call for a very different progressivism in which teachers would take the lead in building a more democratic and egalitarian society for all. Count's speeches were published as Dare the School Build a New Social Order? *(New York: John Day Co., 1932). Chapter 2 of the book appears here.*

Counts, George S. *Dare the School Build a New Social Order?* Carbondale: Southern Illinois University Press; London: Feffer & Simons, Inc., 1932. Reprinted by permission of Martha L. Counts.

1. There is the fallacy that man is born free. As a matter of fact, he is born helpless. He achieves freedom, as a race and as an individual, through the medium of culture. The most crucial of all circumstances conditioning human life is birth into a particular culture. By birth one becomes a Chinese, an Englishman, a Hottentot, a Sioux Indian, a Turk, or a 100 percent American. Such a range of possibilities may appear too shocking to contemplate, but it is the price that one must pay in order to be born. Nevertheless, even if a given soul should happen by chance to choose a Hottentot for a mother, it should thank its lucky star that it was born into the Hottentot culture rather than entirely free. By being nurtured on a body of culture, however backward and limited it may be comparatively, the individual is at once imposed upon and liberated. The child is terribly imposed upon by being compelled through the accidents of birth to learn one language rather than another, but without some language, man would never become man. Any language, even the most poverty-stricken, is infinitely better than none at all. In the life cycle of the individual, many choices must of necessity be made, and the most fundamental and decisive of these choices will always be made by the group. This is so obvious that it should require no elaboration. Yet this very obvious fact with its implications, is commonly disregarded by those who are fearful of molding the child.

One of the most important elements of any culture is a tradition of achievement along a particular line—a tradition which the group imposes upon the young and through which the powers of the young are focused, disciplined, and developed. One people will have a fine hunting tradition, another a maritime tradition, another a musical tradition, another a military tradition, another a scientific tradition, another a baseball tradition, another a business tradition, and another even a tradition of moral and religious prophecy. A particular society of the modern type has a vast number of different traditions, all of which may be bound together and integrated more or less by some broad and inclusive tradition. One might argue that the imposing of these traditions upon children involves a severe restriction upon their freedom. My thesis is that such imposition, provided the tradition is vital and suited to the times, releases the energies of the young, sets up standards of excellence, and makes possible really great achievement. The individual who fails to come under the influence of such a tradition may enjoy a certain kind of freedom, but it is scarcely a kind of freedom that anyone would covet for either himself or his children. It is the freedom of mediocrity, incompetence, and aimlessness.

2. There is the fallacy that the child is good by nature. The evidence from anthropology, as well as from common observation, shows that on entering the world the individual is neither good nor bad; he is merely a bundle of potentialities which may be developed in manifold directions. Guidance is, therefore, not to be found in child nature, but rather in the culture of the group and the purposes of living. There can be no good individual apart from some conception of the character of the *good* society; and the good society is not something that is given by nature: it must be fashioned by the hand and brain of man. This process of building a good society is to a very large degree an educational process. The nature of the child must of course be taken into account in the organization of any educational program, but it cannot furnish the materials and the guiding principles of that program. Squirm and wriggle as we may, we must admit that

the bringing of materials and guiding principles from the outside involves the molding of the child.

3. There is the fallacy that the child lives in a separate world of his own. The advocates of freedom often speak of the adult as an alien influence in the life of the child. For an adult to intrude himself or his values into the domain of boys and girls is made to take on the appearance of an invasion by a foreign power. Such a dualism is almost wholly artificial. Whatever may be the view of the adult, the child knows but one society; and that is a society including persons of all ages. This does not mean that conflicts of interest may not occur, or that on occasion adults may not abuse and exploit children. It does mean that in a proper kind of society, the relationship is one of mutual benefit and regard in which the young repay in trust and emulation the protection and guidance provided by their elders. The child's conception of his position in society is well-expressed in the words of Plenty-coups, the famous Crow chieftain, who spoke thus of his boyhood: "We followed the buffalo herds over the beautiful plains, fighting a battle one day and sending out a war-party against the enemy the next. My heart was afire. I wished so to help my people, to distinguish myself, so that I might wear an eagle's feather in my hair. How I worked to make my arms strong as a grizzly's, and how I practiced with my bow! A boy never wished to be a man more than I." Here is an emphatic and unequivocal answer to those who would raise a barrier between youth and age. Place the child in a world of his own and you take from him the most powerful incentives to growth and achievement. Perhaps one of the greatest tragedies of contemporary society lies in the fact that the child is becoming increasingly isolated from the serious activities of adults. Some would say that such isolation is an inevitable corollary of the growing complexity of the social order. In my opinion, it is rather the product of a society that is moved by no great commanding ideals and is consequently victimized by the most terrible form of human madness—the struggle for private gain. As primitive peoples wisely protect their children from the dangers of actual warfare, so we guard ours from the acerbities of economic strife. Until school and society are bound together by common purposes, the program of education will lack both meaning and vitality.

4. There is the fallacy that education is some pure and mystical essence that remains unchanged from everlasting to everlasting. According to this view, genuine education must be completely divorced from politics, live apart from the play of social forces, and pursue ends peculiar to itself. It thus becomes a method existing independently of the cultural milieu and equally beneficient at all times and in all places. This is one of the most dangerous of fallacies and is responsible for many sins committed in different countries by American educators traveling abroad. They have carried the same brand of education to backward and advanced races, to peoples living under relatively static conditions and to peoples passing through periods of rapid and fundamental transition. They have called it Education with a capital *E*, whereas in fact it has been American education with a capital *A* and a small *e*. Any defensible educational program must be adjusted to a particular time and place, and the degree and nature of the imposition must vary with the societal situation. Under ordinary conditions, the process of living suffices in itself to hold society together, but when the forces of disintegration become sufficiently powerful, it may well be that a fairly large measure of deliberate control is desirable and even essential to social survival.

5. There is the fallacy that school should be impartial in its emphases, that no bias should be given instruction. We have already observed how the individual is inevitably molded by the culture into which he is born. In the case of the school, a similar process

operates and presumably is subject to a degree of conscious direction. My thesis is that complete impartiality is utterly impossible, that the school must shape attitudes, develop tastes, and even impose ideas. It is obvious that the whole of creation cannot be brought into the school. This means that some selection must be made of teachers, curricula, architecture, methods of teaching. And in the making of the selection, the dice must always be weighted in favor of this or that. Here is a fundamental truth that cannot be brushed aside as irrelevant or unimportant; it constitutes the very essence of the matter under discussion. Nor can the reality be concealed beneath agreeable phrases. Professor Dewey states in his *Democracy and Education* that the school should provide a *purified* environment for the child. With this view I would certainly agree; probably no person reared in our society would favor the study of pornography in the schools. I am sure, however, that this means stacking the cards in favor of the particular system of value which we may happen to possess. It is one of the truisms of the anthropologist that there are no maxims of purity on which all people would agree. Other vigorous opponents of imposition unblushingly advocate the "cultivation of democratic sentiments" in children or the promotion of child growth in the direction of "a better and richer life." The first represents definite acquiescence in imposition; the second, if it does not mean the same thing, means nothing. I believe firmly that democratic sentiments should be cultivated and that a better and richer life should be the outcome of education, but in neither case would I place responsibility on either God or the order of nature. I would merely contend that as educators we must make many choices involving the development of attitudes in boys and girls and that we should not be afraid to acknowledge the faith that is in us or mayhap the forces that compel us.

6. There is the fallacy that the great object of education is to produce the college professor, that is, the individual who adopts an agnostic attitude towards every important social issue, who can balance the pros against the cons with the skill of a juggler, who sees all sides of every question and never commits himself to any, who delays action until all the facts are in, who knows that all the facts will never come in, who consequently holds his judgment in a state of indefinite suspension, and who before the approach of middle age sees his powers of action atrophy and his social sympathies decay. With Peer Gynt he can exclaim:

> Ay, think of it—wish it done—will it to boot,—
> But do it—! No, that's past my understanding!

This type of mind also talks abut waiting until the solutions of social problems are found, when as a matter of fact there are no solutions in any definite and final sense. For any complex social problem worthy of the name there are probably tens and even scores, if not hundreds, of "solutions," depending upon the premises from which one works. The meeting of a social situation involves the making of decisions and the working out of adjustments. Also it involves the selection and rejection of values. If we wait for a solution to appear like the bursting of the sun through the clouds or the resolving of the elements in an algebraic equation, we shall wait in vain. Although college professors, if not too numerous, perform a valuable social function, society requires great numbers of persons who, while capable of gathering and digesting facts, are at the same time able to think in terms of life, make decisions, and act. From such persons will come our real social leaders.

7. There is the closely related fallacy that education is primarily intellectualistic in its processes and goals. Quite as important is that ideal factor in culture which gives

meaning, direction, and significance to life. I refer to the element of faith or purpose which lifts man out of himself and above the level of his more narrow personal interests. Here, in my judgment, is one of the great lacks in our schools and in our intellectual class today. We are able to contemplate the universe and find that all is vanity. Nothing really stirs us, unless it be that the bath water is cold, the toast burnt, or the elevator not running; or that perchance we miss the first section of a revolving door. Possibly this is the fundamental reason why we are so fearful of molding the child. We are moved by no great faiths; we are touched by no great passions. We can view a world rushing rapidly towards collapse with no more concern than the outcome of a horse race; we can see injustice, crime, and misery in their most terrible forms all about us and, if we are not directly affected, register the emotions of a scientist studying white rats in a laboratory. And in the name of freedom, objectivity, and the open mind, we would transmit this general attitude of futility to our children. In my opinion, this is a confession of complete moral and spiritual bankruptcy. We cannot, by talk about the interests of children and the sacredness of personality, evade the responsibility of bringing to the younger generation a vision which will call forth their active loyalties and challenge them to creative and arduous labors. A generation without such a vision is destined, like ours, to a life of absorption in self, inferiority complexes, and frustration. The genuinely free man is not the person who spends the day contemplating his own navel, but rather the one who loses himself in a great cause or glorious adventure.

8. There is the fallacy that the school is an all-powerful educational agency. Every professional group tends to exaggerate its own importance in the scheme of things. To this general rule the teachers offer no exception. The leaders of Progressive Education in particular seem to have an over-weening faith in the power of the school. On the one hand, they speak continually about reconstructing society through education; and on the other, they apparently live in a state of perpetual fear lest the school impose some one point of view upon all children and mold them all to a single pattern. A moment's reflection is sufficient to show that life in the modern world is far too complex to permit this: The school is but one formative agency among many, and certainly not the strongest at that. Our major concern consequently should be, not to keep the school from influencing the child in a positive direction, but rather to make certain that every progressive school will use whatever power it may possess in opposing and checking the forces of social conservatism and reaction. We know full well that, if the school should endeavor vigorously and consistently to win its pupils to the support of a given social program, unless it were supported by other agencies, it could act only as a mild counterpoise to restrain and challenge the might of less enlightened and more selfish purposes.

9. There is the fallacy that ignorance rather than knowledge is the way of wisdom. Many who would agree that imposition of some kind is inevitable seem to feel that there is something essentially profane in any effort to understand, plan, and control the process. They will admit that the child is molded by his environment, and then presumably contend that in the fashioning of this environment we should close our eyes to the consequences of our acts, or at least should not endeavor to control our acts in the light of definite knowledge of their consequences. To do the latter would involve an effort to influence deliberately the growth of the child in a particular direction—to cause him to form this habit rather than that, to develop one taste rather than another, to be sensitive to a given ideal rather than its rival. But this would be a violation of the "rights of the child," and therefore evil. Apparently his rights can be protected only if our influence upon him is thoroughly concealed under a heavy veil of ignorance. If the

school can do no better than this, it has no reason for existence. If it is to be merely an arena for the blind play of psychological forces, it might better close its doors. Here is the doctrine of *laissez-faire*, driven from the field of social and political theory, seeking refuge in the domain of pedagogy. Progressive Education wishes to build a new world but refuses to be held accountable for the kind of world it builds. In my judgment, the school should know what it is doing, in so far as this is humanly possible, and accept full responsibility for its acts.

10. Finally, there is the fallacy that in a dynamic society like ours the major responsibility of education is to prepare the individual to adjust himself to social change. The argument in support of this view is fairly cogent. The world is changing with great rapidity; the rate of change is being accelerated constantly; the future is full of uncertainty. Consequently, the individual who is to live and thrive in this world must possess an agile mind, be bound by no deep loyalties, hold all conclusions and values tentatively, and be ready on a moment's notice to make even fundamental shifts in outlook and philosophy. Like a lumberjack riding a raft of logs through the rapids, he must be able with lightning speed to jump from one insecure foundation to another, if he is not to be overwhelmed by the onward surge of the cultural stream. In a word, he must be as willing to adopt new ideas and values as to install the most up-to-the-minute labor-saving devices in his dwelling or to introduce the latest inventions in his factory. Under such a conception of life and society, education can only bow down before the gods of chance and reflect the drift of the social order. This conception is essentially anarchic in character, exalts the irrational above the rational forces of society, makes of security an individual rather than a social goal, drives every one of us into an insane competition with his neighbors, and assumes that man is incapable of controlling in the common interest the creatures of his brain. Here we have imposition with a vengeance, but not the imposition of the teacher or the school. Nor is it the imposition of the chaos and cruelty and ugliness produced by the brutish struggle for existence and advantage. Far more terrifying than any indoctrination in which the school might indulge is the prospect of our becoming completely victimized and molded by the mechanics of industrialism. The control of the machine requires a society which is dominated less by the ideal of individual advancement and more by certain far-reaching purposes and plans for social construction. In such a society, instead of the nimble mind responsive to every eddy in the social current, a firmer and more steadfast mentality would be preferable.

⇥ THE SOCIAL FRONTIER, 1934

In October 1934, in the midst of the Great Depression, the most politically minded of the progressive educators launched a new journal, The Social Frontier. *Under George Count's leadership, the Social Frontier included such other progressives as William H. Kilpatrick, Harold Rugg, Harrison Elliott, and the venerable John Dewey among its directors. The journal's editors were clear in their goals, calling on teachers and progressive educators to engage in active political agitation for a more socially democratic school and to play a role in the reconstruction of American society. An editorial from the first issue of the journal gives a good sense of the urgency with which these educators faced the issues raised by the Great Depression. A subsequent article by John Dewey represents his own call to teachers to enlist in the crusade for social reconstruction.*

Orientation—The Editors

The Social Frontier assumes that the age of individualism in economy is closing and that an age marked by close integration of social life and by collective planning and control is opening. For weal or woe, it accepts as irrevocable this deliverance of the historical process. It intends to go forward to meet the new age and to proceed as rationally as possible to the realization of all possibilities for the enrichment and refinement of human life. It will nurse no fantasies of returning to the simple household and neighborhood economy of the time of Thomas Jefferson; it will seek no escape from the responsibilities of today, either by longing for a past now gone beyond recovery or by imagining a future bearing the features of Utopia. It proposes to take seriously the affirmation of the Declaration of Independence that "all men are created equal" and are entitled to "life, liberty, and the pursuit of happiness." Also it proposes, in the light of this great humanist principle applied to the collective realities of industrial civilization, to pass every important educational event, institution, theory, and program under critical review. Finally, it will devote its pages positively to the development of the thought of all who are interested in making education discharge its full responsibility in the present age of social transition. Its editorial staff and board of directors hope that it will help fight the great educational battles—practical and theoretical—which are already looming above the horizon. And they trust that it will engage in the battles of the twentieth and not of the eighteenth century.

The Social Frontier acknowledges allegiance to no narrow conception of education. While recognizing the school as society's central educational agency, it refuses to *limit* itself to a consideration of the work of this institution. On the contrary, it includes within its field of interest all of those formative influences and agencies which serve to induct the individual—whether old or young—into the life and culture of the group. It regards education as an aspect of a culture in process of evolution. It therefore has no desire to promote a restricted and technical professionalism. Rather does it address itself to the task of considering the broad role of education in advancing the welfare and interests of the great masses of the people who do the work of society—those who labor on farms and ships and in the mines, shops, and factories of the world.

Can Education Share In Social Reconstruction?—John Dewey

That upon the whole schools have been educating for something called the *status quo* can hardly be doubted by observing persons. The fallacy in this attempt should be equally evident. There is no *status quo*—except in the literal sense in which Andy explained the phrase to Amos: a name for the "mess we are in." It is not difficult, however, to define that which is called the *status quo*; the difficulty is that the movement of actual events has little connection with the name by which it is called.

For the alleged *status quo* is summed up in the phrase "rugged individualism." The assumption is—or was—that we are living in a free economic society in which every individual has an equal chance to exercise his initiative and his other abilities, and that the legal and political order is designed and calculated to further this equal liberty on the part of all individuals. No grosser myth ever received general currency. Economic freedom has been either nonexistent or precarious for large masses of the population. Because of its absence and its tenuousness for the majority, political and cultural freedom has been sapped; the legally constituted order has supported the idea of a *beati possidentes.*

There is no need here to review the historic change from a simple agrarian order, in which the idea of equal opportunity contained a large measure of truth, to a complex industrial order with highly concentrated economic and political control. The point is that the earlier idea and theory persisted after it had lost all relevance to actual facts, and was then used to justify and strengthen the very situation that had undermined it in practice. What, then, is the real *status quo?* Is it the condition of free individuality postulated by the ruling theoretical philosophy, or is it the increasing encroachment of the power of a privileged minority, a power exercised over the liberties of the masses without corresponding responsibility?

It would not be difficult to make out a case for a positive and sweeping answer in favor of the latter alternative. Let me quote, as far as schools are concerned, from Roger Baldwin. "On the whole, it may be said without question that the public schools have been handed over to the keeping of the militant defenders of the *status quo*—the Daughters of the American Revolution, the American Legion, the Fundamentalists, the Ku Klux Klan, and the War Department. Look at rites and flag saluting by law in most states; compulsory reading of the Protestant Bible in eighteen states, contrary to the provision for the separation of church and state; compulsory teaching of the Constitution by prescribed routine; making a crime of the teaching of evolution in three states; special oaths of loyalty not required of other public servants in ten states; loyalty oaths required of students as a condition of graduation in many cities; history textbooks revised under pressure to conform to prejudice; restriction or ban on teachers' unions affiliated with the labor movement; laws protecting tenure beaten or emasculated; compulsory military training in both high schools and colleges, with inevitable pressure on students and teachers by the military mind." To these forms of outward and overt pressure may be added—as indeed Mr. Baldwin does add—more powerful, because more subtle and unformulated, pressures that act constantly upon teachers and students.

It might seem, then, that, judged by the present situation, *limitation* upon the efforts of teachers to promote a new social order—in which the ideal of freedom and equality of individuals will be a fact and not a fiction—tremendously outweighs the element of *possibility* in their doing so. Such is not the case, however, great as are the immediate odds against effort to realize the possibility. The reason is that the actual *status quo* is in a state of flux; there is no *status quo,* if by that term it means something stable and constant. The last forty years have seen in every industrialized society all over the world a steady movement in the direction of social control of economic forces. Pressure for this control of capital—or, if you please, for its "regimentation"—is exercised mostly through political agencies and voluntary organizations. *Laissez-faire* has been dying of strangulation. Mr. Hoover, who gave currency to the phrase "rugged individualism" while President, acted repeatedly and often on a fairly large scale for governmental intervention and regulation of economic forces. The list of interferences with genuine educational freedom that has been cited is itself a sign of an effort, and often a conscious one, to stem a tide that is running in the opposite direction—that is, toward a collectivism that is hostile to the idea of unrestricted action on the part of those individuals who are possessed of economic and political power because of control [of the nation's resources] and the possibility of educational effort for establishing a new social order is fairly evident. Teachers and administrators often say they must "conform to conditions" rather than do what they would personally prefer to do. The proposition might be sound if conditions were fixed or even reasonably stable. But they are not. . . .

In spite of the lethargy and timidity of all too many teachers, I believe there are enough teachers who will respond to the great task of making schools active and militant participants in creation of a new social order, provided they are shown not merely the general end in view but also the means of its accomplishment . . . Laying the bases, intellectual and moral, for a new social order is a sufficiently novel and inspiring ideal to arouse a new spirit in the teaching profession and to give direction to a radically changed effort. Those who hold such an ideal are false to what they profess in words when they line up with reactionaries in ridicule of those who would make the profession a reality. That task may well be left to educational fascists.

CHAPTER 8

SCHOOLS IN THE COLD WAR ERA, 1950-1970

❖ Introduction

❖ National Defense Education Act, 1958

❖ The *Scott, Foresman Readers*, 1955

❖ H. G Rickover, *Education for All Children: What We Can Learn from England*, 1962

❖ Herbert Kohl, *Thirty-Six Children*, 1967

❖ John Holt, *How Children Fail*, 1964

❖ Supreme Court of the United States, *Engel v. Vitale*, 1962

Introduction

By the 1950s, progressive education, in most of its many guises, had lost its energy. As Lawrence Cremin saw it, "By the 1950s, the enthusiasm, the vitality, and the drive were gone; all that remained were the slogans" (p. 181). The loss of drive came on many fronts. The administrative progressives' effort to reform schools through top-down dictates had been frustrated because so many of the top positions had been captured by people with little vision. Bureaucrats replaced reformers, while the business-based reformers like James Jackson Storrow found activities like organizing General Motors more rewarding than organizing the schools. As for the militant teachers, from Margaret Haley to Ella Flagg Young to George Counts, the anticommunism of the Cold War ended whatever opportunities they had once had to tie teacher union organizing to the quest for a socialist and democratic society. The new generation of teacher union organizers that emerged in the 1950s carefully separated the movement from any controversial social changes and focused instead on bread-and-butter issues such as salary and working conditions. This move speeded their drive to organize, but separated them from efforts to improve the society in which children lived. Finally, as Counts had warned, the child-centered advocates fell victim to their own class limitations and to social concerns about well-educated youth.

At the same time, all of these movements came face to face with a major crisis in the United States: the launching of the Soviet satellite Sputnik. The fact that the Soviet Union was able to launch a satellite in 1957, before the United States, was a psychic shock unimaginable today. But that this event would awaken school reform efforts should be of little surprise in a nation that turns to its schools to solve significant social problems. In the case of Sputnik, the result was a resurgence of interest in schools, especially in their capacity to train scientists and engineers who could surpass the Russians—in space and in the more mundane matters of the Cold War. Suddenly, John Dewey and the progressive educators—diverse as they had been—were seen as the enemy, soft and mushy-headed sentimentalists who had let the nation's schools fall dangerously behind the rigorous and tough-minded schools of the Russian enemy.

One result of the Sputnik crisis was the National Defense Education Act, passed by Congress in 1958. The title of the act indicates both the urgency and the focus of federal education policy in the 1950s. The NDEA, as it was forever known, provided a major boost to efforts within the National Science Foundation to support school curricula as well as scientific research. The result was a significant expansion of the laboratory materials available to teachers as well as improvements in the quality of science textbooks. NDEA scholarships also supported a generation of college students who might otherwise have had difficulty financing higher education.

For school critics such as Navy Admiral Hyman Rickover, more needed to be done. For him the solution was clear—wipe away the vestiges of progressivism and replace them with a tough basic education that would produce the leaders the nation needed. Rickover's *Education and Freedom,* a republication of his testimony before Congress, was both a direct attack on progressive education and a call for America to return to a more traditional curriculum taught in more traditional ways. Rickover and his allies were not, however, debating with progressive educators. They were simply putting the last nails into the coffin of a movement which—except in its educational testing phase, which had conveniently forgotten its progressive roots—had run its course.

Not everyone responded to the 1950s as Admiral Rickover and his educational colleagues did. A new generation of educational critics also emerged during this decade. Although they differed significantly among themselves, these critics did hark back to the concerns of the earlier child-centered educators. Herb Kohl, at the beginning of his long career as an education reformer, was appalled at the antichild atmosphere he found in the New York City Public Schools when he first entered the classroom. He called for an education that began by exploring the wonderful curiosity of children and for the creation of classrooms and school systems founded on respect for each child. John Holt began with many similar observations. But where Kohl focused on changing schools, Holt gave up on them. His *How Children Fail* and subsequent books and lectures provided some of the philosophical foundation for both alternative schools and a growing home-school movement.

Later in the Cold War era, another issue reappeared in the school debates with a vengeance. While the nation has always debated the proper relationship between religion and public education, the issue had not come to the forefront of the debates since the 1920s, when the famous trial of high school biology teacher John T. Scopes took place in Dayton, Tennessee. Scopes was charged with teaching evolution—against state law—and his trial sparked a national debate. The decades of quiet following this event came to an end in 1962 when the United States Supreme Court ruled in *Engel v. Vitale* that the New York state policy requiring students to recite a prayer at the beginning of the school day was unconstitutional. The following year, the Court expanded its ruling in *Abington v. Schempp,* stating that all required prayers as well as the devotional reading of the Bible in school was unconstitutional. While the Court carefully protected objective teaching about religion from its ban, the charge that the Court was "banning God from the schools" fanned the flame of a resistance campaign. A battle in part about who controls the content of public culture, in part about the proper relationship of personal piety and values to the educational process, the storm over religion in the schools that began with *Engel v. Vitale* continued for the remainder of the century.

✦ NATIONAL DEFENSE EDUCATION ACT, 1958

The NDEA was a significant development in a campaign that had begun during the Civil War to provide federal aid to the states to support schools. Ironically, while the NDEA represented a significant expansion in federal aid, it was couched in terms that diverted attention from the actual result. The act was a direct response to the launch of the Sputnik satellite by the Soviet Union. The goal was very American—to use the schools to address the problem—by providing better curriculum materials, better teachers, and better financing for future scientists and engineers. At the same time, the framers of the act went to great lengths to assure all concerned that federal aid did not mean federal control of the schools, but only federal assistance.

General Provisions

The Congress hereby finds and declares that the security of the Nation requires the fullest development of the mental resources and technical skills of its young men and women. The present emergency demands that additional and more adequate educational opportunities be made available. The defense of this Nation depends upon the mastery of modern techniques developed from complex scientific principles. It depends as well upon the discovery and development of new principles, new techniques, and new knowledge.

We must increase our efforts to identify and educate more of the talent of our Nation. This requires programs that will give assurance that no student of ability will be denied an opportunity for higher education because of financial need; [and that] will correct as rapidly as possible the existing imbalances in our educational programs which have led to an insufficient proportion of our population educated in science, mathematics, and foreign languages, and trained in technology.

The Congress reaffirms the principle and declares that the States and local communities have and must retain control over and primary responsibility for public education. The national interest requires, however, that the Federal Government give assistance to education for programs, which are important to our defense.

To meet the present educational emergency requires additional effort at all levels of government. It is therefore the purpose of this Act to provide substantial assistance in various forms to individuals, and to States and their subdivisions, in order to insure trained manpower of sufficient quality and quantity to meet the national defense needs of the United States.

Federal Control of Education Prohibited

Nothing contained in this Act shall be construed to authorize any department, agency, officer, or employee of the United States to exercise any direction, supervision, or control over the curriculum, program of instruction, administration, or personnel of any educational institution or school system. . . .

Financial Assistance for Strengthened Science, Mathematics, and Modern Language Instruction

There are hereby authorized to be appropriated $70,000,000 for the fiscal year ending June 30, 1959, and for each of three succeeding fiscal years, for (1) making payments to State educational agencies under this title for the acquisition of equipment (suitable for use in providing education in science, mathematics, or modern foreign language) and for minor remodeling described in paragraph (1) of Section 303(a), and (2) making loans authorized in Section 305. There are also authorized to be appropriated $5,000,000 for the fiscal year ending June 30, 1959, and for each of the three succeeding fiscal years, for making payments to State educational agencies under this title to carry out the programs described in paragraph (5) of section 303(a). . . .

Science Information Service

The National Science Foundation shall establish a Science Information Service. The Foundation, through such Service, shall (1) provide, or arrange for the provision of, indexing, abstracting, translating, and other services leading to a more effective dissemination of scientific information, and (2) undertake programs to develop new or improved methods, including mechanized systems, for making scientific information available.

Science Information Council

a. The National Science Foundation shall establish, in the Foundation, a Science Information Council (hereafter in this title referred to as the "Council") consisting of the Librarian of Congress, the director of the National Library of Medicine, the director of the Department of Agriculture library, and the head of the Science Information Service, each of whom shall be ex officio members, and fifteen members appointed by the Director of the National Science Foundation. The Council shall annually elect one of the appointed members to serve as chairman until the next election. Six of the appointed members shall be leaders in the fields of fundamental science, six shall be leaders in the fields of librarianship and scientific documentation, and three shall be outstanding representatives of the lay public who have demonstrated interest in the problems of communication. Each appointed member of such Council shall hold office for a term of four years, except that (1) any member appointed to fill a vacancy occurring prior to the expiration of the term for which his predecessor was appointed shall be appointed only for the remainder of such term, and (2) that of the members first appointed, four shall hold office for a term of three years, four shall hold office for a term of two years, and three shall hold office for a term of one year, as designated by the Director of the National Science Foundation at the time of appointment. No appointed member of the Council shall be eligible for reappointment until a year has elapsed since the end of his preceding term.

b. It shall be the duty of the Council to advise, to consult with, and to make recommendations to, the head of the Science Foundation Service. The Council shall meet at least twice each year, and at such other times as the majority thereof deems appropriate.

c. Persons appointed to the Council shall, while serving on business of the Council, receive compensation at rates fixed by the National Science Foundation, but not to exceed $50 per day, and shall also be entitled to receive an allowance for actual and necessary travel and subsistence expenses while so serving away from their places of residence. . . .

❖ THE SCOTT, FORESMAN READERS, 1955

From the time of the New England Primer *in the 1700s and the* McGuffey's Readers *from the 1830s to the 1920s, textbook publishing has been a big business. The textbooks that emerged in the United States after World War II were no exception. No company was more successful in marketing its products than Scott, Foresman and Company. Their readers, which began with the famous stories of Dick and Jane and their dog Spot—and which a generation of Americans used to learn to read—continued through the elementary grades. Like all textbooks, the* Scott, Foresman Readers *reflected their times. They marked a turn away from progressivism to a more traditional pedagogy. In response to the Cold War, they were also filled with patriotic stories. Indeed, looking back from the perspective of half a century, one is struck in reading these stories with how similar they are to the* McGuffey's Readers *of a century before, linking literacy with learning to be a patriotic American citizen. The two examples that follow illustrate the tone and content of these readers.*

"How a Song Named a Flag," pages 184–194 from *the New Basic Readers: More Times and Places,* Grade Four, 1955

In the year 1814, a large new flag waved over the fort guarding the city of Baltimore.

"It's a grand flag," said Mary Pickersgill, who had made it. "It's a strong flag, too," Mary boasted. "Those broad stripes will never tear apart. I fastened them thread by thread, to hold together forever, like our United States."

Caroline Pickersgill regarded the flag with shining eyes and echoed her mother's words. "Yes, it's a grand flag," she said. Her own skillful sewing had helped make the brilliant banner in the Pickersgill flag shop.

The huge flag was about thirty-three feet long and twenty-seven feet wide. This was the largest flag that Mary Pickersgill had ever made. It could be seen from both land and sea.

In the streets of Baltimore, the citizens looked up thankfully at the huge flag waving over the fort. "As long as it waves, we'll be safe," they thought.

One day a small ship was sailing past the fort. On it was a young man who forgot all else as he admired the bright banner. How magnificent it looked against the sky!

At the sight, Francis Scott Key bared his head. "A star-spangled banner!" he said to himself. Then he added a wish, "Long may it wave."

The United States was again at war with England. The nearby city of Washington had been attacked and some Americans had been captured.

Among these prisoners was an old doctor whom everyone loved. He was being held on an enemy ship. Naturally many Americans were anxious for Dr. Beans's safety.

Francis Scott Key was sailing to rescue the prisoner. Key's ship carried a flag of truce to protect it from being fired upon by the enemy ships. But first he must find the ship on which Dr. Beans was held.

At last the English warships were found. The officer in charge of them permitted Dr. Beans to go aboard the truce ship at once. But the truce ship was forced to stay with the English fleet, which was preparing for a surprise attack on the fort that guarded

Baltimore. Dr. Beans, Francis Scott Key, and another American aboard the truce ship spent a dreary week of anxious waiting.

Finally the English fleet sailed to attack, and the United States truce ship was taken along.

The truce ship was held back of the warships. The three Americans on deck took turns watching the battle through a powerful spyglass.

When the warships first started to bomb the fort, no guns answered from the shore. The three loyal watchers groaned. Then the enemy fleet moved up closer. Immediately, the guns of the fort roared violently.

The warships moved back, badly damaged. Francis Scott Key felt encouraged. All day long he stood on the ship's deck. His eyes were glued to the Stars and Stripes, still waving over the fort.

Before midnight the enemy renewed their attack. Again, the Americans on the deck of the distant truce ship watched the firing. By the light of the bursting bombs they saw their star-spangled flag clearly.

Just before dawn, the bombing ceased, and Francis Scott Key waited anxiously to see the fort. At daybreak he cried in triumph, "It's there! The flag is still there!"

In the meantime, under cover of darkness, the enemy fleet had sailed away. Now the truce ship was free to return to Baltimore. On the way, Key was busy writing something on a piece of paper.

"Listen!" he cried, showing the paper to his companions. He sang the words on it to an old, familiar tune. His friends joined in and sang, too.

> 'Tis the star-spangled banner.
> Oh, long may it wave
> O'er the land of the free
> And the home of the brave.

People all over the country began singing Francis Scott Key's song. People still sing it. It is called "The Star-Spangled Banner."

"A Boy and His Book," pages 189–94, *The New Basic Readers: More Items and Places,* Grade Four, 1955

Pigeon Creek was a lonely place when the pioneers began to settle in Indiana. But as young Abraham Lincoln tramped across a field, he was thinking how much he loved his new home in the Indiana wilderness.

The Lincoln cabin was roughly built. At night from his bed in the loft, the lad could see the sky through the cracks between the logs. Great white stars shone down on him. Sometimes the yellow moon lighted his room like a bright candle. Sometimes, on warm summer nights, cooling raindrops fell gently over his face. In winter, feathery flakes of snow fell on his pillow.

Today the sturdy youth was hurrying home with good news. A school was starting nine miles from Pigeon Creek. Abe meant to go and get some book learning.

Early the next morning, Abe and his older sister, Sally, got ready for the long walk to school. Nancy, their mother, saw that they were neat and clean. Then she sent them off with a loving pat.

"Now go and learn all you can," she told them. And away they went. They were both dressed in clothing made entirely by their mother. She had even made Abe's coonskin cap. His boots were made from bearskin.

After a few days of school, Sally tired of the daily eighteen-mile walk. She did not go any more. But young Abraham considered no distance too great if only he could learn to spell and write and to read books.

About a month later, the school closed so that the pupils could help with the spring planting. Abe was much disappointed. He knew, however, that the pioneer farmers of Indiana needed all the help they could get to plow their fields and to raise and harvest their crops.

Abe was big and sturdy for a boy of his age. He tried his best to do a man's work. But as he worked, he never stopped thinking about books. He never stopped wishing that he knew what they contained.

The next year, a strange illness brought sorrow to the community at Pigeon Creek. The illness was so terrible that many people died. Abe's mother was one of them.

For a long time after her death, the boy did not go to school. He spent all his time helping Sally with the housework or hunting and fishing.

Then one day Mr. Lincoln brought home a new wife with three children of her own.

The new wife was a good mother to Abe and Sally. She knew how much Abe wanted book learning and sent him back to school. But in the Indiana wilderness, school was open for just a few weeks during the winter season. And Abe was often absent while he helped his father chop wood or pull fodder.

In those few weeks of school, the boy learned reading, writing, spelling, and some arithmetic. He liked reading best of all. But books were scarce in Pigeon Creek.

The Lincoln family owned only two books—a Bible and an arithmetic. The Bible was hard to read, and Abe often stumbled over the words. The arithmetic was easier. He studied it from cover to cover.

Abe borrowed every book anyone would lend him. He read each one until he knew it almost by heart.

One cold day he tramped five miles over rough fields to help a farmer pull cornstalks for fodder. When he came in to dinner at noon, he saw a book on a table.

"Could I borrow it?" he asked.

Abe's eyes sparkled with pleasure when he left with the book tucked under his arm. At home he swallowed his supper quickly. Then he stretched out flat on the floor with his borrowed book. He read until midnight by the light of the crackling fire.

When Abe went up to his bed in the loft, he tucked the book between two logs of the wall. At dawn, when he reached for it, his fingers touched something wet and cold.

The book was soaked with snow that had blown in through the cracks. Now it was ruined! The only honest thing he could do was to go and tell the owner. The boy did not hesitate. He set out without waiting for breakfast or combing his hair.

Abe told the farmer his sad story. "Oh, please, sir," he said anxiously, "I'll pull fodder or do anything you say to make up for your spoiled book."

"Well," drawled the farmer, "I reckon two days' work will pay for it. Pull fodder for two days and keep the book."

So Abe toiled for two days. He did not mind that his back ached and his hands were stiff with cold. The precious book was his! It was a story about George Washington.

Years afterwards, Abraham Lincoln often told about the Washington book. "It helped me become president of the United States," he always said.

✦ H. G. Rickover, Education for All Children: What We Can Learn from England, 1962

Navy Admiral Hyman Rickover gained national fame as the "father of the nuclear submarine." A crusty, tough-talking career officer in the Navy, Rickover had assembled a team of scientists, engineers, and Navy officers that had produced a nuclear-fueled submarine well ahead of schedule. In the 1960s, based on this experience, Rickover—although he continued on active duty as leader of the nuclear fleet—also turned his attention to the nation's schools. In a series of speeches and publications, he became a fierce critic of progressive pedagogy, blaming John Dewey and his fellow progressives for all that was wrong with education and demanding a return to the tough-minded, curriculum-centered pedagogy of an earlier time for the nation's youth. While other critics of progressivism, such as Mortimer J. Adler, offered more nuanced views, Rickover, in part because of his plain-spokenness and in part because of his Navy hero aura, became the best known advocate for a return to the basics. The interchange with Representative Clarence Cannon at the end of this article was part of Rickover's testimony before the U.S. House of Representatives Committee on Appropriations, which Cannon chaired.

You can inform yourself about *anything* in two ways; by *personal* experience and by *studying* the experience of others. Personal experience is necessarily limited by the kind of life you lead and the kind of work you do. But study of the experience of others is limited only by the time you can find to study, to read, to correspond, or to talk with experts. Now, anybody can read books. They are available in public libraries and if your own library hasn't got what you want they will even order it for you—free of charge. When he was a young man, Lincoln remarked: "The things I want to know are in books; my best friend is the man who'll get me a book I ain't read."

We are fortunate that we all have so many friends in our local library.

What you get out of books depends, of course, on how well you choose your authors, how reliable they are. I myself get most of my knowledge of education from official sources: from expressions by education authorities as to what objectives they believe the schools should pursue; writings of educators, which give one a good clue to how well or how badly they are educated, and how informed they are on their subject; also school curricula, examination questions and answers, the value given by outsiders to particular school diplomas and higher degrees, and so on. I am fortunate to be in contact by correspondence with eminent scholars and educators here and abroad who are kind enough to give me the benefit of their own wide practical experience and of a reasoned judgment in educational matters that ultimately rests upon their high intelligence and broad general and professional education.

The Value of Outsiders' Judgment

All this, I know, has no value whatsoever in the eyes of educational officialdom. Like most bureaucracies, this huge organization would like to escape lay criticism and ties to do so by constantly using the stereotyped argument that only "professionals" or "inside" critics can judge the performance of other professionals and anyway, nobody can judge the schools unless he has personally inspected every school in the country, sat in every classroom of every school, and listened to every child in every classroom of every school.

Now these are splendid gimmicks if all that the educators want is to save themselves the trouble to answer criticism of the schools. The most effective critics have almost always been outsiders—individuals working on their own, individuals who have no access to public funds that finance junkets of educators around the world. These days, they rarely obtain a foundation grant.

Dewey versus "Book Learning"

But I wonder sometimes whether this is merely a gimmick or whether the educators really mean it. I would feel much better if I thought it was only a gimmick, but what I am afraid of is that they actually believe what they say. This is what worries me so much, because if they do believe it, then they are denying the validity of our entire educational system, because all education is based on what humanity has learned throughout history. If you can only learn from what is going on *today,* then obviously we should do away with our educational system and just have our children make field trips to the firehouse and city hall.

It seems to me that the educators are in their own adult lives following the precepts Dewey used for *elementary school children* in his Chicago Laboratory School. He felt that children learned more by practical experience than out of books. Hence, his dogma that children should be "learning by doing." For instance, he had ten- and eleven-year-olds spend endless hours *reinventing* such things as how to make cotton, flax, and wool cloth, how to card wool, and so on. "You can concentrate the history of all mankind into the evolution of flax, cotton, and wool fibers into clothing," said Dewey. But would this not give you an utterly materialistic, worm's eye view of history and of man? And can modern children afford to devote so much time to learning the primitive origins of a manufacturing process that is unlikely to be important in their lives unless they all become managers of textile mills? At that, a manager could grasp the principle of primitive looms in half an hour from a book.

Ordinarily, mistrust of "book learning" is to be found only among uneducated people who do not themselves read books and whose schooling has not carried them from concrete things to abstract concepts. And so, quite naturally, they feel that to *know,* a person should have personally seen, heard, and touched the things he talks about; and before he can *criticize* anything, he must prove he can do the things he criticizes better himself.

Many people believe that unless a critic can demonstrate a better way, his criticism isn't "constructive." Doesn't the person who reports a fire perform a valuable service, even though the fire department puts it out? You sometimes hear people remark disparagingly of an art or literary critic—to take just one example—that they'd like to see this critic paint a better picture or write a better book. This way of thinking confuses *ability to judge art* with *artistic talent,* but the two are different. If it were not so, no layman could discriminate between good and bad art, or for that matter between a good and a bad doctor, lawyer, or teacher. The "professionals" would then have it all their own way. Many an administrator uses this stratagem of requiring his subordinates never to criticize unless it is "constructive," the administrator himself, of course, being the one who decides what is and what is not "constructive" criticism.

Judging Schools by Their Graduates

For myself, besides study and reading, correspondence and discussion, I have learned much about education through experience gained on my job with novel engineering development projects. Also, my many years in Washington have given me a unique opportunity to observe how greatly the United States is handicapped because we simply do not have enough people with the educational qualifications essential to keep us progressing satisfactorily. The lack is both in general or liberal education, and in the specialized education needed by professionals and technicians.

As a practical man, I am not much interested in the mystique or esoterics of education which fascinate so many of our professional educators. I freely admit I judge schools by their products. Literally thousands of these products pass through my hands and those of my leading scientists and engineers when we interview young people who apply for positions as designers and builders of nuclear reactors or as officers and men to operate our nuclear ships. I find the percentage so qualified to be deplorably small. Those selected we must send to special schools set up and run by our own naval reactors group. These schools do not teach reactor technology alone; they also have to teach many basic subjects which abroad have already been taught in the regular schools. My "school system" of six schools enrolls about 2,500 students at different levels from high school to graduate university. So I can claim some personal experience with educating young Americans.

Mr. Cannon:	If I may be frank with you, Admiral Rickover. Isn't nuclear propulsion a narrowly specialized field? Can you judge American education solely by the educational qualifications of persons who want to work in this field?
Admiral Rickover:	How can I, who am engaged in a specialty—nuclear propulsion—qualify as a critic of education? It so happens that this specialty has in it all the elements that go into modern technology. When you find out what it takes to accomplish an engineering project for developing atomic energy, you know what it takes to do almost any other new development job. The educational qualifications of the people who do the technical work and of those who direct it as administrators are roughly the same. In fact, our nuclear project is a pretty good touchstone of the effectiveness of our schools. It calls for flexibility and toughness of mind, for understanding the basic principles in physics, chemistry, and all types of engineering. Also for what I'd like to call an impersonal "scientific" attitude toward the work that must be done. This means, first of all, a readiness to go back to fundamental principles, for it is these that must be applied in a novel way to develop a new item such as a nuclear reactor. It requires readiness to shed accustomed routines—nothing new can be created by routine methods. It means on the part of nontechnical administrators, who are set above the technical people doing the actual development work, that they must forget their organizational "status" when it comes to dealing with technical problems. Because here they are inferior in knowledge to the experts who are organizationally their subordinates. It isn't easy

for people whose jobs give them power, not to use this power but to respect the imperatives of science and engineering and to bow to the judgment of technical subordinates in *all* technical matters.

→ HERBERT KOHL, THIRTY-SIX CHILDREN, 1967

For all of the national debates about school reform, the day-to-day reality of many schools remained much the same through the generations. Herb Kohl, who has become one of the nation's most respected commentators on the educational scene, began his career as a young graduate of Columbia University's Teachers College working in a school in Harlem. As Kohl reports, the school was only a few blocks from his home and his college, but—as generations of teachers have seen—miles away in terms of culture and the experiences of students and teachers. Kohl's first book, Thirty-Six Children, *became a bestseller, much respected for the harsh but clear light it shone on the reality of schools in urban America in the 1960s. His account of his first days on the job remains a classic description of what many experience upon entering the teaching profession.*

My alarm clock rang at seven-thirty, but I was up and dressed at seven. It was only a fifteen-minute bus ride from my apartment on 90th Street and Madison Avenue to the School on 119th Street and Madison.

There had been an orientation session the day before. I remembered the principal's words. "In times like these, this is the most exciting place to be, in the midst of ferment and creative activity. Never has teaching offered such opportunities . . . we are together here in a difficult situation. They are not the easiest children, yet the rewards are so great—a smile, a loving concern, what an inspiration, a felicitous experience."

I remembered my barren classroom, no books, a battered piano, broken windows and desks, falling plaster, and an oppressive darkness.

I was handed a roll book with thirty-six names and thirty-six cumulative record cards, years of judgments already passed upon the children, their official personalities. I read through the names, twenty girls and sixteen boys, the 6–1 class, though I was supposed to be teaching the fifth grade and had planned for it all summer. Then I locked the record cards away in the closet. The children would tell me who they were. Each child, each new school year, is potentially many things, only one of which the cumulative record card documents. It is amazing how "emotional" problems can disappear, how the dullest child can be transformed into the keenest, and the brightest into the most ordinary, when the prefabricated judgments of other teachers are forgotten.

The children entered at nine and filled up the seats. They were silent and stared at me. It was a shock to see thirty-six black faces before me. No preparation helped. It is one thing to be liberal and talk, another to face something and learn that you're afraid.

The children sat quietly, expectant. *Everything must go well; we must like each other.*

Hands went up as I called the roll. Anxious faces, hostile, indifferent, weary of the ritual, confident of its outcome.

The smartest class in the sixth grade, yet no books.

"Write about yourselves, tell me who you are." (I hadn't said who I was, too nervous.)

Kohl, Herbert. *Thirty-Six Children.* New York: The New American Library, Inc., 1967. Reprinted by permission of Penquin Putnam.

Slowly they set to work, the first directions followed—and if they had refused?

Then arithmetic, the children working silently, a sullen, impenetrable front. *To talk to them, to open them up this first day.*

"What would you like to learn this year? My name is Mr. Kohl."

Silence. The children looked up at me with expressionless faces, thirty-six of them crowded at thirty-five broken desks. *This is the smartest class?*

Explain: They're old enough to choose, enough time to learn what they'd like as well as what they have to.

Silence, a restless movement rippled through the class. *They don't understand? There must be something that interests them, that they care to know more about.*

A hand shot up in the corner of the room.

"I want to learn more about volcanoes. What are volcanoes?"

The class seemed interested. I sketched a volcano on the blackboard, made a few comments, and promised to return.

"Anything else? Anyone else interested in something?"

Silence, then the same hand.

"Why do volcanoes form?"

And during the answer:

"Why don't we have a volcano here?"

A contest. The class savored it, I accepted. Question, response, question. I walked toward my inquisitor, studying his mischievous eyes, possessed and possessing smile. I moved to congratulate him, my hand went happily toward his shoulder. I dared because I was afraid.

His hands shot up to protect his dark face, eyes contracted in fear, body coiled, ready to bolt for the door and out, down the stairs into the streets.

"But why should I hit you?"

They're afraid, too!

Hands relaxed, he looked torn and puzzled. I changed the subject quickly and moved on to social studies—How We Became Modern America.

"Who remembers what America was like in 1800?"

A few children laughed; the rest barely looked at me.

"Can anyone tell me what was going on about 1800? Remember, you studied it last year. Why don't we start specifically? What do you think you'd see if you walked down Madison Avenue in those days?"

A lovely hand, almost too thin to be seen, tentatively rose.

"Cars?"

"Do you think there were cars in 1800? Remember that was over a hundred and fifty years ago. Think of what you learned last year and try again. Do you think there were cars then?"

"Yes . . . no . . . I don't know."

She withdrew, and the class became restless as my anger rose.

At last another hand.

"Grass and trees?"

The class broke up as I tried to contain my frustration.

"I don't know what you're laughing about—it's the right answer. In those days, Harlem was farmland, with fields and trees and a few houses. There weren't any roads or houses like the ones outside, or streetlights or electricity. There probably wasn't even a Madison Avenue."

The class was outraged. It was inconceivable to them there was a time their Harlem didn't exist.

"Stop this noise and let's think. Do you believe that Harlem was here a thousand years ago?"

A pause, several uncertain "noes."

"It's possible that the land was green, then. Why couldn't Harlem also have been green a hundred and fifty or two hundred years ago?"

No response. The weight of Harlem and my whiteness and strangeness hung up in the air as I droned on, lost in my righteous monologue. The uproar turned into sullen silence. A slow, nervous drumming began at several desks; the atmosphere closed as intelligent faces lost their animation. Yet I didn't understand my mistake, the children's rejection of me and my ideas. Nothing worked, I tried to joke, command, play—the children remained joyless until the bell, then quietly left for lunch.

There was an hour to summon energy and prepare for the afternoon, yet it seemed futile. What good are plans, clever new methods and materials, when the children didn't—wouldn't—care or listen? Perhaps the best solution was to prepare for hostility and silence, become the cynical teacher, untaught by his pupils, ungiving himself, yet protected.

At one o'clock, my tentative cynicism assumed, I found myself once again unprepared for the children who returned and noisily and boisterously avoided me. Running, playing, fighting—they were alive as they tore about the room. I was relieved, yet how to establish order? I fell back on teacherly words.

"You've had enough time to run around. Everybody please go to your seats. We have work to begin."

No response. The boy who had been so scared during the morning was flying across the back of the room pursued by a demonic-looking child wearing black glasses. Girls stood gossiping in little groups, a tall boy fantasized before four admiring listeners, while a few children wandered in and out of the room. I still knew no one's name.

"Sit down, we've got to work. At three o'clock you can talk all you want to."

One timid girl listened. I prepared to use one of the teacher's most fearsome weapons and last resources. Quickly white paper was on my desk, the blackboard erased, and numbers from 1 to 10 and 11 to 20 appeared neatly in two columns.

"We're now going to have an *important* spelling test. Please, young lady"—I selected one of the gossipers—"what's your name? Neomia, pass out the paper. When you get your paper, fold it in half, put your heading on it, and number carefully from one to ten and eleven to twenty, exactly as you see it on the blackboard."

Reluctantly the girls responded, then a few boys, until after the fourth, weariest, repetition of the directions the class was seated and ready to begin—I thought.

Rip, a crumpled paper flew onto the floor. Quickly I replaced it; things had to get moving.

Rip, another paper, rip. I got the rhythm and began quickly, silently, replacing crumpled papers.

"The first word is *anchor.* The ship dropped an *anchor. Anchor.*"

"A what?"

"Where?"

"Number two is *final. Final* means last, *final.* Number three is *decision.* He couldn't make a *decision* quickly enough."

"What *decision?*"

"What was number two?"

"*Final.*"

I was trapped.

"Then what was number one?"

"*Anchor.*"

"I missed a word."

"Number four is *reason.* What is the *reason* for all this noise?"

"Because it's the first day of school."

"Yeah, this is too hard for the first day."

"We'll go on without any comments whatever. The next word is _____."

"What number is it?

"_____ *direction.* What *direction* are we going? *Direction.*"

"What's four?"

The test seemed endless, but it did end at two o'clock. What next? Once more I needed to regain my strength and composure, and it was still the first day.

"Mr. Kohl, can we please talk to each other about the summer? We won't play around. Please, it's only the first day."

"I'll tell you what, you can talk, but on the condition that everyone, I mean *every single person in the room,* keeps quiet for one whole minute."

Teacher still had to show he was strong. To prove what? The children succeeded in remaining silent on the third attempt; they proved they could listen. Triumphant, I tried more.

"Now let's try for thirty seconds to think of one color."

"You said we could talk!"

"My head hurts, I don't want to think anymore."

"It's not fair!"

It wasn't. A solid mass of resistance coagulated, frustrating my need to command. The children would not be moved.

"You're right, I'm sorry. Take ten minutes to talk and then we'll get back to work."

For ten minutes the children talked quietly; there was time to prepare for the last half-hour. I looked over my lesson plans: Reading, 9 to 10; Social Studies, 10 to 10:45, etc., etc. How absurd academic time was in the face of the real day. *Where to look?*

"You like it here, Mr. Kohl?"

I looked up into a lovely, sad face.

"What do you mean?"

"I mean do you like it here, Mr. Kohl, what are you teaching us for?"

What?

"Well, I . . . not now. Maybe you can see me at three and we can talk. The class has to get back to work. All right, everybody back to your seats, get ready to work."

She had her answer and sat down and waited with the rest of the class. They were satisfied with the bargain. Only it was I who failed then; exhausted, demoralized, I only wanted three o'clock to arrive.

"It's almost three o'clock and we don't have much time left."

I dragged the words out, listening only for the bell.

"This is only the first day, and of course we haven't got much done. I expect more from you during the year . . ."

The class sensed the maneuver and fell nervous again.

"Take out your notebooks and open to a clean page. Each day except Friday you'll get homework."

My words weighed heavy and false; it wasn't my voice but some common tyrant or moralizer, a tired old man speaking.

"There are many things I'm not strict about, but homework is the one thing I insist upon. In my class *everybody always* does homework. I will check your work every morning. Now copy the assignment I'm putting on the blackboard, and then when you're finished, please line up in the back of the room."

What assignment? What lie now? I turned to the blackboard, groping for something to draw the children closer to me, for something to let them know I cared. *I did care!*

"Draw a picture of your home, the room you live in. Put in all the furniture, the TV, the windows, and doors. You don't have to do it in any special way but keep in mind that the main purpose of the picture should be to show someone what your house looks like."

The children laughed, pointed, then a hand rose, a hand I couldn't attach to a body or face. They all looked alike. I felt sad, lonely.

"Do you have to show your house?"

Two boys snickered. *Are there children ashamed to describe their homes?—have I misunderstood again?* The voice in me answered again.

"Yes."

"I mean . . . what if you can't draw, can you let someone help you?"

"Yes, if you can explain the drawing yourself."

"What if your brother can't draw?"

"Then write a description of your apartment. Remember, *everybody always* does homework in my classes."

The class copied the assignment and lined up, first collecting everything they'd brought with them. The room was as empty as it was at eight o'clock. Tired, weary of discipline, authority, school itself, I rushed the class down the stairs and into the street in some acknowledged state of disorder.

The bedlam on 119th Street, the stooped and fatigued teachers smiling at each other and pretending *they* had had no trouble with their kids, relieved my isolation. I smiled, too, assumed the comfortable pose of casual success, and looked down into a mischievous face, the possessed eyes of the child who had thought I would hit him, Alvin, who kindly and thoughtfully said: "Mr. Kohl, how come you let us out so early today? We just had lunch . . ."

Crushed, I walked dumbly away, managed to reach the bus stop and make my way home. As my weariness dissolved, I only remembered of that first day Alvin and the little girl who asked if I liked being "there."

The books arrived the next morning before class. There were twenty-five arithmetic books from one publisher and twelve from another, but in the entire school there was no complete set of sixth-grade arithmetic books. A few minutes spent checking the first day's arithmetic assignment showed me that it wouldn't have mattered if a full set had existed, since half the class had barely mastered multiplication, and only one child, Grace, who had turned in a perfect paper, was actually ready for sixth-grade arithmetic. It was as though, encouraged to believe that the children couldn't do arithmetic judging from the school's poor results in teaching it, the administration decided not to waste any money on arithmetic books, thereby creating a vicious circle that made it even more impossible for the children to learn.

The situation was almost as dismal in reading—the top of the sixth grade had more than half of its members reading on fourth-grade level and only five or six children actually able to read through a sixth-grade book. There were two full sets of sixth-grade readers available, however, and after the arithmetic situation I was grateful for anything. Yet accepting these readers put me in an awkward position. The books were flat and uninteresting. They only presented what was pleasant in life, and even then limited the pleasant to what was publicly accepted as such. The people in the stories were all middle-class, and their simplicity, goodness, and self-confidence were unreal. I couldn't believe in this foolish ideal and knew that anyone who had ever bothered to observe human life couldn't believe it. Yet I had to teach it, and through it make reading important and necessary. Remembering the children, their anxiety and hostility, the alternate indifference, suspicion, and curiosity they approached me with, knowing how essential it is to be honest with children, I felt betrayed by the books into hypocrisy. No hypocrite can win the respect of children, and without respect one cannot teach.

One of the readers was a companion to the social studies unit on the growth of the United States and was full of stories about family fun in a Model T Ford, the first wireless radio in town, and the joys of wealth and progress. The closest the book touched upon human emotion or the real life of children was in a story in which children accepted a new invention before their parents did, even though the adults laughed at the children. Naturally, everything turned out happily.

The other reader was a miscellany of adventure stories (no human violence or antagonists allowed, just treasure hunts, animal battles, close escapes), healthy poems (no love except for mother, father, and nature), and a few harmless myths (no Oedipus, Electra, or Prometheus). I also managed to get twenty dictionaries in such bad condition that the probability of finding any word still intact was close to zero.

The social studies texts (I could choose from four or five) praised industrial America in terms that ranged from the enthusiastic to the exorbitant. Yet the growth of modern industrial society is fascinating, and it was certainly possible to supplement the text with some truth. I decided to work with what was given me and attempt to teach the sixth-grade curriculum as written in the New York City syllabus, ignoring as long as possible the contradictions inherent in such a task.

The class confronted me, surrounded by my motley library, at nine that second morning and groaned.

"Those phoney books?"

"We read them already, Mr. Kohl."

"It's a cheap, dirty, bean school."

My resolve weakened, and I responded out of despair.

"Let me put it straight to you. These are the only books here. I have no more choice than you do, and I don't like it any better. Let's get through them and maybe by then I'll figure out how to get better ones."

The class understood and accepted the terms. As soon as the books were distributed, the first oral reading lesson began. Some children volunteered eagerly, but most of the class tried not to be seen. The children who read called out the words, but the story was lost. I made the lesson as easy as possible by helping children who stumbled, encouraging irrelevant discussion, and not letting any child humiliate himself. It was bad enough that more than half the class had to be forced to use books they couldn't read.

The lesson ended, and a light-skinned boy raised his hand.

"Mr. Kohl, remember that ten minutes you gave us yesterday? Couldn't we talk again now? We're tired after all this reading."

I wasn't sure how to take Robert's request. My initial feeling was that he was taking advantage of me and trying to waste time. I felt, along with the official dogma, that no moment in school should be wasted—it must all be preplanned and structured. Yet why shouldn't it be "wasted"? Hadn't most of the class wasted years in school, not merely moments?

I remembered my own oppressive school days in New York City, moving from one subject to another without a break, or at most, with a kind teacher letting us stand and stretch in unison; I remember reading moving into social studies into arithmetic. How hateful it seemed then. Is it a waste to pause, talk, or think between subjects? As a teacher I, too, needed a break.

"You're right, Robert, I'm tired too. Everybody can take ten minutes to do what you want, and then we'll move on to social studies."

The class looked fearful and amazed—freedom in school, do what you want? For a few minutes they sat quietly and then slowly began to talk. Two children walked to the piano and asked me if they could try. I said of course, and three more children joined them. It seemed so easy; the children relaxed. I watched closely and suspiciously, realizing that the tightness with time that exists in the elementary school has nothing to do with the quantity that must be learned or the children's needs. It represents the teacher's fear of loss of control and is nothing but a weapon used to weaken the solidarity and opposition of the children that too many teachers unconsciously dread.

After the ten minutes, I tried to bring the children back to work. They resisted, tested my determination. I am convinced that a failure of will at that moment would have been disastrous. It was necessary to compel the children to return to work, not due to my "authority" or "control" but because they were expected to honor the bargain. They listened, and at that moment I learned something of the toughness, consistency, and ability to demand and give respect that enables children to listen to adults without feeling abused or brutalized and, therefore, becoming defiant.

I tried *How We Became Modern America* again. It was hopeless. The children acted as if they didn't know the difference between rivers, islands, oceans, and lakes; between countries, cities, and continents; between ten years and two centuries. Either their schooling had been hopeless, or there was a deeper reason I did not understand underlying the children's real or feigned ignorance. One thing was clear, however, they did not want to hear about the world and, more specifically, modern America from me. The atmosphere was dull as I performed to an absent audience.

"The steam engine was one of the most important . . . Alvin, what was I talking about?"

"Huh?"

He looked dull, his face heavy with resignation, eyes vacant, nowhere . . .

The morning ended on that dead note, and the afternoon began with an explosion. Alvin, Maurice, and Michael came dashing in, chased by a boy from another class who stuck his head and fist in the room, rolled his eyes, and muttered, "Just you wait, Chipmunk."

As soon as he disappeared, the three boys broke up.

"Boy, is he dumb. You sure psyched him."

"Wait till tomorrow in the park."

The other children returned, and I went up to the three boys and said as openly as I could, "What's up?"

They moved away. Alvin muttered something incomprehensible and looked at the floor. As soon as they reached the corner of the room, the laughter began again. Maurice grabbed Michael's glasses and passed them to Alvin. Michael grabbed Alvin's pencil and ran to the back of the room as one of the girls said to me:

"Mr. Kohl, they're bad. You ought to hit them."

Refusing that way out, I watched chaos descend once more. Only this time, being more familiar with the faces and feeling more comfortable in the room, I discerned some method in the disorder. Stepping back momentarily from myself, forgetting my position and therefore my need to establish order, I observed the children and let them show me something of themselves. There were two clusters of boys and three of girls. There were also loners watching shyly or hovering eagerly about the peripheries of the groups. One boy sat quietly drawing, oblivious to the world. As children entered the room they would go straight to one group or another, hover, or walk over to the boy who was drawing and watch silently. Of the two boys' groups, one was whispering conspiratorially, while the other, composed of Alvin, Maurice, Michael, and two others, was involved in some wild improbable mockery of tag. Alvin would tag himself and run. If no one was watching him, he'd stop, run up to one of the others, tag himself again, and the chase was on—for a second. The pursuer would invariably lose interest, tag himself, and the roles would be switched until they all could collide, laughing, slapping palms, and chattering. The other group paid no attention—they were talking of serious matters. They looked bigger, older, and tougher.

There wasn't time to observe the girls. The tag game seemed on the verge of violence and, frightened, I stepped back into the teacherly role, relaxed and strengthened with my new knowledge of the class, and asked in a strong quiet voice for the homework. I felt close to the children—observing them, my fear and self-consciousness were forgotten for a moment. It was the right thing. The girls went to their desks directly, while the boys stopped awkwardly and made embarrassed retreats to their seats.

I am convinced that the teacher must be an observer of his class as well as a member of it. He must look at the children, discover how they relate to each other and the room around them. There must be enough free time and activity for the teacher to discover the children's human preferences. Observing children at play and mischief is an invaluable source of knowledge about them—about leaders and groups, fear, courage, warmth, isolation. Teachers consider the children's gym or free play time their free time too, and usually turn their backs on the children when they have most to learn from them.

I went through a year of teacher training at Teachers College, Columbia, received a degree, and heard no mention of how to observe children, nor even a suggestion that it was of value. Without learning to observe children and thereby knowing something of the people one is living with five hours a day, the teacher resorts to routine and structure for protection. The class is assigned seats, the time is planned down to the minute, subject follows subject—all to the exclusion of human variation and invention.

I witnessed the same ignorance of the children in a private school I once visited, only it was disguised by a progressive egalitarian philosophy. The teachers and students were on a first-name basis; together, they chose the curriculum and decided upon the schedule. Yet many of the teachers knew no more of their classes than the most rigid public-school teachers. They knew only of their pupils and their mutual relationships in contexts where the teacher was a factor. It was clear to me, watching the children when the teacher left the room, that the children's preferences "for the teachers" were not the same as their human preferences (which most likely changed every week). That is not an academic point, for observation can open the teacher to his pupils' changing needs, and can often allow him to understand and utilize internal dynamic adjustments that the children make in relation to each other, rather than impose authority from without.

After the first few days of the year, my students are free to move wherever they want in the room, my role being arbiter when someone wants to move into a seat whose occupant does not want to vacate or when health demands special consideration. I have never bothered to count the number of continual, self-selected seat changes in my classes, yet can say that they never disrupted the fundamental fabric of the class. Rather, they provided internal adjustments and compensations that avoided many possible disruptions. Children fear chaos and animosity. Often they find ways of adjusting to difficult and sensitive situations (when free to) before their teachers are aware they exist.

Only fourteen of the thirty-six children brought in homework that second afternoon, and twelve of them were girls. One of the boys, I noticed, was the quiet artist. Here was a critical moment that plunged me back into the role of participant and destroyed my objective calm. What was the best reaction to the children's lack of response, especially after I'd been so pompous and adamant about homework the first day? How many of the twenty-two missing homeworks were the result of defiance (perhaps merited), of inability, of shame at what the result might reveal? Was there a simple formula: *Good = do homework* and another *Bad = not do homework?* Or would these formulas themselves negate the honesty and sincerity that could lead the children to find a meaningful life in school? At that moment in the classroom, I had no criteria by which to decide and no time to think out my response. It would have been most just to react in thirty-six different ways to the thirty-six different children, but there was no way for me to be most just at that moment. I had to react intuitively and immediately, as anyone in a classroom must. There is never time to plot every tactic. A child's responses are unpredictable, those of groups of children even more so, unless through being brutalized and bullied they are made predictable. When a teacher claims he knows exactly what will happen in his class, exactly how the children will behave and function, he is either lying or brutal.

That means that the teacher must make mistakes. Intuitive, immediate responses can be right and magical, can express understanding that the teacher doesn't know he has, and lead to reorganizations of the teacher's relationship with his class. But they can also be peevish and petty, or merely stupid and cruel. Consistency of the teacher's response is frequently desirable, and the word *consistency* is a favorite of professors at teacher training institutions. Consistency can sometimes prevent discovery and honesty. More, consistency of response is a function of the consistency of a human personality, and that is, at best, an unachievable ideal.

I've said many stupid, unkind things in my classroom, hit children in anger, and insulted them maliciously when they threatened me too much. On the other hand, I've also said some deeply affecting things, moved children to tears by unexpected kindnesses, and made them happy with praise that flowed unashamedly. I've wanted to be consistent and have become more consistent. That seems the most that is possible, a slow movement toward consistency tempered by honesty. The teacher has to live with his own mistakes, as his pupils have to suffer them. Therefore, the teacher must learn to perceive them as mistakes and find direct or indirect ways to acknowledge his awareness of them and of his fallibility to his pupils.

The ideal of the teacher as a flawless moral exemplar is a devilish trap for the teacher as well as a burden for the child. I once had a pupil, Narciso, who was over-burdened by the perfection of adults, and especially of teachers. His father demanded he believe in this perfection as he demanded Narciso believe in and acquiesce to absolute authority. It was impossible to approach the boy for his fear and deference. I had terrified him. He wouldn't work or disobey. He existed frozen in silence. One day he happened to pass by a bar where some other teachers and I were sitting having beers. He was crushed; *teachers don't do that.* He believed so much in what his father and some teachers wanted him to believe that his world collapsed. He stayed away from school for a while, then returned. He smiled, and I returned the smile. After a while he was at ease in class and could be himself; delightful, and defiant, sometimes brilliant, often lazy, an individual reacting in his unique way to what happened in the classroom.

It is only in the world of Dick and Jane, Tom and Sally, that the *always* right and righteous people exist. In a way, most textbooks, and certainly the ones I had to use in the sixth grade, protect the pure image of the teacher by showing the child that some-where in the ideal world that inspires books all people are as "good" as the teacher is supposed to be! It is not insignificant that it is teachers and not students who select school readers, nor that, according to a friend of mine who edits school texts, the books were written for the teachers and not for children for this very reason.

⇥ John Holt, How Children Fail, 1964

While Herb Kohl's response to the difficulty he experienced in his first days as a teacher was to devote his life to improving schools, others have reacted with less optimism. John Holt's How Children Fail, *another educational classic from the early 1960s, was the first of a series of books from an author who eventually came to believe that public schools could not be reformed. Holt believed that other efforts, including home school-ing, were more likely to produce real success in the lives of children. Whether or not one accepts all of Holt's later thinking, his description of why children fail, or why schools fail children, is a valid reminder of what needs to change in American education.*

School tends to be a dishonest as well as a nervous place. We adults are not often hon-est with children, least of all in school. We tell them, not what we think, but what we feel they ought to think; or what other people feel or tell us they ought to think. Pressure groups find it easy to weed out of our classrooms, texts, and libraries whatever facts, truths, and ideas they happen to find unpleasant or inconvenient. And we are not even as truthful with children as we could safely be, as the parents, politicians, and pressure groups would let us be. Even in the most noncontroversial areas, our teaching, the books, and the textbooks we give children present a dishonest and distorted picture of the world.

The fact is that we do not feel an obligation to be truthful to children. We are like the managers and manipulators of news in Washington, Moscow, London, Peking, and Paris, and all the other capitals of the world. We think it our right and our duty, not to tell the truth, but to say whatever will best serve our cause—in this case, the cause of

---

making children grow up into the kind of people we want them to be, thinking whatever we want them to think. We have only to convince ourselves (and we are very easily convinced) that a lie will be "better" for the children than the truth, and we will lie. We don't always need even that excuse; we often lie only for our own convenience.

Worse yet, we are not honest about ourselves, our own fears, limitations, weaknesses, prejudices, motives. We present ourselves to children as if we were gods, all-knowing, all-powerful, always rational, always just, always right. This is worse than any lie we could tell about ourselves. I have more than once shocked teachers by telling them that when kids ask me a question to which I don't know the answer, I say, "I haven't the faintest idea"; or that when I make a mistake, as I often do, I say, "I goofed again"; or that when I am trying to do something I am no good at, like paint in water colors or play a clarinet or bugle, I do it in front of them so they can see me struggling with it, and can realize that not all adults are good at everything. If a child asks me to do something that I don't want to do, I tell him that I won't do it because I don't want to do it, instead of giving him a list of "good" reasons sounding as if they had come down from the Supreme Court. Interestingly enough, this rather open way of dealing with children works quite well. If you tell a child that you won't do something because you don't want to, he is very likely to accept that as a fact which he cannot change; if you ask him to stop doing something because it drives you crazy, there is a very good chance that, without further talk, he will stop, because he knows what that is like.

We are, above all, dishonest about our feelings, and it is this sense of dishonesty of feeling that makes the atmosphere of so many schools so unpleasant. The people who write books that teachers have to read say over and over again that a teacher must love all the children in a class, all of them equally. If by this they mean that a teacher must do the best he can for every child in a class, that he has an equal responsibility for every child's welfare, an equal concern for his problems, they are right. But when they talk of love, they don't mean this; they mean feelings, affection, the kind of pleasure and joy that one person can get from the existence and company of another. And this is not something that can be measured out in little spoonfuls, everyone getting the same amount.

In a discussion of this in a class of teachers, I once said that I liked some of the kids in my class much more than others and that, without saying which ones I liked best, I had told them so. After all, this is something that children know, whatever we tell them; it is futile to lie about it. Naturally, these teachers were horrified. "What a terrible thing to say!" one said. "I love all the children in my class exactly the same." Nonsense; a teacher who says this is lying, to herself or to others, and probably doesn't like any of the children very much. Not that there is anything wrong with that; plenty of adults don't like children, and there is no reason why they should. But the trouble is they feel they should, which makes them feel guilty, which makes them feel resentful, which in turn makes them try to work off their guilt with indulgence and their resentment with subtle cruelties—cruelties of a kind that can be seen in many classrooms. Above all, it makes them put on the phony, syrupy, sickening voice and manner, and the fake smiles and forced, bright laughter that children see so much of in school, and rightly resent and hate.

As we are not honest with them, so we won't let children be honest with us. To begin with, we require them to take part in the fiction that school is a wonderful place and that they love every minute of it. They learn early that not to like school or the teacher is *verboten,* not to be said, not even to be thought. I have known a child, otherwise healthy, happy, and wholly delightful, who at the age of five was being made sick with worry by the fact that she did not like her kindergarten teacher. Robert Heinemann worked for a number of years with remedial students whom ordinary schools were hopelessly unable to deal with. He found that what choked up and froze the minds of these children was, above all else, the fact that they could not express, they could hardly even acknowledge, the fear, shame, rage, and hatred that school and their teachers had aroused in them. In a situation in which they were able and felt free to express these feelings to themselves and others, they were able once again to begin learning. Why can't we say to children what I used to say to fifth graders who got sore at me, "The law says you have to go to school; it doesn't say you have to like it, and it doesn't say you have to like me, either." This might make school more bearable for many children.

Children hear all the time, "Nice people don't say such things." They learn early in life that for unknown reasons they must not talk about a large part of what they think and feel, are most interested in, and worried about. It is a rare child who, anywhere in his growing up, meets even one older person with whom he can talk openly about what most interests him, concerns him, worries him. This is what rich people are buying for their troubled kids when for $25 per hour they send them to psychiatrists. Here is someone to whom you can speak honestly about whatever is on your mind, without having to worry about his getting mad at you. But do we have to wait until a child is snowed under by his fears and troubles to give him this chance? And do we have to take the time of a highly trained professional to hear what, earlier in his life, that child might have told anybody who was willing to listen sympathetically and honestly? The workers in a project called Streetcorner Research, in Cambridge, Massachusetts, have found that nothing more than the opportunity to talk openly and freely about themselves and their lives, to people who would listen without judging, and who were interested in them as human beings rather than as problems to be solved or disposed of, has totally remade the lives and personalities of a number of confirmed and seemingly hopeless juvenile delinquents. Can't we learn something from this? Can't we clear a space for honesty and openness and self-awareness in the lives of growing children? Do we have to make them wait until they are in a jam before giving them a chance to say what they think?

Behind much of what we do in school lie some ideas, that could be expressed roughly as follows: (1) Of the vast body of human knowledge, there are certain bits and pieces that can be called essential, that everyone should know; (2) the extent to which a person can be considered educated, qualified to live intelligently in today's world and be a useful member of society, depends on the amount of this essential knowledge that he carries about with him; (3) it is the duty of schools, therefore, to get as much of this essential knowledge as possible into the minds of children. Thus we find ourselves trying to poke certain facts, recipes, and ideas down the gullets of every child in school, whether the morsel interests him or not, even if it frightens him or sickens him, and even if there are other things that he is much more interested in learning.

These ideas are absurd and harmful nonsense. We will not begin to have true education or real learning in our schools until we sweep this nonsense out of the way. Schools should be a place where children learn what they most want to know, instead of what we think they ought to know. The child who wants to know something remembers it and uses it once he has it; the child who learns something to please or appease someone else forgets it when the need for pleasing or the danger of not appeasing is past. This is why children quickly forget all but a small part of what they learn in school. It is of no use or interest to them; they do not want, or expect, or even intend to remember it. The only difference between bad and good students in this respect is that the bad students forget right away, while the good students are careful to wait until after the exam. If for no other reason, we could well afford to throw out most of what we teach in school because the children throw out almost all of it anyway.

The notion of a curriculum, an essential body of knowledge, would be absurd even if children remembered everything we "taught" them. We don't and can't agree on what knowledge is essential. The man who has trained himself in some special field of knowledge or competence thinks, naturally, that his specialty should be in the curriculum. The classical scholars want Greek and Latin taught; the historians shout for more history; the mathematicians urge more math and the scientists more science; the modern language experts want all children taught French, or Spanish, or Russian; and so on. Everyone wants to get his specialty into the act, knowing that as the demand for his special knowledge rises, so will the price that he can charge for it. Who wins this struggle and who loses depends not on the real needs of children or even of society, but on who is most skillful in public relations, who has the best educational lobbyists, who best can capitalize on events that have nothing to do with education, like the appearance of Sputnik in the night skies.

The idea of the curriculum would not be valid even if we could agree what ought to be in it. For knowledge itself changes. Much of what a child learns in school will be found, or thought, before many years, to be untrue. I studied physics at school from a fairly up-to-date text that proclaimed that the fundamental law of physics was the law of conservation of matter—matter is not created or destroyed. I had to scratch that out before I left school. In economics at college, I was taught many things that were not true of our economy then, and many more that are not true now. Not for many years after I left college did I learn that the Greeks, far from being a detached and judicious people surrounded by chaste white temples, were hot-tempered, noisy, quarrelsome, and liked to cover their temples with gold leaf and bright paint; or that most of the citizens of Imperial Rome, far from living in houses in which the rooms surrounded an atrium, or central court, lived in multistory tenements, one of which was perhaps the largest building in the ancient world. The child who really remembered everything he heard in school would live his life believing many things that were not so.

Moreover, we cannot possibly judge what knowledge will be most needed forty, or twenty, or even ten years from now. At school, I studied Latin and French. Few of the teachers who claimed then that Latin was essential would make as strong a case for it now; and the French might better have been Spanish, or better yet, Russian. Today the schools are busy teaching Russian; but perhaps they should be teaching Chinese, or Hindi, or who-knows-what? Besides physics, I studied chemistry, then perhaps the most popular of all science courses; but I would probably have done better to study biology, or ecology, if such a course had been offered (it wasn't). We always find out, too late, that we don't have the experts we need, that in the past we studied the wrong things; but this is bound to remain so. Since we can't know what knowledge will be most needed in the future, it is senseless to try to teach it in advance. Instead, we should try to turn out people who love learning so much and learn so well that they will be able to learn whatever needs to be learned.

How can we say, in any case, that one piece of knowledge is more important than another, or indeed, what we really say, that some knowledge is essential and the rest, as far as school is concerned, worthless? A child who wants to learn something that the school can't and doesn't want to teach him will be told not to waste his time. But how can we say that what he wants to know is less important than what we want him to know? We must ask how much of the sum of human knowledge anyone can know at the end of his schooling. Perhaps a millionth. Are we then to believe one of these millionths is so much more important than another? Or that our social and national problems will be solved if we can just figure out a way to turn children out of schools knowing two millionths of the total, instead of one? Our problems don't arise from the fact that we lack experts enough to tell us what needs to be done, but out of the fact that we do not and will not do what we know needs to be done now.

Learning is not everything, and certainly one piece of learning is as good as another. One of my brightest and boldest fifth graders was deeply interested in snakes. He knew more about snakes than anyone I've ever known. The school did not offer herpetology; snakes were not in the curriculum; but as far as I was concerned, any time he spent learning about snakes was better spent than in ways I could think of to spend it; not least of all because, in the process of learning about snakes, he learned a great deal more about many other things than I was able to "teach" those unfortunates in my class who were not interested in anything at all. In another fifth-grade class, studying Romans in Britain, I saw a boy trying to read a science book behind the cover of his desk. He was spotted, and made to put the book away, and listen to the teacher; with a heavy sigh he did so. What was gained here? She traded a chance for an hour's real learning about science for, at best, an hour's temporary learning about history—much more probably no learning at all, just an hour's worth of daydreaming and resentful thoughts about school.

It is not subject matter that makes some learning more valuable than others, but the spirit in which the work is done. If a child is doing the kind of learning that most children do in school, when they learn at all—swallowing words, to spit back at the teacher on demand—he is wasting his time, or rather, we are wasting it for him. This learning will not be permanent, or relevant, or useful. But a child who is learning naturally, following his curiosity where it leads him, adding to his mental model of reality whatever he needs and can find a place for, and rejecting without fear or guilt what he does not need, is growing—in knowledge, in the love of learning, and in the ability to learn. He is on his way to becoming the kind of person we need in our society, and that our "best" schools and colleges are *not* turning out, the kind of person who, in Whitney Griswold's words, seeks and finds meaning, truth, and enjoyment in everything he does. All his life he will go on learning. Every experience will make his mental model of reality more complete and more true to life, and thus make him more able to deal realistically, imaginatively, and constructively with whatever new experience life throws his way.

We cannot have real learning in school if we think it is our duty and our right to tell children what they must learn. We cannot know, at any moment, what particular bit of knowledge or understanding a child needs most, will most strengthen and best fit his model of reality. Only he can do this. He may not do it very well, but he can do it a hundred times better than we can. The most we can do is try to help, by letting him know roughly what is available and where he can look for it. Choosing what he wants to learn and what he does not is something he must do for himself.

There is one more reason, and the most important one, why we must reject the idea of school and classrooms as places where, most of the time, children are doing what some adult tells them to do. The reason is that there is no way to coerce children without making them afraid, or more afraid. We must not try to fool ourselves into thinking that that is not so. The would-be progressives, who until recently had great influence over most American public school education, did not recognize this—and still do not. They thought, or at least talked and wrote as if they thought, that there were good ways and bad ways to coerce children (the bad ones mean, harsh, cruel, the good ones gentle, persuasive, subtle, kindly), and that if they avoided the bad and stuck to the good they would do no harm. This was one of their greatest mistakes, and the main reason why the revolution they hoped to accomplish never took hold.

The idea of painless, nonthreatening coercion is an illusion. Fear is the inseparable companion of coercion, and its inescapable consequence. If you think it your duty to make children do what you want, whether they will or not, then it follows inexorably that you must make them afraid of what will happen to them if they don't do what you want. You can do this in the old-fashioned way, openly and avowedly, with the threat of harsh words, infringement of liberty, or physical punishment. Or you can do it in the modern way, subtly, smoothly, quietly, by withholding the acceptance and approval which you and others have trained the children to depend on; or by making them feel that some retribution awaits them in the future, too vague to imagine but too implacable to escape. You can, as many skilled teachers do, learn to tap with a word, a gesture, a look, even a smile, the great reservoir of fear, shame, and guilt that today's children carry around inside them. Or you can simply let your own fears, about what will happen to you if the children don't do what you want, reach out and infect them. Thus the children will feel more and more that life is full of dangers from which only the goodwill of adults like you can protect them, and that this goodwill is perishable and must be earned anew each day.

The alternative—I can see no other—is to have schools and classrooms in which each child in his own way can satisfy his curiosity, develop his abilities and talents, pursue his interests, and from the adults and older children around him get a glimpse of the great variety and richness of life. In short, the school should be a great smorgasbord of intellectual, artistic, creative, and athletic activities, from which each child could take whatever he wanted, and as much as he wanted, or as little. When Anna was in the sixth grade, the year after she was in my class, I mentioned this idea to her. After describing very sketchily how a school might be run, and what the children might do, I said, "Tell me, what do you think of it? Do you think it would work? Do you think the kids would learn anything?" She said, with utmost conviction, "Oh, yes, it would be wonderful!" She was silent for a minute or two, perhaps remembering her own generally unhappy schooling. Then she said thoughtfully, "You know, kids really like to learn; we just don't like being pushed around."

No, they don't; and we should be grateful for that. So let's stop pushing them around, and give them a chance.

✦ SUPREME COURT OF THE UNITED STATES, ENGEL V. VITALE, 1962

Few decisions in the history of the Supreme Court have created such long lasting animosity as Engel v. Vitale *in 1962 and the Court's subsequent 1963 decision in* Abington School Board v. Schempp. *The* Engel *case only banned a state-written prayer, but*

Abington *expanded the field to include all official prayers and the devotional reading of the Bible. While* Abington *was, therefore, significantly broader, the fact that* Engel *came first made it the target of debate. Many believed that these rulings represented not only the exclusion of faith, but the exclusion of what they had long seen as the properly dominant Protestant-European-Christian faith from the education of their children. All of the debates about cultural domination versus cultural inclusion came to a head here. At the same time, for others, the issue was much simpler—they wanted the right to affirm their own faith and piety at the beginning of the school day. The overlap of so many issues and fundamental debates about the nature of the unifying culture of the United States in these cases—shown clearly in the majority and minority opinions that follow—meant that resolution would never be easy or final.*

Majority Opinion: Mr. Justice Black delivered the opinion of the Court.

The respondent Board of Education of Union Free School District No. Nine, New Hyde Park, New York, acting in its official capacity under state law, directed the School District's principal to cause the following prayer to be said aloud by each class in the presence of a teacher at the beginning of each school day:

"Almighty God, we acknowledge our dependence upon Thee, and we beg Thy blessings upon us, our parents, our teachers, and our Country."

This daily procedure was adopted on the recommendation of the State Board of Regents, a governmental agency created by the State Constitution to which the New York Legislature has granted broad supervisory, executive, and legislative powers over the State's public school system. These state officials composed the prayer which they recommended and published as a part of their "Statement on Moral and Spiritual Training in the Schools," saying: "We believe that this Statement will be subscribed to by all men and women of good will, and we call upon all of them to aid in giving life to our program."

Shortly after the practice of reciting the Regents' prayer was adopted by the School District, the parents of ten pupils brought this action in a New York State Court, insisting that use of this official prayer in the public schools was contrary to the beliefs, religions, or religious practices of both themselves and their children. Among other things, these parents challenged the constitutionality of both the state law authorizing the School District to direct the use of prayer in Public Schools and the District's regulation ordering the recitation of this particular prayer on the ground that these actions of official governmental agencies violate that part of the First Amendment of the Federal Constitution which commands that "Congress shall make no law respecting an establishment of religion"—a command which was "made applicable to the State of New York by the Fourteenth Amendment of the said Constitution." The New York Court of Appeals, over the dissents of Judges Dye and Fuld, sustained an order of the lower state courts which had upheld the power of New York to use the Regents' prayer as a part of the daily procedures of its public schools so long as the schools did not compel any pupil to join in the prayer over his or his parents' objection. We granted *certiorari* to review this important decision involving rights protected by the First and Fourteenth Amendments.

We think that by using its public school system to encourage recitation of the Regents' prayer, the State of New York has adopted a practice wholly inconsistent with the Establishment Clause. There can, of course, be no doubt that New York's program of daily classroom invocation of God's blessings as prescribed in the Regents' prayer is a religious activity. It is a solemn avowal of divine faith and supplication for the blessings of the Almighty. The nature of such a prayer has always been religious, none of the respondents has denied this, and the trial court expressly so found:

> The religious nature of prayer was recognized by Jefferson and has been concurred in by theological writers, the United States Supreme Court, and State courts and administrative officials, including New York's Commissioner of Education. A committee of the New York Legislature has agreed.
> The Board of Regents as *amicus curiae,* the respondents, and intervenors all concede the religious nature of prayer, but seek to distinguish this prayer because it is based on our spiritual heritage.

The petitioners contend among other things that the state laws requiring or permitting use of the Regents' prayer must be struck down as a violation of the Establishment Clause because that prayer was composed by governmental officials as a part of a governmental program to further religious beliefs. For this reason, petitioners argue, the State's use of the Regents' prayer in its public school system breaches the constitutional wall of separation between Church and State. We agree with that contention since we think that the constitutional prohibition against laws respecting an establishment of religion must at least mean that in this country it is no part of the business of government to compose official prayers for any group of the American people to recite as a part of a religious program carried on by government.

It is a matter of history that this very practice of establishing governmentally composed prayers for religious services was one of the reasons which caused many of our early colonists to leave England and seek religious freedom in America. The Book of Common Prayer, which was created under governmental direction and which was approved by Acts of Parliament in 1548 and 1549, set out in minute detail the accepted form and content of prayer and other religious ceremonies to be used in the established, tax-supported Church of England. The controversies over the Book and what should be its content repeatedly threatened to disrupt the peace of that country as the accepted forms of prayer in the established church changed with the views of the particular ruler that happened to be in control at the time. Powerful groups representing some of the varying religious views of the people struggled among themselves to impress their particular views upon the Government and obtain amendments of the Book more suitable to their respective notions of how religious services should be conducted in order that the official religious establishment would advance their particular religious beliefs. Other groups, lacking the necessary political power to influence the Government on the matter, decided to leave England and its established church and seek freedom in America from England's governmentally ordained and supported religion.

It is an unfortunate fact of history that when some of the very groups which had most strenuously opposed the established Church of England found themselves sufficiently in control of colonial governments in this country to write their own prayers into law, they passed laws making their own religion the official religion of their respective colonies. Indeed, as late as the time of the Revolutionary War, there were established churches in at least eight of the thirteen former colonies and established religions in at least four of the other five. But the successful Revolution against English political domination was shortly followed by intense opposition to the practice of establishing religion by law. This opposition crystallized rapidly into an effective political force in

Virginia, where the minority religious groups such as Presbyterians, Lutherans, Quakers, and Baptists had gained such strength that the adherents to the established Episcopal Church were actually a minority themselves. In 1785–1786, those opposed to the established Church, led by James Madison and Thomas Jefferson, who, though themselves not members of any of these dissenting religious groups, opposed all religious establishments by law on grounds of principle, obtained the enactment of the famous "Virginia Bill for Religious Liberty" by which all religious groups were placed on an equal footing so far as the State was concerned. Similar though less far-reaching legislation was being considered and passed in other States.

By the time of the adoption of the Constitution, our history shows that there was a widespread awareness among many Americans of the dangers of a union of Church and State. These people knew, some of them from bitter personal experience, that one of the greatest dangers to the freedom of the individual to worship in his own way lay in the Government's placing its official stamp of approval upon one particular kind of prayer or one particular form of religious services. They knew the anguish, hardship, and bitter strife that could come when zealous religious groups struggled with one another to obtain the Government's stamp of approval from each King, Queen, or Projector that came to temporary power. The Constitution was intended to avert a part of this danger by leaving the government of this country in the hands of the people rather than in the hands of any monarch. But this safeguard was not enough. Our Founders were no more willing to let the content of their prayers and their privilege of praying whenever they pleased be influenced by the ballot box than they were to let these vital matters of personal conscience depend upon the succession of monarchs. The First Amendment was added to the Constitution to stand as a guarantee that neither the power nor the prestige of the Federal Government would be used to control, support, or influence the kinds of prayer the American people can say—that the people's religions must not be subjected to the pressures of government for change each time a new political administration is elected to office. Under that Amendment's prohibition against governmenal establishment of religion, as reinforced by the provisions of the Fourteenth Amendment, government in this country, be it state or federal, is without power to prescribe any law, any particular form of prayer which is to be used as an official prayer in carrying on any program of governmentally sponsored religious activity.

There can be no doubt that New York's state prayer officially establishes the religious beliefs embodied in the Regents' prayer. The respondents' argument to the contrary, which is largely based upon the contention that the Regents' prayer is "nondenominational" and the fact that the program, as modified and approved by state courts, does not require all pupils to recite the prayer but permits those who wish to do so to remain silent or be excused from the room, ignores the essential nature of the program's constitutional defects. Neither the fact that the prayer may be denominationally neutral nor the fact that its observance on the part of the students is voluntary can serve to free it from the limitations of the Establishment Clause, as it might from the Free Exercise Clause, of the First Amendment, both of which are operative against the States by virtue of the Fourteenth Amendment. Although these two clauses may in certain instances overlap, they forbid two quite different kinds of government encroachment upon religious freedom. The Establishment Clause, unlike the Free Exercise Clause, does not depend upon any showing of direct governmental compulsion and is violated by the enactment of laws which establish an official religion whether those laws operate directly to coerce nonobservant individuals or not. This is not to say, of course, that laws officially prescribing a particular form of religious worship do not involve coercion of such individuals. When the power, prestige, and financial support of government is placed behind a particular religious belief, the indirect coercive pressure upon religious minorities to conform to the prevailing, officially approved religion is plain. But the purposes underlying the Establishment Clause go much further than that. Its first and most immediate purpose rested on the belief that a union of government and religion tends to destroy government and to degrade religion. The history of governmentally established religion, both in England and in this country, showed that whenever government had allied itself with one particular form of religion, the inevitable result had been that it had incurred the hatred, disrespect, and even contempt of those who held contrary beliefs. That same history showed that many people had lost their respect for any religion that had relied upon the support of government to spread its faith. The Establishment Clause thus stands as an expression of principle on the part of the Founders of our Constitution that religion is too personal, too sacred, too holy, to permit its "unhallowed perversion" by a civil magistrate. Another purpose of the Establishment Clause rested upon an awareness of the historical fact that governmentally established religions and religious persecutions go hand in hand. The Founders knew that only a few years after the Book of Common Prayer became the only accepted form of religious services in the established Church of England, an Act of Uniformity was passed to compel all Englishmen to attend those services and to make it a criminal offense to conduct or attend religious gatherings of any other kind—a law which was consistently flouted by dissenting religious groups in England and which contributed to widespread persecutions of people like John Bunyan who persisted in holding "unlawful [religious] meetings . . . to the great disturbance and distraction of the good subjects of this kingdom . . ." And they knew that similar persecutions had received the sanction of law in several of the colonies in this country soon after the establishment of official religions in those colonies. It was in large part to get completely away from this sort of systematic religious persecution that the Founders brought into being our Nation, our Constitution, and our Bill of Rights with its prohibition against any governmental establishment of religion. The New York laws officially prescribing the Regents' prayer are inconsistent both with the purposes of the Establishment Clause and with the Establishment Clause itself.

It has been argued that to apply the Constitution in such a way as to prohibit state laws respecting an establishment of religious services in public schools is to indicate a hostility toward religion or toward prayer. Nothing, of course, could be more wrong. The history of man is inseparable from the history of religion. And perhaps it is not too much to say that since the beginning of that history, many people have devoutly believed that "More things are wrought by prayer than this world dreams of." It was doubtless largely due to men who believed this that there grew up a sentiment that caused men to leave the cross-currents of officially established state religions and religious persecution in Europe and come to this country, filled with the hope that they could find a place in which they could pray when they pleased to the God of their faith in the language they chose. And there were men of this same faith in the power of prayer who led the fight for adoption of our Constitution and also for our Bill of Rights with the very guarantees of religious freedom that forbid the sort of governmental activity which New York has attempted here. These men knew that the First Amendment, which tried to put an end to governmental control of religion and of prayer, was not written to destroy either. They knew that it was written to quiet well-justified fears, which nearly all of them felt arising out of an awareness that governments of the past had shackled men's tongues to make them speak only the religious thoughts that government wanted them to speak and to pray only to the God that government wanted them to pray to. It is neither sacrilegious nor antireligious to say that each separate government in this country should stay out of the business of writing or sanctioning official prayers and leave that purely religious function to the people themselves and to those the people choose to look to for religious guidance.

It is true that New York's establishment of its Regents' prayer as an officially approved religious doctrine of that State does not amount to a total establishment of one particular religious sect to the exclusion of all others—that, indeed, the governmental endorsement of that prayer seems relatively insignificant when compared to the governmental encroachments upon religion which were commonplace two hundred years ago. To those who may subscribe to the view that because the Regents' official prayer is so brief and general there can be no danger to religious freedom in its governmental establishment, however, it may be appropriate to say in the words of James Madison, the author of the First Amendment:

"It is proper to take alarm to the first experiment in our liberties . . . Who does not see that the same authority which can establish Christianity, in exclusion of all other Religions, may establish with the same ease any particular sect of Christians, in exclusion of all other Sects? That the same authority which can force a citizen to contribute three pence only of his property for the support of any one establishment, may force him to conform to any other establishment in all cases whatsoever?"

The judgment of the Court of Appeals of New York is reversed and the cause remanded for further proceedings not consistent with this opinion.

Dissent: Mr. Justice Stewart, dissenting.

A local school board in New York has provided that those pupils who wish to do so may join in a brief prayer at the beginning of each school day, acknowledging their dependence upon God and asking His blessing upon them and upon their parents, their teachers, and their country. The Court today decides that in permitting this brief nondenominational prayer the school board has violated the Constitution of the United States. I think this decision is wrong.

The Court does not hold, nor could it, that New York has interfered with the free exercise of anybody's religion. For the state courts have made clear that those who object to reciting the prayer must be entirely free of any compulsion to do so, including any "embarrassments and pressures." Cf. *West Virginia State Board of Education v. Barnette, 319 U.S. 624.* But the Court says that in permitting school children to say this simple prayer, the New York authorities have established "an official religion."

With all respect, I think the Court has misapplied a great constitutional principle. I cannot see how an "official religion" is established by letting those who want to say a prayer say it. On the contrary, I think that to deny the wish of these school children to join in reciting this prayer is to deny them the opportunity of sharing in the spiritual heritage of our Nation.

The Court's historical review of the quarrels over the Book of Common Prayer in England throws no light for me on the issue before us in this case. England had then and has now an established church. Equally unenlightening, I think, is the history of the early establishment and later rejection of an official church in our own States. For we deal here not with the establishment of a state church, which would, of course, be constitutionally impermissible, but with whether school children who want to begin their day by joining in prayer must be prohibited from doing so. Moreover, I think that the Court's task, in this as in all areas of constitutional adjudication, is not responsibly aided by the uncritical invocation of metaphors like the "wall of separation," a phrase nowhere to be found in the Constitution. What is relevant to the issue here is not the history of an established church in sixteenth-century England or in eighteenth-century America, but the history of the religious traditions of our people, reflected in countless practices of the institutions and officials of our government.

At the opening of each day's Session of the Court we stand, while one of our officials invokes the protection of God. Since the days of John Marshall, our Crier has said, "God save the United States and this Honorable Court." Both the Senate and the House of Representatives open their daily Sessions with prayer. Each of our Presidents, from George Washington to John F. Kennedy, has, upon assuming his Office, asked the protection and help of God.

For example, on April 30, 1789, President George Washington said:

> It would be peculiarly improper to omit in this first official act my fervent supplications to that Almighty Being who rules over the universe, who presides in the councils of nations, and whose providential aids can supply every human defect, that His benediction may consecrate to the liberties and happiness of the people of the United States a Government instituted by themselves for these essential purposes, and may enable every instrument employed in its administration to execute with success the functions allotted to his charge. In tending this homage to the Great Author of every public and private good, I assure myself that it expresses your sentiments not less than my own, nor those of my fellow-citizens at large less than either. No people can be bound to acknowledge and adore the Invisible Hand which conducts the affairs of men more than those of the United States . . .
>
> Having thus imparted to you my sentiments as they have been awakened by the occasion which brings us together, I shall take my present leave; but not without resorting once more to the benign Parent of the Human Race in humble supplication that, since He has been pleased to favor the American people with opportunities for deliberating in perfect tranquility, and dispositions for deciding with unparalleled unanimity on a form of government for the security of their union and the advancement of their happiness, so His divine blessing may be equally *conspicuous* in the enlarged views, the temperate consultations, and the wise measures on which the success of this Government must depend.

On March 4, 1797, President John Adams said:

> And may that Being who is supreme over all, the Patron of Order, the Fountain of Justice, and the Protector in all ages of the world of virtuous liberty, continue His blessing upon this nation and its Government and give it all possible success and duration consistent with the ends of His providence.

On March 4, 1805, President Thomas Jefferson said:

> I shall need, too, the favor of that Being in whose hands we are, who led our fathers, as Israel of old, from their native land and planted them in a country flowing with all the necessaries and comforts of life; who has covered our infancy with His providence and our riper years with His wisdom and power, and to whose goodness I ask you to join in supplications with me that He will so enlighten the minds of your

servants, guide their councils, and prosper their measures that whatsoever they do shall result in your good, and shall secure to you the peace, friendship, and approbation of all nations.

On March 4, 1809, President James Madison said:

But the source to which I look . . . is in . . . my fellow-citizens, and in the counsels of those representing them in the other departments associated in the care of the national interests. In these my confidence will under every difficulty be best placed, next to that which we all have been encouraged to feel in the guardianship and guidance of that Almighty Being whose power regulates the destiny of nations, whose blessings have been so conspicuously dispensed to this rising Republic, and to whom we are bound to address our devout gratitude for the past, as well as our fervent supplications and best hopes for the future.

On March 4, 1865, President Abraham Lincoln said:

Fondly do we hope, fervently do we pray, that this mighty scourge of war may speedily pass away. Yet, if God wills that it continue until all the wealth piled up by the bondsman's two hundred and fifty years of unrequited toil shall be sunk, and until every drop of blood drawn with the lash shall be paid by another drawn with the sword, as was said three thousand years ago, so still it must be said "the judgments of the Lord are true and righteous altogether."
With malice toward none, with charity for all, with firmness in the right as God gives us to see the right, let us strive on to finish the work we are in, to bind up the nation's wounds, to care for him who shall have borne the battle and for his widow and his orphan, to do all which may achieve and cherish a just and lasting peace among ourselves and with all nations.

On March 4, 1885, President Grover Cleveland said:

And let us not trust to human effort alone, but humbly acknowledging the power and goodness of Almighty God, who presides over the destiny of nations, and who has at all times been revealed in our country's history, let us invoke His aid and His blessing upon our labors.

On March 5, 1917, President Woodrow Wilson said:

I pray God I may be given wisdom and the prudence to do my duty in the true spirit of this great people.

On March 4, 1933, President Franklin D. Roosevelt said:

In this dedication of a Nation we humbly ask the blessing of God. May He protect each and every one of us. May He guide me in the days to come.

On January 21, 1957, President Dwight D. Eisenhower said:

Before all else, we seek, upon our common labor as a nation, the blessings of Almighty God. And the hopes in our hearts fashion the deepest prayers of our whole people.

On January 20, 1961, President John F. Kennedy said:

The world is very different now . . . And yet the same revolutionary beliefs for which our forebears fought are still at issue around the globe—the belief that the rights of man come not from the generosity of the state but from the hand of God . . . With a good conscience our only sure reward, with history the final judge of our deeds, let us go forth to lead the land we love, asking His blessing and His help, but knowing that here on earth God's work must truly be our own.

The Court today says that the state and federal governments are without constitutional power to prescribe any particular form of words to be recited by any group of the American people on any subject touching religion. One of the stanzas of "The Star-Spangled Banner," made our National Anthem by the Act of Congress in 1931, contains these verses:

> Blest with victory and peace, may the heav'n rescued land
> Praise the Pow'r that hath made and preserved us a nation!
> Then conquer we must, when our cause it is just,
> And this be our motto, "In God is our Trust."

In 1954, Congress added a phrase to the Pledge of Allegiance to the Flag so that it now contains the words "one Nation *under God*, indivisible, with liberty and justice for all." In 1952, Congress enacted legislation calling upon the President each year to proclaim a National Day of Prayer. Since 1865, the words "In God We Trust" have been impressed on our coins.

Countless similar examples could be listed, but there is no need to belabor the obvious. It was all summed up by this Court just ten years ago in a single sentence: "We are a religious people whose institutions presuppose a Supreme Being" *Zorach v. Clauson,* 343 U.S. 306, 313.

I do not believe that this Court, or the Congress, or the President has by the actions and practices I have mentioned established an "official religion" in violation of the Constitution. And I do not believe the State of New York has done so in this case. What each has done has been to recognize and to follow the deeply entrenched and highly cherished spiritual traditions of our Nation—traditions which come down to us from those who almost two hundred years ago avowed their "firm Reliance on the Protection of divine Providence" when they proclaimed the freedom and independence of this brave new world.

I dissent.

CHAPTER 9

CIVIL RIGHTS, INTEGRATION, AND SCHOOL REFORM, 1954-1980

Introduction

Contrary to more simplistic versions of history, the civil rights movement did not burst on the American scene with the Supreme Court's 1954 *Brown v. Board of Education* decision. That decision represented the culmination of years of activity by civil rights organizations.

African Americans and white allies understood that separate-but-equal schooling never meant equal. The Legal Defense Fund of the National Association for the Advancement of Colored People—the NAACP—led by lawyers such as Thurgood Marshall, began a slow and systematic process of challenging both inequality and separation in the 1930s. At the same time, a grassroots civil rights movement of African-American parents, teachers, and various allies began to raise the issue of school segregation across the country. Septima Clark, one of the great leaders of the civil rights movement of the 1950s, reports her own experiences of teaching and being fired in the segregated South prior to the *Brown* decision. I have included the story of how she was fired as a public school teacher when she joined the NAACP in Charleston, South Carolina in the 1950s from her biography, *Ready from Within* (Trenton, New Jersey: Africa World Press 1990). Clark went on to prepare a generation of teachers for Freedom Schools across the South from her base at the Highlander Center in Tennessee.

While it is important to view it in context, it is true that few Supreme Court decisions have had the impact of the 1954 *Brown v. Board of Education* decision, which declared racial segregation in public schools to be unconstitutional. Prior to *Brown* a decade of Court decisions, focusing primarily on higher education, were brought by the NAACP Legal Defense Fund. Yet *Brown* itself was only the beginning of a continuing struggle to end segregation and discrimination in education. The first significant test came in the crisis at Little Rock (Arkansas) Central High School in 1957. Daisy Bates, one participant in the Little Rock struggle, remembers what things were like in Arkansas in the 1950s. Many similar crises would follow in the succeeding decades.

It is important to read the school desegregation literature in this chapter and elsewhere in light of earlier works, however. While an end to *legal* segregation in schools (*de jure* segregation) was gained through the *Brown* decision, the reality of segregated, and unequal, schooling (*de facto* segregation) continues to the present.

It is also important to note the degree to which the American civil rights movement turned to the schools to provide the solution for many larger issues of social inequity. This was a deeply American point of focus. As with other issues noted throughout this volume, leaders of the civil rights movement of the 1950s believed that if the schools could treat children as equals—if segregation could end and a quality education could be provided for every child—then some large strides would have been made towards creating a larger society of freedom and justice for all.

In 1971, the United States Supreme Court ruled that the schools of Charlotte and surrounding Mecklenburg County in North Carolina could not continue a de facto pattern of segregation. The Court ordered that the school districts end segregation by busing students across district lines, triggering a new era for school desegregation. For the first decade and a half after the Court's *Brown* decision, desegregation efforts focused on the South. After 1970, the focus of desegregation shifted to the urban North. During the 1970s, no city received more attention in its struggle with school desegregation than Boston. Long seen as the bastion of Northern liberalism, capital of the only state in the union to support the liberal nominee of the Democratic Party, George McGovern's 1972 presidential bid, Boston's long history of racism was well-hidden from the national media. At the same time, Boston's many world-class universities gave it a reputation as the "Athens of America." Yet few noted the fact that only a handful of the graduates of the Boston Public Schools ever attended these universities; in fact, too many students in the Boston Public Schools received a very poor-quality education, indeed. Boston's national reputation changed quite significantly, however, when the Federal District Court ordered the complete desegregation of the Boston Public Schools in 1974.

In fact, the issue of segregation and unequal school opportunities, linked to other issues of corruption and a class-divided school system, had plagued Boston and most of its northern counterparts for generations. In spite of the fact that Massachusetts was the first in the nation to legally desegregate the public schools in 1855, by the 1890s, some schools in Boston's Lower Roxbury neighborhood were known informally to citizens and the School Committee alike as the "colored schools." The city's failure to annex new suburbs in the twentieth century—as it had in the nineteenth—also meant that the continued migration of whites away from the city center created a pattern of "white flight" as early as the 1930s. By the 1950s, the schools in the city's northern half, whether in African-American Roxbury or in white South Boston, East Boston, or Charlestown, were generally operating in old, overcrowded buildings with poor teaching and poorer resources.

Boston's African-American community was not passive in the face of this situation. In 1963, the Education Committee of the Boston Branch of the NAACP, chaired by Ruth Batson, petitioned the School Committee for change. This was but the first of many petitions and pleas to improve the quality and end the segregation of the Boston schools.

In 1967, Jonathan Kozol, recently fired after a short-lived career as a teacher in the virtually all African-American Gibson School, published *Death at an Early Age* (Boston: Houghton Mifflin Company, 1967). This powerfully written book described Kozol's experience with the Boston Public Schools in the early 1960s and the school system's role, as the cover said, in the "destruction of the hearts and minds of Negro Children in the Boston Public Schools." While Kozol was teaching, and later writing his book, a coalition of local leaders (led by future state representative and candidate for mayor, Mel King—an African American—and a sitting member of the School Committee, Arthur Gartland—a European-American) began grassroots efforts to elect a new School Committee. In the 1965 elections for School Committee, the new coalition was soundly defeated by a second emerging coalition; this one was led by Louise Day Hicks and others who took racist positions to defend the status quo. During the following decade, leaders in the African-American community and their white allies used a variety of tactics to try to change the racist and antichild public schools. Only as a last resort did they turn to the federal courts, filing what would become the *Morgan v. Hennigan* case in 1972.

Septima Clark, Ready from Within, ca. 1950

Septima Clark is one of the great heroes of the civil rights movement. The story of her life in the South, including her firing as a teacher in a segregated school because of her membership in the NAACP, provides a powerful example of the issues southern African-American educators faced in the years before the Brown *decision. Clark was an exceptional human being, and her story therefore cannot be considered typical. But the struggles she endured and the choices she made in the years leading up to the* Brown *decision and during the subsequent flowering of the civil rights movement are representative of the experiences of many African-American activists, especially in the field of education.*

My name is Septima Poinsette Clark. I was born at 105 Wentworth Street in Charleston, South Carolina, on May 3, 1898. When I was seven, my parents moved to Henrietta Street. 26 Henrietta Street. After I grew up, I moved to different places in South Carolina to teach, but I always had the home I bought here in Charleston. This German that my brother was working with had that house for sale. It wasn't but a thousand and five hundred dollars. I was able to get it in 1927 with my little bit of money and get it all paid for. So we had our own house at 17 Henrietta Street, the street I had grown up on.

I moved back to Charleston in 1947, and that is the part of my story I want to tell about first. Later on I will go back and tell about my growing up and the early years of my teaching.

I want to start my story with the end of World War II because that is when the civil rights movement really got going, both for me personally and for people all over

Brown, Cynthia Stokes, ed. *Septima Clark and the Civil Rights Movement: Ready from Within.* Trenton: Africa World Press, 1990. Reprinted by permission of Africa World Press.

the South. After World War II, the men were coming home from fighting in Europe and Africa, and they weren't going to take segregation any more.

In 1947, I got a job in Charleston teaching seventh grade at the newest school in the system, the Henry P. Archer School. But soon my assignment was changed, and I was put in charge of a group of problem pupils in grades four through seven. Each period these children would come to me from their homerooms, and we did what was actually remedial reading. It was challenging work, and we made considerable progress.

I hadn't been in Charleston long before I got involved in civic activities. Among other organizations I had a special interest in the work of the Young Women's Christian Association. There was a dual system in Charleston, with separate white and black "Y's." Soon after I returned to Charleston, I became chairman of the black Y's committee on administration. My courage was soon to be tested. It came about this way.

At the time, the judge of the United States Court for the eastern district of South Carolina was a Charlestonian named Julius Waties Waring. He was the same judge who had decreed that the salaries of schoolteachers in South Carolina, black and white, had to be equalized. I knew him principally because of that decision; since he was Charleston born and bred, I saw his name in the newspapers frequently.

I knew that Judge Waring had grown up in the upper-class area of Charleston and had married an aristocratic girl. He was a personal friend of both the U.S. senators from South Carolina, one of whom just spouted racist rhetoric. When Waring was appointed U.S. judge, he was considered a person who would protect the southern way of life.

But Judge Waring transformed himself as he sat in his judge's chair. I heard him say once: "You know, a judge has to live with his conscience. I would sit in the courtroom, and I would see black men coming in that I knew were decent men, and they were considered bums and trash because they were black. And I would see white men that I knew were bums, and they were considered gentlemen. I just couldn't take it any longer."

When I returned to Charleston, black people still could not vote in the Democratic primary elections. There weren't many blacks who were registered voters, but those who were registered Democrats could not vote in the primary election, where you elect the candidates your party will run in the final election.

The rule to keep blacks out of primary elections was made way back in 1896, just before I was born. The legislature passed that law as part of setting up segregation in South Carolina. The U.S. Supreme Court finally ruled against white primaries in 1944, but southern states were still following their own rules.

A number of black people had gotten to the place where their children were going north to college, and they were coming back talking about the injustices we had in Charleston, where we could not vote in the Democratic primary. It had gotten to the place where the younger generation felt very bad about it.

After Judge Waring realized how wrong it was to keep blacks out of the primary, he decided to change it. In 1947, he ruled that blacks must be permitted to vote in the next primary, and he told the leaders of the Democratic Party that the court would hold them personally responsible for carrying out this ruling.

Several days before the election, some of the whites made a statement that if blacks attempted to vote in the primary, then blood would be running down the streets like water. Judge Waring said to them, and had the press print it, that "If that happens,

I'll put you in jail, and you'll stay there for the rest of your life. These people have a right to vote, and so they will vote."

You know, that was a quiet election. Election Day used to be a terrible thing around Charleston. Guns were always out. During the election just before this one, a young white reporter was killed. There would always be some death. But Judge Waring stopped that.

Just reading about Judge Waring, I became really enthused about him. I thought, "This is a wonderful man to come forth and say that blacks should vote." At the YWCA we were going to have a special day, and I thought, "Now, if Judge Waring could say that, his wife might be able to say something to Negro women." In 1945, Judge Waring had divorced his first wife and had married Elizabeth Avery, a native of Detroit.

Another lady from the Y and I went to Mrs. Waring's house at 9 o'clock one night to ask her to speak. She was very glad to do it. But somehow or other the newspaper got hold of it, and all hell broke forth. Evidently somebody saw us going into that house, and they decided that this could not be.

I started getting obscene phone calls. I'd pick up the telephone, and they'd say, "Who in the hell do you think you are? You are a damn fool to ask Judge Waring's wife to speak." I'd say, "Thank you," and put down the phone.

Right away I decided that I'd better go and tell Mrs. Waring that if black people would ask her not to speak, would she let me know, but if white people would ask her not to speak, would she decide that she was going to speak regardless.

I went down to the Warings' house again. Judge Waring told me, "Now, Septima, the thing to do is to put somebody at each one of the places where you turn the lights on. You're going to have to have a man standing there, because if the Klan comes in, the first thing they're going to do is turn your lights out, and then you'll have a terrible time."

That's what I did. I got men to stand by all the lights in the hall of the YWCA. But no Klan came, only two or three white men. Mrs. Waring called the white people in Charleston decadent and low-down. I think she did it because they were mean. The reporters were there, and Mrs. Waring passed out a copy of her speech, saying, "Take this speech and put it in the paper just as it is. Don't change a word."

They printed that speech word for word. For three days after that meeting, the town talked about Mrs. Waring and what she had said.

After that, the Warings were terribly harassed and persecuted. Their friends abandoned them. Not one white person would have their dinner with them, or even drink tea with them. The white hairdressers refused to wash Mrs. Waring's hair. And when Judge Waring went to get his hair cut, a guard had to go with him and sit until he got his hair cut. They had to guard him day and night.

The Warings reached out to their black friends. Of course, a lot of blacks wouldn't go to the Warings' house. The Warings invited them to teach one night, and they wouldn't go. A few of us went to dinner. I had to say to myself that if these people invite me, surely I should go. Why should I be one who says not to go? All of these things you had to make up in your mind to do because too many of the blacks were against your going to the Warings' anyway. I had to make a decision to go regardless of what happened.

When I went to Judge Waring's home to dinner I, too, felt real worried. I always had to have my hair straightened, and I tried to have a new dress. Mrs. Waring told me that wasn't necessary. I was glad she could tell me that, but I thought it had to be.

At the Warings' I met many of the mulatto people of Charleston, and I wasn't considered too well by that group because they were very fair-skinned people with straight hair. My mother was a washerwoman, and my father had been a slave, so I wasn't considered one of them. But because of the way I could talk about the things I knew about, the injustices, they listened. By that time I had been to several universities, and I had studied a good bit about history, the history of government, and economics. These things had made an impression on me. I don't know whether they ever learned to like me too well, but they listened to me.

I was very happy for the kinds of people that I could meet at Mrs. Waring's house. I couldn't meet them otherwise. They would not have come to my house. I wasn't good enough. Neither could I go to their house. I couldn't even play cards or bridge with them, not at all. But this was the kind of caste and class thing that we had in Charleston.

I had a feeling that if I could eat at Judge Waring's house, at any white person's house, then they should be able to drink a cup of tea or do something at my house. So I invited Judge and Mrs. Waring and two others to have tea with me one afternoon, and they did come. My mother was sick in bed at the time, and I had taken her meal to her bedside. But she couldn't eat; she was too worried about it. My neighbors on my street were also worried. They said, "As long as Septima Clark have them white people coming to her house, we're gonna always have trouble."

Then my principal got worried about it, too. He saw me coming out of Mrs. Waring's house from dinner one Sunday, and he said, "That's a dangerous thing to do. How in the world could you do it?"

At a faculty meeting at my school, they all told me how wrong they thought it was for me to go to the Warings' house. They said it just proved what white people were saying, that the real reason that blacks wanted integration was to socialize with whites.

I waited until they finished. Then I asked the principal if I could ask him a question.

"I would like to ask you if anyone decided for you whom you would marry."

"No, of course not," he replied. "I decided for myself."

Then I asked one of the women teachers, "Did anyone tell you what kind of car to buy and how much to pay for it?"

"No," she said, "I did that myself. It's my car. Why shouldn't I have made those decisions?"

Then I turned to a teacher who put a big emphasis on clothes; she was probably our best-dressed teacher.

"Did anybody tell you what type of dresses to buy and what stores to buy them at?" I asked.

"Of course not," she replied, a bit indignantly.

"Well, I can see that you all make decisions for yourselves," I told them. "The principal decided what woman he wished to marry, and I think that no one should tell a man or woman who to marry. And you—" I pointed to the first woman I questioned, "selected the car you bought, and I'm sure you had a perfect right to do that, just as you—" I pointed to the woman who loved to dress beautifully, "have every right to select your own clothes. In the same way," I looked them in the eyes, "I think that I have a right to select my own friends. I feel that nobody has a right to tell me who my friends must be any more than I have a right to tell the principal who his wife will be, or you what kind of car to buy, or you what sort of clothes you should wear."

The meeting closed, but I knew they were quite angry with me. After that there were many times, I'm sure, when it was hard for them to say a pleasant word to me or about me, all because of my associations with the Warings.

The Warings did not get to finish out their years here in Charleston. They moved to New York City in 1950. They did that because when Mrs. Waring was sitting on a couch in their living room, someone threw a block of cement through the window. It nearly hit her, but it didn't. Then when she went to get some letters mimeographed, the woman refused and said, "Please don't come in here, because if you do you're going to ruin my business, and I won't be able to stay here any longer." Judge Waring used to go and hold court in the upper part of New York and in California, down at San Diego. When those courts were cancelled, he decided that they had better get out of here, which they did.

They lived in New York City until they died in 1968. He was buried in January, and she died in November. He had two hundred blacks and twelve whites at his funeral, and she had nine of us at hers. She said she didn't want none of the hypocrites at her funeral, and she didn't have any. They were both buried in Charleston, right up in Magnolia Cemetery overlooking the harbor.

They had one laugh from the grave, though. They gave his retirement money to the College of Charleston, and it has to be used for a black student to live on campus. Of course, at that time the College of Charleston did not allow black people to go there. It took the college until 1976 to spend that money. Now black students can live on the campus. That has come out of Judge Waring's will. . . .

In 1952, there was a childhood education meeting in Washington, D.C., and a worker from the black Y in Charleston, a Mrs. Anna Kelly, went to that meeting. There were some things that she wanted to discuss with both blacks and whites, and she couldn't discuss them down here because we couldn't have a black and white meeting together. Teachers couldn't meet together, and neither could community people. They had to meet separately.

At that meeting, Mrs. Kelly asked where in the South blacks and whites could meet together and talk over the problems that they talked about in that workshop. People told her that there was only one place—at the Highlander Folk School near Chattanooga.

Mrs. Kelly decided to go there in the summer of '53, and she asked me would I sit on the desk of the YWCA while she was away. When she came back, she said, "Oh, that's a wonderful place. You don't even have to spend a nickel. You go up there, and they feed you, and they sleep you, and they ride you, and so everything is wonderful."

I decided I should go to a place like that, so the next summer I went up, and I found what she said was true. I even found that blacks and whites were sleeping in the same room—that surprised me.

That's when I met Myles Horton and his wife Zilphia. Myles used to open the workshops by asking the people what they wanted to know, and he would close it with, "What you going to do back home?"

Zilphia played an accordion, and she would always lead the singing. She was a very good singer, and she had the songs of the people of the mountains, of the low country, of the labor unions, and whatever group. When she died, we really missed her.

Myles and Zilphia came to Charleston when we were having a testimonial for Judge Waring. Judge Waring had become the most hated fellow below Broad Street in

Charleston; the white people learned to dislike him greatly. They said they disliked him because he married a Yankee woman. To marry a Yankee in their face was terrible. He also was hated because he had opened the Democratic primary to black people. For that, the black people of Charleston gave him a testimonial. That night we had large numbers of people at a school we were able to get. Afterwards Zilphia stayed at my house, and Mrs. Waring stayed at one of the other black women's house.

I kept up my contacts with Myles and Zilphia and the Highlander Folk School. While I was at Highlander for the first time, the Supreme Court decided that segregation shall be no more. We were really happy over that, and I felt wonderful. But I didn't yet have the feeling that this thing was really a part of me.

I went to Highlander twice the first summer in '54, and the following summer I used my car to transport three groups of six persons each to Highlander workshops. At the end of that summer, we held a workshop to develop leadership, which I was directing. That was when I met Rosa Parks.

At that time Mrs. Parks lived in Montgomery, Alabama. Her husband was a barber, and he used to shave and cut hair for all of the high-class whites. Rosa was working with the youth group of the National Association for the Advancement of Colored People, or the N, double A, C, P, for short.

Rosa got to Highlander because she knew Virginia Durr, a great friend of Myles Horton, the director of the Highlander. Rosa and Virginia got to know each other by Rosa being a seamstress and Virginia's husband being the only lawyer in Montgomery who would take the legal cases brought by the NAACP. Working with the NAACP, Rosa was under fire. Virginia stayed under fire because she was a white woman who dared to take sides with blacks.

First Virginia Durr wrote a letter and asked that we send money for Rosa to come up to Highlander, which we did. Then Virginia took Rosa to Atlanta and saw her on a bus to Highlander.

We had a large group of people at that workshop. It was a two-week workshop on the United Nations. We knew that Rosa had been working with the youth group in Montgomery, so at the meeting I asked Rosa to tell how she was able to get the Freedom Train to come to Montgomery and get this youth group to go through the Freedom Train. She wouldn't talk at all at first.

People at the workshop knew only a little bit about the Freedom Train. It was being sent by the government around the country from Washington, D.C. as a lesson in democracy. It carried an exhibit of the original U.S. Constitution and the Declaration of Independence. Anyone could go inside for free, but segregation was not permitted.

One night up there in the bedroom (there were about six beds in one dormitory) everyone started singing and dancing, white kids and all, and they said, "Rosa, how in the world did you deal with that Freedom Train?"

Then she said, "It wasn't an easy task. We took our children down when the Freedom Train came, and the white and black children had to go in together. They wouldn't let them go in otherwise, and that was a real victory for us." But she said, "After that, I began getting obscene phone calls from people because I was president of the youth group. That's why Mrs. Durr wanted me to come up here and see what I could do with this same youth group when I went back home."

The next day in the workshop I say, "Rosa, tell these people how you got that Freedom Train to come to Montgomery." She hated to tell it. She thought that certainly somebody would go back and tell the white people. A teacher from Montgomery came at the same time, and she say she couldn't let them know she was coming to Highlander, because if these white people knew then she would have lost her job, too.

Anyway, Rosa got up and told that group about it. We, had somebody there from the United Nations, and they said to her, "If anything happens, you get in touch with me, and I'll be sure to see that you have your rights."

After the workshop, Rosa was afraid to go from Highlander to Atlanta. Myles sent me with her. She was afraid that somebody had already spoken, and she didn't know what was going to happen. I went with her to Atlanta and saw her in a bus going down to Montgomery. She felt much better then.

I guess she kept thinking about the things at the workshop. At the end of the workshops we always say, "What do you plan to do back home?" Rosa answered that question by saying that Montgomery was the cradle of the Confederacy, that nothing would happen there because blacks wouldn't stick together. But she promised to work with those kids, and to tell them that they had the right to belong to the NAACP, that they had the right to do things like going through the Freedom Train. She decided that she was going to keep right on working with them.

Three months after Rosa got back to Montgomery, on December 1, 1955, she refused to get up from her seat on the bus. When I heard the news, I said, "Rosa? Rosa?" She was so shy when she came to Highlander, but she got enough courage to do that.

Rosa hadn't planned at Highlander that she was going to refuse to get up out of her seat. That evidently came to her that day after she got done at work. But many people at the Highlander workshop told about the discrimination on the buses. I guess practically every family around Montgomery had had trouble with people getting on buses. They'd had a hard time. They had a number of cases where bus drivers had beaten 15-year-olds who sat up to the front or refused to get up from their seat and give it to whites coming in. That was the kind of thing they had, and they had taken it long enough.

Now I had that all the time here in Charleston. I was living down on Henrietta Street. I caught the bus going to my school about a mile up. The Navy Yard men would be going to work at the same time. I would sit in that section that's designed for blacks. But if a white man came up, and the white section is all filled in, I'd have to stand up and give him my seat and stand up the rest of the way. I'd just get up and give him my seat. I knew I had to do it or be arrested. I'd sit in the back but when that front got crowded they'd come to the back and you had to get up and give them your seat. That's what they call justice. I had to do that for a long time until Rosa refused, and then that changed.

I don't know why it was, but it seems like that did not make me angry. I always felt that there would be a time when I could work on things. I never felt that getting angry would do you any good other than hurt your own digestion—keep you from eating, which I liked to do. . . .

By the time that Rosa Parks refused to get up and give her seat to a white man, I had gotten into some trouble of my own back in Charleston. I began to realize that I might be dismissed from my position as an elementary teacher because I belonged to that same organization Rosa Parks did—the National Association for the Advancement of Colored People, the NAACP.

Let me go way back and tell you how I first heard about the NAACP. It started in 1909 in New York City, but I didn't hear of it until 1918. I was about twenty years old, and I was teaching on Johns Island, one of the islands off the coast of Charleston. That

Presbyterian convention came to Johns Island, and I went down to the meeting. The man started talking about an organization that was to help people unjustly treated. It was just a dollar a year, so I joined while I was there on Johns Island.

Soon after that something happened that really led me to the NAACP. It was in the summer time, and I was working here in Charleston. We had a Jewish woman on King Street who had a watch in her apron pocket. We didn't have frigidaires then, and a boy was putting ice in her icebox. She thought he took her watch out of her apron pocket, and she had him arrested. The artist who was the head of the NAACP in Charleston found [out] about it, and when we searched, we found that her watch had gone to the laundry in her apron pocket and that boy was unjustly arrested. We got together, and we told her what big harm she had done to this boy. We said that some-body would call him jailbird and perhaps cause him to fight and that he had lost many weeks by spending that time in jail.

I felt real bad about that incident. I said, "Well, I must really get into the organi-zation because we've got to see that things like this won't happen again." I became very fond of the NAACP, and from that time on I worked with it.

There weren't too many black people who considered the NAACP worthwhile. They were still afraid, you know, so it was a very small group at first. But after many years of work by its lawyers, the United States Supreme Court ruled, in 1954, that racial segregation in public schools was unconstitutional. After that decision, the school authorities in South Carolina passed out questionnaires to every teacher requiring us to list all the organizations we belonged to. I refused to overlook my membership in the NAACP, as some of the teachers did. I listed it.

The next year the South Carolina legislature passed a law that said that no city or state employee could belong to the NAACP. You see, our legislature was joining others across the Deep South in a systematic campaign to wipe out the NAACP.

Our supervisor of Negro teachers was horribly concerned about it. She knew that she was going to lose her job because she was a member, and she did not want to give it up. She just got terribly ill in her mind. She became senile soon, and she died not too long after that, before they took her job away.

It wasn't too long before I got my letter of dismissal. The Board of Education wrote me that it would not be renewing my contract to teach remedial reading at the Henry Archer School. My goodness, somehow or other it really didn't bother me.

But it bothered my family. My sister said that when people called her she felt like she had something in her stomach, just like butterflies, working around. She was teach-ing then. I said, "You just let me answer the phone and tell the people I'm a member and I've been dismissed. I don't mind at all."

My mother had died by the time I was dismissed, but I know she would have said, "I told you so." She never joined the NAACP, nor my sister Edith. My brother Peter hasn't either. They weren't fighters. They didn't feel as if they could fight for freedom or for justice. They just didn't have that kind of feeling.

One hundred and sixty-nine teachers came from Washington and Baltimore to get our jobs, and there weren't but forty-two of us dismissed. Those teachers came down here because they had to have one year experience before they could teach in Baltimore or Washington. They came thinking they could get those jobs.

But they didn't get them. Other people already here got those jobs. Most of those forty-two teachers who were fired went to New York and Boston and other places in the North. A few of them came back and were able to get jobs teaching.

I never did try. I felt that they never would let me have one anyway because they considered me a Communist because I worked with the Highlander Folk School. I had been to Highlander two years before I was dismissed here. I know they felt that I was really a Communist then, I was too much of a head woman, a controversial leader, and I couldn't get any job here.

I feel the big failure in my life was trying to work with the black teachers to get them to realize, when that law was passed in South Carolina, that it was an unjust law. But there were such a few jobs that they didn't see how they could work against the law. I had the feeling that if all of them would say, "We are members of the NAACP," that the legislature would not have said, "All of you will lose your jobs," because that would mean thousands of children out on the streets at one time.

But I couldn't get them to see that. I signed my name to seven-hundred twenty-six letters to black teachers, asking them to tell the state of South Carolina that it was unjust to rule that no city or state employee could belong to the NAACP. If whites could belong to the Ku Klux Klan, then surely blacks could belong to the NAACP.

I don't know why I felt that the black teachers would stand up for their rights. But they wouldn't. Most of them were afraid and became hostile. Only twenty-six of them answered my letter, and I wrote them that we should go and talk with the superintendent. Eleven decided that they would go talk to the superintendent, but when it was time to go, there were only five of us. The superintendent did everything he could before he would see us. He was writing out some plans on a board. Finally he talked, and the only thing he did was to let us know that we were living far ahead of our time. That's what he said.

I considered that one of the failures of my life because I think that I tried to push them into something that they weren't ready for. From that day on I say, "I'm going to have to get the people trained. We're going to have to show them the dangers or the pitfalls that they are in, before they will accept." And it took many years.

You always have to get the people with you. You can't just force them into things. That taught me a good lesson, because when I went into Mississippi and Alabama, I stayed behind the scene and tried to get the people in the town to push forward, and then I would come forth with ideas. But I wouldn't do it at first because I knew it was detrimental. That was a weakness of mine that I felt I had to strengthen. The people in the masses, though, do better than the teachers. They come out. They're willing to fight anyhow.

You know, I had to go away for twenty years from Charleston. I couldn't get a job here, nowhere in South Carolina. Not only that, but the black teachers here, my sorority, Alpha Kappa Alpha, gave me a testimonial. Alpha Kappa Alpha is an organization of black women college graduates. Do you know that at that party my [sorority sisters] would not stand beside me and have their picture made with me? If they had, they would have lost their jobs.

I can't say that I kept from being frightened about this whole episode. For three solid months after I took a new job at Highlander Folk School, I couldn't sleep. Night after night I stayed up listening to the tape of the workshop that we had conducted during the day. One morning, it must have been a September morning, I felt a kind of a free feeling in my mind, and I said, "Now I must have been right." I was able to fall asleep and to sleep after that. I decided that I had worried about the thing enough.

Supreme Court of the United States, Brown v. Board of Education of Topeka, Kansas, 1954

The United States Supreme Court's decision in the Brown v. Board of Education *case was unusual for the Court in two ways. First, it directly overturned a previous Court decision: the 1896* Plessy v. Ferguson *decision in which the Court had decided that segregation on the basis of race was legal.* Brown *was also a unanimous decision; indeed, Chief Justice Earl Warren worked hard to achieve the compromises necessary for a unanimous decision because he believed that the full Court should be behind such a dramatic order. It is hard for people living a half-century after the* Brown *decision to understand how controversial the order was when the Court handed it down. On the other hand, it is essential that we see* Brown *as just one step on a very long road. Years of local organizing and legal action had gone into building the judicial base and the community support that made* Brown *possible. Many more years of legal action, civil rights activity, and local organizing across the country would be necessary to implement* Brown. *Still, the case is a marker of great significance in the history of education, and worth reading with special attention.*

Mr. Chief Justice Warren delivered the opinion of the Court.

These cases come to us from the States of Kansas, South Carolina, Virginia, and Delaware. They are premised on different facts and different local conditions, but a common legal question justifies their consideration together in this consolidated opinion.

In each of the cases, minors of the Negro race, through their legal representatives, seek the aid of the courts in obtaining admission to the public schools of their community on a nonsegregated basis. In each instance, they had been denied admission to schools attended by white children under laws requiring or permitting segregation according to race. This segregation was alleged to deprive the plaintiffs of the equal protection of the laws under the Fourteenth Amendment. In each of the cases other than the Delaware case, a three-judge federal district court denied relief to the plaintiffs on the so-called "separate but equal" doctrine announced by this Court in *Plessy v. Ferguson*, 163 U.S. 537. Under that doctrine, equality of treatment is accorded when the races are provided substantially equal facilities, even though these facilities be separate. In the Delaware case, the Supreme Court of Delaware adhered to that doctrine, but ordered that the plaintiffs be admitted to the white schools because of their superiority to the Negro schools.

The plaintiffs contend that segregated public schools are not "equal" and cannot be made "equal," and that hence they are deprived of the equal protection of the laws. Because of the obvious importance of the question presented, the Court took jurisdiction. Argument was heard in the 1952 Term, and reargument was heard this Term on certain questions propounded by the Court.

Reargument was largely devoted to the circumstances surrounding the adoption of the Fourteenth Amendment in 1868. It covered exhaustively consideration of the Amendment in Congress, ratification by the states, then existing practices in racial segregation, and the views of proponents and opponents of the Amendment. This discussion and our own investigation convince us that, although these sources cast some light, it is not enough to resolve the problem with which we are faced. At best, they are inconclusive. The most avid proponents of the post-War Amendments undoubtedly intended them to remove all legal distinctions among "all persons born or naturalized in the

United States." Their opponents, just as certainly, were antagonistic to both the letter and the spirit of the Amendments and wished them to have the most limited effect. What others in Congress and the state legislatures had in mind cannot be determined with any degree of certainty.

An additional reason for the inconclusive nature of the Amendment's history, with respect to segregated schools, is the status of public education at that time. In the South, the movement toward free common schools, supported by general taxation, had not yet taken hold. Education of white children was largely in the hands of private groups. Education of Negroes was almost nonexistent, and practically all of the race were illiterate. In fact, any education of Negroes was forbidden by law in some states. Today, in contrast, many Negroes have achieved outstanding success in the arts and sciences as well as in the business and professional world. It is true that public school education at the time of the Amendment had advanced further in the North, but the effect of the Amendment on Northern States was generally ignored in the congressional debates. Even in the North, the conditions of public education did not approximate those existing today. The curriculum was usually rudimentary; ungraded schools were common in rural areas; the school term was but three months a year in many states; and compulsory school attendance was virtually unknown. As a consequence, it is not surprising that there should be so little in the history of the Fourteenth Amendment relating to its intended effect on public education.

In the first cases in this Court construing the Fourteenth Amendment, decided shortly after its adoption, the Court interpreted it as proscribing all state-imposed discriminations against the Negro race. The doctrine of "separate but equal" did not make its appearance in this Court until 1896 in the case of *Plessy v. Ferguson, supra*, involving not education but transportation. American courts have since labored with the doctrine for over half a century. In this Court, there have been six cases involving the "separate but equal" doctrine in the field of public education. In *Cumming v. County Board of Education,* 175 U.S. 528, and *Gong Lum v. Rice,* 275 U.S. 78, the validity of the doctrine itself was not challenged. In more recent cases, all on the graduate school level, inequality was found in that specific benefits enjoyed by white students were denied to Negro students of the same educational qualifications. *Missouri ex rel. Gaines v. Canada,* 305 U.S. 337; *Sipuel v. Oklahoma,* 332 U.S. 631; *Sweatt v. Painter,* 339 U.S. 629; *McLaurin v. Oklahoma State Regents,* 339 U.S. 637. In none of these cases was it necessary to reexamine the doctrine to grant relief to the Negro plaintiff. And in *Sweatt v. Painter, supra,* the Court expressly reserved decision on the question whether *Plessy v. Ferguson* should be held inapplicable to public education.

In the instant case, that question is directly presented. Here, unlike *Sweatt v. Painter,* there are findings below that the Negro and white schools involved have been equalized, or are being equalized, with respect to buildings, curricula, qualifications and salaries of teachers, and other "tangible" factors. Our decision, therefore, cannot turn on merely a comparison of these tangible factors in the Negro and white schools involved in each of the cases. We must look instead to the effect of segregation itself on public education.

In approaching this problem, we cannot turn the clock back to 1868 when the Amendment was adopted, or even to 1896 when *Plessy v. Ferguson* was written. We must consider public education in the light of its full development and its present place in American life throughout the Nation. Only in this way can it be determined if segregation in public schools deprives these plaintiffs of the equal protection of the laws.

Today, education is perhaps the most important function of state and local governments. Compulsory school attendance laws and the great expenditures for education both demonstrate our recognition of the importance of education to our democratic society. It is required in the performance of our most basic public responsibilities, even service in the armed forces. It is the very foundation of good citizenship. Today it is a principal instrument in awakening the child to cultural values, in preparing him for later professional training, and in helping him to adjust normally to his environment. In these days, it is doubtful that any child may reasonably be expected to succeed in life if he is denied the opportunity of an education. Such an opportunity, where the state has undertaken to provide it, is a right which must be made available to all on equal terms.

We come then to the question presented: Does segregation of children in public schools solely on the basis of race, even though the physical facilities and other "tangible" factors may be equal, deprive the children of the minority group of equal educational opportunities? We believe that it does.

In *Sweatt v. Painter, supra,* in finding that a segregated law school for Negroes could not provide them equal educational opportunities, this Court relied in large part on "those qualities which are incapable of objective measurement but which make for greatness in a law school." In *McLaurin v. Oklahoma State Regents, supra,* the Court, in requiring that a Negro admitted to a white graduate school be treated like all other students, again resorted to intangible considerations: ". . . his ability to study, to engage in discussions and exchange views with other students, and, in general, to learn his profession." Such considerations apply with added force to children in grade and high schools. To separate them from others of similar age and qualifications solely because of their race generates a feeling of inferiority as to their status in the community that may affect their hearts and minds in a way unlikely ever to be undone. The effect of this separation on their educational opportunities was well-stated by a finding in the Kansas case by a court which nevertheless felt compelled to rule against the Negro plaintiffs:

> Segregation of white and colored children in public schools has a detrimental effect
> upon the colored children. The impact is greater when it has the sanction of the law;
> for the policy of separating the races is usually interpreted as denoting the inferiority
> of the negro group. A sense of inferiority affects the motivation of a child to learn.
> Segregation with the sanction of law, therefore, has a tendency to [retard] the
> educational and mental development of negro children and to deprive them of some
> of the benefits they would receive in a racial[ly] integrated school system.

Whatever may have been the extent of psychological knowledge at the time of *Plessy v. Ferguson,* this finding is amply supported by modern authority. Any language in *Plessy v. Ferguson* contrary to this finding is rejected.

We conclude that in the field of public education, the doctrine of "separate but equal" has no place. Separate educational facilities are inherently unequal. Therefore, we hold that the plaintiffs and others similarly situated for whom the actions have been brought are, by reason of the segregation complained of, deprived of the equal protection of the laws guaranteed by the Fourteenth Amendments. This disposition makes unnecessary any discussion whether such segregation also violates the Due Process Clause of the Fourteenth Amendment.

Because these are class actions, because of the wide applicability of this decision, and because of the great variety of local conditions, the formulation of decrees in these cases presents problems of considerable complexity. On reargument, the consideration of appropriate relief was necessarily subordinated to the primary question—the constitutionality of segregation in public education. We have now announced that such segregation is a denial of the equal protection of the laws. In order that we may have the full assistance of the parties in formulating decrees, the cases will be restored to the docket, and the parties are requested to present further argument on Questions 4 and 5 previously propounded by the Court for the reargument this Term. The Attorney General of the United States is again invited to participate. The Attorneys General of the states requiring or permitting segregation in public education will also be permitted to appear as *amici curiae* upon request to do so by September 15, 1954, and submission of briefs by October 1, 1954.

It is so ordered.

KENNETH B. CLARK, HOW CHILDREN LEARN ABOUT RACE, 1950

The Supreme Court's reasoning in the Brown *case was based on many considerations, but one of the most important was Kenneth Clark's research on the impact of segregation on the self-image and learning potential of African-American children. Clark had presented his findings at a White House Conference in 1950. While he faced significant challenges later in the century, Clark's study showing the harmful impact of "separate but equal" schooling influenced the Court, and much of American society, to conclude that there could be no such thing as separate and equal; that legally enforced separation was inherently unequal. Clark published his findings in 1955, but they had already made their most significant impact through the Supreme Court's 1954 decision.*

Are children born with racial feelings? Or do they have to learn, first, what color they are and, second, what color is "best"?

Less than fifty years ago, some social theorists maintained that racial and religious prejudices are inborn—that they are inherent and instinctive. These theorists believed that children do not have to learn to dislike people who differ from them in physical characteristics; it was considered natural to dislike those different from oneself and to like those similar to oneself.

However, research over the past thirty years has refuted these earlier theories. Social scientists are now convinced that children learn social, racial, and religious prejudices in the course of observing, and being influenced by, the existence of patterns in the culture in which they live. Students of the problem are now facing these questions:

1. How and when do children learn to identify themselves with some people and to differentiate themselves from others?
2. How and when do children acquire racial attitudes and begin to express these attitudes in their behavior?
3. What conditions in the environment foster the development of these racial attitudes and behavior?
4. What can be done to prevent the development and expression of destructive racial prejudices in children?

Until quite recently, there were differences in opinion concerning the age at which children develop and express racial prejudices. Some observers (in the tradition of those who believed that prejudices are inborn) said that even infants express racial preferences and that therefore such preferences play little or no role in the life of the child until the early teens. They pointed out that children of different races have been observed playing together and sometimes developing close friendships; this fact, they thought, showed that young children are unaware of racial or religious differences.

Within the past two decades, social scientists have made a series of studies of this problem. They indicate, on the one hand, that there is no evidence that racial prejudices are inborn; and, on the other hand, that it is equally false to assume that the child remains unaffected by racial considerations until his teens or preteens.

Racial attitudes appear early in the life of children and affect the ideas and behavior of children in the first grades of school. Such attitudes—which appear to be almost inevitable in children in our society—develop gradually.

According to one recent study, white kindergarten children in New York City show a clear preference for whites and a clear rejection of Negroes. Other studies show that Negro children in the kindergarten and early elementary grades of a New England town, in New York City, in Philadelphia, and in two urban communities in Arkansas know the difference between Negroes and whites; realize they are Negro or white; and are aware of the social meaning and evaluation of racial differences.

The development of racial awareness and racial preferences in Negro children has been studied by the author and his wife. To determine the extent of consciousness of skin of color in these children between three and seven years old, we showed the children four dolls all from the same mold and dressed alike; the only difference in the dolls was that two were brown and two were white. We asked the children to choose among the dolls in answer to certain requests:

1. "Give me the white doll."
2. "Give me the colored doll."
3. "Give me the Negro doll."

These children reacted with strong awareness of skin color. Among three-year-old Negro children in both northern and southern communities, more that 75 percent showed that they were conscious of the difference between "white" and "colored." Among older children, an increasingly greater number made the correct choices.

These findings clearly support the conclusion that racial awareness is present in Negro children as young as three years old. Furthermore, this knowledge develops in stability and clarity from year to year, and by the age of seven, it is a part of the knowledge of all Negro children. Other investigators have shown that the same is true of white children.

Some children whose skin color is indistinguishable from that of white people, but who are nonetheless classified as Negroes by the society, have difficulty in making a correct racial identification of themselves at an age when other children do so. Soon, however—by the age of five or six—the majority of these children also begin to accept the social definition of themselves, even though this differs from their observance of their own skin color.

There is now no doubt that children learn the prevailing social ideas about racial differences early in their lives. Not only are they aware of race in terms of physical characteristics such as skin color, but also they are generally able to identify themselves in terms of race. . . .

The problem of the development and awareness of religious ideas and identification in children involves more subtle and complex distinctions which understandably require a longer period of time before they are clearly understood.

It is much more difficult for children to know if they are Catholic, Protestant, or Jewish than it is to know if they are white or Negro. In one study (Radke, Trager, and Davis), children were shown pictures of a church with a cross, and of a building clearly marked as a synagogue. The investigators asked the children their reactions to these pictures. Only a minority of children between the ages of five and eight made stable and accurate identification of themselves in terms of religion. Less than half the Jewish children in this age group identified themselves as Jews, while only 30 percent of the Catholic children and less than 27 percent of the white Protestant children made correct religious identifications. The relatively high percentage of Jewish children who identified themselves as Jews indicates that for these children there is an earlier awareness of religious identification and probably of minority status.

In these tests, no Negro child identified himself in religious terms. This fact probably indicates that for the Negro child at these ages, the dominant factor in self-identification is skin color. The impact of their minority status as determined by skin color is so great that it precludes more abstract bases for self-identification.

A study of seven- and eight-year-old Jewish boys (by Hartley, Rosenbaum, and Schwartz) found that these boys had a generalized preference for all things "Jewish." The children responded to all questions concerning self-identification and preference with such comments as: "Because I am Jewish." "Because I like Jewish . . ." "Because they are Jewish, like me." "Because I like to play with Jewish people."

This undifferentiated preference for Jewishness was found by Radke to be appreciably less among Jewish children of ten and eleven, and even less in thirteen- and fourteen-year-olds. It is possible that as these children mature, their increased contact with the larger culture results in a decreased interest in Jewishness as such. It is also possible that this tendency reflects an increase in rejection of Jewishness—indicating the children's growing awareness of the minority status of Jews in America.

The same social scientists have studied small groups of Jewish, Catholic, Negro, and white Protestant children in New York City. These children were asked to respond to the simple question, "What are you?" Jewish children on all age levels answered by the term "Jewish," rarely identifying themselves in terms of nationality or color. On the other hand, a considerable proportion of the non-Jewish children identified themselves in terms of nationality rather than religion.

Non-Jewish children between the ages of $3\frac{1}{2}$ and $4\frac{1}{2}$ were usually not certain what religion they belonged to. Some non-Jewish white children in this age group said that they were Jewish; the fact that they were enrolled in a Jewish neighborhood center may have accounted for their mistaken belief that they were Jewish. At this stage of development, a non-Jewish child in a Jewish setting may conceive of himself as Jewish, and vice-versa. These results suggest that the problem of religious identification involves a level of abstract thinking of which preschool children are generally incapable.

These investigators also studied the meaning of such terms as *Jewish* and *Catholic* for children between the ages of four and ten. They found that at these ages, the concepts are understood in terms of concrete activities. Jewish children mentioned

"Going to shul," "Not eating bacon," or "Talking Jewish." Catholic children mentioned "Going to church," "Taking communion," or "To speak as a Catholic."

Certain conclusions arise from the many independent investigations of the development of racial awareness and identification in children. By the age of four, Negro and white children are generally aware of differences in skin color and can identify themselves correctly in terms of such differences. Jewish children are not consistently aware of their Jewishness until around the age of five. The average Catholic or Protestant child does not begin to identify himself in religious terms until around seven or eight. Thus, it appears that the concrete and perceptible fact of skin color provides a basis for earlier self-identification and preferences in American children than the more abstract factor of the family religion.

A child gradually learns what status the society accords to his group. The tendency of older Jewish children to show less preference for Jewishness than younger Jewish children suggests that they have learned that Jews do not have a preferred status in the larger society, and that these children have accordingly modified their self-appraisal. This effect of the awareness of the status of one's own group is even more clearly apparent in the case of Negro children.

In addition to Negro children's awareness of differences in skin color, the author and his wife studied the ability of these children to identify themselves in racial terms. . . . We asked the children to point out the doll "which is most like you." Approximately two-thirds of all the children answered correctly. Correct answers were more frequent among the older ones. (Only 37 percent of the three-year-olds but 87 percent of the seven-year-olds responded accurately.) Negro children of light skin color had more difficulty in choosing the brown doll than Negro children of medium-brown or dark-brown skin color. This was true for older as well as younger children.

Many personal and emotional factors probably affected the ability of these Negro children to select the brown doll. In an effort to determine their racial preferences, we asked the children the following four questions:

1. "Give me the doll that you like to play with" or "the doll you like best."
2. "Give me the doll that is the nice doll."
3. "Give me the doll that looks bad."
4. "Give me the doll that is a nice color."

The majority of these Negro children at each age indicated an unmistakable preference for the white doll and a rejection of the brown doll.

Studies of the development of racial awareness, racial identification, and racial preference in both Negro and white children thus present a consistent pattern. Learning about races and racial differences, learning one's own racial identity, learning which race is to be preferred and which rejected—all these are assimilated by the child as part of the total pattern of ideas he acquires about himself and the society in which he lives. These acquired patterns of social and racial ideas are interrelated both in development and in function. The child's first awareness of racial differences is found to be associated with some rudimentary evaluation of these differences. Furthermore, as the average child learns to evaluate these differences according to the standards of the society, he is at the same time required to identify himself with one or another group. This identification necessarily involves a knowledge of the status assigned to the group with which he identifies himself, in relation to the status of other groups. The child therefore cannot learn what racial group he belongs to without being involved in a larger pattern of emotions, conflict, and desires which are part of his growing knowledge of what society thinks about his race.

Many independent studies enable us to begin to understand how children learn about race, how they identify themselves and others in terms of racial, religious, or nationality differences, and what meaning these differences have for the growing child. Racial and religious identification involves the ability of the child to identify himself with others of similar characteristics and to distinguish himself from those who appear to be dissimilar.

The fact that young Negro children would prefer to be white reflects their knowledge that society prefers white people. White children are generally found to prefer their white skin—an indication that they, too, know that society like whites better. It is clear, therefore, that the self-acceptance or self-rejection found so early in a child's developing complex of racial ideas reflects the awareness and acceptance of the prevailing racial attitudes in his community.

Some children as young as three years of age begin to express racial and religious attitudes similar to those held by adults in their society. The racial and religious attitudes of sixth graders are more definite than the attitudes of preschool children, and hardly distinguishable from the attitudes of high school students. Thereafter, there is an increase in the intensity and complexity of these attitudes, until they become similar (at least, as far as words go) to the prevailing attitudes held by the average adult American.

The racial ideas of children are less rigid, more easily changed, than the racial ideas of adults. It is probable, too, that racial attitudes and behavior are more directly related among adults. The racial and religious attitudes of a young child may become more positive or more negative as he matures. The direction these attitudes will take, their intensity and form of expression, will be determined by the type of experiences that the child is permitted to have. One student of this problem says that, although children tend to become more tolerant in their general social attitudes as they grow older, they become less tolerant in their attitudes toward the Negro. This may reflect the fact that the things children are taught about the Negro and the experiences they are permitted to have usually result in the development of racial intolerance.

School Desegregation in the South: Little Rock, 1957

Daisy Bates, *The Long Shadow of Little Rock,* 1962

Daisy Bates, editor of a newspaper in the African-American community in Little Rock, Arkansas, and president of the Arkansas chapter of the NAACP in 1957, was a major actor in the desegregation of Little Rock High School. She tells of the experience she shared with the students and others in her book, The Long Shadow of Little Rock *(1962). Clearly she and her coworkers never expected the massive resistance to the federal court orders that occurred in Little Rock and elsewhere. Yet when it appeared, they faced it with courage. Bates's account provides a moving personal glimpse of the desegregation struggle.*

Bates, Daisy. *The Long Shadow at Little Rock.* Fayetteville: The University of Arkansas Press, 1962. Reprinted by permission of the University of Arkansas Press.

It was Labor Day, September 2, 1957. The nine pupils who had been selected by the school authorities to enter Central High School—Carlotta Walls, Jefferson Thomas, Elizabeth Eckford, Thelma Mothershed, Melba Pattillo, Ernest Green, Terrance Roberts, Gloria Ray, and Minnijean Brown—were enjoying the last day of their summer vacation . . . About mid-afternoon, young Jefferson Thomas was on his way home from the pool and stopped at my house for a brief visit. While Jeff was raiding the refrigerator, a news flash came over the radio that the Governor would address the citizens of Arkansas that night.

"I wonder what he's going to talk about," said Jeff. The youngster then turned to me and asked, "Is there anything they can do—now that they lost in court? Is there any way they can stop us from entering Central tomorrow morning?"

"I don't think so," I said.

About seven o'clock that night, a local newspaper reporter rang my doorbell. "Mrs. Bates, do you know that national guardsmen are surrounding Central High?"

L. C. [Bates] and I stared at him incredulously for a moment. A friend who was visiting us volunteered to guard the house while we drove out to Central. L. C. gave him the shotgun. We jumped into our car and drove to Central High . . . Men in full battle dress—helmets, boots, and bayonets—were piling out of the trucks and lining up in front of the school.

As we watched, L. C. switched on the car radio. A newscaster was saying, "National guardsmen are surrounding Central High School. No one is certain what this means. Governor Faubus will speak later this evening. . . ."

I don't recall all the details of what Governor Faubus said that night. But his words electrified Little Rock. By morning, they shocked the United States. By noon the next day, his message horrified the world.

Faubus's alleged reason for calling out the troops was that he had received information that caravans of automobiles filled with white supremacists were heading toward Little Rock from all over the state. He therefore declared Central High School off limits to Negroes. For some inexplicable reason, he added that Horace Mann, a Negro high school, would be off limits to whites.

Then, from the chair of the highest office of the State of Arkansas, Governor Orval Eugene Faubus delivered the infamous words, "blood will run in the streets," if Negro pupils should attempt to enter Central High School.

In a half dozen ill-chosen words, Faubus made his contribution to the mass hysteria that was to grip the city of Little Rock for several months.

The citizens of Little Rock gathered on September 3 to gaze upon the incredible spectacle of an empty school building surrounded by two-hundred fifty National Guard troops. At about eight fifteen in the morning, Central students starting passing through the line of national guardsmen—all but the nine Negro students.

I had been in touch with their parents throughout the day. They were confused, and they were frightened. As the parents voiced their fears, they kept repeating Governor Faubus's words that "blood would run in the streets of Little Rock" should their teenage children try to attend Central—the school to which they had been assigned by the school board?

On the afternoon of the same day, September 3, when the school was scheduled to open, Superintendent [Virgil] Blossom called a meeting of leading Negro citizens and parents of the nine children . . . [and] instructed the parents *not* to accompany their children the next morning when they were scheduled to enter Central. "If violence breaks out," the Superintendent told them, "it will be easier to protect the children if the adults aren't there."

During the conference, Superintendent Blossom had given us little assurance that the children would be adequately protected. As we left the building, I was aware of how deeply worried the parents were, although they did not voice their fears.

About ten o'clock that night, I was alone in the downstairs recreation room.

I sat huddled in my chair, dazed, trying to think, yet not knowing what to do. I don't recall how much time went by . . . before some neighbors entered. One of them was the Reverend J. C. Crenshaw, President of the Little Rock branch of the NAACP.

"Maybe," I said, "maybe we could round up a few ministers to go with the children tomorrow. Maybe then the mob wouldn't attack them. Maybe with the ministers by their side—"

I called a white minister, Reverend Dunbar Ogden, Jr., President of the Interracial Ministerial Alliance. I did not know Mr. Ogden. I explained the situation, then asked if he thought he could get some ministers to go with the children to school the next morning.

Tensely, I waited for his return call. When it came, he sounded apologetic. The white ministers he had talked to had questioned whether it was the thing to do. Some of the Negro ministers had pointed out that the Superintendent of Schools had asked that no Negro adults go with the children, and that in view of this, they felt they shouldn't go. Then he added gently, "I'll keep trying—and, God willing, I'll be there."

Next I called the city police. I explained to the officer in charge that we were concerned about the safety of the children and that we were trying to get ministers to accompany them to school the next morning. I said that the children would assemble at eight thirty at Twelfth and Park Avenue. I asked whether a police car could be stationed there to protect the children until the ministers arrived.

The police officer promised to have a squad car there at eight o'clock. "But you realize," he warned, "that our men cannot go any closer than that to the school. The school is off limits to the city police while it's 'occupied' by the Arkansas National Guardsmen."

By now it was two thirty in the morning. Still, the parents had to be called about the change in plan. At three o'clock I completed my last call, explaining to the parents where the children were to assemble and the plan about the ministers. Suddenly I remembered Elizabeth Eckford. Her family had no telephone. Should I go to the Union Station and search for her father? Someone had once told me that he had a night job there. Tired in mind and body, I decided to handle the matter early in the morning. I stumbled into bed.

A few hours later, at about eight fifteen in the morning, L. C. and I started driving to Twelfth Street and Park Avenue. On the way I checked out in my mind the possibilities that awaited us . . .

The bulletin over the car radio interrupted. The voice announced: "A Negro girl is being mobbed at Central High . . ."

"Oh my God!" I cried. "It must be Elizabeth! I forgot to notify her where to meet us!"

L. C. jumped out of the car and rushed to find her. I drove on to Twelfth Street. There were the ministers—two white—Mr. Ogden and Reverend Will Campbell, of the National Council of Churches, Nashville, Tennessee—and two colored—the Reverend Z. A. Driver, of the African Methodist Episcopal Church, and the Reverend Harry Bass, of the Methodist Church. With them also was Mr. Ogden's twenty-one-year-old son, David. The children were already there. And, yes, the police had come as promised. All of the children were there—all except Elizabeth.

Elizabeth, whose dignity and control in the face of jeering mobsters had been filmed by television cameras and recorded in pictures flashed to newspapers over the world, had overnight become a national heroine . . . The first day that her parents agreed she might come out of seclusion, she came to my house, where the reporters awaited her. Elizabeth was very quiet, speaking only when spoken to. I took her to my bedroom to talk before I let the reporters see her. I asked her how she felt now. Suddenly all her pent-up emotion flared.

"Why am I here?" she said, turning blazing eyes on me. "Why are you so interested in my welfare now? You didn't care enough to notify me of the change of plans—"

Little by little, Elizabeth came out of her shell. Up to now she had never talked about what happened to her at Central. Once when we were alone in the downstairs recreation room of my house, I asked her simply, "Elizabeth, do you think you can talk about it now?"

She remained quiet for a long time. Then she began to speak.

"You remember the day before we were to go in, we met Superintendent Blossom at the school board office. He told us what the mob might say and do, but he never told us we wouldn't have any protection. He told our parents not to come because he wouldn't be able to protect the children if they did.

"That night I was so excited I couldn't sleep. The next morning I was about the first one up. While I was pressing my black-and-white dress—I had made it to wear on the first day of school—my little brother turned on the TV set. They started telling about a large crowd gathered at the school. The man on TV said he wondered if we were going to show up that morning.

"Before I left home, Mother called us into the living room. She said we should have a word of prayer. Then I caught the bus and got off a block from the school. I saw a large crowd of people standing across the street from the soldiers guarding Central. As I walked on, the crowd suddenly got quiet. Superintendent Blossom had told us to enter by the front door. I looked at all the people and thought, 'Maybe I will be safer if I walk down the block to the front entrance behind the guards.'

"At the corner, I tried to pass through the long line of guards around the school so as to enter the grounds behind them. One of the guards pointed across the street. So I pointed in the same direction and asked whether he meant for me to cross the street and walk down. He nodded 'yes.' So, I walked across the street, conscious of the crowd that stood there, but they moved away from me.

"For a moment all I could hear was the shuffling of their feet. Then someone shouted, 'Here she comes, get ready!' I moved away from the crowd on the sidewalk and into the street. If the mob came at me I could then cross back over so the guards could protect me.

"The crowd moved in closer and then began to follow me, calling me names. I still wasn't afraid. Just a little bit nervous. Then my knees started to shake all of a sudden and I wondered whether I could make it to the center entrance a block away. It was the longest block I ever walked in my whole life.

"Even so, I still wasn't too scared, because all the time I kept thinking that the guards would protect me.

"When I got in front of the school, I went up to a guard again. But this time he just looked straight ahead and didn't move to let me pass him. I didn't know what to do. Then I looked and saw the path leading to the front entrance was a little further ahead. So I walked until I was right in front of the path to the front door.

"I stood looking at the school—it looked so big! Just then the guards let some white students through.

"The crowd was quiet. I guess they were waiting to see what was going to happen. When I was able to steady my knees, I walked up to the guard who had let the white students in. He, too, didn't move. When I tried to squeeze past him, he raised his bayonet and then the other guards moved in and they raised their bayonets.

"They glared at me with a mean look and I was very frightened and didn't know what to do. I turned around and the crowd came toward me.

"They moved closer and closer. Somebody started yelling, 'Lynch her! Lynch her!'

"I tried to see a friendly face somewhere in the mob—someone who maybe would help. I looked into the face of an old woman and it seemed a kind face, but when I looked at her again, she spat on me.

"They came closer, shouting, 'No nigger bitch is going to get in our school. Get out of here!'

"I turned back to the guards but their faces told me I wouldn't get any help from them. Then I looked down the block and saw a bench at the bus stop. I thought, 'If I can only get there, I will be safe.' I don't know why the bench seemed a safe place to me, but I started walking toward it. I tried to close my mind to what they were shouting, and kept saying to myself, 'If I can only make it to the bench, I will be safe.'

"When I finally got there, I don't think I could have gone another step. I sat down and the mob crowded up and began shouting all over again. Someone hollered, 'Drag her over to this tree! Let's take care of that nigger.' Just then a white man sat down beside me, put his arm around me and patted my shoulder. He raised my chin and said, 'Don't let them see you cry.'

"Then, a white lady—she was very nice—she came over to me on the bench. She spoke to me but I don't remember what she said. She put me on the bus and sat next to me. She asked my name and tried to talk to me, but I don't think I answered. I can't remember much about the bus ride, but the next thing I remember I was standing in front of the School for the Blind, where Mother works."

In addition to Mrs. Bates's account, the Eyes on the Prize Civil Rights Reader *reports the transcript of a roundtable discussion set up by NBC News one month into the desegregation effort. This report from the fall of 1957 features six students; four—Sammy Dean Parker, Kay Bacon, Robin Woods, and Joseph Fox are white, and two—Ernest Green and Minnijean Brown—are black. Mrs. Ricketts was the moderator.*

Mrs. Ricketts: Do you think it is possible to start working this out on a more sensible basis than violent demonstration?

Sammy:	No, I don't, because the South has always been against racial mixing and I think they will fight this thing to the end . . . We fight for freedom—that's one thing. And we don't have any freedom any more.
Ernest:	Sammy, you said that you don't have any freedom. I wonder what do you mean by it—that you don't have any freedom? You are guaranteed your freedom in the Bill of Rights and your Constitution. You have the freedom of speech—I noticed that has been exercised a whole lot in Little Rock. The freedom of petition, the freedom of religion, and the other freedoms are guaranteed to you. As far as freedom, I think that if anybody should kick about freedoms, it should be us. Because I think we have been given a pretty bad side on this thing as far as freedom.
Sammy:	Do you call those troops freedom? I don't. And I also do not call when you are being escorted into the school every morning.
Ernest:	You say why did the troops come here? It is because our government—our state government—went against the federal law . . . Our country is set up so that we have forty-eight states and no one state has the ability to overrule our nation's government. I thought that was what our country was built around. I mean, that is why we fight. We fought in World War II together—the fellows that I know died in World War II, they died in the Korean War. I mean, why should my friends get out there and die for a cause called "democracy" when I can't exercise my rights—tell me that.
Robin:	I agree with Ernest.
Joe:	Well, Sammy, I don't know what freedom has been taken away from you, because the truth there—I know as a senior myself—the troops haven't kept me from going to my classes or participating in any school activity. I mean, they're there just to keep order in case—I might use the term *hotheads*—get riled up. But I think as long as—if parents would just stay out of it for themselves, I think it would be a whole lot better. I think the students are mature enough to figure it out for themselves . . . As far as I'm concerned, I'll lay the whole blame of this trouble in Governor Faubus's lap.
Sammy:	I think we knew before this ever started that some day we were going to have to integrate the schools. And I think that our Governor was trying to protect all of us when he called out the National Guard— and he was trying to prepare us, I think.
Ernest:	Well, I have to disagree . . . I know a student that's over there with us, Elizabeth, and that young lady, she walked two blocks, I guess— as you all know—and the mob was behind her. Did the troops break up the mob?
Robin:	And when Elizabeth had to walk down in front of the school, I was there and I saw that. And may I say, I was very ashamed—I felt like crying—because she was so brave when she did that. And we just weren't behaving ourselves—just jeering her. I think if we had had any sort of decency, we wouldn't have acted that way. But I think if

	everybody would just obey the Golden Rule—do unto others as you would have others do unto you—might be the solution. How would you like to have to . . . walk down the street with everybody yelling behind you like they yelled behind Elizabeth?
Mrs. Ricketts:	Sammy, why do these children not want to go to school with Negroes?
Sammy:	Well, I think it is mostly race mixing.
Mrs. Ricketts:	Race mixing? What do you mean?
Sammy:	Well, marrying each other.
Minnijean:	Hold your hand up. I'm brown, you are white. What's the difference? We are all of the same thoughts. You're thinking about your boy—he's going to the Navy. I'm thinking about mine—he's in the Air Force. We think about the same thing.
Sammy:	I'll have to agree with you.
Ernest:	Well, getting back to this intermarriage and all that. I don't know [where] people get all that. Why do I want to go to school? To marry with someone? I mean, school's not a marriage bureau . . . I'm going there for an education. Really, if I'm going there to socialize, I don't need to be going to school. I can stand out on the corner and socialize, as far as that.
Minnijean:	Kay, Joe, and Robin—do you know anything about me, or is it just that your mother has told you about Negroes?
Mrs. Ricketts:	Have you ever really made an effort to try to find out what they're like?
Kay:	Not until today.
Sammy:	Not until today.
Mrs. Ricketts:	And what do you think about it after today?
Kay:	Well, you know that my parents and a lot of the other students and their parents think that the Negroes aren't equal to us. But—I don't know. It seems like they are, to me.
Sammy:	These people are—we'll have to admit that.
Ernest:	I think, like we're doing today, discussing our different views . . . if the people of Little Rock . . . would get together, I believe they would find out a different story—and try to discuss the thing instead of getting out in the street and kicking people around and calling names—and all that sort of thing. If . . . people got together it would be smoothed over.
Ray:	I think that if . . . our friends had been getting in this discussion today, I think that maybe some of them—not all of them—in time, they would change their mind. But probably some of them would change their mind today.
Sammy:	I know now that it isn't as bad as I thought it was—after we got together and discussed it.
Kay:	We [Sammy and I] both came down here today with our mind set on it [that] we weren't going to change our mind, that we were fully against integration. But I know now that we're going to change our mind.
Mrs. Ricketts:	What do your parents say to that?
Kay:	I think I'm going to have a long talk with my parents.

School Desegregation in the North: Boston, 1965

Jonathan Kozol, *Death at an Early Age*, 1967

Jonathan Kozol, who has become well-known to education audiences for his later books, including Ordinary Resurrections *(2000) and* Savage Inequalities *(1991), was a young college graduate just hired by the Boston Public Schools when he began his career at the predominantly African-American Gibson School in Roxbury in 1965. His traumatic experience paints a vivid picture of the Boston schools before desegregation.*

Perhaps a reader would like to know what it is like to go into a new classroom in the same way that I did and to see before you suddenly, and in terms you cannot avoid recognizing, the dreadful consequences of a year's wastage of real lives.

You walk into a narrow and old wood-smelling classroom and you see before you thirty-five curious, cautious, and untrusting children, aged eight to thirteen, of whom about two-thirds are Negro. Three of the children are designated to you as special students. Thirty percent of the class is reading at the Second-Grade level in a year and in a month in which they should be reading at the height of Fourth-Grade performance or at the beginning of the Fifth. Seven children out of the class are up to par. Ten substitutes or teacher changes. Or twelve changes. Or eight. Or eleven. Nobody seems to know how many teachers they have had. Seven of their lifetime records are missing: symptomatic and emblematic at once of the chaos that has been with them all year long. Many more lives than just seven have already been wasted, but the seven missing records become an embittering symbol of the lives behind them which, equally, have been lost or mislaid. (You have to spend the first three nights staying up until dawn trying to reconstruct these records out of notes and scraps.) On the first math test you give, the class average comes out to 36. The children tell you with embarrassment that it has been like that since fall.

You check around the classroom. Of forty desks, five have tops with no hinges. You lift a desktop to fetch a paper, and you find that the top has fallen off. There are three windows. One cannot be opened. A sign on it written in the messy scribble of a hurried teacher or some custodial person warns you: DO NOT UNLOCK THIS WINDOW IT IS BROKEN. The general look of the room is as a bleak-light photograph of a mental hospital. Above the one poor blackboard, gray rather than really black, and hard to write on, hangs from one tack, lopsided, a motto attributed to Benjamin Franklin: *Well begun is half done.* Everything, or almost everything like that, seems a mockery of itself.

Into this grim scenario, drawing on your own pleasures and memories, you do what you can do to bring some kind of life. You bring in some cheerful and colorful paintings by Joan Miro and Paul Klee. While the paintings by Miro do not arouse much interest, the ones by Klee become an instantaneous success. One picture in particular, a watercolor titled "Bird Garden," catches the fascination of the entire class. You slip it out of the book and tack it up on the wall beside the doorway, and it creates a traffic jam every time the children have to file in or file out. You discuss with your students some of the reasons why Klee may have painted the way he did, and you talk about the

---

From Kozol, Jonathan, *Death at an Early Age*. Boston: Houghton Mifflin, 1967. Reprinted by permission of Jonathan Kozol.

things that can be accomplished in a painting which could not be accomplished in a photograph. None of this seems to be above the children's heads. Despite this, you are advised flatly by the Art Teacher that your naiveté has gotten the best of you and that the children cannot possibly appreciate this. Klee is too difficult. Children will not enjoy it. You are unable to escape the idea that the Art Teacher means herself instead.

For poetry, in place of the recommended memory gems, going back again into your own college days, you make up your mind to introduce a poem of William Butler Yeats. It is about a lake isle called Innisfree, about birds that have the funny name of "linnets" and about a "bee-loud glade." The children do not all go crazy about it, but a number of them seem to like it as much as you do, and you tell them how once, three years before, you were living in England and you helped a man in the country to make his home from wattles and clay. The children become intrigued. They pay good attention, and many of them grow more curious about the poem than they appeared at first. Here again, however, you are advised by older teachers that you are making a mistake: Yeats is too difficult for children. They can't enjoy it, won't appreciate it, wouldn't like it. You are aiming way above their heads . . . Another idea comes to mind and you decide to try out an easy and well-known and not very complicated poem of Robert Frost. The poem is called "Stopping By the Woods on a Snowy Evening." This time, your supervisor happens to drop in from the School Department. He looks over the mimeograph, agrees with you that it's a nice poem, then points out to you—tolerantly, but strictly—that you have made another mistake. "Stopping By Woods" is scheduled for Sixth Grade. It is not "a Fourth-Grade poem," and it is not to be read or looked at during the Fourth Grade. Bewildered as you are by what appears to be kind of idiocy, you still feel reproved and criticized and muted and set back, and you feel that you have been caught in the commission of a serious mistake.

On a series of other occasions, the situation is repeated. The children are offered something new and something lively. They respond to it energetically, and they are attentive and their attention does not waver. For the first time in a long while, perhaps, there is actually some real excitement and some growing and some thinking going on within that one small room. In each case, however, you are advised sooner or later that you are making a mistake. Your mistake, in fact, is to have impinged upon the standardized condescension on which the entire administration of the school is based. To hand Paul Klee's pictures to the children of this classroom, and particularly in a twenty-dollar volume, constitutes a threat to this school system. It is not different from sending a little girl from the Negro ghetto into an art class near Harvard Yard. Transcending the field of familiarity of the administration, you are endangering its authority and casting a blow at its self-confidence. The way the threat is handled is by a continual and standardized underrating of the children: They can't do it, couldn't do it, wouldn't like it, don't deserve it . . . In such a manner, many children are tragically and unjustifiably held back from a great many of the good things that they might come to like or admire and are pinned down instead to books the teacher knows and to easy tastes that she can handle. This includes, above all, of course, the kind of material that is contained in the Course of Study.

Try to imagine, for a child, how great the gap between the outside world and the world conveyed within this kind of school must seem: A little girl, maybe Negro, comes in from a street that is lined with car-carcasses. Old purple Hudsons and one-wheel-missing Cadillacs represent her horizon and mark the edges of her dreams. In the kitchen of her house, roaches creep and large rats crawl. On the way to school, a wino totters. Some teenage white boys slow down their car to insult her, and speed on. At school, she stands frozen for fifteen minutes in a yard of cracked cement that overlooks a hillside on which trash has been unloaded and at the bottom of which the New York, New Haven, and Hartford railroad rumbles past. In the basement, she sits upon broken or splintery seats in filthy toilets and she is yelled at in the halls. Upstairs, when something has been stolen, she is told that she is the one who stole it and is called a liar and forced abjectly to apologize before a teacher who has not the slightest idea in the world of who the culprit truly was. The same teacher, behind the child's back, ponders audibly with imagined compassion: "What can you do with this kind of material? How can you begin to teach this kind of child?"

Gradually going crazy, the child is sent after two years of misery to a pupil adjustment counselor who arranges for her to have some tests and considers the entire situation and discusses it with the teacher and finally files a long report. She is, some months later, put onto a waiting list some place for once-a-week therapy, but another year passes before she has gotten anywhere near to the front of a long line. By now she is fourteen, has lost whatever innocence she still had in the back seat of the old Cadillac, and, within two additional years, she will be ready and eager for dropping out of school.

Once at school, when she was eight or nine, she drew a picture of a rich-looking lady in an evening gown with a handsome man bowing down before her, but she was told by an insensate and wild-eyed teacher that what she had done was junk and garbage and the picture was torn up and thrown away before her eyes. The rock and roll music that she hears on the Negro station is considered "primitive" by her teachers, but she prefers its insistent rhythms to the dreary monotony of school. Once, in Fourth Grade, she got excited at school about some writing she had never heard about before. A handsome green book, brand new, was held up before her and then put into her hands. Out of this book her teacher read a poem. The poem was about a Negro—a woman who was a maid in the house of a white person—and she liked it. It remained in her memory. Somehow, without meaning to, she found that she had done the impossible for her: she had memorized that poem. Perhaps, horribly, in the heart of her, already she was aware that it was telling about her future: fifty dollars a week to scrub floors and bathe little white babies in the suburbs after an hour's streetcar ride. The poem made her want to cry. The white lady, the lady for whom the maid was working, told the maid she loved her. But the maid in the poem wasn't going to tell any lies in return. She knew she didn't feel any love for the white lady and she told the lady so. The poem was shocking to her, but it seemed bitter, strong and true. Another poem in the same green book was about a little boy on a merry-go-round. She laughed with the class at the question he asked about a Jim Crow section on a merry-go-round, but she also was old enough to know that it was not a funny poem, really, and it made her valuably sad. She wanted to know how she could get hold of that poem, and maybe that whole book. The poems were moving to her . . .

This was a child in my class. Details are changed somewhat, but it is essentially one child. The girl was one of the three unplaced special students in that Fourth Grade room. She was not an easy girl to teach, and it was hard even to keep her at her seat on many mornings, but I do not remember that there was any difficulty at all in gaining and holding onto her attention on the day that I brought in that green book of Langston Hughes.

Of all of the poems of Langston Hughes that I read to my Fourth Graders, the one that the children liked most was a poem that has the title "Ballad of the Landlord." The poem is printed along with some other material in the back part of this book. This poem may not satisfy the taste of every critic, and I am not making any claims to immortality for a poem just because I happen to like it a great deal. But the reason this poem did have so much value and meaning for me and, I believe, for many of my students, is that it not only seems moving in an obvious and immediate human way but that it *finds* its emotion in something ordinary. It is a poem which really does allow both heroism and pathos to poor people, sees strength and awkwardness, and attributes to a poor person standing on the stoop of his slum house every bit as much significance as William Wordsworth saw in daffodils, waterfalls, and clouds. At the request of the children, later on I mimeographed that poem and, although nobody in the classroom was asked to do this, several of the children took it home and memorized it on their own. I did not assign it for memory, because I do not think that memorizing a poem has any kind of special value. Some of the children just came in and asked if they could recite it. Before long, almost every child in the room had asked to have a turn.

All of the poems that you read to Negro children obviously are not going to be by or about Negro people. Nor would anyone expect that all poems which are read to a class of poor children ought to be grim or gloomy or heartbreaking or sad. But when, among the works of many different authors, you do have the will to read children a poem by a man so highly renowned as Langston Hughes, then I think it is important not to try to pick a poem that is innocuous, being like any other poet's kind of poem, but I think you ought to choose a poem that is genuinely representative and then try to make it real to the children in front of you in the way that I tried. I also think it ought to be taken seriously by a teacher when a group of young children come in to him one morning and announce they have liked something so much that they have memorized it voluntarily. It surprised me and impressed me when that happened. It was all I needed to know to confirm for me the value of reading that poem and the value of reading many other poems to children which will build upon, and not attempt to break down, the most important observations and very deepest foundations of their lives.

One morning in the spring, as I was putting work up on the blackboard, the Reading Teacher came into my room to chat with me. There still were a few minutes before the children would come in. It was a bright, cheerful morning and she was in a bright and cheerful mood. Before her, on the table beside my desk, were several piles of new books from the library and piles of mimeographed poetry, including the poems by Frost and Langston Hughes. On the back of the door that led into the room was the chart that gave my class's math and spelling scores. The math grades stopped suddenly at the score of 36, then there was a week's jump to 60, and the grade after that was 79.

Deleted from those averages, however, were the scores of five or six pupils who were so hopelessly behind that it seemed no longer meaningful even to include their average in a final grade, since they actually could score no grade at all. Among those children, thus excluded from our final reckonings, was the boy I have called Edward. Edward, that week, was still learning to add nine and three and to subtract six from eight. I also was trying hard to teach him to tell time. Some of the children who were doing well in math would take turns working with him. At moments when some kind of small victory was made, his helper would bring him back up to my desk to show me what he had learned. When I saw how much could be done even in such a short time and in such grimy circumstances, I used to wonder about the judgment of those who said that a boy like Edward could not be taught within a normal room. He was having a hard time still, and his day was a steady stream of disappointments. But he was learning something. He was learning to tell time.

While she still stood there, chatting, beside the doorway, and while I was hurrying to get all the morning's work up on the board, the Reading Teacher looked out at the sunshine and she said to me happily: "Spring is a wonderful season for a teacher, Johnny." She looked at me, and she added: "It's a time when all of the hard gains of the year's work come to view."

I knew what she meant by this, and I knew that it was partly out of habit that she said it. But partly, once again, I was bothered by the tone of what she said. It suggested to me that she was unaware of too much of the pain and too much of the waste around us in this school, and it was clear from the sound of her voice that she allowed herself no sense at all of the extent of the tragedy which this year had been for many children. A few days before, I had taken my children to the zoo, and Edward, gazing in wonderment and envy at the monkey in the cage, had said to me unhesitantly: "I wish I could be him." The same day, a toy snake I had given him broke in two somehow, and he instantly collapsed on the ground and began squirming on his belly and writhing in pain. He wept and screamed. At length I bought him another toy snake, and he picked it up in his hand and stopped crying. An occurrence of that sort seemed characteristic of his school career. Yet he, like Stephen, like Frederick, had been receiving regular rattannings down in the cellar all year long. I wondered if the Reading Teacher was thinking of him, too, when she told me that spring was a wonderful season for a teacher.

On a day a week later, about fifteen minutes before lunchtime, I was standing in front of the class, and they were listening to a record I had brought in. The record was a collection of French children's songs. We had been spending the month reading and talking about Paris and about France. As lunchtime drew near, I decided to let the children listen to the music while they were having their meal. While the record was playing, a little signal on the wall began to buzz. I left the room and hurried to the Principal's office. A white man whom I had never seen before was sitting by the Principal's desk. This man, bristling and clearly hostile to me, as was the Principal, instantly attacked me for having read to my class and distributed at their wish the poem I have talked about that was entitled "Ballad of the Landlord." It turned out that he was the father of one of the white boys in the class. He was also a police officer. The mimeograph of the poem, in my handwriting, was waved before my eyes. The Principal demanded to know what right I had to allow such a poem—not in the official Course of Study—to be read and memorized by the children in my class. I said I had not asked anyone to memorize it, but that I would defend the poem and its use against her or anyone on the basis that it was a good poem. The Principal became incensed with my answer and blurted out that she did not consider it a work of art. I remember that I knew right away I was not going to give in to her. I replied, in my own anger, that I had spent a good many years studying poetry and that I was not going to accept her judgment about a poem that meant that much to me and to my pupils. Although I did not say it in these words, it was really a way of telling her that I thought myself a better judge of poetry than she. I hope that I am.

The parent attacked me, as well, for having forced his son to read a book about the United Nations. I had brought a book to class, one out of sixty or more volumes, that told about the U.N. and its Human Rights Commission. The man, I believe, had mistaken "human rights" for "civil rights" and he was consequently in a patriotic rage. The Principal, in fairness, made the point that she did not think there was anything really wrong with the United Nations, although in the report that she later filed on the matter, she denied this for some reason and said, instead, "I then spoke and said that I felt there was no need for this material in the classroom." The Principal's report goes on to say that, after she dismissed me to my own room, she assured the parent that "there was not another teacher in the district who would have used this poem or any material like it. I assured him that his children would be very safe from such incidents."

As the Principal had instructed, I returned to my class, where the children had remained quiet and had not opened up their lunch because I had not told them to, and they were patiently waiting for me to come back. We had our lunch and listened to more music and did the rest of our lessons, and at quarter to two, just before school ended, the Principal called me back again. She told me I was fired. This was about eight days before the end of school. I asked her whether this was due to the talk we had had earlier, but she said it was not. I asked her if it was due to an evaluation, a written report, which I had sent in on the compensatory program about a week before. This was a report that I had written, as all teachers had, in answer to a request from the School Department and in which I had said that the program seemed to me to be very poor. I was told, at the time I passed it in, that the Principal had been quite angry. But again she said it was not that. I asked her finally if my dismissal was at her request, and she said, No, it came from higher up, and she didn't know anything about it except that I should close up my records and leave school and not come back. She said that I should not say goodbye to the children in my class. I asked her if she really meant this, and she repeated it to me as an order.

I returned to my class, taught for ten more minutes, then gave assignments for the following morning as if I would be there and saw the children file off. After all but one were gone, that one, a little girl, helped me to pile up the books and posters and pictures with which I had tried to fill the room. It took an hour to get everything out, and when it was all in my car, it filled up the back seat and the space behind it and the floor, as well as the floor and half the seat in front. Outside my car, on the sidewalk, I said goodbye to this one child and told her that I would not be back again. I told her I had had a disagreement with the Principal and I asked her to say goodbye to the other children. I regretted very much now that I had not disobeyed the Principal's last order and I wished that I could have had one final chance to speak to all my pupils. The little girl, in any case, took what I had said with great solemnity and promised that she would relay my message to the other children. Then I left the school.

The next morning, an official who had charge of my case at the School Department contradicted the Principal by telling me that I was being fired at her wish. The woman to whom I spoke said the reason was the use of the poem by Langston Hughes, which was punishable because it was not in the Course of Study. She also said something to me at the time that had never been said to me before, and something that represented a much harder line on curriculum innovation than I had ever seen in print. No literature, she said, which is not in the Course of Study can *ever* be read by a Boston teacher without permission from someone higher up. When I asked her about this in more detail, she said further that no poem, anyway, by any Negro author can be considered permissible if it involves suffering. I thought this a very strong statement and I asked her several times again if that was really what she meant. She insisted that it was.

I asked if there would be many good poems left to read by such a standard. Wouldn't it rule out almost all great Negro literature? Her answer evaded the issue. No poetry that described suffering was felt to be suitable. The only Negro poetry that could be read in the Boston schools, she indicated, must fit a certain kind of standard or canon. The kind of poem she meant, she said by example, might be a poem that "accentuates the positive," or "describes nature" or "tells of something hopeful." Nothing was wanted of suffering, nothing that could be painful, nothing that might involve its reader in a moment of self-questioning or worry. If this is an extremely conservative or eccentric viewpoint, I think that it is nonetheless something which has to be taken seriously. For an opinion put forward in the privacy of her office by a School Department official who has the kind of authority that the woman had must be taken to represent a certain segment of educational opinion within the Boston school system, and, in some ways, it seems more representative even than the carefully written and carefully prepared essays of such a lady as the Deputy Superintendent. For in those various writings, Miss Sullivan unquestionably has had one ear tuned to the way they were going to come across in print and sound in public, whereas, in the office of a central bureaucratic person such as the lady with whom I now was talking, you receive an absolutely innocent and unedited experience in what a school system really feels and believes.

The same official went on a few minutes later to tell me that, in addition to having made the mistake of reading the wrong poem, I also had made an error by bringing in books to school from the Cambridge Public Library. When I told her that there were no books for reading in our classroom, except for the sets of antiquated readers, and that the need of the children was for individual reading which they would be able to begin without delay, she told me that that was all very well, but still this was the Boston school system, and that meant that you must not use a book that the Cambridge Library supplied. She also advised me, in answer to my question, that any complaint from a parent means automatic dismissal of a teacher anyway, and that this, in itself, was therefore sufficient grounds for my release. When I repeated this later to some Negro parents, they were embittered and startled. For they told me of many instances in which they had complained that a teacher whipped their child black and blue or called him a nigger openly, and yet the teacher had not been released. It seemed obvious to them, as it seems to me, and would to anyone, that a complaint from a white police officer carries more weight in the Boston school system than the complaint of the mother of a Negro child.

I asked this official finally whether I had been considered a good teacher and what rating I had been given. She answered that she was not allowed to tell me. An instant later, whimsically reversing herself, she opened her files and told me that my rating was good. The last thing she said was that deviation from a prescribed curriculum was a serious offense and that I would never be permitted to teach in Boston again. The words she used were these: "You're out. You cannot teach in the Boston schools again. If you want to teach, why don't you try a private school someday?" I left her office, but before I left the building, I stopped at a table and I took out a pad of paper and wrote down what she had said.

The firing of a "provisional teacher" from a large public school system is not generally much of an event. As Mr. Ohrenberger was to say later, it happens commonly.

When the firing is attributed to something as socially relevant and dramatically specific as a single poem by a well-known Negro poet, however, it is not apt to go unnoticed; and, in this case, I was not ready to let it go unnoticed. I telephoned one of the civil rights leaders of Roxbury and told him what had happened. He urged me to call Phyllis Ryan, press spokesman for the Boston chapter of CORE. Mrs. Ryan decided to set up a press conference for the same day. That afternoon, sitting at the side of the Negro minister who had begun and carried on a lonely vigil for so many days outside the Boston School Committee, I described what had just happened.

The reaction of the reporters seemed, for the most part, as astonished as my own, and the direct consequence of this was that Miss Sullivan and Mr. Ohrenberger were obliged in a hurry, and without checking carefully, to back up the assertions of their own subordinates. The consequences of this, in turn, was that both of them allowed themselves to repeat and to magnify misstatements. Mr. Ohrenberger came out with a statement that I had been "repeatedly warned" about deviation from the Course of Study. Miss Sullivan's statement on my dismissal was much the same as Mr. Ohrenberger's, adding, however, a general admonition about the dangers of reading to Negro children poems written in bad grammar. Although Langston Hughes "has written much beautiful poetry," she said, "we cannot give directives to the teachers to use literature written in native dialects." It was at this time that she also made the statement to which I have alluded earlier: "We are trying to break the speech patterns of these children, trying to get them to speak properly. This poem does not present correct grammatical expression and would just entrench the speech patterns we want to break." I felt it was a grim statement.

The reactions of a large number of private individuals were recounted in the press during the following weeks, and some of them gave me a better feeling about the city in which I grew up than I had ever had before. One school employee who asked, for his safety, to remain anonymous, gave a statement to the press in which he reported that the atmosphere at school on the civil rights subject was like the atmosphere of a Gestapo. I believe that the person in question was a teacher in my school, but the fact that he had felt it necessary to keep his name anonymous, and his position unspecified, made his statement even more revelatory than if his name and position had appeared.

Another thing that reassured me was the reaction of the parents of the children in my class and in the school. I did not have any means of contacting them directly, but dozens of CORE members went out into the neighborhood, knocked at doors, and told parents very simply that a teacher had been fired for reading their children a good poem written by a Negro. A meeting was called by the chairman of the parent group, a woman of great poise and courage, and the parents asked me if I would come to that meeting and describe for them what had gone on. I arrived at it late and I was reluctant to go inside, but when I did go in, I found one of the most impressive parent groups that I had ever seen gathered in one hall. Instead of ten or eleven or twelve or fifteen or even twenty or thirty, which was the number of parents that usually could be rallied for a meeting on any ordinary occasion during the year, there were in the church building close to two hundred people, and I discovered that several of my pupils were in the audience as well as over half the parents of the children in my class.

I do not want to describe all the things that were said that night, what statements of strong loyalty came forward from those mothers and fathers, or how they developed, step by step, the plan of protest which they would put into effect on the following morning and which was to be the subject of intensive press attention for a good many days to come. Looking back on it, I am sure that it was one of the most important and most valuable and most straightforward moments in my life. A white woman who was present, and who has observed race relations in Roxbury for a long while, said to me after the meeting: "I hope that you understand what happened tonight between you and those parents. Very few white people in all of their lives are ever going to be given that kind of tribute. You can do anything in your life—and I don't know what plans you have. But you will never have a better reason to feel proud."

I believed that what she said was true. It is hard to imagine that any other event in my life can matter more.

In the days after that meeting, there were a number of demonstrations at the school, which had a disruptive effect on certain classes. Whether this is a good thing or a bad thing, many people may not be sure. The question is whether it is a real loss to miss one or two or even three or four days of school when none of the days that you are spending in school is worth much anyway. The Art and Reading Teachers, as well as many of the other older teachers, I was told, went on teaching and talking and grading as if in total oblivion of the turmoil breaking all around them and as if they had no idea that anything out of the ordinary might be going on. On the Monday after my firing, the parents of many students in my class kept their children home from school and went up to sit all day at their children's desks themselves. The action brought the Deputy Superintendent to the school building, and she cajoled and pleaded with the parents to give up their protest but, for once perhaps in her career, diplomacy of that type just did not work. Although the parents consented at least to leave the building at her request, they did not give up the demonstration and they returned to the school two days later to carry out a longer and larger protest. At length, it took a member of the School Committee, Mr. Eisenstadt, to persuade the parents to give up their sit-in at the school. He achieved this purpose by promising them a thorough investigation into the entire matter. Before he began the investigation, however, he told me on the telephone and he told the press as well that he felt the firing was completely justified. His announcement of such a prejudgment, along with his expressed intention to investigate anyway, seemed to me to place him in an ambiguous position, and I did not therefore expect a great deal from the investigation he now was about to undertake.

NAACP BOSTON BRANCH, STATEMENT TO THE BOSTON SCHOOL COMMITTEE, JUNE 11, 1963

Ruth Batson, who was the Chairman of the Education Committee of the NAACP, Boston Branch, in 1963, is currently completing her own history of the desegregation of the Boston Public Schools. In 1963, Batson was a well-known community and civil rights leader who was part of a group that steadily challenged the inequality and the poor education offered to the children of Boston's small African-American community. The statement speaks for itself.

Madame Chairman, Members of the Boston School Committee:

The National Association for the Advancement of Colored People is an organization dedicated to the elimination of discrimination and prejudice from all phases of American life. Our goal is First-Class Citizenship, and we will settle for nothing less. All immigrants to the American shores have suffered from discrimination, but in most cases, as soon as they lost their identifying accents, they were able to blend into the American culture and enjoy the fruits of our democratic system. The Negro, brought here in chains, bears visible identification of his race, and we have spent our lives tearing down wall after wall of resistance raised in our path, because of our color.

One of the most frustrating and devastating obstacles confronting us is the lack of educational opportunity. Education constitutes our strongest hope for pulling ourselves out of the inferior status to which society has assigned us. For a boy of eight or nine years, who is receiving an inferior education today, will feel the effects at age thirty-five, forty-five, and until he dies, as he struggles, as a father, to rear and educate his children. His lack of educational opportunity will make it impossible for him to motivate his children properly, and thus, this burden is inherited by each succeeding generation. Since, you, our School Committee, are the caretakers of our educational school system, a job which each of you sought voluntarily, we are here tonight to express our dissatisfaction, to air our complaints, and to make certain demands in connection with our schools.

I know that the word *demand* is a word that is disliked by many public officials, but I am afraid that it is too late for pleading, begging, requesting, or even reasoning. The NAACP's concern with the plight of Negro pupils in the Boston schools is of long duration. Please allow me a few minutes to review. Several years ago, because of many complaints of a varying nature from parents, I received permission from the then superintendent, Dr. Haley, to visit and interview certain principals. I interviewed six principals of predominantly Negro schools. Three of these principals refused to acknowledge the existence of any problems. They tossed off the complaints parents had made and, in general, inferred that the NAACP was making a "mountain out of a molehill." One principal acknowledged that it could be true that his graduates, 99 percent Negro, might have difficulty in high school when competing with students from all over Boston, because, he stated, "Negroes do not make their kids learn." He said further that we should be like Jewish parents, who see that their children learn. Another principal told me that she just didn't think that Negroes could learn at the same rate as white children. She had just left a school in Roslindale which was an all-white school, and felt that she could come to this conclusion. Another principal, very pleasant and affable, said that he saw no differences in children, and that he was sure that his attitude was reflected in his staff. Time has proven that this rather nonchalant attitude did not produce the results desired by the complaining parents.

We are here because the claim from the community is too anxious to be ignored, the dissatisfaction and complaints too genuine and deep-seated to be passed over lightly, and the injustices present in our school system hurt our pride, rob us of our dignity, and produce results which are injuries not only to our future, but to that of our city, our commonwealth, and our nation.

Paul Parks, a member of the Education Committee of the NAACP, has produced certain facts that call for serious attention. Mr. Parks' research brings out that there are 13 schools in Boston with predominantly Negro populations. The youngest of these buildings was built in 1937. The rest were built in 1932, 1912, 1910, 1909, 1922, 1906, 1900, 1870, and 1868. According to the Sargent Report of May 1962, at least four of these buildings have been recommended to be abandoned because of health and safety reasons. Eight have been recommended to be renovated in order to meet present educational requirements.

We then make this charge . . . There is segregation in fact in our Boston Public School System. To be sure, the May 17, 1954 Supreme Court decision dealt with deliberate segregation, but there can be no misinterpretation of the language used in that decision which stated that the "separation of children solely on the basis of race generates a feeling of inferiority that may affect their hearts and minds in a way unlikely ever to be undone." The steady migration of Negroes to Boston has intensified this problem. The 1960 census showed a total Negro population of 112,000. 63,000 of that total live in Boston, and 57,000 live in the Roxbury-Dorchester section of Boston. Our schools' population as of last Spring was 93,000, and of that, approximately 14,000 are Negroes.

The NAACP's position on northern school segregation is clear . . . We must work to reduce and eliminate school segregation wherever it exists. In the discussions of segregation in fact in our public schools, we do not accept residential segregation as an excuse for countenancing this situation. We feel that it is the responsibility of school officials to take an affirmative and positive stand on the side of the best possible education for all children. This "best possible education" is not possible where segregation exists. Inadequate educational standards, unequal facilities, and discriminatory educational practices exist wherever there is school segregation.

Therefore, we state that it is imperative that the Boston School Committee take immediate steps to eliminate and reduce segregation from our school system. We recognize that some of the methods advised pose problems when related to younger children; therefore, we recommend that the immediate concentration be centered on our Jr. High Schools. There should be a review of the Open Enrollment plan which would allow transfers without the present limitations. This plan should be accompanied by rezoning designed deliberately to integrate our schools. Site selections and additions to existing school buildings must be planned to achieve integration. Segregation in fact is a problem existing in all urban communities today. This problem must be acknowledged and faced up to by all citizens and public officials. . . .

The unjust conditions created by segregation should also come under our scrutiny tonight. There are many conditions that must be corrected as we move forward to give to Negro students what rightfully belongs to them.

We are indebted to the many known and unknown dedicated principals and teachers who have seen their duty clearly and have performed in the true spirit of their profession. We acknowledge and honor their presence in our system. However, too many others approach the Negro schools with their minds poisoned by stereotyped, preconceived notions of Negro people. They believe that Negroes are lazy, stupid, and inferior. This attitude does not go unnoticed by the youngest Negro child . . . for at an early age, our youngest become skilled in their ability to recognize prejudice. This recognition is always accompanied by resentment, hostility, and a feeling of humiliation. This is an unhealthy situation which cannot create an atmosphere in which the teacher is at his or her best, or where the child can perform at his highest level. We realize that teachers in these schools do teach under difficult conditions, and these conditions should be remedied in order to encourage teachers not only to remain in these districts, but to improve the quality of their teaching. Training programs should be expanded to establish a liaison between the school administration and colleges from which we get our teachers so that they can start their teaching careers able to distinguish myth from reality. Such a program should create an understanding of the child in congested Negro school districts, which would be [an] invaluable aid to well-meaning teachers who want to do a good job wherever they are assigned.

We also urge that permanent teachers be assigned to grades 1–3 and that the size of these classes be reduced to 25. I know that it is not necessary to stress the importance of a good beginning. Our teachers should have at their disposal sufficient supplies . . . books and other materials.

We should use books and other visual aids that include illustrations of people of all races. To use material depicting only white people is unrealistic in today's world. Please do not minimize the importance of this statement. It is important that the Negro child see recognition of himself as a person of worth, and it is important that the white child see people of other races in a positive setting. This material is available and is being used in other school systems.

The statement often made by school officials to refute charges of discrimination—that we have a uniform curriculum—concerns thoughtful people. We know that needs vary from district to district. We know that many of our predominantly Negro schools are located in the older, underprivileged sections of Boston. We acknowledge that many of our children come from deprived homes. Many of our parents, handicapped by lack of training or formal education, are consumed with the day-to-day struggle of just trying to make ends meet. For many reasons that go hand-in-hand with deprivation, inadequate and dilapidated overcrowded housing, discrimination, bitterness, and frustration, our schools must consider the plight of the pupil in these congested Negro areas. As a good teacher gears her program to the individual child, the school administration must gear its curriculum to the individual districts. We must have concentrated developmental reading programs in these schools in grades 1–8. In each school, the programs for the gifted and the slow learners should be expanded and taught by qualified, specially trained teachers. The needs of the average child in this setting must not be overlooked. The curriculum must be enriched to enable this child to compete in a society where the removal of the barriers of segregation will force them to compete with those who have not been handicapped as they have been.

Because ghetto living produces children with problems, we cannot emphasize too strongly the importance of the school adjustment counselors and the need for more such programs.

The vocational program should be expanded to include grade 7, and Negro children should be counseled by people who believe that America is the land of opportunity for all. To steer Negro students into certain trades or into certain training programs because the counselor believes other programs out of their reach is unfair, and this happens often in our schools. We are disturbed by the small number of our youngsters who take advantage of the cooperative programs. This, we feel, is the result of poor guidance programs, and the fact that many are discouraged from attending schools outside of their assigned school districts. This discouraging of students in the Industrial Arts courses prohibits them from gaining an entry into union and apprenticeship programs. We should see that all students, Negro and white, have the opportunity during specially observed weeks and in assemblies, to hear and see people of all races who have achieved in many fields. The value of this type of learning experience cannot be over-emphasized and should be planned. This is something that can be accomplished without affecting our school budget, and the dividends are great.

We feel that there should be no discrimination in the hiring or assigning of teachers. We take note of the fact there is no Negro school principal in our system and ask you to examine the reasons for this.

We recommend that you accept in toto the section of the Sargent Report that refers to Roxbury and North Dorchester. This portion of the survey, we feel, will achieve maximum integration in this section of Boston.

We also urge that you review the system of intelligence testing in our schools. The Boston school system mainly uses a group test to determine the intelligence and capability of a child to learn. When we realize that many of the Negro children coming to Boston are from rural communities, we feel that a group test is unfair and does not give a true picture of ability. As a result of this kind of testing, many Negro children are declared slow learners and unteachable.

We are aware of the problems confronting this school administration. We, like any citizens, are vitally concerned with good sound educational policies. Our demands tonight have centered around de facto segregation and its evil effects because we know that this issue has not been faced by Boston school officials. This issue must be dealt with, if we are to move along with the plans and blueprints that proclaim a New Boston.

In the selection of a new superintendent, we see an opportunity to tackle a problem that is facing every major Northern city today. We regret that you chose to reject the proposal of the committee to aid in your selection, but we are encouraged by Dr. Hunt's role as consultant. In all frankness, we must say that we have seen no one with the present school administration who has demonstrated knowledge or ability to help in this problem. We feel strongly that the school committee should not limit itself to any section of this nation in its quest for the right person to fill this position. We do not believe that this man has to be a super man, as indicated by a writer recently. We do believe, however, that he must be a person experienced in dealing with the problems of an urban community, who is sensitive to the needs of minority groups, who sees the community as an ally, and who is morally committed to the doctrine of the Fatherhood of God and the Brotherhood of Man.

We demand the right to discuss this selection in detail with Dr. Hunt, and we demand that every applicant be examined thoroughly in regard to his background in the area of human relations. It might seem that we have placed the entire responsibility for the solving of these problems on your shoulders. Let me say that the community is also concerned and stands ready to work along with you. The school administration and the community must join forces [to] erase the faulty image they have of each other and work together if we are to be successful. You might question the ability of the community to rise to the occasion, and I answer that just as we rise to the occasion to pay our taxes (for which we get small return) . . . we will rise to the occasion to see that our children are no longer shortchanged in the education they receive.

Ruth Batson, Chairman, Education Committee
NAACP, Boston Branch

Elizabeth Price, Barbara Erna Ballantyne, Melvin King, Paul Parks

CHAPTER 10

❧

RIGHTS AND OPPORTUNITIES IN AMERICAN EDUCATION, 1965-1980

Introduction

The initial focus of the civil rights movement in schools was on school integration and quality education for African-American children. In time, however, the movement affected wider and wider spheres of activity. By the mid-1960s, and for the decade that followed, few Americans were unaffected by the civil rights movement, and fewer still lacked opinions, positive or negative, on these developments. Civil rights leaders properly remind members of other groups that many of the rights won during the 1960s and 1970s were won first through the civil rights movement and only later expanded to include a wider circle of citizens.

The federal government became a major player in school reform as part of Lyndon Johnson's War on Poverty. Of course, the War on Poverty was itself a direct outgrowth of the civil rights movement. If not for the pressure of civil rights activities all across the country, it is doubtful that either the president or Congress would have initiated the Great Society programs, including dramatically expanded federal aid to education. Johnson's speeches as he proposed and, three months later, signed the Elementary and Secondary Education Act of 1965 reveal the change of thinking that occurred as a result of civil rights activism.

As the 1960s wore on, the war in Vietnam came to overshadow all other aspects of the times. Schools were not exempt from the firestorm that swept the land. While the most significant antiwar demonstrations took place on college campuses, high schools—and even elementary schools—were not immune. The case of *Tinker v.*

Des Moines Independent Community District is particularly noted in legal history for its significance in expanding the rights of high school students. The specific issue involved three young people who wore black armbands to their schools in Des Moines, Iowa to protest the war. Reading the case, one gains a sense of the changing educational scene in the late 1960s, as well as of the divided judicial—and national—views on how society should respond to these changes.

Following the civil rights movement, which focused largely on African Americans, many other groups also began to demand their rights in society and in the schools. While women of all races, Latinos, and American Indians had certainly fought for their rights throughout American history, they had been relatively quiet during the post-World War II era. The civil rights movement sparked them to life again. Earlier documents in this book revealed the expanded roles women filled as they entered the teaching profession in large numbers early in the nineteenth century. Many women teachers in the turn-of-the-twentieth-century progressive era became militant advocates for their right to have input in the schools where they taught as well as just compensation for their efforts. Nineteenth-century American Indians fought wars and resisted the efforts of European-American soldiers and missionaries to school them in the ways of an alien culture. During the 1960s and 1970s, they and other previously marginalized groups in American society initiated a dramatic resurgence of militancy and successful advocacy. While none of the groups won total victories, and American schools and the larger society remained discriminatory in many ways, some very significant changes were won during these years. The documents included here describe some of the changes of these dramatic years, including:

- Title IX of the Elementary and Secondary Education Act, added in 1972, which expanded opportunities for women and girls in schools by requiring any educational institution that received federal money—by 1972, virtually all schools in the country—to provide equal resources and opportunities for women.
- Public Law 94–142, which provided equality of opportunity for students with disabilities. While never enforced to the satisfaction of its advocates, PL 94–142 and similar state legislation ended the virtual exclusion of students with mental or physical disabilities from American schools.
- The community control movement developed among many groups in many different parts of the country. The example provided here—in which Chicago's Mexican-American community successfully demanded a far greater level of autonomy in running their schools—is just one of many possible examples. While the New York City Public schools were virtually paralyzed by the issue during the 1968–69 school year, they were not alone: community control struggles were taking place in many places.
- One of the most dramatic examples of expanded civil rights and community control occurred within the American Indian community. The federally funded but Navajo-controlled Rough Rock Demonstration School remains a model of self-directed education.

Many more worthy examples exist, but these four should provide a flavor of the times.

THE ELEMENTARY AND SECONDARY EDUCATION ACT AND THE GREAT SOCIETY, 1965

The civil rights movement had a significant impact on federal legislation in the 1960s. Soon after his inauguration in 1961, John F. Kennedy began to lobby for a federal role in improving the nation's schools. However, it was Kennedy's successor, Lyndon B. Johnson, who called for a national "War on Poverty," and who coined the phrase "The Great Society" for his wide-reaching social program. Johnson believed that education was the key to improved economic opportunity. As the president never tired of saying, "Poverty has many roots, but the tap root is ignorance." Improved schooling was thus the key to the whole effort.

The Kennedy-Johnson commitment to ending poverty and improving schools did not spring from nothing. The civil rights movement exerted one of the strongest influences on presidential policies and decisions during the 1960s. Moreover, Lyndon Johnson had begun his career as a schoolteacher in rural Texas. He brought a personal passion to the debate, as is evidenced in the two speeches that follow. By the mid-1960s, Johnson was advocating a significant national effort to improve the educational experience of every citizen in a way no president before—or since—has done. Johnson's initial Special Message to Congress, "Toward Full Educational Opportunity," was submitted on January 12, 1965. He signed the act, which included all of the major provisions he had requested, on April 11 of the same year—just three months later, with a speed rarely seen in federal legislation.

Lyndon B. Johnson, Towards Full Educational Opportunity, January 12, 1965

To the Congress of the United States:

In 1787, the Continental Congress declared in the Northwest Ordinance: "schools and the means of education shall forever be encouraged."

America is strong and prosperous and free because for one hundred and seventy eight years, we have honored that commitment.

In the United States today:

- One quarter of all Americans are in the nation's classroom.
- High school attendance has grown 18-fold since the turn of the century—6 times as fast as the population.
- College enrollment has advanced 80-fold. Americans today support a fourth of the world's institutions of higher learning and a third of its professors and college students.

In the life of the individual, education is always an unfinished task.

And in the life of this nation, the advancement of education is a continuing challenge.

There is a darker side to education in America;

- One student in every three now in the fifth grade will drop out before finishing high school—if the present rate continues.

- Almost a million young people will continue to quit school each year—if our schools fail to stimulate their desire to learn.
- Over one hundred thousand of our brightest high school graduates each year will not go to college—and many others will leave college—if the opportunity for higher education is not expanded.

The cost of this neglect runs high—both for the youth and the nation.

- Unemployment of young people with an eighth grade education or less is four times the national average.
- Jobs filled by high school graduates rose by 40 percent in the last ten years. Jobs for those with less schooling decreased by nearly 10 percent.

We can measure the cost in even starker terms. We now spend about $450 a year per child in our public schools. But we spend $1,800 a year to keep a delinquent youth in a detention home, $2,500 a year for a family on relief, $3,500 a year for a criminal in state prison.

The growing numbers of young people reaching school age demand that we move swiftly even to stand still.

- Attendance in elementary and secondary schools will increase by 4 million in the next five years; 400,000 new classrooms will be needed to meet this growth. But almost 1/2 million of the nation's existing classrooms are already more than 30 years old.
- The post-World War II boom in babies has now reached college age. And by 1970, our colleges must be prepared to add 50 percent more enrollment to their presently overcrowded facilities.

In the past, Congress has supported an increasing commitment to education in America. Last year, I signed historic measures passed by the Eighty-eighth Congress to provide:

- facilities badly needed by universities, colleges, and community colleges;
- major new resources for vocational training;
- more loans and fellowships for students enrolled in higher education;
- enlarged and improved training for physicians, dentists, and nurses.

I propose that the Eighty-ninth Congress join me in extending the commitment still further. I propose that we declare a national goal of *Full Educational Opportunity*.

Every child must be encouraged to get as much education as he has the ability to take.

We want this not only for his sake—but for the nation's sake.

Nothing matters more to the future of our country: not our military preparedness—for armed might is worthless if we lack the brain power to build a world of peace; not our productive economy—for we cannot sustain growth without trained manpower; not our democratic system of government—for freedom is fragile if citizens are ignorant.

We must demand that our schools increase not only the quantity but the quality of America's education. For we recognize that nuclear-age problems cannot be solved with horse-and-buggy learning. The *three R's* of our school system must be supported by the three T's—*teachers* who are superior, *techniques* of instruction that are modern, and *thinking* about education which places it first in all our plans and hopes.

Specifically, four major tasks confront us:

- to bring better education to millions of disadvantaged youth who need it most;
- to put the best educational equipment and ideas and innovations within reach of all students;
- to advance the technology of teaching and the training of teachers;
- to provide incentives for those who wish to learn at every stage along the road to learning.

Our program must match the magnitude of these tasks. The budget on education which I request for fiscal year 1966 will contain a total of $4.1 billion. This includes $1.1 billion to finance programs established by the Eighty-eighth Congress. I will submit a request for $1.5 billion in new obligational authority to finance the programs described in this message. This expenditure is a small price to pay for developing our nation's most priceless resource.

In all that we do, we mean to strengthen our state and community education systems. Federal assistance does not mean federal control—as past programs have proven. The late Senator Robert Taft declared: "Education is primarily a state function—but in the field of education, as in the fields of health, relief, and medical care, the Federal Government has a secondary obligation to see that there is a basic floor under those essential services for all adults and children in the United States."

In this spirit, I urge that we now push ahead with the number one business of the American people—the education of our youth in preschools, elementary and secondary schools, and in the colleges and universities.

Lyndon B. Johnson, Remarks in Johnson City, Texas, upon Signing the Elementary and Secondary Education Bill, April 11, 1965

For too long, political acrimony held up our progress. For too long, children suffered while jarring interests caused stalemate in the efforts to improve our schools. Since 1946, Congress tried repeatedly, and failed repeatedly, to enact measures for elementary and secondary education.

Now, within the past 3 weeks, the House of Representatives, by a vote of 263 to 153, and the Senate, by a vote of 73 to 18, have passed the most sweeping educational bill ever to come before Congress. It represents a major new commitment of the Federal Government to quality and equality in the schooling that we offer our young people. I predict that all of those of both parties of Congress who supported the enactment of this legislation will be remembered in history as men and women who began a new day of greatness in American society.

By passing this bill, we bridge the gap between helplessness and hope for more than 5 million educationally deprived children.

We put into the hands of our youth more than 30 million new books, and into many of our schools their first libraries.

We reduce the terrible time lag in bringing new teaching techniques into the nation's classrooms.

We strengthen state and local agencies which bear the burden and the challenge of better education.

And we rekindle the revolution—the revolution of the spirit against the tyranny of ignorance.

As a son of a tenant farmer, I know that education is the only valid passport from poverty.

As a former teacher—and, I hope, a future one—I have great expectations of what this law will mean for all of our young people.

As President of the United States, I believe deeply no law I have signed or will ever sign means more to the future of America.

To each and every one who contributed to this day, the nation is indebted.

Supreme Court of the United States, Tinker, et al. v. Des Moines Independent Community School District, 1969

While the U. S. Supreme Court had dealt with a number of cases, dating back to the 1940s, having to do with the free speech rights of teachers and professional staff in schools, few similar cases had been heard in the courts regarding students' rights. It is not surprising that the student protests of the late 1960s would create new legal precedents. In this case, three students, with the support of their parents, wore black armbands to school to protest the war in Vietnam. They did this in spite of the fact that the school district, fearing such a protest, had recently declared armbands against school rules, warning that any student who wore one would be asked to remove it and, if he or she refused to do so, they would be suspended. The three students refused to remove their armbands and the school district suspended them. The federal District Court ruled in favor of the school district. In the opinion provided here, the Supreme Court sided with the students, seven to two. The divided opinions of the justices provide an especially valuable window into their thinking on several issues, including the rights of students to speak their minds in school.

Mr. Justice Fortas delivered the opinion of the Court.

Petitioner John F. Tinker, fifteen years old, and petitioner Christopher Eckhardt, sixteen years old, attended high schools in Des Moines, Iowa. Petitioner Mary Beth Tinker, John's sister, was a thirteen-year-old student in junior high school.

In December 1965, a group of adults and students in Des Moines held a meeting at the Eckhardt home. The group determined to publicize their objections to the hostilities in Vietnam and their support for a truce by wearing black armbands during the holiday season and by fasting on December 16 and New Year's Eve. Petitioners and their parents had previously engaged in similar activities, and they decided to participate in the program.

The principals of the Des Moines schools became aware of the plan to wear armbands. On December 14, 1965, they met and adopted a policy that any student wearing an armband to school would be asked to remove it, and if he refused he would be suspended until he returned without the armband. Petitioners were aware of the regulation that the school authorities adopted.

On December 16, Mary Beth and Christopher wore black armbands to their schools. John Tinker wore his armband the next day. They were all sent home and suspended from school until they would come back without their armbands. They did not return to school until after the planned period for wearing armbands had expired—that is, until after New Year's Day.

This complaint was filed in the United States District Court by petitioners, through their fathers, under section 1983 of Title 42 of the United States Code. It prayed for an injunction restraining the respondent school officials and the respondent members of the board of directors of the school district from disciplining the petitioners, and it sought nominal damages. After an evidentiary hearing, the District Court dismissed the complaint. It upheld the constitutionality of the school authorities' action on the ground that it was reasonable in order to prevent disturbance of school discipline. 258 F. Supp. 971 (1966). The court referred to but expressly declined to follow the Fifth Circuit's holding in a similar case that the wearing of symbols like the armbands cannot be prohibited unless it "materially and substantially interfere[s] with the requirements of appropriate discipline in the operation of the school." *Burnside v. Byars,* 363 F. 2d 744, 749 (1966).

On appeal, the Court of Appeals for the Eighth Circuit considered the case *en banc.* The court was equally divided, and the District Court's decision was accordingly affirmed, without opinion. 383 F. 2d 988 (1967). We granted certiorari. 390 U.S. 942 (1968).

The District Court recognized that the wearing of an armband for the purpose of expressing certain views is the type of symbolic act that is within the Free Speech Clause of the First Amendment. See *West Virginia v. Barnette,* 319 U.S. 624 (1943); *Stromberg v. California,* 283 U.S. 359 (1931). *Cf. Thornhill v. Alabama,* 310 U.S. 88 (1940); *Edwards v. South Carolina,* 373 U.S. 229 (1963); *Brown v. Louisiana,* 383 U.S. 131 (1966). As we shall discuss, the wearing of armbands in the circumstances of this case was entirely divorced from actually or potentially disruptive conduct by those participating in it. It was closely akin to "pure speech" which, we have repeatedly held, is entitled to comprehensive protection under the First Amendment. *Cf. Cox v. Louisiana,* 379 U.S. 536, 555 (1965); *Adderley v. Florida,* 385 U.S. 39 (1966).

First Amendment rights, applied in light of the special characteristics of the school environment, are available to teachers and students. It can hardly be argued that either students or teachers shed their constitutional rights to freedom of speech or expression at the schoolhouse gate. This has been the unmistakable holding of this court for almost fifty years. In *Meyer v. Nebraska,* 262 U.S. 390 (1923), and *Bartels v. Iowa,* 262 U.S. 404 (1923), this Court, in opinions by Mr. Justice McReynolds, held that the Due Process Clause of the Fourteenth Amendment prevents States from forbidding the teaching of a foreign language to young students. Statutes to this effect, the Court held, unconstitutionally interfere with the liberty of teacher, student, and parent. See also *Pierce v. Society of Sisters,* 268 U.S. 510 [*507] (1925); *West Virginia v. Barnette,* 319 U.S. 624 (1943); *McCollum v. Board of Education,* 333 U.S. 203 (1948); *Wieman v. Updegraff,* 344 U.S. 183, 195 (1952) (concurring opinion); *Sweezy v. New Hampshire,* 354 U.S. 234 (1957); *Shelton v. Tucker,* 364 U.S. 479, 487 (1960); *Engel v. Vitale,* 370 U.S. 421 (1962); *Keyishian v. Board of Regents,* 385 U.S. 589, 603 (1967); *Epperson v. Arkansas, ante,* p. 97 (1968).

In *West Virginia v. Barnette, supra,* this Court held that under the First Amendment, the student in public school may not be compelled to salute the flag. Speaking through Mr. Justice Jackson, the Court said:

"The Fourteenth Amendment, as now applied to the States, protects the citizen against the State itself and all of its creatures—Boards of Education not excepted. These have, of course, important, delicate, and highly discretionary functions, but none that they may not perform within the limits of the Bill of Rights. That they are educating the young for citizenship is reason for scrupulous protection of Constitutional freedoms of the individual, if we are not to strangle the free mind at its source and teach youth to discount important principles of our government as mere platitudes." 319 U.S. at 637.

On the other hand, the Court has repeatedly emphasized the need for affirming the comprehensive authority of the States and of school officials, consistent with fundamental constitutional safeguards, to prescribe and control conduct in the schools. See *Epperson v. Arkansas, supra,* at 104; *Meyer v. Nebraska, supra,* at 402. Our problem lies in the area where students in the exercise of the First Amendment rights collide with the rules of the school authorities.

The problem posed by the present case does not relate to regulation of the length of skirts or the type of clothing, to hair style, or deportment. *Cf. Ferrell v. Dallas Independent School District*, 392 F. 2d 697 (1968); *Pugsley v. Sellmeyer,* 158 Ark. 247, 250 S. W. 538 (1923). It does not concern aggressive, disruptive action or even group demonstrations. Our problem involves direct, primary First Amendment rights akin to "pure speech."

The school officials banned and sought to punish petitioners for a silent, passive expression of opinion, unaccompanied by any disorder or disturbance on the part of petitioners. There is here no evidence whatever of petitioners' interference, actual or nascent, with the schools' work or of collision with the rights of other students to be secure and to be let alone. Accordingly, this case does not concern speech or action that intrudes upon the work of the schools or the rights of other students.

Only a few of the 18,000 students in the school system wore the black armbands. Only five students were suspended for wearing them. There is no indication that the work of the schools or any class was disrupted. Outside the classrooms, a few students made hostile remarks to the children wearing armbands, but there were no threats or acts of violence on school premises. The District Court concluded that the action of the school authorities was reasonable because it was based upon their fear of a disturbance from the wearing of the armbands. But, in our system, undifferentiated fear or apprehension of disturbance is not enough to overcome the right to freedom of expression. Any departure from absolute regimentation may cause trouble. Any variation from the majority's opinion may inspire fear. Any word spoken, in class, in the lunchroom, or on the campus, that deviates from the views of another person may start an argument or cause a disturbance. But our Constitution says we must take this risk, *Terminiello v. Chicago,* 337 U.S. 1 (1949); and our history says that it is this sort of hazardous freedom— this kind of openness—that is the basis of our national strength and of the independence and vigor of Americans who grow up and live in this relatively permissive, often disputatious, society.

In order for the State in the person of school officials to justify prohibition of a particular expression of opinion, it must be able to show that its action was caused by something more than a mere desire to avoid the discomfort and unpleasantness that always accompany an unpopular viewpoint. Certainly where there is no finding and no showing that engaging in the forbidden conduct would "materially and substantially interfere with the requirements of appropriate discipline in the operation of the school," the prohibition cannot be sustained. *Burnside v. Byars, supra,* at 749.

In the present case, the District Court made no such finding, and our independent examination of the record fails to yield evidence that the school authorities had reason to anticipate that the wearing of the armbands would substantially interfere with the work of the school or impinge upon the rights of other students. Even an official memorandum prepared after the suspension that listed the reasons for the ban on wearing the armbands made no reference to the anticipation of such disruption.

On the contrary, the action of the school authorities appears to have been based upon an urgent wish to avoid the controversy which might result from the expression, even by the silent symbol of armbands, of opposition to this Nation's part in the conflagration in Vietnam. It is revealing, in this respect, that the meeting at which the school principals decided to issue the contested regulation was called in response to a student's statement to the journalism teacher in one of the schools that he wanted to write an article on Vietnam and have it published in the school paper. (The student was dissuaded.)

It is also relevant that the school authorities did not purport to prohibit the wearing of all symbols of political or controversial significance. The record shows that students in some of the schools wore buttons relating to national political campaigns, and some even wore the Iron Cross, traditionally a symbol of Nazism. The order prohibiting the wearing of armbands did not extend to these. Instead, a particular symbol— black armbands worn to exhibit opposition to this Nation's involvement in Vietnam— was singled out for prohibition. Clearly, the prohibition of expression of one particular opinion, at least without evidence that it is necessary to avoid material and substantial interference with schoolwork or discipline, is not constitutionally permissible.

In our system, state-operated schools may not be enclaves of totalitarianism. School officials do not possess absolute authority over their students. Students in school as well as out of school are "persons" under our Constitution. They are possessed of fundamental rights which the State must respect, just as they themselves must respect their obligations to the State. In our system, students may not be regarded as closed-circuit recipients of only that which the State chooses to communicate. They may not be confined to the expression of those sentiments that are officially approved. In the absence of a specific showing of constitutionally valid reasons to regulate their speech, students are entitled to freedom of expression of their views. As Judge Gewin, speaking for the Fifth Circuit, said, school officials cannot suppress "expressions of feelings with which they do not wish to contend." *Burnside v. Byars, supra,* at 749.

In *Meyer v. Nebraska, supra,* at 402, Mr. Justice McReynolds expressed this Nation's repudiation of the principle that a State might so conduct its schools as to "foster a homogeneous people." He said:

"In order to submerge the individual and develop ideal citizens, Sparta assembled the males at seven into barracks and intrusted their subsequent education and training to official guardians. Although such measures have been deliberately approved by men of great genius, their ideas touching the relation between individual and State were wholly different from those upon which our institutions rest; and it hardly will be affirmed that any legislature could impose such restrictions upon the people of a State without doing violence to both letter and spirit of the Constitution."

This principle has been repeated by this Court on numerous occasions during the intervening years. In *Keyishian v. Board of Regents,* 385 U.S. 589, 603, Mr. Justice Brennan, speaking for the Court, said:

"The vigilant protection of constitutional freedom is nowhere more vital than in the community of American schools. *Shelton v. Tucker* [364 U.S. 479], at 487. The classroom is peculiarly the 'marketplace of ideas.' The Nation's future depends upon leaders trained through wide exposure to that robust exchange of ideas which discovers truth 'out of a multitude of tongues, [rather] than through any kind of authoritative selection.'"

The principle of these cases is not confined to the supervised and ordained discussion which takes place in the classroom. The principal use to which the schools are dedicated is to accommodate students during prescribed hours for the purpose of certain types of activities. Among those activities is personal intercommunication among the students. This is not only an inevitable part of the process of attending school; it is also an important part of the educational process. A student's rights, therefore, do not embrace merely the classroom hours. When he is in the cafeteria, or on the playing field, or on the campus during the authorized hours, he may express his opinions, even on controversial subjects like the conflict in Vietnam, if he does so without "materially and substantially interfer[ing] with the requirements of appropriate discipline in the operation of the school" and without colliding with the rights of others. *Burnside v. Byars, supra,* at 749. But conduct by the student, in class or out of it, which for any reason—whether it stems from time, place, or type of behavior—materially disrupts classwork or involves substantial disorder or invasion of the rights of others is, of course, not immunized by the constitutional guarantee of freedom of speech. *Cf. Blackwell v. Issaquena County Board of Education,* 363 F. 2d 749 (C.A. 5th Cir. 1966).

In *Hammond v. South Carolina State College,* 272 F. Supp. 947 (D.C.S.C. 1967), District Judge Hemphill had before him a case involving a meeting on campus of three-hundred students to express their views on school practices. He pointed out that a school is not like a hospital or a jail enclosure. *Cf. Cox v. Louisiana,* 379 U.S. 536 (1965); *Adderley v. Florida,* 385 U.S. 39 (1966). It is a public place, and its dedication to specific uses does not imply that the constitutional rights of persons entitled to be there are to be gauged as if the premises were purely private property. *Cf. Edwards v. South Carolina,* 372 U.S. 229 (1963); *Brown v. Louisiana,* 383 U.S. 131 (1966).

Under our Constitution, free speech is not a right that is given only to be so circumscribed that it exists in principle but not in fact. Freedom of expression would not truly exist if the right could be exercised only in an area that a benevolent government has provided as a safe haven for crackpots. The Constitution says that Congress (and the States) may not abridge the right to free speech. This provision means what it says. We properly read it to permit reasonable regulation of speech-connected activities in carefully restricted circumstances. But we do not confine the permissible exercise of First Amendment rights to a telephone booth or the four corners of a pamphlet, or to supervised and ordained discussion in a school classroom.

If a regulation were adopted by school officials forbidding discussion of the Vietnam conflict, or the expression by any student of opposition to it anywhere on school property except as part of a prescribed classroom exercise, it would be obvious that the regulation would violate the constitutional rights of students, at least if it could not be justified by a showing that the students' activities would materially and substantially disrupt the work and discipline of the school. *Cf. Hammond v. South Carolina State College,* 272 F. Supp. 947 (D.C.S.C. 1967) (orderly protest meeting on state college campus); *Dickey v. Alabama State Board of Education,* 273 F. Supp. 613 (D.C.M.D. Ala. 1967) (expulsion of student editor of college newspaper). In the circumstances of the present case, the prohibition of the silent, passive "witness of the armbands," as one of the children called it, is no less offensive to the Constitution's guarantees.

As we have discussed, the record does not demonstrate any facts which might reasonably have led school authorities to forecast substantial disruption of or material interference with school activities, and no disturbances or disorders on the school premises in fact occurred. These petitioners merely went about their ordained rounds in school. Their deviation consisted only in wearing on their sleeve a band of black cloth, not more than two inches wide. They wore it to exhibit their disapproval of the Vietnam hostilities and their advocacy of a truce, to make their views known, and, by their example, to influence others to adopt them. They neither interrupted school activities nor sought to intrude in the school affairs or the lives of others. They caused discussion outside of the classrooms, but no interference with work and no disorder. In the circumstances, our Constitution does not permit officials of the State to deny their form of expression.

We express no opinion as to the form of relief which should be granted, this being a matter for the lower courts to determine. We reverse and remand for further proceedings consistent with this opinion.

Dissent: Mr. Justice Black, dissenting.

The Court's holding in this case ushers in what I deem to be an entirely new era in which the power to control pupils by the elected "officials of state-supported public schools" in the United States is in ultimate effect transferred to the Supreme Court. The Court brought this particular case here on a petition for certiorari urging that the First and Fourteenth Amendments protect the right of school pupils to express their political views all the way "from kindergarten through high school." Here the constitutional right to "political expression" asserted was a right to wear black armbands during school hours and at classes in order to demonstrate to the other students that the petitioners were mourning because of the death of United States soldiers in Vietnam and to protest that war, which they were against. Ordered to refrain from wearing the armbands in school by the elected school officials and the teachers vested with state authority to do so, apparently only seven out of the school system's eighteen-thousand pupils deliberately refused to obey the order. One defying pupil was Paul Tinker, 8 years old, who was in the second grade; another, Hope Tinker, was 11 years old and in the fifth grade; a third member of the Tinker family was 13, in the eighth grade; and a fourth member of the same family was John Tinker, 15 years old, an 11th-grade high school pupil. Their father, a Methodist minister without a church, is paid a salary by the American Friends Service Committee. Another student who defied the school order and insisted on wearing an armband in school was Christopher Eckhardt, an 11th-grade pupil and a petitioner in this case. His mother is an official in the Women's International League for Peace and Freedom.

As I read the Court's opinion, it relies upon the following grounds for holding unconstitutional the judgment of the Des Moines school officials and the two courts below. First, the Court concludes that the wearing of armbands is "symbolic speech" which is "akin to 'pure speech'" and therefore protected by the First and Fourteenth Amendments. Secondly, the Court decides that the public schools are an appropriate place to exercise "symbolic speech" as long as normal school functions are not "unreasonably" disrupted. Finally, the Court arrogates to itself, rather than to the State's elected officials charged with running the schools, the decision as to which school disciplinary regulations are "reasonable."

Assuming that the Court is correct in holding that the conduct of wearing armbands for the purpose of conveying political ideas is protected by the First Amendment, cf., e.g., *Giboney v. Empire Storage and Ice Co.,* 336 U.S. 490 (1949), the crucial remaining questions are whether students and teachers may use the schools at their whim as a platform for the exercise of free speech—"symbolic" or "pure"—and whether the courts will allocate to themselves the function of deciding how the pupils' school day will be spent. While I have always believed that under the First and Fourteenth Amendments neither the State nor the Federal Government has any authority to regulate or censor the content of speech, I have never believed that any person has a right to give speeches or engage in demonstrations where he pleases and when he pleases. This Court has already rejected such a notion. In *Cox v. Louisiana,* 379 U.S. 536, 554 (1965), for example, the Court clearly stated that the rights of free speech and assembly "do not mean that everyone with opinions or beliefs to express may address a group at any public place and at any time."

While the record does not show that any of these armband students shouted, used profane language, or were violent in any manner, detailed testimony by some of them shows their armbands caused comments, warnings by other students, the poking of fun at them, and a warning by an older football player that other, nonprotesting students had better let them alone. There is also evidence that a teacher of mathematics had his lesson period practically "wrecked" chiefly by disputes with Mary Beth Tinker, who wore her armband for her "demonstration." Even a casual reading of the record shows that this armband did divert students' minds from their regular lessons, and that talk, comments, etc., made John Tinker "self-conscious" in attending school with his armband. While the absence of obscene remarks or boisterous and loud disorder perhaps justifies the Court's statement that the few armband students did not actually "disrupt" the classwork, I think the record overwhelmingly shows that the armbands did exactly what the elected school officials and principals foresaw they would, that is, took the students' minds off their classwork and diverted them to thoughts about the highly emotional subject of the Vietnam war. And I repeat that if the time has come when pupils of state-supported schools, kindergartens, grammar schools, or high schools, can defy and flout orders of school officials to keep their minds on their own schoolwork, it is the beginning of a new revolutionary era of permissiveness in this country fostered by the judiciary. The next logical step, it appears to me, would be to hold unconstitutional laws that bar pupils under twenty-one or eighteen from voting, or from being elected members of the boards of education.

The United States District Court refused to hold that the state school order violated the First and Fourteenth Amendments. 258 F. Supp. 971. Holding that the protest was akin to speech which is protected by the First and Fourteenth Amendments, that court held that the school order was "reasonable" and hence constitutional. There was at one time a line of cases holding "reasonableness" as the Court saw it to be the test of a "due process" violation. Two cases upon which the Court today heavily relies for striking down this school order used this test of reasonableness, *Meyer vs. Nebraska,* 262 U.S. 390 (1923) and *Bartels v. Iowa,* 262 U.S. 404 (1923). The opinions in both cases were written by Mr. Justice McReynolds; Mr. Justice Holmes, who opposed this reasonableness test, dissented from the holdings, as did Mr. Justice Sutherland. This constitutional test of reasonableness prevailed in this Court for a season. It was this test that brought on President Franklin Roosevelt's well-known Court fight. His proposed legislation did not pass, but the fight left the "reasonableness" constitutional test dead on the battlefield, so much that this Court in *Ferguson v. Skrupa,* 372 U.S. 726, 729, 730, after a thorough review of the old cases, was able to conclude in 1963: "There was a time when the Due Process Clause was used by this Court to strike down laws which were thought unreasonable, that is, unwise or incompatible with some particular economic or social philosophy. . . .

"The doctrine that prevailed in *Lochner, Coppage, Adkins, Burns,* and like cases—that due process authorizes courts to hold laws unconstitutional when they believe the legislature has acted unwisely—has long since been discarded."

The *Ferguson* case totally repudiated the old reasonableness-due process test, the doctrine that judges have the power to hold laws unconstitutional upon the belief of judges that they "shock the conscience" or that they are "unreasonable," "arbitrary," "irrational," "contrary to fundamental 'decency,'" or some other such flexible term without precise boundaries. I have many times expressed my opposition to the concept on the ground that it gives judges power to strike down any law they do not like. If the majority of the Court today, by agreeing to the opinion of my brother Fortas, is resurrecting that old reasonableness-due process test, I think the constitutional change should be plainly, unequivocally, and forthrightly stated for the benefit of the bench and bar. It will be a sad day for the country, I believe, when the present-day Court returns to the McReynolds due process concept. Other cases cited by the Court do not, as implied, follow the McReynolds reasonable doctrine. *West Virginia v. Barnette,* 319 U.S. 624, clearly rejecting the "reasonableness test," held that the Fourteenth Amendment made the First applicable to the States, and that the two forbade a State to *compel* little schoolchildren to salute the United States flag when they had religious scruples against doing so. Neither *Thornhill v. Alabama,* 310 U.S. 88; *Stromberg v. California,* 283 U.S. 359; *Edwards v. South Carolina,* 372 U.S. 229; nor *Brown v. Louisiana,* 383 U.S. 131, related to schoolchildren at all, and none of these cases embraced Mr. Justice McReynolds's reasonableness test; and *Thornhill, Edwards,* and *Brown* relied on the vagueness of the state statutes under scrutiny to hold them unconstitutional. *Cox v. Louisiana,* 379 U.S. 536, 555 and *Adderley v. Florida,* 385 U.S. 39, cited by the Court as a "compare," indicating, I suppose, that these two cases are no longer the law, were not rested to the slightest extent on the *Meyer* and *Bartels* "reasonableness-due-process-McReynolds" constitutional test.

I deny, therefore, that it has been the "unmistakable holding of this Court for almost fifty years" that "students" and "teachers" take with them into the "schoolhouse gate" constitutional rights to "freedom of speech or expression." Even *Meyer* did not hold that. It makes no reference to "symbolic speech" at all; what it did was to strike down as "unreasonable" and therefore unconstitutional a Nebraska law barring the teaching of the German language before the children reached the eighth grade. One can well agree with Mr. Justice Holmes and Mr. Justice Sutherland, as I do, that such a law was no more unreasonable than it would be to bar the teaching of Latin and Greek to pupils who have not reached the eighth grade. In fact, I think the majority's reason for invalidating the Nebraska law was that it did not like it, or in legal jargon, that it "shocked the Court's conscience," "offended its sense of justice," or was "contrary to fundamental concepts of the English-speaking world," as the Court has sometimes said.

See, e.g., *Rochin v. California*, 342 U.S. 165, and *Irvine v. California*, 347 U.S. 128. The truth is that a teacher of kindergarten, grammar school, or high school pupils no more carries into a school with him a complete right to freedom of speech and expression than an anti-Catholic or anti-Semite carries with him a complete freedom of speech and religion into a Catholic church or Jewish synagogue. Nor does a person carry with him into the United States Senate or House, or into the Supreme Court, or any other court, a complete constitutional right to go into those places contrary to their rules and speak his mind on any subject he pleases. It is a myth to say that any person has a constitutional right to say what he pleases, where he pleases, and when he pleases. Our Court has decided precisely the opposite. See, *e.g., Cox v. Louisiana,* 379 U.S. 536, 555; *Adderley v. Florida*, 385 U.S. 39.

In my view, teachers in state-controlled public schools are hired to teach there. Although Mr. Justice McReynolds may have intimated to the contrary in *Meyer v. Nebraska, supra,* certainly a teacher is not paid to go into school and teach subjects the State does not hire him to teach as a part of its selected curriculum. Nor are public school students sent to the schools at public expense to broadcast political or any other views to educate and inform the public. The original idea of schools, which I do not believe is yet abandoned as worthless or out of date, was that children had not yet reached the point of experience and wisdom which enabled them to teach all of their elders. It may be that the Nation has outworn the old-fashioned slogan that "children are to be seen not heard," but one may, I hope, be permitted to harbor the thought that taxpayers send children to school on the premise that at their age they need to learn, not teach.

The true principles on this whole subject were in my judgment spoken by Mr. Justice McKenna for the Court in *Waugh v. Mississippi University* in 237 U.S. 589, 596–597. The State had there passed a law barring students from peaceably assembling in Greek letter fraternities and providing that students who joined them could be expelled from school. This law would appear on the surface to run afoul of the First Amendment's freedom of assembly clause. The law was attacked as violative of due process and of the privileges and immunities clause and as a deprivation of property and of liberty, under the Fourteenth Amendment. It was argued that the fraternity made its members more moral, taught discipline, and inspired its members to study harder and to obey better the rules of discipline and order. This Court rejected all the "fervid" pleas of the fraternities' advocates and decided unanimously against these Fourteenth Amendment arguments. The Court in its next-to-the-last paragraph made this statement which has complete relevance for us today:

"It is said that the fraternity to which complainant belongs is a moral and of itself a disciplinary force. This need not be denied. But whether such membership makes against discipline was for the State of Mississippi to determine. It is to be remembered that the University was established by the State and is under the control of the State, and the enactment of the statute may have been induced by the opinion that *membership in the prohibited societies divided the attention of the students and distracted from that singleness of purpose which the State desired to exist in its public educational institutions*. It is not for us to entertain conjectures in opposition to the views of the State and annul its regulations upon disputable considerations of their wisdom or necessity." (Emphasis supplied.)

It was on the foregoing argument that this Court sustained the power of Mississippi to curtail the First Amendment's right of peaceable assembly. And the same reasons are equally applicable to curtailing in the States' public schools the right to complete freedom of expression. Iowa's public schools, like Mississippi's university, are operated to give students an opportunity to learn, not to talk politics by actual speech, or by "symbolic" speech. And, as I have pointed out before, the record amply shows that public protest in the school classes against the Vietnam War "distracted from that singleness of purpose which the State [here Iowa] desired to exist in its public educational institutions." Here the Court should accord Iowa educational institutions the same right to determine for themselves to what extent free expression should be allowed in its schools as it accorded Mississippi with reference to freedom of assembly. But even if the record were silent as to protests against the Vietnam War distracting students from their assigned class work, members of this Court, like all other citizens, know, without being told, that the disputes over the wisdom of the Vietnam War have disrupted and divided this country as few other issues ever have. Of course students, like other people, cannot concentrate on lesser issues when black armbands are being ostentatiously displayed in their presence to call attention to the wounded and dead of the war, some of the wounded and the dead being their friends and neighbors. It was, of course, to distract the attention of other students that some students insisted up to the very point of their own suspension from school that they were determined to sit in school with their symbolic armbands.

Change has been said to be truly the law of life, but sometimes the old and the tried and true are worth holding. The schools of this Nation have undoubtedly contributed to giving us tranquility and to making us a more law-abiding people. Uncontrolled and uncontrollable liberty is an enemy to domestic peace. We cannot close our eyes to the fact that some of the country's greatest problems are crimes committed by the youth, too many of school age. School discipline, like parental discipline, is an integral and important part of training our children to be good citizens—to be better citizens. Here a very small number of students have crisply and summarily refused to obey a school order designed to give pupils who want to learn the opportunity to do so. One does not need to be a prophet or the son of a prophet to know that after the Court's holding today, some students in Iowa schools and indeed in all schools will be ready, able, and willing to defy their teachers on practically all orders. This is the more unfortunate for the schools since groups of students all over the land are already running loose, conducting break-ins, sit-ins, lie-ins, and smash-ins. Many of these student groups, as is all too familiar to all who read the newspapers and watch the television news programs, have already engaged in rioting, property seizures, and destruction. They have picketed schools to force students not to cross their picket lines and have too often violently attacked earnest but frightened students who wanted an education that the pickets did not want them to get. Students engaged in such activities are apparently confident that they know far more about how to operate public school systems than do their parents, teachers, and elected school officials. It is no answer to say that the particular students here have not reached such high points in their demands to attend classes in order to exercise their political pressures. Turned loose with lawsuits for damages and injunctions against their teachers as they are here, it is nothing but wishful thinking to imagine that young, immature students will not soon believe it is their right to control the schools rather than the right of the States that collect the taxes to hire the teachers for the benefit of the pupils. This case, therefore, wholly without constitutional reasons in my judgment, subjects all the public schools in the country to the whims and caprices of their loudest-mouthed, but maybe not their brightest, students. I, for one, am not fully persuaded that school pupils are wise enough, even with this Court's expert help from Washington, to run the 23,390 public school systems in our 50 states. I wish, therefore, wholly to disclaim any purpose on my part to hold that the Federal Constitution compels the teachers, parents, and elected school officials to surrender control of the American public school system to public school students. I dissent.

Dissent: Mr. Justice Harlan, dissenting.

I certainly agree that state public school authorities in the discharge of their responsibilities are not wholly exempt from the requirements of the Fourteenth Amendment respecting the freedoms of expression and association. At the same time, I am reluctant to believe that there is any disagreement between the majority and myself on the proposition that school officials should be accorded the widest authority in maintaining discipline and good order in their constitutions. To translate that proposition into a workable constitutional rule, I would, in cases like this, cast upon those complaining the burden of showing that a particular school measure was motivated by other than legitimate school concerns—for example, a desire to prohibit the expression of an unpopular point of view, while permitting expression of the dominant opinion.

Finding nothing in this record which impugns the good faith of respondents in promulgating the armband regulation, I would affirm the judgment below.

TITLE IX, THE EDUCATION AMENDMENTS OF 1972

Sometimes, a very short statement makes a very large difference. This is certainly true in Title IX, an education amendment passed by the Congress and signed by President Richard Nixon in 1972. Congress spent more than two years of debate leading up to the passage of Title IX. The then U.S. Department of Health, Education, and Welfare, which was charged with implementing the act, spent another three years developing the interpretative regulations before they were published in 1975. It is likely that some of those who voted for the act expected little from it. In fact, most of the detailed language of the legislation lists all of the types of cases to which it would not apply, including admission to private colleges, military academies, and student housing facilities. Nevertheless, because of patient and determined advocacy over the years after its passage, Title IX brought more and more changes to every aspect of American education, from more nearly equal sports facilities, to new initiatives to encourage women to participate in nontraditional programs, to very different portraits of women in textbooks.

No person in the United States shall, on the basis of sex, be excluded from participation, be denied the benefits of, or be subjected to discrimination under any education program or activity receiving federal financial assistance.

For purposes of this title, an educational institution means any public or private preschool, elementary, or secondary school, or any institution of vocational, professional, or higher education, except that in the case of an educational institution composed of more than one school, college, or department which are administratively separate units, such term means each such school, college, or department.

PUBLIC LAW 94-142, EDUCATION FOR ALL HANDICAPPED CHILDREN ACT, 1975

Perhaps the last group petitioning Congress to recognize their civil rights in the 1960s and 1970s were people with handicaps. While schools have still not met the goal of offering fully equal treatment to all students regardless of handicap, Public Law 94–142 made an extraordinary difference in schools. Prior to the law (and its predecessors in a few states), many students with handicapping conditions were simply excluded from school or separated into special classes, often in the symbolic basements of the schools, which were properly described as warehouses. Because of the costs associated with implementing the law, the implementation of Public Law 94–142 has aroused continual debate in many school districts across the country.

Be it enacted by the Senate and House of Representatives of the United States of America in Congress assembled, That this Act may be cited as the "Education for All Handicapped Children Act of 1975."

Statement of Findings and Purpose
Section 3 (a) Section 601 of the Act (20 U.S.C. 1401) is amended by inserting "(a)" immediately before "This title" and by adding at the end thereof the following new subsections:

(b)   The Congress finds that—

(1) there are more than eight million handicapped children in the United States today;

(2) the special educational needs of such children are not being fully met;

(3) more than half of the handicapped children in the United States do not receive appropriate educational services which would enable them to have full equality of opportunity;

(4) one million of the handicapped children in the United States are excluded entirely from the public school system and will not go through the educational process with their peers;

(5) there are many handicapped children throughout the United States participating in regular school programs whose handicaps prevent them from having a successful educational experience because their handicaps are undetected;

(6) because of the lack of adequate services within the public school system, families are often forced to find services outside the public school system, often at great distance from their residence and at their own expense;

(7) developments in the training of teachers and in diagnostic and instructional procedures and methods have advanced to the point that, given appropriate funding, State and local educational agencies can and will provide effective special education and related services to meet the needs of handicapped children;

(8) State and local educational agencies have a responsibility to provide education for all handicapped children, but present financial resources are inadequate to meet the special educational needs of handicapped children; and

(9) it is in the national interest that the Federal Government assist State and local efforts to provide programs to meet the educational needs of handicapped children in order to assure equal protection of the law.

(c)   It is the purpose of this Act to assure that all handicapped children have available to them, within the time periods specified in section 612(2) (B), a free appropriate public education which emphasizes special education and related services designed to meet their unique needs, to assure that the rights of handicapped children and their parents or guardians are protected, to assist States and localities to provide for the education of all handicapped children, and to assess and assure the effectiveness of efforts to educate handicapped children.

(d)   The heading for section 601 of the Act (20 U.S.C. 1401) is amended to read as follows: "Short title; statement of findings and purpose."

Viva La Raza! Community Control in Chicago, 1974

In the late 1960s and early 1970s, the community control movement became a signifi-cant part of the school reform drive in many communities of color across the United States. For many, a decade of integrated schooling had begun to sour them on its val-ues. Some African-American and Latino leaders began to ask if it was not better to allow the schools in their communities to remain segregated, but under the control of the local communities. As can be imagined, such a program spawned unusual political alliances. The most famous community control movement took place in New York City. The New York City teachers strike, in which the local branch of the American Federation of Teachers virtually brought the schools to a standstill for weeks, ultimately defeated the most powerful aspects of community control in New York. Nevertheless, the issue arose in many communities. The following report on the development of a Mexican-American movement in Chicago is one example of the effort to secure com-munity control.

In 1970, our own Chicano school system was born. The Crusade had been holding lib-eration summer classes for several years (that summer, 325 pupils attended). Then, at the September 16 celebration, Corky Gonzales announced before a crowd of ten thou-sand Raza that a year-round Chicano school would open during the next month. It would cover the years from kindergarten through college, and it was accredited. The school would be named Tlatelolco, after the famous town of ancient Mexico and the present-day plaza in Mexico City (also called Plaza de las Tres Culturas), where one thousand innocent citizens became martyrs of justice when they were massacred by government forces in 1968.

The new school, housed in the Crusade building, is a bilingual, bicultural school and unlike any other school in the country today. Its whole purpose is, in Corky's words, to offer "education that opens your eyes, not washes your brain." The first seven years of the school represent the seven cultures of Mexico. Instead of passing from one *grade* to the next, children move from one *tribe* to another and learn the culture of that tribe.

The teachers not only teach the students but also learn from them. This is one of the most important principles of the Crusade school, and one of the things that makes

From *Via La Raza: The Stuggle of the Mexican-American People,* By Elizabeth Sutherland Martínez and Enriqueta Longeaux y Vásquez. Garden City, New York: Doubleday & Company, Inc., 1974. Reprinted by permission of Elizabeth Sutherland Martínez and Enriqueta Longeaux y Vásquez.

it very different from the regular school system. Under this principle, everybody is both a teacher and a student—and the teacher isn't there for the money or professional status, but out of love for La Raza and especially the youth.

That first year, one of the best loved teachers was Ricardo Romero. Ricardo is the toughest of men, and the most gentle. He knows his history by memory, inside and out, and he also takes his classes on field trips where they can relate what they learn from him to the real situation—today, for example, a trip to a courthouse where they see with their own eyes how the U.S. legal system operates. Ricardo, by the way, did not go beyond the sixth grade of school. Other classes went to visit Raza businesses, to see other schools so they could compare, to look at the rich section of town and learn what causes the differences in the public schools. In one trip, the class visited the welfare office and learned what a person goes through when applying for welfare.

That first year, the Tlatelolco school had 130 students at all levels. The next year it took twice as many, and there are still hundreds on the waiting list. As Corky Gonzales stated in an interview published in the Chicano newspaper *La Voz del Pueblo:* "Tlatelolco is a model for schools across the country. We're getting people from all over the country now, coming to see how we're doing it . . . The schools want to send what they consider problem kids to us . . . We feel that independent schools for Chicanos will be starting to develop all over the country."

To visit Tlatelolco and see the faces of the children is to know that this school is giving a real education. Their faces tell us that these young people are growing in knowledge, free to express that growth, and happy in the discovery and development of what they are. Tlatelolco is meeting the real educational needs of our people, and only we ourselves can do that. No one else can do it for us.

One of the best examples of what will be coming out of the Chicano school system is the Ballet Chicano de Aztlán. At one time, Mexican folk dancing was something that only a select few could learn because you had to pay for lessons, and more Anglos were studying it than Chicanos. Then the Crusade sent fourteen young people to Mexico City, where they spent six weeks of dedicated and concentrated study. When they returned, they taught all the young people—down to the age of three—how to dance. Out of this learning and teaching came the Ballet Chicano, under the direction of Enrique Montoya, which gave its first performance on September 16, 1970. Since then, the ballet has performed at many schools and colleges.

One of the most popular dances of the Ballet Chicano is the dance of Adelita. This famous figure of the Mexican Revolution is represented by twenty girls in modern dress, wearing black and red, with black boots to the knee, their hair sleek, packs and rifles on their backs. They move in a combination of dancing and marching, often aiming the rifles in different directions. The new Adelita is a good example of how the Crusade school draws upon our heritage and adapts it to today's struggle. There is no separation of "the arts" from the revolution.

That night, a birthday party was taking place at one of the apartments in a building next door to the Crusade, where Tlatelolco teachers—including Luis Martinez—lived. Around midnight, a police car parked across the street. An unidentified youth went up to the car and asked the officers inside what they were doing there. They asked him for identification and put him in the car for "jaywalking" when he couldn't produce it. Luis Martinez and several other Chicanos then went over to the car from the apartments. While they tried to convince the police to free the youth, the boy ran out of the car and escaped.

According to police, Officer Stephen Snyder then tried to get out of the car, and Luis kicked the door against him. Then Luis ran to a parking lot with Snyder after him. According to Snyder, he was shot at three times, and then killed Luis. People were sniping at the police from the apartments. More police came, the apartments were searched, and many people were arrested. About 2:00 A.M. a huge explosion blew apart a section of the apartment building. Police said it was caused by dynamite inside. They also claimed to have found many guns there.

But our people did not believe this story. The Crusade stated that it had witnesses and evidence proving Luis was executed in cold blood. Corky Gonzales said Luis was shot in the back, not from the front, as police claimed. According to Ernesto Vigil, Luis didn't run away. When last seen, he was walking backward, away from Snyder, without a gun and with his hands up, saying, "Leave me alone, man, I don't want no hassle." There is also the fact that Snyder was suspended three years earlier for hitting a sixteen-year-old whom he had arrested. Chicanos know how rarely an officer is suspended for brutality, so it must have been serious.

As for the explosion, Crusaders said it was caused by something fired at or thrown into the building by police. Why would Crusaders blow up their own building? And if there was sniper fire from the Chicanos, why hadn't officials mentioned bullet holes in any of the police cars? Crusaders also pointed out that the police had changed their story of what happened several times.

But even the police didn't deny that there was police brutality that night. The chief just wouldn't answer questions about it. Almost a hundred people were arrested in connection with the incident, including juveniles in their homes who said they were just watching TV. Many violations of civil rights were reported by Chicanos and many Crusaders said they were beaten for no reason.

> today,
> history and time
> as we have known it,
> came to an end.   today
> is the birth of
> a new history of man,
> AZTLÁN.

DILLON PLATERO, THE ROUGH ROCK DEMONSTRATION SCHOOL, NAVAJO NATION, 1970

In March of 1970, a unique academic convention of scholars, Native students, and tribal representatives met at Princeton University. The convocation heard a range of presentations on Indian matters. Indian Voices: The First Convocation of American Indian Scholars *is a record of the papers presenters gave at panels and discussions held at the Convocation. Dillon Platero, Director of the Rough Rock Demonstration School in Chinle, Arizona, reported on the school. The Rough Rock Demonstration School represents a different type of community control, and a very significant shift in the culture of Indian schooling that had begun in the 1960s with federal funding and local Navajo energy and control.*

Indian Voices: The First Convocation of American Indian Scholars. San Francisco: The Indian Historian Press, 1970. Reprinted by permission of the Indian Historian Press.

In 1965, like-minded persons from the Navajo tribe, governmental agencies, and institutions of higher learning came together and were able to propose, and get funded, an experimental school. A demonstration school if you will, which would show to the many skeptics that Navajo people could run their own educational affairs, *now*. Unfortunately, the mechanics of establishing such a school made it necessary to place a dual staff in an existing Bureau of Indian Affairs boarding school, with the result being an obvious source of friction. What resulted was essentially two schools operating in one plant and with one student body. With allegiance thus divided, with the federal employees responsible for functioning under their rules and regulations, however well-meaning, and the demonstration staff seeing their responsibility to the people of the community and their children, misunderstandings, friction, and ill-will were inevitable. The school was not then successful and its supporters agonized over this apparent failure, as the decision to terminate the project was seriously considered. However, everyone understood what had happened. The principle underlying the experiment was felt still to be sound. Only the manner of attempted implementation needed improvement.

And so we tried again, this time with a more experienced administrator and in a locale where only the demonstration school would be functioning. A new facility was turned over to the Navajo people, only the broadest restrictions were imposed as to its use. A private, nonprofit corporation was formed as the legal entity which could accept funds from government agencies, as well as from private sources for the operation of the Rough Rock Demonstration School. This was accomplished in the spring of 1966 and in July 1 of that year, the experiment began anew.

From the very beginning, cooperation and even more importantly, freedom, have characterized our relationships with other involved agencies. Rough Rock now truly became responsible for its own school. With the election of a five-member board of education in June, 1966, the governing body was ready to begin functioning by the time the school came into being.

The Navajo people of Rough Rock wanted to accomplish two things: (1) the development of educational experiences comparable to those offered in the federal and state schools, in order to equip Indian children with knowledge of English, and the subject areas usually taught in any elementary school in the state of Arizona; (2) the development of educational experiences in Navajo-oriented subjects in order to enrich our children's academic work and enhance their total educational program.

When Rough Rock first began operation, the community had been used to having their school serve children from the ages of six through the highest grade taught. Not even a kindergarten program existed, to say nothing of a nursery school. In 1966–67, for the first time, a Head Start unit was established, affiliated with the Demonstration School. These children were among the most enthusiastic in the entire community. Our gravest problem is how to keep the class to a reasonable size. The office of Navajo Economic Opportunity set up a unit to provide for 20 children; in its first year, average daily attendance in that was 20.9. In 1967–68 it was 19.7; in 1968–69, it was 22.8. In response to increasing pressure from local parents to extend the entrance age downward, Rough Rock began a nursery school, accommodating two-, three-, and four-year-olds. The kindergarten program bridges the gap between this group and the regular school-age children. Just last week, our nursery school had an average daily attendance of 26.4, and it has recently been as high as 29.6. A third preschool section currently is our kindergarten class, with an average daily attendance of about 25. Serving as a transition between the less highly structured nursery school and the more formally constituted beginning phase (our school is ungraded), kindergarten at Rough Rock functions as do kindergartens in other parts of the country. There are two notable exceptions; (1) instruction is in the Navajo language; (2) emphasis is placed on the relevancy of education to the childrens' Navajo home milieu.

In this fashion, the child's self-image and feeling of worthy personhood is not shattered so mercilessly as often happens, when the difference between what is actual life and what is taught in school strikes the child at the age of six. School at Rough Rock is an extension of the child's normal world, in which he is competent to communicate and react in fashions sanctioned by his community and culture. Recently, the community has also begun a child care center for infants. It's so new that no general statement can be made about it.

Rough Rock is a bilingual school. We believe this term embraces the concept of fluency in two media of communication: in our case, in Navajo and in English. This is a little different from the usual "bilingual" programs at other schools, that merely treat the language other than English as a necessary evil. All students receive instruction in the Navajo language one period a day. The school was thus firmly committed to the concept of equality of value of the two most commonly used languages in the community. At the same time, thought was seriously being given to actually providing instruction in Navajo to certain children for certain periods of time. In 1968–69, our "Follow-Through" students, at the early primary grade level, began receiving all their teaching in Navajo, with exception of a daily English lesson. Today we have six classes being taught in the Navajo language, in addition to our kindergarten and nursery school. As the children gain confidence in their ability to handle the intricacies of school learning, Navajo gives way as the basic medium of instruction, and English replaces it by the end of the third-grade age level.

The Rough Rock community, through their elected school board, hold to the philosophy that we teach the Navajo language for the reason that proficiency in it is a tool needed by our children and a skill worthy of formal educational efforts. Just as there is a wide range of fluency in the speaking of English, so in Navajo some handle the language better than others. All too often in the past, the Navajo child has been removed from his home environment at an early age and thrown into a completely alien cultural milieu and language. Great efforts were made to inhibit the speaking of such Navajo as he already knew, which not only stunted the quality of his native tongue, but actually made him ashamed of himself and of his language, as something inferior to English. The result was often a person who was fluent in neither language—one who was handicapped linguistically. Once the parents of Rough Rock actually had control of their school, the Navajo language ceased to be considered as a patois to be eliminated, or suppressed, and instead took its rightful place as the co-language of the school, a place it continues to hold with dignity.

Navajo culture is taught daily at Rough Rock. But we recognize that there is no clear-cut dichotomy, with Navajo culture occupying one compartment and non-Indian culture another. Recognizing and accepting the inevitability of our children's biculturalness, the school board emphasizes the values found in each and helps our students understand that neither is "right" nor "wrong" as such.

The school board also realizes that our children's familiarity with Navajo culture needs to be systematically expanded, and the non-Indian culture taught as well. The early primary grade levels find what is probably the best teaching done in this area, inasmuch as these children all have Navajo-speaking teachers whose knowledge of Navajo culture is better than any non-Navajo's could possibly be. Speakers from the community who have special knowledge of various aspects of Navajo culture spend an entire day at the school, lecturing to the older students on their specialty, once a week. These presentations are followed with vocabulary study, composition, and consideration of the specific topic during the following five days, in the social studies classes and homerooms.

Such extensive and systematic teaching of Navajo language and culture calls for both texts and teaching aids. In this respect, the school's Navajo Curriculum Center has proved to be invaluable. Rough Rock has found that there are teachers of Navajo language and culture . . . and others, who merely think they can teach. Too often a person not professionally trained to teach has attempted to provide instruction only to find himself running out of pedagogic steam within a few weeks. This is one explanation for our school's attempt to hire as many Navajo teachers as possible: They have both the knowledge of Navajo language and culture and the professional acumen to organize and present their subject. During the past three and a half years, the Navajo Curriculum Center has published such texts as Black Mountain Boy for intermediate grades, several beginning readers, and a book of Navajo biographies for older students. Emphasis at the present time is being placed on getting more works in the Navajo language. The center has also completed materials explaining the school, and the principles upon which it is founded, and such ancillary teaching aids as film strips, puppets, and dramatic presentations.

We need leadership, of course. And in cooperation with the Navajo Community College, the Chinle Public School District, and Arizona State University, we have had four teacher aides in full-time training for the past year. These are people who spent several years as practical aides in our classrooms and showed such potential for the teaching profession that the opportunity was given them to upgrade their skills and prepare for entrance into the profession. We have also been able to provide rotating employment opportunities for parents in the community whose lack of special, non-Indian skills makes it impractical to engage them on a full-time basis. The U.S. Office of Education has provided funds for this purpose.

Since the school began in 1966, Rough Rock has had dormitory parent aides. They have functioned as less experienced instructional aides and have the same benefits as our classroom parent aides. It is recognized that a most sensitive point with parents is the way their children are treated in the dormitories. At Rough Rock, our community parents have nearly all had the opportunity to actually work in the dorms and find out for themselves what is involved in group living with large numbers of children. The dormitory program itself may slowly go out of business, but right now, the Navajo communities don't have facilities such as would normally be found in cities.

Community development is an integral part of the demonstration project. All too often, people equate the activities of the project solely with that of operating an elementary school. Our entire community development building, built of adobe with local labor, is a service to our total population, as well as to our school and our students. For example, the postal facilities serve the entire community with mail service that was not available before the demonstration project began. The personnel office serves the entire community as well as the school. The community recreation office, office of community development director, office of special services, all serve the entire community. The funds expended for these largely non-school-related functions cannot justifiably be considered legitimate expenses in the education of children. The old bureaucratic accountancy method of figuring cost per pupil for education cannot be utilized at Rough Rock.

Our adult education program has been functioning since the first day that Rough Rock Demonstration School began operation. The courses stress basic English, as well as Navajo. Basic Navajo is also taught to the non-Indians employed at the school. Also taught are health, home economics, tribal and national government, and dealing with governmental agencies. This past fall, the Adult Basic Education Center was established, serving our more traditional Navajo people, as well as our youth who have had some elementary and secondary education but who dropped out. Dormitory parent aides and classroom parent aides receive regular instruction in the Adult Basic Education Center as part of their work at the school.

An extensive arts and crafts program was conducted during the first years at the school. However, as the types of skills multiplied and the number of practitioners increased, it was possible to phase out this aspect of activity. Now such work is pursued largely in the homes of various persons trained in 1966–68. Our emphasis is now upon the development of marketing.

Navajo people will not abandon their traditional cultural ways and devote themselves to living by non-Indian standards. Thus, the role of the medicine man in Navajo life has received new respect from conventional physicians. Most people felt, when we went looking for help, that the medicine man is the Navajo religion. They know nothing about Navajo religion, and less about Navajo healing ceremonies. Finally, we went to the people in the National Institute of Mental Health. All the doctors sort of smiled at each other. Pretty soon, though, after a couple of meetings, they said, well, let's go out to Rough Rock. They spent a little time there, and they contacted about everyone who had anything to do with medicine men. They finally processed a proposal, which received favorable action. The program was funded for a three-year period. Now it is beginning to make sense that it is a viable program, and it does help in the area of mental health. The Navajo medicine man is very effective with people who talk Navajo and understand the culture. Right now, about 95 percent or more of the Navajo people who go to Vietnam, or into the service, receive ritual help from the Navajo medicine man so that they are safe and sound, healthy, mentally capable of going into the various services. It makes them happy.

There was a time when indigenous medical practice was condemned by culturally egocentric non-Indians, who could not bring themselves to admit that any way of living could possibly contain merit, if it differed from their own lifeways. Now the trend has been reversed, as non-Indian medicine learns more about the incredibly complex mechanisms of the human mind. Many public health physicians have come to realize that the traditional medicine man has the key to the healing of many types of maladies which can afflict Navajo people. Thus, a feeling of mutual respect is arising as a result of cooperation between the two types of medical practitioners. The school's medicine man training program provides for apprenticeships on a one-to-two basis, with prominent medicine men relaying to their students the intricacies of their healing arts.

The preservation of our ancient and effective healing arts is one of the remarkable results of this program . . . one might say a bonus in educational achievement.

However, we feel that the knowledge of the Navajo Way is, in itself, not enough. There should also be fundamental knowledge on the part of the medicine man of the types of maladies which will better respond to non-Indian medicine. Such patently organic ailments as broken bones, wounds, burns, etc., and the onset of such diseases as cancer, tuberculosis, etc., may well be referred by medicine men to Public Health physicians who are then able to bring their expertise into play. As a part of our medicine man training program, there is in-service training by public health services, of both the medicine men and their apprentices, in basic physiology. It is another type of adult education, but one that brings together in mutual respect the different practices aimed at a single result: optimum health for the Navajo people.

The uses of existing leadership and the consistent training of new leadership is the keynote for the success of Rough Rock. It is to be emphasized that the Rough Rock Community School Board controls policy and has the decision-making power. I could stand here and be fired right now, and may not know it, but the school board has that power. They hire and fire teachers. They make the policies of the school. Recently, they made the decision to make Rough Rock into a high school, so that we are working on this now.

Of particular interest in this discussion are the basic principles used:

(1)   The work to be accomplished must be recognized by Indian people as being needed. Only after a realization of need for change by Indian people, can such change be effective.

(2)   Indian people must be afforded recognition as competent human beings whose decisions (and rationale for them) merit the respect of all. An end to paternalism is demanded—though not to the services, which were brought and paid for hundreds of years ago. Here is a fine distinction that too often is completely overlooked by persons who would turn Indians into copies of non-Indian peoples. For example, on the Navajo reservation, the federal government is responsible for providing educational opportunities for our children. This is no largess that has been handed down to us. It is part of the spoils of war which was written into the Treaty of 1868 between the United States government and the Navajo Nation.

(3)   Indian people must be involved with the efforts their community is making to improve their lot. Such involvement can take many forms, such as participation on a Parents Advisory Committee, service on the school board, work as a dormitory aide, work as a classroom parent aide, helping supervise an off-reservation field trip, or addressing a convocation of scholars, as have several of our local leaders. Following these basic principles, Rough Rock has been an example.

The acceptance and consideration of objective criticism is a necessary part of an experiment, or any program. Indeed, there have been evaluations of Rough Rock. We have one objective evaluation, however, which we think very highly of. It is in the best traditions of self-criticism in a positive and objective way—pointing out the weaknesses but also pointing out the strengths and proposing such measures as will correct specific situations. The Navajo people themselves made the evaluation, and continue the process of evaluation. They go into a school system such as Rough Rock and spend a great deal of time talking to students, asking what they think of the curriculum, courses, subject matter, what they think of the people, the teachers. You don't have to interpret.

Finally, we at Rough Rock feel that this demonstration project has great significance for other areas and peoples. Concepts which were first put into practice at Rough Rock have been seized upon as worthy of emulation by federal schools, and by state institutions as well. Noteworthy was the establishment of Navajo Community College, which is predicated upon the same principles as is Rough Rock Demonstration School, but serving an older clientele.

Emphasizing the need for Indian people to solve Indian education problems has been the Dine Biolta Association, a recently founded, nonprofit corporation of Navajo educators and others interested in Indian education, which limits its voting membership to Navajo people. This dynamic group plans a summer workshop to train Navajo teachers for work in bilingual schools. Although college credit will be given, all instruction and administration will be handled by Indian people, for Indian people, to benefit Indian children.

In Ramah, New Mexico, the local people have formed their own corporation for operating a school. Rough Rock was studied before planning the Ramah program. The Bureau of Indian Affairs' project TRIBE is an outgrowth of the Rough Rock program. This could provide guidelines for a type of local control within the total federal school system. Thus far, the results have been meager. There is one small school at Blackwater. However, the fact that this massive bureaucracy would move at all in an attempt to provide some way for greater local control is a tribute to the effectiveness of Rough Rock in proving that Indian people are ready *now* for such responsibilities.

Both bilingual and bicultural education have recently found much more favor and even entrance into formerly "Closed" curricula in Bureau and public schools. An example of the latter may be seen in the Navajo language programs at Gallup, New Mexico public schools. The mere providing of educational opportunities for kindergarten age children (not to be confused with the long-established beginners' classes) is a step long advocated but even to this day not implemented in the majority of public schools in our state.

This combination—extension of early childhood education to younger students, along with instruction, heavily utilizing the Navajo language—produces a great forward step in raising the educational level of our Indian people on our reservation. A less tangible but real benefit from the very existence of Rough Rock Demonstration School has been a spirit of competition engendered which cannot help but be beneficial.

While there is no point in the denigration of different school systems, the mere existence of this Demonstration School has served as a catalyst to other schools and has stirred them into action. Rough Rock stands as a symbol of *doing*, rather than merely *talking*.

Indian people need to be doers, rather than objects to which things are done. They need to be masters of their own destinies, a dream that has been constant with American people ever since this nation was founded—a dream that Indian people, whose nationhood predates America itself, are now fulfilling for themselves, thus returning to their ancient and original rights as the first and only true Americans.

CHAPTER 11

REFORM EFFORTS OF THE 1980S AND 1990S

Introduction

With the election of Ronald Reagan as president in 1980, the Great Society era was clearly over. Reagan had pledged to abolish the federal Department of Education. More substantially, the Reagan revolution involved cutting all of the nonmilitary functions of the federal government so that they would revert to the states, or—for most of the social programs that had expanded in the previous two decades, including education—simply shrink or disappear. Reagan engineered the massive transfer of funds from the poor and middle class to the rich, which became his lasting legacy, by cutting many of the services that had opened doors of opportunity for poor and working-class Americans during the previous era. Given such a philosophy of governance, it was a surprise to many observers when Reagan's Secretary of Education, Terrell Bell, created the National Commission on Excellence in Education. The Commission's 1983 report, *A Nation at Risk: The Imperative for Educational Reform* (Washington, D.C.: U.S. Government Printing Office, 1983) brought significantly more national attention to school reform than any act of the Carter-era Department of Education; indeed, it called more attention to school reform than virtually any federal action in education since Richard Nixon had signed Public Law 94–142 in the early 1970s. To say the report "burst on the scene" is not an overstatement. The report's authors framed their call for school reform as a matter of national crisis. While careful to avoid offending the sensibilities of their federal patrons by calling for federal funds (a logical assumption given their martial rhetoric), they did fuel a significant range of state spending, state and local reform efforts, and a national debate about "school reform" that has lasted to the end of the century. Ironically, while the authors of the report did not end the continued cuts in federal spending for education, they probably did save the structure of the federal Department itself.

While President Reagan was reportedly appalled by the report and the limits it placed on his ability to maneuver for further cuts in education, the most vocal critics of the report were on the left. While grateful for the attention to school issues and for the call for change, the heirs of the progressive education movement feared that the rhetoric of *A Nation at Risk,* and the many further reports it generated, would focus on punishing students, punishing teachers, and sometimes punishing parents, but would leave most of the rest of the society with little responsibility to remediate the problems. One of the most cogent arguments for a more humane and generous stance on the issue of school reform came from Ann Bastian and her colleagues in the Report of the New World Foundation, *Choosing Equality: The Case for Democratic Schooling* (New York: The New World Foundation, 1985). A selection from the book's introduction, which is included here, summarizes the arguments of those who sought a much broader definition of school reform.

One of the issues that dominated the educational debates of the late twentieth century is multiculturalism. How can schools attract and reflect increasing diversity in their student bodies? How can schools celebrate the contributions to American culture that many different ethnic groups have made? How can schools counter discrimination by race, class, or gender that has so long been a part of the American story? These and other questions have caused the flowering of multicultural curricula, which attempt to educate students about the many contributions people of diverse heritage have made to our nation and culture. At the same time, this multicultural approach has provoked heated debate; a surprising range of people defend a single cultural norm or national story and see any other approach as dangerously divisive.

From the many things written about multiculturalism—from many different perspectives—two are presented here to provide some of the flavor of this debate. The debate begins with a focus on what schools should be teaching and quickly expands to a reflection on the fundamental nature of the "good society" and what kind of culture the United States should encourage in the twenty-first century.

Sonia Nieto's *Affirming Diversity: The Sociopolitical Context of Multicultural Education* (New York: Longman, 1992) makes the case for multicultural education as clearly as any single document. On the other side of the debate, noted historian Arthur M. Schlesinger, Jr., argues in *The Disuniting of America* (Knoxville, Tenn.: Whittle Direct Books, 1991) that multiculturalism is both a distortion of history and a political project with dangerous consequences for the nation's future. In the comparison of Nieto and Schlesinger the debate about multicultural education can be seen as clearly as anywhere.

Other voices and other debates also marked the last two decades of the twentieth century. *A Nation at Risk* was the first report among many to come in the following two decades that criticized schools and called for reform. A major movement to institute national educational standards began during the presidency of George Bush and expanded under Bill Clinton. At the same time, others critiqued the critics. David C. Berliner and his colleagues have argued in *The Manufactured Crisis* that all the talk about school reform has masked the successes of the schools.

Finally, the volume closes with a short piece by Herb Kohl. Kohl reminds educators, historians, and students of education that hope is essential if one is to continue the enterprise of education.

NATIONAL COMMISSION ON EXCELLENCE IN EDUCATION, A NATION AT RISK: THE IMPERATIVE FOR EDUCATIONAL REFORM, 1983

It is hard to imagine the surprise and the energy surrounding A Nation at Risk *when the report first appeared in 1983. Few federal reports have stirred as much debate. In part, the debate was so intense because a number of other reports appeared within the following year, such as* Making the Grade: Report of the Twentieth-Century Fund Task Force on Federal Elementary and Secondary Education Policy. *A number of individual scholars, including Ernest Boyer, Theodore Sizer, Mortimer J. Adler, Sarah Lawrence Lightfoot, Seymour Sarason, and John Goodlad wrote their own telling reports at about the same time. Education was in the news. Debates about education were in the air. And the* Nation at Risk *report, along with its many successors, continues to influence school policy to the present.*

Our Nation is at risk. Our once unchallenged preeminence in commerce, industry, science, and technological innovation is being overtaken by competitors throughout the world. This report is concerned with only one of the many causes and dimensions of the problem, but it is the one that undergirds American prosperity, security, and civility. We report to the American people that while we can take justifiable pride in what our schools and colleges have historically accomplished and contributed to the United States and the well-being of its people, the educational foundations of our society are presently being eroded by a rising tide of mediocrity that threatens our very future as a Nation and a people. What was unimaginable a generation ago has begun to occur— others are matching and surpassing our educational attainments.

If an unfriendly foreign power had attempted to impose on America the mediocre educational performance that exists today, we might well have viewed it as an act of war. As it stands, we have allowed this to happen to ourselves. We have even squandered the gains in student achievement made in the wake of the Sputnik challenge. Moreover, we have dismantled essential support systems which helped make those gains possible. We have, in effect, been committing an act of unthinking, unilateral educational disarmament.

Our society and its educational institutions seem to have lost sight of the basic purposes of schooling, and of the high expectations and disciplined effort needed to attain them. This report, the result of 18 months of study, seeks to generate reform of our educational system in fundamental ways and to renew the Nation's commitment to schools and colleges of high quality throughout the length and breadth of our land.

That we have compromised this commitment is, upon reflection, hardly surprising, given the multitude of often conflicting demands we have placed on our Nation's schools and colleges. They are routinely called on to provide solutions to personal, social, and political problems that the home and other institutions either will not or cannot resolve. We must understand that these demands on our schools and colleges often exact an educational cost as well as a financial one.

On the occasion of the Commission's first meeting, President Reagan noted the central purpose of education in American life when he said, "Certainly there are few areas of American life as important to our society, to our people, and to our families as our schools and colleges." This report, therefore, is as much an open letter to the

American people as it is a report to the Secretary of Education. We are confident that the American people, properly informed, will do what is right for their children and for the generations to come.

The Risk

History is not kind to idlers. The time is long past when America's destiny was assured simply by an abundance of natural resources and inexhaustible human enthusiasm, and by our relative isolation from the malignant problems of older civilizations. The world is indeed one global village. We live among determined, well-educated, and strongly motivated competitors. We compete with them for international standing and markets, not only with products but also with the ideas of our laboratories and neighborhood workshops. America's position in the world may once have been reasonably secure with only a few exceptionally well-trained men and women. It is no longer.

The risk is not only that the Japanese make automobiles more efficiently than Americans and have government subsidies for development and export. It is not just that the South Koreans recently built the world's most efficient steel mill, or that American machine tools, once the pride of the world, are being displaced by German products. It is also that these developments signify a redistribution of trained capability throughout the globe. Knowledge, learning, information, and skilled intelligence are the new raw materials of international commerce and are today spreading throughout the world as vigorously as miracle drugs, synthetic fertilizers, and blue jeans did earlier. If only to keep and improve on the slim competitive edge we still retain in world markets, we must dedicate ourselves to the reform of our educational system for the benefit of all—old and young alike, affluent and poor, majority, and minority. Learning is the indispensable investment required for success in the "information age" we are entering.

Our concern, however, goes well beyond matters such as industry and commerce. It also includes the intellectual, moral, and spiritual strengths of our people which knit together the very fabric of our society. The people of the United States need to know that individuals in our society who do not possess the levels of skill, literacy, and training essential to this new era will be effectively disenfranchised, not simply from the material rewards that accompany competent performance, but also from the chance to participate fully in our national life. A high level of shared education is essential to a free, democratic society and to the fostering of a common culture, especially in a country that prides itself on pluralism and individual freedom.

For our country to function, citizens must be able to reach some common understandings on complex issues, often on short notice and on the basis of conflicting or incomplete evidence. Education helps form these common understandings, a point Thomas Jefferson made long ago in his justly famous dictum:

> I know no safe depository of the ultimate powers of the society but the people themselves; and if we think them not enlightened enough to exercise their control with a wholesome discretion, the remedy is not to take from but to inform their discretion.

Part of what is at risk is the promise first made on this continent: All, regardless of race or class or economic status, are entitled to a fair chance and to the tools for developing their individual powers of mind and spirit to the utmost. This promise means that all children by virtue of their own efforts, competently guided, can hope to attain the mature and informed judgment needed to secure gainful employment and to manage their own lives, thereby serving not only their own interests but also the progress of society itself.

Indicators of the Risk

The educational dimensions of the risk before us have been amply documented in testimony received by the Commission. For example:

- International comparisons of student achievement, completed a decade ago, reveal that on 19 academic tests, American students were never first or second, and, in comparison with other industrialized nations, were last seven times.
- Some 23 million American adults are functionally illiterate by the simplest tests of everyday reading, writing, and comprehension.
- About 13 percent of all 17-year-olds in the United States can be considered functionally illiterate. Functional illiteracy among minority youth may run as high as 40 percent.
- Average achievement of high school students on most standardized tests is now lower than 26 years ago, when Sputnik was launched.
- Over half the population of gifted students do not match their tested ability with comparable achievement in school.
- The College Board's Scholastic Aptitude Test (SAT) demonstrates a virtually unbroken decline from 1963 to 1980. Average verbal scores fell over 50 points and average mathematics scores dropped nearly 40 points.
- College Board achievement tests also reveal consistent declines in recent years in such subjects as physics and English.
- Both the number and proportion of students demonstrating superior achievement on the SATs (i.e., those with scores of 650 or higher) have also dramatically declined.
- Many 17-year-olds do not possess the "higher-order" intellectual skills we should expect of them. Nearly 40 percent cannot draw inferences from written material; only one-fifth can write a persuasive essay; and only one-third can solve a mathematics problem requiring several steps.
- There was a steady decline in science achievement scores of U.S. 17-year-olds as measured by national assessments of science in 1969, 1973, and 1977.
- Between 1975 and 1980, remedial mathematics courses in public 4-year colleges increased by 72 percent and constitute one-quarter of all mathematics courses taught in those institutions.
- Average tested achievement of students graduating from college is also lower.
- Business and military leaders complain that they are required to spend millions of dollars on costly remedial education and training programs in such basic skills as reading, writing, spelling, and computation. The Department of the Navy, for example, reported to the Commission that one-quarter of its recent recruits cannot read at the ninth-grade level, the minimum needed to simply understand written safety instructions. Without remedial work they cannot even begin, much less complete, the sophisticated training essential in much of the modern military.

These deficiencies come at a time when the demand for highly skilled workers in fields is accelerating rapidly. For example:

- Computers and computer-controlled equipment are penetrating every aspect of our lives—homes, factories, and offices.
- One estimate indicates that by the turn of the century, millions of jobs will involve laser technology and robotics.
- Technology is radically transforming a host of other occupations. They include health care, medical science, energy production, food processing, construction, and the building, repair, and maintenance of sophisticated scientific, educational, military, and industrial equipment.

Analysts examining these indicators of student performance and the demands for new skills have made some chilling observations. Educational researcher Paul Hurd concluded at the end of a thorough national survey of student achievement that within the context of the modern scientific revolution, "We are raising a new generation of Americans that is scientifically and technologically illiterate." In a similar vein, John Slaughter, a former Director of the National Science Foundation, warned of "a growing chasm between a small scientific and technological elite and a citizenry ill-informed, indeed uninformed, on issues with a science component."

But the problem does not stop there, nor do all observers see it the same way. Some worry that schools may emphasize such rudiments as reading and computation at the expense of other essential skills such as comprehension, analysis, solving problems, and drawing conclusions. Still others are concerned that an overemphasis on technical and occupational skills will leave little time for studying the arts and humanities that so enrich daily life, help maintain civility, and develop a sense of community. Knowledge of the humanities, they maintain, must be harnessed to science and technology if the latter are to remain creative and humane, just as the humanities need to be informed by science and technology if they are to remain relevant to the human condition. Another analyst, Paul Copperman, has drawn a sobering conclusion. Until now, he has noted:

> Each generation of Americans has outstripped its parents in education, in literacy, and in economic attainment. For the first time in the history of our country, the educational skills of one generation will not surpass, will not equal, will not even approach, those of their parents.

It is important, of course, to recognize that *the average citizen* today is better educated and more knowledgeable than the average citizen of a generation ago—more literate, and exposed to more mathematics, literature, and science. The positive impact of this fact on the well-being of our country and the lives of our people cannot be overstated. Nevertheless, *the average graduate* of our schools and colleges today is not as well-educated as the average graduate of 25 or 35 years ago, when a much smaller proportion of our population completed high school and college. The negative impact of this fact likewise cannot be overstated.

Hope and Frustration

Statistics and their interpretation by experts show only the surface dimension of the difficulties we face. Beneath them lies a tension between hope and frustration that characterizes current attitudes about education at every level.

We have heard voices of high school and college students, school board members, and teachers; of leaders of industry, minority groups, and higher education; of parents and State officials. We could hear the hope evident in their commitment to quality education and in their descriptions of outstanding programs and schools. We could also hear the intensity of their frustration, a growing impatience with shoddiness in many walks of American life, and the complaint that this shoddiness is too often reflected in our schools and colleges. Their frustration threatens to overwhelm their hope.

What lies behind this emerging national sense of frustration can be described as both a dimming of personal expectations and the fear of losing a shared vision for America.

On the personal level, the student, the parent, and the caring teacher all perceive that a basic promise is not being kept. More and more young people emerge from high school ready neither for college nor for work. This predicament becomes more acute as the knowledge base continues its rapid expansion, the number of traditional jobs shrinks, and new jobs demand greater sophistication and preparation.

On a broader scale, we sense that this undertone of frustration has significant political implications, for it cuts across ages, generations, races, and political and economic groups. We have come to understand that the public will demand that educational and political leaders act forcefully and effectively on these issues. Indeed, such demands have already appeared and could well become a unifying national preoccupation. This unity, however, can be achieved only if we avoid the unproductive tendency of some to search for scapegoats among the victims, such as the beleaguered teachers.

On the positive side is the significant movement by political and educational leaders to search for solutions—so far centering largely on the nearly desperate need for increased support for the teaching of mathematics and science. This movement is but a start on what we believe is a larger and more educationally encompassing need to improve teaching and learning in fields such as English, history, geography, economics, and foreign languages. We believe this movement must be broadened and directed toward reform and excellence throughout education.

Excellence in Education

We define *excellence* to mean several related things. At the level of the *individual learner,* it means performing on the boundary of individual ability in ways that test and push back personal limits, in school and in the workplace. Excellence characterizes a *school or college* that sets high expectations and goals for all learners, then tries in every way possible to help students reach them. Excellence characterizes a *society* that has adopted these policies, for it will then be prepared through the education and skill of its people to respond to the challenges of a rapidly changing world. Our Nation's people and its schools and colleges must be committed to achieving excellence in all these senses.

We do not believe that a public commitment to excellence and educational reform must be made at the expense of a strong public commitment to the equitable treatment of our diverse population. The twin goals of equity and high-quality schooling have profound and practical meaning for our economy and society, and we cannot permit one to yield to the other either in principle or in practice. To do so would deny young people their chance to learn and live according to their aspirations and abilities. It also would lead to a generalized accommodation to mediocrity in our society on the one hand or the creation of an undemocratic elitism on the other.

Our goal must be to develop the talents of all to their fullest. Attaining that goal requires that we expect and assist all students to work to the limits of their capabilities. We should expect schools to have genuinely high standards rather than minimum ones, and parents to support and encourage their children to make the most of their talents and abilities.

The search for solutions to our educational problems must also include a commitment to life-long learning. The task of rebuilding our system of learning is enormous and must be properly understood and taken seriously: Although a million and a half new workers enter the economy each year from our schools and colleges, the adults working today will still make up about 75 percent of the workforce in the year 2000. These workers, and new entrants into the workforce, will need further education and retraining if they—and we as a Nation—are to thrive and prosper.

The Learning Society

In a world of ever-acceleating competition and change in the conditions of the workplace, of ever-greater danger, and of ever-larger opportunities for those prepared to meet them, educational reform should focus on the goal of creating a Learning Society. At the heart of such a society is the commitment to a set of values and to a system of education that affords all members the opportunity to stretch their minds to full capacity, from early childhood through adulthood, learning more as the world itself changes. Such a society has as a basic foundation the idea that education is important not only because of what it contributes to one's career goals, but also because of the value it adds to the general quality of one's life. Also at the heart of the Learning Society are educational opportunities extending far beyond the traditional institutions of learning, our schools and colleges. They extend into homes and workplaces; into libraries, art galleries, museums, and science centers; indeed, into every place where the individual can develop and mature in work and life. In our view, formal schooling in youth is the essential foundation for learning throughout one's life. But without life-long learning, one's skills will become rapidly dated.

In contrast to the ideal of the Learning Society, however, we find that for too many people, education means doing the minimum work necessary for the moment, then coasting through life on what may have been learned in its first quarter. But this should not surprise us because we tend to express our educational standards and expectations largely in terms of "minimum requirements." And where there should be a coherent continuum of learning, we have none, but instead an often incoherent, outdated patchwork quilt. Many individual, sometimes heroic, examples of schools and colleges of great merit do exist. Our findings and testimony confirm the vitality of a number of notable schools and programs, but their very distinction stands out against a vast mass shaped by tensions and pressures that inhibit systematic academic and vocational achievement for the majority of students. In some metropolitan areas, basic literacy has become the goal rather than the starting point. In some colleges, maintaining enrollment is of greater day-to-day concern than maintaining rigorous academic standards. And the ideal of academic excellence as the primary goal of schooling seems to be fading across the board in American education.

Thus, we issue this call to all who care about America and its future: To parents and students; to teachers, administrators, and school board members; to colleges and industry; to union members and military leaders; to governors and State legislators; to the President; to members of Congress and other public officials; to members of learned and scientific societies; to the print and electronic media; to concerned citizens everywhere. America is at risk.

We are confident that America can address this risk. If the tasks we set forth are initiated now and our recommendations are fully realized over the next several years, we can expect reform of our Nation's schools, colleges, and universities. This would also reverse the current declining trend—a trend that stems more from weakness of purpose, confusion of vision, underuse of talent, and lack of leadership, than from conditions beyond our control.

The Tools at Hand

It is our conviction that the essential raw materials needed to reform our educational system are waiting to be mobilized through effective leadership:

- the natural abilities of the young that cry out to be developed and the undiminished concern of parents for the well-being of their children;
- the commitment of the Nation to high retention rates in schools and colleges and to full access to education for all;
- the persistent and authentic American dream that superior performance can raise one's state in life and shape one's own future;
- the dedication, against all odds, that keeps teachers serving in schools and colleges, even as the rewards diminish;
- our better understanding of learning and teaching and the implications of this knowledge for school practice, and the numerous examples of local success as a result of superior effort and effective dissemination;
- the ingenuity of our policymakers, scientists, State and local educators, and scholars in formulating solutions once problems are better understood;
- the traditional belief that paying for education is an investment in ever-renewable human resources that are more durable and flexible than capital plant and equipment, and the availability in this country of sufficient financial means to invest in education;
- the equally sound tradition, from the Northwest Ordinance of 1787 until today, that the Federal Government should supplement State, local, and other resources to foster key national educational goals; and
- the voluntary efforts of individuals, businesses, and parent and civic groups to cooperate in strengthening educational programs.

These raw materials, combined with the unparalleled array of educational organizations in America, offer us the possibility to create a Learning Society, in which public, private, and parochial schools; colleges and universities; vocational and technical schools and institutes; libraries; science centers, museums, and other cultural institutions; and corporate training and retraining programs offer opportunities and choices for all to learn throughout life. . . .

Our final word, perhaps better characterized as a plea, is that all segments of our population give attention to the implementation of our recommendations. Our present plight did not appear overnight, and the responsibility for our current situation is widespread. Reform of our educational system will take time and unwavering commitment. It will require equally widespread, energetic, and dedicated action. For example, we call upon the National Academy of Sciences, National Academy of Engineering, Institute of Medicine, Science Service, National Science Foundation, Social Science Research Council, American Council of Learned Societies, National Endowment for the Humanities, National Endowment for the Arts, and other scholarly, scientific, and learned societies for their help in this effort. Help should come from students themselves; from parents, teachers, and school boards; from colleges and universities; from local, State, and Federal officials; from teachers' and administrators' organizations; from industrial and labor councils; and from other groups with interest in and responsibility for educational reform.

It is their America, and the America of all of us, that is at risk; it is to each of us that this imperative is addressed. It is by our willingness to take up the challenge, and our resolve to see it through, that America's place in the world will be either secured or forfeited. Americans have succeeded before, and so we shall again.

ANN BASTIAN, NORM FRUCHTER, MARILYN GITTELL, COLIN GREER, AND KENNETH HASKINS, CHOOSING EQUALITY: THE CASE FOR DEMOCRATIC SCHOOLING, 1985

Many people praised A Nation at Risk, *and many were critical. A few reports emerged from other perspectives, asking fundamentally different questions about the nature of the risk to education and the social values that schools should reflect.* Choosing Equality *represents a thoughtful critique of* A Nation at Risk. *It also poses a series of important questions about the relationship of education to the larger social good.*

When the question is asked, "What should we do about the public schools?" it almost always means, "What should public schools do?" For the past two years, this has been the fundamental issue in the intense national debate over school reform. Beyond the focus on teacher morale or academic standards, we are probing the purposes of schooling, sorting out which needs schools should meet and what expectations they should fulfill.

For the general public, the debate expresses a rising fear about declining school performance and, perhaps more basically, fear about the future for youth in our society. This concern seems a natural product of recurring economic and social insecurity. The country is in the midst of profound structural shifts in technology, in job and income distribution, in family life and in government commitments. These shifts intensify existing inequities and threaten familiar patterns of individual mobility and community cohesion. Yet the debate also expresses hope. People turn to the schools as a social tool, one of few institutions which are public and local, for adapting to new demands and for protecting the coming generation.

Underlying the impulses to fear and hope is an unspoken tension between priorities for school change. We see this as a tension between two divergent goals for public education: a desire for schools to serve the competitive demands of a stratified society, and a desire for schools to play a socially integrative and democratic role, serving the right of all children to develop to their fullest potential. Some people do not see these as incompatible functions; other deny that they require different kinds of schooling. Yet, choices are being made, and in the current wave of school reform, democratic values of education have not been the central concern.

When we look beyond the universal call for excellence, we find new standards for achievement, but not new strategies for ensuring that all children will have the appropriate means to meet them. We find a new emphasis on accountability, but not institutional reforms which open the schools to those they serve. We find new tests for performance, but not analysis which measures the total school experience—including the patterns of inequality, rigidity, and exclusion which remain fundamental barriers to learning for millions of American schoolchildren.

This essay attempts to explore the tension between elitist and democratic goals in education in the present debate. Clearly, we feel that the democratic concepts of schooling should govern the direction of change and, in particular, that the massive school failure experienced in low-income communities should be of primary concern. We believe that equality in education is the inalienable right of all Americans. We believe that schools belong to citizens, not as clients but as owners of a public institution. And we believe that equality and participation in the educational process are essential conditions of educational excellence.

Yet we are also aware that our beliefs require a much firmer vision of what constitutes quality schooling and what is necessary to make quality a [more] universal commitment than has emerged in the debate thus far. This essay has, therefore, a threefold purpose: to understand where the current thrust for school change is leading, to examine alternative frameworks and approaches for restructuring our schools, and to consider what constituencies can be set in motion so that reform enlarges the democratic promise of education.

We are presenting an image of the opportunities for change, not a blueprint or formula which can ensure progressive outcomes in school reform. The agenda for democratic schooling will itself be incomplete until a more active and cohesive citizens' movement develops in education. What we propose are ways of viewing the options which would help break through the polarities of equity and excellence and move beyond the limits of past reform or present reaction. We try to connect what happens in the classroom to organizational and institutional contexts. We discuss the multiple levels of structural change necessary to achieve fundamental change. We explore the political processes which set priorities for education, and thus decide what we expect or tolerate in school performance.

There is the danger, of course, that such a sweeping statement of needs and issues may suggest all-or-nothing solutions. Our intent, however, is not to assert that anything short of wholesale reform can't make a difference. Rather, we try to envision long-term goals for change which place immediate struggles for school improvement in an ongoing process, so that today's demands are consistent with an overall vision for change, so that today's advocates can build isolated victories into broader challenges. Settling for piecemeal reform does have serious limitations: the problem of winning skirmishes and losing the war. Nonetheless, systematic change can proceed in stages, if we recognize that the basic conflicts between democratic and elitist purposes in schooling are not resolved because we have gained new ground.

In surveying these multiple dimensions of school reform, we have developed the following basic arguments.

The Mission of Schooling

The opening rounds of the school debate have been dominated by a neoconservative consensus which, by design or by default, identifies excellence with an elitist concept of meritocracy. The thrust has been to reinforce competitive structures of achievement, modeled on and serving the economic marketplace. This perspective misconstrues the crisis in education, which in our view is twofold: There is a catastrophic failure to provide decent schools and adequate skills to low-income students; there is also a chronic failure to provide reasoning and citizenship skills among all students. Moreover, school failure in the bottom tiers and narrow achievement throughout the system, cited to justify meritocratic practices, are in fact the result of such practices.

In establishing a framework for progressive alternatives, it is necessary to project a concept of education in which quality and equality are mutually inclusive standards. We must answer the questions: How do we measure equality? What defines democratic education?

Three Myths of School Performance

In further challenging the meritocratic framework, we examine three popular beliefs which underlie the neoconservative side of the school debate. These myths serve to narrow the vision of reform and to lower the expectations placed on education, particularly its role in meeting social needs and promoting capacities for citizenship.

Myth One is that today's school failures represent a recent development, in contrast with a "golden age" of public schooling which once served well both the elite and mass of students. But in our view, the gulf between elite and mass goals and methods of education has been a constant feature of our education system; today's failures express the tradition of a historically stratified system.

Myth Two is that the equity reforms attempted in the '60s and '70s have proven either diverting or damaging to the quest for excellence. In fact, the reforms enacted were not fully egalitarian, were actively subverted in their implementation, and have remained marginal to the education system. The reform era achieved a shift from exclusive meritocracy to inclusive meritocracy, but it did not transform the schools. Our choices are not limited to embracing either deficient reform or an elitist backlash; we can also choose to pursue more fundamental change.

Myth Three is that national economic growth and individual mobility are contingent on establishing more rigorous standards of education competition. Yet current economic trends contradict the notion that education will fuel economic recovery and broadly distribute economic rewards. The employment functions of schooling do not constitute a sufficient mechanism or rationale for structuring educational goals.

School Practice: Ingredients of Effective Instruction

If we seek to address the crisis of inequality which has meant school failure for the poor, and seek to improve the citizenship capacities of all students, we must refocus the debate over classroom reforms. Prevailing prescriptions for school improvement tend to swing between hard and soft approaches—poles expressed by calls to restore authority and toughen standards or, conversely, by the reflex to defend the neglect and lowered expectations that too often pass for "appropriate" education. These approaches ignore what is deeply flawed in the traditional structures of the learning environment: the neglect of critical inquiry, the isolation of teachers and segregation of students, inappropriate uses of time and testing, rigidity in response to diverse needs, the fragmentation and denial of supportive services.

Technological approaches, for stressing reward-or-punish models of accountability for both teachers and students, offer more of the same. Yet there are alternative models which tell us a great deal about the ingredients of effective instruction. Common to each is the construction of flexible, collaborative and human-scale school environments, and a clear commitment to equality of need. These models indicate that a systematic restructuring of school organization is necessary, in mainstream education as much as in programs to meet special needs, in suburban as well as ghetto schools.

School Constituencies: Directions for Change

To secure progressive changes in instruction, it is essential to go beyond the classroom focus and to challenge the arrangements of institutional power which subvert responsive education. School systems are typically constructed to deny parents, teachers, and communities a positive role in guiding school practice. These frontline constituencies are vital both as resources for school improvement and as activists for democratic priorities in the reform process. But it is often the case, particularly in the most deprived school systems, that parents are regularly excluded from participating in school affairs and even blamed for student failure. Teachers are frequently viewed as custodians and technicians, denied control over their working conditions and their professional development by the lack of supportive resources, by bureaucratic professionalism, by autocratic management. And schools, especially the worst schools, remain isolated from and often antagonistic toward the communities they serve.

The educational value of schools which empower their constituents and function as community institutions can be clearly demonstrated. Pursuing this goal on a broad scale, however, quickly raises the problem of making such reforms tangible, not token. We look at four topical issues which are proving important in defining our concept of the school as an open institution: voucher or optional enrollment systems, the Effective Schools Movement, community-based campaigns, and youth service programs.

Governance and Funding: Toward Progressive Federalism

Progressive reforms in the structure of education will not go far without addressing the fundamental governance and funding mechanisms which set the bottom lines for school priorities. In the face of conservative attempts to reduce government commitments, and with policy increasingly in the hands of bureaucrats and professionals, it is important to rethink our goals for federal, state, and local authority in education. We propose a concept of progressive federalism, altering the role of each level of government to promote the redistribution of resources and power in school institutions.

We advocate that the local school become the center of decision making, involving parents and communities, as well as frontline educators, in control over budget and policy. Recognizing state government as the pivotal arena for school change, we argue for a more strategic effort to reform funding formulas and standards; we project an activist state role in redressing the pervasive disparities in school revenues and in promoting local governance. We look to a federal role which enlarges both funding and mandates for educational equality. In formulating these potentials for progressive federalism, we affirm our belief that public education is not wholly bound by the powerful influences of social and economic stratification; the public sector can be shaped to serve democratic purposes, even as it contends with structural inequalities in society at large.

Today's Agenda

Taken as a whole, this essay rejects the notion of a one best reform or a one best school system. This essay is an effort to clarify the choices before us and the steps that promote or deter democratic purposes in education. Reviewing the major issues of the current debate, we look not only to specific proposals, but to the context in which they are offered: Are they seen as panaceas or as leverage points for restructuring? Do they substitute for fundamental changes or move toward them? Do they preempt the empowerment of school constituents or enlarge their capacities to shape policy in practice?

The school debate of the 1980s is far from over. While we question many of the initiatives launched in the name of excellence, the current excellence movement has at least focused public attention on the conditions of schooling. A broader vision of alternatives is being forged, in defense of past gains and in support of new models. This essay seeks to further enlarge our sense of opportunity and possibility by looking beyond the alarm over the school crisis, by moving toward a democratic conception of the public school mission, and by posing the priorities for change that democratic education demands.

Sonia Nieto, Affirming Diversity: The Sociopolitical Context of Multicultural Education, 1992

James Banks is often called the father of multicultural education. Certainly he has been a towering figure in the field for many years. A number of other scholars have also developed their own views on multicultural education. As with any topic in education, there are almost as many definitions of multicultural education as there are writers discussing the subject. Sonia Nieto from the University of Massachusetts at Amherst provides a clear definition of multicultural education and a compelling case for its value.

Multicultural education cannot be understood in a vacuum, but rather must be seen in its personal, social, historical, and political context. Assuming that multicultural education is "the answer" to school failure is simplistic at best, for it overlooks important social and educational issues that affect daily the lives of students. Educational failure is too complex and knotty an issue to be "fixed" by any single program or approach. However, if broadly conceptualized and implemented, multicultural education can have a substantive and positive impact on the educational experience of most students. That is the thesis of this book.

I have come to this understanding as a result of many experiences, including my childhood and my life as a student, teacher, researcher, and parent. As a young child growing up in Brooklyn, New York, during the 1940s, I was able to experience firsthand the influence that poverty, discrimination, and the perception of one's culture and language as inferior can have. Speaking only Spanish when I entered the first grade, I was immediately confronted with the arduous task of learning a second language while my already quite developed native language was all but ignored. Some 40 years later, I still recall the frustration of groping for words I did not know to express thoughts I could very capably say in Spanish. Equally vivid are memories of some teachers' expectations that because of our language and cultural differences, my classmates and I would not do well in school. This explains my fourth-grade teacher's response when mine was the only hand to go up when she asked if anybody in the class wanted to go to college. "Well, that's O.K.," she said, "because we always need people to clean toilets."

I also recall teachers' perceptions that there was something wrong with speaking a language other than English. "Is there anybody in this class who started school without speaking English?" my tenth-grade homeroom teacher asked loudly, filling out one of the endless forms that teachers are handed by the central office. By this time, my family had moved to what was at the time a working-class and primarily European-American neighborhood. My classmates looked in hushed silence as I, the only Puerto Rican in the class, raised my hand timidly. "Are you in a special English class?" he asked in front of the entire class. "Yes," I said, "I'm in Honors English." Although there is nothing wrong with being in a special class for English as a second language (ESL), I felt fortunate that I was able to respond in this way. I had learned to feel somewhat ashamed of speaking Spanish and wanted to make it very clear that I was intelligent in spite of it. Many students in similar circumstances who are in bilingual and ESL classes feel guilty and inferior to their peers.

Those first experiences with society's responses to cultural differences did not, of course, convince me that something was wrong with the *responses*. Rather, I assumed, as many of my peers did, that there was something wrong with *us*. We learned to feel ashamed of who we were, how we spoke, what we ate, and everything else that was "different" about us. "Please," I would beg my mother, "make us hamburgers and hot dogs for dinner." Luckily, she never paid attention and kept right on cooking rice, beans, platanos, and all those other good foods that we grew up with. She and my father also continued speaking Spanish to us, in spite of our teachers' pleas to speak to us only in English. And so, alongside the messages at school and in the streets that being Puerto Rican was not something to be proud of, we learned to keep on being who we were. As the case studies point out, these conflicting messages are still being given to many young people.

Immigration is not a phenomenon of the past. In fact, the experience of immigration is still fresh in the minds of a great many people in our country. It is an experience that begins anew every day that planes land, ships reach our shores, and people make their way on foot to our borders. Many of the students in our schools, even if they themselves are not immigrants, have parents or grandparents who were. The United States is thus not only a nation of immigrants as seen in some idealized and romanticized past; it is also a living nation of immigrants even today.

The pain and alienation of the immigrant experience, however, have rarely been confronted in our schools. This experience includes the forced immigration of enslaved Africans, and the colonization of American Indians and Mexicans from within. Because schools have traditionally perceived their role to be that of an assimilating agent, the isolation and rejection that come hand-in-hand with immigration and colonization have simply been left at the schoolhouse door. Curriculum and pedagogy, rather than using the lived experiences of students as a foundation, have been based on what can be described as an alien and imposed reality. The rich experiences of millions of our students, their parents, grandparents, and neighbors have been kept strangely quiet. Although we almost all have an immigrant past, very few of us know or even acknowledge it.

What the research reported in this book suggests to me is that we need to make this history visible by making it part of the curriculum, instruction, and educational experience in general. Whether through the words of Manuel, who claims that he cannot be an American because it would mean forsaking his Cape Verdean background, or those of Vanessa, who knows nothing about her European-American past and even feels uncomfortable discussing it, it has become clear that the immigrant experience is an important point of departure for beginning our journey into multicultural education. This journey needs to begin with teachers, who themselves are frequently unaware of or uncomfortable with their own ethnicity. By going through a process of reeducation about their own backgrounds, their families' pain, and their rich legacy of stories, teachers can lay the groundwork for students to reclaim their own histories and voices.

As an adult, I have come to the conclusion that no child should have to go through the painful dilemma of choosing between family and school and of what inevitably becomes a choice between belonging and succeeding. The costs for going through such an experience are high indeed, from becoming a "cultural schizophrenic" to developing doubts about one's self-worth and dignity. This is nowhere more poignantly described than Richard Rodriguez's painful recollection of growing up as a "scholarship boy," an academically promising student who is doomed to lose his family, culture, and language in the process. His conclusion is that one's public and private worlds cannot be reconciled:

> My awkward childhood does not prove the necessity of bilingual education. My story discloses instead an essential myth of childhood—inevitable pain. If I rehearse here the changes in my private life after my Americanization, it is finally to emphasize the public gain. The loss implies the gain.

Because of his wrenching loss of language and culture, Rodriguez decides that bilingual/multicultural education and affirmative action are all policies that cannot work because they in effect delay the inevitable loss. My conclusion is quite the opposite: *The loss implies the pain.* Just as the title of an important book on the issue asserts (*Minority Education: From Shame to Struggle*), our society must move beyond causing and exploiting students' shame to using their cultural and linguistic differences to struggle for an education that is more in tune with society's rhetoric of equal and high-quality education for all students. That is the fundamental lesson I have relearned while doing the research for this book.

Some Assumptions

It is necessary to clarify a number of assumptions embedded in the text. The first concerns who is included in multicultural education. My perspective is that multicultural education is for everyone regardless of ethnicity, race, language, social class, religion, gender, or sexual preference. My framework for multicultural education is thus a very broad and inclusive one. Nevertheless, although I refer in the text to many kinds of differences, I am particularly concerned with race, ethnicity, and language. These are the major issues that provide a lens through which I view multicultural education. This perspective is probably based on a number of reasons, not the least of which is my own experience. Another reason concerns the very history of multicultural education. A direct outgrowth of the civil rights movement, multicultural and bilingual education was developed as a response to inequality in education based on racism, ethnocentrism, and language discrimination. Although I believe it is imperative to include other differences, for me it is necessary to approach an understanding of multicultural education with a firm grounding in these three areas.

This brings up another dilemma related to inclusion. It is easier for some educators to embrace a very inclusive and comprehensive framework of multicultural education because they have a hard time facing racism. They may prefer to deal with issues of class, exceptionality, or religious diversity because, for them, these factors may be easier to confront. Racism is an excruciatingly difficult issue for most of us. Given our history of exclusion and discrimination, this is not surprising. Nevertheless, I believe it is only through a thorough investigation of discrimination based on race and other differences related to it that we can understand the genesis as well as the rationale for multicultural education. I will also refer to gender, social class, and exceptionality because these areas provide other important lenses with which to view inequality in education. However, because no one book can possibly give all of these issues the central importance they deserve, I have chosen to focus on race, ethnicity, and language.

Another assumption that guides this book is that teachers should not be singled out as the villains in the failure of so many students. Although some teachers do indeed bear the responsibility for having low expectations, being racist and elitist in their interactions with students and parents, and providing educational environments that discourage many students from learning, most do not do so consciously. Most teachers are sincerely concerned about their students and want very much to provide the best education they can. Nevertheless, they are often at the mercy of decisions made by others far removed from the classroom. In addition, they have little to do with developing the policies and practices in operation in their schools and frequently do not even question them.

Teachers are also the products of educational systems that have a history of racism, exclusion, and debilitating pedagogy. As such, they put into practice what they themselves have been subjected to and thus perpetuate structures that may be harmful to many of their students. Furthermore, the disempowerment felt by so many teachers is a palpable force in many schools. Finally, schools cannot be separated from communities or from our society in general. Oppressive forces that limit opportunities in the schools are a reflection of such forces in the society at large. Thus, the purpose of this book is not to point a finger, but to provide a forum for reflection and discussion so that teachers take responsibility for their actions, challenge the actions of schools and society that affect their students' education, and help effect positive change.

Overview

Multicultural education cannot be understood in a vacuum. Yet it is often presented as somehow divorced from the policies and practices of schools and from the society in which we live. The result is a fairyland kind of multicultural education disassociated from the lives of teachers, students, and their communities. The premise of this book is quite different: No educational philosophy or program is worthwhile unless it focuses on two primary concerns:

- Raising the achievement of all students and thus providing them with an equal and equitable education
- Giving students the opportunity to become critical and productive members of a democratic society

To the extent that it remains education to help students get along, or to help them feel better about themselves, or to "sensitize" them to one another, without tackling the central but far more difficult issues of stratification, empowerment, and inequity, multicultural education becomes another approach that simply scratches the surface of educational failure. Although we may all want our students to get along and to be sensitive to and respect one another, this by itself will make little difference when it comes to the options they have as a result of their schooling. Because the choices they make are inexorably affected by social and political forces in schools and society, it is necessary to consider them in our understanding of multicultural education.

Equal education in this context goes beyond providing the same resources and opportunities for all students, although this alone would be a crucial step in affording a better education for a wide variety of students. By remaining at this level, however, it completely misses the point that education is a two-way process. That is, education must involve the interaction of students with teachers and schools, not simply the action of teachers and schools on students. Equal education thus also means that the skills, talents, and experiences that all students bring to their education need to be considered valid starting points for further schooling. *Equity* is a more comprehensive term because it includes equal educational opportunities while at the same time demanding fairness and the real possibility of *equality of outcomes* for a broader range of students. Throughout this book, multicultural education will be considered as fundamental to educational equity.

ARTHUR M. SCHLESINGER, JR., THE DISUNITING OF AMERICA, 1991

While many educators rallied to the cause of multicultural education, others became more and more critical. Few issues have cut so deeply to the core questions of the nature and purpose of schooling and the fundamental nature of the American story. Arthur M. Schlesinger, advisor to President John F. Kennedy and well-known liberal icon, surprised many with the vehemence of his attack on multicultural education. For Schlesinger, multiculturalism can quickly lead to division and separation; he wants none of it.

The attack on the common American identity is the culmination of the cult of ethnicity. That attack was mounted in the first instance by European Americans of non-British origin ("unmeltable ethnics") against the British foundations of American culture; then, latterly and massively, by Americans of non-European origin against the European foundations of that culture. As Theodore Roosevelt's foreboding suggests, the European immigration itself palpitated with internal hostilities, everyone at everybody else's throats—hardly the "monocultural" crowd portrayed by ethnocentric separatists. After all, the two great "world" wars of the 20th century began as fights among European states. Making a single society out of this diversity of antagonistic European peoples is a hard enough job. The new salience of non-European, nonwhite stocks compounds the challenge. And the non-Europeans, or a least their self-appointed spokesmen, bring with them a resentment, in some cases a hatred, of Europe and the West provoked by generations of Western colonialism, racism, condescension, contempt, and cruel exploitation.

Will not this rising flow of non-European immigrants create a "minority majority" that will make Europeans obsolete by the 21st century? This is the fear of some white Americans and the hope (and sometimes the threat) of some nonwhites.

Immigrants were responsible for a third of population growth during the 1980s. More arrived than in any decade since the second of the century. And the composition of the newcomers changed dramatically. In 1910, nearly 90 percent of immigrants came from Europe. In the 1980s, more than 80 percent came from Asia and Latin America.

Still, foreign-born residents constitute only about 7 percent of the population today, as against nearly 15 percent when the first Roosevelt and Wilson were worrying about hyphenated Americans. Stephan Thernstrom doubts that the minority majority will ever arrive. The black share in the population has grown rather slowly—9.9 percent in 1920, 10 percent in 1950, 11.1 percent in 1970, 12.1 percent in 1990. Neither Asian Americans nor Hispanic Americans go in for especially large families; and family size in any case tends to decline as income and intermarriage increase. "If today's immigrants assimilate to American ways as readily as their predecessors at the turn of the century—as seems to be happening," Thernstrom concludes, "there won't be a minority majority issue anyway."

America has so long seen itself as the asylum for the oppressed and persecuted—and has done itself and the world so much good thereby—that any curtailment of immigration offends something in the American soul. No one wants to be a Know-Nothing. Yet uncontrolled immigration is an impossibility; so the criteria of control are questions the American democracy must confront. We have shifted the basis of [immigration policy] administration three times this century—from national origins in 1924, to family reunification in 1965, to needed skills in 1990. The future of immigration policy depends on the capacity of the assimilation process to continue to do what it has done so well in the past: to lead newcomers to an acceptance of the language, the institutions, and the political ideals that hold the nation together.

Is Europe really the root of all evil? The crimes of Europe against lesser breeds without the law (not to mention even worse crimes—Hitlerism and Stalinism—against other Europeans) are famous. But these crimes do not alter other facts of history: that Europe was the birthplace of the United States of America, that European ideas and culture formed the republic, that the United States is an extension of European civilization, and that nearly 80 percent of Americans are of European descent.

When Irving Howe, hardly a notorious conservative, dared write, "The Bible, Homer, Plato, Sophocles, Shakespeare are central to our culture," an outraged reader ("having graduated this past year from Amherst") wrote, "Where on Howe's list is the *Quran,* the *Gita,* Confucius, and other central cultural artifacts of the peoples of our nation?" No one can doubt the importance of these works, nor the influence they have had on other societies. But on American society? It may be too bad that dead white European males have played so large a role in shaping our culture. But that's the way it is. One cannot erase history.

These humdrum historical facts, and not some dastardly imperialist conspiracy, explain the Eurocentric slant in American schools. Would anyone seriously argue that teachers should conceal the European origins of American civilization? or that schools should educate the 20 percent and ignore the 80 percent? Of course the 20 percent and their contributions should be integrated into the curriculum, too, which is the point of cultural pluralism.

But self-styled "multiculturalists" are very often ethnocentric separatists who see little in the Western heritage beyond Western crimes. The Western tradition, in this view, is inherently racist, sexist, "classist," hegemonic; irredeemably repressive, irredeemably oppressive. The spread of Western culture is due not to any innate quality but simply to the spread of Western power. Thus the popularity of European classical music around the world—and, one supposes, of American jazz and rock, too—is evidence not of wide appeal but of "the pattern of imperialism, in which the conquered culture adopts that of the conqueror."

Such animus toward Europe lay behind the well-known crusade against the Western Civilization course at Stanford ("Hey-hey, ho-ho, Western Culture's got to go!"). According to the National Endowment for the Humanities, students can graduate from 78 percent of American colleges and universities without taking a course in the history of Western civilization. A number of institutions—among them Dartmouth, Wisconsin, Mount Holyoke—require courses in third-world or ethnic studies, but not in Western civilization. The mood is one of divesting Americans of the sinful European inheritance and seeking redemptive infusions from non-Western cultures.

One of the oddities of the situation is that the assault on the Western tradition is conducted very largely with analytical weapons forged in the West. What are the names invoked by the coalition of latter-day Marxists, deconstructionists, poststructuralists, radical feminists, Afrocentrists? Marx, Nietzsche, Gramsci, Derrida, Foucault, Lacan, Sartre, de Beauvoir, Habermas, the Frankfurt "critical theory" school—Europeans all. The "unmasking," "demythologizing," "decanonizing," "dehegomizing" blitz against Western culture depends on methods of critical analysis unique to the West—which surely testifies to the internally redemptive potentialities of the Western tradition.

Even Afrocentrists seem to accept subliminally the very Eurocentric standards they think they are rejecting. "Black intellectuals condemn Western civilization," Professor Pearce Williams says, "yet ardently wish to prove it was founded by their ancestors." And, like Frantz Fanon and Leopold Senghor, whose books figure prominently on their reading lists, Afrocentric ideologues are intellectual children of the West they repudiate. Fanon, the eloquent spokesman of the African wretched of the earth, had French as his native tongue and based his analyses on Freud, Marx, and Sartre. Senghor, the prophet of Negritude, wrote in French, established the Senegalese educational system on the French model and, when he left the presidency of Senegal, retired to France.

Western hegemony, it would seem, can be the source of protest as well as of power. Indeed, the invasion of American schools by the Afrocentric curriculum, not to mention the conquest of university departments of English and comparative literature by deconstructionists, poststructuralists, etc., are developments that by themselves refute the extreme theory of "cultural hegemony." Of course, Gramsci had a point.

Ruling values do dominate and permeate any society; but they do not have the rigid and monolithic grip on American democracy that academic leftists claim. . . .

It is time to adjourn the chat about hegemony. If hegemony were as real as the cultural radicals pretend, Afrocentrism would never have got anywhere, and the heirs of William Lyons Phelps would still be running the Modern Language Association.

Is the Western tradition a bar to progress and a curse on humanity? Would it really do America and the world good to get rid of the European legacy?

No doubt Europe has done terrible things, not least to itself. But what culture has not? History, said Edward Gibbon, is little more than the register of the crimes, follies, and misfortunes of mankind. The sins of the West are no worse than the sins of Asia or of the Middle East or of Africa.

There remains, however, a crucial difference between the Western tradition and the others. The crimes of the West have produced their own antidotes. They have provoked great movements to end slavery, to raise the status of women, to abolish torture, to combat racism, to defend freedom of inquiry and expression, to advance personal liberty and human rights.

Whatever the particular crimes of Europe, that continent is also the source—the *unique* source—of those liberating ideas of individual liberty, political democracy, the rule of law, human rights, and cultural freedom that constitute our most precious legacy and to which most of the world today aspires. These are *European* ideas, not Asian, nor African, nor Middle Eastern ideas, except by adoption.

The freedoms of inquiry and of artistic creation, for example, are Western values. Consider the differing reactions to the case of Salman Rushdie: what the West saw as an intolerable attack on individual freedom, the Middle East saw as a proper punishment for an evildoer who had violated the mores of his group. Individualism itself is looked on with abhorrence and dread by collectivist cultures in which loyalty to the group overrides personal goals—cultures that, social scientists say, comprise about 70 percent of the world's population.

There is surely no reason for Western civilization to have guilt trips laid on it by champions of cultures based on despotism, superstition, tribalism, and fanaticism. In this regard, the Afrocentrists are especially absurd. The West needs no lectures on the superior virtue of those "sun people" who sustained slavery until Western imperialism abolished it (and, it is reported, sustain it to this day in Mauritania and the Sudan), who still keep women in subjection and cut off their clitorises, who carry out racial persecutions not only against Indians and other Asians but against fellow Africans from the wrong tribes, who show themselves either incapable of operating a democracy or ideologically hostile to the democratic idea, and who, in their tyrannies and massacres, their Idi Amins and Boukassas, have stamped with utmost brutality on human rights.

Certainly the European overlords did little enough to prepare Africa for self-government. But democracy would find it hard in any case to put down roots in a tribalist and patrimonial culture that, long before the West invaded Africa, had sacralized the personal authority of chieftains and ordained the submission of the rest. What the West would call corruption is regarded through much of Africa as no more than the prerogative of power. Competitive political parties, an independent judiciary, a free press, the rule of law are alien to African traditions.

It was the French, not the Algerians, who freed Algerian women from the veil (much to the irritation of Frantz Fanon, who regarded deveiling as symbolic rape); as in India it was the British, not the Indians, who ended (or did their best to end) the horrible custom of *suttee*—widows burning themselves alive on their husbands' funeral pyres. And it was the West, not the non-Western cultures, that launched the crusade to abolish slavery—and in doing so encountered mighty resistance, especially in the Islamic world (where Moslems, with fine impartiality, enslaved whites as well as blacks). Those many brave and humane Africans who are struggling these days for decent societies are animated by Western, not by African, ideals. White guilt can be pushed too far.

The Western commitment to human rights has unquestionably been intermittent and imperfect. Yet the ideal remains—and movement toward it has been real, if sporadic. Today it is the *Western* democratic tradition that attracts and empowers people of all continents, creeds, and colors. When the Chinese students cried and died for democracy in Tiananmen Square, they brought with them not representations of Confucius or Buddha, but a model of the Statue of Liberty.

The great American asylum, as Crevecoeur called it, open, as Washington said, to the oppressed and persecuted of all nations, has been from the start an experiment in a multiethnic society. This is a bolder experiment than we sometimes remember. History is littered with the wreck of states that tried to combine diverse ethnic or linguistic or religious groups within a single sovereignty. Today's headlines tell of imminent crisis or impending dissolution in one or another multiethnic polity—the Soviet Union, India, Yugoslavia, Czechoslovakia, Ireland, Belgium, Canada, Lebanon, Cyprus, Israel, Ceylon, Spain, Nigeria, Kenya, Angola, Trinidad, Guyana . . . The list is almost endless. The luck so far of the American experiment has been due in large part to the vision of the melting pot. "No other nation," Margaret Thatcher has said, "has so successfully combined people of different races and nations within a single culture."

But even in the United States, ethnic ideologues have not been without effect. They have set themselves against the old American ideal of assimilation. They call on the republic to think in terms not of individual but of group identity and to move the polity from individual rights to group rights. They have made a certain progress in transforming the United States into a more segregated society. They have done their best to turn a college generation against Europe and the Western tradition. They have imposed ethnocentric, Afrocentric, and bilingual curricula on public schools, well designed to hold minority children out of American society. They have told young people from minority groups that the Western democratic tradition is not for them. They have encouraged minorities to see themselves as victims and to live by alibis rather than to claim the opportunities opened for them by the potent combination of black protest and white guilt. They have filled the air with recrimination and rancor and have remarkably advanced the fragmentation of American life.

Yet I believe the campaign against the idea of common ideals and a single society will fail. Gunnar Myrdal was surely right: For all the damage it has done, the upsurge of ethnicity is a superficial enthusiasm stirred by romantic ideologues and unscrupulous hucksters whose claim to speak for their minorities is thoughtlessly accepted by the media. I doubt that the ethnic vogue expresses a reversal of direction from assimilation to apartheid among the minorities themselves. Indeed, the more the ideologues press the case for ethnic separatism, the less they appeal to the mass of their own groups. They have thus far done better in intimidating the white majority than in converting their own constituencies.

"No nation in history," writes Lawrence Fuchs, the political scientist and immigration expert in his fine book *The American Kaleidoscope,* "had proved as successful as the United States in managing ethnic diversity. No nation before had ever made diversity itself a source of national identity and unity." The second sentence explains the success described in the first, and the mechanism for translating diversity into unity has been the American Creed, the civic culture—the very assimilating, unifying culture that is today challenged, and not seldom rejected, by the ideologues of ethnicity.

A historian's guess is that the resources of the Creed have not been exhausted. Americanization has not lost its charms. Many sons and daughters of ethnic neighborhoods still want to shed their ethnicity and move to the suburbs as fast as they can—where they will be received with far more tolerance than they would have been seventy years ago. The desire for achievement and success in American society remains a potent force for assimilation. Ethnic subcultures, Stephen Steinberg, author of *The Ethnic Myth,* points out, fade away "because circumstances forced them to make choices that undermined the basis for cultural survival."

Others may enjoy their ethnic neighborhoods but see no conflict between foreign descent and American loyalty. Unlike the multiculturalists, they celebrate not only what is distinctive in their own backgrounds but what they hold in common with the rest of the population.

The ethnic identification often tends toward superficiality. The sociologist Richard Alba's study of children and grandchildren of immigrants in the Albany, New York, area shows the most popular "ethnic experience" to be sampling the ancestral cuisine. Still, less than half the respondents picked that, and only 1 percent ate ethnic food every day. Only one-fifth acknowledged a sense of special relationship to people of their own ethnic background; less than one-sixth taught their children about their ethnic origins; almost none was fluent in the language of the old country. "It is hard to avoid the conclusion," Alba writes, "that ethnic experience is shallow for the great majority of whites."

If ethnic experience is a good deal less shallow for blacks, it is because of their bitter experience in America, not because of their memories of Africa. Nonetheless most blacks prefer "black" to "African American," fight bravely and patriotically for their country, and would move to the suburbs, too, if income and racism would permit.

As for Hispanic Americans, first-generation Hispanics born in the United States speak English fluently, according to a Rand Corporation study; more than half of second-generation Hispanics give up Spanish altogether. When *Vista,* an English-language monthly for Hispanics, asked its readers what historical figures they most admired, Washington, Lincoln, and Theodore Roosevelt led the list, with Benito Juarez trailing behind as fourth, and Eleanor Roosevelt and Martin Luther King, Jr. tied for fifth. So much for ethnic role models.

Nor, despite the effort of ethnic ideologues, are minority groups all that hermetically sealed off from each other, except in special situations, like colleges, where ideologues are authority figures. The wedding notices in any newspaper testify to the increased equanimity with which people these days marry across ethnic lines, across religious lines, even, though to a smaller degree, across racial lines. Around half of Asian-American marriages are with non-Orientals, and the Census Bureau estimates one million interracial—mostly black-white—marriages in 1990 as against 310,000 in 1970.

The ethnic revolt against the melting pot has reached the point, in rhetoric at least, though not, I think, in reality, of a denial of the idea of a common culture and a single society. If large numbers of people really accepted this, the republic would be in serious trouble. The question poses itself: how to restore the balance between *unum* and *pluribus?*

The old American homogeneity disappeared well over a century ago, never to return. Ever since, we have been preoccupied in one way or another with the problem, as Herbert Croly phrased it 80 years back in *The Promise of American Life,* "of preventing such divisions from dissolving the society into which they enter—of keeping such a highly differentiated society fundamentally sound and whole." This required, Croly believed, "an ultimate bond of union." There was only one way by which solidarity could be restored, "and that is by means of a democratic social ideal . . ."

The genius of America lies in its capacity to forge a single nation from peoples of remarkably diverse racial, religious, and ethnic origins. It has done so because democratic principles provide both the philosophical bond of union and practical experience in civic participation. The American Creed envisages a nation composed of individuals making their own choices and accountable to themselves, not a nation based on inviolable ethnic communities. The Constitution turns on individual rights, not on group rights. Law, in order to rectify past wrongs, has from time to time (and in my view, often properly so) acknowledged the claims of groups; but this is the exception, not the rule.

Our democratic principles contemplate an open society founded on tolerance of individuals with differences and on mutual respect. In practice, America has been more open to some than to others. But it is more open to all today than it was yesterday and is likely to be even more open tomorrow than today. The steady movement of American life has been from exclusion to inclusion.

Historically and culturally, this republic has an Anglo-Saxon base; but from the start the base has been modified, enriched, and reconstituted by transfusions from other continents and civilizations. The movement from exclusion to inclusion causes a constant revision in the texture of our culture. The ethnic transfusions affect all aspects of American life—our politics, our literature, our music, our painting, our movies, our cuisine, our customs, our dreams. . . .

The American identity will never be fixed and final; it will always be in the making. Changes in the population have always brought changes in the national ethos and will continue to do so; but not, one must hope, at the expense of national integration. The question America confronts as a pluralistic society is how to vindicate cherished cultures and traditions without breaking the bonds of cohesion—common ideals, common political institutions, common language, common culture, common fate—that hold the republic together.

Our task is to combine due appreciation of the splendid diversity of the nation with due emphasis on the great unifying Western ideas of individual freedom, political democracy, and human rights. These are the ideas that define the American nationality—and that today empower people of all continents, races, and creeds.

"What then is the American, this new man? . . . Here individuals of all nations are melted into a new race of men." Still a good answer—still the best hope.

David C. Berliner and Bruce J. Biddle, The Manufactured Crisis, 1995

While talk of school reform—and the implicit critique of the American education system—dominated the last decades of the twentieth century, some educators began to ask dif-

ferent questions. Was so much reform necessary? Was so much really wrong with the schools? David Berliner and Bruce Biddle offered a new perspective in their book, charging that the crisis in the schools is manufactured—developed not to improve schools, but to dismantle them.

This book was written in outrage.

Throughout much of recent history, our federal government seemed to be willing to promote the interests of public education. Advocates who favored public schools appeared regularly in both the White House and Congress; various programs to support the needs of our schools passed into law over the years; and although we knew that those schools continued to face many problems, our political leaders seemed to be aware of those problems and to be willing to respect the results of research on education in their pronouncements. Thus, like many other Americans, we came to believe that in their discussions of education, our federal leaders were, within limits, well-intentioned and honest people.

Events in the last decade have certainly challenged these beliefs. In 1983, the Reagan White House began to make sweeping claims attacking the conduct and achievements of America's public schools—claims that were contradicted by evidence we knew about. We thought at first this might have been a mistake, but these and related hostile and untrue claims were soon to be repeated by many leaders of the Reagan and Bush administrations. The claims were also embraced in many documents issued by industrialists and business leaders and were endlessly repeated and embroidered on by the press. And, as time passed, even leading members of the education community—including a number of people whom we knew personally—began to state these lies as facts.

Slowly, then, we began to suspect that something was not quite right, that organized malevolence might actually be underway. We were, however, busy people, and it took us a while to begin to act on our suspicions. Though we had been friends for some years, our first acts were independent ones. David began to make speeches in which he challenged some of the false claims that were being made about schools and their effects, and Bruce began to write essays about the various ways in which federal politicians and their allies were throttling research and misusing evidence about education.

Eventually, we discovered that we were worried about the same things, and we decided to do a book together; then our education truly began. The more we poked into our story, the more nasty lies about education we unearthed; the more we learned about how government officials and their allies were ignoring, suppressing, and distorting evidence; and the more we discovered how Americans were being misled about schools and their accomplishments. This, then, has been the source of our outrage. We also began to wonder why this was happening—why were some people in Washington so anxious to scapegoat educators, what were they really up to, what problems were they trying to hide, what actions did they want to promote or prevent?

We also learned that the answers to these questions are not simple. Some of those who have accepted hostile myths about education have been genuinely worried about our schools, some have misunderstood evidence, some have been duped, and some have had other understandable reasons for their actions. But many of the myths seem also to have been told by powerful people who—despite their protestations—were pursuing a political agenda designed to weaken the nation's public schools, redistribute support for those schools so that privileged students are favored over needy students, or even abolish those schools altogether. To this end, they have been prepared to tell lies, suppress evidence, scapegoat educators, and sow endless confusion. We consider this conduct particularly despicable.

This book, then, is designed to set the record straight about these events; to examine the evidence and correct the hostile myths that have been told about our schools; to explore why they were told and what the myth-tellers were up to; to examine the real problems of education that have too often been masked; and to explore what might be done about those problems.

Thinking About Education in a Different Way

Headlines, news articles, and television news reports have recently portrayed a grim picture of children and their schools, a picture consistent enough to frighten thoughtful and caring people into concern for the future of their nation. Take, for example, the following news reports:

- In a typical year during the 1980s, minors aged fourteen to nineteen accounted for 43.4 percent of all criminal offenses. Fifty-four percent of all murder cases in the nation involved jobless youth.
- A junior high school gang of six extorts $2,500 from 120 classmates.
- Forty-four high school students go wild and raid five shops for merchandise.
- High school girls turn to prostitution for entertainment, curiosity, and as a source of revenue—police report their rate is up 262 percent.
- Fourteen-year-old student, repeatedly tormented and beaten by school thugs, hangs himself.
- Teen tortured by two gang members. Victim burned by cigarettes on hands and back.
- Group of students report feeling "refreshed" after beating up another child.
- Ten percent of the nation's middle schools request police guards for their graduation ceremonies.

With reports like these so commonplace, it is easy to understand why so many people worry so much about schooling and youth. But in this case, the people who have the worrying to do are not Americans. These are all reports from the *Japanese* media about the awful world of *Japanese* youth and the terrible failure of *Japanese* public schooling!

Were you surprised? We suspect that most American readers would automatically think that these statements concerned *American* youth and *American* schools. After all, every week our media seem to supply us with yet another frightening story about the dreadful state of education in our country. In contrast, Americans regularly read and hear glowing reports of Japanese schools and their students' performance on international tests of achievement. Negative stories about Japanese schools are rarely found in our press or on our TV screens. Thus, Americans have been prevented from learning that the Japanese educational system also has enormous problems. In fact, if one judges by American values and standards, Japanese schools are often brutal, overly competitive places.

Perhaps you will find this hard to believe. This may be because, like many other Americans, you have not been told about the thousands of elementary and junior high school students in Japan who refuse to attend school because of persistent problems of bullying—often directed against those with a foreign upbringing or against those who get outstanding grades or who have physical disabilities. Nor have Americans been made aware of the coercive overregulation of students and their families by many Japanese schools. For example, one Japanese school has a policy about the number of pleats permitted in a girl's skirt, violation of which results in the suspension of the child unless the mother comes to school to beg forgiveness. Another school's policy on hair color and curls requires those who do not have straight black hair to obtain a note from a physician stating that they have a genetic problem. Other schools have policies that encourage cruelty by teachers; students have been given electric shocks for low grades, have died because they were locked in unventilated sheds as punishment for smoking, or have been beaten for using a hairdryer "illegally." Americans are also not often told about the gifts of money that Japanese parents frequently pay to teachers to ensure good grades and good letters of recommendation for their children.

You may think our judgments are harsh, but we are not alone in condemning Japanese schools for brutality and for promoting overachievement. A decade ago, a select committee of *Japanese* educators reported to their own prime minister and his council of advisors that

> Bullying, suicides among school children, dropping out from school, increasing delinquency, violence both at home and at school, heated entrance exam races, overemphasis on scholastic ratings, and torture of children by some teachers are the result of the pathological mechanisms that have been established in Japan's educational system.

Manufacturing a Crisis in Education

> Seldom in the course of policymaking in the U.S. have so many firm convictions held by so many been based on so little convincing proof.

> —Clark Kerr
> *President Emeritus of the University of California (1991)*

Given the serious problems of Japanese education, why have so many Americans come to believe that *American* education is so deficient and that we should look to the Japanese to find out how to run our schools? The answer is that for more than a dozen years, this groundless and damaging message has been proclaimed by major leaders of our government and industry and has been repeated endlessly by a compliant press. Good-hearted Americans have come to believe that the public schools of their nation are in a crisis state because they have so often been given this false message by supposedly credible sources.

To illustrate, in 1983, amid much fanfare, the White House released an incendiary document highly critical of American education. Entitled *A Nation at Risk,* this work was prepared by a prestigious committee under the direction of then Secretary of Education Terrell Bell and was endorsed in a speech by President Ronald Reagan. It made many claims about the "failures" of American education, how those "failures" were confirmed by "evidence," and how this would inevitably damage the nation. (Unfortunately, none of the supposedly supportive "evidence" actually appeared in *A Nation at Risk,* nor did this work provide citations to tell Americans where that "evidence" might be found.)

But leaders in this disinformation campaign were not content merely to attack American schools. *A Nation at Risk* charged that American students never excelled in international comparisons of student achievement and that this failure reflected systematic weaknesses in our school programs and lack of talent and motivation among American educators. Thus, it came as little surprise when the White House soon sent a team of Americans to Japan to discover and report on why Japanese education was so "successful." Following this visit, the then Assistant Secretary of Education, Chester Finn, a leader of the team, said of the Japanese:

> They've demonstrated that you can have a coherent curriculum, high standards, good discipline, parental support, a professional teaching force and a well-run school. They have shown that the average student can learn a whole lot more.

This enthusiasm was echoed by others on the team. According to team member Herbert Walberg, an educational researcher, features of the Japanese system could be adopted in America and would help to solve the many "problems" of American education. Walberg suggested, "I think it's portable. Gumption and willpower, that's the key."

This was far from the end of White House criticisms of American education. Indeed, the next decade witnessed a veritable explosion of documents and pronouncements from government leaders—two American presidents, Ronald Reagan and George Bush, secretaries of education, assistant secretaries, and chiefs and staff members in federal agencies—telling Americans about the many "problems" of their public schools. As in *A Nation at Risk,* most of these claims were said to reflect "evidence," although the "evidence" in question either was not presented or appeared in the form of simplistic, misleading generalizations.

During the same years, many leaders in industry claimed in documents and public statements that American education was in deep trouble, that as a result our country was falling behind foreign competitors, and that these various charges were all confronted by "evidence" (which somehow was rarely presented or appeared in simple, misleading formats). And these many charges, documents, and pronouncements from leaders of government and industry, often seconded by prominent members of the educational community, were dutifully reported and endlessly elaborated upon by an unquestioning press.

So it is small wonder that many Americans have come to believe that education in our country is now in a deplorable state. Indeed, how could they have concluded anything else, given such an energetic and widely reported campaign of criticism, from such prestigious sources, attacking America's public schools? To the best of our knowledge, no campaign of this sort had ever before appeared in American history. Never before had an American government been so critical of the public schools, and never had so many false claims been made about education in the name of "evidence." We shall refer to this campaign of criticism as the Manufactured Crisis.

The Manufactured Crisis was not an accidental event. Rather, it appeared within a specific historical context and was led by identifiable critics whose political goals could be furthered by scapegoating educators. It was also supported from its inception by an assortment of questionable techniques—including misleading methods for analyzing data, distorting reports of findings, and suppressing contradictory evidence. Moreover, it was tied to misguided schemes for "reforming" education—schemes that would, if adopted, seriously damage American schools.

Unfortunately, the Manufactured Crisis has had a good deal of influence—thus, too many well-meaning, bright, and knowledgeable Americans have come to believe some of its major myths, and this has generated serious mischief. Damaging programs for educational reform have been adopted, a great deal of money has been wasted, effective school programs have been harmed, and morale has declined among educators.

But myths need not remain unchallenged; in fact, they have become shaky when they are exposed to the light of reason and evidence. When one actually *looks* at the evidence, one discovers that most of the claims of the Manufactured Crisis are, indeed, myths, half-truths, and sometimes outright lies. Thus, as our first major task, we undertake, through reason and displays of relevant evidence, to dispel some of the mischief of the Manufactured Crisis—to place the crisis in context, to counter its myths, to explain why its associated agenda will not work, to set the record straight.

But accomplishing only this first task would leave many questions unanswered. One of the worst effects of the Manufactured Crisis has been to divert attention away from the *real* problems faced by American education—problems that are serious and that are escalating in today's world. To illustrate, although many Americans do not realize it, family incomes and financial support for schools are *much* more poorly distributed in our country than in other industrialized nations. This means that in the United States, very privileged students attend some of the world's best private and public schools, but it also means that large numbers of students who are truly disadvantaged attend public schools whose support is far below that permitted in other Western democracies. Thus, opportunities are *not* equal in America's schools. As a result, the achievements of students in schools that cater to the rich and the poor in our country are also far from equal.

In addition, America's school system has expanded enormously since World War II and now serves the needs of a huge range of students. This increased diversity has created many opportunities—but also many dilemmas—and debates now rage over how to distribute resources and design curricula to meet the needs of students from diverse backgrounds, with many different skills and interests. Problems such as these *must* be addressed if Americans are to design a school system that truly provides high standards and equal opportunities for all students.

Our second major task, then, is to direct attention away from the fictions of the Manufactured Crisis and toward the real problems of American schools.

HERBERT KOHL, THE DISCIPLINE OF HOPE, 1998

Herb Kohl's first day as a teacher is recorded in chapter 8 in this volume, within the selection from his best known book, Thirty-Six Children. *By 1998, Kohl was a seasoned veteran, looking back on three decades of effort to improve the lives of children in schools. Kohl pleads with educators to maintain their hope in the face of tremendous obstacles. His statement is a fitting conclusion to this study—and a reminder that essential chapters are yet to be added to the history of schooling in the United States.*

These are not easy times in which to keep hope alive in poor or even middle-class communities. The most common question I am asked these days is whether the schools are

Kohl, Herbert. *The Discipline of Hope: Learning from a Lifetime of Teaching.* New York: Simon and Schuster, 1998.

worse now than they were when I began teaching. My answer is no; they are just about as bad. But now there are more local efforts to provide decent schools, based on the notion that all children can learn, than I have ever seen before. Unfortunately, the world beyond the school is much harsher toward children, much more cynical about the future, and much more indifferent to those children who do not have privilege, support, or special gifts that will enable them to succeed. The ordinary child, my child, your child, our children have a much harder time of it than I have ever seen before, and their needs are not being met by most schools.

And yet I have hope—hope that we will look intelligently at what *is* working, especially for poor children, and learn from those special places how to shape learning for children in the spirit of hope. I hope that we as adults will then make it our business to transform society into the place of hope that we have prepared them for.

A common characteristic of all these schools and educational programs, which I call schools and classrooms of hope, is that staff, parents, and community are in common accord that every child can learn. They all see their role as making the doable possible, and this is reflected in how their students come to believe in themselves as learners. This is in contrast with the majority of schools for the poor, where the staff is demoralized and projects the belief that only a small number of the children can learn. In such schools, the community and parents are often considered the enemies; this turns the school into a sad, isolated place that perpetuates failure.

Schools of hope are places where children are honored and well-served. They have a number of common characteristics, no matter where they are to be found across the country. They are safe and welcome places, comfortable environments that have a homey feel. They are places where students can work hard without being harassed, but also places where the joy of learning is expressed in the work of the children and in their sense of being part of a convivial learning community. They are places where the teachers and staff are delighted to work and are free to innovate, while at the same time they are willing to take responsibility for their students' achievement. If you look to children in schools like these, they express a pride of place and sense of ownership that are also manifest in how the rest of the community regards the school. Parents feel welcome and often have a role in school governance. Community volunteers are abundant. Hope, projected primarily through the children's learning, is also manifest in how the physical environment of the school is treated with respect.

We do have many schools of hope across the country, and many teachers who try to build classrooms of hope within more hostile and indifferent schools. It is essential to seek out these places, to support them, and to learn from them. Simply acknowledging that there are places where public education works is not a formula for school change. Besides, particular formulas do not work anyway. You have to know the community you serve, know what you want to teach or need to teach. You have to understand the times in which you work and your responsibilities as a citizen to fight for your children. Most of all, you have to love to be there with them, have to be delighted in their presence and feel the awe at their growth that any gardener does in experiencing the unfolding of a beautiful flower or the emergence of a delicious fruit or vegetable. It takes hard, careful, loving work to nurture hope and bring learning into the school—but what a birthing, what a pleasure, what fun despite all the struggles. And because teaching is so full of love, so hope-centered, and so difficult, it is also one of the most painful vocations. Despite the best teaching and the most passionate learning, this society has a way of wasting young talent. To teach well and care about children has a double edge that keeps one militant as well as romantic, that tempers what you know children can do with worry about what might happen to them after school, on the streets, in the job market, and in their own personal lives. . . .

With these, as with all of the challenges of teaching and learning, I'm looking forward to beginning again. There's no end to the delights and joys of teaching, no limit to the challenges we will continue to face in order to serve children well, and no limit to the creativity and love adults can and should bring to helping children grow through teaching, which is, at its heart, the discipline of hope.

FOR FURTHER READING

Basic Background Information for Studying the History of American Education

Lawrence A. Cremin's three-volume history remains the most comprehensive discussion of schooling in the United States:

Cremin, Lawrence A. *American Education: The Colonial Experience, 1607–1783.* New York: Harper & Row, 1970.

———. *American Education: The National Experience, 1783–1876.* New York: Harper & Row, 1980.

———. *American Education: The Metropolitan Experience, 1876–1980.* New York: Harper & Row, 1988.

In addition, a number of excellent studies provide a strong framework for studying the history of schooling in the United States, including:

Hoffman, Nancy. *Women's "True" Profession: Voices from the History of Teaching.* Old Westbury, N.Y.: The Feminist Press, 1981.

Spring, Joel. *The American School, 1642–1996.* New York: McGraw-Hill, 2001.

———, *American Education.* New York: McGraw-Hill, 2000.

Takaki, Ronald. *A Different Mirror: A History of Multicultural America.* Boston: Little, Brown, 1993.

Urban, Wayne, and Wagoner, Jennings, Jr. *American Education: A History.* New York: McGraw-Hill, 2000.

Chapter 1: The School in Colonial America, 1620–1770

Axtell, James. *The Invasion Within: The Contest of Cultures in Colonial North America.* New York: Oxford University Press, 1985.

Bailyn, Bernard. *Education in the Forming of American Society.* Chapel Hill: University of North Carolina Press, 1960.

Best, John Hardin, ed. *Benjamin Franklin on Education.* New York: Teachers College Press, 1967.

Calam, John. *Parsons and Pedagogues: The Society for the Propagation of the Gospel Adventure in American Education.* New York: Columbia University Press, 1971.

Ford, Paul Leicester, ed. *The New England Primer.* New York: Teachers College Press, 1962.

Franklin, Benjamin. *The Autobiography of Benjamin Franklin.* New York: New American Library, 1961.

Jennings, Francis. *The Invasion of America: Indians, Colonialism, and the Cant of Conquest.* New York: W. W. Norton, 1976.

Morison, Samuel Eliot. *The Intellectual Life of Colonial New England.* Ithaca: Cornell University Press, 1936, 1956.

Szasz, Margaret Connell. *Indian Education in the American Colonies, 1607–1783.* Albuquerque: University of New Mexico Press, 1988.

Chapter 2: The American Revolution and Schools for the New Republic, 1770–1820

Bailyn, Bernard. *The Ideological Origins of the American Revolution.* Cambridge: Harvard University Press, 1967.

Commager, Henry Steele. *Noah Webster's American Spelling Book.* New York: Teachers College Press, 1962.

Kaestle, Carl F. *Pillars of the Republic: Common Schools and American Society, 1780–1860.* New York: Hill and Wang, 1983.

Lee, Gordon C. *Crusade Against Ignorance: Thomas Jefferson on Education.* New York: Teachers College Press, 1961.

Rudolph, Frederick, ed. *Essays on Education in the Early Republic.* Cambridge: Harvard
    University Press, 1965.

Chapter 3: The Common School Movement, 1820–1860

Cremin, Lawrence A., ed. *The Republic and the School: Horace Mann on the Education of
    Free Men.* New York: Teachers College Press, 1957.
Glenn, Charles Leslie, Jr. *The Myth of the Common School.* Amherst: The University of
    Massachusetts Press, 1988.
Kaestle, Carl F. *The Evolution of an Urban School System: New York City, 1750–1850.*
    Cambridge: Harvard University Press, 1973.
Kaestle, Carl F. *Pillars of the Republic: Common Schools and American Society, 1780–1860.*
    New York: Hill and Wang, 1983.
Kaestle, Carl F., and Vinovskis, Marias. *Education and Social Change in Nineteenth-Century
    Massachusetts.* New York: Cambridge University Press, 1980.
Katz, Michael. *The Irony of Early School Reform.* Cambridge: Harvard University Press, 1968.
Lannie, Vincent P. *Public Money and Parochial Education: Bishop Hughes, Governor Seward,
    and the New York School Controversy.* Cleveland: Case Western Reserve University
    Press, 1968.
Messerli, Jonathan. *Horace Mann: A Biography.* New York: Alfred A. Knopf, 1972.
Schultz, Stanley K. *The Culture Factory: Boston Public Schools, 1789–1860.* New York:
    Oxford University Press, 1973.
Sklar, Kathryn Kish. *Catharine Beecher: A Study in American Domesticity.* New Haven, Conn:
    Yale University Press, 1973.
Solomon, Barbara Miller. *In the Company of Educated Women: A History of Women and
    Higher Education in America.* New Haven, Conn.: Yale University Press, 1985.

Chapter 4: Schooling Moves West, 1835–1860

American Book Company. *McGuffey's Fifth Eclectic Reader.* Cincinnati: American Book
    Company, 1836, 1920.
American Book Company. *McGuffey's Sixth Eclectic Reader.* Cincinnati: American Book
    Company, 1836, 1920.
Berkhofer, Robert F., Jr. *Salvation and the Savage: An Analysis of Protestant Missions and
    American Indian Response, 1787–1862.* University of Kentucky Press, 1965.
Brown, Dee. *Bury My Heart at Wounded Knee: An Indian History of the American West.* New
    York: Henry Holt, 1970.
Fraser, James W. *Pedagogue for God's Kingdom: Lyman Beecher and the Second Great
    Awakening.* Lanham, Md.: University Press of America, 1985.
Kaufman, Polly Welts. *Women Teachers on the Frontier.* New Haven: Yale University
    Press, 1984.
See also Sklar and Solomon, Chapter 3.

Chapter 5: Slavery, Reconstruction, and the Schools of the South, 1820–1903

Anderson, James D. *The Education of Blacks in the South, 1860–1935.* Chapel Hill: University
    of North Carolina Press, 1988.
Boylan, Anne M. *Sunday School: The Formation of an American Institution, 1790–1880.* New
    Haven, Conn.: Yale University Press, 1988.
Bullock, Henry Allen. *A History of Negro Education in the South: From 1619 to the Present.*
    New York: Praeger, 1970.
Butchart, Ronald E. *Northern Schools, Southern Blacks, and Reconstruction: Freedmen's
    Education, 1862–1875.* Westport, Conn.: Greenwood Press, 1980.
Douglass, Frederick. *Life and Times of Frederick Douglass, Written by Himself.* Hartford,
    Conn.: Park Publishing, 1991.

DuBois, W. E. B. *The Souls of Black Folk.* Greenwich, Conn.: Fawcett Publications, 1953, 1964.

DuBois, W. E. B. *Black Reconstruction: An Essay Towards a History of the Part Which Black Folk Played in the Attempt to Reconstruct Democracy in America, 1860–1880.* New York: Russell and Russell, 1935.

Franklin, John Hope, and Moss, Alfred A., Jr. *From Slavery to Freedom: A History of African Americans,* 7th ed. New York: Alfred A. Knopf, 1994.

Genovese, Eugene D. *Roll, Jordan, Roll: The World the Slaves Made.* New York: Vintage Books, 1972.

Jones, Jacqueline. *Soldiers of Light and Love: Northern Teachers and Georgia Blacks, 1865–1873.* Chapel Hill: University of North Carolina Press, 1980.

McAfee, Ward M. *Religion, Race, and Reconstruction: The Public School in the Politics of the 1870s.* Albany, N.Y.: State University of New York Press, 1998.

McFeely, William S. *Frederick Douglass.* New York: Simon & Schuster, 1991.

Raboteau, Albert J. *Slave Religion: The "Invisible Institution" in the Antebellum South.* New York: Oxford University Press, 1978.

Washington, Booker T. *Up from Slavery: An Autobiography.* New York: Doubleday-Page, 1901.

Webber, Thomas L. *Deep Like the Rivers: Education in the Slave Quarter Community, 1831–1865.* New York: W. W. Norton, 1978.

Chapter 6: Growth and Diversity in Schools and Students 1880–1960

Adams, David Wallace. *Education for Extinction: American Indians and the Boarding School Experience, 1875–1928.* Lawrence: University Press of Kansas, 1995.

Allen, Paula Gunn. *The Sacred Hoop: Recovering the Feminine in American Indian Traditions.* Boston: Beacon Press, 1992.

Antin, Mary. *The Promised Land.* Boston: Houghton Mifflin, 1911.

Axtell, James. *The European and the Indian: Essays in the Ethnohistory of Colonial North America.* New York: Oxford University Press, 1981.

Burns, J. A. *The Catholic School System in the United States: Its Principles, Origin, and Establishment.* New York: 1908.

Dog, Mary Crow, with Erdoes, Richard. *Lakota Woman.* New York: Harper, 1990.

Franklin, Barry M. *From "Backwardness" to "At-Risk": Childhood Learning Difficulties and the Contradictions of School Reform.* Albany: State University of New York Press, 1994.

Gonzalez, Gilbert. *Chicano Education in the Era of Segregation.* Philadelphia: Balch Institute Press, 1990.

Lazerson, Marvin. *Origins of the Urban School: Public Education in Massachusetts, 1870–1915.* Cambridge: Harvard University Press, 1971.

Low, Victor. *The Unimpressible Race: A Century of Educational Struggle by the Chinese in San Francisco.* San Francisco: East/West Publishing, 1982.

McCluskey, Neil G., S.J. *Catholic Education in America: A Documentary History.* New York: Teachers College Press, 1964.

Prucha, Francis Paul, ed. *Documents of United States Indian Policy,* 2nd ed., expanded. Lincoln: University of Nebraska Press, 1990.

———. *The Great Father: The United States Government and the American Indians,* 2 vols. Lincoln: University of Nebraska Press, 1984.

Ravitch, Diane. *The Great School Wars: New York City, 1805–1973.* New York: Basic Books, 1974.

Rury, John L. *Education and Women's Work: Female Schooling and the Division of Labor in Urban American, 1870–1930.* Albany: State University of New York Press, 1991.

Sanders, James W. *The Education of an Urban Minority: Catholics in Chicago, 1833–1965.* New York: Oxford University Press, 1977.

————. Boston Catholics and the School Question, 1825–1907. In James W. Fraser, Henry L. Allen, and Sam Barnes, eds., *From Common School to Magnet School: Selected Essays in the History of Boston's Schools.* Boston: Boston Public Library, 1979.

San Miguel, Guadalupe, Jr. *"Let All of Them Take Heed": Mexican Americans and the Campaign for Educational Equality in Texas, 1910–1981.* Austin: University of Texas Press, 1987.

Takaki, Ronald. *Strangers from a Different Shore: A History of Asian Americans.* New York: Penguin Books, 1989.

Walsh, Catherine. *Pedagogy and the Struggle for Voice: Issues of Language, Power, and Schooling for Puerto Ricans.* New York: Bergin and Garvey, 1991.

Chapter 7: The Progressive Era, 1890–1950

Bowers, C. A. *The Progressive Educator and the Depression: The Radical Years.* New York: Random House, 1969.

Counts, George S. *Dare the School Build a New Social Order?* Edited and with an introduction by Wayne Urban. Carbondale: Southern Illinois University Press, 1978.

Cremin, Lawrence A. *The Transformation of the School: Progressivism in American Education, 1876–1957.* New York: Random House, 1961.

Cuban, Larry. *How Teachers Taught: Constancy and Change in American Classrooms, 1890–1990,* 2nd ed. New York: Teachers College Press, 1993.

Dewey, John. *Democracy and Education.* New York: Macmillan, 1916.

————. *The Child and the Curriculum.* Chicago: The University of Chicago Press, 1902.

————. *The School and Society.* Chicago: University of Chicago Press, 1900.

Graham, Patricia Albjerg. *Progressive Education: From Arcady to Academe.* New York: Teachers College Press, 1967.

Katz, Michael B. *Class, Bureaucracy, and Education: The Illusion of Educational Change in America.* New York: Praeger, 1975.

Labaree, David F. *The Making of an American High School.* New Haven, Conn.: Yale University Press, 1988.

Murphy, Marjorie. *Blackboard Unions: The AFT and the NEA, 1900–1980.* Ithaca: Cornell University Press, 1990.

Reese, William J. *The Origins of the American High School.* New Haven, Conn.: Yale University Press, 1995.

Reese, William J. *Power and the Promise of School Reform: Grass-Roots Movement During the Progressive Era.* Boston: Routledge & Kegan Paul, 1986.

Smith, Joan K. *Ella Flagg Young: Portrait of a Leader.* Ames, Ia.: Educational Studies Press, 1979.

Tyack, David. *The One Best System: A History of American Urban Education.* Cambridge: Harvard University Press, 1974.

Tyack, David, and Hansot, Elisabeth. *Managers of Virtue: Public School Leadership in America, 1820–1980.* New York: Basic Books, 1982.

Tyack, David; Lowe, Robert; and Hansot, Elisabeth. *Public Schools in Hard Times: The Great Depression and Recent Years.* Cambridge: Harvard University Press, 1984.

Westbrook, Robert. *John Dewey and American Democracy.* Ithaca: Cornell University Press, 1991.

Wrigley, Julia. *Class Politics and Public Schools: Chicago, 1900–1950.* New Brunswick, N.J.: Rutgers University Press, 1982.

Urban, Wayne J. *Why Teachers Organized.* Detroit: Wayne State University Press, 1982.

Chapter 8: Schools in the Cold War Era, 1950–1970

Andryszewski, Tricia. *School Prayer: A History of the Debate.* Springfield, N.J.: Enslow Publishers, 1997.

Dudley, Mack E. *Engel v. Vitale (1962): Religion and the Schools,* New York: Twenty-First Century Books/Henry Holt, 1995.

Fitzgerald, Frances. *America Revised: History Schoolbooks in the Twentieth Century.* New York: Vintage Books, 1979.

Kliebard, Herbert M. *The Struggle for the American Curriculum, 1893–1958.* Boston: Routledge & Kegan Paul, 1986.

Kohl, Herbert. *Thirty Six Children.* New York: New American Library, 1967.

Mirel, Jeffrey. *The Rise and Fall of an Urban School System: Detroit, 1907–1981.* Ann Arbor: University of Michigan Press, 1993.

Ravitch, Diane. *The Troubled Crusade: American Education, 1945–1980.* New York: Basic Books, 1983.

Spring, Joel. *The Sorting Machine: National Educational Policy Since 1945.* New York: McKay, 1976.

Trace, Arthur S. *What Ivan Knows That Johnny Doesn't.* New York: Random House, 1961.

See also Cuban, Chapter 7.

Chapter 9: Civil Rights, Integration, and School Reform, 1954–1980

Carson, Clayborne; Garrow, David J.; Gill, Gerald; Harding, Vincent; and Hine, Darlene Clark. *The Eyes on the Prize Reader: Documents, Speeches, and Firsthand Accounts from the Black Freedom Struggle, 1954–1990.* New York: Penguin Books, 1991.

Coleman, James S., et al. *Trends in School Segregation, 1968–1973.* Washington, D.C.: Urban Institute, 1975.

Coleman, James S.; Campbell, Ernest Q.; Hobson, Carol J.; McPortland, James; Mood, Alexander M.; Weinfeld, Fredrick D., and York, Robert L. *Equality of Educational Opportunity.* Washington, D.C.: U. S. Government Printing Office, 1966.

Cronin, Joseph M. *The Control of Urban Schools: Perspectives on the Power of Educational Reformers.* New York: Free Press, 1973.

Kluger, Richard. *Simple Justice.* New York: Alfred A. Knopf. 1976.

Kozol, Jonathan. *Death at an Early Age: The Destruction of the Hearts and Minds of Negro Children in the Boston Public Schools.* Boston: Houghton Mifflin, 1967.

Myrdal, Gunnar. *An American Dilemma: The Negro Problem and Modern Democracy.* New York: Harper & Row, 1944.

Orfield, Gary. *The Reconstruction of Southern Education: The Schools and the 1964 Civil Rights Act.* New York: Wiley Interscience, 1969.

Washington, James M., ed. *A Testament of Hope: The Essential Writings and Speeches of Martin Luther King, Jr.* New York: HarperCollins, 1991.

Chapter 10: Rights and Opportunities in American Education, 1965–1980

Berke Joel S., and Kirst, Michael W. *Federal Aid to Education: Who Benefits? Who Governs?* Lexington, Mass.: D. C. Heath, 1972.

Fellman, David. *The Supreme Court and Education,* 3rd ed. New York: Teachers College Press, 1976.

Graham, Hugh Davis. *Uncertain Triumph: Federal Educational Policy in the Kennedy and Johnson Years.* Chapel Hill: University of North Carolina Press, 1984.

Jordan, Barbara C., and Rostow, Elispeth D. *The Great Society: A Twenty Year Critique.* Austin, Tex.: Lyndon Baines Johnson Library, 1986.

Porter, Rosalie Pedalino. *Forked Tongue: The Politics of Bilingual Education.* New York: Basic Books, 1990.

Silberman, Charles E. *Crisis in the Classroom: The Remaking of American Education.* New York: Random House, 1970.

Wollenberg, Charles. *All Deliberate Speed: Segregation and Exclusion in California Schools, 1855–1975.* Berkeley: University of California Press, 1976.

Chapter 11: Reform Efforts of the 1980s and 1990s

Apple, Michael. *Cultural Politics and Education.* New York: Teachers College Press, 1996.

Apple, Michael. *Official Knowledge: Democratic Education in a Conservative Age.* New York: Routledge, 1993.

Asante, Molefi Kete. *Afrocentricity.* Trenton, N.J.: Africa World Press, 1988.

Bell, Terrell. *The Thirteenth Man: A Reagan Cabinet Memoir.* New York: The Free Press, 1988.

Berliner, David C., and Biddle, Bruce J. *The Manufactured Crisis: Myths, Fraud, and the Attack on America's Schools.* Reading, Mass.: Addison-Wesley, 1995.

Chubb J., and Moe, T. *Politics, Markets, and America's Schools.* Washington, D.C.: Brookings Institution, 1990.

Cornbleth, Catherine, and Waugh, Detter. *The Great Speckled Bird: Multicultural Politics and Education Policy Making.* New York: St. Martin's Press, 1995.

Foster, Michele. *Black Teachers on Teaching.* New York: The New Press, 1997.

Fraser, James W. *Between Church and State: Religion and Public Education in a Multicultural America.* New York: St. Martin's, 1999.

Giroux, Henry. *Border Crossings: Cultural Workers and the Politics of Education.* New York: Routledge, 1992.

Kozol, Jonathan. *Savage Inequalities: Children in America's Schools.* New York: Crown, 1991.

McLaren, Peter. *Revolutionary Multiculturalism: Pedagogies of Dissent for the New Millennium.* Boulder, Colo.: Westview Press, 1997.

Meier, Deborah. *The Power of Their Ideas.* Boston, Beacon Press, 1995.

Nieto, Sonia. *Affirming Diversity: The Sociopolitical Context of Multicultural Education.* New York: Addison-Wesley Longman, 2000.

Ogbu, John A. Variability in Minority School Performance: A Problem in Search of an Explanation. *Anthropology and Education Quarterly,* vol. 18 (1987), pp. 312–34.

Sarason, Seymour B. *Revisiting "The Culture of the School and the Problem of Change."* New York: Teachers College Press, 1996.

Schlesinger, Arthur, Jr. *The Disuniting of America: Reflections on a Multicultural Society.* Whittle Direct Books, 1991.

For the most up-to-date information on continuing school reform efforts in the new century, check these websites:

Education Week: www.edweek.org

U.S. Department of Education: www.ed.gov

SOURCES

Note: I have listed the source of the document actually used in the preparation of this text. Where I have taken the document from a more recent source, both the original and the more recent source are indicated with the original source listed first.

Chapter One: The School in Colonial America, 1620-1770

Virginia Council [London], "Instructions to Governor of Virginia," 1636
Susan M. Kingsbury, ed., *Virginia County Records*. The Records of the Virginia Company of London: The Court Book. From the Manuscript in the Library of Congress. 4 volumes. Washington, D.C.: Government Printing Office, 1906-1935, Vol. III, pp. 14-15.
From Robert H. Bremner, ed., *Children and Youth in America: A Documentary History, Volume I: 1600-1865*. Cambridge: Harvard University Press, 1970, p. 75.

Virginia Statutes on the Education of Indian Children Held Hostage, 1656
Susan M. Kingsbury, ed., *Virginia County Records*. The Records of the Virginia Company of London: The Court Book. From the Manuscript in the Library of Congress. 4 volumes. Washington, D.C.: Government Printing Office, 1906-1935, Vol. I, p. 396.
From Robert H. Bremner, ed., *Children and Youth in America: A Documentary History, Volume I: 1600-1865*. Cambridge: Harvard University Press, 1970, p.75.

South Carolina Statute on Conversion of Slaves to Christianity, 1711
J. Brevard, ed., *Digest of the Public Statute Law of South Carolina*. Charleston, 1814, Vol. II, p. 229.
From Robert H. Bremner, ed., *Children and Youth in America: A Documentary History, Volume I: 1600-1865*. Cambridge: Harvard University Press, 1970, p. 97.

Missionary Report on Baptism of Slaves, 1719
William L. Saunders, ed., *The Colonial Records of North Carolina (1662-1776)*. 10 volumes. Raleigh: P.M. Hale, etc., 1886-1890, Vol. II (1886), pp. 331-333.
From Robert H. Bremner, ed., *Children and Youth in America: A Documentary History, Volume I: 1600-1865*. Cambridge: Harvard University Press, 1970, p. 97.

Virginia's Cure, or an Advisive Narrative Concerning Virginia, 1662
R. G., *Virginia's Cure, or An Advisive Narrative Concerning Virginia*. London, 1662, pp. 5-6, 9, 10-11.
From Robert H. Bremner, ed., *Children and Youth in America: A Documentary History, Volume I: 1600-1865*. Cambridge: Harvard University Press, 1970, p. 90.

Sir William Berkeley to the Lords' Commissioners on Foreign Plantations, 1671
W. W. Hening, ed., *Statutes at Large of Virginia (1619-1782)*. 13 volumes. Richmond: Samuel Pleasants, 1809-1823, Vol. II, p. 517.
From Robert H. Bremner, ed., *Children and Youth in America: A Documentary History, Volume I: 1600-1865*. Cambridge: Harvard University Press, 1970, p. 90.

Massachusetts' Old Deluder Satan Law, 1647
Nathaniel Shurtleff, ed. *Records of the Governor and Company of Massachusetts Bay, 1628-1686*. 5 volumes. Boston: W. White, 1853-1854, Vol. II, p. 203.
From Robert H. Bremner, ed., *Children and Youth in America: A Documentary History, Volume I: 1600-1865*. Cambridge: Harvard University Press, 1970, p. 81.

Benjamin Franklin, Autobiography, 1714–1718
Benjamin Franklin, *The Works of Benjamin Franklin*, with Notes and a Life of the Author by Jared Sparks. London: Benjamin Franklin Stevens, 1882, pp. 9-10, 14-16.

The New England Primer, *1727*
The New England Primer. Boston: Printed and Sold By John Perkins, 1768. MHS Neg. #1313, #1314, #1315, #1316, #1319, and #1490.

Chapter Two: The American Revolution and Schools for the New Republic, 1770-1820

Thomas Jefferson, A Bill For the More General Diffusion of Knowledge, 1799
Paul Leicester Ford, ed., *The Writings of Thomas Jefferson, Volume III, 1781-1784*. New York: G. P.
    Putnam's Sons, 1894, pp. 242-243, 251, 253-255.
Thomas Jefferson, Notes on the State of Virginia, 1783
Thomas Jefferson, *Notes on the State of Virginia*. London: John Stockdale, 1787, pp. 136-137, 143,
    146-149.
Benjamin Rush, Thoughts Upon the Mode of Education Proper in a Republic, 1786
Benjamin Rush, *Essays Literary, Moral & Philosophical*. Philadelphia: Samuel F. Bradford, 1798, pp. 2-20.
Benjamin Rush, Thoughts Upon Female Education, 1787
Benjamin Rush, M.D., *Thoughts Upon Female Education, accommodated to the Present State of Society,
    Manners and Government*. Boston: John W. Folsom, 1791, pp. 3-14 from an original copy at the
    Massachusetts Historical Society.
Noah Webster, On the Education of Youth in America, 1790
Noah Webster, *A Collection of Essays and Fugitive Writings on Moral, Historical, Political and Literary
    Subjects*. Boston: L. Thomas and E. T. Andrews, 1790, pp. 3-11, 15-18, 22-30, 36, from an original
    copy at the Massachusetts Historical Society.
U.S. Congress, The Northwest Ordinance, 1787
United States Congress, "An Ordinance for the Government of the Territory of the United States north-west
    of the river Ohio," July 13, 1787, in *Public Statutes at Large of the United States of America*, edited by
    Richard Peters. Boston: Little, Brown, and Company, 1856, Vol. I, pp. 52-53.
U.S. Congress, Civilization Fund Act, 1819
United States Congress, "An Act making provision for the civilization of the Indian tribes adjoining the
    frontier settlements," March 3, 1819, in *Public Statutes at Large of the United States of America*, edited
    by Richard Peters. Boston: Little, Brown, and Company, 1856, Vol. III, pp. 516-517.

Chapter Three: The Common School Movement, 1820-1860

*Horace Mann, Tenth and Twelfth Annual Reports to the Massachusetts Board of Eduction, 1846 and
    1848*
Horace Mann, *Annual Reports on Education*. Boston: Lee and Shepard, 1872, pp. 533-536, 544-550,
    650-651, 701-706, 715-717, 731, 734-737, 753-754, from an original copy at the Massachusetts
    Historical Society.
Catharine E. Beecher, An Essay on the Education of Female Teachers, 1835
Catharine Beecher, "An Essay on the Education of Female Teachers". New York: Van Nostrand & Dwight,
    1835. From an original in the Lane Theological Seminary collection at the Library of McCormack
    Theological Seminary, Chicago.
The Common School Journal, Debate Over Plan to Abolish the Board of Education, 1840
The Common School Journal, Boston, August 1, 1840, Vol. II, No. 15, pp. 225-240. From an original copy
    of the Journal, Gutman Library, Harvard Graduate School of Education.
Petition of the Catholics of New York for a Portion of the Common School Fund, 1840
Lawrence Kehoe, ed., *Complete Works of the Most Rev. John Hughes, D.D., Archbishop of New York*. 2 vol-
    umes. New York: Lawrence Kehoe, 1865, Vol. I, pp. 102-107.
The Desegregation of the Boston Public Schools, 1846-1855
"Report to the Primary School Committee, June 15, 1846, on the Petition of Sundry Colored Persons for
    the Abolition of the Schools for Colored Children," Boston, 1846, p. 2 and 28-30; "Sarah C. Roberts v.
    The City of Boston, 5 Mass. Reports," 1849, pp. 200-201, 206-210; "Argument of Charles Sumner Esq.
    Against the Constitutionality of Separate Colored Schools in the Case of Sarah C. Roberts vs. The City
    of Boston," Boston, 1849, pp. 4-30, selections; "An Act in amendment of An Act concerning Public
    Schools," Chapter 256, Massachusetts Acts and Resolves, 1854-1855, Boston, 1855, pp. 674-675.
From Robert H. Bremner, ed., *Children and Youth in America: A Documentary History, Volume I:
    1600-1865*. Cambridge: Harvard University Press, 1970, pp. 528-535.

Chapter Four: Schooling Moves West, 1835-1860

Selections from McGuffey's Sixth Eclectic Reader, 1836
McGuffey's Sixth Eclectic Reader. Cincinnati: Van Antwerp, Bragg & Co., 1879, pp. 115-118, 128-129.
Calvin E. Stowe, Report on Elementary Public Instruction in Europe, 1836
"Report on Elementary Public Instruction in Europe, made to the Thirty-Sixth General Assembly of the
    State of Ohio, December 19, 1837 by C. E. Stowe," reprinted, Boston: Dutton and Wentworth, State

Printers, 1838, pp. 17-21, 51-54. Copy of the Report in the Archives of the Massachusetts Historical Society, Boston, Massachusetts.

Board of National Popular Education, Correspondence, 1849-1850
"Second Annual Report of the General Agent of the Board of National Popular Education," Cleveland: Steam Press of M. C. Younglove & Co, 1849, pp. 29-32.
"Third Annual Report of the General Agent of the Board of National Popular Education," Cleveland: Steam Press of M. C. Younglove & Co, 1850, pp. 35-39.

Mary Augusta Roper, Letter From Mill Point, Michigan, 1852-1854
From the Archives of the Board of National Popular Education, Connecticut State Historical Archives.
Cited in Polly Welts Kaufman, *Women Teachers on the Frontier*. New Haven, CT: Yale University Press, 1984, pp. 160-165.

The Speech of Red Jacket, the Seneca Chief, to a Missionary, circa 1830
John McIntosh, *History of the North American Indians; Their Origin, with a Faithful Description of their manners and customs, both civil and military, their religions, languages, dress, and ornaments . . .*, New Haven: H. Mansfield, 1859. Copy in the Harvard College Library, Cambridge, Massachusetts.

Chapter Five: Slavery, Reconstruction and the Schools of the South, 1820-1903

Frederick Douglass, The Narrative of the Life of Frederick Douglass: An American Slave, 1845
Frederick Douglass, *Narrative of the Life and Times of Frederick Douglass, Written by Himself.* Boston: Published at the Anti-Slavery Office, 1845, pp. 33-34, 36-44, from an original copy at the Massachusetts Historical Society.

The New England Freedmen's Aid Society—Official Records, 1862-1872
Minutes. February 1, 1862, February 7, 1862, and September 10, 1862. Volume of Minutes, 1862-74. Ms. N-10 New England Freemen's Aid Society Records.
Annual Meeting. 1872. Volume of Minutes, 1862-74. Ms. N-10 New England Freemen's Aid Society Records.

The New England Freedmen's Aid Society—Correspondence, 1865-1874
N. E. Brackett. Letters to Edward D. Cheney, March 14, 1865 and September 29, 1869. Ms. N-10 New England Freemen's Aid Society Records.
N. E. Brackett. Letter to Caroline Alfred, January 8, 1874. Ms. N-10 New England Freemen's Aid Society Records.

Charlotte Forten, The Journal of Charlotte Forten, 1862
Brenda Stevenson, ed. *The Journals of Charlotte Forten Grimke.* New York: Oxford University Press, 1988, pp. 380-383, 387-394, 397-401, 404-407.

Booker T. Washington, The Future of the American Negro, 1899
Booker T. Washington, *The Future of the American Negro.* Boston: Small, Maynard & Company, 1899, pp. 16-41.

W.E.B. DuBois, The Souls of Black Folk, 1903
W. E. B. DuBois, *The Souls of Black Folk.* Chicago: A. C. McClurg & Co., 1903, pp. 41-59, 88-109.

Chapter Six: Growth and Diversity in Schools and Students, 1880-1960

Third Plenary Council of Baltimore, 1884
Acta et Decreta Concilii Plenarii Baltimorensis Tertii. Baltimorae: Typis Joannis Murphy et sociorum, MDCCCLXXXVI, pp. 104; [English text pp. lxxviii-lxxix, lxxxii-lxxxvi.]

Mary Antin, The Promised Land, 1912
Mary Antin, *The Promised Land.* Boston: Houghton Mifflin Company, 1912, pp. 198-215.

Lewis Meriam, The Problem of the Indian Administration, 1928
Lewis Meriam, et al., *The Problem of Indian Administration.* Baltimore: Johns Hopkins University Press, 1928, pp. 8-9, 11-14, 32-37.

The Asian Experience in California, 1919-1920
"California and the Oriental: Japanese, Chinese, and Hindus, Report of State Board of Control of California to Gov. Wm. D. Stephens, June 19, 1920, revised to January 1, 1922,". Sacramento: California State Printing Office, 1922, pages 213-215, 221-233. Copy in the Harvard College Library, Cambridge, Massachusetts.

Beatrice Griffith, American Me, 1948
Beatrice Griffith, *American Me.* Boston: Houghton Mifflin Company, 1948, pp. 144-169.

Teaching Children of Puerto Rican Background in the New York City Schools, 1954

Board of Education of the City of New York, "Teaching Children of Puerto Rican Background in New York City Schools: Suggested Plans and Procedures," June 28, 1954, pages 1-2, 6, 9-10, 13, 25-26.

Chapter Seven: The Progressive Era, 1890-1950

James Jackson Storrow, **Son of New England,** *1932*
Henry Greenleaf Pearson, *Son of New England: James Jackson Storrow*. Boston: Thomas Todd Company, 1932, pp. 43-53.
Margaret Haley, **Why Teachers Should Organize,** *1904*
Margaret A. Haley, "Why Teachers Should Organize," National Educational Association, *Addresses and Proceedings*. St. Louis, 1904, pp. 145-152.
Ella Flagg Young, **Isolation in the School,** *1901*
Ella Flagg Young, *Isolation in the School*. Chicago: University of Chicago Press, 1901, pp. 24, 88-92, 106-111.
Grace C. Strachan, **Equal Pay for Equal Work,** *1910*
Grace C. Strachan, *Equal Pay for Equal Work*. New York: B. F. Buck, 1910, pp. 117-122.
Cora Bigelow, ***World Democracy and School Democracy,*** *1918*
Cora Bigelow, "World Democracy and School Democracy." Boston: *Boston Teachers Newsletter*, December, 1918, pages 10-11.
John Dewey, **The School and Society,** *1899*
John Dewey, *The School and Society*. Chicago: University of Chicago Press, 1899, pp. 6-29.
Lewis M. Terman, **National Intelligence Tests,** *1919*
Lewis M. Terman, *The Intelligence of School Children*. Boston: Houghton Mifflin Company, 1919, pp. 1-21.
George Counts, **Dare the School Build A New Social Order?** *1932*
George S. Counts, *Dare the School Build a New Social Order?* New York: The John Day Company, 1932, pp. 13-27.
The Social Frontier, *1934*
The Social Frontier: A Journal of Educational Criticism and Reconstruction, October, 1934, Vol. I, No. 1, pp. 3-5, 11-12.

Chapter Eight: Schools in the Cold War Era, 1950-1970

National Defense Education Act, **1958**
Laws of the 85th Congress 2nd Session, P. L. 85-864, pp. 1896-1897, 1903-1904, 1918-1919.
The Scott, Foresman Readers, **1955**
The New Basic Readers: More Times and Places, Grade Four. Chicago: Scott, Foresman & Company, 1955, pp. 184-194.
H.G. Rickover, **Education for All Children: What We Can Learn From England,** *1962*
H. G. Rickover, USN, "Education for All Children: What We Can Learn from England," *Hearings Before the Committee on Appropriations, House of Representatives, Eighty-Seventh Congress, Second Session*. Washington: U.S. Government Printing Office, 1962, pp. 3-5.
Herbert Kohl, **Thirty-Six Children,** *1967*
Herbert Kohl, *36 Children*. New York: New American Library, 1967, pp. 13-25.
John Holt. **How Children Fail.** *1964*
John Holt, *How Children Fail*. New York: Pitman Publishing Company, 1964, pp. 211-223.
Supreme Court of the United States, **Engel v. Vitale,** *1962*
U. S. Supreme Court, *Engel, et al. v. Vitale, et al.*, No. 468, Supreme Court of the United States 370 U. S. 421; 82 S. Ct. 1261; 1962.

Chapter Nine: Civil Rights, Integration, and School Reform, 1954-1980

Septima Clark, **Ready From Within,** *1990*
Cynthia Stokes Brown, ed. *Septima Clark and the Civil Rights Movement: Ready from Within*. Trenton: Africa World Press, 1990.
Supreme Court of the United States, **Brown v. Board of Education of Topeka, Kansas, 1954**
U.S. Supreme Court, *Brown, et al. v. Board of Education of Topeka, et al.*, No. 1, Supreme Court of the United States 347 U.S. 483; 1954.
Kenneth B. Clark, How Children Learn About Race, 1950

Kenneth B. Clark, "How Children Learn About Race," in Clayborne Carson, David J. Garrow, Gerald Gill, Vincent Harding, Darlene Clark Hine, eds. The Eyes on the Prize Civil Rights Reader. New York: Penguin Books, 1991, pp. 74-81.
Also published as *Prejudice and Your Child*. Boston: Beacon Press, 1955.
School Desegregation in the South: Little Rock, 1957
Daisy Bates. *The Long Shadow at Little Rock*. Fayetteville: The University of Arkansas Press, 1962.
In Clayborne Carson, David J. Garrow, Gerald Gill, Vincent Harding, Darlene Clark Hine, eds. *The Eyes on the Prize Civil Rights Reader*. New York: Penguin Books, 1991, pp. 97-106.
School Desegregation in the North: Boston, 1963-1968
Ruth Batson, NAACP Statement to the Boston School Committee, 1963, original transcript in Clayborne Carson, David J. Garrow, Gerald Gill, Vincent Harding, Darlene Clark Hine, eds., *The Eyes on the Prize Civil Rights Reader*. New York: Penguin Books, 1991, pp. 596-601.
Jonathan Kozol, *Death at an Early Age: The Destruction of the Hearts and Minds of Negro Children in the Boston Public Schools*. Boston: Houghton Mifflin, 1967, pp. 190-207 from the original paperback Bantam edition, 1968.

Chapter Ten: Rights and Opportunities in American Education 1965-1980

The Elementary and Secondary Education Act and the Great Society, 1965
Lyndon B. Johnson, "Special Message to the Congress Toward Full Educational Opportunity, January 12, 1965," and "Remarks in Johnson City, Texas, Upon Signing the Elementary and Secondary Education Bill, April 11, 1965," *Public Papers of the Presidents, Lyndon B. Johnson, 1965, Book I*, Washington, D. C., 1966, pp. 25-27 and 413-414.
Supreme Court of the United States, **Tinker, et al. v. Des Moines Independent Community School District, 1969**
U. S. Supreme Court, *Tinker, et al. v. Des Moines Independent Community School District, et al.*, No. 21, Supreme Court of the United States 393 U. S. 503; 1969.
Title IX, Women's Educational Equality Act, 1972
Laws of the 92nd Congress, P. L. 92-318, "Title IX, Women's Educational Equity Act, 1974" June 23, 1972.
Public Law 94-142, Education for All Handicapped Children Act, 1975
Laws of the 94th Congress, P. L. 94-142, "Education for All Handicapped Children Act, 1975," November 29, 1975, pp. 774-774.
Viva La Raza! Community Control in Chicago, 1974
Elizabeth Sutherland Martinez and Enriqueta Longeaux y Vasquez, *Viva La Raza! The Struggle of the Mexican-American People*. Garden City, New York: Doubleday & Company, 1974, pp. 259-263.
Dillon Platero, The Rough Rock Demonstration School, Navajo Nation, 1970
Dillon Platero, remarks recorded in *Indian Voices: The First Convocation of American Indian Scholars*. San Francisco: The Indian Historian Press, 1970, pp. 132-140.

Chapter Eleven: Reform Efforts of the 1980s and 1990s

National Commission on Excellence in Education, **A Nation At Risk: The Imperative For Educational Reform, 1983**
National Commission on Excellence in Education, "A Nation At Risk: The Imperative for Educational Reform." Washington, D.C.: U. S. Government Printing Office, 1983, pp. 5-23.
Ann Bastian, et al., **Choosing Equality: The Case for Democratic Schooling,** *1985*
Ann Bastian, Norm Fruchter, Marilyn Gittell, Colin Greer, Kenneth Haskins, *Choosing Equality: The Case for Democratic Schools*. New York: The New World Foundation, 1985, pp. 1-7.
Sonia Nieto, **Affirming Diversity: The Sociopolitical Context of Multicultural Education,** *1992*
Sonia Nieto, *Affirming Diversity: The Sociopolitical Context of Multicultural Education*. New York: Longman, 1992, pp. xxiii-xxviii, 1-2.
Arthur M. Schlesinger, Jr., **The Disuniting of America,** *1991*
Arthur Schlesinger, Jr., *The Disuniting of America: Reflections on a Multicultural Society*. New York: Whittle Direct Books, 1991, pp. 70-83.
David C. Berliner and Bruce J. Biddle, **The Manufactured Crisis,** *1995*
David C. Berliner and Bruce J. Biddle, *The Manufactured Crisis: Myths, Fraud, and the Attack on America's Schools*. Reading, MA: Addison-Wesley, 1995. pp. xi-xii, 1-5.
Herbert Kohl, The Discipline of Hope, 1998
Herbert Kohl, *The Discipline of Hope: Learning from a Lifetime of Teaching*. New York: Simon & Schuster, 1998, pp. 331-333.

INDEX

Achievement, 214, 323
Act of Uniformity, 250
Adams, John, 18, 252
Administrative progressives, 182,
    183–87
Adult education, at Rough Rock,
    315–16
Affirming Diversity, 320, 332–36
African American literacy. *See also*
    Literacy
    development of, 107–9
    Douglass's account, 109–13
    DuBois's vision for, 128–39
    Forten journal excerpt, 117–22
    New England Freedman's Aid
        Society role, 113–17
    Washington's vision for, 122–28
African Americans
    in Boston schools, 80–88,
        279–88, 288–92
    civil rights movement (*see* Civil
        rights movement)
    colleges for, 133, 134, 136–39
    common school movement and,
        51–52
    educational traditions of, 1
    in Harlem classroom, 232–41
    inferiority learned, 269–73
Afrocentrism, 338, 339
Aldermen, 20–21
Alien land laws, 163
Alpha Kappa Alpha, 265
American Creed, 340, 342
American Federation of Teachers,
    310
Americanization campaign, 164,
    165–66
American Me, 167–75
Antin, Mary, 141, 145–53
Armbands, 298–308
Asian immigrants, 159–67
Astronomy, 33
Atlanta Compromise, 129

Baby talk, 41
Bacon, Kay, 277, 279
"Ballad of the Landlord," 282, 284
Ballet Chicano de Aztlán, 311
Baptism of slaves, 6
Bartels v. Iowa, 304–5
Bastian, Ann, 328–32
Bates, Daisy, 273–77
Batson, Ruth, 288–92
Beecher, Catharine, 49, 61–66, 90
Beecher, Lyman, 89, 91–94
Berkeley, William, 7–8
Berliner, David C., 342–47
Bible. *See also* Christianity;
    Religion
    in frontier schools, 99–100
    Mann's support for use in
        schools, 59–60
    Rush's view of use in schools,
        29, 33–34

Webster's view of use in
    schools, 37–38
Biddle, Bruce J., 342–47
Bilingual programs, 176–77, 314, 318
"Bill for the More General Diffusion
    of Knowledge," 19–24
Binet, Alfred, 208
Binet-Simon intelligence scale, 208,
    211
Blossom, Virgil, 274–75
Boarding schools, Meriam report
    on, 154–58
Board of Education (Massachusetts),
    66–74
Board of National Popular
    Education, 90, 98–104
Bookkeeping, 33
Book of Common Prayer, 248, 250,
    251
Books
    biases of, 237, 241
    Rickover's emphasis on, 229–30
    shortage in Boston school, 286
    shortage in Harlem school, 237
    Webster's comments on, 40–41
Boston
    as abolitionist center, 113
    desegregation in, 80–88, 256–57
    Irish immigration to, 50–51
    Kozol's classroom experience,
        279–88
    NAACP statement to School
        Committee, 256–57,
        288–92
    progressive school reforms in,
        183–87
Boston Latin School, 3, 9
Brooks, Stratton D., 186
Brown, Minnijean, 278, 279
Brownell, George, 9
Brown v. Board of Education deci-
    sion, 255–56, 266–69
Bureaucracy, 69, 229–31
Burnside v. Byars, 299, 301
Busing, 256

California
    Asian immigrants to, 159–67
    Griffith's study of schools in,
        167–75
Carroll, John, 142
Catholic children, religious aware-
    ness of, 271, 272
Catholicism
    decree for parish schools, 141,
        142–45
    opposition to Protestant
        influence in schools,
        50–51, 74–80
Chicago Teachers Federation, 187
Chicano schools, 310–12
Child labor, 146–47, 155
Chinese Exclusion Act, 159–60
Choosing Equality, 328–32

Christianity. *See also* Bible;
    Religion
    Catholic vs. Protestant
        influence, 50–51,
        74–80
    in colonial schools, 8, 10–16
    common school movement and,
        49
    in frontier schools, 99–100
    for Indians and slaves, 2, 4, 5, 6,
        104–6
    Mann's support for, 59–60
    prayer in schools, 246–54
    proselytizing among Japanese
        immigrants, 166
    in Rush's view of education,
        28–31, 33–34
Churches, segregated, 131
Church of England, 248, 250
Civilization Fund Act of 1819, 19,
    46–47
Civil rights movement
    Brown v. Board of Education
        decision, 255–56,
        266–69
    Clark's participation in, 257–65
    expansion of, 293–94
    Johnson administration
        initiatives, 295–98
    Little Rock Central High School
        integration, 256,
        273–79
    multicultural education's roots
        in, 334–35
    NAACP statement to Boston
        School Committee,
        256–57, 288–92
    overview of desegregation
        victories, 255–57
Clark, Kenneth B., 269–73
Clark, Septima, 255, 257–65
Cleveland, Grover, 253
Close supervision, 193
Coercion, 246
Colby, Bainbridge, 159–60
Cold War, 222–23
Collectivist cultures, 339
College of Charleston, 261
Colonial schools
    origins of, 1–4
    religion in, 8, 10–16
Columbian Orator, The, 111
Common school movement
    Mann's view of, 52–61
    overview of, 48–52
Commonwealth v. Davis, 83–84
Community control movement, 294,
    310–12
Community development, at Rough
    Rock, 315–16
Consistency, 240–41
Contrabands, 113
Corporal punishment, 39
Cotton, 204